DATE DUE

NO 27 00			
MY 31 '01			
AE 1 1 '01			
OC 19 01			
DE 4 02			
JE 2 '03			
DE 17 04			
AP 17 06			
NO 27 07			

ss Cataloging-in-Publication Data

y, processing, and the law

ndex.
ISBN 0-13-603408-X
1. Juvenile justice, Administration of--United States,
2. Juvenile courts--United States.   I. Title.
KF9779.C425   1998
345.73'08--dc21

98-37318
CIP

Editorial/Production Supervision,
   Interior Design, and Electronic Paging: *Naomi Sysak*
Acquisitions Editor: *Neil Marquardt*
Cover Photo: *Tim Macpherson, Tony Stone Images*
Cover Design: *Miguel Ortiz*
Manufacturing Buyer: *Ed O'Dougherty*
Managing Editor: *Mary Carnis*
Marketing Manager: *Frank Mortimer, Jr.*
Director of Production: *Bruce Johnson*

Printed in the United States of America

10 9 8 7 6 5 4

ISBN 0-13-603408-X

Prentice-Hall International (UK) Limited, *London*
Prentice-Hall of Australia Pty. Limited, *Sydney*
Prentice-Hall of Canada, Inc., *Toronto*
Prentice-Hall Hispanoamericana, S. A., *Mexico*
Prentice-Hall of India Private Limited, *New Delhi*
Prentice-Hall of Japan, Inc., *Tokyo*
Pearson Education Asia Pte. Ltd., *Singapore*
Editora Prentice-Hall do Brasil, Ltda., *Rio de Janeiro*

THE JUVENILE JUSTICE SYSTEM
Delinquency, Processing, and the Law

SECOND EDITION

Dean Champion
Minot State University

PRENTICE HALL
UPPER SADDLE RIVER, NJ 07458

Riverside Community College
Library
4800 Magnolia Avenue
Riverside, CA 92506

MAY '00

CONTENTS

Chapter 4
Juveniles and the Police 111

Chapter 5
Intake and Preadjudicatory Processing 147

Chapter 6
Classification and Preliminary Treatment: Waivers and Other Alternatives   191

Chapter 7
Prosecutorial Decision Making in Juvenile Justice   239

Chapter 8
The Adjudicatory Process: Dispositional Alternatives   279

Chapter 9
The Legal Rights of Juveniles   333

Chapter 10
Nominal Sanctions: Warnings, Diversion, and Standard Probation 381

Chapter 11
Juvenile Probation and Community-Based Alternatives 403

My appreciation is extended to those who provided some of the photos for this book. These include Corky Stromme, Chief of Security, North Dakota State Penitentiary; Lt. Darrell Theurer, North Dakota State Penitentiary; and Jarrett Wold, Jennia Green, Jordan Hendershot, Eric Pinnick, and Zach Schultz of Minot, North Dakota.

FOREWORD

The Juvenile Justice System: Delinquency, Processing, and the Law is a contemporary presentation of the juvenile justice system in its entirety. It examines the nature of delinquency, classifications of juvenile offenders, and alternative explanations for juvenile misconduct. This book draws on literature largely from the most current sources, although many classical works are not neglected.

Because the law changes with frequency, it is imperative to have a book that treats juvenile law in an up-to-date fashion. Current cases are cited that bear directly on juvenile rights in different contexts. Landmark Supreme Court cases are included, although persuasive decisions from various federal circuits and state courts are presented as means of portraying future juvenile justice trends. This reflects a legalistic perspective, and in this context, the book should have relevance and appeal for all instructors who teach this course. The processing of juvenile offenders is contingent, in part, upon how delinquent behavior is defined. An integral feature of this book is the distinction between status offenses and delinquent offenses. This difference has significant consequences for all juveniles affected.

The history of juvenile courts is described, including crucial events that have influenced the course of juvenile justice. Increasingly, juveniles are extended rights commensurate with the rights of adults. An indication of this trend is the growing use of waivers (certifications or transfers) to criminal court. This option is intended to expose more serious juvenile offenders to more severe punishment forms compared with the possible punishments that juvenile judges may impose. Unfortunately, the spreading use of waivers has not always achieved the intended result of more severe penalties for juveniles, since many juveniles who are waived to criminal courts receive minimal punishments if punished at all.

One explanation is that most juveniles who are transferred to criminal court are not necessarily the most serious, dangerous, or violent juvenile offenders. Often, waived juveniles include many who are charged with minor infractions and who appear before juvenile judges repeatedly for status offenses such as truancy, curfew violations, or incorrigibility. Juvenile judges attempt to remedy this situation by transferring their jurisdiction over these juveniles to criminal courts, where their recidivism, no matter how minor, may be dealt with more severely. Interestingly, once juveniles have been waived to criminal court jurisdiction, their age functions as a mitigating factor. Quite often, this factor reduces the seriousness or severity of their punishment. Cases against many of these juveniles are dropped or are reduced to less serious allegations. Thus many juveniles who are tried as adults receive sentences that are comparatively less severe than those that would otherwise be contemplated and imposed by juvenile judges. However, one potential penalty that receives increasing attention is the death penalty applied to juveniles. Current case law about imposing the death penalty as a punishment for juveniles is examined, and several juvenile death penalty cases are described.

Juveniles are not only classified according to type of offense, but they are also tracked according to the nature of offenses committed across years. Delinquency is defined and measured according to several popular indices: the *Uniform Crime Reports* and the *National Crime Victimization Survey*. Each of these measures is defective in various respects, and it is unlikely that any single resource discloses the true amount of delinquency in the United States.

Although this book does not explore in-depth delinquent behavior per se, it does offer a brief examination of several of the more popular explanations for delinquent conduct. Thus several theories of delinquency are described and evaluated. These theoretical explanations of delinquent conduct are linked with various types of treatment programs for juvenile offenders as they are processed by the juvenile justice system.

The major components of the juvenile justice system are featured, including the interface with police and police discretion, the distinction drawn between status offenders and delinquents, the prosecutorial decision-making process, the adjudicatory phase, and finally, corrections. Corrections is presented in a broad context, with each correctional component described. Correctional strategies ranging from diversion to full-fledged incarceration are featured, together with pros and cons of each program. One interesting feature is a section devoted to recidivism among juveniles, depending on the nature of the treatment program described. Thus community-based correctional programs are assessed, together with probation and parole alternatives for managing a growing juvenile offender aggregate. Electronic monitoring and home confinement are described as strategic and technological means of coping with growing numbers of juvenile offenders, where existing juvenile justice budgets have not been enhanced accordingly.

CHAPTER 1

AN INTRODUCTION TO JUVENILE JUSTICE IN THE UNITED STATES

INTRODUCTION

THE HISTORY OF JUVENILE COURTS

WHO ARE JUVENILE OFFENDERS?

PARENS PATRIAE

MODERN INTERPRETATIONS OF *PARENS PATRIAE*

JUVENILE AND CRIMINAL COURTS: SOME PRELIMINARY DISTINCTIONS

ALTERNATIVE PHILOSOPHIES FOR MANAGING JUVENILE OFFENDERS

KEY TERMS

QUESTIONS FOR REVIEW

SUGGESTED READINGS

INTRODUCTION

Raul Felix, 17, made a wrong turn in a Los Angeles suburb and was shot to death by two carloads of gang members in Southgate, California. Felix had just dropped off his date and was on his way home. He was looking for a freeway when two cars of youths forced his car into a laundry parking lot. Guns blazed from the other cars and the youths sped away. Felix was hit numerous times in the head and chest, while a passenger dropped down on the floorboard of the car and remained unharmed. Neither Felix nor his friend were gang members. The killing was unprovoked and pointless. But it was just another day in South Central LA. (Associated Press, "Teen Who Made Wrong Turn Killed," *Minot (ND) Daily News*, September 17, 1996:A2)

It happened in Richmond, California. A group of children, ranging in age from 4 to 8, victimized a six-week-old infant during an attempt to steal a bicycle. The children entered a dwelling one evening undetected in an effort to steal various items, including a bicycle that one of the youths knew was there. A babysitter was in another area of the home and did not hear the boys enter. The boys knocked over a crib containing the six-week-old baby and commenced to beat and kick it. One of the youths said he "thought it was a doll." Nearly killing the infant in their unprovoked attack, the boys laughed when they discovered it was a live baby. They continued to beat and kick it. The racket caused the babysitter to investigate and she was able to drive away the boys. She rushed the infant to the local Children's Hospital, where a spokesperson said that the baby was in critical condition. The boys were subsequently apprehended and held for questioning. What should the punishment be for the actions of these boys? Should children under the age of 7, an age drawn under common law below which culpability is presumed nonexistent, be held accountable as other juveniles for committing violent acts? How should these boys be adjudicated, if at all, by a juvenile court? What would you recommend? (Adapted from Associated Press, "Police: Baby Beaten by Group of Kids," *Minot (ND) Daily News*, April 24, 1996:A2)

It happened in Manchester, New Hampshire. Several girls ranging in age from 4 to 13 were lured to a boy's home to play Nintendo and other video games. Ice cream was also used as an inducement. Once at the boy's home, the girls were threatened with a large knife and raped. Mothers in the neighborhood determined that at least 10 girls had been ravaged by the boy, who turned out to be 10 years old. The 10-year-old was taken into custody by police and charged with rape and other sexual assault charges. Some of the girls told police that the boy told them that they "wouldn't go to heaven" if they ever told their parents about him. Detectives were investigating an additional six complaints against the boy, according to Captain Glenn Leidemer, head of the police department's juvenile division. If adjudicated delinquent on the rape charges, how should the 10-year-old boy be punished? Should the boy be charged as an adult, for committing an "adult" offense? How would you decide punishment for this boy if he is determined guilty by the juvenile court judge? What would you do? (Adapted from Associated Press, "Ten-Year-Old Boy Charged with Rape," *Minot (ND) Daily News,* August 22, 1996:A2)

There is no doubt about it. Juvenile delinquency is becoming increasingly violent. Greater access to firearms, greater reliance on gang associations for friendships and ego-building, less control over one's emotional state, deteriorating traditional family values, loss of parental control over growing numbers of incorrigible youths, and more frequent school disorder and disruption suggest that something is seriously wrong with the youth of American society. Whether juvenile violence is evidenced by a drive-by or freeway shooting, a drug deal turned deadly, gang fighting, bullying or menacing on school property, or increasing numbers of teen rapes, many experts believe that growing numbers of youths are simply *out of control.* Further, serious offenses are deserving of more serious punishments. More drastic measures are needed to turn the tide of rising teenage violence.

There are diverse attitudes about juvenile violence (Hanke, 1996). Not everyone agrees about which solutions are best to reduce or eliminate this violence. A clear and universally acceptable mandate about what should be done with delinquent youths, in the form of a consistent standard of punishment or treatment, does not exist. Surveys of public opinion about juvenile violence suggest that those juveniles who commit violent acts should be tried as adults and accept their punishment. "If they commit the crime, they can do the time" (Stalans and Henry, 1994). Other critics believe that youths ought to be treated rather than punished, a philosophy that has been pervasive in the United States for the past two centuries (Gittens, 1994). Although it has been faulted by critics in many respects, the juvenile justice system is an essential component of American jurisprudence. Currently, mechanisms are in place for dealing with both violent and nonviolent juvenile offenders. The constellation of mechanisms for this purpose is referred to as the juvenile justice system.

The Juvenile Justice System

The *juvenile justice system* consists of a more or less integrated network of agencies, institutions, organizations, and personnel that process juvenile offenders. This network is made up of law enforcement agencies, prosecutors, and courts; corrections, probation, and parole services; and public and private community-based treatment programs that provide youths with diverse services. This definition is qualified by the phrase *more or less integrated,* because the concept of juvenile justice has different meanings for individual states and the federal government. Also, in some jurisdictions, the diverse components of the juvenile justice system are closely coordinated, while in other jurisdictions, these components are at best loosely coordinated, if they are coordinated at all.

A Process or System?

Many criminologists and criminal justice professionals express a preference for *process* rather than *system* when they refer to juvenile justice. This is because system connotes a condition of homeostasis, equilibrium, or internal balance among system components. In contrast, process focuses on the different actions and contributions of each of these components in dealing with juvenile offenders at various stages of the "processing" through the juvenile justice system. Furthermore, system implies coordination among elements in an efficient production process; but in reality, communication and coordination among juvenile agencies, organizations, and personnel in the juvenile justice system are often inadequate or nonexistent.

Further clouding the concept of juvenile justice is the fact that different criteria are used to define the broad classes of juveniles among local, state, and federal jurisdictions. Within each of these jurisdictions, certain mechanisms exist for redefining particular juveniles as adults so that they may be legally processed by the adult counterpart to juvenile justice, the criminal justice system. Despite these definitional ambiguities and systemic interfaces among jurisdictions, most scholars who investigate juveniles understand what is meant by juvenile justice. As with pornography, these scholars and investigators recognize the juvenile justice process whenever they see its components, even if they may not always be able to define it precisely.

About This Book

This book is about the juvenile justice system. Because of the multifaceted nature of this system or process, the wide variety of characteristics of its intended clients, and its interrelatedness with the criminal justice system, we may acquire a better understanding of its nature, purposes, and development if we can place it within a historical framework. Thus the first part of this chapter describes the historical emergence of juvenile justice in the United States. Key events are noted, and their significance and influence on contemporary juvenile agencies and organizations are discussed. Early versions of juvenile justice were affected by and patterned substantially after early English common law and the role of kings and their agents in public affairs; we will trace the origins of our system in English law. Interestingly, certain functions and objectives of contemporary juvenile justice systems have their origins in fifteenth-century England, although particular ideas about how youths of all ages were to be defined, judged, punished, or treated also existed in biblical times.

This historical introduction is followed by a description of the juvenile court. This is a relatively recent concept. It is both pivotal and pervasive in most juvenile justice systems. Coexisting with juvenile courts are criminal courts designed to adjudicate adult offenders. Several important characteristics of both types of courts will be described, together with some of their differences. One feature that distinguishes these courts from one another is the age range of the clientele over which each exercises jurisdiction. The matters dealt with by these court systems vary as well. Some of these major differences are highlighted.

Throughout the juvenile justice system in both colonial and modern times is the pervasive doctrine of *parens patriae*. This doctrine originated from early English common law in the twelfth century. Meaning literally the *parent of the country, parens patriae* referred originally to the fact that the king of England was both a sovereign and a guardian of persons under legal disability, including children (Black, 1990:1114). This concept has been particularly influential regarding juvenile court practices as contrasted with criminal courts. In recent decades there have been numerous reforms throughout the juvenile justice system, and the *parens patriae* doctrine has become both transformed and limited as it applies to youths.

Finally, alternative managerial philosophies exist that favor various modes of juvenile control. Some of these philosophies are in direct conflict, and all have competing implications for affected juveniles. A description of these philosophies is in order at the outset, since all currently available juvenile services and programs have been variously influenced by them. As we will see, no consensus exists presently among juvenile justice scholars and researchers about which philosophy is best or most useful. The result is a programmatic Tower of Babel, replete with conflicting values, interests, and aims with regard to the goals and purposes of the juvenile justice system.

This conflict is highlighted by competing juvenile justice reforms which have been attempted over the last 100 years. Moral entrepreneurs emphasized religion as an integrating and rehabilitative medium for wayward youths, while domestic reformers proclaimed that placing children in model homes would solve delinquency problems. Charitable reformers established cultural centers in impoverished neighborhoods, while progressive reformers suggested psychological adjustment as a cure for deviance. All of these reformers failed to anticipate that clients themselves would resist these different forms of assistance and intervention. In a glib manner, reformers did not question their assumption that by reforming individuals, they could change society. In many respects, these reformers were wrong (Schneider, 1992).

THE HISTORY OF JUVENILE COURTS

Juvenile courts are a relatively recent U.S. creation. However, modern American juvenile courts have various less formal European antecedents. In biblical times, Roman law vested parents with the almost exclusive responsibility for disciplining their offspring. One's age was the crucial determinant of whether youths were subject to parental discipline or to the more severe penalties invoked for adult law violators. While the origin of this cutting point is unknown, the age of 7 was used in Roman times to separate infants from those older children who were accountable to the law for their actions. During the Middle Ages, English **common law** established under the monarchy adhered to the same standard. In the United States, several state jurisdictions currently apply this distinction and consider all children below the age of 7 to be not accountable for any criminal acts they may commit.

Under the laws of England during the sixteenth century, **shires** (counties) and other political subdivisions were organized to carry out the will of the king or queen. Each shire had a **reeve**, or chief law enforcement officer. In later years, the term *shire* was combined with the term *reeve* ("shire-reeve") to create the word *sheriff,* a term that is now applied to the chief law enforcement officer of most U.S. counties. While reeves enforced both criminal and civil laws and arrested law violators, other functionaries, called **chancellors**, acted on the sovereign's behalf and dispensed justice according to his or her wishes. These chancellors held court and settled disputes that included simple property trespass, property boundary disagreements, and assorted personal and property offenses, including public drunkenness, thievery, and vagrancy. The courts conducted by chancellors were known as **chancery courts** or **courts of equity**. Today, some jurisdictions in the United States (e.g., Tennessee) have chancery courts where property boundary disputes and contested wills may be adjudicated by chancellors. These courts have other jurisdiction as well, although they deal primarily with equity cases (e.g., breaches of contract, specific performance actions, and child custody cases).

In eighteenth-century England, no distinctions were made with regard to age or gender when punishments were administered. Youthful offenders age 7 or older were subject to the same harsh types of punishment imposed on adults. Stocks and pillories, whipping posts, branding, "ducking stools," and other forms of corporal punishment were meted out to juveniles as well as to adult male and female offenders for many different types of crimes. **Banishment** was used in some instances as a means of punishing more serious offenders. The death penalty was invoked frequently, often for petty crimes. Incarceration of offenders was particularly sordid, as women, men, and youths were confined together in jails for lengthy periods. No attempts were made to classify these offenders by gender or age, and all prisoners slept on hay loosely thrown on wooden floors.

These eighteenth-century jails were patterned largely after **workhouses** that were common nearly two centuries earlier. In 1557, for example, **Bridewell Workhouse** was established in London. Although the manifest aim of such places was to punish offenders, Bridewell and similar facilities were created primarily for the purpose of providing cheap labor to satisfy mercantile interests and demands. Interestingly, jailers and sheriffs profitted greatly from leasing their inmates to various merchants as semiskilled and skilled labor (American Correctional Association, 1983). Authorities claimed that the work performed by inmates for mercantile interests was largely therapeutic and rehabilitative, although in reality the profit motive was the primary incentive for operating such houses. Exploitation of inmates for profit in these and other workhouses was perpetuated by jailers and sheriffs for many decades, and the general practice was accepted by an influential constituency of merchants and entrepreneurs.

At the time Bridewell Workhouse thrived, English legislators had already created various statutes known as the **Poor Laws**. In part, these laws targeted relationships between debtors and creditors and prescribed sanctions for those unable to pay their debts. Debtors' prisons—a product of life during this period—were places where debtors were incarcerated until such time as they could pay their debts or fines. Debtors needed to work to earn the money required to pay off their debts, but imprisonment prevented them from doing so. Consequently, they would be incarcerated indefinitely—or until someone, perhaps a relative or influential friend, could pay their debts for them. Many died in prisons because of their failure to pay their debts.

The Poor Laws were directed at the poor or socioeconomically disadvantaged. In 1601, additional statutes were created that provided constructive work for youths deemed by the courts to be vagrant, incorrigible, truant, or neglected. In general, education was not an option for these youths—it was an expensive commodity available almost exclusively to children from the upper social strata, and it provided a major means of achieving even higher status over time. For the masses of poor, education was usually beyond their reach; they spent most of their time earning money to pay for life's basic necessities. They had little or no time to consider education as a feasible life option (Sanders, 1945).

Many youths during this time became apprentices, usually to master craftsmen, in a system of involuntary servitude. This servitude was patterned in part after the **indentured servant system. Indentured servants** entered voluntarily into contractual agreements with various merchants and business owners to work for them for extended periods of up to seven years. This seven-year work agreement was considered by all parties to be a mutually beneficial way of paying for the indentured servant's passage from England to the colonies. In the case of youthful apprentices, however, their servitude, for the most part, was compulsory. Furthermore, it usually lasted until they reached adulthood or age 21.

During the colonial period, English influence on penal practices was apparent in most New England jurisdictions. Colonists relied on familiar traditions for administering laws and sanctioning offenders. It is no coincidence, therefore, that much criminal procedure in American courts today traces its origins to legal customs and precedents inherent in British jurisprudence during the seventeenth and eighteenth centuries. However, relatively little attention was devoted to the legal status of juveniles during this period and to how to manage them.

In other parts of the world during the same era, certain religious interests were gradually devising institutions that catered primarily to youthful offenders. For example, in Italy, a corrective facility was established in 1704 to provide for unruly youths and other young people who violated criminal laws. This facility was the **Hospital of Saint Michael**, constructed in Rome at the request of the Pope. The institution was misleadingly named, however, since the youths it housed were not ill. Rather, they were assigned various tasks and trained to perform semiskilled and skilled labor—useful tools that would enable them to find employment more easily after their release from Saint Michael. During rest periods and evening hours, youths were housed in individual cells (Griffin and Griffin, 1978).

Reforms relating to the treatment and/or punishment of juvenile offenders occurred slowly. Shortly after the Revolutionary War, religious interests in the United States moved forward with various proposals designed to improve the plight of the oppressed, particularly those who were incarcerated in prisons and jails. In 1787, the Quakers in Pennsylvania established the **Philadelphia Society for Alleviating the Miseries of the Public Prisons**. This largely philanthropic society was comprised of prominent citizens, religious leaders, and philanthropists who were appalled by existing prison and jail conditions. Adult male, female, and juvenile offenders continued to be housed in common quarters and treated like animals. The High Street Jail in Philadelphia was one eyesore that particularly attracted the society's attention. Because members of the Quaker faith visited this and other jail facilities regularly to bring food, clothing, and religious instruction to inmates, they were in strategic positions to observe the totality of circumstances in which those confined found themselves.

In 1790, the society's efforts were rewarded. An older Philadelphia jail facility constructed in 1776 was overhauled and refurbished. It was named the **Walnut Street Jail**. This facility has considerable historical significance for corrections, since it represented the first real attempt by jail authorities to classify and segregate offenders according to age, gender, and seriousness of crime. The Walnut Street Jail was innovative in at least three respects. First, it pioneered what is now known as **solitary confinement**. Sixteen large solitary cells were constructed to house prisoners on an individual basis during evening hours. Second, prisoners were segregated from other prisoners according to the seriousness of their offenses. More hardened criminals were placed with others like them. First offenders or petty offenders were similarly grouped together. Third, women and children were maintained in separate rooms during evening hours, apart from their male counterparts.

Additionally, the Walnut Street Jail was, to a degree, rehabilitative. It sought to train its inmates for different types of labor, such as sewing, shoemaking, or carpentry. Unskilled laborers were assigned tasks such as beating hemp for ship caulking. Most prisoners received modest wages for their skilled or unskilled labor, although much of this pay was used to offset their room and board expenses. Finally, religious instruction was provided to inmates by Quaker teachers. This provision underscores the dramatic influence of religion in the shaping of prison policies and practices relating to inmate treatment and benefits.

During the early nineteenth century, as more families gravitated toward large cities such as New York, Philadelphia, Boston, and Chicago to find work, increasing numbers of children were "at large," most often left unsupervised by working parents who could not afford child care services. Lacking familial controls, many of these youths committed acts of vandalism and theft. Others were simply idle, without visible means of support, and were designated as vagrants. Again, religious organizations intervened to protect unsupervised youths from the perils of life in the streets. Believing that these youths would subsequently turn to lives of crime as adults, many reformers and philanthropists sought to "save" them from their plight. Thus, in different cities throughout the United States, various groups were formed to find and control these youths by offering them constructive work programs, healthful living conditions, and above all, adult supervision. Collectively, these efforts became widely known as the **childsaving movement**. **Childsavers** came largely from the middle and upper classes, and their assistance to youths took many forms. Food and shelter were provided to children who were in trouble with the law or who were simply idle. Private homes were converted into settlements where social, educational, and other important activities could be provided for needy youths.

The **New York House of Refuge** was established in New York City in 1825 by the Society for the Prevention of Pauperism (Cahalan, 1986:101).

Subsequently imitated in other communities, the House of Refuge was an institution largely devoted to managing status offenders, such as runaways or incorrigible children. Compulsory education and other forms of training and assistance were provided to these children. However, the strict, prisonlike regimen of this organization was not entirely therapeutic for its clientele. Many of the youthful offenders who were sent to such institutions, including the House of Reformation in Boston, were offspring of immigrants. Often, they rebelled when exposed to the discipline of these organizations, and many of these youths eventually pursued criminal careers as a consequence (Ferdinand, 1986). It would appear that at least some of these humanitarian and philanthropic efforts by childsavers and others had adverse consequences for many affected juveniles.

Up until the late 1830s, there was little or no pattern to the division of labor among parental, religious, and state authorities (Musick, 1995). As private interests continued to include larger numbers of juveniles within the scope of their supervision, various jurisdictions sought to regulate and institutionalize these assorted juvenile assistance, treatment, and/or intervention programs. In many communities, city councils sanctioned the establishment of facilities to accommodate youths who were either delinquent, dependent, or neglected. As more formal state control over youths evolved through legislation, it became increasingly clear that the early English concept of *parens patriae* was becoming institutionalized.

In 1839, a decision in a state case invested juvenile authorities with considerable parental power. *Ex parte Crouse* (1839) was a case involving a father who attempted to secure the release of his daughter from the Philadelphia House of Refuge. The girl had been committed to the Philadelphia facility by the court because she was considered unmanageable. She was not given a trial by jury. Rather, her commitment was made arbitrarily by a presiding judge. A higher court rejected the father's claim that parental control of children is exclusive, natural, and proper, and it upheld the power of the state to exercise necessary reforms and restraints to protect children from themselves and their environments. Although this decision was only applicable to Pennsylvania citizens and their children, other states took note of it and sought to invoke similar controls over errant children in their jurisdictions. In effect, children (at least in Pennsylvania) were temporarily deprived of any legal standing to challenge decisions made by the state in their behalf.

Throughout the remainder of the nineteenth century, different types of institutions were established to supervise unruly juveniles. At roughly midcentury, **reform schools** were created in several jurisdictions. One of the first state-operated reform schools was opened in Westboro, Massachusetts in 1848 (US Department of Justice, 1976). By the end of the century, all states had reform schools of one sort or another. All of these institutions were characterized by strict discipline, absolute control over juvenile behavior, and compulsory work at various trades. Another common feature was that they were controversial.

The primary question raised by reform school critics was: Do reform schools reform? Since many juveniles continued their delinquent conduct after being released from these schools and eventually became adult offenders, their reform or rehabilitative value was seriously questioned. The Civil War exacerbated the problem of unruly youths, since many families were broken up. Orphans of dead soldiers were commonplace in the post–Civil War period. Such children were often committed to reform schools regardless of whether they had committed criminal offenses. Many status offenders were sent to reform schools simply because they were vagrants. Many of these children did not need to be reformed; rather, they needed homes and noninstitutional care.

Few legal challenges of state authority were made by complaining parents, because of the awesome power of the state and its control over juvenile matters. However, an Illinois case (*O'Connell v. Turner*) in 1870 paved the way for special courts for juveniles and an early recognition of their rights. A youth, Daniel O'Connell, was declared vagrant and in need of supervision and committed to the Chicago Reform School for an unspecified period. O'Connell's parents challenged this court action, claiming that his confinement for vagrancy was unjust and untenable. Existing Illinois law vested state authorities with the power to commit any juvenile to a state reform school as long as a "reasonable justification" could be provided. In this instance, vagrancy was a reasonable justification. The Illinois Supreme Court distinguished between misfortune (vagrancy) and criminal acts in arriving at its decision to reverse Daniel O'Connell's commitment. In effect, the court nullified the law by declaring that reform school commitments of youths could not be made by the state if the "offense" was simple misfortune. They reasoned that the state's interests would be better served if commitments of juveniles to reform schools were limited to those committing more serious criminal offenses rather than those who were victims of misfortune.

Three decades later, on July 1, 1899, the Illinois legislature established the first juvenile court by passing the **Act to Regulate the Treatment and Control of Dependent, Neglected and Delinquent Children**, or the **Illinois Juvenile Court Act**. This act provided for limited courts of record, where notes might be taken by judges or their assistants, to reflect judicial actions against juveniles. The jurisdiction of these courts, subsequently designated as *juvenile courts*, would include all juveniles under the age of 16 who were found in violation of any state or local law or ordinance. Also, provision was made for the care of dependent and/or neglected children who had been abandoned or who otherwise lacked proper parental care, support, or guardianship. No minimum age was specified that would limit the jurisdiction of juvenile court judges. However, the act provided that judges could impose secure confinement on juveniles 10 years of age or over by placing them in state-regulated juvenile facilities, such as the state reformatory or *State Home for Juvenile Female Offenders*. Judges were expressly prohibited from confining any juvenile under 12 years of age in a jail or police station. Extremely young juveniles would be assigned probation officers who would look after their needs and placement on a temporary basis.

During the next 10 years, 20 states passed similar acts to establish juvenile courts. By the end of World War II, all states had created juvenile court systems. However, considerable variation existed among these court systems, depending on the jurisdiction. Not all of these courts were vested with a consistent set of responsibilities and powers.

While Illinois is credited with establishing the first juvenile court system in the United States, an earlier juvenile justice apparatus was created in Massachusetts in 1874. Known as the **children's tribunal**, it was used exclusively as a mechanism for dealing with children charged with crimes; it was kept separate from the system of criminal courts for adults (Hahn, 1984:5). Some years later, Colorado implemented an education law in 1899 known as the Compulsory School Act. Although this act was targeted primarily at youths who were habitually absent from school, it also encompassed juveniles who wandered the streets during school hours without obvious business or occupation. These youths, termed *juvenile disorderly persons*, were legislatively placed within the purview of truant officers and law enforcement officers, who could detain them and hold them for further action by other community agencies (Champion, 1990a:402; Hahn, 1984). While both Massachusetts and Colorado created these different mechanisms specifically for dealing with juvenile offenders, they were not true juvenile courts equivalent with those established in Illinois.

Feld (1993c) says that the juvenile court has evolved from an informal welfare agency into a scaled-down, second-class criminal court as a result of a series of reforms that have diverted less serious offenders from juvenile court and moved more serious offenders to criminal courts for processing. Several policy responses that Feld recommends as options include (1) restructuring the juvenile courts to fit their original therapeutic purposes, (2) accepting punishment as the purpose of delinquency proceedings but coupling it with criminal procedural safeguards, or (3) abolishing juvenile courts altogether and trying young offenders in criminal courts, with certain substantive and procedural modifications. These and other juvenile justice reforms have been recommended by various experts and are explored later in the book (Cohn, 1994; Feld, 1993a–c).

WHO ARE JUVENILE OFFENDERS?

Depending on the jurisdiction, **juvenile offenders** are classified and defined according to several different criteria (Hale et al., 1991). According to the 1899 Illinois act that created **juvenile courts**, the jurisdiction of such courts would extend to all juveniles under the age of 16 who were found in violation of any state or local law or ordinance (Gittens, 1994). About a fifth of all states, including Illinois, place the upper age limit for juveniles at either 15 or 16. In the remaining states, the upper limit for juveniles is 17 (except for Wyoming, where it is 18). Ordinarily, the jurisdiction of juvenile courts includes all **juveniles** between the ages of 7 and 18 (Black, 1990:867). At the federal level, juveniles are considered to be persons who have not attained their eighteenth birthday (18 U.S.C., Sec. 5031, 1997).

The Age Jurisdiction of Juvenile Courts

While fairly uniform upper age limits for juveniles have been established in all U.S. jurisdictions (either under 16, under 17, or under 18 years of age), there is no uniformity concerning applicable lower age limits. As we have seen, English common law placed juveniles under age 7 beyond the reach of criminal courts, since it was believed that those under age 7 were incapable of formulating criminal intent. However, many juvenile courts throughout the United States have no specified lower age limits for those juveniles within their purview. Although no juvenile court will march a 3-year-old before a judge for adjudication, many of these courts exert almost absolute control over the lives of young children or infants of any age. This control often involves placement of children or infants in foster homes or under the supervision of community service or human welfare agencies that can meet their needs. Neglected, unmanageable, abused, or other children in need of supervision are placed in the custody of these various agencies, at the discretion of juvenile judges. Thus juvenile courts generally have broad discretionary powers over most persons under the age of 18.

The Treatment and Punishment Functions of Juvenile Courts

The idea that for juvenile courts to exercise jurisdiction over juveniles, these youths must be "offenders" and must have committed offending acts (conceivably illegal acts or crimes) is misleading. A significant proportion of youths who appear before juvenile judges have not violated any criminal laws (Feld, 1993c). Rather, their *status* as juveniles renders them subject to juvenile court control, provided that certain circumstances exist. These circumstances may be the quality of their adult supervision, if any. Other circumstances may be that they run away from home, are truant from school, or loiter on certain city streets during evening hours. Runaways, truants, or loiterers are considered **status offenders**, since their actions would not be criminal acts if committed by adults.

Additionally, children who are physically, psychologically, or sexually abused by parents or other adults in their homes are brought within the scope of juvenile court authority. However, the majority of youthful offenders who appear before juvenile courts are those who have violated state or local laws or ordinances. These youths are juvenile delinquents. Federal law says that juvenile delinquency is the violation of any law of the United States by a person prior to his eighteenth birthday, which would have been a crime if committed by an adult (18 U.S.C., Sec. 5031, 1997). In law, juveniles are referred to as **infants**. A legal definition of a *juvenile delinquent* is any infant of not more than a specified age who has violated criminal laws or engages in disobedient, indecent, or immoral conduct, and is in need of treatment, rehabilitation, or supervision (Black, 1990:777).

It is evident from these definitions that juvenile courts may define juveniles and juvenile delinquency more or less broadly, and that for many jurisdictions a delinquent act is whatever these courts say it is. Despite U.S. Supreme Court proclamations to the contrary, juvenile court judges continue to determine which juvenile rights will be observed or ignored (Sanborn, 1994b). This ambiguity is unsettling to many critics of the juvenile justice system, who feel that the authority of juvenile judges is too broad and ought to be restricted. Incorrigibility, for instance, most often arises in everyday disputes between parents and children. The courts, thus far, have mediated these disputes largely in favor of adults. At least some critics contend that juvenile courts should not intervene in less-than-life-threatening events that arise from normal parent–child relations (Guggenheim, 1985a,b). However, the vast bulk of incorrigibility charges that result in court-imposed sanctions on juveniles involve ordinary parent–child disputes. For some critics, these disputes are not appropriately a part of the business of U.S. courts (Schneider, 1992). Other experts contend, however, that society has thrust upon children a degree of pseudomaturity, such as is manifested by juvenile court plea bargaining and other criminal court–like procedures (Sanborn, 1993). It is important at the outset to understand that much of this state authority originated under the early English doctrine of *parens patriae.*

PARENS PATRIAE

As indicated earlier, *parens patriae* is a concept that originated with the English sovereign during the twelfth century. It means literally "parent of the country." Applied to juvenile matters, *parens patriae* means that the sovereign is in charge of, makes decisions about, or has responsibility for all matters involving juvenile conduct. Within the scope of early English common law, parental authority was primary in the early upbringing of children. However, as children advanced to age 7 and beyond, they acquired some measure of responsibility for their actions. Accountability to parents was shifted gradually to accountability to the state whenever youths 7 years of age or older violated the law. In the name of the sovereign, chancellors in various districts adjudicated matters involving juveniles and the offenses they committed. Juveniles had no legal rights or standing in any court. They were the sole responsibility of the sovereign or his or her agents. Their future often depended largely on chancellor decisions. In effect, children were wards of the court, and the court was vested with the responsibility to safeguard their welfare.

Chancery courts of twelfth- and thirteenth-century England and later years performed many tasks, including the management of children and their affairs, as well as the management of the affairs of the mentally ill and incompetent. Therefore, an early division of labor was created, involving a three-way relationship among the child, the parent, and the state (Blustein, 1983). The underlying thesis of *parens patriae* was that the parents are merely the agents of society in the area of childrearing, and that the state has a primary and legitimate interest in the upbringing of its children. Thus *parens patriae* created a type of fiduciary or trustlike parent–child relation, with the state able to exercise the right of intervention to delimit parental rights (Blustein, 1983).

Since children could become wards of the court and subject to their control, a key concern for many chancellors was for the future welfare of these children. The welfare interests of chancellors and their actions led to numerous rehabilitative and/or treatment measures. Some of these measures included placement of children in foster homes or their assignment to various work tasks for local merchants. Parental influence in these child placement decisions was minimal. In the context of *parens patriae*, it is fairly easy to trace this early philosophy of child management and its influence to subsequent events in the United States, such as the childsaver movement, houses of refuge, and reform schools (Watkins, 1987). The latter developments were both private and public attempts to rescue children from their hostile environments and to meet some or all of their needs through various forms of institutionalization.

MODERN INTERPRETATIONS OF *PARENS PATRIAE*

Parens patriae in the 1990s is very much alive throughout all juvenile court jurisdictions in the United States, although some erosion of this doctrine has occurred during the past three or four decades (Ellsworth, Kinsella, and Massin, 1992). The persistence of this doctrine is evidenced by the wide range of dispositional options available to juvenile court judges and others involved in earlier stages of offender processing in the juvenile justice system. Most of these dispositional options are either nominal or conditional, meaning that the confinement of any juvenile for most offenses is regarded as a last resort. Nominal or conditional options involve relatively mild sanctions (e.g., verbal warnings or reprimands, diversion, probation, making financial restitution to victims, performance of community service, participation in individual or group therapy, or involvement in educational programs), and these sanctions are intended to reflect the rehabilitative ideal that has been a major philosophical underpinning of *parens patriae* (Mershon, 1991).

However, the strong treatment or rehabilitative orientation inherent in *parens patriae* is not acceptable to some juvenile justice experts (Schwartz, 1992). Contemporary juvenile court jurisprudence stresses individual accountability for one's actions. Consistent with a growing trend in the criminal justice system toward "just deserts" and justice, a similar trend is being observed throughout the juvenile justice system (Champion and Mays, 1991). This **get-tough movement** is geared toward providing law violators with swifter, harsher, and more certain justice and punishment than the previously dominant rehabilitative philosophy of American courts.

For juveniles, this means greater use of nonsecure and secure custody and incarcerative sanctions in state group homes, industrial schools, or reform schools. For those juveniles charged with violent offenses, this means transferring larger numbers of them to the jurisdiction of criminal courts for adults, where more severe sanctions such as life imprisonment or the death penalty may be imposed (Bishop, Frazier, and Henretta, 1989). Not all authorities agree that this is a sound trend, however. Based on selected public opinion polls, some experts suggest that while many people favor a separate juvenile justice system different from that for adults, they exhibit a strong preference for a system that sentences most juveniles to specialized treatment or counseling programs in lieu of incarceration, even for repeat offenders (Steinhart, 1988).

Influencing the *parens patriae* doctrine are the changing rights of juveniles. Since the mid-1960s, juveniles have acquired greater constitutional rights commensurate with those enjoyed by adults in criminal courts. Some professionals believe that as juveniles are vested with greater numbers of constitutional rights, a gradual transformation of the juvenile court is occurring toward one of greater criminalization (Feld, 1993a–c; Grissom, 1991; Johnson and Secret, 1995). Interestingly, as juveniles obtain a greater range of constitutional rights, they become more immune to the influence of *parens patriae*. Quite simply, juvenile judges are gradually

BOX 1.1   ATTORNEYS FOR KIDS?

The Case of a Call for Justice in Juvenile Courtrooms

Few experts believed that it would ever come to this. Thousands of juvenile defendants throughout juvenile courts in the United States are increasingly in need of legal counsel. Juvenile court judges are meting out increasingly severe punishments in response to escalating juvenile violence. The get-tough movement has finally made it to juvenile court.

According to a *Call for Justice* report, juvenile defendants in all parts of the country regularly appear in juvenile courts, either without legal counsel or with overworked and underpaid counsel whose effectiveness is questionable. Experts say that the juvenile court is responding accordingly to the present get-tough philosophy by imposing tougher penalties on juveniles for their offending. Although most juvenile courts are empowered to provide juveniles with counsel if these juveniles and their families are indigent, thousands of juveniles appear each year without counsel. Thus, their freedom is jeopardized to a great degree by the simple absence of counsel where counsel ought to be provided.

The *Call for Justice* report was funded by the Office of Juvenile Justice and Delinquency Prevention in 1992. It was prepared by the American Bar Association and two advocacy organizations, the Youth Law Center and the Juvenile Law Center in Philadelphia. Robert Schwartz, principal investigator with the Juvenile Law Center, said that the "next few years will be telling. Youth face the prospect of much longer sentences, mandatory minimum sentences, and time in adult jails or prisons...the need for access to quality defense attorneys for juveniles has never been greater." Other experts agree with Schwartz.

The facts are that in many cases, juvenile defense lawyers work at least 500 cases at a time. In many cases, children in juvenile court met their counsels when they sat down at the counsel table during detention hearings. The strain of defending so many youths at once is such that most lawyers stay around for less than two years. Thus, most lawyers who represent juvenile clients are inexperienced. There are serious gaps in the training of juvenile counsel, say various reports. About half of all public defender offices lack the money or resources to send even new lawyers to training programs so that they can master the unique problems that emerge in juvenile court proceedings.

Should attorneys be required in *all* juvenile court proceedings? What are the implications of the greater formalization of juvenile courts? Should there be one court handling both adult and juvenile cases?

Source: Associated Press, "Report: Children Need Legal Representation," *Minot (ND) Daily News,* January 1, 1996:A5.

losing much of their former, almost absolute, autonomy over juveniles and their life chances.

Another factor is the gradual transformation of the role of prosecutors in juvenile courts. As prosecutors become more involved in pursuing cases against juvenile defendants, the entire juvenile justice process is perceived by some experts as weakening the delinquency prevention role of juvenile courts. Thus, more aggressive prosecution of juvenile cases is perceived as moving away from delinquency prevention for the purpose of deterring youths from future adult criminality. The intentions of prosecutors in most cases are to ensure that youths are entitled to due process, but the social costs may be to label these youths in ways that will propel them toward adult criminality rather than away from it (Ellsworth, Kinsella, and Massin, 1992).

JUVENILE AND CRIMINAL COURTS: SOME PRELIMINARY DISTINCTIONS

Some of the major differences between juvenile and criminal courts are indicated below. These generalizations are more or less valid in most jurisdictions in the United States.

1. *Juvenile courts are civil proceedings exclusively designed for juveniles, whereas criminal courts are proceedings designed to try adults charged with crimes.* In criminal courts, adults are targeted for criminal court actions, although some juveniles may be tried as adults in these same courts. The civil–criminal distinction is important because a civil adjudication of a case does not result in a criminal record. In criminal courts, either a judge or jury finds a defendant guilty or not guilty. In the case of guilty verdicts, offenders are convicted and acquire criminal records. These **convictions** follow adult offenders for the rest of their lives. However, when juveniles are tried in juvenile courts, their juvenile court adjudications are sealed or expunged and forgotten once they become adults.

2. *Juvenile proceedings are informal, whereas criminal proceedings are formal. Attempts are made in many juvenile courts to avoid the formal trappings that characterize criminal proceedings.* Juvenile judges frequently address juveniles directly and casually. Formal criminal procedures are not followed relating to the admissibility of evidence or testimony, and hearsay from various witnesses is considered together with hard factual information and evidence.

3. *In 80 percent of all states, juveniles are not entitled to a trial by jury unless the juvenile court judge approves. In all criminal proceedings, defendants are entitled to a trial by jury if these desire one, and if the crime or crimes they are accused of committing carry incarcerative penalties of up to six or more months.* Judicial approval of a jury trial for juveniles in most jurisdictions is one of the remaining legacies of the parens patriae doctrine in contemporary

juvenile courts. At least 11 states have legislative mandated jury trials for juveniles in juvenile courts if they are charged with certain offenses and if they request such jury trials (Maguire and Pastore, 1996).

4. *Juvenile court and criminal court proceedings are adversarial.* Juveniles may or may not wish to retain or be represented by counsel (*In re Gault*, 1967). In almost every case, juvenile court prosecutors allege various infractions or law violations against juveniles, and these charges may be rebutted by juveniles or others. If juveniles are represented by counsel, these defense attorneys are permitted to offer a defense for the charges alleged. Criminal courts are obligated to provide counsel for anyone charged with a crime if defendants cannot afford to retain their own counsel (*Argersinger v. Hamlin*, 1972). Virtually every state currently has provisions for furnishing defense attorneys to indigent juveniles who must appear in juvenile court.

5. *Criminal courts are **courts of record**, whereas transcripts of most juvenile proceedings are made only if the judge decides.* **Court reporters** record all testimony presented in most criminal court action. All state criminal trial courts are courts of record, where either a tape-recorded transcript of proceedings is maintained or a written record is kept. Thus, if appeals by either the defense or prosecution are brought before appellate courts later, these transcripts of proceedings may be presented by either side as proof of errors committed by the judge or other violations of one's due process rights. Original convictions may be reversed or they may be allowed to stand, depending on whatever the records disclose about the propriety of the proceedings. In juvenile courts, recorded transcriptions of proceedings are not required by law in most jurisdictions (*In re Gault*, 1967). However, some juvenile court judges may have the resources and/or interest to provide for such transcriptions, particularly if serious offenses against certain juveniles have been alleged (Feld, 1988c; Schwartz, 1992).

6. *The **standard of proof** used for determining one's guilt in criminal proceedings is **beyond a reasonable doubt**. This same standard is applicable in juvenile courts where violations of criminal laws are alleged and incarceration in a juvenile facility is a possible punishment. However, the less rigorous civil standard of **preponderance of the evidence** is used in most other juvenile court matters (In re Gault, 1967).*

7. *The range of penalties juvenile court judges may impose is limited, whereas in most criminal courts, the range of penalties may include either life-without-parole sentences or the death penalty. The jurisdiction of juvenile court judges over youthful offenders usually ends whenever these juveniles reach adulthood.* Under certain circumstances (e.g., cases of mentally ill or mentally retarded juvenile offenders), juvenile court judges may retain their jurisdiction over older offenders for longer periods, although this is relatively rare. In California, juveniles may be sent to the California Youth Authority, a secure facility for youthful offenders, until they reach the age of 25 (Camp and Camp, 1995c).

This brief comparison shows that criminal court actions are more serious and have more significant long-term consequences for offenders than do juvenile court proceedings. It is possible, for instance, for a juvenile to be adjudicated delinquent 10 times or more by the same juvenile court judge within a relatively short time period. These delinquency adjudications are not necessarily additive in the sense that five or more of them will

---

BOX 1.2 MORE JUVENILES TO BE TRIED AS ADULTS

The Cases of Catarino "Ray" Martinez and Juan Guerrero

It happened in Fargo, North Dakota. A woman, Cherryl Tendeland, was shot in the head while sitting in an automobile driven by her husband and another friend. The Tendelands were returning to their home following an evening religious service.

At least four youths were charged with the November 15, 1995 shooting. Earlier, on December 13, 1995, Michael Paul Charbonneau, 17, was charged in adult court with murder and being an accomplice to an attempted robbery. A friend, Barry Garcia, 17, the alleged triggerman, was charged on December 11, 1995 with murder, aggravated assault, and attempted robbery. On December 20, 1995, two other youths, Catarino "Ray" Martinez, 17, and Juan Guerrero, 16, both of Moorhead, Minnesota, faced the same charges stemming from the November 15 incident.

Prosecutors alleged that Garcia and Charbonneau got out of a car driven by Martinez, intending to rob the Tendelands. Instead, Garcia fired a shotgun blast through the window of the Tendeland car, striking and killing Cherryl Tendeland instantly. Guerrero and Martinez were both charged with criminal street gang activity. They were transferred to a state mental hospital to undergo psychological tests. These youths are in the early wave of youths made vulnerable to a new state law mandating transfers of youths to criminal court if they have committed serious offenses, such as murder or attempted murder or robbery. Ultimately, Garcia was convicted of murder and given a life-without-parole sentence. Other participants were also convicted and given lighter prison terms.

What should be the earliest age at which a youth should be transferred to criminal court? Does transferring dangerous juvenile offenders to criminal court really mean more severe punishment for them? To what extent should the juvenile court preserve its jurisdiction over such youths, despite the heinous nature of their offending? Are transfers and waivers effective deterrents to juvenile delinquency?

Source: Adapted from Associated Press, "Heading to Adult Court," *Minot (ND) Daily News,* December 21, 1995:B1.

result in commitment to a state industrial school or group home. However, certain juveniles who appear before judges with frequency are likely to sustain harsher punishments within the relatively lenient range of juvenile court sanctions. Many juveniles who are recidivists and continue to commit offenses are of the petty variety. They tend to engage in petty theft, vandalism, or occasional drug use.

In the case of adult recidivists, legislative action in most jurisdictions has mandated that these offenders be subject to **habitual offender statutes**, where sufficient subsequent convictions will lead to one's being classified as an **habitual offender**. If adults are convicted of violating habitual offender statutes (e.g., they are convicted of three or more serious crimes at different points in time), they are subject to a mandatory penalty of life imprisonment (California Little Hoover Commission, 1994; Flango, 1994b; Florida Office of the Auditor General, 1994; Virginia Commission on Youth, 1994b). But because of severe prison overcrowding, these habitual offender statutes are infrequently invoked, since incarcerating all habitual offenders would greatly aggravate the present prison overcrowding problem. In any case, the habitual offender penalty exists and can be imposed as a punishment for adult recidivists.

Juveniles are not immune from habitual offender laws. In jurisdictions such as Colorado, there are habitual offender laws written especially for juveniles. For instance, Colorado has a *Serious Habitual Offender/Directed Intervention* (SHO-DI) Program, which seeks to identify a very small percentage of juveniles who commit a disproportionate amount of serious, repeat offenses (Colorado Springs Police Department, 1988). System alerts are issued whenever an exceptional juvenile offender comes into contact with police. In these cases, habitual serious juveniles are given priority in case filing, prosecution, disposition, and treatment. In many cases, their dispositions are harsher and of longer durations than those of other juvenile offenders who are neither recidivists nor serious or violent.

The juvenile court continues to be guided by a strong rehabilitative orientation in most jurisdictions, whereas criminal courts are seemingly adopting more punitive sanctions for adult offenders. Although many critics see juvenile courts moving in a similar punitive or just-deserts direction in the treatment and adjudication of juveniles, many youths are still directed toward treatment-oriented *punishments* rather than incarcerated in secure juvenile facilities. Of course, overcrowding exists in juvenile facilities to almost the same extent as it exists for most prisons and jails in the United States. Thus it is in the best interests of the state to provide alternatives to incarceration for both adult and juvenile offenders (Ellsworth, Kinsella, and Massin, 1992). These alternatives are not necessarily the right alternatives, but they are expedient and practical ones under the present circumstances.

However, juvenile courts have acquired several features of criminal courts. In many juvenile court jurisdictions, juveniles may be offered plea bargains from prosecutors in exchange for some type of leniency. Interestingly, the use of plea bargaining in juvenile courts is for essentially the same purpose as in criminal courts. Case processing is facilitated through plea bargaining. Cases can be concluded without lengthy or protracted juvenile court proceedings. The system moves more quickly if charges against juveniles are not contested (Sanborn, 1993). Sanborn suggests another motive behind more extensive use of juvenile plea bargaining. In an increasing number of jurisdictions, plea bargaining is used by juvenile court prosecutors as a means of building up a juvenile's case file and record in order to justify transferring the juvenile to criminal court later, if new offenses are committed (Sanborn, 1993).

ALTERNATIVE PHILOSOPHIES FOR MANAGING JUVENILE OFFENDERS

As the different components of the juvenile justice process are presented in subsequent chapters, it will become apparent that this process has been shaped at various times by different philosophies about how juveniles should be treated and managed. In some respects, the contrasting philosophies about how juveniles should be treated tend to parallel several of the philosophies applicable to the management and treatment of adult offenders. These include (1) the medical model, (2) the rehabilitation model, (3) the community reintegration model, (4) the prevention/control model, (5) the just-deserts model, (6) the reality therapy model, and (7) the justice model.

The Medical Model

The **medical model** assumes that juvenile delinquency is a disease subject to treatment. It is otherwise known as the *treatment model*. The treatment or medical model seeks to locate the cause of the disease (delinquency) and then prescribe medication (a treatment program) as a cure. According to this model, incarcerating offenders is ineffective as a means of preventing future criminal behaviors.

The medical model or treatment model was officially recognized in 1870 by the Declaration of Principles promulgated by the National Prison Association (later known as the American Correctional Association) (McAnany, Thomson, and Fogel, 1984). At the time these principles were officially recognized, criminal justice authorities believed that criminals suffered illnesses brought on by malnutrition and psychological maladies.

Controlled diets and psychiatric treatments were used extensively as "medicine" to effect cures of criminal behaviors.

The medical model has much broader application than that associated with disease identification and an appropriate medical prescription. The "treatment" may be individual or group therapy and unrelated to medicine entirely. For instance, advocates of the medical model promote group encounters, family therapy, or individual therapy as "cures" for antisocial or delinquent behavior (Lombardo and DiGiorgio-Miller, 1988). However, purely medical remedies may be in order for adolescent sex offenders. Psychiatric strategies such as Jungian therapy are also prescribed in selected instances involving the treatment of female adolescent prostitutes (Gerdes, Gourley, and Cash, 1995).

The Rehabilitation Model

The most common model about how juvenile offenders ought to be managed is the **rehabilitation model**. Like the medical model, the rehabilitation model underscores the ineffectiveness of secure confinement for juvenile offenders. Alternatively, the rehabilitation model stresses experiences that enable youths to overcome various social and psychological handicaps that have placed them in their delinquent status. These experiences or strategies may be educational or social remedies (Krisberg et al., 1993). Ideally, it would be most favorable to isolate such problem children in their early years. Such at-risk youths could be targeted for early intervention programs that would assist them in becoming integrated into school activities and social groups (Lattimore, Visher, and Linster, 1995). In a sense, the rehabilitation model incorporates various aspects of the treatment or medical model, since the treatments ordinarily prescribed in the context of the medical model are analogous to various rehabilitative experiences (Gerdes, Gourley, and Cash, 1995).

Presently there is an argument about whether juveniles have the right to be rehabilitated. Often secure facilities for juveniles are accused of merely warehousing them rather than treating them effectively for any social or emotional problems they may have (Alexander, 1995). Unfortunately, the effectiveness of juvenile rehabilitation programs often depends on the funding allocated. Currently, there are inadequate funds in many jurisdictions for implementing effective rehabilitation programs for youths (Alexander, 1995).

The Community Reintegration Model

Some investigators believe that youths who commit delinquent acts have become alienated from their communities or estranged from society.

Therefore, it is important to assist these youths to become reintegrated into their communities. Institutionalization is not the answer. Rather, some alternative to incarceration that will keep youths in their communities will be of greater value in helping them to overcome their delinquent propensities. The **community reintegration model** is designed to provide experiences for selected delinquent youths while they remain within their communities and participate in everyday events such as attending school and other activities (Krisberg et al., 1993). Temporary placement in residential treatment centers within communities preserves the general concept of community reintegration (Gerdes, Gourley, and Cash, 1995). One's youthfulness and immaturity are factors that often limit one's reasoning ability in deciding whether to be law-abiding or delinquent. Reintegrative programs, therefore, are designed to enable certain youths to acquire maturity over time and exhibit moral growth. Some experts favor reintegrative programs for this reason (Geiger, 1996).

The Prevention/Control Model

The **prevention/control model** attempts to deal with or repress delinquency before juveniles have an opportunity to commit delinquent acts or to advance to more serious offenses (Packer, 1968). Using intervention strategies for youths at risk in their early years has been suggested as a delinquency prevention action (Greenwood, 1986b; Hurley, 1985). For juveniles who have already been adjudicated as delinquent, wilderness experiences and other outdoor educational programs are means whereby they may be subject to limited control by others. Under the close supervision of adults in a nonthreatening atmosphere, many youths may acquire skills to cope with their various problems and develop better self-concepts (Greenwood, 1986d). Residential placement programs introduce an element of control as well. For instance, Goodstein and Sontheimer (1987) report the variable effectiveness of 10 residential institutions for juveniles in a Pennsylvania jurisdiction. Recidivism appeared to depend on the length of placement in such institutions. Over time, the propensity to engage in delinquent conduct decreases substantially for most juveniles. Thus, in this instance, such residential placements were deemed more or less useful depending on a youth's length of stay.

The Just-Deserts Model

In recent years, juvenile justice critics have recommended that more stringent means be employed for dealing with juvenile offenders (Springer, 1987). The **just-deserts model** stresses offender accountability, regardless of the offense committed (Baron and Hartnagel, 1996). Rehabilitation and treatment are not rejected outright, but these are secondary to punishment commensurate with offense seriousness. This is particularly true for those juveniles who have committed capital murder, although not everyone agrees that juvenile murderers should be barred from rehabilitation programs (Reinharz, 1996). Increasingly, juvenile courts and the juvenile justice process generally are subjecting juvenile offenders to more stringent treatments or corrective measures, reflecting the just-deserts philosophy (Feld, 1987c; McDermott and Laub, 1987). Juvenile court judge options are continuing to be geared toward imposing probation as a sentence, but with conditions as punishments. These conditions include community service work, victim restitution, participation in individual or group therapy, drug or alcohol treatment programs, or some other constructive activity. Those youths who are subjected to such experiences appear to be less inclined toward recidivism and more favorably affected than those youths who are extended considerable leniency by the system (Harris, 1988; Rossum, Koller, and Manfredi, 1987).

The Reality Therapy Model

The **reality therapy model** is seemingly the juvenile equivalent to *shock probation* sometimes administered to adults as a sentence (Vito, 1984). Shock probation is an incarcerative sentence imposed by the judge which involves a short stay in a jail or prison for up to 130 days. If offenders have behaved well during that period, they are brought back to court for resentencing. Judges will often sentence them to probation for the remainder of their statutory sentence. The shock of confinement, in some instances, functions as a cure for further criminal behavior. In short, these offenders have experienced what it is like to be confined. In a sense, they are shocked into conforming to the law to avoid further incarceration.

For juveniles, similar experiences, not necessarily incarcerative ones, are proposed in various programs (Fuller and Norton, 1993). For example, studies of juvenile offenders in Kansas and Maryland have involved youths heavily in visits to prisons, discussions with incarcerated offenders, and other reality experiences (Locke et al., 1986; Mitchell and Williams, 1986). Exposing these youths to the realities of prison life seemed helpful in decreasing recidivism rates among study participants. Of course, some programs are designed to confine youths temporarily in secure juvenile facilities to achieve the same effect (Greenwood, 1986b).

The Justice Model

A leading proponent of the **justice model** is David Fogel (Fogel and Hudson, 1981). The justice model advocates fair and reasonable treatment of those convicted of crimes or adjudicated as delinquent. It does not reject rehabilitation, but rather, it conceives rehabilitation to be functional to the extent that one's participation in rehabilitative programs is voluntary. With an aim toward fairness in treatment, the justice model must necessarily embrace due process, which emphasizes safeguards extended to juveniles at all stages of their processing by the juvenile justice system (Feld, 1993a–c).

Application of the justice model to juveniles is inconsistent. Although juveniles have achieved several significant constitutional rights as an important part of due process, they have not as yet been extended the full range of rights, guarantees, and protections of the constitution normally available to adults in criminal courts. The doctrine of *parens patriae* continues to influence what happens to youths as they face adjudicatory proceedings on one or more charges. *Parens patriae* and due process are, to a degree, incompatible. As Shireman notes, "It is not clear precisely how we are to move in the future in efforts to achieve essential and evident fairness and still retain the 'idealistic prospect' of an intimate, informal protective proceeding. There is much yet to be done" (Fogel and Hudson, 1981:148).

Each of these philosophies of juvenile treatment has key priorities. Increasingly important in the management of juvenile offenders is their **acceptance of responsibility** for offenses they commit. It is true that juveniles are being treated more like adults each year, as they are extended greater constitutional rights. However, the *parens patriae* doctrine is still quite influential in affecting their life chances in juvenile courts. In subsequent chapters it will be apparent that each model has exerted some impact on intervention programs and other strategies that are employed throughout the juvenile justice process as means of dealing with youthful offender behaviors. Of those presented above, the justice, just deserts, and reality therapy models seem most frequently used in contemporary juvenile programs. No single theme is dominant, however, as many programs continue to provide a wide variety of therapy, group and individual counseling, and rehabilitation for many of the juveniles who enter the juvenile justice system.

Too Many Juvenile Rights?

Is there such a thing as too many rights for juveniles? As juveniles acquire more rights through local juvenile court decision making, legislative action, and U.S. Supreme Court statements, they also acquire additional responsibilities. Some experts believe that their youthfulness and immaturity make it difficult for many juveniles to bear this additional burden that society and lawmakers provide in the interest of due process.

BOX 1.3 PRETEEN VIOLENCE

The Case of the 11-Year-Old Rapists

Scene 1: It happened in Dallas, Texas. A 40-year-old autistic woman who had the mental capacity of an 8-year-old had been living with her mother in a Dallas apartment until late 1995, when her mother died. A cousin of the woman and his girlfriend moved in with her shortly after her mother's death. The girlfriend had two sons, ages 11 and 12.

After a few months had passed, the autistic woman appeared to have bruises about her face and arms. It was apparent that she was being hurt in some way, although her cousin was uncertain as to the causes. Subsequently, it was learned that the two boys had systematically sexually assaulted the woman, raped her repeatedly on numerous occasions, beat her with a toilet plunger and other weapons, and had even invited some of their boyfriends over to join in what they called "parties." These "beating parties" became routine for several boys, including the girlfriend's sons. The boys ordered the woman to remove her clothes, and when she refused, they would punch her in the face and beat her with belts and the wooden handle of a toilet plunger. At least one of the youths then sexually assaulted the woman. Investigating officers, including Sgt. Ross Salvarino, said "At their age, I don't know how it could enter their minds, something as inhuman and cruel as this."

How should such young boys be punished? What rehabilitative efforts might prove useful in dealing with such a problem? What are the responsibilities of the cousin and girlfriend for the safety of the autistic woman?

Scene 2: The place is San Diego, California. Picture an 11-year-old boy in school, suddenly complaining about not feeling well to school nurses. The mother is called and arrives to pick up her ailing son. At home, the boy retires to his room where he proceeds to shave his head, grab his father's .22 caliber rifle, put on a ski mask, and don a monk's robe. Next, the boy goes on a shooting spree, shooting people at random with the rifle, wounding several. Lawrence Misa, a pedestrian, was shot in the hand when he attempted to get the rifle away from the 11-year-old. Wounded in the melee was a security guard. The boy was subsequently subdued and held in juvenile detention to await further investigation.

What kinds of penalties should be imposed on 11-year-olds for such erratic behavior? How can such behavior be explained? Who is to blame for this behavior? How responsible are the parents for the behaviors of their children?

Sources: Adapted from Associated Press, "Police: Boys Pummeled, Raped Woman during Beating 'Parties,'" *Minot (ND) Daily News*, February 29, 1996:A2; Associated Press, "Eleven-Year-Old Boy Dons Robe, Shaves Head before Shooting Spree," *Minot (ND) Daily News*, February 29, 1996:A2.

Accompanying these rights is a greater need for attorney involvement and representation in juvenile matters. In the 1950s, the presence of defense attorneys in juvenile courts was peculiar. In the 1990s, the presence of attorneys in juvenile courts is expected and commonplace. Like a double-edged sword, this has both good and bad implications. Attorney representation means that one's full range of rights will be observed by all parties, including intake officers, juvenile court prosecutors, and judges. Unequal or disparate decision making according to one's race or ethnicity or gender is minimized by a defense attorney's presence. However, advocates of *parens patriae* believe that attorneys tend to formalize juvenile proceedings, and that such formalization has certain adverse consequences for certain juveniles.

Formality means rigid application of rules. Rigid rule application means less flexibility on the part of all court actors relating to a juvenile's case. Thus judges may sometimes impose harsher dispositions and conditions on juveniles adjudicated delinquent because defense attorneys are there to monitor their conduct. If defense attorneys were not present, the judges might tend to be more lenient with certain juvenile offenders. Therefore, juveniles might receive harsher treatment as the result of greater defense attorney involvement, simply because the setting is more formalized and formal rules must be followed precisely. Under more relaxed, nonadversarial proceedings where juvenile court judges are left to their own subjective judgments, they might be inclined to be more lenient with adjudicated youths. This is a great dilemma confronting juvenile court experts. How can the individuality of juvenile court proceedings be preserved while extending juveniles due process rights? The very idea of individualizing juvenile justice according to the principle of *parens patriae* is inherently discriminatory. Yet many proponents of *parens patriae* contend that such individualized judicial decision making and discretion are essential to preserving the value of the juvenile court as a rehabilitative tool. Due process proponents reject individualized decision making by judges as discriminatory, inherently wrong, and corrected only by application of the sound legal principle of due process.

Most experts believe that juveniles ought to be treated fairly and equally. Due process is believed to be the legal means whereby juveniles can expect such fair treatment under the law. But one's discretion is influenced by the presence or absence of formality. In later chapters we will see how the juvenile courtroom has become increasingly formalized. Indeed, we will see how the entire juvenile justice process has become increasingly formal, resembling in some cases criminal proceedings for adults (Feld, 1993a).

KEY TERMS

Acceptance of responsibility

Banishment

Beyond a reasonable doubt

Bridewell Workhouse

Chancellors

Chancery courts

Children's tribunals

Childsavers

Childsaving movement

Common law

Community reintegration model

Convictions

Court of record

Court reporters

Courts of equity

Get-tough movement

Habitual offender

Habitual offender statutes

Hospital of Saint Michael

Houses of Refuge

Illinois Juvenile Court Act

Indentured servants

Indentured servant system

Infants

Just-deserts model

Justice model

Juvenile courts

Juvenile delinquents

Juvenile justice system

Juvenile offenders

Juveniles

Medical model

New York House of Refuge

Parens patriae

Philadelphia Society for Alleviating the Miseries of the Public Prisons

Poor Laws

Prevention/control model

Reality therapy model

Reeve

Reform schools

Rehabilitation model

Shire

Shock probation

Solitary confinement

Standard of proof

Status offenders

Treatment model

Walnut Street Jail

Workhouses

QUESTIONS FOR REVIEW

1. What is *parens patriae*? How is this doctrine related to juvenile rehabilitation and treatment? What evidence is there that this doctrine continues to be influential in juvenile courts today?

2. What is the *juvenile justice system*? What are its various components? Why do some critics believe that it should be called a process rather than a system? Explain.

3. What are *houses of refuge*? When were they first established in the United States? What do houses of refuge have to do with the childsaver movement?

4. What were some of the common punishments administered to both adult and juvenile offenders during colonial times? What are Poor Laws? What are their functions?

5. Who were *indentured servants*? How were juveniles used originally with the indentured servant concept?

6. What is the significance for juveniles of the Walnut Street Jail in Philadelphia, Pennsylvania? Discuss.

7. Briefly identify several important developments during the nineteenth century that led to the eventual establishment of juvenile courts.

8. What is *juvenile delinquency*? How are juveniles defined? What kinds of cases are likely to come before juvenile court judges? Are these cases always connected with delinquency? Explain.

9. What is a *status offender*? How do status offenders differ from delinquent offenders?

10. How does acquiring greater constitutional rights for juveniles conflict with the doctrine of *parens patriae*?

SUGGESTED READINGS

Angenent, Huub and Anton de Man. *Background Factors of Juvenile Delinquency*. New York: Peter Lang, 1996.

Klein, Malcolm W. *The American Street Gang: Its Nature, Prevalence, and Control*. New York: Oxford University Press, 1995.

Leonard, Kimberly Kempf, Carl E. Pope, and William H. Feyerherm (eds.). *Minorities in Juvenile Justice*. Thousand Oaks, CA: Sage, 1995.

Spergel, Irving A. *The Youth Gang Problem: A Community Approach*. New York: Oxford University Press, 1995.

Tedisco, James N. and Michele A. Paludi. *Missing Children: A Psychological Approach to Understanding the Causes and Consequences of Stranger and Non-stranger Abduction of Children*. Albany, NY: State University of New York Press, 1996.

CHAPTER 2

MEASURING DELINQUENCY:
TYPES OF OFFENDERS AND TRENDS

INTRODUCTION

The car approached the couple walking down the street. It was 10:30 P.M. on a cool summer evening in Columbia, South Carolina. As the couple neared a streetcorner they stopped and conversed, and the car accelerated toward them. Two gun barrels protruded from the open car windows. As the car passed the couple, gunfire erupted. The fusillade cut down the couple where they stood and they died instantly from numerous bullet wounds. The car sped out of sight. An eyewitness wrote down the car's license number and called police. A subsequent investigation led to the arrest of three teenage girls, members of a street gang known as Los Lobos (the wolves). Eventually, two girls confessed to the murders and guns were confiscated, linking them to the double murder. The ages of the girls—13 and 15. The third girl, 17, drove the car on the night of the shooting. All three girls were transferred to the jurisdiction of a criminal court, where they would be prosecuted as adults. Brenda and Janice, the 13- and 15-year-olds, were convicted of murder and sentenced to life without parole. The third girl, Donna, was given 30 years in exchange for her testimony against Brenda and Janice.

An 8-year-old boy, Donald, was taken into custody by police after setting fire to a neighbor's barn. The barn and some livestock were destroyed, causing about $30,000 in damages. The boy was released to his parents. When Donald was 11, he struck another student with a brick on the playground at school. The victim required 20 stitches and was out of school for a week. Donald was released to his parents and placed on probation by the school authorities. Between Donald's twelfth and thirteenth years, he was chronically truant, missing two or three school days a week, without explanation or parent/teacher approval. Again, he was placed on probation by school authorities, suspended for a period of time, and given other verbal reprimands. Over the years, Donald's behavior became increasingly serious. Donald was involved in school theft, burglaries of homes in his neighborhood, and assaults against various neighbors and other students at school. He had been in juvenile court a dozen times by the time he reached age 18. When Donald was 19, he and two other youths robbed a liquor store. Donald shot the liquor store manager in the head, killing him. Donald was charged with murder, convicted, and sentenced to death. He was executed in Florida in 1996.

Flo wanted to fit in. She was not particularly attractive and was unpopular in school. Nobody asked her to school functions and she had no particular extracurricular interests. She became increasingly rebellious at home, arguing frequently with her mother and father. They insisted that she see a counselor at school, and eventually, she had a complete psychiatric examination. The psychiatrist could only say that she was manic-depressive, and he prescribed some medication for her mood swings. One night her parents couldn't find her. She had told them that she was going to a movie downtown and would be back later. When she didn't return, her parents became worried. The next day when she still didn't return home, the parents notified police. A search was conducted and some schoolmates were interviewed. No one knew where she was. However, a Trailways Bus Company clerk remembered her boarding a bus for Chicago, about 100 miles away from her home in Indiana. At the time of her disappearance, Flo was 13 years old. By the time Flo was 20, she had been a prostitute and drug addict for six years, living on New York streets. In Chicago, she was a child adrift, without any means of supporting herself. A runaway with no desire to return to her home, Flo met a man who dealt in drugs and prostitution. She worked for him for two years, eventually moving to New York, where she continued in the same business. One morning, New York police found her body in an alleyway. She had overdosed on heroin. No one knew who she was or where she was from. She was buried in a pauper's grave as "Jane Doe." Her parents never knew of her death. One consolation known only to Flo was that she had numerous sexual encounters with anonymous men who showered her with favors and temporary attention and affection over the years.

Are Brenda, Janice, Donna, Donald, and Flo exceptions? Are children destined to commit particular crimes? Do youths gradually escalate from less serious to more serious offenses? What interventions may have led to different outcomes in each of the three scenarios above? Did these cases have to happen?

Youths aged 13 to 18 make up about 10 percent of the U.S. population. However, members of this same age group account for 20 percent of all arrests annually (Famighetti, 1996; Maguire and Pastore, 1996). Such an overrepresentation of juveniles among those arrested for crimes in the United States has attracted the attention and interest of many organizations and agencies. Is there currently a crime wave of youthful offenders? Is juvenile violence increasing? Is there anything we can do about it?

In this chapter we examine delinquency and how it is defined, both officially and unofficially. Each jurisdiction has different policies that pertain to the treatment and punishment of juvenile offenders. Numerous programs have been designed to manage the juvenile offender population and are in various stages of implementation throughout the United States today. No single program seems to have universal appeal. Widely different juvenile audiences are targeted by each of these programs, and the successfulness of each is measured according to several types of standards. Because some of these programs are preventive in nature and involve interventions with children designated at risk in their early years, it is often impossible to calculate their long-term value and effectiveness (U.S. General Accounting Office, 1996).

For many years the juvenile justice system has included within its jurisdiction youths who represent a wide variety of offense categories. Not all of these categories involve crimes. Thus an important distinction is made between youthful offenders who engage in serious offenses and those who are involved in less serious activities known as status offenses. Recently, efforts have been undertaken in different jurisdictions to separate more serious offenders from less serious ones, and the deinstitutionalization of status offenses (DSO) or removal of certain types of less serious juveniles from the authority of the juvenile court has occurred. This process is described.

We also examine primary sources of information about juvenile offenders, including *Uniform Crime Reports* and the *National Crime Victimization Survey*. These official sources of information are flawed in various respects. However, they do portray offense trends in different jurisdictions. Although the accuracy of this information is suspect, it nevertheless is used by agencies and organizations as a measure or gauge of program effectiveness. The strengths and weaknesses of these sources are described, together with certain criticisms that each has received. In addition to these official sources, unofficial information about juvenile offenses is provided by juveniles themselves in the form of self-reports. Juveniles are questioned about their offending activities, and on the basis of anonymous responses, comparisons of these self-report data are made against that provided by official sources. However, self-reports may not be perfectly accurate indicators of delinquent activity, either. We examine the value of such self-report information.

In the final portion of this chapter we discuss the general questions of whether juveniles who are adjudicated for minor offenses progress eventually to more serious offense activity. Does career escalation occur among juvenile offenders? Are youths committing more violent acts over successive years? Also, are there major differences in the nature of juvenile offending behavior that might be attributable to gender? (Heimer, 1996) These and similar questions are highlighted.

DELINQUENCY: DEFINITIONS AND DISTINCTIONS

Juveniles

The jurisdiction of juvenile courts depends on the established legislative definitions of juveniles among the various states. The federal government has no juvenile court. Rather, federal cases involving juveniles infrequently are heard in federal district courts, but adjudicated juveniles are housed in state or local facilities if the sentences involve incarceration. Ordinarily, upper and lower age limits are prescribed. However, these age limits are far from uniform among jurisdictions. As we saw in Chapter 1, common law has been utilized by some jurisdictions to set the minimum age of juveniles at 7, although no state is obligated to recognize the common law as it pertains to youths. In fact, some states have no lower age limits that would otherwise function to limit juvenile court jurisdiction. Table 2.1 shows upper age limits for most U.S. jurisdictions. Those states with the lowest maximum age for juvenile court jurisdiction include Connecticut, New York, and North Carolina. In these states, the lowest maximum age for juvenile court jurisdiction is 15. Those states having the lowest maximum age of 16 for juvenile court jurisdiction are Georgia, Illinois, Louisiana, Massachusetts, Michigan, Missouri, South Carolina, and Texas. All other states and the federal government use age 18 as the minimum age for criminal court jurisdiction (Butts, 1996a:64–87). Under the *Juvenile Justice and Delinquency Prevention Act of 1974, juveniles are persons who have not attained their eighteenth birthday* (18 U.S.C., Sec. 5031, 1997).

Juvenile offenders who are especially young (under age 7 in most jurisdictions) are often placed within the control of community agencies such as departments of human services or social welfare. These children frequently have little or no responsible parental supervision or control. In many cases, the parents themselves may have psychological problems or

TABLE 2.1

Age at Which Criminal Courts Gain Jurisdiction of Young Offenders

Age of offender when under criminal court jurisdiction (years)	States
16	Connecticut, New York, North Carolina
17	Georgia, Illinois, Louisiana, Massachusetts, Missouri, South Carolina, Texas
18	Alabama, Alaska, Arizona, Arkansas, California, Colorado, Delaware, District of Columbia, Florida, Hawaii, Idaho, Indiana, Iowa, Kansas, Kentucky, Maine, Maryland, Michigan, Minnesota, Mississippi, Montana, Nebraska, Nevada, New Hampshire, New Jersey, New Mexico, North Dakota, Ohio, Oklahoma, Oregon, Pennsylvania, Rhode Island, South Dakota, Tennessee, Utah, Vermont, Virginia, Washington, West Virginia, Wisconsin, Federal districts
19	Wyoming

Source: Butts et al., 1996. Data Source: Linda A. Szymanski, *Upper Age of Juvenile Court Jurisdiction Statutes Analysis*, Pittsburgh, PA: National Center for Juvenile Justice, March 1987.

suffer from alcohol or drug dependencies. Youths from such families may be abused and/or neglected and in need of supervision and other forms of care or treatment. Under common law in those states where common law applies, *it is presumed that persons under the age of 7 are incapable of formulating criminal intent.* Although this presumption may be rebutted, in most cases, it isn't. Thus, if a 6-year-old child kills someone, deliberately or accidentally, he or she will probably be *treated* rather than *punished.*

Juvenile Delinquency

Juvenile delinquency is defined by federal law as the violation of a law of the United States by a person prior to his eighteenth birthday, which would have been a crime if committed by an adult (18 U.S.C., Sec. 5031, 1997). A broader, legally applicable definition of *juvenile delinquency* is *a violation of any state or local law or ordinance by anyone who has not yet achieved the age of majority* (adapted from Black, 1990:428). Black (1990:428) refers to a juvenile delinquent as a **delinquent child**. The **age of majority** depends on the defining jurisdiction, as shown in Table 2.1.

The most liberal definition of juvenile delinquency is *whatever the juvenile court believes should be brought within its jurisdiction.* This definition vests juvenile court judges and other juvenile authorities with broad discretionary powers to define almost *any* juvenile conduct as delinquent conduct (Watkins, 1987). To illustrate the implications of such a definition for any juvenile, consider the following scenarios.

Scenario 1. A 13-year-old female juvenile has recently been apprehended and charged with murder. She is accused of being a serial killer who has allegedly murdered 12 elderly women in different parts of the community over a six-month period. These women lived alone and were dependent on others for various services. This female juvenile would run errands for these women, including trips to the store for food and medicines. She would use various rodent poisons mixed with different foods to kill her victims. The last woman she attempted to poison did not die but simply became ill. Diagnosed by doctors as having ingested poison, the woman reported the female juvenile as the only likely subject to have had an opportunity to poison her. The juvenile was questioned by police and eventually admitted her guilt and involvement in the murders of the other elderly women. The juvenile has been examined by psychiatrists and awaits adjudication by the juvenile court judge.

Scenario 2. A 14-year-old male juvenile has been reported to police several times by observant neighbors who claim that he wanders about the neighborhood daily unsupervised and without purpose. Investigations by authorities disclose that his parents are alcoholics, often in drunken stupors for much of the day, who exert little or no control over his behaviors. The youth is supposed to be attending school, but school records indicate unusually large numbers of absences. The youth has appeared in juvenile court on six different occasions, largely because of his lack of school attendance and loitering behavior. The juvenile court judge has formally ordered him to attend school during regular daytime hours, after repeated warnings to his parents to ensure his school attendance. He now faces the juvenile court judge and is charged with violating a court order.

Scenario 3. A 12-year-old female juvenile has been taken into custody by authorities on a charge of lewd conduct. Neighbors and others visiting her neighborhood have complained that she has been deliberately exhibiting herself in the nude through a front-room window near the sidewalk. The passersby who inform police of her exhibitionist behavior include several adults, some with younger children. Police investigate and observe her nude in the front-room window. They arrest her and take her to juvenile hall for processing. She now faces the juvenile court judge on lewd conduct charges.

These and a thousand other scenarios could be presented. Are all of these scenarios the same? No. Are all of these scenarios of equivalent seriousness? No. Can each of these scenarios result in an adjudication of *delinquency* by a juvenile court judge? Yes. Whether juveniles are a juvenile serial murderess, a juvenile exhibitionist, or a juvenile loiterer/truant, they may be lumped into one large category as delinquent. This fact has prompted many professionals and others to consider whether juvenile courts are sufficiently discriminatory about the cases brought before them. Some juvenile offending is more serious than other types of juvenile offending. Breaking windows or letting the air out of someone's automobile tires is less serious than armed robbery, rape, or murder. The variability in juvenile offense seriousness has caused many jurisdictions to channel less serious cases away from juvenile courts and toward various community agencies where the juveniles involved can receive assistance rather than punishment (Fuller and Norton, 1993).

Most U.S. jurisdictions restrict their definitions of juvenile delinquency to *any act committed by a juvenile which, if committed by an adult, would be considered a crime* (Rogers and Mays, 1987:566). This is our working definition and will apply in all subsequent chapters. However, we cannot ignore those jurisdictions where juveniles are charged with non-crimes or behaviors that are considered offenses and where they are defined as such strictly on the basis of their *status* as juveniles. **Status**

BOX 2.1 TEEN CRIME TRENDS

Crime Is Rising among Teens

Serious crime in the United States fell during 1995 for a fourth consecutive year since 1991. Experts believe that the end of the "crime wave" of the 1980s has occurred. For instance, the most significant declines are:

Homicide:	-8 percent
Rape:	-8 percent
Robbery:	-7 percent
Assault:	-3 percent
Burglary:	-5 percent
Car theft:	-6 percent

In the nine largest U.S. cities, crime fell substantially. For instance, in New York City, homicides declined by 25 percent, to 1170 in 1995, while Chicago boasted an 11 percent decline in homicides, to 824. The Clinton administration has cited the Crime Bill as a major causal factor here, according to unofficial sources. More police officers placed on city streets have a deterrent effect, according to Clinton administration officials. U.S. Attorney General Janet Reno has said: "We will continue to put more cops on the beat, get guns off the street, and put violent criminals behind bars."

Some experts, such as James Fox at Northeastern University in Boston, say that there are both good and bad trends in the 1995 crime statistics. For instance, Fox says that homicides committed by youths age 14 to 17 rose 22 percent during 1995, while homicides among adults declined by 18 percent for the same period. Professor Fox says that "the bad news is that we have 39 million kids under 10 years of age now. They'll be teenagers before you can say 'juvenile crime wave.' If current trends persist, there will likely be a bloodbath that will make 1995 look like the good old days." Other experts share his pessimism.

How reliable are crime statistics? Do we really know much about crimes that go unreported? What precautions might we suggest when interpreting crime trends?

Source: Adapted from Kevin V. Johnson, "Homicide, Rape, Robbery: The Numbers Are Fewer," *USA Today,* May 6, 1996:9A.

offenses are any acts committed by juveniles that would (1) bring the juveniles to the attention of juvenile courts and (2) not be crimes if committed by adults. Typical status offenses are running away from home, truancy, and curfew violations. Adults would not be arrested for running away from home, unexcused absence from school, or walking the streets after some curfew time for juveniles. However, if juveniles engage in these behaviors in particular cities, they may eventually be included within the broad *delinquency* category, together with more serious juvenile offenders who are charged with armed robbery, forcible rape, murder, aggravated assault, burglary, larceny, vehicular theft, or illicit drug sales.

STATUS OFFENDERS AND DELINQUENT OFFENDERS

Status offenders are of interest to both the juvenile justice system and the criminal justice system. While status offenses such as runaway behavior, truancy, or curfew violations are crimes, many experts believe that there are several adverse concomitants of status offenses. One result is the belief by some experts that status offenders progress to more serious types of offending over time. However, there is little empirical support for this view.

Runaways

By year end 1994, there were 201,459 **runaways** reported to police (Maguire and Pastore, 1996:404). This represents less than 1 percent of all offenses charged that year. Over half of these runaways are 15 to 17 years of age. *Runaways consist of those youths who leave their homes, without permission or their parents' knowledge, and who remain away from home for prolonged periods ranging from several days to several years.* Many runaways are eventually picked up by police in different jurisdictions and returned to their homes. Others return of their own free will and choice. Some runaways remain permanently missing, although they are probably a part of growing number of homeless youths roaming faraway city streets throughout the United States.

Runaway behavior is complex and difficult to explain, although researchers tend to agree that many runaways generally have serious mental health needs (Famularo et al., 1992). Many of these youths seek out others like them for dependency and emotional support. Some runaways regard others like them as role models and peers, and often, delinquency among them occurs and increases through such peer modeling (Benda and Whiteside, 1995; Lindstrom, 1996). Studies of runaways indicate that many boys and girls have psychological and/or familial adjustment problems and have been physically and sexually abused by their parents or close relatives (Famularo et al., 1992; Florida Governor's Juvenile Justice and Delinquency Prevention Advisory Committee, 1994). Evidence suggests

that many runaways engage in theft or prostitution to finance their independence away from home and are exploited (Flowers, 1994). Although all
runaways are not alike (Zimet et al., 1995), there have been attempts to profile them (Posner, 1992; Sharlin and Mor-Barak, 1992).

Depending on how authorities and parents react to children who have
been apprehended after running away, there may be positive or adverse
consequences (Washington State Task Force on Juvenile Issues, 1992).
Empathy for runaways and their problems is important for instilling positive feelings within them (Alaska Department of Health and Social Services
Division of Family and Youth Services, 1992). Various runaway shelters
have been established to offer runaways a nonthreatening residence and
social support system in various jurisdictions. The Covenant House, origi-
nating in New York City during the 1960s, provides various services to runaway youths (Ritter, 1987). Similar homes have been established in
Houston, Fort Lauderdale, Toronto, Canada, and Guatemala. These shelters
often locate particular services for runaways that will help meet their
needs. Many children accommodated by these shelters report that they
have been physically and sexually abused by family members (Janus, 1995;
Posner, 1994). Thus there is some coordination of these homes with various law enforcement agencies to investigate these allegations and assist
parents in making their homes safer for their children (Collins et al., 1993).

Truants and Curfew Violators

Other types of status offenders are truants and curfew and liquor law violators. **Truants** *are those who absent themselves from school without either
school or parental permission.* **Curfew violators** *are those youths who
remain on city streets after specified evening hours when they are prohibited from loitering or not being in the company of a parent or guardian.* By
year end 1994, there were 105,888 youths charged with curfew violation in
the United States (Maguire and Pastore, 1996:404). This is less than 1
percent of all offenses reported to police that year. Because of the fragmen-
tation of record keeping in the nation's school districts, figures about the
amount of truancy are either unreliable or unavailable, or both. Some
research shows that these offenders differ from runaways in that they are
more serious offenders (Alaska Department of Health and Social Services
Division of Family and Youth Services, 1992; Collins et al., 1993). Truants
and liquor law violators may be more inclined to become **chronic offenders**
and to engage in more serious, possibly criminal behaviors. Truancy and
violating curfew are regarded by some experts as indicative of undisci-
plined offenses. Analyses of self-reported information by juveniles in
other studies suggests that escalation to more serious juvenile offenses does

not necessarily occur. Rather, panels of boys studied over a lengthy time period revealed a pattern of stable or constant juvenile misbehaviors rather than a progression to more serious juvenile offenses (Posner, 1992; Sharlin and Mor-Barak, 1992).

Juvenile and Criminal Court Interest in Status Offenders

Regarding status offenders, juvenile courts are most interested in chronic or persistent offenders, such as those who habitually appear before juvenile court judges. Repeated juvenile court involvement may eventually be followed by adult criminality (Benda, 1987). Among many juvenile justice reformers, it is often assumed that status offenders will have low rates of recidivism. However, a study was conducted of 932 juveniles in Wisconsin

---

BOX 2.2 THE HIGH COST OF GRAFFITI

The Case of the Oahu Taggers

It happened in Honolulu, Hawaii. The main drag, H-1, is Oahu's major "interstate" highway. One of these major highways is called the Moanalua Freeway. Road signs are plentiful as one traverses these thoroughfares. But almost all of these signs are blemished in one way or another with graffiti. It seems that no state can escape it. Not even Hawaii.

The Hawaii State Department of Transportation has estimated that graffiti damage, even to a small sign, can cost $100 to repair or replace. A large, oversized sign can cost as much as $100,000. This is serious money. Highway experts say that during a one-month period, it cost an estimated $11,000 to reclean (read: "remove graffiti from") the Moanalua Freeway. But the costs don't stop there. Once a sign has been damaged by graffiti two or more times, it must be replaced. Replacement costs of highway signs are staggering. This is because the fluid needed to clean the graffiti strips the signs of their reflective coating, which makes them hard to see at night. Graffiti "taggers" with spray paint cans do much to obscure signs and make them unreadable. Especially at night, certain signs warn motorists of sharp curves or other road hazards. Thus graffiti contributes indirectly to fatal highway accidents.

What should police officers do to prevent or deter taggers from defacing road signs? What should the penalties be for defacing road signs? How should taggers be punished?

Source: Adapted from "Cost High for Graffiti on Road Signs," *Honolulu Observer,* August 4, 1996:A20.

---

correctional facilities during the period 1965–1967. Of these juveniles, 166 were status offenders. These youths were studied as long as they remained in the juvenile justice system, and they were also observed for a 10-year period as adults. About 33 percent of these youths were returned to training schools after their first releases, largely because they committed new delinquent acts. Furthermore, 38 percent were subsequent convicted as adults for serious felonies (Benda, 1987). Additional support for the Benda research has been reported by Greenwood (1986c) and Tonry and Morris (1986), in that a clear connection is believed to exist between juvenile criminal activity and adult criminal careers.

The chronicity of juvenile offending seems to be influenced by the amount of contact youths have with juvenile courts (Minnesota Criminal Justice Statistical Analysis Center, 1989). Greater contact with juvenile courts is believed by some experts to **stigmatize** youths and cause them either to be labeled or acquire **stigmas** as delinquents or deviants (Florida Governor's Juvenile Justice and Delinquency Prevention Advisory Committee, 1994). Therefore, diversion of certain types of juvenile offenders from the juvenile justice system has been advocated and recommended to minimize **stigmatization** (Fuller and Norton, 1993). However, not everyone agrees that diversion functions to reduce personal stigmatization or labeling. Despite the controversy concerning diverting youths away from the juvenile justice system for informal processing, diversion programs of various kinds have increased substantially in most jurisdictions during the 1980s and 1990s (Fuller and Norton, 1993).

One increasingly popular strategy is to remove certain types of offenses from the jurisdiction of juvenile court judges (Blackmore, Brown, and Krisberg, 1988). Because status offenses are less serious compared with juvenile delinquents who commit crimes, status offenders have been targeted by many state legislatures for removal from juvenile court jurisdiction. The removal of status offenses from the discretionary power of juvenile courts is a part of what is known as the **deinstitutionalization of status offenses** (DSO).

THE DEINSTITUTIONALIZATION OF STATUS OFFENSES

The U.S. Congress passed the **Juvenile Justice and Delinquency Prevention Act of 1974** (JJDPA) in response to a national concern about growing juvenile delinquency and youth crime. This act authorized the establishment of the **Office of Juvenile Justice and Delinquency Prevention** (OJJDP), which has been extremely helpful and influential in matters of disseminating information about juvenile offending and prevention and as a general data source.

The fourth division of the act is the *State Relations and Assistance Division*. This division addresses directly the matter of removing juveniles, especially status offenders, from secure institutions (facilities similar to adult prisons), jails, and lockups. The second division, *Research and Program Development*, is concerned with examining how juvenile courts process juvenile offenders. Individual states and local jurisdictions are encouraged to devise ways of separating juvenile delinquents from status offenders and removing status offenders from the jurisdiction of juvenile courts. The act suggests that status offenders should be processed by agencies and organizations other than juvenile courts, such as social or human services agencies and bureaus.

Changes and Modifications in the JJDPA

In 1977 Congress modified the act by declaring that juveniles should be separated by both sight and sound from adult offenders in detention and correctional facilities. Also in 1977, states were given five years to comply with the DSO mandate. Nonoffenders, such as dependent and neglected children, were also included. Congress relaxed certain JJDPA rules and gave states additional latitude regarding their placement options for status offenders and nonoffenders, including no placement.

In 1980, Congress prohibited states from detaining juveniles in jails and lockups. Congress also directed that states should examine their secure confinement policies relating to minority juveniles and to determine reasons and justification for the disproportionately high rate of minority confinement. Congress also created an exception to DSO by declaring that juveniles who violated a valid court order could be placed in secure confinement for a period of time.

By 1992, Congress directed that any participating state would have up to 25 percent of its formula grant money withheld to the extent that the state was not in compliance with each of the JJDPA mandates. Thus it is clear that state compliance with these provisions of the JJDPA was encouraged and obtained by providing grants-in-aid to various jurisdictions wishing to improve their juvenile justice systems and facilities (Bilchik, 1995).

Deinstitutionalization Defined

The deinstitutionalization of status offenses (DSO) involves the removal of status offenders from secure institutions (Holden and Kapler, 1995). Schneider (1984a:410) says that deinstitutionalization means "the removal from secure institutions and detention facilities of youths whose only infractions are...running away from home, incorrigibility, truancy, and curfew violations." Three versions of DSO are described by Schneider (1984a:410-411): (1) decarceration, (2) diverting dependent and neglected children, and (3) divestiture of jurisdiction.

Decarceration. ***Decarceration*** *means to remove certain types of juveniles from secure institutions, such as industrial schools.* Juveniles charged with status offenses often remain with the jurisdiction of juvenile courts and can be subjects of petitions by interested parties. Although secure confinement of these youths is not desirable under the act, different state jurisdictions can remove these youths involuntarily from their homes and place them in secure facilities, put them on probation, require them to attend treatment or service programs, and subject them to other behavioral restraints. Under decarceration, states are encouraged to remove status offenders from secure facilities.

A majority of the states have implemented decarceration policies relating to status offenders. Pennsylvania, for example, does not place status offenders in secure facilities. However, predominantly rural states, such as Montana and North Dakota, continue to incarcerate some status offenders. One reason is that juvenile court judges see incarceration of these youths as an appropriate punishment and potential cure for their status offending. Another reason is that these state legislatures have not devised alternative strategies for treating status offenders through other state agencies or services (Krisberg et al., 1993). A third reason is that, often, facilities simply do not exist in remote rural areas to meet status offender needs and provide the services they require. Thus the only alternative for their treatment is to be locked up in secure juvenile facilities. A major problem with this action is that it places status offenders in direct contact with juvenile delinquents. Delinquents are more serious types of offenders. Therefore, there is some justification for the belief that combining status offenders with delinquent offenders in secure confinement is particularly detrimental to the well-being and rehabilitation of status offenders.

Diverting Dependent and Neglected Children. A second type of DSO deals with **dependent and neglected children** (Schneider, 1984a:411). While the juvenile court continues to exercise jurisdiction over dependent and neglected youths, diversion programs are established to receive these children directly from law enforcement officers, schools, parents, or even self-referrals. These diversion programs provide crisis intervention services for youths, and their aim is to return juveniles eventually to their homes. However, more serious offenders may need more elaborate services provided by shelter homes, group homes, or even foster homes.

Divestiture of Jurisdiction. The third type of deinstitutionalization is **divestiture of jurisdiction**. Under full divestiture, juvenile courts cannot detain, petition, adjudicate, or place youths on probation or in institutions for committing any status offense. Schneider (1984a:41l) notes that under full divestiture, all services are provided by nonjustice agencies on a strictly voluntary basis. She indicates that by 1984, the states of Washington and Maine had legislatively mandated divestiture laws for all juvenile courts and removed all status offenders from them. Since then, most other jurisdictions have enacted similar types of divestiture statutes (Colley and Culbertson, 1988).

Early proponents of DSO believed that custodial confinement of status offenders would harden them, thus increasing their likelihood of committing future, more serious offenses (U.S. Senate Judiciary Committee, 1984). This belief has not received widespread support among researchers (Datesman and Aickin, 1985). Another belief about DSO was that it would greatly diminish the number of cases brought before juvenile courts throughout the United States as well as the numbers of detainees in juvenile secure facilities (Schneider, 1984a). Each of these beliefs has been refuted to a degree by studies of DSO in selected jurisdictions. Five experiences with DSO have been highlighted by various researchers as significant.

1. *DSO has failed to reduce substantially the number of status offenders in secure confinement, especially in local facilities.* Supporting this experience is a study by Logan and Rausch (1985). They studied a DSO program implemented in Connecticut from December 1976 to December 1977. On the basis of a survey of the state's automated juvenile court data base, they found that the juvenile gross incarceration rate actually increased after DSO. Independent of the DSO program, juvenile courts appeared to switch from institutional to noninstitutional procedures for removing juveniles from homes to secure facilities. However, more recent evidence suggests that greater numbers of jurisdictions have adopted deinstitutionalization policies and that the actual numbers of institutionalized status offenders is decreasing (Bilchik, 1995:31). In 1995 only 10 states had provisions for holding status offenders in secure facilities for periods of 24 hours or longer. Circumstances used by a minority of states to justify incarcerating status offenders include whether the offender poses a risk to himself/herself or others; is a risk not to appear at subsequent court proceedings; or is a risk to leave or to be taken from the jurisdiction (Bilchik, 1995:29).

2. **Net-widening**, *pulling youths into the juvenile justice system who would not have been involved before, has increased as one result of DSO.* Washington as well as several other jurisdictions has drawn larger numbers of status offenders into the net of the juvenile justice system after DSO was implemented.

BOX 2.3 PUNISHMENTS FOR PARENTS OF ERRANT CHILDREN

The Case of the Provenzino Family

It happened in St. Clair Shores, Michigan. Alex Provenzino is a 16-year-old who was caught burglarizing churches and growing a 4-foot marijuana plant in his bedroom. Alex's plight began when he was arrested in 1995 on charges of burglarizing churches in St. Clair Shores, Michigan, a Detroit suburb. He was placed on probation. The juvenile court placed Alex on probation again, but this time the court included the proviso that Alex must be supervised closely by his parents. Subsequently, he assaulted his father with some golf clubs and was arrested again. Again, he was placed on probation. In September 1995, Alex was arrested again, this time for breaking into at least six homes in his neighborhood.

Police investigated and obtained a search warrant for the Provenzino home. While conducting their search of the premises, they found a 4-foot-tall marijuana plant growing in Alex's bedroom, together with a quantity of stolen property, including a gun, knife, and strong box. Under questioning, Alex admitted to stealing $3500 from a local church collection box.

This time, the juvenile court judge ordered Alex placed in secure confinement in a juvenile detention center. The parents were ordered to pay $155 per day for Alex's maintenance at the center. Besides, charges were filed against the Provenzinos for failing to supervise Alex adequately while he was on probation. A trial was held and a jury found the Provenzinos guilty of failing to control Alex under a new Michigan parental-responsibility ordinance. The Provenzinos were ordered to pay a fine of $100 and court costs of $1000. Additionally, the parents must continue to pay the $155-per-day maintenance fee for Alex's secure confinement.

Anthony Provenzino, Alex's father, blamed the juvenile justice system for its failure to lock up Alex when he first ran afoul of the law. Both parents contended at their trial that they did their best to contain their son and his antics. The attorney for the Provenzinos, William Bufalino, said that the Provenzinos are paying every day for the consequences of their son's crimes. He said, "These 'bad parents' are paying every day, paying court costs. They are paying for the sins of their son. They are not paying for their sins. They don't have any." Some experts disagree.

Punishing the parents for the illegal conduct of their children is not a new concept. It is very much a part of the juvenile court laws of several states. Howard Davidson of the American Bar Association's Center on Children and the Law in Washington said that the number of states utilizing parental punishment for youth misconduct is increasing. He added that this fact is not widely known, primarily because of the fact that often, juvenile court proceedings are closed to the public and parental sanctions are not reported to local news agencies.

Should parents bear the responsibility for paying for their children's misconduct? Should there be limits on the liability incurred by such parents? What sorts of monetary punishments should be imposed on children who violate the law? Is parental punishment a deterrent to delinquency?

Source: Adapted from Associated Press, "Parents Convicted of Failing to Control Their Teen-Age Son," *Minot (ND) Daily News*, May 10, 1996:A4.

Net-widening may occur as follows. Originally, juvenile courts adjudicated both status and delinquent offenders. However, law enforcement officers seldom bothered to do much more than give status offenders verbal warnings and wrist slaps whenever they were confronted. Many juvenile court judges issued stern reprimands to status offenders and returned them to the custody of their parents. Once DSO was mandated, juvenile courts lost control over status offenders and these offenders acquired a new legal definition. Various community agencies were then established to provide community-based services for these status offenders as noninstitutional actions. Because of the existence of these new services, many law enforcement officers directed youths to them for treatment. Many of these remanded youths would have received verbal warnings from police previously. Therefore, DSO created a new class of juvenile offender as well as new action alternatives for law enforcement officers to follow. The ultimate result was to drag more youths into the net to serve certain juvenile justice ends.

3. ***Relabeling****, defining youths as delinquent or as emotionally disturbed who in the past would have been defined and handled as status offenders, has occurred in certain jurisdictions following DSO.* This particular consequence has been initiated, in part, by police officers who appear resentful over their loss of discretion relating to status offenders (Schneider and Schram, 1986). For instance, it is easy for a police officer to relabel a juvenile curfew violator or loiterer as a larceny or burglary suspect and detain the youth for a lengthy period. In many instances, juvenile court judges themselves have been resistant to these DSO reforms for similar reasons (e.g., loss of discretion over status offenders) (Colley and Culbertson, 1988). Krause and McShane (1994) have observed relabeling in California in the 1990s. In San Bernardino County, for instance, Krause and McShane found that large numbers of minors whose referral offense would have been disposed of routinely had been held in custody in juvenile hall and placed outside their parents' homes. This has occurred largely through relabeling, or police redefinitions of nonserious offending as serious offending.

4. *DSO has had little, if any, impact on recidivism rates among status offenders.* More than a few jurisdictions report that removing status offenders from juvenile court jurisdiction or not institutionalizing them will decrease their recidivism. For instance, Gottfredson and Barton (1993) studied 927 youths who were removed from a Maryland training school known as the Montrose Training School. When the training school was closed, some youths previously confined there were transferred to other secure facilities. Many other youths were deinstitutionalized and released from state custody. When the institutionalized youths were subsequently released as well, their rate of recidivism was compared with the noninstitutionalized aggregate. The noninstitutionalized offenders had a significantly higher rate of recidivism than did those who had remained institutionalized for longer periods.

Data collected from a seven-state (e.g., Colorado, Florida, Minnesota, New Mexico, New York, Ohio, and Oregon) investigation of the deinstituionalization of status offenders has shown that merely removing status offenders from secure institutional confinement does not mean that they will automatically be transferred to an alternative caring environment (Lieb, Fish, and Crosby, 1994). In fact, many of these deinstitutionalized youths were transferred to city streets, where they continued to reoffend. In certain local jurisdictions, such as San Francisco, projects such as the Omega Boys Club have attempted to absorb some of the youths removed from the California Youth Authority (CYA) under DSO (Macallair, 1994). During the mid-1980s, CYA commitments from San Francisco dropped by 58 percent. The Omega Boys Club provided a caring environment for many youths subsequently discharged from the CYA under DSO. In the San Francisco case at least, recidivism rates of Omega youths were quite low compared with those of other jurisdictions. These mixed results from different jurisdictions suggest that strict DSO policies are more complex than they at first appear and that there is a lack of uniformity of outcomes where DSO has been implemented (Altschuler and Luneburg, 1992; J. Conley, 1994).

5. *DSO has generated numerous service delivery problems, including inadequate services, nonexistent services or facilities, or the general inability to provide services within a voluntary system* (Schneider, 1984a:411). Status offenders exhibit diverse characteristics. It is impossible to profile the average status offender. Thus, whenever DSO occurs and community-based service agencies are called upon to accommodate larger numbers of youths diverted from juvenile courts by legislative mandate, these services may be inadequate or simply nonexistent. In some instances, status offenders with special problems may be rejected outright by more than a few of these agencies. For example, delivery services in 13 states under a National Runaway and Homeless Youth Program were examined in 1983. Three hundred fifty-three staff members, youths, and parents were interviewed, and it was found that for most of these programs, the centers did not accept youths who were or appeared to be psychotic, violent, or addicted to drugs or alcohol (U.S. General Accounting Office, 1983). Thus it would seem that those most in need of these very services are being denied them by agency personnel.

At least one voice among critics regards DSO unfavorably. Kearon (1989) opposes DSO largely on theoretical grounds. He directs his criticism particularly toward how runaways have been treated in the aftermath of DSO. Kearon contends that adolescent street abuse cannot be reduced appreciably as long as DSO is the prevailing philosophy of the state. The state must regain its legitimate control over runaways, asserts Kearon, to shield the runaways from their most self-destructive urges. He encourages use of secure incarcerative facilities for short-term periods, especially for those youths who have run away from open facilities and require treatment in a secure setting. He believes that the state can mandate such treatment. He suggests up to three-day stays for some runaways to remind them of the court's authority. More lengthy stays in confinement of up to 30 days or more in intensive care would be needed for those offenders with drug or alcohol dependencies and psychological problems. For many youths he recommends long-term confinement from 12 to 18 months to ensure that proper intervention treatment may be provided.

Other experts favor the institutionalization of certain types of status offenders. In Utah, for example, a survey of juvenile court personnel was conducted to determine their thinking about DSO and its implications (Norman and Burbidge, 1991). Most respondents said that they believed that the juvenile crime problem was becoming increasingly serious over time and that more punitive measures should be implemented. They believed that their DSO policies were not working and that more punitive measures should be established for status offenders as well as delinquents.

Regardless of the relative merits of DSO and the ambiguity of research results concerning its short- and long-term effects, there is no doubt that DSO is widespread nationally and has become the prevailing juvenile justice policy (Holden and Kapler, 1995). DSO has set in motion numerous programs in all jurisdictions to better serve the needs of a growing constituency of status offenders. This necessarily obligates growing numbers of agencies and organizations to contemplate new and innovative strategies, rehabilitative, therapeutic, and/or educational, to cope with these youths with diverse needs. Greater cooperation between the public, youth services, and community-based treatment programs is required to facilitate developing the best program policies and practices.

THE *UNIFORM CRIME REPORTS AND NATIONAL CRIME VICTIMIZATION SURVEY*

Two official sources of information about both adult and juvenile offenders are *Uniform Crime Reports* and *National Crime Victimization Survey*.

Uniform Crime Reports

Uniform Crime Reports (UCR) is published annually by the Federal Bureau of Investigation (FBI) in Washington, DC. *UCR* is a compilation of arrests for various offenses according to several time intervals. Periodic reports of arrests are issued quarterly to interested law enforcement agencies. All rural and urban law enforcement agencies are requested on a voluntary basis to submit statistical information about 29 different offenses. Most of these agencies submit arrest information, and thus *UCR* represents over 15,000 law enforcement agencies throughout the United States.

Crime in *UCR* is classified into two major categories, Part I and Part II offenses. Part I offenses are considered the most serious, and eight serious felonies are listed. These include murder and nonnegligent manslaughter, forcible rape, robbery, aggravated assault, burglary, larceny-theft, motor vehicle theft, and arson. Table 2.2 lists the eight major **index offenses** (Part I offenses) and their definition.

Table 2.3 shows **index crimes** for 1994. The first eight offenses are major offenses classified as felonies. *Felonies* are *violations of criminal laws that are punishable by terms of imprisonment of one year or longer in state or federal prisons or penitentiaries*. These offenses are known as index offenses because they provide readers with a sample of key or index crimes that can be charted quarterly or annually, according to different jurisdictions and demographic and socioeconomic dimensions (e.g., city size, age, race, gender, urban–rural). Thus the crime categories listed are not intended to be an exhaustive compilation. However, it is possible to scan these representative crime categories to obtain a general picture of crime trends across years or other desired time segments.

Table 2.3 shows various index offenses, including both felonies and misdemeanors, according to the age of arrestees. The second grouping of offenses in Table 2.3, beginning with "other assaults" and ending with "runaways," portrays both misdemeanors and status offenses. *Misdemeanors* are *violations of criminal laws that are punishable by incarcerative terms of less than one year in city or county jails*. Status offenses listed, including runaway behavior, truancy, and violation of curfew, are not considered crimes, although they are reported together with criminal offenses to give a more complete picture of arrest activity throughout the United States. These offenses listed are not an exhaustive compilation. Rather, a sample listing of crimes based on arrests is provided.

Because of the age breakdown presented in Table 2.3, it is possible to examine juvenile arrest statistics for different offenses and age categories. For example, by inspecting Table 2.3, we can determine that juveniles under age 18 accounted for about 18.6 percent of all arrests in 1994. For

TABLE 2.2

Uniform Crime Report, Part I: Crimes and Their Definition

Crime	Definition
Murder and nonnegligent manslaughter	Willful (nonnegligent) killing of one human being by another
Forcible rape	Carnal knowledge of a female, forcibly and against her will; assaults or attempts to commit rape by force or threat of force are included
Robbery	Taking or attempting to take anything of value from the care, custody, or control of a person or persons by force or threat of force or violence and/or by putting the victim in fear
Aggravated assault	Unlawful attack by one person upon another for the purpose of inflicting severe or aggravated bodily injury
Burglary	Unlawful entry into a structure to commit a felony or theft
Larceny-theft	Unlawful taking, carrying, leading, or riding away of property from the possession or constructive possession of another, including shoplifting, pocket picking, purse snatching, and thefts from motor vehicle parts or accessories
Motor vehicle theft	Theft or attempted theft of a motor vehicle, including automobiles, trucks, buses, motorscooters, and snowmobiles
Arson	Any willful or malicious burning or attempt to burn, with or without intent to defraud, a dwelling house, public building, motor vehicle or aircraft, and the personal property of another

Source: U.S. Department of Justice, Federal Bureau of Investigation, *Crime in the United States* (Washington, DC: U.S. Government Printing Office, 1997).

violent crimes, those under age 18 accounted for 19.4 percent of these. For property crimes, juveniles accounted for 15 percent of all arrests. Specific crime categories may be consulted as well. For instance, 3102 juveniles were arrested in 1994 for murder or nonnegligent manslaughter. About 412,000 juveniles were arrested that same year for larceny-theft.

Besides this factual information about juvenile offenders, *UCR* may also be used to gauge the incidence of arrests across youthful age categories. We can inspect Table 2.3 and determine that for runaways, arrests increase for juveniles and peak at about ages 13 to 14. For subsequent years, numbers of arrests for runaway behavior decrease. For curfew violations and loitering, the peak year for juveniles appears to be 16. Thereafter, declines in arrests are observed. Interestingly, liquor law violations involving juveniles

TABLE 2.3

Arrests by Offense Charged and Age, United States, 1994[a]

Offense charged[b]	Total, all ages	Under 15	Under 18	18 and older	Ages Under 10	10 to 12	13 to 14	15	16	17	18	19
Total	11,877,188	780,979	2,209,675	9,667,513	37,130	176,289	567,560	428,697	489,089	510,640	520,831	505,122
Percent	100	6.6	18.6	81.4	0.3	1.5	4.8	3.6	4.1	4.3	4.4	4.3
Murder and nonnegligent manslaughter	18,497	379	3,102	15,395	3	31	345	535	912	1,276	1,418	1,418
Forcible rape	29,791	1,863	4,859	24,932	103	442	1,318	892	993	1,111	1,217	1,158
Robbery	146,979	13,543	47,094	99,885	245	2,478	10,820	10,008	11,753	11,790	10,653	8,701
Aggravated assault	449,716	23,190	70,030	379,686	1,043	5,261	16,886	13,219	15,993	17,628	17,853	17,030
Burglary	319,926	47,481	115,681	204,245	3,135	11,833	32,513	22,232	23,413	22,555	20,223	15,889
Larceny-theft	1,236,311	185,811	412,349	823,962	9,145	51,765	124,901	76,459	77,418	72,661	62,806	49,702
Motor vehicle theft	166,260	21,867	73,265	92,995	206	2,592	19,069	17,986	18,087	15,325	11,698	8,718
Arson	16,764	6,289	9,268	7,496	1,153	2,041	3,095	1,224	964	791	531	488
Violent crime	644,983	38,975	125,085	519,898	1,394	8,212	29,369	24,654	29,651	31,805	31,145	28,307
Percent	100	6.0	19.4	80.6	0.2	1.3	4.6	3.8	4.6	4.9	4.8	4.4
Property crime	1,739,261	261,448	610,563	1,128,698	13,639	68,231	179,578	117,901	119,882	111,332	95,258	74,797
Percent	100	15.0	35.1	64.9	0.8	3.9	10.3	6.8	6.9	6.4	5.5	4.3
Total crime index[c]	2,384,244	300,423	735,648	1,648,596	15,033	76,443	208,947	142,555	149,533	143,137	126,403	103,104
Percent	100	12.6	30.9	69.1	0.6	3.2	8.8	6.0	6.3	6.0	5.3	4.3
Other assaults	991,881	72,514	171,642	820,239	3,731	18,961	49,822	32,005	33,602	33,521	31,173	31,652
Forgery and counterfeiting	93,003	927	7,013	85,990	33	184	710	981	2,057	3,048	4,199	4,512
Fraud	330,752	4,409	18,594	312,158	127	657	3,625	4,082	4,120	5,983	8,969	11,896
Embezzlement	11,614	92	803	10,811	8	22	62	60	211	440	574	631
Stolen property; buying, receiving, possessing	134,930	10,751	36,218	98,712	240	1,890	86,621	7,376	8,714	9,377	9,690	8,078
Vandalism	259,579	60,250	122,085	137,494	6,074	17,782	36,394	21,415	21,381	19,039	13,965	11,017
Weapons; carrying, possessing, etc.	213,494	16,661	52,200	161,294	611	3,424	12,626	9,963	12,199	13,337	14,213	12,554
Prostitution and commercialized vice	86,818	120	1,013	85,805	10	18	92	129	289	475	1,317	1,900
Sex offenses (except forcible rape and prostitution)	81,887	7,506	14,418	67,469	658	2,081	4,767	2,442	2,230	2,240	2,205	2,183
Drug abuse violations	1,118,348	21,830	131,220	987,126	266	2,281	19,283	24,103	36,747	48,540	60,142	57,786
Gambling	15,845	242	1,493	14,352	2	24	216	299	423	529	531	537
Offenses against family and children	92,133	1,475	4,234	87,899	98	293	1,084	815	978	966	2,009	2,207
Driving under the influence	1,079,533	329	10,573	1,068,960	117	24	188	534	2,708	7,002	15,769	22,312
Liquor laws	424,452	10,083	94,030	330,422	153	832	9,098	14,001	27,520	42,426	60,029	59,868
Drunkenness	571,420	2,065	14,778	556,642	120	197	1,748	2,298	3,606	6,809	12,831	14,090
Disorderly conduct	601,002	48,868	137,328	463,674	1,741	10,752	36,375	27,057	30,178	31,225	30,639	27,148
Vagrancy	21,413	925	3,657	17,756	19	154	752	773	946	1,013	1,072	860
All other offenses (except traffic)	3,046,100	99,318	343,669	2,702,431	5,396	20,348	73,574	61,382	81,918	101,051	124,694	132,388
Suspicion	11,395	551	1,712	9,683	39	128	384	396	385	380	407	399
Curfew and loitering law violations	105,888	31,609	105,888	×	537	4,552	26,520	24,667	28,098	21,514	×	×
Runaways	201,459	90,031	201,459	×	2,117	15,242	72,672	51,634	41,246	18,548	×	×

Source: Maguire and Pastore, 1996. Data source: U.S. Department of Justice, Federal Bureau of Investigation, *Crime in the United States 1994* (Washington, DC: U.S. Government Printing Office, 1995), pp. 227–228.

Table 2.3 (cont'd)

Arrests by Offense Charged and Age, United States, 1994[a]

20	21	22	23	24	Ages 25 to 29	30 to 34	35 to 39	40 to 44	45 to 49	50 to 54	55 to 59	60 to 64	65 and older
459,948	433,449	419,027	420,909	406,399	1,761,357	1,713,145	1,298,615	796,890	433,908	277,419	120,448	70,677	79,369
3.9	3.6	3.5	3.5	3.4	14.8	14.4	10.9	6.7	3.7	1.9	1.0	0.6	0.7
1,215	1,097	938	803	706	2,538	1,847	1,342	856	533	271	164	113	136
1,156	1,065	990	1,107	1,001	4,674	4,617	3,382	2,023	1,120	621	334	216	251
6,808	5,946	5,398	5,130	4,740	19,712	15,823	9,621	4,432	1,745	658	255	118	145
16,115	16,485	16,315	16,741	16,195	72,265	70,262	52,262	31,176	17,003	8,763	4,920	2,862	3,435
11,818	10,234	9,497	9,258	8,385	38,079	35,507	24,140	12,426	5,180	2,017	805	355	432
39,440	34,473	31,926	31,928	30,636	140,027	141,593	109,829	68,611	36,125	18,320	10,259	6,854	11,433
6,516	5,510	4,989	4,642	4,217	17,153	13,812	8,348	4,133	1,848	761	305	132	213
341	283	263	264	245	1,178	1,268	1,069	665	407	238	99	80	77
25,294	24,593	23,641	23,781	22,642	99,189	92,549	66,607	38,487	20,401	10,313	5,673	3,309	3,967
3.9	3.8	3.7	3.7	3.5	15.4	14.3	10.3	6.0	3.2	1.6	0.9	0.5	0.6
58,115	50,500	46,675	46,092	43,483	196,437	192,180	143,386	85,835	43,560	21,336	11,468	7,421	12,155
3.3	2.9	2.7	2.7	2.5	11.3	11.0	8.2	4.9	2.5	1.2	0.7	0.4	0.7
83,409	75,093	70,316	69,873	66,125	295,626	284,729	209,993	124,322	63,961	31,649	17,141	10,730	16,122
3.5	3.1	2.9	2.9	2.8	12.4	11.9	8.8	5.2	2.7	1.3	0.7	0.5	0.7
30,938	33,605	35,257	36,524	36,465	163,495	160,971	117,939	67,879	35.759	17,997	9,173	5,401	6,011
4,308	4,174	4,115	4,088	4,086	17,829	16,234	11,234	6,046	2,856	1,226	540	258	285
13,192	13,559	14,146	14,739	14,606	63,001	57,461	43,331	27,414	15,181	7,271	3,425	1,900	2,067
599	556	553	499	519	2,042	1,716	1,295	799	513	260	123	62	70
6,440	5,754	5,158	4,833	4,503	18,057	14,875	10,417	5,761	2,708	1,237	616	282	303
8,347	7,804	6,898	6,664	6,200	24,811	21,565	14,552	7,794	3,853	1,872	917	481	754
10,361	10,462	9,449	8,650	7,827	28,035	21,742	15,325	9,676	5,663	3,282	1,735	1,047	1,273
2,275	2,727	2,953	3,501	3,876	20,017	20,712	13,527	6,851	2,962	1,429	786	460	512
2,058	2,127	2,244	2,227	2,167	11,056	12,191	9,903	6,695	4,483	2,853	1,849	1,333	1,895
51,330	48,063	45,564	45,455	43,839	190,382	183,565	133,141	73,403	32,406	12,773	5,170	2,270	1,837
533	466	389	433	389	1,770	1,880	1,775	1,563	1,191	970	726	601	598
2,383	2,731	2,916	3,256	3,465	16,778	19,310	15,461	8,913	4,419	1,980	989	534	548
27,223	38,711	40,866	44,180	43,818	195,657	201,508	161,847	111,111	70,710	41,984	23,910	14,628	14,726
47,987	14,628	11,150	9,477	8,012	29,069	27,355	22,918	16,126	9,964	6,035	3,657	2,112	2,035
14,841	19,260	18,959	18,928	18,599	87,057	101,426	90,333	65,154	40,160	24,643	13,776	8,502	8,083
24,627	26,244	23,791	23,202	20,985	81,732	76,119	56,300	33,277	18,142	9,664	5,078	3,083	3,643
677	580	591	647	602	2,930	3,265	2,747	1,739	1,009	541	227	141	128
128,076	126,545	123,337	123,304	119,931	510,184	484,602	365,026	221,462	117,530	59,593	30,525	16,798	18,436
344	360	375	429	385	1,829	1,919	1,551	905	438	160	85	54	43
×	×	×	×	×	×	×	×	×	×	×	×	×	×
×	×	×	×	×	×	×	×	×	×	×	×	×	×

This table represents data from all law enforcement agencies submitting complete reports for 12 months in 1994. Population figures represent U.S. Bureau of the Census July 1, 1994 estimates.
[a]10,654 agencies; 1994 estimated population 207,624,000.
[b]Because of rounding, percents may not add to total. Violent crimes are offenses of murder and nonnegligent manslaughter, forcible rape, robbery, and aggravated assault. Property crimes are offenses of burglary, larceny-theft, motor vehicle theft, and arson.
[c]Includes arson.

show a progressively upward trend across years. The sheer numbers of arrests for liquor law violations increase dramatically between ages 10 to 18.

National Crime Victimization Survey

Compared with *UCR*, the ***National Crime Victimization Survey*** (*NCVS*) is conducted annually by the U.S. Bureau of the Census. It is a random survey of approximately 60,000 dwellings, about 127,000 persons age 12 or over, and approximately 50,000 businesses. Subsamples of persons are questioned by interviewers who compile information about crime victims. Those interviewed are asked whether they have had different types of crime committed against them during the past six months or year. Through statistical manipulations, the amount of crime throughout the general population may be estimated.

NCVS provides what is known as *victimization data. A victimization is the basic measure of the occurrence of a crime and is a specific criminal act that affects a single victim. An* **incident** *is a specific criminal act that may involve one or more victims.* Because *NCVS* reflects an amount of crime allegedly perpetrated against a large sample of victims, it is believed more accurate than *UCR* as a national crime estimate. Thus whenever comparisons of crime from *UCR* are made against *NCVS*, the latter reports from two to four times the amount of crime as indicated by law enforcement agency arrest figures in *UCR*. But because of certain flaws inherent in both estimates of national crime, experts believe that both reports are underestimates of the true amount of crime in the United States.

Strengths of These Measures

One strength shared by both of these indicators of crime in the United States is the sheer numbers of offenses reported. Few, if any, alternative sources of information about crime in the United States exhibit such voluminous reporting. Furthermore, regional and seasonal reports of criminal activity are provided. *UCR* also reports the proportion of different types of crime that are cleared by arrest. ***Cleared by arrest*** *means that someone has been arrested and charged with a particular crime.*

Another favorable feature of both *UCR* and *NCVS* is that numbers of arrests and reported crimes can be compared across years. Although irregularities exist in both documents that are attributable to diverse factors, the information reported by both sources is most often interpreted as "generally" indicative of national crime trends. Therefore, *UCR* reports percentage increases or decreases in the amount of different types of crime for many different jurisdictions and over various time periods. And although *NCVS* does not purport to survey all crime victims, the randomness inherent in the selection of the target respondents is such that generalizations about the U.S. population are considered reasonably valid.

A primary advantage of *NCVS* over *UCR* is that victims offer interviewers information about crimes committed against them. In many instances, these respondents disclose that they do not report these crimes to police. The reasons for not reporting crimes to police vary, although these victims often believe that the police cannot do much about their victimization anyway. If tools are missing from one's pickup truck, for example, it is unlikely that police will be able to retrieve these tools. Therefore, victims don't bother reporting these incidents. Perhaps they do not believe the stolen property is worth the time taken to complete the extensive paperwork often involved at police headquarters when reports of stolen property are made. Perhaps their own carelessness resulted in misplacing their property, and theft may not have been involved. In physical injury cases resulting from aggravated assault or rape, some victims may be afraid to report these crimes because of fear of reprisals from the perpetrators. Sometimes, rape victims are too embarrassed to report these incidents, or they may feel that they were partially to blame. Furthermore, in some of these cases, family members or close friends may be "guilty parties," and victims may be reluctant to press for criminal charges against them.

Weaknesses of These Measures

Certain limitations of *UCR* and *NCVS* are well documented (Baumer, 1994; Steffensmeier and Harer, 1991; Wells and Rankin, 1995). Focusing on *UCR* first, we may cite some of the more important weaknesses of these statistics.

1. *UCR figures do not provide an annual per capita measure of crime frequency. Population increases are not taken into account directly, and thus reported arrests across years may be suspect.* To overcome this problem, researchers must calculate annual general population increase and contrast this figure against reported numbers of arrests.

2. *Not all law enforcement agencies report crime to the FBI, and those that do may fail to report crime uniformly.* Because law enforcement agencies are not compelled to submit annual information to the FBI, some agencies fail to report their arrest activity. Also, crimes of the same name vary in definition among jurisdictions.

3. *UCR only reports arrests, not the actual amount of crime. Based on self-reported information from criminals and others, including victimization records from the NCVS, many criminals escape detection and arrest for a large number of crimes they commit.* Thus *UCR* shows only a record of those who happen to

get caught; and not all of those who are apprehended are subsequently convicted of those crimes. Charges are dropped, prosecutors fail to establish their cases against certain defendants, or suspects are eventually released without pursuing their cases beyond the initial arrest.

4. *When arrests are reported in UCR, only the most serious offenses are often reported.* Thus, if a robbery suspect is apprehended, he may possess burglary tools, a concealed weapon, and stolen property. He may have caused physical injuries to victims. All of these events are crimes, although only *robbery* will be recorded in the law enforcement agency's report to the FBI. Therefore, there is much basis for the belief that these official reports of crime are at best underestimates.

5. *Arrest activity in UCR may be attributable to fluctuations in police activity rather than actual fluctuations in criminal activity.* It may be that an incumbent city official running for another term of office insists that police officers in his jurisdiction become more visible by effecting more arrests. Thus police officers are instructed to crack down on criminals. One result is that many suspicious persons are arrested on weak evidence, and these are subsequently released. However, the politician may cite record numbers of arrests in his city as proof that police are combating crime more effectively. In reality, no actual change in the amount of crime has occurred.

6. *Although they only make up a fraction of national criminal activity, federal crimes are not reported in UCR.* Thus if the figures in *UCR* are used for evaluating an agency's effectiveness, it would be impossible to assess various federal law enforcement agencies, including the FBI itself, and whether certain federal crimes are increasing or decreasing in frequency annually.

   NCVS has also been criticized. Among the criticisms of *NCVS* are the following:

1. *NCVS (as well as UCR) seems to emphasize street crimes and to deemphasize corporate crimes.* Whenever persons are interviewed, they are questioned about theft, burglary, robbery, assaults, and other types of street crime. It is seldom the case that they report fraudulent actions against them by different businesses or organizations. The savings and loan scandal of the late 1980s involved many innocent victims. Yet most of the criminal activity accompanying this scandal did not appear in *NCVS.*

2. *Self-reported information contained in NCVS is often unreliable. Some of those interviewed may not be able to identify certain actions as crimes.* For instance, date-rapes may be classified as assaults. Also, persons may not be able to remember clearly certain criminal events. Fear of reprisals from criminals may compel some victims not to disclose their victimizations to interviewers.

3. *Some victimization data reported in NCVS may be either exaggerated or more liberally reported.* For various reasons, interviewees may lie to interviewers in disclosing details of crimes committed against them. In some instances involving

child sexual abuse, more families seem more willing to discuss these crimes in succeeding years. Thus the incidence of child sexual abuse may not be increasing; rather, admissions of its existence may be more frequent because of the greater publicity and attention it has received in recent years.

Despite these and other criticisms, *UCR* and *NCVS* provide valuable data for interested professionals. The fact that virtually all law enforcement agencies rely to some extent on these annual figures as valid indicators of criminal activity in the United States suggests that their utility in this regard is invaluable. Supplementing this information are other, more detailed, reports of selected offense activity. The U.S. Department of Justice Bureau of Justice Statistics publishes an incredible amount of information annually about different dimensions of crime and offender characteristics and behavior. This supplemental information, together with the data provided by *UCR* and *NCVS*, may be combined to furnish us with a more complete picture of crime in the United States. Several alternative data sources are discussed in the following section.

OTHER SOURCES

One of the best compendiums of data specifically about juveniles and juvenile court adjudications is the **National Juvenile Court Data Archive** (Butts, 1996a:10). While the federal government has collected data pertaining to juveniles since 1926, the data were dependent on the voluntary completion of statistical forms by juvenile courts in a limited number of U.S. jurisdictions. In 1975, however, the Office of Juvenile Justice and Delinquency Prevention (OJJDP) assumed responsibility for acquiring court dispositional records and publishing periodic reports of juvenile offenses and adjudicatory outcomes (National Center for Juvenile Justice, 1988:1–2).

By 1996, the National Juvenile Court Data Archive contained over 700,000 annual automated case records of juveniles in various states. Numerous data sets are currently available to researchers and may be accessed for investigative purposes. These data sets are nonuniform, although they ordinarily contain information such as age at referral, gender, race, county of residence, offense(s) charged, date of referral, processing characteristics of the case (e.g., incarceration and manner of handling), and the case disposition.

Another compendium of offender characteristics of all ages is the ***Sourcebook of Criminal Justice Statistics*** published annually by the Hindelang Criminal Justice Research Center and supported by grants from the U.S. Department of Justice (Maguire and Pastore, 1996). This is perhaps the most comprehensive source that we have discussed, since it accesses numerous governmental documents and reports annually to keep readers abreast of the latest crime figures. Among other things, it describes justice system employment and spending, jail and prison management and prisoner issues, judicial misconduct and complaints, correctional officer characteristics, crime victim characteristics and victimization patterns, delinquent behavior patterns and trends, and considerable survey information. Literally hundreds of tables are presented that summarize much of the information reported by various private and governmental agencies. Useful annotated information is provided to supplement the tabular material.

Statistics pertaining to juvenile offenders include juvenile admissions and discharges from public and private incarcerative facilities, average length of stay of juveniles in these facilities, a profile of juvenile custody facilities, demographic information about juveniles detained for lengthy terms, criminal history or prior records of juveniles, illegal drug and alcohol use among juveniles, waiver information, and offense patterns according to socioeconomic and demographic factors. Each annual sourcebook is somewhat different from those published in previous years, although much of the material in subsequent editions has been updated from previous years.

Self-Report Information

Although these official sources of crime and delinquency are quite useful, a common criticism is that they tend to underestimate the amount of offense behaviors that actually occur in the United States. For many years, those interested in studying juvenile offense behaviors have frequently relied on data derived from self-reports. ***Self-reports*** *are surveys of youths (or adults) based on disclosures they might make about the types of offenses they have committed and how frequently they have committed them* (Elliott, 1994a). High school students or others may be asked to complete a confidential questionnaire where lists of offenses are provided. Ordinarily, simple checklists are given to students and they are asked to identify those behaviors they have done, not necessarily those for which they have been apprehended. Considered "unofficial" sources of information about delinquency and delinquency patterns, these self-disclosures are considered by many professionals to be more accurate than official sources. An example of such a checklist is shown in Figure 2.1.

In his 1993 address to the American Society of Criminology, Delbert Elliott described aggregate data derived from self-reports and the first eight waves of questionnaires in the National Youth Survey, a prospective longitudinal study involving a national probability sample of 1725 youths. The utility of self-reporting was amply illustrated. These self-reports disclosed, for instance, that the prevalence of serious violent offending among juveniles is substantially higher than otherwise reported by different official sources;

the onset of serious violent offending occurs at earlier ages; evidence of career escalation (e.g., progressing from less serious to more serious offending) is stronger than believed previously; that serious violent offending represents only a small proportion of all juvenile offending annually; and that a small subset of serious violent offenders accounts for a majority of all serious violent offending (Elliott, 1994a). Thornberry, Loeber, and Huizinga (1991) have also been able to detect career escalation among juveniles by using self-reports. Thus official sources may be less reliable as indicators of progressive delinquency among those processed by the juvenile justice system.

The *unofficial* nature of such self-reporting is misleading, however, since the **National Youth Survey** (Menard, 1987) and a **Monitoring the Future Survey** (Osgood et al., 1987) are among several national surveys administered either annually or at other intervals through various organizations and agencies to large numbers of high school students. For instance, the Institute for Social Research at the University of Michigan regularly solicits information nationally from over 3000 high school students (Osgood et al., 1987). Although these surveys are not supported fully by government grants or other public funding, their importance as official sources should not be underestimated. The credibility of such information is highly regarded among juvenile justice professionals, and this is indicated, in part, by the frequency with which such data are cited in the literature by others.

Self-reported data about juvenile offenses suggests that a sizable gap exists between official reports of delinquent conduct and information disclosed through self-reports. In short, self-report disclosures by teenagers

FIGURE 2.1 Hypothetical Checklist for Self-Report Disclosures of Delinquent or Criminal Conduct among High School Students

"How often during the past six months have you committed the following offenses?" Check whichever best applies to you.

OFFENSE	0 times	1 time	2 times	3 times	4 or more times
Smoked marijuana	___	___	___	___	___
Stole something worth $50 or less	___	___	___	___	___
Got drunk on beer or wine	___	___	___	___	___
Got drunk on hard liquor	___	___	___	___	___
Used crack or cocaine	___	___	___	___	___

Source: Compiled by author

reveal far greater delinquency than is reported by either *UCR* or *NCVS*. However, since *NCVS* information is also a form of self-disclosure, some investigators have found greater compatibility between delinquency self-reporting and *NCVS* than between delinquency self-reporting and *UCR*, which reports only arrest information (Menard, 1987). In any case, self-reports of delinquency or status offense conduct have caused researchers to refer to these undetected offending behaviors as **hidden delinquency**.

These data sources have enabled researchers to assess whether there are changing offending patterns among juveniles over the years. Much descriptive information exists that characterizes violent juvenile offenders as well as professional conjecturing about the many potential causal factors that seem to cause violence. One concern of certain critics of DSO, for instance, is whether status offenders actually escalate to more serious types of offending behavior. Can useful trends be charted over the years that enable us to anticipate appropriate interventions for violence-prone juveniles or those likely to escalate to more serious offenses? Additionally, researchers are interested in whether significant differences exist between male and female juvenile offenders, apart from certain typical offense behaviors associated with each. Is female delinquency increasing? If so, what can be done about it? We examine these topics in the following section.

VIOLENCE AND NONVIOLENCE: CAREER ESCALATION?

What is the nature of violent crime among juveniles? Are juveniles likely to escalate to more serious offenses during their youthful years as they become more deeply involved in delinquent conduct? Are there certain kinds of juvenile offenders who are more or less susceptible to intervention programs and treatments as means of reducing or eliminating their propensity to engage in delinquent conduct? Are schools new battlezones for gang warfare and other forms of violence? (Hoffman, 1996) Certainly the media have helped to heighten our awareness of the presence and violence of youth gangs in various cities. Startling information about extensive drug and alcohol use among juveniles is frequently broadcasted or reported. Is there currently an unstoppable juvenile crime wave throughout the United States?

School Violence

Violence among schoolchildren has received increased attention in recent years (Hanke, 1996; Levine, 1996). The media suggest that school violence is pervasive. However, a study of 3364 high school seniors drawn from 113 public and 19 private schools across the United States revealed that between 1982 and 1988, school victimizations occurred at relatively low rates (Hanke,

1996). The rate of victimization varied considerably by race and gender. Boys were victimized more frequently than girls, and non-whites were victimized more frequently than whites. Most victimizations were single occurrences, with dangerous weapons used in only limited instances. Verbal threats not involving injury or weapons were most commonly observed. These victimizations were detected through the use of self-reports, where juveniles were asked whether they had been the victims of others at school.

Other researchers have reported more serious and frequent violence, especially in schools with larger proportions of at-risk youth (Levine, 1996). Miami high school students reported both serious and frequent victimization. In many of these victimizations, dangerous weapons such as firearms were used to effect the **victimization**.

Gang Violence

Of particular interest to juvenile justice professionals is the increased incidence of gang formation and membership behavior in recent years (Chicago Police Department, 1988; Wang, 1996). The gang phenomenon seems widespread throughout the United States rather than localized in major city centers. Gangs are found in most jurisdictions and seem to organize along racial or ethnic lines, often for mutual protection against other gangs (Wang, 1996). Of course, gang formation and membership would function to heighten the awareness of community residents that their communities were being infested with lawless juveniles (Hagedorn, 1988). Thus there are not necessarily increasing numbers of juvenile delinquents running rampant in cities. There may be more visible organizational activity among those juveniles already there.

Kids Who Kill

Juveniles who commit homicide are relative rare. Of the 18,497 homicide arrests reported by *UCR* in 1994, only 379 of these involved juveniles under age 15. And about 17 percent of all homicide arrests involved persons under age 18 (Maguire and Pastore, 1996:404). An increasing amount of youth violence, including homicide, is linked to gang membership (Sheley and Wright, 1995; Spergel, 1995).

Apart from gang-related killings, many youths kill one or more of their family members, such as their mothers or fathers. Studies of youths who kill their parents show that they are often severely physically or sexually abused, and that they are particularly sensitive to stressors in the home environment (Heide, 1992, 1993). Many juvenile murderers have chemical dependencies for which they require treatment (Smith, 1994).

One of the most horrifying murders in the 1990s was the murder of a 3-year-old by two 10-year-olds in England. A toddler was led from a shopping mall by two other children. Later, they battered the 3-year-old with sticks and left his body on railroad tracks. Video surveillance cameras in the shopping center helped police to identify the young culprits and apprehend them. They confessed, although police remain baffled as to why they committed this terrible act of murder (Smith, 1994). While explanations of juvenile violence, including homicide, often include child maltreatment, these youths did not manifest the characteristics of "typical" juvenile murderers (Bumby, 1994; Smith, 1994).

Some juvenile murders are sexually motivated and occur when victims threaten to tell others (Myers, 1994). But even something as specific as sexually motivated juvenile murder is poorly misunderstood by the experts. A wide variety of explanations is provided for explaining or rationalizing adolescent murders, although any excuse is rarely accepted as mitigating (Myers, 1994; Stalans and Henry, 1994). Most often cited as mitigating factors in juvenile homicides are troubled family histories and social backgrounds, psychological disturbances, mental retardation, indigence, and substance abuse (Robinson and Stephens, 1992). Treatments often include psychotherapy, psychiatric hospitalization, institutional placement, and psychopharmacological agents (Myers, 1992).

Juvenile Violence Trends

Violence committed by juveniles has increased during the last few decades. Between 1988 and 1994, the juvenile violent crime index soared (Snyder, Sickmund, and Poe-Yamagata, 1996:14). Figure 2.2 shows juvenile arrest rates for these years. Further, if juvenile arrest rates continue to escalate, juvenile arrest rates for violent crimes will more than double by the year 2010 (Snyder, Sickmund, and Poe-Yamagata, 1996:15). Figures 2.3 and 2.4 show both projections of the growth of the ages 15 to 17 and arrests of juveniles for violent offenses through 2010.

Career Escalation

Concerning **career escalation**, there is little agreement among professionals that delinquents gravitate toward more serious offenses as they get older (Walker, 1995). Datesman and Aickin (1985) have reported no career escalation observed among 687 youths they studied in a family court in Delaware. Also, Hartstone and Hansen (1984) have found little evidence to support the idea that youths progress to more violent crimes during their teenage years. Random samples of 114 juvenile offenders who were

FIGURE 2.2   Arrests per 100,000 Juveniles Ages 10–17 in 1974–1994

From 1975 through 1988 the juvenile arrest rates for violent crimes remained relatively constant, but these rates have climbed rapidly in recent years

Arrest per 100,00 juveniles ages 10–17

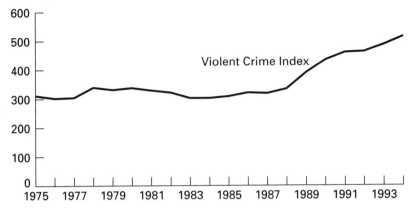

Note: 1993 and 1994 arrest rates were estimated by the National Center for Juvenile Justice by using data presented in *Crime in the United States* reports and population data from the U.S. Bureau of the Census.

Source: From Snyder, Sickmund, and Poe-Yamagata, 1996:14. Data sources: FBI, *Age-Specific Arrests Rates for Selected Offenses 1965–1992* (1994), *Crime in the United States 1993* (1995), and *Crime in the United States 1994* (1995); Bureau of the Census, *Resident Population of States 1992–1994* (1995) (machine-readable data file), and *Current Population Reports*, Series P-25 (1995).

arrested for violent crimes were investigated as a part of a U.S. government-funded Violent Juvenile Offender Research and Development Program. These youths had an average of 10.5 delinquency petitions and 5.7 formal adjudications against them, as well as even higher levels of delinquency than official documents revealed, according to self-reported information. Essentially, there was no escalation among these youths to indicate that they started out as nonviolent offenders and progressed eventually to violent ones. Lab (1984) reaches similar conclusions in his investigation of over 6000 subjects from three different birth cohorts in 1942, 1949, and 1952. Most of the juveniles he examined tended to commit minor offenses, and no pattern of escalation was disclosed. For the most part, those juveniles who began a pattern of delinquent activity tended to continue the same type of activity over time rather than to change to some more violent behaviors.

However, among 863 youths studied in a Las Vegas, Nevada, juvenile court, some career escalation to more serious offenses was observed by

FIGURE 2.3   Population of Juvenile Ages 15 to 17 through 2010

The population of juveniles ages 15–17 declined from the mid-1970s to 1991, then began to rise, and is projected to increase 31% by 2010

Population ages 15–17 in thousands

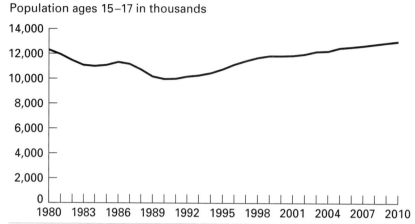

Source: From Snyder, Sickmund, and Poe-Yamagata, 1996:15. Data sources: FBI, *Age-Specific Arrest Rates and Race-Specific Arrest Rates for Selected Offenses 1965–1992* (1994); Bureau of the Census, "U.S. Population Estimates by Age, Sex, Race and Hispanic Origin: 1980 to 1991," *Current Population Reports* (1993), and "U.S. Population Estimates by Age, Sex, Race and Hispanic Origin: 1992–2050," *Current Population Reports* (1995).

Shelden, Horvath, and Tracy (1989). Furthermore, male offenders seemed more likely than female officers to escalate to more serious offending behaviors. In both of these studies, however, the subjects studied were status offenders. Although some investigators have found that some connection exists between criminal careers and earlier patterns of juvenile offending, other investigators do not particularly believe that widespread escalation occurs among juvenile offenders during their juvenile years (U.S. General Accounting Office, 1995a). Interestingly, some support has been found for greater career escalation from delinquency to adult criminality among females compared with males in selected jurisdictions (Rosenbaum, 1987; Shelden, 1987). Using self-report data from eight survey waves between 1976 and 1989, Elliott (1994b) has also found evidence of escalation toward greater violent offending among juvenile offenders.

FEMALE VERSUS MALE DELINQUENCY: CATALOGING THE DIFFERENCES

Of the total number of juveniles held in either public or private secure facilities annually, approximately 8 percent are female (Camp and Camp,

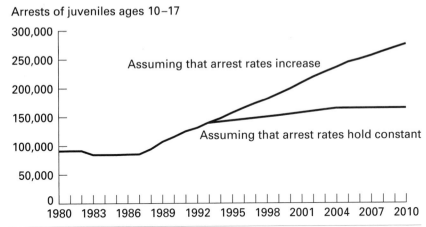

FIGURE 2.4 Violent Crimes and Arrest Trends through 2010

If Violent Crime Index arrest rates for juveniles ages 10–17 increase in the future as they did from 1983–1992, arrests will more than double by 2010

Arrests of juveniles ages 10–17

Assuming that arrest rates increase

Assuming that arrest rates hold constant

Source: From Snyder, Sickmund, and Poe-Yamataga, 1996:15. Data sources: FBI, *Age-Specific Arrest Rates and Race Specific Arrest Rates for Selected Offenses 1965–1992* (1994); Bureau of the Census, "U.S. Population Estimates by Age, Sex, Race and Hispanic Origin: 1980 to 1991," *Current Population Reports* (1993), and "U.S. Population Estimates by Age, Sex, Race and Hispanic Origin: 1992–2050," *Current Population Reports* (1995).

1995c:9). About 14 percent of all youths in juvenile community correctional programs are female (Camp and Camp, 1995c:9). These figures indicate that females are committed at a lower rate than males, and females are also returned to their communities at a greater rate after serving comparatively shorter secure confinement terms (Maguire and Pastore, 1996).

During 1994, female juveniles accounted for about 14 percent of all juvenile violent crime arrests (Snyder, Sickmund, and Poe-Yamagata, 1996:11). However, females are catching up with and surpassing their male counterparts in their rate of serious offending. Between 1985 and 1994, for example, there was a 40 percent increase in juvenile female offending generally compared with a 25 percent increase in male juvenile offending for the same period (Snyder, Sickmund, and Poe-Yamagata, 1996:11). There was a 128 percent increase among juvenile females for violent crimes compared with a 69 percent increase for male juvenile offenders. Table 2.4 shows percent changes for male and female juveniles for several different comparative periods. Interestingly, sex offense arrests have declined over the years for both males and females. Also, liquor-related offenses have declined for both genders (e.g., driving while intoxicated, public drunkenness, liquor law violations). Female juveniles have had a 115 percent increase in robbery arrests and a 137

TABLE 2.4

Comparison of Male and Female Arrests, 1985–1994[a]

| | Percent change in arrest | | | | | |
| | 1993–1994 | | 1990–1994 | | 1985–1994 | |
	Female	Male	Female	Male	Female	Male
Total	13	10	31	19	40	25
Crime index total	10	5	25	4	42	12
Violent crime index	12	6	48	23	128	69
Murder	2	-3	29	14	64	158
Forcible rape	6	-8	9	0	8	6
Robbery	15	11	40	31	115	53
Aggravated assault	11	4	52	20	137	90
Property crime index	9	4	23	1	36	4
Burglary	-1	1	16	-3	6	-21
Larceny-theft	11	7	24	5	35	6
Motor vehicle theft	2	-2	22	-11	113	69
Arson	16	18	79	35	82	34
Nonindex offenses	15	14	34	28	38	33
Other assaults	15	13	61	36	143	105
Forgery	16	9	25	7	11	-11
Fraud	30	39	69	106	22	0
Embezzlement	16	44	-25	-20	46	14
Stolen property	3	1	17	-2	56	30
Vandalism	12	5	45	18	54	26
Weapons	3	2	96	53	137	101
Prostitution	-7	19	-35	-14	-72	-28
Sex offense	-25	-10	19	2	-3	-1
Drug abuse	50	41	101	87	31	72
Gambling	46	34	103	92	145	96
Against the family	13	9	66	63	72	72
Driving under influence	7	11	-29	-31	-38	-43
Liquor law violations	9	8	-17	-20	-5	-14
Drunkenness	7	7	-22	-27	-37	-37
Disorderly conduct	19	15	61	37	110	64
Vagrancy	33	15	60	33	46	38
All other offenses (except traffic)	17	13	38	30	30	21
Curfew	33	26	75	59	83	45
Runaways	7	7	19	17	18	19

[a]Because the absolute number of female arrests is less than male arrests, a larger percentage increase in female arrests does not necessarily imply a larger increase in the actual number of arrests. For example, while the percentage increase in female arrests for robbery was greater than the male increase between 1985 and 1994, the increase in the number of arrests was over 7 times greater for males than for females.

Source: Snyder, Sickmund, and Poe-Yamagata, 1996: 11. Data source: U.S. Department of Justice, Federal Bureau of Investigation, *Crime in the United States 1994* (Washington, DC: U.S. Government Printing Office, 1995).

percent increase in aggravated assault arrests between 1985 and 1994. However, male juvenile homicide offenders have greatly outpaced female juvenile homicide offenders. Figure 2.5 shows the great increase and difference between male and female juvenile homicide offenders from 1980 to 1994.

The paternalistic nature of the juvenile justice system as well as the differential handling by police of juvenile female offenders accounts in part for these small figures (Chesney-Lind and Shelden, 1992). Historical observations by Gelsthorpe (1987) indicate that there are four main themes that guide responses to boys and girls in the juvenile justice system nationally. First, it seems that boys are more likely to offend at some point during their adolescence. Those few girls who offend during this period are often considered abnormal in some way (Campbell, 1984). Second, much male offending is property related, while it is assumed that female delinquency is predominantly sexual. Third, female delinquents seem to

FIGURE 2.5   Male–Female Differences in Juvenile Homicide Offending, 1980–1994

Males have outpaced females in terms of growth in the number of juvenile homicide offenders

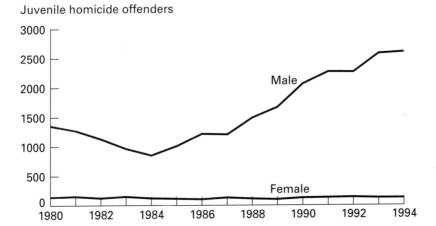

- From 1980 to 1994, about 9 in 10 juvenile homicide offenders were male.
- Over the 15 years since 1980, male and female homicide offending trends have been very different. The number of female homicide offenders increased 29% since 1980, while the number of male offenders has doubled.
- Although the number of female juvenile homicide offenders has increased, the female proportion of juvenile homicide offenders declined from the early 1980s to the early 1990s.

Source: From Snyder, Sickmund, and Poe-Yamagata, 1996:11. Data source: J. Fox, *Supplementary Homicide Reports 1976–1994* (machine-readable data file) (1996).

BOX 2.4   FEMALE DELINQUENCY

The Case of T.B. and the Telephone Repairman

It happened in Milwaukee, Wisconsin. A telephone repairman pulled into a Milwaukee alley to make a telephone call while repairing telephone lines. A drug dealer was standing nearby and suspected that Albert Thompson, the telephone repairman, was an undercover officer investigating illegal drug dealing. Danny Conner, a 20-year-old drug dealer known by the nickname "Crazy," knew undercover cops when he saw them. Acting on his orders, T.B., a 13-year-old girlfriend of Conner, loaded a .25 caliber pistol at Conner's instruction, went to confront Thompson in the alley, walked up to his truck, and tapped on his window. When Thompson looked at T.B., she shot him in the head through the window glass. His body was found slumped over his steering wheel in the truck by a co-worker when he failed to report in. Thompson was still barely alive, but he died five days later.

The drug dealer, Conner, was subsequently arrested, tried, and convicted of murder. He was given a mandatory life sentence for the crime. His girlfriend, 13-year-old T.B., faced murder charges in juvenile court for her role in Thompson's murder. She faced incarceration in a juvenile facility until her twenty-fifth birthday, a sentence of 12 years. She was six months' pregnant when appearing before the juvenile court judge for her disposition following the adjudication of delinquency on the murder charge.

Should T.B. be held in prison beyond her 12-year juvenile disposition? Should she have been tried in criminal court as an adult? What policies should juvenile court judges adopt as juveniles commit more serious offenses at younger ages?

Source: Adapted from Associated Press, "Girl Kills Repairman," *Minot (ND) Daily News,* May 17, 1996:A7.

come from broken homes at a higher rate than their male counterparts; therefore, their delinquency is often attributed to deficient family relationships. Finally, female delinquents seem to be regarded by criminological theory as the result of mental instability and unrational behavior, whereas male juvenile offenders are often regarded as rational and adventurous beings who are simply testing the bounds of their adolescence (Glick and Goldstein, 1995). It is concluded that much of this historical analysis of male and female juvenile differences is mythical and misconceived (Gelsthorpe, 1987).

A similar analysis along political–legal lines has been made by Curran (1984). Curran examined the long-range impact of the women's movement in the United States during the period 1960–1980. A prevailing belief is that the women's movement brought about many changes in both the quality and quantity of female offenses during this period, as well as the way in which women were generally treated in both the criminal and juvenile justice systems. However, Curran disagrees with this view. Rather, he suggests that certain political and legal changes in the United States during the 1960–1980 period furnish a better explanation of how female juvenile offenders have been treated. Further, changes in the rate of female delinquency are probably attributable to these same factors.

Two major events seemed to trigger the general shift from a liberal to a conservative approach to juvenile justice observed in many jurisdictions. First, states passed various acts geared to respond to public perceptions of rising violent crime among juveniles. Second, status offenses were removed from the jurisdiction of juvenile courts in many jurisdictions. High priority was given to "cracking down" on juvenile offenders by district attorneys in many cities. Regarding female juveniles, Curran has identified three major political–legal periods: (1) the "paternalistic" period (1960–1967), during which female delinquents were harshly treated by the courts "for their own good"; (2) a "due process" period (1968–1976), which reflected the impact of various legal decisions, such as *In re Gault* (1967); and (3) a "law-and-order" phase (1977–1980), during which the court adjusted to the new conservatism of the late 1970s (Curran, 1984). Therefore, *presumed* changing rates in female juvenile offending were more attributable to changing policies in the treatment of female juveniles rather than actual increases in the rate of female criminality. However, as we have seen, the nature of female juvenile offending is definitely changing and increasing. While policy changes and juvenile court views toward female offenders have probably occurred during the 1980s and 1990s, increased female juvenile offending has been observed. Female juveniles are presently outpacing their male counterparts in several key offending categories, as evidenced by the material presented in Table 2.4.

Profiling Female Juvenile Delinquents

Profiles of female delinquents have been infrequent. Those that have been conducted parallel in some ways the historical descriptions noted by Gelsthorpe (Chesney-Lind, 1978; Sarri, 1983). For example, Bergsmann (1989:73) says that "young women in trouble with the law are typically 16 years old, live in urban ghettos, are high school dropouts...are victims of sexual abuse, come from single-parent families, have experienced foster care placement, lack adequate work skills...and are predominantly black or Hispanic." These same observations have been made by others (Bergsmann, 1988; Sarri, 1988).

Evidence of stereotyping female juvenile offenders is extensive throughout the juvenile justice system (Bishop and Frazier, 1992). Courts tend to view female juveniles as more "vulnerable" than males, and thus there is a tendency for many juvenile court judges and others to treat them differently for even minor offense behaviors (Chesney-Lind, 1987a,b; Webb, 1984). For example, in 1984, of all juveniles who appeared in juvenile courts, females represented 45 percent of all status offender cases compared with only 19 percent of all delinquency cases. Of these 45 percent, 62 percent were runaways (Bersgmann, 1989:74).

Several case studies of female juvenile delinquents have indicated that many of these girls lack coping skills and good moral judgment (Bartek, Krebs and Taylor, 1993; Chesney-Lind and Shelden, 1992). In many jurisdictions a double standard exists, whereby parents are more likely to call the police when their daughters run away from home, and police are more likely to arrest females for running away (Chesney-Lind and Shelden, 1992; Glick and Goldstein, 1995). Some studies suggest that female delinquents are chronically self-destructive (Dolin, Kelly, and Beasley, 1992; Lewis et al., 1991). Thus greater emphasis should be given to self-development and improvement activities and counseling (Bartek, Krebs, and Taylor, 1993). Furthermore, theories designed to explain delinquency deal primarily with male delinquents rather than females. In several respects, different criteria must be applied in treatment programs designed for female offenders, since male-oriented strategies are often unworkable (Chesney-Lind and Shelden, 1992; Hale et al., 1991). For instance, programs for female juveniles should place greater emphasis on housing, training, employment, and survival skills, recognizing that many of these girls will not or cannot return to their families (Chesney-Lind and Shelden, 1992; Sommers and Baskin, 1994).

In many respects, present problems with female juvenile institutions and treatment programs are similar to adult female treatment program problems and patterns. The juvenile justice system has traditionally been geared to process male offenders in large numbers rather than female offenders. Thus services and programs benefiting female juveniles have often been neglected compared with programs that accommodate male juvenile offenders.

KEY TERMS

Age of majority

Career escalation

Chronic offenders

Cleared by arrest

Curfew violators

Decarceration

Deinstitutionalization of status offenses (DSO)

Delinquency

Delinquent child

Dependent and neglected children

Divestiture of jurisdiction

Felony

Hidden delinquency

Incident

Index crimes

Index offenses

Juvenile Justice and Delinquency Prevention Act of 1974 (JJDPA)

Misdemeanor

Monitoring the Future Survey

National Crime Victimization Survey (NCVS)

National Youth Survey

Net widening

Office of Juvenile Justice and Delinquency Prevention (OJJDP)

Relabeling

Runaways

Self-reports

Sourcebook of Criminal Justice Statistics

Status offendses

Truants

Uniform Crime Reports (UCR)

Victimization

QUESTIONS FOR REVIEW

1. How are juveniles generally defined in most jurisdictions? What seems to be the lowest age of majority for juvenile offenders in some states? Compare the federal definition of juveniles with the state conceptions you have identified.

2. What is *delinquency*? Is there a universally acceptable definition of delinquent conduct in the United States? What are several different interpretations of delinquent conduct among jurisdictions?

3. What are *status offenders*? Are status offenders also delinquents? Why or why not? What are some exceptions?

4. Are status offenders more likely than delinquents to escalate to more serious offenses during their youthful years? How do delinquents differ from status offenders relative to career escalation? What studies can you cite to support your views?

5. What is *DSO*? What are some of the aims of DSO? Are these aims necessarily being realized in most jurisdictions today? Why or why not? Explain.

6. What is *divestiture of jurisdiction*? What types of cases are usually targeted for divestiture? Why? How do judges and police in certain jurisdictions react to divestiture?

7. Describe the information generally presented about juveniles in the *Uniform Crime Reports* and *National Crime Victimization Survey*. What criticisms have been leveled at these official information sources? Are these criticisms valid? Why or why not? Explain.

8. Differentiate between an *incident* and a *victimization*. Why do some investigators feel that *NCVS* is a more accurate reflection of crime and delinquency in the United States than *UCR*?

9. What are *self-reports*? How are self-reports and *NCVS* related? Are self-reports necessarily more valid than official sources of information about delinquency? Why or why not? Explain.

10. What evidence exists that might suggest that females are treated differently than males by juvenile courts? What are some of the reasons traditionally given to explain the nature of female juvenile treatment? Are these reasons necessarily valid?

SUGGESTED READINGS

Alexander, Ruth M. *The "Girl Problem": Female Sexual Delinquency in New York, 1900–1930*. Ithaca, NY: Cornell University Press, 1995.

Gabel, Katherine and Denise Johnston (eds.). *Children of Incarcerated Parents*. New York: Lexington Books, 1995.

Ney, Tara (ed.). *True and False Allegations of Child Sexual Abuse: Assessment and Case Management*. New York: Brunner/Mazel, 1995.

Odem, Mary E. *Delinquent Daughters: Protecting and Policing Adolescent Female Sexuality in the United States: 1885–1920*. Chapel Hill, NC: University of North Carolina Press, 1995.

Rascovsky, Arnaldo. *Filicide: The Murder, Humiliation, Mutilation, Denigration, and Abandonment of Children by Parents*. Northvale, NJ: Jason Aronson, 1995.

Snyder, Howard N. and Melissa Sickmund. *Juvenile Offenders and Victims: A Focus on Violence*. Washington, DC: U.S. Office of Juvenile Justice and Delinquency Prevention, 1995.

CHAPTER 3

AN OVERVIEW OF THE JUVENILE JUSTICE SYSTEM

INTRODUCTION

In November 1989, a 16-year-old Detroit youth was shot to death for his Triple F.A.T. Goose parka and Nike sneakers. In Newark, New Jersey, at least 64 armed robberies in 1989 were attributable to athletic or leather wear. In February 1990, a 19-year-old, Calvin Wash, was shot to death when he ran away after several youths demanded his Cincinnati Bengals jacket. In New York, a security guard was shot to death after youths demanded his three-quarter-length leather jacket. Clothing kills. (Adapted from Nina Darnton, "Street Crimes of Fashion: Bloodshed over Clothes," *Newsweek,* March 5, 1990:58)

It was Valentine's Day in Long Beach, California. A 10-year-old girl put on her bright red dress for school. Her teacher told everyone to wear either red or pink for Valentine's Day. As she exited her school bus and prepared to enter school, a gang of four youths drove by with handguns extended from the car. One of the guns was pointed at the girl's head. She immediately dropped to the ground as bullets zinged overhead. A rival gang, whose colors were blue, was driving through the neighborhood of another gang, whose colors were red. They mistook the 10-year-old school girl for a gang member. She was nearly killed. (Adapted from Susan Pack, "How Safe Are Our Schools?" *Long Beach Press-Telegram,* April 28, 1991:A1)

It was a hot summer afternoon in Chicago. A 5-year-old boy, Eric Morse, was lured by two other boys to their clubhouse, a vacant apartment on the fourteenth floor of an old building in a housing project. Once at the apartment, Eric was grabbed by the two boys and dangled by his legs from the apartment window. The two boys let him drop 14 floors to his death. The two boys were 10 and 11, respectively. When police interviewed them later, they said that Eric refused to steal candy for them from a local store. At most the boys who killed Eric face five years' probation. ("Chicago Tragedy's Tearful Goodbye," *USA Today,* October 20, 1994:3A)

It was another hot summer afternoon in Chicago. Robert "Yummy" Sandifer was hiding from police. He was wanted for murder. He was nicknamed "Yummy" because he loved cookies. He had a rap sheet longer than those of most adult felons: 28 arrests in 18 months. Suddenly, two brothers in Sandifer's gang found him and shot him to death. They were afraid "Yummy" might implicate them in other crimes. Says Pat Tolan, professor of psychology and psychiatry at the University of Illinois at Chicago: "Violence has become so pervasive that 35 percent of a group of Chicago inner-city youths had seen someone shot, stabbed or severely beaten by age 11." (Adapted from Associated Press, "Kids Killing Kids," *Minot (ND) Daily News,* October 21, 1994:A7)

It happened at the Cook County Detention Center. A 10-year-old boy was raped by four boys under age 14. The assault occurred as two boys held the 10-year-old's arms and a group of youngsters watched television nearby. One of the four rapists was serving 30 days for burglary. Another was in for attempted murder. The 10-year-old victim was there on charges of attempting to hold up a doughnut shop. (Adapted from Associated Press, "10-Year-Old Boy Says He Was Raped Twice in Detention Center," *Minot (ND) Daily News,* October 23, 1994:A2)

What should be done with kids who kill or rape other kids? How should violent offenders be processed? What punishments should be imposed for juvenile rapists and youths who commit other violent crimes? In 1994, 2.2 million juveniles were arrested for various crimes in the United States (Maguire and Pastore, 1996:404). Most of these juveniles are taken to jails or lockups where they are detained for brief periods. While approximately 90 percent of these juveniles are either referred to juvenile court jurisdiction or released to parents or guardians within hours following their arrest, the remainder are formally admitted to these jails or other places of confinement to await further action (Maguire and Pastore, 1996).

The juvenile justice system interfaces in several significant ways with the criminal justice system. Because a small portion of the juveniles who are arrested by police will eventually come within the **jurisdiction** of the criminal justice system, it is important to understand the basic elements of *both* systems. This chapter is an overview of both the juvenile justice system and the criminal justice system. A description of the criminal justice system is provided, including the preliminary procedures often followed by law enforcement officers whenever youthful offenders are apprehended. Subsequent to arrest, juveniles must be identified and classified. Depending on the seriousness of the offense(s) alleged, decisions are made by arresting officers, jail personnel, and/or judges whether to release certain juveniles to the custody of their parents or legal guardians, whether to release them to juvenile authorities, or whether to detain them for further action.

Preliminary classifications and dispositions of many juvenile offenders are routine and pose few problems for arresting officers and others. However, a proportion of those taken into custody may require special handling and treatment. They may be mentally or physically ill, under the influence of drugs or alcohol, or dangerous and posing threats to the safety and security of others or even to themselves. Discretionary actions in some of these cases are far from perfunctory. The process of classifying juveniles and establishing where jurisdiction lies is described.

Once jurisdiction is established and it is determined that the juvenile justice system is where certain youthful offenders should be sent, these juveniles are brought to juvenile halls or other juvenile facilities, where they will await further disposition by *intake officers*. Although specific procedures followed in the processing of juveniles vary among jurisdictions, the general intake process will be described. This process involves several alternative actions and may lead to further involvement in the juvenile justice system. Prosecutors in many jurisdictions decide whether to bring juveniles before juvenile courts for formal adjudicatory action by judges. The juvenile court is becoming increasingly adversarial as juveniles acquire greater numbers of constitutional rights commensurate with those enjoyed by adults in the criminal justice system. In this chapter we provide an overview of adjudicatory alternatives available to juvenile court judges and describe the array of punishments that may be imposed on those found delinquent or in need of special care. Finally, a brief overview and description of juvenile corrections is presented.

THE CRIMINAL JUSTICE SYSTEM

The ***criminal justice system*** *is an interrelated set of agencies and organizations designed to control criminal behavior, to detect crime, and to apprehend, process, prosecute, punish, or rehabilitate criminal offenders.* Figure 3.1 is a diagram of the criminal justice system. Actually, the figure includes descriptions of both the criminal and juvenile justice systems, since cases that are considered as being within the jurisdiction of the juvenile justice system are diverted to it. These diversions to juvenile court occur either as the result of arrests by police officers or referrals from various community agencies, after appropriate classifications have been made about the youthful offenders involved. By the same token, some cases that originate in juvenile courts are eventually transferred to the jurisdiction of criminal courts. These actions are waivers, certifications, or transfers, and they are discussed in depth in Chapter 6. Therefore, since juveniles may eventually fall within the jurisdiction of adult criminal courts, it is important that we have some familiarity with these courts and the criminal justice system generally.

The traditional elements of the criminal justice system include *law enforcement, prosecution and courts*, and **corrections**, although lawmaking bodies such as the legislatures of states and the federal government are sometimes included. The word *system* is misleading in a sense, since the various criminal justice components are not as closely integrated and coordinated as a system would indicate. Some experts prefer to use *process* as the better means of depicting how those accused of crimes move through the various phases of the *system* and are *processed*. A system exists, but it is a loosely integrated one. For instance, law enforcement officers seldom ask prosecutors and the courts if they have arrested too many alleged criminals for the system to handle. In turn, prosecutors and the courts seldom ask penal authorities whether there is enough space to accommodate those sentenced to terms of incarceration. Below are descriptions of the various criminal justice system components.

FIGURE 3.1 The Criminal Justice System

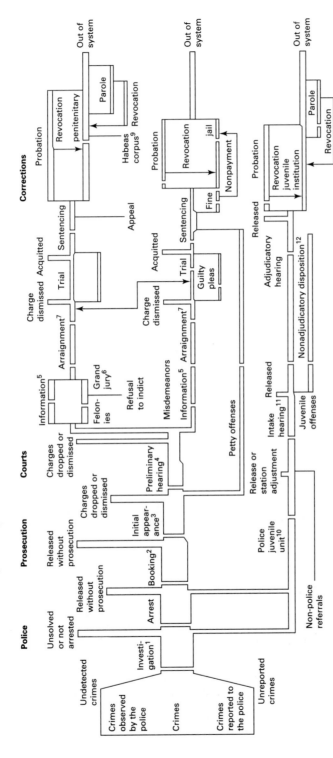

[1] May continue until trial.
[2] Administrative record of arrest. First step at which temporary release on bail may be available.
[3] Before magistrate, commissioner, or justice of the peace. Formal notice of charge, advice of rights. Bail set. Summary trials for petty offenses usually conducted here without further processing.
[4] Preliminary testing of evidence against defendant. Charge may be reduced. No seperate preliminary hearing for misdemeanors in some systems.

[5] Charge filed by prosecutor on basis of information submitted by police or citizens. Alternative to grand jury indictment; often used in felonies, almost always in misdemeanors.
[6] Reviews whether government evidence sufficient to justify trial. Some states have no grand jury system; others seldom use it.
[7] Appearance for plea; defendant elects trial by judge or jury (if available); counsel for indigent usually appointed here in felonies. Often not at all on other cases.

[8] Charge may be reduced at any time prior to trial in return for plea of guilty or for other reasons.
[9] Challenge on constitutional grounds to legality of detention. May be sought at any point in process.
[10] Police often hold informal hearings, dismiss or adjust many cases without further processing.
[11] Probation officer decides desirability of futher court action.
[12] Welfare agency, social services, counseling, medical care, etc., cases where adjudicatory handling not needed.

Source: From the President's Commission of Law Enforcement and Administration of Justice, The Challenge of Crime in a Free Society (Washington, DC: U.S. Government Printing Office, 1967), pp. 8–9.

Legislatures

Criminal laws originate largely as the result of legislative actions in most jurisdictions. *Jurisdiction refers to the power of courts to hear cases*, although we generally define a jurisdiction according to various political subdivisions, including townships, cities, counties, states, or federal districts. Thus when criminals cross state or county lines, they leave the state or local jurisdictions where violations of the law occurred. Under certain circumstances, these jurisdictional boundaries may be crossed by pursuing authorities. At the federal level, any federal agency may enforce certain federal laws in any state, territory, or U.S. possession.

The Congress of the United States passes criminal laws that are enforceable by various federal agencies, including the Federal Bureau of Investigation (FBI), Drug Enforcement Administration (DEA), and the Criminal Investigation Division (CID) of the Internal Revenue Service. State legislatures enact criminal laws that are enforced by state and local law enforcement officers. At the community level, city and county governments determine specific criminal laws, statutes, and ordinances that should be enforced, depending on the circumstances of the locality. Some local ordinances are especially geared to regulate juvenile conduct. Such ordinances include curfews, truancy laws, and incorrigibility provisions, where parents or guardians cannot control the behaviors of their children. Virtually all ordinances aimed at juveniles are status ordinances, since these ordinances are not applicable to adults. Whenever juveniles violate these ordinances or commit prohibited criminal offenses, they fall within the purview of law enforcement.

Law Enforcement

There were 17,358 police and sheriff's departments in 1993, including 12,502 general-purpose local police departments, 3086 sheriff's departments, and 1721 special police agencies (Reaves, 1993:1). These **law enforcement agencies** employ over 604,000 full-time sworn officers with general **arrest** powers and 237,000 nonsworn civilian personnel (Reaves, 1996). The most visible **law enforcement** officers are uniformed police officers in local and state governments. Although federal authorities may become involved in federal crimes allegedly committed by juveniles, most of the time their work is focused on apprehending adult offenders. Often, federal agents and other federal officers who apprehend juveniles will deliver them to local authorities for processing. Direct federal processing of juveniles is relatively rare (Rossum, Koller, and Manfredi, 1987).

Those law enforcement officers who have the most direct contact with juveniles are city police and sheriff's deputies, who patrol the streets, encounter juveniles acting suspiciously or in the act of committing offenses, or respond to citizen reports of disturbances involving juveniles. In certain jurisdictions, special police forces are designated to deal with particular types of juvenile offenders. In Honolulu, Hawaii, for example, the Honolulu Police Department has created a Youth Gang Response System, a collaboration between state and county agencies that emphasizes programs and community services (Chesney-Lind and Matsuo, 1995). Officers assigned to this program seek out all types of juvenile offenders, including truants and runaways, and either return them to school or take them into custody. Of course, in Hawaii and other jurisdictions, police officers may apprehend any juvenile suspected of violating criminal laws.

Whenever juveniles are **taken into custody** by police officers, they may be taken to a local police station and questioned. Police discretion is very important, since officers may make "on-the-spot" decisions either to warn and release juveniles in their initial encounters with them on city streets or take them to a jail or police department for further questioning. Circumstances often dictate which course of action is followed. Juveniles loitering late at night near a store where a burglar alarm has been activated are likely targets for apprehension by police. The police have a right to be suspicious of these juveniles and to investigate the circumstances of their presence in the area until they are satisfied that the youths were not involved in a possible burglary. However, if officers discover contraband, weapons, and/or burglary tools in the youths' possession, these are grounds to detain the juveniles until a more thorough investigation can be conducted.

Police discretion also influences where juveniles are taken if it is decided they should be detained. Extremely young juveniles may be taken directly to juvenile detention facilities in the community and turned over to juvenile officers. These juveniles may or may not be involved in offending activity, but their youthful appearance may indicate the need for adult supervision and parental involvement. This is particularly relevant in the case of extremely young runaways who have violated no criminal laws but who are nevertheless in need of shelter and other forms of assistance. Many male and female juveniles appear older than they really are. They may lie to police and give false names, addresses, and ages. Police have a right to detain these juveniles until their identity can be determined and whether they have violated any criminal laws (*Schall v. Martin*, 1984). This is known as **preventive detention**, and it is designed, in part, to protect juveniles from harming themselves or others, especially if they are considered dangerous or mentally disturbed. Juveniles who are detained pending further action may eventually fall within the discretion of prosecutors and juvenile courts.

BOX 3.1   MOTHER TURNS IN OWN SON FOR MURDER

The Case of Davon Murdock

On Monday, July 28, 1996, a 13-year-old girl was gang-raped by two 15-year-olds, a 17-year-old, and a 12-year-old. There were other unidentified participants. When an 82-year-old woman sought to intervene and save the girl from being raped, the old woman, Viola McClain, known affectionately throughout the neighborhood as "everybody's mama," was shot to death.

Police were able to locate suspects early in the investigation and piece together what had happened. The 13-year-old girl was taken from her own home and forced into an abandoned dwelling, a neighborhood eyesore that had been the subject of numerous complaints to city officials. There behind the boarded-up windows, the girl was raped and tortured for two hours. In an attempt to kill her, some of the gang attempted to burn down the house, setting fire to a mattress used in the attack. When neighbors smelled the smoke, Viola McClain's grandson, 33-year-old Dumar Stokes, walked toward the abandoned dwelling and saw some boys running from it. "What's going on?" he said. "We can do whatever we want to," said one of the boys. "If you don't get out of our way, we'll smoke you." Stokes told his grandmother, Viola, what was happening and went to get a gun. In the meantime, Viola went outside to confront the boys and was shot to death by them.

Six persons were arrested on the rape and murder charges. One was still missing, however. His name was Davon Murdock and he was only 12 years old. Less than 5 feet tall and weighing less than 100 pounds, no one would ever suspect Murdock of rape and murder. Los Angeles Police Chief Willie Williams put Davon's picture on the television nightly news and requested neighborhood help in locating Davon. When Davon's mother saw her son's picture on television, she immediately brought him to police headquarters and turned him in. It turned out that Davon was the main suspect in the incident, despite the fact that older kids were present.

If Davon is guilty of this crime, what should be his punishment? Should youths as young as 12 years of age receive life-without-parole sentences? Are kids this young and younger emotionally and socially responsible to be charged with murder? At what age should the line be drawn?

Source: Adapted from Michael Fleeman, "Crimes, Suspect's Age Shock Neighborhood," *Honolulu Advertiser*, August 4, 1996:A7.

Prosecution and the Courts

When criminal suspects and others are arrested by law enforcement officers or are otherwise taken into custody, they are usually booked. ***Booking*** *involves obtaining descriptive information from those arrested, including* *their names, addresses, occupations (if any), next of kin, photographs, and fingerprints.* Booking varies in formality among jurisdictions. Essentially, the booking process is a formality as well as an account or written report of the arrest or detention. Police may consult other law enforcement agencies through a computer network to determine whether those arrested have prior records of arrests or crimes. Interested agencies such as the Bureau of Justice Statistics within the U.S. Department of Justice may collect this statistical information later to profile those admitted to jails and other places of confinement.

Figure 3.1 shows other stages of processing in the criminal justice system subsequent to the arrest and booking of suspects. Note that one early discretionary action is to divert certain offenders directly to the juvenile justice system. For adult offenders, however, they will likely move forward to the **initial appearance** stage. The initial appearance of **defendants** or those charged with crimes is before a magistrate or other court official, usually to advise defendants of the charges against them and to determine the amount of bail necessary to obtain their release. ***Bail*** or a ***bail bond*** *is a surety in the form of money or property that may be posted by either a bonding company or others, including defendants themselves, to obtain their temporary release from custody and to ensure their subsequent appearance at trial.*

Under the Eighth Amendment, only those entitled to bail may receive it. Bail is not an absolute right under the constitution. Ordinarily, those not entitled to bail are either considered very dangerous to others or highly likely to flee the jurisdiction to avoid prosecution for their crimes. Because of serious jail overcrowding problems and other considerations, bail is often waived in minor cases, and defendants are **released on their own recognizance** (ROR). These persons usually have ties within the community, are employed, and are not considered dangerous or likely to flee.

During the interim following the defendant's initial appearance, prosecutors, who represent the state's interests, must decide whether to pursue formal charges against these persons. Evidence of criminal activity collected by police officers (e.g., eyewitness reports, confessions, weapons, fingerprints) is carefully examined, and consideration is given to the seriousness of the alleged criminal activity and prior record of the defendant, if any. If defendants are represented by counsel, interactions may occur between prosecutors and defense counsels where agreements are reached known as plea bargains. ***Plea bargains*** *are preconviction agreements between defendants and the state whereby defendants enter guilty pleas to certain criminal charges in exchange for some state benefit such as sentencing leniency* (McDonald, 1985). Probably over 90 percent of all criminal convictions are secured through **plea bargaining** in most U.S. jurisdictions at both the state and federal levels. In many instances, if the cases against certain defendants are weak, prosecutors may elect to drop the charges and excuse these defendants from further processing.

Depending on the circumstances, prosecutors may follow through with charges against defendants and take their cases to trial. Using this worst-case scenario (for the defendant), defendants who either do not plea bargain or persist in a plea of "not guilty" will eventually be arraigned. *An* ***arraignment*** *is a proceeding where (1) a list of specific charges is made available to defendants and their attorneys, (2) a formal plea to the charges is entered by the defendant, and (3) a trial date is established.* Prior to being arraigned, however, those charged with especially serious crimes will be entitled to a **preliminary examination** or **preliminary hearing**, a proceeding where both the prosecutor and defense counsel may present some evidence against and on behalf of the defendant. Preliminary hearings establish whether probable cause exists. ***Probable cause*** *is the determination or reasonable suspicion that a crime has been committed and that the defendant probably committed it. These hearings are not trials and do not establish one's guilt or innocence.* They are intended to determine whether sufficient evidence exists to proceed further (i.e., probable cause).

The preliminary hearing is important also because it is an opportunity for judges and others to hear some of the evidence both in the defendant's favor and derogatory to the defendant. In some respects, as Figure 3.1 specifies, this is a preliminary testing of the evidence. Two types of evidence are **exculpatory** and **inculpatory** respectively, meaning that the evidence may help to show the defendant's innocence (exculpatory) or guilt (inculpatory). At this stage, prosecutors sometimes decide to withdraw charges against defendants. Also at this stage, the presiding magistrate may conclude that insufficient evidence exists against the defendant to proceed any further. Thus the criminal charges either may be dropped or dismissed outright. Figure 3.1 shows this particular phase sandwiched between the initial appearance and arraignment.

Note in Figure 3.1 also that upward and downward branches of the process following the preliminary hearing include **informations**. A brief explanation of these branches is in order. First, informations, sometimes known as **criminal informations**, are *formal charges against defendants brought by prosecutors acting on their own authority*. Typically, informations may be brought against any defendant for minor crimes or misdemeanors. This is reflected by the lower branch stemming from preliminary hearings. However, if the crime is a felony, this follows the upper branch.

While preliminary hearings or preliminary examinations are used in most jurisdictions for an early test of the evidence against defendants for the purpose of establishing whether probable cause exists to proceed further, about half of all states use **grand juries** to bring charges against defendants charged with serious offenses. Grand juries are investigative bodies of citizens selected from residents of the jurisdiction. Because of great variation among jurisdictions relating to the size and functions of grand juries, it is difficult to specify a universally applicable definition of them. Federal grand juries, for instance, consist of from 16 to 23 members and serve for 90- or 120-day periods. Besides the issuance of criminal informations against defendants by prosecutors, grand juries may also issue charges against defendants. These charges are either **indictments** or **presentments**.

Indictments, also known as **true bills**, are the functional equivalent of criminal informations brought by prosecutors. Ordinarily, prosecutors present evidence to grand juries for their consideration. Defendants and their attorneys are barred from grand jury proceedings. Thus, in these one-sided affairs, it is fairly easy for prosecutors to present convincing cases against defendants and rationales for why they should be charged with crimes. When grand juries issue indictments, they are in effect saying, "We believe that probable cause has been established that a crime or crimes have been committed and John Doe (or the person or persons named in the indictment) probably committed the crimes." If the grand jury feels that insufficient evidence has been presented by prosecutors against defendants, these juries may issue **no bills** or **no true bills**. A no bill results in charges being dismissed against defendants, since probable cause was not established that the person or persons named in the indictment committed the crimes alleged. Since grand jury proceedings are so one-sided, however, no bills or no true bills are exceptional.

In certain cases under investigation, grand juries hear evidence or allegations against one or more suspects. Perhaps local law enforcement officers or federal authorities such as the FBI are conducting undercover surveillance or sting operations of organized criminal activity, illegal gambling operations, or vehicular theft rings and "chop-shops" (facilities where stolen vehicles are dismembered or altered so that they may be resold to others as new cars or newly titled automobiles and cannot easily be traced). If the undercover activities of law enforcement officers became known to those allegedly engaged in these criminal activities, this would be to the criminals' advantage and they could possibly escape detection. Therefore, rather than make early arrests of suspects, law enforcement officers gather evidence over fairly lengthy time periods in order to build strong cases against targeted law violators. Eventually, this evidence is accumulated by grand juries, which on their own, issue presentments or charges against those allegedly conducting the illegal activities. The media in various jurisdictions have popularized these undercover law enforcement activities as **sting operations**.

Summarizing these procedures briefly, grand juries issue either indictments or presentments against various suspects, depending on whether the evidence is submitted by prosecutors who request grand jurors to indict specific persons (indictments) or whether the grand jury, acting on its own authority, believes that crimes have been committed and specific persons committed those crimes. In either case, indictments and presentments are formal and written accusations detailing alleged criminal activity against one or more defendants. If the grand juries investigate and determine that insufficient evidence exists against certain defendants, they simply issue no true bills and actions against alleged wrongdoers are terminated. Also, prosecutors, acting on their own authority, may bring informations against suspects for minor, misdemeanor offenses.

In those jurisdictions utilizing both grand juries and preliminary examinations or hearings, defendants charged with crimes may waive their right to a preliminary hearing and have their case bound over to grand juries for further action. However, if suspects exercise their right to the preliminary examination, grand jury action is unnecessary. In sum, the purpose of both preliminary examinations (hearings) and grand jury action is to establish probable cause that a crime was committed and the defendant probably committed it. In neither instance is guilt or innocence proved.

The term **jury** is confusing to those unfamiliar with the criminal justice system. Because grand juries issue indictments or presentments against defendants, some persons believe immediately that those indicted must obviously be guilty of the crimes alleged, since a "jury" issued an indictment against them. This isn't so. Those juries charged with determining one's guilt beyond a reasonable doubt are known as **petit juries**. The petit juries, more commonly known as "juries," are the citizens selected to hear evidence in trials. Thus an important distinction exists between grand juries, who decide probable cause questions and whether further action should be taken against defendants, and petit juries, who decide the issue of guilt using the *beyond a reasonable doubt* standard in all criminal cases.

After a trial date is established from the point of arraignment, defendants may elect to have either a **bench trial** or a **jury trial**, depending on the seriousness of the crimes alleged. Bench trials are conducted exclusively by the judge who presides and determines the defendant's guilt or innocence. Jury trials or trials by jury involve determinations of one's guilt or innocence by a jury of one's peers. These peers are selected by various methods from the community or jurisdiction where the trial occurs. All citizens charged with a crime are entitled to a jury trial as a matter of right under the U.S. Constitution if the possible statutory incarcerative term accompanying the alleged offense is six months or longer (*Duncan v. Louisiana*, 1968). There are some exceptions to this provision, however.

Trials are adversarial proceedings where a defendant's guilt or innocence is established. Jury trials vary in size among jurisdictions. In some states, for instance, juries may consist of six jurors. Traditionally, jury size in the majority of states and in federal district courts in criminal trials is 12 jurors. In these jury trials, if jurors cannot agree on a verdict, the jury is considered deadlocked or "hung" and a **mistrial** is declared. Most jurisdictions, including the federal district courts, require that juries must be unanimous, regardless of their finding. However, in a few states, such as Louisiana and Oregon where jury size is 12, majority verdicts of 9–3 or 10–2 are permitted (*Johnson v. Louisiana*, 1972; *Apodaca v. Oregon*, 1972).

The minimum jury size for any criminal trial in any U.S. jurisdiction has been fixed by the U.S. Supreme Court at six, although no upper limit on jury size has ever been determined (*Williams v. Florida*, 1970). In cases where the jury consists of six jurors, their verdict must be unanimous. It is unconstitutional to permit majority verdicts of 5–1 or 6–2 in these minimally sized juries (*Burch v. Louisiana*, 1979). In those events where jurors cannot agree, a simple mistrial is declared. At this point it is the prosecutor's option to resurrect the case against the defendant again and bring it to another trial later. The 1990 federal trial of Washington, DC, Mayor Marion Barry, Jr. was an example of jury disagreement. Originally tried on multiple charges (14) involving drug possession and use and perjury, Barry was found guilty of one misdemeanor charge of simple cocaine possession and acquitted of one misdemeanor charge, but the jury could not agree on his guilt or innocence on the remaining 12 charges. Federal prosecutors at first advised the media that they would seek to retry Barry on the remaining charges in a new trial, but a few weeks after this announcement, the U.S. Attorney's Office stated that it had no further plans to prosecute Barry for the original crimes alleged.

When defendants are convicted of one or more crimes, they must face sentencing. Criminal court judges consider all circumstances and information available, and on the basis of their experience and judgment, together with statutory provisions mandated by legislatures, they impose sentences. Sentences do not necessarily involve incarceration. In many states, judges are permitted wide latitude in the sentences they may give convicted offenders. Judges consider factors such as one's leadership role in the crime and whether physical injuries were inflicted on victims during the crime's commission. Such circumstances are **aggravating circumstances** and they intensify the punishment convicted offenders receive. Other factors are considered, including whether offenders furnished helpful information to police that enabled them to apprehend others connected with the crime. An offender's youthfulness would be considered as well. Whether offenders were mentally ill when they committed their crimes would also be important.

These factors are considered **mitigating circumstances**, and they often result in lessening the severity of punishment imposed by the judge.

Because of serious prison and jail overcrowding problems in most jurisdictions, however, judges often impose probation as a punishment. *Probation is a conditional nonincarcerative sentence in which the offender is under the management of probation department personnel or probation officers.* Probation is most often used for first offenders who have been convicted of minor crimes. However, evidence of its growing use in the United States annually for more serious crimes (e.g., felony probation) is well documented (Champion, 1988). Regardless of whether convicted offenders receive probation or a sentence involving incarceration for designated terms, offenders move to the final component of the criminal justice process—corrections.

Corrections

Corrections consists of all agencies and personnel who deal with convicted offenders after court proceedings. As noted earlier, some convicted offenders may receive probation or conditional sentences in lieu of incarceration. Use of probation is widespread in the United States. In 1996 over 3 million offenders were on probation (U.S. Department of Justice, 1996). Table 3.1 shows the numbers of offenders on probation and parole in the United States at year end 1995.

Other offenders may be confined in jails or prisons, again depending on the seriousness of their offenses, the jurisdiction where the conviction occurred, and the availability of jail or prison space. In 1996 1,585,400 offenders were in either jails or prisons in the United States (Gilliard and Beck, 1996:1). Generally, jails are short-term facilities and are locally operated by city or county governments (Mays and Thompson, 1991). In a few instances, jails are state operated. Most jail functions include but are not limited to detaining those arrested for various offenses and who are awaiting trial, maintaining witnesses in protective custody pending their testimony in court, providing confinement for short-term, petty offenders serving sentences of less than one year, and accommodating overflow from state or federal prisons in instances where chronic prison overcrowding exists (Mays and Thompson, 1991). Ordinarily, jails are not equipped for long-term confinement of prisoners. They have few, if any, recreational facilities and few services. As we have seen, jails are often sites where juveniles are taken when they are first apprehended. Various dispositional arrangements are made pertaining to them once police officers and others have investigated the circumstances of their arrests.

TABLE 3.1

Adults on Probation, 1995[a]

Region and jurisdiction	Beginning probation population, 1/1/95	During 1995 Entries	Exits	Ending probation population, 12/31/95	Percent change in probation population, during 1995	No. on probation on 12/31/95 per 100,000 adult residents
U.S. total	2,981,400	1,501,589	1,381,636	3,090,626	3.7	1,593
Federal[b]	42,309	18,601	22,404	38,506	*	20
State	2,939,091	1,482,988	1,359,232	3,052,120	3.8	1,573
Northeast	526,375	232,686	214,444	544,620	3.5	1,402
Connecticut	53,453	37,135	36,081	54,507	2.0	2,201
Maine[c]	8,638	†	†	8,641	‡	923
Massachusetts	46,670	36,611	37,601	43,680	-6.4	941
New Hampshire	4,323	3,432	3,408	4,347	0.6	509
New Jersey	125,299	59,376	57,552	127,123	1.5	2,125
New York	163,613	45,061	35,175	173,499	6.0	1,276
Pennsylvania	99,524	39,764	32,465	106,823	7.3	1,166
Rhode Island	18,179	9,813	9,314	18,678	2.7	2,483
Vermont	6,676	3,494	2,848	7,322	9.7	1,672
Midwest	642,924	341,567	316,851	671,094	4.4	1,472
Illinois[c]	104,664	63,862	61,723	109,489	4.6	1,258
Indiana[d]	83,555	†	†	83,555	*	1,936
Iowa	15,902	10,456	9,779	16,579	4.3	783
Kansas[c]	17,256	11,831	7,726	16,547	-4.1	884
Michigan[c]	142,640	68,000	62,338	148,377	4.0	2,110
Minnesota[c]	81,972	55,911	57,131	83,778	2.0	2,490
Missouri[c]	36,295	21,887	18,453	40,595	11.8	1,030
Nebraska	18,639	15,485	14,697	19,427	4.2	1,627
North Dakota	2,036	1,474	1,219	2,291	12.5	486
Ohio[c]	90,190	68,077	59,558	99,603	10.4	1,201
South Dakota	3,874	4,393	4,643	3,624	-6.5	693
Wisconsin[c]	45,901	20,191	19,584	47,269	3.0	1,254
South	1,214,375	618,343	573,402	1,254,817	3.3	1,846
Alabama[c]	31,284	4,696	4,498	31,416	0.4	990
Arkansas	19,606	8,431	5,656	22,381	14.2	1,220
Delaware	15,507	7,395	6,555	16,347	5.4	3,036
District of Columbia	11,306	4,733	5,777	10,262	-9.2	2,334
Florida[c]	247,014	146,989	133,585	255,550	3.5	2,367
Georgia[c]	140,694	69,102	67,228	142,453	1.3	2,699
Kentucky	11,417	5,582	5,500	11,499	0.7	398
Louisiana	33,604	11,431	11,282	33,753	0.4	1,088
Maryland	76,940	35,530	41,441	71,029	-7.7	1,884
Mississippi	9,042	3,511	2,958	9,595	6.1	496
North Carolina	90,418	49,804	42,301	97,921	8.3	1,815
Oklahoma[c]	26,285	14,195	13,029	27,866	6.0	1,161
South Carolina	40,005	16,643	14,482	42,166	5.4	1,545
Tennessee	34,896	20,431	18,594	36,733	5.3	931
Texas	396,276	200,365	181,144	415,497	4.9	3,119
Virginia	24,089	19,394	19,219	24,264	0.7	485
West Virginia[c]	5,992	111	153	6,085	1.6	433
West	555,417	290,392	254,535	581,589	4.7	1,397
Alaska	2,899	960	1,296	2,563	-11.6	619
Arizona[c]	34,365	15,514	10,728	32,532	-5.3	1,076
California	277,655	142,560	133,229	286,986	3.4	1,259
Colorado[c]	39,065	25,042	21,840	42,010	7.5	1,519
Hawaii	13,088	6,620	6,385	13,323	1.8	1,518
Idaho	5,770	6,110	5,711	6,169	6.9	757
Montana	5,656	2,022	1,833	5,845	3.3	922
Nevada	9,410	6,043	5,377	10,076	7.1	890
New Mexico	8,063	7,727	7,514	8,276	2.6	698
Oregon	38,086	13,397	11,758	39,725	4.3	1,695
Utah	7,714	4,136	3,372	8,478	9.9	664
Washington[c]	110,279	58,476	43,640	122,306	10.9	3,048
Wyoming	3,367	1,785	1,852	3,300	-2.0	960

Source: U.S. Department of Justice, 1996:5.

[a]Counts are subject to revision. Final counts will be published in *Correctional Populations in the United States, 1995.* *, not calculated; †, not available ‡ less than 0.05%.

[b]Defined as persons received for probation directly from court. The decrease resulted from a review of the statistical database by the Administrative Office of the U.S. Courts, which identified and closed cases that had been coded incorrectly.

[c]Because of nonresidents or incomplete data, the population on December 31, 1995, does not equal the population on January 1, 1995, plus entries, minus exits.

[d]Data are for 12/31/94.

Prisons are long-term facilities. Most prisons have recreational yards, hospitals, work programs, and a host of other facilities to accommodate inmates who are confined for lengthy periods. Prisons are usually reserved for more serious offenders who have received incarcerative sentences of one year or longer from judges. It is highly unusual for those convicted of misdemeanors and sentenced to short incarcerative terms to be placed in prisons. There simply is no space available in most jurisdictions to accommodate them. Priority is usually given to long-term and more dangerous offenders, although each jurisdiction exhibits differences in the composition of its prison population. In certain areas where chronic prison overcrowding exists, it is not unusual for the courts to order prison inmates confined to local jail facilities to serve a portion of their incarcerative terms. This is a primary means of alleviating prison overcrowding, although it often creates or contributes to chronic jail overcrowding in the process. However, state authorities pay city and county governments an attractive sum per diem per prisoner, substantially more than these governments would spend on their own jail inmates. Thus the profit motive explains some jail overcrowding in certain jurisdictions.

In many jurisdictions, inmates of prisons and jails may be released short of serving their full sentences. This is usually accomplished through parole. ***Parole** is a conditional release from incarceration for a designated duration, usually the remainder of one's original sentence.* Thus, if offenders were sentenced to 10 years' incarceration, they might be eligible for parole after serving four or five years. A **parole board** would consider their parole eligibility and grant them early release from prison. In parole situations, parolees are supervised by parole officers. In 1988, about 700,000 offenders were on parole in the United States (U.S. Department of Justice, 1996:5). Table 3.2 shows the number of parolees in the United States at year end 1995.

Besides parole, prisoners might obtain early release through an accumulation of **good-time credits**. These are usually statutorily prescribed days off for good behavior, provided inmates comply with prison rules and commit no serious infractions. In federal prisons, for example, federal inmates may accumulate 54 days per year as *good time* off their original sentences. Usually, good time is calculated at the rate of so many days per months served.* An example of how good time can influence one's sentence is the case of Lawrence Singleton, an ex-merchant seaman who was convicted in 1979 of raping and mutilating Mary Vincent. Mary Vincent

---

*For the U.S. Federal Bureau of Prisons, federal prisoners must serve at least 85 percent of their sentences. The remaining time, 15 percent, is used to calculate good time. Each year consists of 365 days: 365 days × 0.15 = 54. Thus 54 days per year is approximately 15 percent. This good time is deducted from one's maximum sentence for every year served, provided that inmates do not violate prison rules and are not involved in prison disturbances, such as riots or fights.

TABLE 3.2

Adults on Parole, 1995[a]

Region and jurisdiction	Beginning parole population, 1/1/95	During 1995 Entries	Exits	Ending parole population, 12/31/95	Percent change in parole population, during 1995	No. on parole on 12/31/95 per 100,000 adult residents
U.S. total	690,371	411,369	391,298	700,174	1.4	361
Federal[b,c]	61,430	29,491	22,552	59,136	*	30
State	628,941	381,878	368,746	641,038	1.9	330
Northeast	173,882	77,451	67,082	184,122	5.9	474
Connecticut	1,146	1,934	1,847	1,233	7.6	50
Maine[c]	40	1	2	41	2.5	4
Massachusetts[c]	4,755	3,727	3,702	4,639	-2.4	100
New Hampshire[c]	835	702	762	785	-6.0	92
New Jersey	41,802	17,198	11,589	47,411	13.4	793
New York	53,832	27,158	25,422	55,568	3.2	409
Pennsylvania	70,355	25,814	22,935	73,234	4.1	799
Rhode Island	525	597	529	593	13.0	79
Vermont	592	320	294	618	4.4	141
Midwest	82,478	62,155	56,698	87,364	5.9	192
Illinois	26,695	22,706	19,860	29,541	10.7	339
Indiana	3,409	5,310	5,120	3,599	5.6	83
Iowa	3,696	1,665	1,826	3,535	-4.4	167
Kansas	6,291	3,741	3,938	6,094	-3.1	325
Michigan	12,846	9,078	8,062	13,862	7.9	197
Minnesota	1,904	2,581	2,368	2,117	11.2	63
Missouri[c]	12,592	5,352	5,278	13,023	3.4	330
Nebraska	771	718	828	661	-14.3	55
North Dakota	94	209	189	114	21.3	24
Ohio	6,453	5,332	5,203	6,582	2.0	79
South Dakota	662	590	564	688	3.9	132
Wisconsin[c]	7,065	4,873	3,462	7,548	6.8	200
South	253,731	101,722	111,741	243,309	-4.1	358
Alabama	7,235	1,525	1,525	7,235	0	228
Arkansas	5,224	4,108	4,477	4,855	-7.1	265
Delaware	1,029	40	259	810	-21.3	150
District of Columbia	6,574	2,702	2,580	6,696	1.9	1,523
Florida[c]	20,573	3,769	9,649	13,746	-33.2	127
Georgia[c]	17,505	10,862	9,479	19,434	11.0	368
Kentucky	4,380	3,256	3,379	4,257	-2.8	147
Louisiana	17,112	9,793	7,877	19,028	11.2	613
Maryland	14,795	11,921	10,968	15,748	6.4	418
Mississippi[c]	1,519	840	847	1,510	-0.6	78
North Carolina	20,159	11,530	13,188	18,501	-8.2	343
Oklahoma	2,604	661	909	2,356	-9.5	98
South Carolina	6,077	1,522	1,702	5,897	-3.0	216
Tennessee	9,353	3,357	3,859	8,851	-5.4	224
Texas	108,563	24,425	29,899	103,089	-5.0	774
Virginia	9,649	10,766	10,227	10,188	5.6	204
West Virginia	1,380	645	917	1,108	-19.7	79
West	118,850	140,550	133,225	126,243	6.2	303
Alaska	412	439	392	459	11.4	111
Arizona	4,351	5,693	5,935	4,109	-5.6	136
California	85,082	118,948	112,223	91,807	7.9	403
Colorado	2,463	3,021	2,460	3,024	22.8	109
Hawaii	1,650	668	629	1,689	2.4	192
Idaho[c]	931	539	676	862	-7.4	106
Montana	710	431	386	755	6.3	119
Nevada	3,529	1,787	1,856	3,460	-2.0	306
New Mexico	1,078	815	775	1,118	3.7	94
Oregon	14,264	6,160	5,405	15,019	5.3	641
Utah	2,417	1,818	1,504	2,731	13.0	214
Washington	1,650	75	850	875	-47.0	22
Wyoming	313	156	134	335	7.0	97

Source: U.S. Department of Justice, 1996:5.

[a]Counts are subject to revision. Final counts will be published in *Correctional Populations in the United States, 1995*. *, not calculated.
[b]Defined as persons received for probation supervision upon release from prison. Includes supervised release, parole, military parole, special parole, and mandatory release. The decrease resulted from a review of the statistical database by the Administrative Office of the U.S. Courts, which identified and closed cases that had been coded incorrectly.
[c]Because of nonresidents or incomplete data, the population on December 31, 1995, does not equal the population on January 1, 1995, plus entries, minus exits.

was a 16-year-old hitchhiking in San Francisco, California when Singleton picked her up and drove her to a remote location. He raped her repeatedly, beat her, and then cut off both her arms at the elbows. He dumped her in a ditch and left her to die. However, she lived and eventually identified him as her assailant. He was convicted for his crimes under California law and received the maximum term of 14 years, 4 months in prison. Had Singleton served the entire sentence, he would not have been released from prison until 1995. However, he walked out of prison a free man on April 25, 1987. Singleton was not paroled. The California Department of Corrections had to release him, since he had accumulated a sufficient amount of good time credit to warrant unconditional early release. Singleton died later in Florida from natural causes.

There are many correctional options available for judges to impose besides probation and incarceration. A vast array of intermediate punishments has been described by McCarthy and McCarthy (1997). **Intermediate punishments** *are sanctions that exist somewhere between incarceration and probation on the continuum of criminal penalties* (McCarthy and McCarthy, 1997). Intermediate punishments might include electronic monitoring, house arrest or home confinement, or community-based correctional alternatives such as halfway houses or intensive supervised probation or parole. Many of these options are available to juvenile as well as adult offenders.

This brief overview was designed to describe generally the criminal justice process or system outlined in Figure 3.1. In-depth discussions of each phase of this system may be found in general criminal justice textbooks or in specialized works about law enforcement, the police, prosecutors, the courts, sentencing systems, corrections, or probation and parole. As was noted at the beginning of this section, it is important that we should be somewhat familiar with the criminal justice process, since many juveniles fall within its jurisdiction annually.

Some people believe it unusual for juvenile courts to willingly relinquish control over juveniles and pass these youths to the jurisdiction of criminal courts. Although much more will be presented about why certain youths are transferred to criminal courts from the jurisdiction of juvenile courts, it is sufficient for the present to indicate that criminal courts have available a broader array of punishments as well as more severe punishments, including the death penalty (Streib, 1987). For certain youthful offenders, one view is that these severe punishments ought to be considered as optional. In juvenile courts, the death penalty and life-without-parole are beyond the jurisdiction of juvenile court judges.

Literally thousands of juveniles are transferred to the jurisdiction of U.S. criminal courts each year (Champion and Mays, 1991). In 1994, for

BOX 3.2   NEW LAWS AND JUVENILE TRANSFER HEARINGS

The Case of Trying Younger Juveniles in Criminal Courts

A few days after New Year's Day, 1996, a motel clerk was stabbed to death early one morning by several adults and a 17-year-old juvenile. The murder and robbery, which netted the perpetrators about $450, took place in Minot, North Dakota. About five months earlier, North Dakota enacted a new law making it possible for youths as young as 14 years of age to be transferred to criminal court to face criminal charges as adults. The implication is that more severe punishments, including life-without-parole sentences or the death penalty (in states where the death penalty might be imposed) could be invoked by judges where juries find the offenders guilty beyond a reasonable doubt.

In the Minot case, considerable evidence existed to show that the men and the juvenile, later identified as David George Sisson, 17, committed the murder. Sisson admitted to the crime and implicated the others. According to the new state law, if a juvenile is 14 or older and the juvenile court finds probable cause that the juvenile committed murder, the juvenile's case is *automatically transferred* to criminal court. All criminal proceedings become open to the public if the case is transferred, and the juvenile's identity is made public. The law had only been on the books for five months at the time of the motel clerk's death. At least two other juveniles had been transferred to criminal court on murder charges by the time of the Minot incident.

However, according to *Kent v. United States* (1966), *all* juveniles are entitled to a **transfer hearing** before their cases can be transferred to criminal court. This means that the 17-year-old is entitled to a hearing before any transfer is possible. But in this type of case, when transfers are automatic, hearings are still required. They involve **reverse waiver hearings**, since the laws are written to transfer such youths automatically when capital offenses are alleged against them.

In September 1996, a Minot man, David George Sisson, 18 years of age, pleaded guilty to the murder of the motel clerk. The other three participants earlier pleaded guilty and received 10-year sentences in exchange for their testimony against the man who stabbed the motel clerk to death. In the case of Sisson, he was sentenced to 45 years in prison and will be eligible for parole after serving 29 years.

Should the age at which juveniles can be charged with adult crimes be lowered even more than 14 years of age? What about juveniles who commit drive-by shootings and kill innocent passersby when these juveniles are 9, 10, or 11 years of age? What should be the minimum age at which youths should be held accountable in criminal court for adults?

Source: Adapted from Luke Shockman, "Transfer Hearing Set for Stabbing Suspect," *Minot (ND) Daily News*, January 10, 1996:C1; and Associated Press, "Sisson Pleads Guilty," *Minot (ND) Daily News*, September 20, 1996:A1, A8.

instance, 12,300 youths were transferred to the jurisdiction of criminal courts from juvenile courts (Butts, 1996a:6). This influx of juveniles into the criminal justice system annually is consistent with the general trend toward more punitive responses to delinquency, a manifestation of the get-tough policy in action (Bishop, Frazier, and Henretta, 1989). Interestingly, it is not always juvenile court judges or prosecutors who initiate these transfers. Rather, in many states, including Illinois, New York, and California, transfers of certain youthful offenders are legislatively mandated for certain types of crimes (Sagatun, McCollum, and Edwards, 1985). Known in some jurisdictions as **automatic transfer laws**, juveniles age 16 or 17 may be automatically transferred to criminal court jurisdiction on charges of rape, murder, or robbery (Grisso, 1996). Thus, for better or worse, juveniles must sometimes face particularly serious consequences for the serious offenses they commit in their youthful years.

In the remainder of this chapter we examine the juvenile justice system and provide an overview of a juvenile's movement through it. Later chapters provide more detailed coverage of each of these stages. We begin this discussion at the point where youths have been arrested and taken into custody by law enforcement officers or others.

ARREST AND IDENTIFICATION

Referrals

Following the diagram in Figure 3.1, many juvenile encounters with the juvenile justice system are prompted by referrals from police officers (Butts, 1996a). *Referrals are notifications made to juvenile court authorities that a juvenile requires the court's attention.* Referrals may be made by anyone, such as concerned parents, school principals, teachers, neighbors and others. However, over 90 percent of all referrals to juvenile court are made by law enforcement officers (Butts, 1996a:5). Arrest and being taken into custody constitute the first of three major processing points that indicate different degrees of entry into the juvenile justice system for juveniles. The other entry points include probation disposition and court disposition. Each of these entry points involves the exercise of discretion from various actors in the juvenile justice system.

Juveniles in Jails

It has been estimated that over 500,000 juveniles are locked up in adult jails in the United States annually (Maguire and Pastore, 1996). Only about 10 percent of these are actually held for serious offenses. About 20 percent are status offenders. Many youths have been jailed for short periods, merely on suspicion, even though they haven't committed offenses of any kind. States such as Illinois have passed laws preventing police officers from detaining juveniles in adult jails for periods of more than six hours (Huskey, 1990:122). These laws are a part of the **jail removal initiative**, whereby states are encouraged to rid their jails of juveniles. For example, in 1988 in Illinois, more than 1200 juveniles spent more than six hours in jails and **lockups**, while more than 100 were in jail for nearly three weeks (Huskey, 1990:122). Most of these jailed youths were nonviolent offenders. Huskey (1990:122) notes that 700 of those jailed included status offenders, and about 1000 were between the ages of 10 and 13.

Despite the passage of new laws to minimize or eliminate the placement of juveniles in adult jails or lockups, juveniles continue to be represented significantly among jail populations annually. In 1995, for instance, an average daily count of jail inmates showed that an average of 7888 juveniles were held, if even for brief periods (Gilliard and Beck, 1996:13).

There is a very good reason to restrict or prevent the confinement of juveniles in adult jails and lockups. Being locked up in jail is a frightening experience for most everyone, especially juveniles. Some juveniles are severely traumatized by the incarceration experience. The trauma is sufficient to cause many of them to attempt suicide. Some of them succeed. In 1994, for instance, 35 jurisdictions reported 45 juvenile deaths (Camp and Camp, 1995c:28). Of these, 16 were suicides and 12 were homicides. Huskey (1990:122) reports incidents of suicide in Kentucky and Indiana involving youths who were only in custody for a few hours. In an Indiana jail, for example, a 17-year-old girl hung herself with her pantyhose in a jail cell after being held for less than two hours on a shoplifting charge of stealing a $2 bottle of suntan lotion. She was awaiting the arrival of her parents. Apparently, this experience was too humiliating for her. In a Kentucky jail, a 15-year-old boy was incarcerated for *30 minutes* for refusing to go on a job interview. He was found in his cell dead a short while later, having used a bedsheet to hang himself from some high bars. Besides these and other jail suicides by juveniles, there are other tragic events suffered by youthful offenders in U.S. jails, including included rape and aggravated assault. At the beginning of this chapter, one of the scenarios involved the rape of a 10-year-old in a juvenile facility by several other children under the age of 14. No particular secure facility is immune from such tragedies.

The Ambiguity of Adolescence and Adulthood

Police have broad discretionary powers in their encounters with the public and dealing with street crime (Kalinich and Senese, 1987; Ryan and Williams, 1986). Although some evidence suggests that police have shifted their policing priorities away from juveniles toward more serious adult offenders for various reasons (e.g., cases against juveniles are often dismissed or judges issue nothing more than verbal warnings to them and return them to the custody of their parents), police arrests and detentions of juveniles in local jails remain the major conduit of a juvenile's entry into the juvenile justice system (Dale, 1988:46; Mixdorf, 1989:106).

Many juveniles are clearly juveniles. It is difficult to find youths age 13 or under who physically appear 18 or older. Yet Dale (1988) and others indicate that nearly 10 percent of all juveniles locked up in adult jails annually are 13 years old or younger. For juveniles in the 14 to 17 age range, visual determination of one's juvenile or nonjuvenile status is increasingly difficult. Thus at least some justification exists for why police officers take many youthful offenders to jails initially for identification and questioning. Furthermore, the U.S. Supreme Court has given some teeth to the constitutionality of jailing juveniles under preventive detention in the case of *Schall v. Martin* (1984). In this particular case, a juvenile was detained by police on serious charges, refused to give his name or other identification, and was deemed by those in charge to be dangerous, either to himself or to others. His preventive detention was upheld by the U.S. Supreme Court as not violative of his constitutional right to due process. Prior to the Supreme Court ruling, however, many states had laws that permitted both pretrial and preventive detention of suspects (Gottlieb and Rosen, 1984). Although pretrial detention presupposes a forthcoming trial of those detained and preventive detention does not, both terms are often used interchangeably or even in tandem, as in *preventive pretrial detention* (Gottlieb, 1984).

Other ways that juveniles can enter the juvenile justice system include referrals from or complaints by parents, neighbors, victims, and others (social work staff, probation officers) unrelated to law enforcement. Dependent or neglected children may be reported to police initially. Following up on these complaints, police officers may take youths into custody until arrangements for their care can be made. Under the new Illinois juvenile detention law, apprehended youths or those taken into custody must eventually be transferred to a community-based program or to an approved juvenile detention home (Huskey, 1990:122). A further provision of the Illinois law is that children under the age of 10 may not be held in an adult jail. However, it is inevitable that *some* youths under the age of 10 will be held briefly in any jail, since there may be no facilities other than jails immediately available where officers can hold them briefly for questioning to determine their age and identity.

Being Taken into Custody and Being Arrested

Also, being *taken into custody* and being *placed under arrest* are not equivalent procedures. They have different meanings for law enforcement officers. Whenever juveniles are taken into custody, they are *not* necessarily *arrested*, and they may not necessarily be arrested subsequently. Being *taken into custody* is precisely what it means. Officers take certain youths into custody to determine the best course of action in any particular situation. Some youths who are taken into custody might include those suffering from child sexual abuse or physical abuse inflicted by parents or others, runaways, or missing children. Youths who wander the streets may also be apprehended by police and taken into custody if they are suspected of being truant. In fact, certain jurisdictions, such as Newark, New Jersey, have truancy task forces as police units that conduct sweep operations, roadblocks, bus stops and searches, and other inspections where teens might frequent to catch truants and return them to school (Skolnick and Bayley, 1986). Such activities have been reported as mildly successful in certain types of crime prevention.

Whenever youths are arrested, this means that they are suspected of committing a crime. Charges may be placed against arrested youths once they have been classified and it is determined who should have jurisdiction over them. The fact that a juvenile is 16 or 17 may not be significant in those jurisdictions with automatic transfer laws. New York, Illinois, and several other states have provisions that direct officers to place their juvenile arrestees within the jurisdiction of the criminal justice system. Again, these automatic transfer laws apply and are ordinarily limited to especially serious crimes such as murder, robbery, or rape, and whenever the alleged offender is either 16 or 17 years of age (Sagatun, McCollum, and Edwards, 1985).

CLASSIFICATION AND PRELIMINARY DISPOSITION

Whenever youths have been taken into custody and are determined to require special care, are needy or dependent, or are otherwise unsupervised by adults or guardians, social welfare agencies or human service organizations may be identified as destinations for their removal from jails. Verification of a youth's identity and contacts with parents may result in verbal warnings by police and return of the youth to the parents. These actions are preliminary dispositions. Status offenders, including truants, runaways, or curfew violators, may be disposed of similarly. Figure 3.2 shows a more elaborate view of the juvenile justice system and provides additional details not illustrated in Figure 3.1.

FIGURE 3.2   The Juvenile Justice System

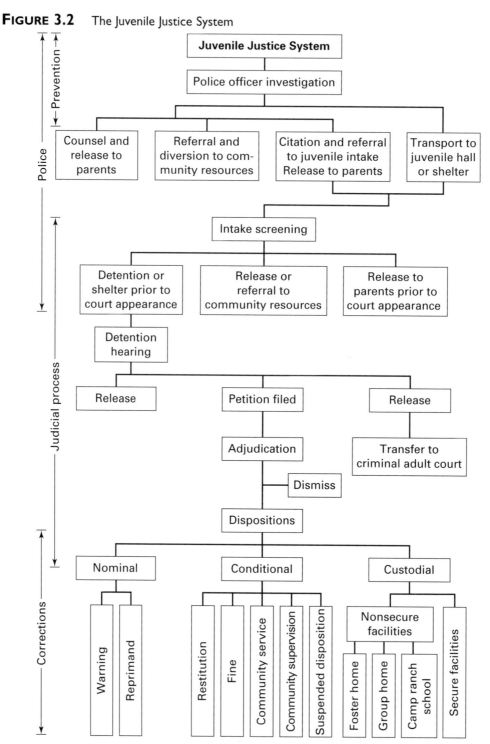

Source: From the National Advisory Committee on Criminal Justice Standards and Goals, *Juvenile Justice and Delinquency Prevention* (Washington, DC: U.S. Government Printing Office, 1967), p. 9.

Appropriate classifications of juveniles are crucial at all stages of juvenile justice processing. However, classification is particularly important whenever youths are first taken into custody. If it is true that less frequent contact with the juvenile justice system is better for juveniles in terms of decreasing their potential of reoffending, it is logical to conclude that those least worthy of exposure to the system should be withheld from it. Truants, runaways, curfew violators—status offenders—are particularly vulnerable in this scenario's context. However, Baird (1984, 1985) observes that often, intuitive systems of classifying youths are used by juvenile professionals at various stages. He says that "juveniles differ considerably in terms of type of offense, likelihood of recommitting crimes, emotional needs, educational levels, vocational skills, honesty, and other factors." Runaways in particular are often characterized as having poor preexisting family relations, where many of these youths have been physically and sexually abused. They lack self-esteem and are easy prey to persons on the street who will exploit them in various ways (Welsh et al., 1995).

Responses of police to runaways and others are affected by their perceptions of youths, departmental structure and policy regarding juvenile operations, statutory constraints, and community characteristics and dispositional alternatives (Maxson, Little, and Klein, 1988). Smaller and more geographically isolated communities may tend to have fewer sophisticated social services available compared with urban areas to accommodate those youths who have been apprehended by police "on suspicion" but who have not otherwise violated the law.

For the 10 percent of the youths taken into custody by law enforcement officers who have committed serious crimes, their preventive detention is expected. However, there are potential legal issues and problems arising from detaining youthful offenders in adult jails for any significant time interval (Dale, 1988:46). While a direct route to juvenile detention facilities is the desired course of action for apprehended youths where serious offenses are alleged, jurisdiction must first be established.

ESTABLISHING JURISDICTION

Jurisdiction is more than political boundaries or geographical landmarks outlining county lines and territories. As we have already seen, jurisdiction is the power of courts to decide cases. If automatic transfer laws are in effect in various jurisdictions, the matter of jurisdiction is settled. Sixteen- and 17-year-olds who commit or are alleged to have committed crimes such as murder, rape, or robbery are automatically transferred to the jurisdiction of criminal courts for adults. These youths may contest such transfers of jurisdiction to criminal courts through reverse waiver actions. One's potential punishment would be comparatively less severe in juvenile court compared with the maximum punishments that could be imposed for the same offenses in criminal courts.

Depending on the jurisdiction, however, the majority of alleged or suspected juvenile delinquents will be advanced further into the juvenile justice system. Some status offenders, especially recidivists, will also be funneled further into the system. Youths who police and others regard at the outset as serious enough to warrant further action may or may not be released to parental custody. Some youths may be maintained in juvenile detention facilities temporarily to await further action. Other youths may be released in their parent's custody, but the youths may be required to reappear later to face further action. These youths will eventually be subjected to an interview with an intake officer.

INTAKE

Intake varies in formality among jurisdictions (Worling, 1995). *Intake is a screening procedure conducted by a court officer or a probation officer, where one or several courses of action are recommended.* Some jurisdictions conduct **intake hearings**, where comments and opinions are solicited from significant others such as the police, parents, neighbors, or victims. In other jurisdictions, intake proceedings are quite informal, usually consisting of a dialogue between the juvenile and the intake officer. These are important proceedings, regardless of their degree of formality. Intake is a major screening stage in the juvenile justice process, where further action against juveniles may be contemplated or required.

Intake officers are either court-appointed officials who hear complaints against juveniles and attempt early resolutions of them, or they are more often juvenile probation officers who perform intake as a special assignment. In many small jurisdictions, juvenile probation officers may perform diverse functions, including intake, enforcement of truancy statutes, and juvenile placements. While the intake process will be examined more thoroughly in Chapter 5, a brief overview of this step follows.

Intake officers consider youths' attitudes, demeanor, age, offense seriousness, and a host of other factors. Has the juvenile had frequent prior contact with the juvenile justice system? If the offenses alleged are serious, what evidence exists against the offender? Should the offender be referred to certain community social service agencies, receive psychological counseling, receive vocational counseling and guidance, acquire educational or technical training and skills, be issued a verbal reprimand, be placed on some type of diversionary status, or be returned to parental custody?

Interviews with parents and neighbors may be conducted as a part of an intake officer's information gathering.

Assisting intake officers are various guidelines and policies in certain jurisdictions. For instance, in Clark County Juvenile Court in Las Vegas, Nevada, dispositions of juveniles by intake officers are influenced by both legal and nonlegal variables, including the present offense, number of charges and prior petitions, the youth's attitude, grades in school, school status, gender, race, and social class (Shelden and Horvath, 1987). In some instances, a judge's punishment ideology has been cited by intake officers as an important consideration. However, an examination of 456 juvenile courts, 257 judges, and 480 probation officers throughout the United States showed that a judge's philosophy has little impact on the intake decision (Hassenfeld and Cheung, 1985).

In most jurisdictions, intake normally results in one of five actions, depending, in part, on the discretion of intake officers:

1. Dismissal of the case, with or without a verbal or written reprimand
2. Remanding youths to the custody of their parents
3. Remanding youths to the custody of their parents, with provisions for or referrals to counseling or special services
4. Diverting youths to an alternative dispute resolution program, if one exists in the jurisdiction
5. Referring youths to the juvenile prosecutor for further action and possible filing of a delinquency petition

There are few universally acceptable standards currently in place in most jurisdictions that define the competencies of intake officers. Therefore, these officers must assume a tremendous responsibility as screening agents and the decisions they make about youths they confront. Budgetary constraints and an absence of licensing such officers in most jurisdictions means that many untrained, but interested, juvenile justice professionals attempt to diagnose a juvenile's problems at this early stage and provide appropriate treatments. If certain juveniles suffer from mental disorders, regardless of their etiology, how can their problems be diagnosed effectively at the time of intake? If intake officers believe that certain youths should have psychological counseling or diagnostic testing to determine whether they actually have psychological disturbances, which agencies should provide these services?

No agency currently has reliable national figures about how many youths suffer from one or more types of mental problems or disorders. One of the most controversial issues in juvenile corrections today is which agencies should be responsible for certain types of offender treatment. This presupposes that agencies exist to provide needed psychiatric services if needed. In reality, relatively few jurisdictions have a broad spectrum of social and psychological services for juveniles (Ellsworth, Kinsella, and Massin, 1992). Whenever children are sent to one agency or another for treatment, they may be rejected and sent to yet other agencies. Thus, children in need of treatment become **turnstile children** who fall between the cracks (Hartstone, 1985:79–80). Intake officers must walk the fine line between "doing what is best for the child" in the context of *parens patriae*, and pushing juveniles further into the system as a means of subjecting them to potential punishment in the context of a generalized societal expectation of "just deserts." This dilemma seems pervasive among many of those working with juveniles at all stages of offender processing (Hurst, 1990b:49).

ALTERNATIVE PROSECUTORIAL ACTIONS

Cases referred to juvenile prosecutors for further action are usually, though not always, more serious cases. Exceptions might include those youths who are chronic recidivists or technical program violators and nonviolent property offenders (e.g., status offenders, vandalism, petty theft, public order offenders) (U.S. General Accounting Office, 1995a). This is not to say that property offending is not serious. It is. But compared with aggravated assault, rape, murder, and armed robbery, property crimes and other nonviolent acts rank much lower in seriousness (Kansas Juvenile Justice Task Force, 1995; Worling, 1995).

Not unlike their criminal court counterparts, juvenile court prosecutors have broad discretionary powers. If they wish, they may drop prosecutions of cases against alleged offenders. Much depends on the docket load or case activity of their own juvenile courts. Prosecutors further screen cases by diverting some of the most serious ones to criminal court through waiver, transfer, or **certification. Prosecutorial waivers** are used for this purpose. Some cases are diverted out of the juvenile justice system for informal processing (Feld, 1995). Less serious cases that should remain within juvenile court jurisdiction are pursued, although like police officers, prosecutors are aware that many juvenile court judges seldom do much to seriously punish youths until the youths are five- or six-time offenders (Snyder, Sickmund, and Poe-Yamagata, 1996).

Either prosecutors file petitions or act on the petitions filed by others. *Petitions are official documents filed in juvenile courts on the juvenile's behalf, specifying reasons for the youth's court appearance. These documents assert that juveniles fall within the categories of dependent or*

The Beauty Shop Murder and Travis Crabtree

It happened in Dallas, Texas. A 15-year-old boy, Travis Crabtree, was indicted on murder charges stemming from a fatal holdup occurring on March 14, 1996. Crabtree had drawn a floor plan of the beauty shop in advance. The beauty shop was owned by 76-year-old Seeta Haddadi. Step-by-step instructions discovered in Crabtree's possession following the robbery-murder left little doubt in their mind that Crabtree was the assailant.

The checklist prepared by Crabtree gave him guidance at every stage of the robbery and murder he had planned. Included in his written plans was the instruction to "kill the victim." He did. He entered the beauty salon on March 14, 1996, ordered all employees and customers to the back, locked the front door, checked for security cameras, and then robbed the place. The sixth item on his "instruction sheet" was "kill." Crabtree stabbed Mrs. Haddadi to death, because she knew him and could identify him to police later. Crabtree was ordered held as an adult to face premeditated murder charges in a Houston criminal court.

What sort of punishment should Crabtree receive if he is convicted? Should teens as young as 15 receive the death penalty? Is there any type of intervention program that might have deterred Crabtree from doing what he did? What would you do to Crabtree if you were the judge and jury and the facts showed his guilt beyond a reasonable doubt?

Source: Adapted from Associated Press, "Teen Accused of Murder in Salon," *Minot (ND) Daily News*, May 17, 1996:A2.

neglected, status offender, or delinquent, and the reasons for such assertions are usually provided* (McCarthy and McCarthy, 1997). Filing a petition formally places the juvenile before the juvenile court judge in many jurisdictions. But juveniles may come before juvenile court judges in less formal ways.

In some jurisdictions, juveniles who are cited by highway patrolmen or other law enforcement personnel for *driving while intoxicated* (DWI) may appear before the juvenile court judge accompanied by a parent or legal guardian. For juveniles, the DWI standard in many jurisdictions is the mere presence of alcohol on the breath or in the bloodstream. The 0.08 or 0.10 percent alcohol standards relating to blood alcohol levels applicable for adults do not generally apply for juveniles accused of the same offense. An amount of 0.001 percent alcohol for juveniles is sufficient to sustain an accusation of DWI. An officer may cite the juvenile, parents may be notified to pick up their children, and the juvenile must appear in juvenile court later with a responsible adult. The judge has various options, including reprimands of parents as well as fines or other punishments for youths (e.g., loss of driving privileges, restitution to victims). Some research shows that about 50 percent of all cases initiated by police and others against juveniles result in judicial action by juvenile courts (McCarthy, 1987b).

ADJUDICATORY PROCEEDINGS

Jurisdictions vary considerably concerning their juvenile court proceedings. Increasingly, juvenile courts are emulating criminal courts in many respects (Feld, 1993a,b). Most of the physical trappings are present, including the judge's bench, tables for the prosecution and defense, and a witness stand. In some jurisdictions, such as Ocean County, New Jersey, however, these facilities are being redesigned to appear less courtlike and threatening (Kearney, 1989). Manuals are currently available that catalog various pleadings that defense attorneys may enter in juvenile courtrooms, and there is growing interest in the rules of juvenile court procedure (Volenik, 1986). Further, there appears widespread interest in holding juveniles more accountable for their actions than was the case in past years (DiCataldo and Grisso, 1995; Wiebush, 1993).

Besides the more formal atmosphere of juvenile courts, the procedure is becoming increasingly adversarial, where prosecutors and defense attorneys do battle against and on behalf of juveniles charged with various offenses (Feld, 1988a). However, less than 50 percent of the juvenile offenders in jurisdictions such as Minnesota have the assistance of counsel, although they are entitled to counsel (Feld, 1995). Both alleged status offenders and those charged with crimes are entitled to be represented by counsel in their court cases. However, an analysis of 17,195 cases in 1986 from various Minnesota juvenile courts shows that those youths who were represented by counsel tended to receive harsher penalties (e.g., twice as many confinements in secure confinement and longer probationary sentences) compared with youths not represented by counsel (Feld, 1989b). Essentially, the greater the formality imposed on these courts, the greater the punishment imposed on the juveniles by the judges (Feld, 1989a).

In some respects, these sentencing disparities are reminiscent of those disparities prevalent in criminal courts between defendants who plea bargain and forgo trials compared with those defendants who insist on their right to a trial and are convicted anyway. Sentences are generally harsher for those convicted through trial proceedings than for with those defendants who enter guilty pleas in plea bargain agreements involving the same or similar types of charges (Champion, 1988, 1990b). In short, it does not always pay to insist on your full range of legal rights in courts, either criminal or juvenile.

In most jurisdictions, juvenile court judges have almost absolute discretion in how their courts are conducted. Juvenile defendants alleged to have committed various crimes may or may not be granted a trial by jury, if one is requested. Few states permit jury trials for juveniles in juvenile courts, according to legislative mandates. The doctrine of *parens patriae* is very much in evidence in juvenile courtrooms. After hearing the evidence presented by both sides in any juvenile proceeding, the judge decides or adjudicates the matter in an **adjudication hearing**. *An **adjudication** is a judgment or action on the petition filed with the court by others.* If the petition alleges delinquency on the part of certain juveniles, the judge determines whether the juveniles are delinquent or not delinquent. If the petition alleges that the juveniles involved are dependent, neglected, or otherwise in need of care by agencies or others, the judge decides the matter. If the adjudicatory proceeding fails to support the facts alleged in the petition filed with the court, the case is dismissed and the youth is freed. If the adjudicatory proceeding supports the allegations, the judge must sentence the juvenile or order a particular disposition.

DISPOSITIONS

At least 12 **dispositions** are available to juvenile court judges if the facts alleged in petitions are upheld. These are generally grouped into (1) nominal, (2) conditional, or (3) custodial options. The dispositions are generally available, regardless of what is alleged in petitions. Thus status offenders, those alleged to have committed delinquent acts, or those in need of special treatment or care are subject to most, if not all, of these dispositions.

Nominal Dispositions

Nominal dispositions are the least punitive of the three major courses of action available to juvenile court judges. These include either *verbal warnings* or *stern reprimands*. The nature of such verbal warnings or reprimands is exclusively a matter of judicial discretion. Release to the custody of parents or legal guardians completes the juvenile court action against the youth.

Conditional Dispositions

All **conditional dispositions** are probationary options. Youths are placed on probation and required to comply with certain conditions during the probationary period. Conditional options or dispositions usually provide for an act or acts on the part of juveniles to be fulfilled as conditions of the sentence imposed. Or these conditions might be placements in programs or community facilities where assorted treatments may be applied. If juveniles have been adjudicated as delinquent and if the delinquency involved damage to a victim's property or bodily harm, restitution to victims may be required to pay for the property or medical bills. Many jurisdictions provide for community services of various kinds to be performed by juveniles. They may be required to cut lawns in city parks, clean debris from local highways or public areas, or perform other services (e.g., painting, maintenance work, carpentry work).

Youths may be required to take courses or therapy at various community service agencies. If they are alcohol or drug dependent, they may be required to take steps toward recovery from their dependencies. Another option available to judges is to sentence youths to custodial terms and suspend their sentences in favor of probation for a designated period such as six months or one year. In some jurisdictions, youths may be permitted to live at home and attend their schools, but they must wear electronic anklets or wristlets as a part of an *electronic monitoring program*. Such programs are designed to keep electronic tabs on offenders. Offenders wear devices that emit electronic signals that can be received at a central location such as a juvenile probation department. Or youths may be reached by special telephonic devices and must place their electronic wristlets into receptacles that enable the sender to verify the offender's presence at home. *Drive-bys* may also be conducted by juvenile probation officers: The officers drive by juveniles' homes with receivers and are able to determine whether the wearers of these wristlet or anklet electronic devices are on the premises. Electronic monitoring of both adult and juvenile offenders is becoming increasingly popular as an inexpensive method of managing probationers and others in many jurisdictions (McCarthy and McCarthy, 1997).

Custodial Dispositions

Custodial dispositions are classified into nonsecure custody and secure custody. **Nonsecure custody** or **nonsecure confinement** consists of placing certain juveniles into foster homes, group homes, or camp ranches or schools (Altschuler and Armstrong, 1994; Harris et al., 1993). These are temporary measures often designed to make more permanent arrangements for juvenile placement later. Juveniles have freedom of movement, and they can generally participate in school and other youthful activities. If they are living in group homes or are on camp ranches, there are curfews to be observed. It is assumed that if they are in the care of others in foster homes or shelters, such curfews will be implicitly (if not explicitly) enforced.

The **secure custodial** or **secure confinement** option is considered by most juvenile court judges as the last resort for the most serious juvenile offenders (Altschuler and Armstrong, 1994; Krisberg et al., 1993). Some of the reasons for this include overcrowding in secure juvenile facilities, a general reluctance among judges to incarcerate youths because of potential adverse labeling effects, and the potential effectiveness of certain intermediate punishments through community-service agencies. However, independent investigations show that often, excessive numbers of juveniles who are not among the worst juveniles are placed in secure confinement (Wiebush, 1993). Data collected in 1991 from custodial training schools in 14 different states showed that a significant portion (30 percent or more) of youths in custody were found *not* to require long-term residential care (Krisberg et al., 1993). Much of this unnecessary secure placement occurred from the misapplication of risk instruments that tended to overclassify youths. When an objective public safety–oriented placement system was used in lieu of risk instrumentation in these states, a 31 percent average reduction in training school beds across the 14 states occurred. In some states, such as Nebraska, secure confinement reductions of 68 percent occurred, meaning that less serious offenders were removed from industrial schools, making it possible to confine more dangerous offenders.

It would be a mistake to place all the blame for placing large numbers of nonserious offenders in industrial schools on risk instrumentation, however. More often than not, juvenile court judges themselves are at fault. There is a pervasive tendency among juvenile court judges to lock up juveniles according to either legal or extralegal criteria. According to a 50-state survey of juvenile court judge sentencing dispositions issued by the National Conference of State Legislatures (1988), judges in some states may impose weekend confinement in secure facilities for some youths as a punishment. In eight states (Alaska, Arkansas, Illinois, Kansas, Montana, New Mexico, Texas, and Vermont), juvenile courts commit those adjudicated youths to the relevant youth corrections agencies, and those agencies decide what types of placements are appropriate (Anonymous, 1988:5). More effective monitoring of juvenile court decision making has been recommended, together with more objective and rational methods for deciding who should receive institutionalization and who should receive community treatment (Altschuler and Armstrong, 1994; DiCataldo and Grisso, 1995). Curiously, juvenile court judges have continued to make inordinate numbers of secure placement decisions, despite a general national mandate for these judges to use the least restrictive punishment options for juveniles where possible.

JUVENILE CORRECTIONS

In 1995, 102,582 juveniles were in residential and nonresidential correctional programs other than probation (Camp and Camp, 1995c:1). The range of juvenile corrections is almost as broad as that existing for adult offenders convicted of crimes. In fact, since 1992 changes in juvenile court dispositions have been in the direction of increased incarceration of juveniles adjudicated delinquent for violent or other serious offenses without comparable attention to probation, community corrections, or other types of aftercare (Torbet et al., 1996:xvi). Those juveniles adjudicated as delinquent may be placed on probation or in secure confinement, depending on juvenile court judge opinions and evaluations. Depending on juvenile probation officer caseloads in various jurisdictions, this probation may be more or less intense, commensurate with intensive supervised probation for adults. One's placement in different types of probationary programs is dependent on how the youth is originally classified. Interestingly, juvenile court judges have not applied consistent legally relevant variables in much of their decision making about juvenile secure placements. In fact, some research suggests that nonlegal or extralegal variables are quite influential in this regard (Lee, 1996). Hoge, Andrews, and Leschied (1995) studied 338 adolescent boys and girls who were adjudicated delinquent in a large urban U.S. region. They found that personal and situational variables often governed secure confinement decision making rather than legal criteria. More rational legal criteria for secure confinement decision making have been recommended (Zimring and Hawkins, 1995).

Probation, whether or not it is intensive, may be conditional and involve restitution to victims and/or community services. In 1993, there were 254,000 juveniles on probation in various state jurisdictions (Snyder, Sickmund, and Poe-Yamagata, 1996:9). Juveniles may be placed in community-based residential programs or exposed to various therapies and treatments or training (Maloney, Romig, and Armstrong, 1988; Rubin, 1988). A **balanced approach** to probation for juveniles in New Orleans combines protecting the community, equipping juveniles with competencies to live productively and responsibly in the community, and imposing accountability for their offenses (Maloney, Romig, and Armstrong, 1988). Also, there are many types of intermediate punishments, including several community-based interventions (McCarthy and McCarthy, 1997). Some of these interventions are group homes and wilderness experiences (Harris et al., 1993).

Confinement in state industrial schools is the juvenile equivalent of incarceration in a state prison for adults. This type of confinement is considered **hard time** for many juveniles. The California Youth Authority operates various facilities to house growing numbers of juvenile offenders in secure confinement. Lengths of commitment vary for offenders, depending on the seriousness of their adjudication offenses (Maguire and Pastore, 1996). In 1995, there were over 102,582 juveniles in public and private correctional facilities in the United States (Camp and Camp, 1995c:1). Over 90 percent of those in secure confinement in 1995 were male (Camp and Camp, 1995c:7). Not all of these secure placements are necessary, however. Investigations of specific jurisdictions, such as New Hampshire, suggest that approximately 50 percent of the institutional placements are nonessential placements. Therefore, at least 50 percent of these youths in secure confinement could have been managed just as well in noninstitutional programs in their communities, with substantial savings to the state Division for Children and Youth Services (Butts and DeMuro, 1989).

The effectiveness of secure confinement for juveniles depends in part on the classification of juveniles placed in these facilities. Ordinarily, risk assessment instruments are applied to assist experts and youth authorities in making the most beneficial placements of youthful clientele. The *Client Management Classification* (CMC) *System* has been developed and provides a structured way for staff to evaluate offenders and develop supervision strategies based on specific offender types (Baird and Neuenfeldt, 1990). The CMC uses a structured interview and scoring guide to classify offenders into one of four groupings: (1) selective intervention, (2) casework/control, (3) environmental structure, and (4) limit setting. The CMC concept has also been modified to include both incarcerated adults and juveniles through *Strategies for Juvenile Supervision* (SJS) and *Prisoner Management Classification* (PMC) (Baird and Neuenfeldt, 1990).

The California Youth Authority has also devised risk prediction criteria for more effective youth placements in its various programs (National Council on Crime and Delinquency, 1990). Two risk assessment instruments have been developed to assess the probability of recidivism for California Youth Authority juveniles and to assess their potential for future violent behavior. These assessment inventories were tested for reliability and validity during a lengthy follow-up period with experimental and control groups. Scales indicating a high propensity for violent behavior were correlated highly with an aggregate of youth predicted to be dangerous. About 80 percent of those youths with low-risk scores had one or fewer sustained petitions filed against them in the follow-up stage. Thus the scales effectively differentiated between those youths predicted to pose the risk of future violence and those predicted to be low risk (National Council on Crime and Delinquency, 1990).

Finally, when juveniles have served a portion of their incarcerative sentences, they are paroled by a juvenile paroling authority to the supervision of an appropriate state or community agency. In 1995, there were 65,000 juveniles on parole in various state jurisdictions (Camp and Camp, 1995c). In Utah, for instance, a seven-member board, the Utah Youth Parole Authority, makes early-release decisions over large numbers of incarcerated youths monthly. Operated by the Utah Division of Youth Corrections, this board consists of three citizens and four staff members. In one 37-day period, the board conducted approximately 300 parole hearings (Norman, 1986). Although the board appears to be guided by certain eligibility criteria, one's institutional behavior while confined is considered quite important as an indicator of one's future community reintegration (Norman, 1986).

Various jurisdictions have attempted to intensify the supervision youths receive while on parole. In New York, for instance, a pilot supervision program for juvenile parolees, PARJO, was implemented for 368 participants in 1983–1984 (New York State Division of Parole, 1985). Juvenile parole officers were assigned relatively low caseloads and assisted parolees in finding jobs and needed services. The program was considered modestly successful at reducing recidivism among juvenile parolees and decreasing their unemployment rate.

KEY TERMS

Adjudication	*Criminal information*
Adjudication hearing	*Criminal justice system*
Aggravating circumstances	*Custodial dispositions*
Arraignment	*Disposition*
Arrest	*Exculpatory evidence*
Automatic transfer laws	*Good time*
Bail	*Good-time credit*
Bail bond	*Grand jury*
Balanced approach	*Hard time*
Bench trials	*Inculpatory evidence*
Booking	*Informations*
Certification	*Initial appearance*
Conditional dispositions	*Intake*
Corrections	*Intake hearing*
Courts and judges	*Intake officer*

Intake screening

Intermediate punishments

Jails

Jurisdiction

Jury

Jury trials

Law enforcement agencies

Law enforcement officers

Lockups

Mistrial

Mitigating circumstances

No bills

Nominal dispositions

Nonsecure custody, confinement

No true bills

Petit jury

Plea bargain

Plea bargaining

Police discretion

Preliminary examination

Preliminary hearing

Presentment

Pretrial detention

Preventive detention

Prisons

Probable cause

Probation

Referrals

Release on own recognizance (ROR)

Reverse waiver hearings

Secure custody, confinement

Sting operations

Taken into custody

Transfer hearings

Transfers

True bills

Turnstile children

Waiver hearings

Waivers

QUESTIONS FOR REVIEW

1. What is the *criminal justice system*? Why is it important to know about the criminal justice system as a means of better understanding the juvenile justice system?

2. What is *jurisdiction*? How do police officers and others determine which courts have jurisdiction over certain juveniles?

3. Differentiate between *grand juries* and *petit juries*. What are *indictments, presentments*, and *informations*? How does each originate? Do these mean that defendants are guilty of the charges alleged? Why or why not?

4. Distinguish between *true bills* and *no bills*. Who issues such bills? What is their effect?

5. Distinguish between *aggravating circumstances* and *mitigating circumstances*. How do these circumstances respectively affect or influence sentencing of offenders?

6. What is *intake*? Who performs the role of intake officers? Are there ordinarily any special requirements or prerequisites for becoming intake officers?

7. What is a *petition*? Who can file a petition? What is the result of filing a petition with the juvenile court? Do all petitions pertain to juvenile delinquents? Why or why not?

8. What is an *adjudication*? What are three major sentencing options available to juvenile court judges?

9. What are the correctional options for juveniles? Differentiate between *secure confinement* and *nonsecure confinement*. What is *hard time*? Why is it important to juveniles?

10. Differentiate between *criminal informations* and *grand jury indictments*.

SUGGESTED READINGS

Cicourel, Aaron V. *The Social Organization of Juvenile Justice*. New Brunswick, NJ: Transaction, 1995.

Forst, Martin L. *The New Juvenile Justice*. Chicago: Nelson-Hall, 1995.

Mendel, Richard A. *Prevention or Pork? A Hard-Headed Look at Youth-Oriented Anti-crime Programs*. Washington, DC: American Youth Policy Forum, 1995.

Shoemaker, Donald J. *International Handbook on Juvenile Justice*. Westport, CT: Greenwood Press, 1996.

Spergel, Irving A. *The Youth Gang Problem: A Community Approach*. New York: Oxford University Press, 1995.

U.S. General Accounting Office. *Juvenile Justice: Minimal Gender Bias Occurred in Processing Noncriminal Juveniles*. Washington, DC: U.S. General Accounting Office, 1995.

U.S. General Accounting Office. *Juvenile Justice: Representation Rates Varied as Did Counsel's Impact on Court Outcomes*. Washington, DC: U.S. General Accounting Office, 1995.

CHAPTER 4

JUVENILES AND THE POLICE

INTRODUCTION

A white four-door automobile with two youths drives by a convenience store. Gunfire erupts from the vehicle as the store is sprayed with bullets. No one is injured, but the store manager gets a quick look at the car and sees two youths in it. He calls police. Nearby a cruiser is idling at an intersection. A white four-door automobile drives by slowly with two occupants. The police stop the vehicle a few blocks away and make the passengers get out. The police conduct a thorough search of the vehicle and find no weapons. The youths are 16 and 17, respectively. They claim that they have been at a theater about two miles away and are going home. As the police question them, they act nervous. The officers decide to take the youths into custody anyway for further investigation. Eventually, it turns out that the youths were at the theater and were only coincidentally in the neighborhood at about the same time as the shooting. The youths' parents come to the police station and accompany them home.

Three youths are looking in the window of an automobile showroom at 10:00 P.M. in a neighborhood known for its gang presence. A police officer stops and questions the youths, who claim that they are merely looking at a car in the window. They are walking home from a neighbor's house, where they were attending a party. The officer asks for ID and the youths show them school cards. The youths are each 14 years old. There is no curfew in the city for youths of any particular age. The officer decides to take the boys into custody and to jail for further investigation. Later, it turns out that the youths were at a party, just as they said. Their parents come to the police station and accompany them home.

A girl appears to be hitchhiking on an interstate highway. A state trooper pulls over and questions her. She produces a driver's license from another state and says that she is on her way from New York to California. She is 17 years old, according to the license. She says that she ran out of gas down the road, describes her vehicle, and the trooper drives her back to where she says she left her car. The car is not there. The officer is suspicious and takes the girl into custody. The officer calls several numbers given to him by the girl. One number is the home of her parents. The officer gets an answering machine. The officer calls another number, the home of the person she intends to visit in California. He gets another answering machine. He decides to have the girl wait. After six hours, another officer comes in and reports that several vehicles have recently been towed from the interstate highway. One of the cars towed matches the description of the girl's vehicle. It turns out that it is the girl's vehicle and that it is, indeed, out of gas. The girl is charged the towing fee but is allowed to reclaim her vehicle. A nearby service station fills her car with gas and she proceeds on her way without further incident.

Were the police justified in each of the cases above? Did they have a right to stop the white vehicle and determine the identities of its occupants? Should the boys have been taken to jail? What about the three youths who were merely looking in an automobile showroom window at night? Is this against the law? Did the police have the authority to take these boys into custody merely for looking in a showroom window? What about the girl on the interstate highway? Was the trooper justified in taking her into custody for further investigation? Should the girl have been required to pay the towing charges, especially when it turned out that she was telling the truth and had run out of gas?

There are no textbook answers for these questions. Each scenario is different and presents police officers with different problems. Much of their decision making will depend on the demeanor of the youths involved. Much of the discretion police exercise in these situations depends on the **totality of circumstances** in each situation. Probably every police officer in every city or county law enforcement agency in the United States who has ever engaged in neighborhood patrol work has encountered at least one of these situations. In most of these encounters, there are no clear-cut guidelines to follow. Police must exercise their discretion. Failure to act correctly in these situations could have serious consequences.

In this chapter we examine police discretion as it pertains to a wide variety of juvenile conduct. How should police officers react toward youths under different circumstances? When is formal action necessary or strongly suggested? What statutory provisions exist for handling certain types of encounters with juveniles? Under what circumstances should juveniles be arrested and taken into custody to local jails or lockups? These and similar questions are examined here.

Since there have been several significant changes in state and federal laws during the last few decades concerning how juvenile offenders are defined and should be processed, police procedures involving juveniles have been modified greatly. Certain classes of juvenile offenders have been reclassified by law. Most notably, a clear distinction exists between status offenders and delinquent offenders in every jurisdiction. However, police officers are those who interface most often with juveniles on the streets. Because many of these police officer/juvenile encounters are diffuse and it is unclear whether any criminal laws have been violated, police officers must use their discretion when interpreting each situation and the events observed. What is the nature of police response to changing procedures about how certain types of juveniles should be processed? Do police officers generally follow procedures and make the same distinctions between juveniles as the law requires? The implications of deinstitutionalizing status offenders (DSO) for influencing police discretion and conduct are examined.

POLICE DISCRETION: USE AND ABUSE

Few will contest the idea that police officers make up the front line or first line of defense in the prevention and/or control of street crime, although the effectiveness of this line in crime control continues to be questioned (Miller and Braswell, 1993). Police officers are vested with considerable *discretionary powers*, depending on the circumstances, ranging from verbal warnings in confrontations with the public to the application of deadly force (*Tennessee v. Garner*, 1985). **Police discretion** *is the range of behavioral choices police officers have within the limits of their power* (Champion and Rush, 1997). Beyond the formal training that police officers receive from law enforcement agency training academies, police discretion is influenced by many other factors, including the *situation*, as well as the race, ethnicity, gender, socioeconomic status, and age of those confronted (Champion and Rush, 1997). Many of those stopped by police, questioned, and subsequently arrested and detained in jails or other lockup facilities, even for short periods, are juveniles.

The Diffuseness of Police Officer Roles

The public tends to define the police role diffusely, where police are expected to address a wide variety of human problems (Cicourel, 1995). The nature of this police intervention is that the police will intervene in various situations and ensure that matters do not get worse (Cicourel, 1995; New York State Division of Criminal Justice Services, 1994). Thus police training in various jurisdictions is geared to reflect this broad public expectation of the police role (Miller and Braswell, 1993). One training manual for police officers includes at least 476 field situations, including how to deal with domestic disturbances, traffic violations, narcotics, civil disorders, vice, drunkenness, federal offenses, and juveniles (Kenney and More, 1986).

Much of this **situationally based discretion** in confronting crime in the streets and the public is covert. Most of what transpires in the interaction between police officers and suspects is known only to these actors. Thus it is often difficult to enforce consistently high standards of accountability for police to observe in their diverse public encounters (Champion and Rush, 1997). In short, police officers make on-the-spot decisions about whether to move beyond simple verbal warnings or reprimands to more formal actions against those stopped and questioned "on suspicion."

Considering the circumstances or situation, law enforcement officers may be more or less aggressive.

Contributing to the diffuseness of police officer roles in communities is a relatively recent phenomenon known as community policing. **Community policing** *is a major policing reform that broadens the police mission from a narrow focus on crime to a mandate that encourages the police to explore creative solutions for a host of community concerns, including crime, fear of crime, disorder, and neighborhood decay....It rests on the belief that only by working together will people and the police be able to improve the quality of life in the community, with the police not only as enforcers, but also as advisors, facilitators, and supporters of new community-based police-supervised initiatives* (Trojanowicz and Bucqueroux, 1990:3).

One immediate effect of community policing in many neighborhoods is to place greater discretionary power in the hands of police officers, whether they are on foot or in cruisers. An implicit consequence of community policing is to create better relations between the police department and the community, in order for community residents to place greater trust in the police rather than to fear them. In communities where such discretion power shifts occur through planning, police officers may be expected by higher-ups to take a greater interest in youths, even where petty infractions are involved (Trojanowicz and Bucqueroux, 1990:238–239). Police officers may be *punished* for failing to take minor infractions seriously and for not intervening when necessary. Thus they are in a dilemma about whether to get involved in the activities of minor offenders. In more sensitive settings where ethnicity may play an important role, law enforcement officers may be criticized unfairly by citizens simply for doing their jobs (Bond-Maupin, Lujan, and Bortner, 1995; Texas Bill Blackwood Law Enforcement Management Institute, 1994).

For many police officers, stopping and detaining juveniles is not a particularly popular activity (Mixdorf, 1989:106). One reason is that the courts, both juvenile and criminal, are inclined to do little or nothing to juvenile first-offenders or minor offenders (Snyder, 1988; Snyder and Sickmund, 1995). Most juvenile courts wait until youths are five- or six-time offenders before they consider them *chronic offenders* (National Center for Juvenile Justice, 1988). Howard Snyder, Director of Systems Research at the National Center for Juvenile Justice, says that "second appearance[s] [by juveniles] serves as a good bellwether that [they are] coming back....Most of the offenses committed by younger juveniles are relatively minor....There aren't many 13- and 14-year olds committing armed robbery" (Anonymous, 1988:4).

Mixdorf (1989:106) adds that "In law enforcement...police officers now spend less time with juveniles, and many have discontinued preventive activities to focus resources on major crimes that have been committed by adults." Besides the fact that the courts are lenient with minor first offenders, some paperwork is involved whenever juveniles are taken into custody. Many police officers are reluctant to involve themselves in trivial juvenile affairs that may take as much or more time to process than the time it would take to process adult criminals following their arrests.

Nevertheless, police officers in every jurisdiction encounter large numbers of juveniles annually in their community patrols and on their "beats." Because of the informal nature of many of these police officer–juvenile encounters, the *UCR* and other official sources of arrest information fail to disclose the true incidence of all juvenile contacts with the law. According to official sources, however, there were 1,489,700 arrests of youths under age 18 in the United States in 1993, about half of which were petitioned to juvenile courts for further action (Snyder, Sickmund, and Poe-Yamagata, 1996:9). Furthermore, self-reports from juveniles in elementary schools and high schools suggest considerably greater delinquent activity as well as contacts with police that do not necessarily result in arrests or being taken into custody for brief periods (Maguire and Pastore, 1996).

Juvenile Units in Police Departments

In the early years of police–juvenile encounters, police departments operated under a type of siege mentality. In Los Angeles, for example, the "zoot suit" riots of 1943 involved a 10-day attack by civilians on alleged Mexican-American youth gang members (Appier, 1990). Extraordinarily repressive police policies were implemented at that time, and police–juvenile relations were strained for many decades (Appier, 1990).

Subsequently, police departments throughout the nation, particularly larger municipal police departments with 200 or more officers, established specialized juvenile units as a part of their organizational structure to deal with different types of offenders. Even relatively small departments in remote geographical areas have at least one juvenile officer who deals exclusively with juvenile affairs. Despite this specialization, however, *every* police officer who encounters juveniles while policing becomes a juvenile officer temporarily (Rogers and Mays, 1987:314). Not all of the police activities in these juvenile units have been directed at gang violence or violent offenses committed by juveniles, however. Those targeted for active police intervention and assistance have included truants (Martin, Schulze, and Valdez, 1988); runaways and missing children (Forst, 1990); property offenders and those who commit vehicular theft (Florida Statistical Analysis Center, 1993); curfew violators (Texas Bill Blackwood

Law Enforcement Management Institute, 1994); and those committing school-related offenses (New York State Division of Criminal Justice Services, 1994). Police interest in gangs is most often focused on prevention rather than retaliation (Mendel, 1995). Prevention measures by police include profiling gang members; methods used by gangs to recruit new members; neighborhood roots that spawn and perpetuate gang activity; the influence and presence of gang members in prison settings; providing materials and strategies for parents and school authorities to use for coping with gang activities; and examining gang structure (Chicago Crime Commission, 1995).

In Cleveland, Ohio, for example, a study of youth gangs identified denial as a typical official response of law enforcement to the presence of youth gangs (Torok and Trump, 1994:13). One consequence was that many Ohio youths interpreted this police denial of their existence as tacit approval for their operation in virtually any Ohio city, with impunity. Victimization of community residents is promoted as one result of this unbridled gang activity. However, in 1990 a youth/gang unit was established by the Cleveland Police Department. The youth component of this unit investigates nongang-related crimes, which are not normally investigated by detectives. However, members of the gang unit conduct in-depth investigations to identify gang members, obtain information about gang territories, activities, and methods of operation, and to ensure successful prosecution of gang members. They supplement their activities with aggressive street enforcement (Torok and Trump, 1994:14). One innovation is that the youth/gang unit has collaborated with school authorities to establish youth/gang units within the Division of Safety and Security, which is a part of the public school system. This youth/gang unit addresses gang crimes and school rule violations. It consists of four school security officers and a unit coordinator, serving 127 schools and over 73,000 students (Torok and Trump, 1994:14). During the first year of this unit's operation, unit personnel investigated 400 gang-related school incidents, identified over 1000 gang members, and trained 7000 staff members, parents, and youth service providers to recognize and intervene in gang problems.

By 1996, 48 of 51 jurisdictions in the United States had made extensive changes in their laws concerning juveniles who commit violent or serious crimes (Torbet et al., 1996:xv). In turn, these legislative changes have caused numerous police departments to implement programs that will achieve certain delinquency prevention objectives contemplated by these changes. Table 4.1 shows how various legislatures have toughened laws targeting serious and violent juvenile offenders for the years 1992–1995. Actually, the activities of juvenile units or **youth squads** are largely directed toward delinquency prevention (Champion and Rush, 1997; Martin,

Schulze, and Valdez, 1988). These units tend to be **reactive units**, in that they respond to public requests for intervention and assistance whenever offenses committed by juveniles are reported. That is, these officers react to calls from others about crimes that have already been committed or are in progress. Gang fights or break-ins involving youths would activate these juvenile units. In contrast, police officers who patrol city streets are most often **proactive units** involved in contacts with juveniles who may or may not be offenders and/or law violators. These officers are almost constantly on the lookout for suspicious activities. They monitor the streets and investigate potentially troublesome situations.

Youth Gangs and Minority Status

The increased visibility of delinquent gangs organized along ethnic and racial lines in many cities and the violence such gangs manifest have caused police departments to establish task forces of special police officers who do nothing but monitor and investigate gang activities (Arizona Criminal Justice Commission, 1994; Beger, 1994b). Some professionals have classified these gangs as scavenger gangs and corporate gangs (Taylor, 1986). **Scavenger gangs** *form primarily as a means of socializing and for mutual protection, while* **corporate gangs** *emulate organized crime* (Taylor, 1986). While both types of gangs pose dangers to the public, corporate gangs are more profit motivated and rely on illicit activities such as drug trafficking to further their profit interests. Corporate gangs use excessive violence, including murder, to carry out their goals. Often, innocent bystanders are gunned down as victims of gang retaliation against rival gangs and gang members (Taylor, 1986).

Less conventional gangs, such as Skinheads, have been targeted by some youth gang bureaus and other police agencies within departments (Anti-Defamation League of B'Nai-B'Rith, 1995; Arizona Criminal Justice Commission, 1994). For example, Skinheads claimed at least 70,000 members worldwide in 1995. They have a cumulative record of gang violence involving weapons. It is not always cities with large populations where police gang units are deployed. In Alabama, for instance, law enforcement agencies in 46 cities with populations of 10,000 or more have reported substantial gang activities in their jurisdictions (Armor and Jackson, 1995). Alabama officials report that their gang visibility is comparable to that reported by larger cities, especially concerning the amount of female involvement or participation in gangs, the trappings of gang culture, and other critical gang elements. Arizona officials have reported similar gang presence and activity (Arizona Criminal Justice Commission, 1994).

TABLE 4.1

Legislatures That Stiffened Laws Targeting Serious and Violent Juvenile Offenders, 1992–1995

State	J	S	CP	C	V	State	J	S	CP	C	V
Alabama	J				V	Missouri	J	S	CP	C	
Alaska	J			C	V	Montana		S		C	V
Arizona		S		C	V	Nebraska					
Arkansas	J	S	CP	C		Nevada	J			C	
California	J		CP	C	V	New Hampshire	J	S		C	V
Colorado	J	S	CP	C		New Jersey		S		C	
Connecticut	J	S	CP	C	V	New Mexico	J	S	CP		V
Delaware	J	S		C		New York					
District of Columbia	J	S				North Carolina	J			C	
Florida	J	S	CP	C	V	North Dakota	J		CP	C	V
Georgia	J	S	CP	C	V	Ohio	J	S	CP	C	
Hawaii				C		Oklahoma	J			C	
Idaho	J	S	CP	C	V	Oregon	J		CP	C	
Illinois	J	S		C	V	Pennsylvania	J			C	V
Indiana	J	S		C		Rhode Island	J	S			
Iowa	J			C	V	South Carolina	J		CP	C	
Kansas	J		CP	C		South Dakota	J				V
Kentucky	J		CP			Tennessee	J		CP	C	
Louisiana	J	S	CP	C	V	Texas	J	S	CP	C	V
Maine				C		Utah	J			C	V
Maryland	J		CP	C		Vermont					
Massachusetts		S				Virginia	J	S		C	
Michigan		S		C		Washington	J			C	
Minnesota	J	S		C	V	West Virginia	J				
Mississippi	J		CP	C		Wisconsin	J	S	CP	C	
						Wyoming	J		CP	C	V

Source: Torbet et al., 1996:xv. *Data source:* Linda Szymanski, *Special Analysis of the Automated Juvenile Law Archive* (Pittsburgh, PA: National Center for Juvenile Justice, 1996).

[a]Key to types of changes in law or court rule: J, jurisdiction; S, sentencing; CP, correctional programming; C, confidentiality; V, victims. Each change indicated enhances the juvenile and/or criminal justice system's response to serious violent crime.

Police officers who observe juveniles in pairs or larger groupings, particularly in areas known to be gang dominated, may assume that these youths are gang related, and this observation may heighten police officer interest in and activity against them (Brantley, Sorrentino, and Torok, 1994). The nature of this heightened interest and activity may be more

BOX 4.1   BAND DIRECTOR GUNNED DOWN BY TEENS

The Case of the Lords of Chaos

It happened in Fort Myers, Florida. A newly formed gang, the *Lords of Chaos*, were bent on doing something bad. They consisted of a ragtag collection of juvenile gang wannabes, and they considered themselves to be a new *militia*, although no gang member could define what a militia was. This militia needed to attract attention. First, they concocted a plan to blow up a Coca-Cola bottling plant which had closed down. They clustered together some propane tanks in the nearly abandoned building and threw a Molotov cocktail at them. The building nearly disintegrated from the explosion. Later, the boys put on ski masks and committed armed robbery and carjacking outside a restaurant. Among other things, the boys set fire to a Baptist church. Then they spread gasoline around a thatched-roof aviary outside a tropical theme restaurant, set fire to it, and casually watched as dozens of exotic birds burned to death.

The gang, in existence not quite a month, formulated another plan. They would enter Disney World, steal costumes, and shoot at black sightseers. This was to be their version of ethnic or racial cleansing. Before they began their assault on Disney World, however, they engaged in some pranks. Arming themselves with cans of peaches, they headed to a nearby school, where they planned to throw the peach cans through school windows. A band director, Mark Schwebes, intercepted them and confiscated their peaches before they could throw them. The gang swore revenge against Schwebes.

Later that night, they extracted their revenge. They went to Schwebes's home and rang his doorbell. When he answered, Foster Shields, the leader who other gang members referred to as "God," shot Schwebes in the face with a 12-gauge shotgun. Then Shields shot Schwebes in the groin because he thought Schwebes was a homosexual. Not good kids!

Police were flabbergasted when they arrested these boys and learned of the Disney World plans from several gang members. At least five boys were arrested in connection with Schwebes' murder. Foster Shields, 18, was charged with first-degree murder, while several other boys, ages 16, 17, and 18, were arrested and charged with murder, armed robbery, and conspiracy to commit armed robbery.

Fort Myers officials are perplexed, especially since they have been planning several interventions for juvenile delinquency in their community. One official, frightened by this event, said that most of these teens weren't even part of the juvenile justice system he has been working with and wouldn't have been targeted for intervention. He thinks that now, the plan must go into effect sooner to head off similar incidents. "Why didn't we know?" he asked. "Probably because we didn't do the things we needed to do."

How should Fort Myers officials deal with these gang members? Are the "Lords of Chaos" really a gang? Would any intervention have worked to prevent Schwebes's killing? Is juvenile violence escalating?

Source: Adapted from Associated Press, "'Lords of Chaos' Run Amok," *Minot (ND) Daily News*, May 10, 1996:A3.

frequent stopping and questioning certain juveniles on the basis of their appearance and geographical location and whether they are minority youths (Armor and Jackson, 1995; Chicago Crime Commission, 1995).

While some investigators question whether police officers discriminate against certain youths or single them out for stopping and questioning on the basis of racial or ethnic factors (Florida Statistical Analysis Center, 1993), other researchers have found patterns of police behavior that appear discriminatory on racial or ethnic grounds (Bond-Maupin, Lujan, and Bortner, 1995; Florida Supreme Court, 1990). At least in some jurisdictions, minority youth stops, arrest rates, and detentions are at least three times as high as those for white youths (Florida Supreme Court, 1990; Manikas et al., 1990; U.S. Bureau of Justice Statistics, 1988).

However, much police officer activity is centered in high-crime areas, which also tend to be areas inhabited by large numbers of persons of lower socioeconomic status (SES). And those areas with larger numbers of persons of lower socioeconomic status are also those that contain larger concentrations of minorities (Cicourel, 1995; Texas Bill Blackwood Law Enforcement Management Institute, 1994). Thus some selectivity regulates where police officers will concentrate their patrol efforts as well as the youths they target for questioning and those they choose to ignore. Experts believe that this opens to the door to allegations of police officer harassment against certain classes of juvenile offenders on the basis of subjectively determined stereotypical features such as a youth's appearance (D. Conley, 1994; Connecticut Gang Task Force, 1994).

The fact of racial and ethnic disproportionality in the juvenile justice system is underscored by a study undertaken by Darlene Conley in 1994. The juvenile justice system of a western state was investigated. Juvenile courts in six counties were selected as the target for her research. A representative sample of 1777 juvenile cases was drawn, together with 170 in-depth interviews with court personnel, community leaders, defense attorneys, prosecutors, law enforcement officers, parents, youths, and others. The study also included 65 hours of participant observation covering court proceedings and plea bargaining involving adjudicated juveniles. Focus-group interviews with juveniles were also conducted. It was found that blacks were twice as likely as whites to be arrested, five times more likely to be referred to juvenile court, five times more likely to be detained, three times more likely to be charged, 2.5 times more likely to be adjudicated delinquent, and 11 times more likely to be placed in secure confinement for a lengthy period (D. Conley, 1994). Hispanics were also overrepresented in the same counties, although they were not processed as extensively as blacks. Similar findings relative to dissimilar treatment of minority juveniles have been reported elsewhere (Guarino-Ghezzi, 1994).

Female Gang Members

How prevalent are female gangs in the United States? Do female gangs commit types of offenses similar to those committed by male gangs? Contemporary descriptions of female gang members suggest that they typically lack a formal education; have violent experiences at their schools; have seriously dysfunctional family lives; and have social problems including poverty, substance abuse, and gang violence (Molidor, 1996). Interviews with a sample of Texas female gang members indicated that they often join gangs to achieve power and protection, engendering respect from others based on fear, and they often resort to more serious criminal conduct (Molidor, 1996). Often, membership in female gangs is contingent upon one's ethnic or racial status. Family disintegration and community deterioration often lead female gang members to create their own subculture where recognition can more easily be attained (Bankston and Caldas, 1996).

Rosenbaum (1996) studied 70 female gang members who had earlier been committed to the California Youth Authority in 1990. She studied a sample of 70 girls with known gang affiliations. Almost all the girls studied by Rosenbaum had records of violent offending. The girls averaged four arrests, and 62 percent of their commitment offenses were committed with other female gang members. Rosenbaum found that many of these girls joined gangs initially to satisfy needs that they could not satisfy in their home environments. Gang affiliation gave these girls loyalty to friends, fun, and excitement. Furthermore, many of these female gang members were of minority status and resented the white, blond "California girl" image that is often unattainable by minority girls. Thus female gang criminality, at least in southern California, appeared to be comparable to male gang criminality in the level and nature of violence.

Juvenile Response to Police Officer Contacts

Interestingly, how youths behave toward police officers whenever juveniles are stopped and questioned by them seems to make an important difference about what the officers will eventually do. Early research about the appearance and demeanor of youths stopped by police officers and their subsequent actions indicates that youths who were poorly dressed and/or behaved defiantly and belligerently toward police were more likely to be harassed, possibly arrested (Piliavin and Briar, 1964; Tomson and Fielder, 1975). Subsequent research is consistent with these early findings and suggests that cooperative, neatly dressed youths stand a better chance of avoiding being stopped, questioned, or arrested by police (Morash, 1984).

In fact, some police officers insist that a youth's demeanor when responding to police questioning on the street is crucial to whether the youth will be taken into custody, even if temporarily. Therefore, if youths do not display the proper amount of deference toward police officers whenever those youths are stopped and questioned, the youths stand a good chance of being taken to the police station for further questioning (Chicago Crime Commission, 1995; Guarino-Ghezzi, 1994). Interestingly, youths also may be too polite and arouse the suspicions of police officers. Thus there is an elusive "range of politeness" that minimizes a youth's chances of being taken into custody. It is possible to be too polite or not polite enough, so that police officers are sufficiently aggravated or motivated to act. According to experts, police officer discretionary abuse occurs when "juveniles are detained when there is little or no evidence that incarceration is necessary or desirable to meet the generally accepted goals of detention" (Roberts, 1989:150).

Despite statutory safeguards about detaining youths in adult jails for long periods and the division of labor relating to youthful offender processing in any jurisdiction, police officers are free to do pretty much whatever they want relative to juveniles they question who are either acting suspiciously or belligerently. If any pretext exists for assuming that certain youths have been or are engaging in delinquent acts, they are subject to temporary detention by police officers. In many instances, these detention decisions by police are purely arbitrary (Chicago Crime Commission, 1995).

The following is a listing of discretionary actions that may be taken by police officers when encountering youths on the street:

1. *Police officers may ignore the behaviors of youths they observe in the absence of citizen complaints.* The most frequent types of encounters police officers have with juveniles do not stem from complaints filed by others. Rather, police officers observe youths under a wide variety of circumstances. The situation

and circumstances are important, since youths walking down a street in pairs during daylight hours would not attract the same kind of attention as pairs of youths walking the streets late at night. Depending on what the officers regard as serious behaviors, if youths are on skateboards on the sidewalks of the main street of a local community, they may or may not be posing risks to other pedestrians. If youths are playing ball on a vacant lot near other homes in a neighborhood, they may or may not be disturbing others. Police action in each case is probably unwarranted.

2. *Police officers may act passively on someone's complaint about juvenile behaviors.* If a store owner complains that youths are jeopardizing the safety of store customers by riding their skateboards down crowded city streets, police officers may respond by directing youths to other streets for their skateboarding. If neighbors complain that youths are making too much noise playing in a nearby vacant lot, police officers may appear and advise youths to play elsewhere. The intent of police officers in these situations is twofold. First, they want citizens to know they are there doing something. Second, they want citizens to know action has been taken and the problem no longer exists. Police officers continue to view the behaviors they observe as not especially serious. In these instances, police warnings are ordinarily sufficient to satisfy complainants. Since complaints were made by complainants, dispositions of those complaints are usually logged officially. Police officers may or may not choose to name those youths warned. Rather, they may file a generalized report briefly describing the action taken.

3. *Police officers may take youths into custody and release them to parents or guardians without incident.* Those youths who may be acting suspiciously or who are in places where their presence might indicate an intent to do something unlawful (e.g., the youths who were in the uninhabited house to "crash" after their party) are likely to be taken into custody for more extensive questioning. In many instances, these **station adjustments** may result in their release to parents with warnings from police about refraining from suspicious conduct in the future (Champion and Rush, 1997). While these actions are official in the sense that police officers actually took youths into custody for a brief period and made records of these temporary detentions, they do not result in official action or intervention by intake officers or juvenile courts.

4. *Police officers may take youths into custody and refer them officially to community service agencies for assistance or treatment.* Sometimes youths appear to police to be under the influence of drugs or alcohol when they are stopped and questioned. Other youths may not have parents or guardians responsible for their conduct. They may be classified by police officers as runaways. In these cases, police officers arrange for various community services to take custody of these juveniles for treatment or assistance. These youths will be under agency care until arrangements can be made for their placement with relatives or in foster homes. Those youths with chemical dependencies may undergo medical treatment and therapy. In either case, juvenile courts are avoided.

5. *Police officers may take youths into custody, file specific charges against them, and refer them to juvenile intake, where they may or may not be detained.* Only a small percentage of all juveniles detained by police will subsequently be charged with offenses. Conservatively, probably less than 10 percent of all juveniles who have contact with police officers annually engage in serious violent or property offenses (Snyder, Sickmund, and Poe-Yamagata, 1996). Therefore, many youths are taken into custody for minor infractions, and their referrals to juvenile intake may or may not result in short- or long-term confinement. The discretion shifts from police officers to intake officers whether to process certain juveniles further into the juvenile justice system. Those juveniles who are deemed dangerous, violent, or persistent nonviolent are most likely to be subject to detention until adjudication by a juvenile court. Police officers may respond to citizen complaints or actually observe juveniles engaging in illegal conduct. Their likelihood of taking these youths into custody for such wrongdoings alleged or observed is increased accordingly.

6. *Police officers may take youths into custody, file criminal charges against them, and statutorily place them in jails pending their initial appearance, a preliminary hearing, and a subsequent trial.* Some juveniles may be classified as adults for the purpose of transferring them to criminal courts where they might receive harsher punishments. Jurisdictions such as Illinois, Washington, DC, New York, and California are a few of many places where automatic transfer laws exist and where some juveniles are automatically placed within the power of criminal courts rather than juvenile courts. Therefore, police officers *must* act in accordance with certain statutory provisions when handling certain juvenile offenders whenever they effect arrests of youthful suspects. Often, they have no choice in the matter. Changing *get-tough* policies toward violent or serious juvenile offenders are making it more difficult for police to be lenient when confronting juveniles on city streets (Torbet et al., 1996).

Therefore, police discretion is exercised most during the normal course of police patrols or *beats.* Those youths who stand the best chance of being targeted for special police attention include minorities who are acting suspiciously and live in high-crime neighborhoods known as gang territories. Also increasing the likelihood of being taken into custody is the demeanor or behaviors exhibited by youths, whether they are polite or impolite to police officers. Short of any illicit conduct actually observed by or reported to police officers, a youth's appearance and behaviors are key considerations in whether they will be harassed and/or detained temporarily by police. However, comparatively few youths are actually arrested in relation to the actual number of police officer/juvenile encounters on city streets.

ARRESTS OF JUVENILES

As we have seen, police officers need little, if any, provocation to bring juveniles into custody (Champion and Rush, 1997; D. Conley, 1994; Mendel, 1995). Arrests of juveniles are, by degree, more serious than acts of bringing them into custody. Since any juvenile may be taken into custody for suspicious behavior or on any other pretext, all types of juveniles may be detained at police headquarters or at a sheriff's station, department, or jail temporarily. Suspected runaways, truants, or curfew violators may be taken into custody for their own welfare or protection, not necessarily for the purpose of facing subsequent offenses. It is standard policy in most jurisdictions, considering the sophistication of available social services, for police officers and jailers to turn over juveniles to the appropriate agencies as soon as possible after these youths have been apprehended or taken into custody (Guarino-Ghezzi, 1994).

Before police officers turn juveniles over to intake officials or juvenile probation officers for further processing, they ordinarily complete an arrest report, noting the youth's name; address; parent's or guardian's name and address; offenses alleged; circumstances; whether other juveniles were involved and apprehended; the juvenile's prior record, if any; height; weight; age; and other classificatory information. Figure 4.1 is a booking form used by the Long Beach (California) Police Department.

Juvenile–Adult Distinctions

According to the Juvenile Justice and Delinquency Prevention Act of 1974 and its subsequent amendments, juveniles must be separated from adults, both by sight and sound, and treated as juveniles as soon as possible following their apprehension. If juveniles are brought into custody and charged with offenses that might be either felonies or misdemeanors if committed by adults, they may be clearly distinguishable as juveniles. It would be difficult to conclude that an 8-, 9-, or 10-year-old could pass for 18 or older. But many juveniles who are taken into custody may or may not be under 18. Their appearance is deceptive, and if they deliberately wish to conceal information about their identity or age from officers, it is relatively easy for them to do so. This is a common occurrence, since many juveniles are afraid that police will notify their parents. Fear of parental reaction may sometimes be more compelling than the fear youths may have of police officers and possible confinement in a jail.

Because juveniles generally have less understanding of the law than that of adults, especially those who make careers out of crime, they may believe that they will fare better if officers believe that they are adults and

FIGURE 4.1   Affidavit and Application for Filing of Juvenile Court Petition

Affidavit and Application for Filing of Juvenile Court Petition
(Welfare and Institutions Code Section 653)

I,_____
    Officer's/Citizen's Name

_____hereby state that
Officer's Agency & Duty Station or Citizen's Address

_____a minor, DOB_____

_____is within San Diego County   _____resides within San Diego County
_____was within San Diego County   _____committed an offense described within sections
                                               601/602 within San Diego County

and that said minor comes within the provisions of sections 601/602 of the Welfare and Institutions Code of the State of California as evidenced by the case reports dated _____ and consisting of _____ pages, which are attached hereto and incorporated by reference herein. On the basis of this information, the undersigned requests that a Juvenile Court Petition be filed on the above named minor for the offense(s) of

_____
(State the name of the offense and the appropriate statutory authority)

I declare under penalty of perjury that the facts set forth in this affidavit and its attachments are true and correct to the best of my knowledge.

Dated: _____   Signed:_____

Companions referred_____

Companions not referred_____

REPORT OF ACTION AND ENDORSEMENT

The following action was taken on this application: _____
                                                             (JDA No. or Misd. No.)

_____Petition requested under section(s)_____
_____D.A. reject
_____Referred to Traffic Court
_____Referral recorded and handled informally**

_____Active delinquent ward (602 W&I)/Offense reported to Juvenile Court**
_____6 Months' Probation Supervision (654 W&I)**

**Reasons(s):
_____Active to another jurisdiction   _____Family moving
_____Active dependent ward (300 W&I)   _____Referred to community agency
_____Minor offense   _____PC 26 problem
_____No prior referral   _____Administrative exception
_____No prior arrests (2 yr. period)   _____Minor cannot be located
_____Transient   _____Parents handling appropriately
_____Restitution paid/property recovered   _____Low maturity/intellectual level

Other reasons/Additional information (if any):_____
_____
_____
_____

_____   _____   _____   _____
  (Date)   (Please Print)   (Deputy Probation Officer)   (Phone No.)

Prob. 419 (8-87)   Dist: White-Ref. Agency   Canary-Prob. Clerk   Pink-Prob. File not juvenile offenders (Center, 1993; Guarino-Ghezzi, 1994). Perhaps there is a chance they might be released after spending a few hours or even a day or two confined in a jail cell. However, if they are identified positively as juveniles, parents will invariably be notified of their arrest. But these youths often underestimate the resources police have at their disposal to verify information received from those booked after arrests. With proper identification, adults are ordinarily entitled to make bail and obtain early temporary release from jail. If fake IDs are used by juveniles, however, this phony information is easily detected and arouses police officer suspicions and interest in these youths. They will probably be detained as long as it takes to establish their true identities and ages. Furnishing police officers with false information is a rapid way to be placed in preventive detention for an indefinite period. Police officers are entitled to use preventive detention lawfully in such cases (*Schall v. Martin*, 1984).

The Ambiguity of Juvenile Arrests

Little uniformity exists among jurisdictions about how an arrest is defined. There is even greater ambiguity about what constitutes a juvenile arrest. Technically, *an **arrest** is the legal detainment of a person to answer for criminal charges or (infrequently at present) civil demands* (Champion, 1997). Available evidence suggests that increasing numbers of police departments are proactively changing their police–juvenile policies so that decision making regarding juvenile processing will be more rational and effective (Florida Supreme Court, 1990; Kenney, Pate, and Hamilton, 1990; Manikas et al., 1990).

Early research by Klein, Rosensweig, and Bates (1975) focused on juvenile arrest procedures followed by 49 suburban and urban police departments in a large metropolitan county. Over 250 police chiefs and juvenile officers and their supervisors were surveyed, some of whom participated in follow-up, in-depth interviews about juvenile arrests and processing. Among police chiefs, for example, fewer than 50 percent were in agreement that booking juvenile suspects was the equivalent of arresting them. Further, respondents variously believed that arrests involved simple police contact with juveniles and "cautioning" behavior. Others believed that "taking youths into custody" and releasing them to parents constituted an arrest. Less than half of those surveyed appeared thoroughly familiar with juvenile rights under the law and the different restrictions applicable to their processing by police officers. Record keeping and other activities related to juvenile processing by police have not changed much in subsequent years (U.S. Bureau of Justice Statistics, 1988).

Fingerprinting, Photographing, and Booking of Juvenile Suspects

Under the Juvenile Justice and Delinquency Prevention Act of 1974, its subsequent revisions, and recommendations from the National Advisory Committee on Criminal Justice Standards and Goals (1976), significant restrictions have been placed on law enforcement agencies concerning how juveniles are processed and the records that may be maintained that relate to such processing. Under the 1974 act, for instance, status offenders have been separated in treatment from delinquent offenders through deinstitutionalization or DSO. Status offenders should not be taken to jails for temporary detention. Rather, they should be taken to juvenile agencies to endure less formal dispositions. No doubt, one intent of such legislative mandates and committee decision making was to minimize the adverse impact and labeling influence that jailing or partial criminal processing might have on status offenders. Although DSO is fairly common in most jurisdictions, police officer discretion causes a fairly large proportion of status offenders to be handled initially as delinquent offenders anyway. Thus large numbers of status offenders continue to be housed in U.S. jails annually, even though such housing is only for a few hours.

Since most juveniles legally fall within the jurisdiction of juvenile courts that are extensions of civil authority, statutory prohibitions obligate police officers and jail officials to depart from certain procedural steps normally followed when processing adult offenders. For example, it is commonplace for officers to photograph and fingerprint adult offenders. This is an integral part of the booking procedure. Ordinarily, juveniles may not be photographed or fingerprinted by police officers as "common procedure." Rather, photographs and fingerprints of juveniles may be taken after a showing by police officers that their use is either to establish one's identity or for some investigative purpose (e.g., theft of property where fingerprints of the possible thieves have been obtained).

Expungement and Sealing Policies

Historically, once photographs and fingerprints have been taken, they have been destroyed as soon as possible following their use by police (Torbet et al., 1996:xiv). If such records exist in police department files after juveniles have reached the age of their majority, they may have their records *expunged* or *sealed* through expungement orders. **Expungement orders** *are usually issued from judges to police departments and juvenile agencies to destroy any file material relating to one's juvenile offense history.* Policies relating to records expungements vary among jurisdictions. Expungement of one's juvenile record, sometimes known as **sealing records of juveniles**, is a means of preserving and ensuring confidentiality of information that might otherwise prove harmful to adults if disclosed to others such as employers (Center, 1993). Sealing of records is intended as a rehabilitative device, although not all juvenile justice experts believe that sealing one's records and enforcing such confidentiality about one's juvenile past through expungement is always beneficial to the general public. Investigations of state policies about police fingerprinting of juvenile suspects have indicated that these policies are diverse and inconsistent among jurisdictions (Miller, 1995). Further, there continues to be considerable disagreement about how such fingerprint and related information should be used by either juvenile or criminal courts in their subsequent processing of youthful offenders (Miller, 1995).

Since 1992, many jurisdictions have extended the time interval for sealing or expunging one's juvenile record. Most states have increased the number of years that must pass before one's juvenile record can be expunged. Thus one's juvenile record may not be expunged for several years after a person has become an adult. In fact, some states now specify that if *any* juvenile has committed a violent or other serious felony, his or her juvenile record *cannot be sealed or expunged* (Torbet et al., 1996:xiv).

Also since 1992, states have increasingly mandated open proceedings and the release of juvenile records to the public, particular where serious offenses are involved (Torbet et al., 1996:xiv). Furthermore, many states now open juvenile court records to school officials or require that schools be notified whenever a juvenile is taken into custody for a crime of violence or when a deadly weapon is used. Another concomitant is that some states have lowered the age at which juvenile court records may be made available to the public (Torbet et al., 1996:xiv).

Other policy changes have occurred as well. Significant legislative activity has occurred with respect to the disclosure, use, and destruction of juvenile records and the openness of juvenile court proceedings. Information sharing has greatly increased, as many states now make provisions for creating repositories of juvenile court information, usually based on fingerprinting and photographing, expanding the use of the criminal court's use of a defendant's juvenile court record, and establishing youthful sex offender laws for community protection (Torbet et al., 1996:xiv).

STATUS OFFENDERS AND JUVENILE DELINQUENTS

One of the more controversial issues in juvenile justice is how status offenders should be classified and managed. The fact that status offenders are labeled as status offenders contributes significantly to this controversy (Krause and McShane, 1994; Little Hoover Commission, 1990). Such a label implies that all status offenders are somehow alike and should be treated similarly in all jurisdictions. But this implication is about as valid as assuming that all juvenile delinquents are alike and should be treated similarly. If we think about the etiology of runaway behavior compared with the respective etiologies of curfew violation, truancy, incorrigibility, liquor law violation, and sex offenses, it is likely that different sets of explanatory factors account for each type of deviant conduct. Accordingly, different treatments, remedies, or solutions would be required for dealing effectively with each.

Altschuler and Luneburg (1992) and others concur. Those juveniles classified as runaways and incorrigibles in some jurisdictions were less likely to commit more serious offenses later in their teens than were truants, curfew violators, and liquor law violators (Collins et al., 1993; Krause and McShane, 1994). But for some experts, even runaways do not comprise a homogeneous category of status offenders, and distinctions should be made between different kinds of runaway behavior (Thornberry, Tolnay, and Flanagan, 1991; U.S. General Accounting Office, 1991).

In 1974, the Juvenile Justice and Delinquency Prevention Act acknowledged some major differences between status offenders and delinquents by mandating that status offenders should not be institutionalized as though they had committed crimes. Rather, they should be diverted away from the trappings of juvenile courts that seemingly criminalize their behaviors. By managing status offenders less formally and dealing with their behaviors largely through counseling and assistance provided through community-based services, it was reasoned that they would be less likely to define themselves as delinquent and that others would be less likely to define them as delinquent as well. The long-range implication of such differential treatment is that status offenders will not be inclined to progress or escalate to more serious types of offenses as will more serious delinquent offenders who are exposed to the **criminogenic environment** of the juvenile courtroom (U.S. General Accounting Office, 1991).

Between the time the 1974 act was implemented and individual states adopted policies to desintitutionalize status offenders, there has been a 95 percent reduction in the number of status offenders who are placed in some type of secure confinement (U.S. General Accounting Office, 1991). However, a portion of those detained consisted of status offenders who violated court orders, or one or more conditions imposed by juvenile court judges at the time of their status offender adjudications (Beger, 1994a; Crippen, 1990; U.S. General Accounting Office, 1991).

As a category, status offenders exhibit less recidivism compared with those referred to juvenile court for delinquent acts (Butts, 1996a). Further,

BOX 4.2   THE MIDOL CONNECTION

The Case of Kimberly Smartt, the Midol Connection

It happened on September 6, 1996, at suburban Baker Junior High School outside Dayton, Ohio. A student passed a white pill to another student. Authorities observed the transaction and moved in. The students involved were taken into custody and brought to the principal's office. The white pill was retrieved. Cocaine? Crack? Heroin? No, just Midol.

Midol is a nonprescription drug used to alleviate the pain and discomfort of menstruation. When Kimberly Smartt, 14, gave 13-year-old Erica Taylor a Midol tablet, she believed it was a perfectly logical thing to do. Erica had been complaining about stomach cramps and bleeding. Kimberly knew what that meant and gave Erica some of her own medicine.

In the aftermath of the school investigation, Erica Taylor was suspended for 10 days from school for accepting the Midol tablet from Kimberly. Kimberly Smartt was suspended for five months for her role as the "Midol supplier." According to the school's policy about drugs, prescription and nonprescription drugs are not distinguished. Students who are not feeling well are supposed to report to the school office, where they must request permission for appropriate medication. A signed parental permission slip must be on file for these students in order for them to receive required medication. If such statements are not on file, the students will be denied medical relief.

When the media attempted to interview the school superintendent, Steve Clifton, he declined comment. In the meantime, Kimberly Smartt received a letter from Clifton indicating that she would not be permitted back into school until February 12, 1997. "I don't like being treated differently," said Kimberly, referring to the obvious discrepancy in punishment meted out to her compared with Erica Taylor, who was suspended for only 10 days. The charge noted on Kimberly Smartt's school records was "drug transmission." A part of her "sentence" was to undergo extensive drug counseling and education. In the aftermath, Kimberly Smartt's parents filed suit against the school and school officials for discrimination. The school decided to limit Smartt's suspension to 13 days instead of the five months originally imposed. Despite the school's action, Smartt's parents continued with their discrimination suit against the school.

While possession of Midol is not a crime, is this act under these circumstances something requiring police intervention? Is the punishment Kimberly Smartt received fair, given what she did? To what extent should school policy function to regulate the distribution and/or use of nonprescription drugs? What do you think?

Source: Adapted from Associated Press, "Midol 'Distributor' Suspended," *Minot (ND) Daily News*, October 4, 1996:A2.

the earlier juveniles are referred to juvenile court, for whatever reason, the more likely they will be to reoffend and reappear in juvenile courts (Snyder, Sickmund, and Poe-Yamagata, 1996). Therefore, diversionary procedures employed by police officers at their discretion when confronting extremely youthful offenders or those who are not doing anything particularly unlawful would seem to be justified on the basis of existing research evidence (Florida Governor's Juvenile Justice and Delinquency Prevention Advisory Committee, 1994).

But deinstitutionalizing status offenders is seen by some as tantamount to relinquishing juvenile court control over them, and not all experts favor this particular maneuver. A strong undercurrent of *parens patriae* persists, especially pertaining to those status offenders who need supervision and guidance from caring adults (Beger, 1994b; Ford and Linney, 1995). Retaining control over status offenders is one means whereby the juvenile court can compel them to receive needed assistance and/or appropriate treatment. But disagreement exists about the most effective forms of intervention to be provided status offenders (Land, McCall, and Parker, 1994; U.S. General Accounting Office, 1995a). One problem experienced by more than a few juvenile justice systems is inadequate resources for status offenders and others require less drastic interventions as alternatives to incarceration (Chesney-Lind and Matsuo, 1995).

DIVESTITURE AND ITS IMPLICATIONS: NET WIDENING

Divestiture means that juvenile courts relinquish their jurisdiction or authority over certain types of offenders, such as status offenders. Thus if a juvenile court in Tennessee or Oregon were to divest itself of authority over status offenders or children in need of supervision, those processing status offenders, such as police officers, would probably take such offenders to social service agencies or other community organizations designed to deal with these youths (Altschuler and Luneburg, 1992; Rabinowitz, 1992). But it doesn't always work this way in some jurisdictions.

Under divestiture provisions such as those enacted by the Washington State legislature, status offenses were simply removed from the jurisdiction of juvenile courts. Various community agencies and social service organizations would assume responsibility for ensuring that status offenders would receive proper assistance and treatment (Colley and Culbertson, 1988). Referrals to juvenile court, incarceration, and the imposition of formal sanctions are no longer justified on the basis that one is a status offender and should suffer this processing and these punishments.

Relabeling Status Offenses as Delinquent Offenses

But because of police discretion, curfew violation, runaway behavior, and truancy can easily be reinterpreted or *relabeled* as *attempted burglary* or *attempted larceny*. Hanging out or common loitering may be defined by police as behaviors associated with *casing* homes, businesses, and automobiles as future targets for burglary and theft (Krause and McShane, 1994). These acts are sufficiently serious and provocative to bring more juveniles into the juvenile justice system, thereby widening the net. Widening the net occurs whenever juveniles are brought into the juvenile justice system who would ordinarily have been dealt with by police differently prior to divestiture. Prior to divestiture, many status offenders would have received "wrist slaps" and verbal warnings by police instead of being taken into custody. However, when police officers resort to relabeling status offenses as conceivably criminal actions, greater rather than fewer numbers of juveniles will be netted into the juvenile justice system in the postdivestiture period than was the case in the predivestiture period.

In the Washington cities of Yakima and Seattle, police officers were not particularly receptive to the idea that their discretion in certain juvenile matters was abolished by legislative mandate in the late 1970s. In effect, the police officers in these cities literally created a fictitious juvenile delinquency wave in the postdivestiture period, where the rate of delinquency appeared to double overnight. Such an artificial wave was easily accomplished, since these front-line officers merely defined juvenile behaviors differently according to their unchecked discretion. A similar phenomenon occurred in Connecticut during approximately the same period (Logan and Rausch, 1985). The primary implication of their actions seems to be that they perceived divestiture as a criticism of their integrity and discretionary quality in dealing with juvenile matters rather than as a positive move to assist certain youths in avoiding the delinquency label (Lieb, Fish, and Crosby, 1994).

In California, an ambitious DSO provision was implemented on a statewide basis. Again, like Washington, DSO did not necessarily deliver what was intended by deinstitutionalization and divestiture. For example, a study of San Bernardino County by Krause and McShane (1994) examined 123 youths who had had previous involvement with the juvenile justice system and 493 youths who had no prior involvement with it. Both groups of juveniles consisted of nonserious youths who were largely from dysfunctional families. Prior to DSO many of these youths would simply be diverted from the juvenile justice system and subjected to family counseling outside any custodial setting. However, following DSO in San Bernardino County, many of the youths who normally would have been given diversion and family counseling were relabeled, placed in custody in juvenile hall, and placed outside their parents' homes in foster care or group homes. Krause and McShane strongly recommended that San Bernardino County juvenile authorities should seriously reexamine their institutionalization criteria and invoke more effective screening mechanisms to avoid the practice of detaining for prolonged periods those youths who deserve to be diverted instead.

Protecting Status Offenders from Themselves

Besides police officer opposition to divestiture, some experts oppose removing status offenders from the jurisdiction of juvenile courts because the courts are perceived as helpful in shielding children from their most self-destructive urges (Kearon, 1989). Many runaways and truants may have certain mental health or educational needs that can only be met through mandatory participation in a mental health therapy program or educational intervention (Collins et al., 1993; Famularo et al., 1992). Court intervention may be necessary to ensure that juveniles take advantage of these services (Feld,1993a,c; Mershon, 1991). Informal dispositions of status offense cases may not have the legal coercion of a juvenile court order. Thus one's participation in various assistance programs is either voluntary or strongly recommended. However, agency response in accommodating youths with various problems seems selective and discriminatory. Often, those youths most in need of certain agency services are turned away as unqualified (Russell and Sedlak, 1993; Steinberg, Levine, and Singer, 1992). Thus status offender referrals to certain agencies may be unproductive, particularly if the status offenders are psychotic, violent, or drug or alcohol dependent (Little Hoover Commission, 1990; National Council on Crime and Delinquency, 1991).

Parens Patriae versus Due Process

The *parens patriae* philosophy is in increasing conflict with the due process orientation that typifies most juvenile court procedures today. Status offenders represent a juvenile offender class clearly in the middle of this conflict (Feld, 1993a–c; Russell and Sedlak, 1993; Thornberry, Tolnay, and Flanagan, 1991). Reducing admissions of status offenders to various detention centers and treatment facilities is seen by some experts as a reversal of the hardening effect of custodial confinement on these youths (U.S. General Accounting Office, 1991). But removing such youths from detention centers and other places where they might receive mandatory treatment may be detrimental as means of helping them to control their self-destructive urges (Kearon, 1989).

Gender Stereotyping and DSO

A continuing problem of DSO in any jurisdiction is how male and female status offenders are differentially treated by juvenile court judges. For instance, in a survey of 87 juvenile probation officers in a large metropolitan county of a southwestern state, it has been found that female juveniles tend to receive relatively punitive protection from juvenile court judges (Reese and Curtis, 1991). In fact, this differential treatment of females by juvenile courts seems fairly routinized and institutionalized. DSO has failed to change how juvenile court judges dispose of female status offense cases compared with how cases were disposed prior to DSO. It has been suggested that judicial stereotyping of female status offenders is such that many judges act to protect females from the system and society by placing them in restrictive circumstances such as secure confinement, even if their offenses do not warrant such placement. Thus a double standard continues to be applied, despite the best intentions of DSO (Reese and Curtis, 1991). Other researchers concur with Reese and Curtis, as a continuation of protectionist policies toward female status offenders persist in most jurisdictions throughout the United States today (Bishop and Frazier, 1992). Rosenbaum and Chesney-Lind (1994) have also found disparities in processing between male and female juvenile offenders in Hawaiian juvenile courts. However, other research takes issue with this judicial paternalism toward female status offenders and suggests that it is not as serious as reported presently (U.S. General Accounting Office, 1995a).

The Race Card

Do juvenile court judges stereotype status offenders on other factors besides gender? Some jurisdictions report that disproportionately high numbers of black youths are represented in their juvenile justice system. In Georgia, for instance, *race* has had a direct effect on disposition decision making, as well as at the law enforcement, intake, and adjudication decision points (Kurtz, Giddings, and Sutphen, 1993). Closely related to the race variable was socioeconomic status. Thus race and socioeconomic status operated in this instance to predict correctly more adverse consequences for black youths compared with youths who had committed similar offenses, had similar delinquency histories, but were white.

A study prepared for the Virginia Department of Criminal Justice Services investigated 1256 youths processed in Fairfax County, Virginia in the early 1990s. Race was studied as it contributed to disparities in treatment of various juvenile offenders at different stages of juvenile justice processing (Williams and Cohen, 1993). Generally, race did not seem to affect whether incarceration was imposed for youths charged with serious crimes in the initial stages of their processing. If the nature of the offense was serious enough, youths were detained. For those youths charged with felonies, minority incarcerations were significantly higher than incarcerations of white juveniles. Later in their processing, black youths were more likely to have court-appointed counsel or no counsel, while white youths tended to have private counsel. Black male juveniles tended to be adjudicated delinquent more frequently than white offenders and to receive longer incarcerative terms, controlling for adjudication offense and prior record (Williams and Cohen, 1993).

Presently, juvenile justice policy statements have been made declaring differential treatment on the basis of race/ethnicity, gender and socioeconomic status to be illegal, immoral and inadvisable. Such extralegal factors should have no place in determining one's chances in the juvenile justice system, whether one is a delinquent or a status offender (Kurtz, Giddings, and Sutphen, 1993; National Council on Crime and Delinquency, 1991; U.S. General Accounting Office, 1995a).

REDEFINING DELINQUENCY

Police officers might consider taking a more proactive role as interventionists in the lives of juvenile offenders encountered on the street (Brantley and DiRosa, 1994). For instance, Trojanowicz and Bucqueroux (1990:238) say that "young people do not launch long-term criminal careers with a daring bank robbery, an elaborate kidnapping scheme, or a million-dollar dope deal. Yet the traditional police delivery system does not want officers 'wasting' much time tracking down the kid who may have thrown rocks through a few windows at school. Narcotics officers on their way to bust Mr. Big at the dope house cruise right by those fleet-footed 10-year-old lookouts. And a call about a botched attempt by a youngster to hotwire a car would not be much of a priority, especially where far more serious crimes occur every day." These professionals indicate that officers should be encouraged to intervene and to take these petty offenses and juvenile infractions seriously. It is possible for police officers to identify those youngsters most at risk in particular neighborhoods and perhaps do something to assist them to refrain from future lives of crime.

But the nature of systems is such that the actions of particular parts of the system may not function properly or be permitted to function properly in relation to other systemic parts (Guarino-Ghezzi, 1994). It would be difficult, for instance, for Trojanowicz and Bucqueroux to sell their ideas to the police departments of Yakima or Seattle, Washington, at least to the officers on duty there in the 1980s. Whether or not these officers were justified in doing so, they took it upon themselves to intervene in the lives of numerous status offenders after divestiture was enacted and relabeled status offenses as delinquent offenses. This intervention was contrary to the spirit of intervention outlined explicitly by Trojanowicz and Bucqueroux in their description of police actions under community policing policies. More status offenders and petty offenders on the streets of Yakima and Seattle were taken to jails and juvenile halls following divestiture than in previous years. This is quite different from officers acting as interventionists in positive ways and doing things *for* youths rather than *against* them.

There are obvious gaps between different contact points in the juvenile justice system. It is one thing to legislate change and remove status offenders from the jurisdiction of juvenile court judges and police officers. It is quite another thing to expect that juvenile court judges and police officers will automatically relinquish their powers over status offenders. Although many juvenile court judges and police officers won't admit it to others, they do not like having their discretionary powers limited or undermined by legislatures (U.S. General Accounting Office, 1991, 1995a).

Experts have recommended that police departments have separate units to interface with juveniles and manage them. This has already been accomplished in many of the larger city police departments throughout the United States (Brantley and DiRosa, 1994; Torok and Trump, 1994). However, many smaller police departments and sheriff's offices simply lack the staff or facilities to accommodate such special youth units. These luxuries are usually enjoyed only by larger departments. Smaller departments must be content with individual officers who assume responsibilities for managing juvenile offenders and perform related tasks. The majority of initial contacts with juveniles who engage in unacceptable behaviors continue to be made by uniformed police officers while on patrol (Kratcoski and Kratcoski, 1986:220).

Police officers will continue to exhibit interest in those juveniles who violate criminal laws. Offense seriousness and the totality of circumstances will usually dictate their reactions in street encounters with these youths. But most juveniles who are the subjects of police-initiated contacts have committed no crimes. These may be status offenders or those reported to police as **children in need of supervision** (CHINS) (Rabinowitz, 1992). The wise use of discretion by police officers is especially crucial in dealing with status offenders. Fine lines may be drawn by academicians and others to distinguish between offender arrests and temporary detentions resulting from being taken into custody, but the bottom line is usually a record of the contact being entered in a juvenile file (Torok and Trump, 1994).

DELINQUENCY PREVENTION PROGRAMS AND POLICE INTERVENTIONS

Much has been done by police officers to cause negative images of themselves among youths (Milton S. Eisenhower Foundation, 1993). Juveniles are stopped, *often*, in their opinion, simply because they are teenagers walking the streets. They cannot or do not want to understand the point of view of police officers who may see gang "trouble" or the potential for violence or crime resulting from accumulating youths on corners at night. Police officers acquire a professional defensiveness, assuming that their authority will be challenged. In certain cities, this defensiveness is justified, since police cruisers have sometimes been targets of random shootings from alleyways or rooftops.

Community policing is one strategy intended to overcome these negative stereotypes of police officers. During community policing, police officers attempt to become acquainted with the neighbors they wish to protect. These are sometimes dubbed "back to the people" methods. One way in which community policing has been varied in different jurisdictions is by changing police officer patrol styles. Foot patrols have been used in Flint, Michigan, and golf cart patrols have been tried in Tampa, Florida. In each case, officers walk beats or ride golf carts, thus breaking the image of riding dispassionately in a cruiser through the community (Champion and Rush, 1997). Some critics say that these patrol variations have not reduced crime particularly, but these same critics admit that these patrol variations have some public relations value. Perhaps this should be at least one police officer objective—to heighten the officer's public relations image in the neighborhood.

Many experts believe that effective intervention programs designed to prevent delinquent conduct should be started early in a youth's life, probably through school programs. School systems are logical conduits through which intervention programs can be channeled. Large numbers of youths assemble there regularly. A considerable amount of illicit activity, including drug use and abuse and gang violence, are common events for teachers. Many students walk to school. Thus they become susceptible and vulnerable targets for various types of persons, including child sexual abusers, youth gangs, and street people (Anonymous, 1991; New York Commission for the Study of Youth Crime and Violence and the Reform of the Juvenile Justice System, 1994).

1. *TOPS.* Police officers in Rochester, New York, decided to use teens themselves to "police" other teens in the early 1980s (Lipson, 1982). A privately funded program was implemented known as **TOPS** (*Teens on Patrol*). In this project,

BOX 4.3   THE GRAFFITI BUSTER

The Case of the Aqua Avenger

It is happening in Hayward, California. A mysterious person who police have nicknamed the "Aqua Avenger" is going about his deeds late at night, covering unsightly graffiti on interstate highways and road signs. Area residents of Castro Valley and Hayward have many positive things to say about the Avenger. He is covering up vulgarities, gang symbols, and other unsightly images that "taggers" or youthful graffiti artists apply, also during evening hours.

The police aren't impressed. They would prefer that instead of using aqua paint the Aqua Avenger would use "earth tones" to blend in more with the walls that he or she is covering. One City Facilities Department spokesman, Jim Ahrontes, said, "I can see that he's trying to make an effort. I get sick of looking at tagging myself." Further, callers to the Hayward Police Department leave messages saying, "The City of Hayward does not have a graffiti program, so I give this guy a thumbs-up, regardless of whatever color he uses." City officials want the Aqua Avenger caught. They want police to find him and confiscate his paint. Perhaps they should hang out at K-Mart and watch for someone buying 20 gallons of aqua paint.

If the Aqua Avenger is caught, do you think that he or she should be punished or rewarded? What does this say about police enforcement of laws against graffiti on public signs and highways?

Source: Adapted from Associated Press, "Police Looking for 'Aqua Avenger.'" *Minot (ND) Daily News,* July 31, 1996:A2.

police officers selected 125 youths to maintain security and patrol city parks and recreational areas. Interestingly, these teens did a reasonably good job at deterring others from committing delinquent acts in the parks and causing trouble for park patrons. Ultimately, even some of the TOPS became cops and were hired by the Rochester Police Department.

2. *Dickerson's Rangers.* **Dickerson's Rangers** is an antidrug program started in the San Fernando Valley of southern California. This program targets children ages 7 through 13, and it operates in various city parks and recreational centers. Children meet weekly and discuss drug abuse in their schools and communities. Police officers advise them how to resist overtures made by drug dealers or their peers who might use drugs. Field trips are also sponsored that include speakers whose specialties include drug abuse and illicit drug prevention.

3. *Campus Pride.* Various school districts throughout the United States have instituted a program known as **Campus Pride**. This program attempts to remove gang graffiti from school grounds. Police officers can assist school

leaders in identifying gang slogans and symbols, and often, gang members themselves may be ordered by juvenile courts to remove this graffiti. Otherwise, the students act in concert to keep their schools clean of gang graffiti and possible violence. Gang graffiti is often used to mark off certain areas, including schools, as a gang's turf or territory. Acting together, however, students have been able to force gang members out of their turf and other "territories."

4. *Graffiti Removal Initiative Program.* One solution to combat gang recruitment and involvement in the southern California area is the **Graffiti Removal Community Service Program** (Agopian, 1989). Juveniles who are initially apprehended and determined to be affiliated with gangs are assigned to a community service program as a condition of their probation. They must perform an average of 140 hours of community service, which consists of removing graffiti from buildings and other structures in their communities, together with other probationary conditions. According to Agopian, the removal of gang graffiti benefits the community as well as gang members, who hopefully learn that law-abiding behavior and respect for property are expected of them. Agopian reports that during the first two years that the program operated, nearly 90 percent of all participating youths completed this requirement of their probation. Further, rearrests of these youths during the two-year interval were minimal. However, these youths, once released from their probation programs, are placed back in their original environments and subject to the same social pressures and economic conditions that brought them to the attention of police officers initially.

5. *COPY Kids.* **COPY Kids** (*Community Opportunities Program for Youth*) is a police demonstration project that was undertaken in the summer of 1992 in Spokane, Washington (Thurman, Giacomazzi, and Bogen, 1993:554–555). Officers engaged in weekly interactions with 300 economically disadvantaged youths averaging 13 years of age. Their program involved an attempt to assist these youths in improving their self-concepts, self-images, and to promote general law-abiding behavior. Parents were involved as well as a large supporting staff contingent. Youths were given an opportunity to participate in various crafts and jobs where they could acquire several useful skills for subsequent employment. Interviews with parents and workers suggested that these productive activities allowed children to develop a greater sense of responsibility. Particularly encouraging was the fact that these youths developed a more favorable image of police officers and the police department. Limited information existed to show any effects on curbing delinquency among those involved youths, although investigators believed that this plan was a useful deterrent to delinquent conduct.

6. *R.O.C.K.* **R.O.C.K.** (*Reaching Out, Convicts and Kids*) is a program established in Visalia, California by the Tulare County Probation Department in 1992 (Anonymous, 1992a). The program was originally designed to enable troubled youth to refrain from involvement in illegal activities. A nontraditional

program, R.O.C.K. uses convicted felons as volunteers who talk to youths and give them first-hand experiences about what led to their crimes and the effects of these crimes on victims. Workshops are used to establish a foundation of honesty between inmates and youths to facilitate the direction of these youths' behaviors toward law-abiding channels. Education is emphasized, improving familial relations and learning ways of coping with peer pressures that often instigate delinquent conduct. Those youths who experience R.O.C.K. stand a much better chance of avoiding delinquency than those who are antisocial and do not become involved in the program.

7. *D.A.R.E.* The Los Angeles Police Department has implemented a program for intervening with elementary school drug use called **D.A.R.E** (*Drug Abuse Resistance Education*). D.A.R.E. uses police officers familiar with drugs and drug laws who visit schools in their precincts and speak to youths about how to say "no" to drugs. Children are taught how to recognize illegal drugs, different types of drugs, as well as their adverse effects.

8. *TIPS.* **TIPS** (*Teaching Individuals Protective Strategies*) is sponsored by the U.S. Department of Education and is geared to helping youths in schools acquire the reasoning power and ability for responsible decision making. Especially designed for children in grades K–8, TIPS has two principal objectives: (1) to reduce victimization among youths as well as their vulnerability to become victims, and (2) identify potential solutions to problems that involve noncriminal activities. Thus youths in schools are trained to deal with strangers, to become more aware of potentially dangerous social situations, and in how to channel anger or frustration into productive activities. Part of the TIPS program is incorporated into each youth's educational training. Thus far, the results seem successful at reducing youth victimizations by adults or other youths who are otherwise hard-core delinquents.

9. *Project Heavy.* **Project Heavy** is an alternative program located in Los Angeles County. It involves both a peer- and a group-counseling program for children and youths ages 8 to 18, and youth leaders are targeted for change so that they can set good examples for others (Keith, 1989:117). The theory underlying Project Heavy is that youth leaders are admired by other youths. If they can set good conduct examples, more youths will follow these examples and be less inclined to follow those engaging in delinquent conduct.

10. *GREAT.* A program has been implemented in Phoenix, Arizona between community leaders and educators and funded by the Bureau of Alcohol, Tobacco, and Firearms to intervene with gangs on a nationwide basis. **GREAT** (*Gang Resistance Education and Training*) utilizes police officers who visit schools and interact with students on a regular basis over a specified period. Classroom sessions consist of eight one-hour periods where youths can learn to overcome peer pressure relative to drug use and joining delinquent gangs. The weekly topics are diverse, including cultural sensitivity and prejudice, crimes, victims and rights, drugs and neighborhoods, diverse responsibilities, goal setting, and conflict resolution and need fulfillment. This program was designed and

targeted for children in after-school hours. Parental involvement is encouraged, and police organizations sponsor summer activities to give local youths alternative interesting projects.

11. *Alateen.* For many youths who are become a part of the juvenile justice system, youths either have alcohol problems themselves or have parents with alcohol problems. Children may be alcoholics. **Alateen** is the teen counterpart to Alcoholics Anonymous. Police officers can function in an instructive capacity to alert children to the signs of alcoholism among themselves and their friends. They can be of assistance in directing children to others who can offer assistance.

12. *Hire a Gang Leader.* **Hire a Gang Leader** is a delinquency prevention program pioneered in 1975 in El Monte, California. The project was sponsored by members of the local police department. Groups of 10 to 15 gang leaders met with police officers and designed a program to provide job opportunities for gang members who were unemployed. This cooperative effort was successful in several respects. First, it taught gang members that police officers are not always their enemies. Second, it gave them a different view of the police officer role as an "enabler" and facilitator, since there were numerous successful job placements. Police officers benefited, since delinquency rates in the El Monte area dropped in areas where gangs participated in the program (Amandes, 1979).

13. *Chicago Area Project.* Initiated in Chicago during the 1920s by Clifford Shaw and his colleagues at the University of Chicago, the **Chicago Area Project** (CAP) was originally designed to reach out to street gangs and redirect their activities toward more conventional community activities. Shaw promoted *curbstone counseling* and *street work* as a means of working directly with gang members and their leaders (Sorrentino and Whittaker, 1994:8–9). Shaw's assistants, who were trained in counseling and gang jargon and behaviors, would seek out gangs in their hangouts and work with youths. Today, CAP uses a three-pronged strategy—direct service, advocacy, and community involvement—to interest youths in changing their behaviors. Local churches and clubs are used to centralize gang interventions and promote useful programs of interest to youth gangs. Recreation and sports programs have been established for involving youths who otherwise might be attracted to gangs for membership and status. In fact, arrested youths are not always taken to juvenile court. Rather, they are sent to community committees where their actions are evaluated. They are given the option of joining some useful group activity or going to juvenile court. Neighborhood volunteers and CAP counselors work closely with juvenile probation officers and juvenile court officials to maintain continuous contact with even the most chronic youthful violators. Directed at youths ages 10 to 17, CAP has evolved into the Comprehensive Community Based Youth Services Program, with a variety of services, including crisis intervention, emergency foster home placement, job training, and counseling. The continuing project is viewed as successful by its advocates

and others who have seen the results of youth exposure to CAP programs (Sorrentino and Whittaker, 1994:10–11).

14. *Amer-I-Can.* **Amer-I-Can** is a program established in Los Angeles by James Brown, noted professional football player and former gang member, and other interested citizens. Amer-I-Can was originally devised as a method of resolving gang disputes. Jim Brown would act as an intermediary between rival gang members, and in many instances his intervention and action would eliminate gang tensions and hostilities. In some cases his actions did not work. His own chief of staff was shot 11 times by a rival gang member who didn't want Brown's work to succeed. Nevertheless, this setback did not deter Brown from persisting in working with gang members, ex-convicts, inmates, and other troubled youths to manage their lives better. Brown spends his time targeting tough guys and teaching them basic skills, such as how to dress for a job, face a prospective employer, and communicate effectively. Brown believes that education, self-pride, and responsibility are key elements of his program. Brown has even invited gang members to his own home, where he attempts various interventions. Over time, gang members and other troubled youth have accepted Brown's actions in good faith and responded favorably. Currently, former gang members work with special Los Angeles police youth squads and teach them how best to relate to other gang members. In Brown's program, the first lesson Brown teaches is that no one is cursed from birth. Success is for those who want it and take action to get it. Former convicts and gang members teach classes in goal setting, family relationships, and financial responsibility. Brown's program has assisted at least 17,000 inmates in California and more than 4000 in New Jersey, where a similar version of his program has been established. It has a presence in at least 24 schools in Ohio and several other states (Terry, 1997:4–7).

These are only a few of the many programs operating throughout the United States involving police in proactive and positive roles, where they are taking an active interest in preventing delinquent conduct through interacting closely with youths. These programs will not make juvenile offenders desist from delinquent conduct, but will make many of them aware of a positive side of police officers. Further, they will have the positive effect of helping police officers understand juveniles and their motives.

KEY TERMS

Alateen

Amer-I-Can

Arrest

Beats

Campus Pride

Chicago Area Project (CAP)

Children in need of supervision (CHINS)

Community policing

COPY Kids (Community Opportunities Program for Youth)

Corporate gangs

Criminogenic environment

D.A.R.E. (Drug Abuse Resistance Education)

Dickerson's Rangers

Discretionary powers

Expungement orders

Graffiti Removal Initiative Program

GREAT (Gang Resistance Education and Training)

Hire a Gang Leader

Police discretion

Proactive units

Project Heavy

Reactive units

R.O.C.K. (Reaching Out, Convicts and Kids)

Scavenger gangs

Sealing records of juveniles

Situationally based discretion

Station adjustment

TIPS (Teaching Individuals Protective Strategies)

TOPS (Teens on Patrol)

Totality of circumstances

Youth squads

QUESTIONS FOR REVIEW

1. What is *police discretion*? In what ways may police officers abuse their discretion in handling encounters with juveniles?

2. What is *situationally based discretion*? How is the *totality of circumstances* relevant to influencing police discretion? What are some of the extralegal or nonlegal factors that cause police officers to take youths into custody who have not otherwise violated the law?

3. What is *community policing*? How does community policing influence police officer discretion? What type of role should police officers have in relation to juveniles within a community policing framework?

4. Differentiate between *proactive* and *reactive* police work. In what sense is every police officer a juvenile officer?

5. Distinguish between *corporate* and *scavenger* delinquent gangs. What are their respective objectives and ambitions?

6. What are five discretionary options that police may exercise in their encounters with juveniles?

7. What is a *station adjustment*? Relate station adjustments to labeling of juveniles as delinquent.

8. Differentiate between *being taken into custody* and *being arrested.*

9. What are some general limitations and prohibitions about photographing and fingerprinting juveniles in jails or lockups?

10. What is meant by *expungement* or *record sealing*? Why is it important for adults with records of juvenile offenses?

SUGGESTED READINGS

English, T. J. *Born to Kill: America's Most Notorious Vietnamese Gang, and the Changing Face of Organized Crime.* New York: William Morrow, 1995.

Jah, Yusaf and Shah Keyah. *Uprising: Crips and Bloods Tell the Story of America's Youth in the Crossfire.* New York: Scribner, 1995.

Monti, Daniel J. *Wannabe: Gangs in Suburbs and Schools.* Oxford, UK: Blackwell, 1994.

Rivlin, Gary. *Drive-By.* New York: Henry Holt, 1995.

Snell, Cudore L. *Young Men in the Street: Help-Seeking Behavior of Young Male Prostitutes.* Westport, CT: Praeger, 1995.

CHAPTER 5

INTAKE AND PREADJUDICATORY PROCESSING

INTRODUCTION

> *The mother, Mrs. Smith, sat uncomfortably in front of the young juvenile probation officer. The father, Mr. Smith, had taken time from work to make the 1:00 P.M. appointment at the juvenile court. Room 120 was equipped with a desk and five chairs, some file cabinets, and a poor view of the building next door. It was not air-conditioned. As the parents sat and listened, the juvenile probation officer, Mike Jones, spoke to Edward, a young boy who had stolen a wagon from another boy in his neighborhood. "What we seem to have here," Jones said, "is that your son, Edward, has taken something from another child in his neighborhood." "Edward, how old are you?" asked Jones. "Eleven," said Edward. "Do you know that it's wrong to steal from someone else?" asked the officer. "Yes," the boy answered. "You also broke the wagon you stole," Jones said. "Yeah, I know," answered Edward. "What do you think we ought to do about it?" asked Jones. "Do you think that if you pay the boy for the broken wagon—and if you do that and your parents see to it that you earn the money to pay for it...what would you think if we just forget about today?" "That would be good," said Edward. "I'll earn money and pay for his wagon...every penny of it." "Is that OK with you, Mr. and Mrs. Smith? Will you see to it that Edward pays the boy for the broken wagon and that Edward earns the money to pay for it?" "Yes, we'll see that he does that." "Now," said Jones, "if Edward comes before me in the future, I'm going to have him see the judge. And if he sees the judge, the judge isn't going to be as forgiving as I am...in fact, the judge may put Edward in an industrial school for people who steal. Do you want that, Edward?" "No, I don't," Edward replied. "Then you can go. I'm keeping a record of this in my desk here, but it won't go any further. Right now, what you did is between you and me. I'll fix it with the police. But if you do anything like this again...well, there's only so much that I can do. OK? Do we have an agreement? Are you going to go out there and not come back to this place ever again?" "Yes," said Edward. His parents nodded in agreement.*

This informal process over a relatively petty event—the theft of someone's wagon—is an intake hearing. The juvenile probation officer is an intake officer. He has just settled a pending case against Edward Smith. He notified the police and he monitored Edward's progress, ensuring over time that the victim was compensated for his broken wagon. As far as Mike Jones was concerned, Edward Smith would never again come before him.

This chapter is about the intake process. Scenes such as that above are repeated daily, probably in every jurisdiction throughout the United States. Intake officers encounter virtually every sort of juvenile offender imaginable. They must assess the circumstances and make fairly rapid decisions about whether to advance certain youths further into the juvenile justice system. The circumstances are not limited to the allegations or infractions.

Rather, they encompass numerous dimensions, including age of offender, gender, ethnicity or race, type and seriousness of offenses alleged, school records, parental behaviors, and prior records of juveniles, if any. Did the juvenile act alone or in concert with others? Were there victims? Was anyone killed or seriously injured?

Because of the differential training juvenile probation officers receive and the individual orientations they manifest, their behaviors as intake officers may be better understood by paying attention to certain models that are commonly used in dealing with juvenile offenders. Several popular treatment models and orientations are described and discussed. Many of those youths appearing before intake officers are first offenders. Because of the continuing belief by many experts that one major function of juvenile justice is to rehabilitate and redirect one's deviant behaviors toward more legitimate and proper conduct, intake officers give serious consideration to diversion as a nonpunitive option. Several forms of diversion are described, although a more thorough discussion of diversion and diversion programs is presented in Chapter 11.

Intake also functions as one of the first screening mechanisms for filtering only the most serious offenders further into the system and diverting the least serious youths away from it (American Correctional Association, 1992). A major consideration in the diversion decision, therefore, is whether responsible guardianship exists for managing youthful offenders (Mershon, 1991). The importance of this consideration is discussed, and various juvenile offender implications are assessed.

WHAT IS INTAKE?

Beyond the discretionary initiatives available to police officers and others who interface with juveniles who may be violating the law, *intake or an intake screening is the second major step in the juvenile justice process.* **Intake** *is a more or less informally conducted screening procedure whereby intake probation officers or other juvenile court functionaries decide whether detained juveniles should be (1) unconditionally released from the juvenile justice system, (2) released to parents or guardians subject to a subsequent juvenile court appearance, (3) released or referred to one or more community-based services or resources, (4) placed in secure confinement subject to a subsequent juvenile court appearance, or (5) waived or transferred to the jurisdiction of criminal courts.* Many jurisdictions are currently reevaluating the intake process and whether it should be modified (Kansas Juvenile Justice Task Force, 1995; Leiber, 1995; U.S. General Accounting Office, 1995a).

The Discretionary Powers of Intake Officers

The pivotal role played by intake probation officers cannot be underestimated. While police officers are often guided by rules and regulations that require specific actions such as taking juveniles into custody when certain events are observed or reported, the guidelines governing intake actions and decision making are less clearcut. In most jurisdictions, intake proceedings are not open to the public, involve few participants, and do not presume the existence of the full range of a juvenile's constitutional rights. This is not meant to imply that juveniles may not exercise one or more of their constitutional rights during an intake hearing or proceeding, but rather, the informal nature of many intake proceedings is such that one's constitutional rights are not usually the primary issue. The primary formality of these proceedings consists of information compiled by intake officers during their interviews with juvenile arrestees. The long-range effects of intake decision making are often serious and have profound implications for adult offenders (Kapp, Schwartz, and Epstein, 1994). Many jurisdictions have standard forms completed by probation officers during intake interviews. One of these forms is illustrated in Figure 5.1.

Florida Assessment Centers

In Florida, juvenile **assessment centers** have been established as processing points for juveniles who have been taken into custody or arrested. These centers provide comprehensive screenings and assessments of youths; to match various available services to client needs; to promote interagency coordination, and to generate data relevant to resource investment and treatment outcomes (Florida House Committee on Criminal Justice, 1994). Florida intake officers conduct clinical screenings, recommend confinement, make provisions for youth custody and supervision, arrange transportation, and track juveniles as they move throughout the juvenile justice system.

The U.S. Supreme Court has rejected attempts by various interests to extend the full range of due process guarantees for juveniles to intake proceedings, largely because of the informal nature of them (Butts et al., 1996:8; Feld, 1995). Thus there are numerous interjurisdictional variations concerning the intake process and the extent to which one's constitutional rights are safeguarded or protected (Dougherty, 1988:77). Generally, these proceedings are conducted informally, without court reporters and other personnel who are normally equated with formal court decorum. A casually dressed, folksy juvenile probation officer sits at a desk with the juvenile

FIGURE 5.1   Social History Report

Social History Report

Routing Information	Case Identification

TO: _____   CASE NAME: _____

FROM: _____ DATE: _____   SERIAL: _____ STATUS: _____

AREA: _____ OFFICE: _____   BIRTH DATE: _____ SEX: ___ RACE: _____

REPORT REQUESTED BY: _____   JPC ASSIGNED CASE: _____

1. IDENTIFYING DATA
    a. Youth's birthplace:
    b. Youth's birth status:
    c. Other names used:
    d. Youth's address at time of commitment:
    e. With whom living at time of commitment:
    f. Family's relationship to youth:
    g. Legal guardian:
    h. Social security number: Youth: Father: Mother:

2. PERSONS AND AGENCIES INTERVIEWED

3. AGENCIES THAT HAVE WORKED WITH YOUTH AND FAMILY

4. DELINQUENCY HISTORY (USE ONLY AS SUPPLEMENTAL TO COURT REPORT. IDENTIFY ANY PARTICULAR CHRONIC AND/OR PECULIAR PROBLEMS.)

5. DEVELOPMENTAL HISTORY
    a. Early history (Use only when obvious value in detailing youth's problems.)
    b. Medical history (Detail only if pertinent.)
    c. Description of youth (How parents perceive youth, attitudes, and behavior patterns.)

6. FAMILY HISTORY—REVISED
    a. Marital history and youth's previous living situations
    b. Father
    c. Mother
    d. Siblings
    e. Family income
    f. Parents' perception of problem
    g. Impression of family functioning
        (1) How parents relate to youth
        (2) Parents' concept of discipline
        (3) Evaluation of parent role (how they should/do perform as parents)
        (4) JPC's impression of performance and evaluation (identify strengths and weaknesses)
        (5) Family's financial resources, including benefits, veterans, social security, welfare, etc., medical/hospital insurance (Note: Income is reported elsewhere—preadmission history.)

7. COMMUNITY INFORMATION
    a. Placement possibilities, including own home. (Note attitudes, family structural compatibility, and other placement considerations.)
    b. Community attitudes toward placement
        (1) Neighbors
        (2) School officials

8. SCHOOL AND VOCATIONAL HISTORY
    a. School performance
        (1) Last school attended and grade completed
        (2) Level of scholastic performance
    b. Vocational history
        (1) Part-time or full-time jobs held
        (2) Performance evaluation

9. IMPRESSIONS AND RECOMMENDATIONS
    a. Overall evaluation by JPC
    b. Family's willingness to become involved and cooperate
    c. Problem list (JPC's perception of specific problems)
    d. Strengths and assets of family and youth which can be used in dealing with problems.

Source: From Thomas G. Pinnock, *Necessary Information for Diagnosis* (Olympia, VA: Bureau of Juvenile Rehabilitation, Department of Social and Health Sciences, 1976), p. 11.

accused of an infraction or crime, or who is alleged to be in need of special supervision or care. One or both parents may be present at this informal hearing, although it is not unusual for parents or guardians to be absent from such proceedings. Victims may or may not attend, again depending on the jurisdiction.

The Increasing Formalization of Intake

More than a few experts have alleged that because intake is such an important stage of a juvenile's processing, it must be scrupulously monitored so that fairness and equitable treatment of juveniles by intake officers is preserved. A study of the intake process in Iowa provides information about intake proceedings, suggesting that extralegal factors are often at work to influence intake officer decision making. Leiber (1995) investigated a random sample of referrals to juvenile courts in Iowa during the period 1980–1991. Included in his study were 3437 white juveniles, 2784 black juveniles, and 350 Hispanic juveniles. Agency records provided detailed information about how the cases were disposed and processed at different stages, beginning with intake. Leiber found that the ultimate case outcome was influenced mostly by legal factors, such as offense seriousness, prior record of offending, and one's age. However, he found compelling evidence of discrimination in offender processing at the intake stage. Black juveniles tended to receive a larger proportion of recommendations from intake officers for further proceedings in the juvenile justice system. Black juveniles were also far less likely than whites and Hispanics to receive diversion or other lenient outcomes from the intake proceeding.

Often, these disparities in processing juveniles at the intake stage are attributable to the subjective impressions of intake officers. While most of these officers are perhaps well intentioned in their individualization of juvenile treatment, there is some general bias inherent in such individualization. This bias usually occurs as the result of gender, race/ethnic, and socioeconomic factors. A study investigating these phenomena and their impact on juvenile justice decision making for the years 1986–1991 found moderate support for bias in intake processing (U.S. General Accounting Office, 1995a).

Adding fuel to the charge that the intake process is often discriminatory according to race/ethnicity, gender, and socioeconomic status, a study of 1256 youths was undertaken in Fairfax County, Virginia, in the early 1990s (Williams and Cohen, 1993). It was determined that disproportionately more black youths were processed at the point of intake compared with youths of other races and ethnicities. While secure confinement was almost always used for those juveniles where serious offenses were alleged, disproportionately more minority offenders were placed in secure confinement, even controlling for type of offense and prior juvenile record. Further, blacks were less likely than whites to receive lenient dispositions and treatment. Disproportionately lower numbers of blacks were likely to have hearings compared with whites, and more minorities used public defenders. Thus minorities, especially black males, received adverse treatment at the early stages of their processing. All of this adverse treatment had the cumulative effect of maximizing the harshness of their dispositions at later stages.

Regardless of whether any particular jurisdiction exhibits differential, preferential, or discriminatory treatment toward juvenile offenders at *any* stage of their processing, there are those who believe that increased *defense* attorney involvement for at least the most serious juveniles is a necessity. The primary reason for the presence of defense attorney involvement in the early stages of a juvenile's processing is to *ensure that the juvenile's* **due process** *rights are observed.* If there are extralegal factors at work that somehow influence an intake officer's view of a particular juvenile's case, the impact of these extralegal factors can be diffused or at least minimized by the presence of someone who knows the law—a defense attorney. During the 1980s where data were available from reporting states, the amount of attorney use in juvenile proceedings increased substantially (Champion, 1992). Specific states involved in a 10-year examination of juvenile attorney use trends were California, Montana, Nebraska, North Dakota, and Pennsylvania. Attorney use increased systematically during this decade.

Feld (1993a–c, 1995) observes that increased presence of counsel in juvenile proceedings at virtually any stage is bound to have both positive and negative effects. An attorney's presence can preserve due process. Intake officers and other juvenile court actors, including judges, are inclined to apply juvenile law more precisely than under circumstances where defense counsel are not present to represent youthful offenders. Where defense counsel is not present, however, the law might be relaxed to the point where some juveniles' rights are ignored or trivialized. But an attorney's presence in juvenile proceedings *criminalizes* these proceedings to a degree. The fact of needing an attorney for one's defense in juvenile court is suggestive of criminal proceedings and ensuring a criminal defendant's right to due process. In circumstances where defense counsel and prosecutors argue the facts of particular cases, juveniles cannot help but be influenced by this adversarial event.

This experience is sometimes so traumatic that juveniles come to identify with criminals who go through essentially the same process. Many experts believe that youths who identify with criminals will eventually *label* themselves as *criminal* or *delinquent*, and thus they will be harmed from the experience. This is consistent with **labeling theory**, where self-definitions of particular types of persons are acquired by others, such as juveniles identifying with criminals on the basis of how they, the juveniles themselves, are treated and defined by others (Lemert, 1951, 1967a). To the extent that labeling theory adversely influences youths who are either first offenders or have committed only minor infractions, including status offenses, some thought ought to be given to maintaining a degree of informality in intake proceedings (Bazemore, 1993b; Rabinowitz, 1992).

The Need for Greater Accountability

More than a few experts seek greater accountability from those who work with juvenile offenders from intake through adjudication and disposition (Page, 1993). Presently, there are many inconsistent juvenile justice systems throughout the United States. Different types of family courts attempt to apply juvenile law in resolving a wide assortment of familial disputes and juvenile matters. Juvenile courts are increasingly seeking new methods and techniques, such as expanded intake functions and nonadversarial resolution of disputes, not only to create smoother case processing for juvenile courts, but also to provide more efficient, just, and enforceable social solutions to diverse juvenile problems. Accountability for judicial power requires that the court act comprehensively in providing social services either directly or by way of referral (Page, 1993). This accountability involves not only the enforcement of dispositional orders requiring the parties and families to respond, but also the agencies and service providers to function effectively and the court to hold itself responsible for its case processing and management systems (Page, 1993).

INTAKE PROCEEDINGS: WHERE DO WE GO FROM HERE?

Intake Compared with Plea Bargaining

A parallel has been drawn by Dougherty (1988) between what goes on in juvenile intake hearings and criminal plea bargaining. In plea bargaining, prosecutors and defense attorneys will negotiate a guilty plea and a punishment that are acceptable to both parties. Ordinarily, plea bargaining occurs before any formal disposition or trial. Thus the accused waives certain constitutional rights, including the right to a trial by jury, the right to confront and cross-examine witnesses, and the right against self-incrimination. A plea bargain is an admission of guilt to one or more criminal charges, and it is anticipated by those entering guilty pleas that leniency will be extended to them in exchange for their guilty pleas (McDonald, 1985; Stitt and

Siegel, 1986). The theory is that the accused will save the state considerable time and expense otherwise allocated to trials as well as the important prosecutorial burden of proving the defendant's guilt beyond a reasonable doubt. Although some jurisdictions prohibit plea bargaining (e.g., Alaska and selected counties throughout the United States), the U.S. Supreme Court has ruled that plea bargaining is constitutional in any jurisdiction that wishes to use it (*Brady v. United States*, 1970).

For many cases this exchange is reasonable. Crime for crime, other factors being reasonably equal, those convicted offenders who plea bargain fare much better and receive more lenient treatment than those who subject the state to the time and expense of jury trials (Champion, 1988; Champion and Mays, 1991). Plea bargaining is favored by those who believe that it accelerates the criminal justice process. Over 90 percent of all criminal convictions are obtained by prosecutors through plea bargaining (Champion, 1996).

During intake hearings, intake probation officers have almost unlimited discretion regarding specific outcomes for youths, especially those where minor offending is alleged. Apart from certain state-mandated hearings that must precede formal adjudicatory proceedings by juvenile court judges, no constitutional provisions require states to conduct such hearings (U.S. General Accounting Office, 1995a). Intake officers seldom hear legal arguments or evaluate the sufficiency of evidence on behalf of or against youths sitting before them. These proceedings, which most often are informally conducted, usually result in adjustments, where intake officers adjust disputes or allegations informally. Dougherty (1988:78) says that while intake officers may advise juveniles and their parents that they may have attorneys present during such proceedings, these officers also indicate that the presence of attorneys may jeopardize the informal nature of these proceedings and any possible informal resolution of the case that might be made. Thus parents and youths are deliberately discouraged from having legal counsel to assist them at this critical screening stage (Guggenheim, 1985b).

Intake officers, then, are in the business of behavioral prediction. They must make important predictions about what they believe will be the future conduct of each juvenile, depending on their decision. Sometimes personality tests are administered to certain youths to determine their degree of social or psychological adjustment or aptitude. Those considered dangerous, either to themselves or to others, are detained at youth centers or other juvenile custodial facilities until a detention hearing is conducted. Florida Juvenile Assessment Centers administer a battery of tests to juveniles during intake, including clinical screenings by psychiatric professionals (Florida House Committee on Criminal Justice, 1994). For sex offenders in some jurisdictions, other psychological assessments are made and inventories administered, such as the Tennessee Self-Concept Scale, Beck Depression

Inventory, the Rape-Myth Acceptance Scale, the Adversarial Sexual Attitudes Scale, and the Assessing Environments Scale, the Buss–Durkee Hostility Inventory, and the Youth Self-Report (Worling, 1995). On the basis of these and other criteria, decisions are made by intake officers about whether additional steps are necessary in juvenile offender processing.

Intake officers perform these early quasi-judiciary functions and decide the outcomes of certain minor cases based, in part, on their reactions to events or circumstances and the factual information acquired by investigating officers or complainants. If they decide to dismiss any complaint against juveniles, the matter is concluded. If they decide to refer juveniles to community-based services or agencies where they can receive needed treatment in cases such as alcohol or drug dependency, this is their option (Bazemore, 1993a, 1994). They may decide that certain juveniles should be detained in secure facilities to await a subsequent adjudication of their cases by juvenile court judges (Schwartz and Barton, 1994). Therefore, any action they take, other than outright dismissal of charges, that requires juveniles to fulfill certain conditions (e.g., attend special classes or receive therapy from some community agency or mental health facility) is based on their presumption that the juvenile is guilty of the acts alleged by complainants.

If parents or guardians or the juveniles themselves insist that the intervention of an attorney is necessary during such informal proceedings, this effectively eliminates the informality and places certain constraints on intake officers. The coercive nature of their position is such that they may compel youths to receive therapy, make restitution, or comply with any number of other conditions to avoid further involvement in the juvenile justice process. It is relatively easy to file petitions against juveniles and compel them to face juvenile court judges (Leiber, 1995; Williams and Cohen, 1993).

Dougherty (1988:78) sums up the intake scenario and its relation to plea bargaining as follows: "The fact is that both adult plea bargaining and juvenile intake function to negotiate discretionary justice. They both create formal settings, where individuals who are, for all intents and purposes, presumed to be guilty [and] are 'convinced' to agree 'voluntarily' to the officials' resolution of their cases or face the potential harsher consequences of formal processing. Individual rights are at best ignored, or at worst denied. One might argue that the only true beneficiaries of these negotiations are the judges who are relieved of the burden of having to preside over the majority of cases that enter the adult and juvenile justice systems."

Parens Patriae Perpetuated

Some evidence suggests that intake probation officers in many jurisdictions are perpetuating the *parens patriae* philosophy that has been systematically undermined by several important U.S. Supreme Court decisions during the 1960s, 1970s, and 1980s. For example, a study of intake probation officers in a southwestern U.S. metropolitan jurisdiction revealed that probation officers believed that they were the primary source of their juvenile clients' understanding of their legal rights, although these same probation officers did not themselves appear to have a sound grasp or understanding of these same juvenile rights (Lawrence, 1984). In this same jurisdiction, juveniles believed that they clearly understood their legal rights. However, interview data from them suggested that, in general, they tended to have a very poor understanding of their rights. Emerging from this study was a general recommendation that probation officers who perform intake functions should receive more training and preparation for these important roles (Lawrence, 1984). Even juvenile court judges have been criticized by some experts who believe that they often make ineffective decisions about the conditions of one's probation and the social and community services they should receive. In more than a few instances, judges are limited because there are limited social services available in their communities. Thus, even if judges wanted to maximize their effectiveness in placing youths in treatment programs that could help them, their actions would be frustrated by an absence of such programs (Ellsworth, Kinsella, and Massin, 1992).

Studies of intake dispositions in several jurisdictions have found that most intake dispositions tend to be influenced by extralegal factors, such as family, school, and employment (Kurtz, Giddings, and Sutphen, 1993; Rosenbaum and Chesney-Lind, 1994; Wordes, Bynum, and Corley, 1994). The preoccupation of intake probation officers in this jurisdiction with social adjustment factors rather than legalistic ones reflected a strong paternalistic orientation in dispositional decision making. Many intake officers dispose of cases according to what they perceived to be in the *best interests* of the children involved rather than according to legalistic criteria, such as witness credibility, tangible evidence, and one's prior offending record (Page, 1993; Steinberg, Levine, and Singer, 1992).

Intake probation officers are not inundated exclusively with cases that require fine judgment calls and discretionary hair-splitting. Many youths appearing before intake officers are hard-core offenders and recidivists who have been there before (Williams and Cohen, 1993). Also, evidentiary information presented by arresting officers is overwhelming in many cases, and a large portion of these cases tend to be rather serious. Therefore, intake officers will send many of these juveniles to juvenile court and/or arrange for a detention hearing so that they may be confined for their own safety as well as for the safety of others. Increasingly, serious juvenile offenders will be referred to juvenile prosecutors with recommendations that these juveniles should be transferred to the jurisdiction of criminal courts. The theory for this measure is that juveniles who are transferred to criminal courts will be amenable to more severe punishments normally meted out to adult offenders. However, it is questionable at present whether those who are transferred to criminal courts actually receive punishments that are more severe than they would otherwise receive if their cases were adjudicated in juvenile courts (Champion and Mays, 1991). Several explanations for this phenomenon are covered in a later chapter.

Intake, then, is a screening mechanism designed to separate the more serious cases from the less serious ones as juveniles are processed by the system. Intake officers perform classificatory functions, where they attempt to classify informally large numbers of juveniles according to abstract criteria. Clearly, intake is not an infallible process. Much depends on the particular experience and training of individual intake probation officers, juvenile court caseloads, and the nature of cases subject to intake decision making.

The discretionary powers of intake probation officers are in some ways equivalent to prosecutors in criminal courts. Intake officers may direct cases further into the system, they may defer certain cases pending some fulfillment of conditions, or they may abandon cases altogether and dismiss them from further processing. This powerful discretion can be used in both positive and negative ways, however. In response to a growing demand for juvenile justice reforms, numerous juvenile court judges have urged that more objective criteria be used for evaluating youthful offenders in the early stages of their processing, particularly at intake. A study of 43 Florida juvenile court judges found that most favored more objective methods for classifying and disposing of minor cases at the intake stage (Bazemore, 1994). Similar objective criteria have been recommended in other jurisdictions, such as Georgia (Lockhart et al., 1991), Rhode Island (Rhode Island Governor's Justice Commission Statistical Analysis Center, 1992), Nevada (Mershon, 1991), and various other states (Wordes, Bynum, and Corley, 1994).

MODELS FOR DEALING WITH JUVENILE OFFENDERS

Six models for dealing with juvenile offenders are described here. Each of these models is driven by a particular view of juvenile delinquency and what might cause it. The causes of delinquency are many and diverse, and thus not everyone agrees with any particular explanation (Angenent and de Man, 1996). Therefore, not every expert dealing with juvenile offenders agrees that one particular model is most fruitful as a basis for delinquency intervention. Rather, these models serve as a guide to the different types of decisions that are made on behalf of or against specific juvenile offenders. Because each model includes aims or objectives that are related to a degree with the aims or objectives of other models, there is sometimes confusion about model identities. For example, professionals may use a particular model label to refer to orientations that are more properly included in the context of other models. Some professionals say that they do not use any particular model, but rather, they rely on their own intuition for exercising a particular juvenile intervention.

Additionally, some recently developed interventionist activities have combined the favorable features of one model with those of others. These hybrid models are difficult to categorize, although they are believed to be helpful in diverting youths to more productive and nondelinquent activities. One way of overcoming this confusion is to highlight those features of models that most directly reflect the models' aims. The models discussed include (1) the rehabilitation model, (2) the treatment or medical model, (3) the noninterventionist model, (4) the due process model, (5) the "just deserts"/justice model, and (6) the crime control model.

The Rehabilitation Model

Perhaps the most influential model that has functioned to intervene on behalf of first-offender juveniles is the rehabilitation model. *The **rehabilitation model** assumes that delinquency or delinquent conduct is the result of poor friendship or peer choices, poor social adjustments, the wrong educational priorities, and/or a general failure to envision realistic life goals and inculcate appropriate moral values.* In corrections, the rehabilitation model is associated with programs that change offender attitudes, personalities, or character. These programs may be therapeutic, educational, or vocational. At the intake stage, however, there is little, if any, reliance on existing community-based programs or services that cater to certain juvenile needs. Intake officers who use the rehabilitation model in their decision-making activities will often attempt to impart different values and personal goals to juveniles through a type of informal teaching.

At the beginning of this chapter, a youth was described who stole a wagon belonging to another youth. The intake officer assigned this case might have asked the juvenile, "Would you want someone to take something that belonged to you?" "How would you feel about this if your property were taken?" "What are some ways you can earn money to buy a bicycle for yourself rather than steal one?" "Maybe your parents can help you think of things to do for which you can earn extra money to buy things you want." The intake officer doesn't particularly want to involve the youth further in the system. Perhaps the officer's intent is to give certain youths a stern warning and then release them to the supervisory responsibility of their parents. But lessons should be learned, and the exercise of intake should be a learning experience, according to this rehabilitative philosophy.

Although theft is a serious offense, it is far less serious than aggravated assault, rape, armed robbery, or murder. Intake officers rely heavily on their personal experience and judgment in determining the best course of action to follow. The fact that a juvenile is 11 years of age and has committed this single theft offense is an ideal situation where intake officers can exercise strategic discretion and temper their decisions with some leniency. But in the context of *parens patriae* and the rehabilitative framework guiding some of these officers, leniency does not mean outright tokenism or ineffective wrist slapping. Doing nothing may send the wrong message to youths who have violated the law. The same may be said of police officers who encounter youths on streets and engage in *police cautioning* or stationhouse adjustments as alternative means of warning juveniles to refrain from future misconduct (Wilkinson and Evans, 1990). Thus it is believed that the informal intake hearing itself is sufficiently traumatic for most youths so that they will not be eager to reoffend subsequently. Advice, cautioning, and warnings given under such circumstances are likely to be remembered (Kenney, Pate, and Hamilton, 1990).

The Treatment or Medical Model

*The **treatment** or **medical model** assumes that delinquent conduct is like a disease, the causes of which can be isolated and attacked. Cures may be effected by administering appropriate remedies. The treatment model is very similar to the rehabilitation model. Indeed, some experts consider the treatment or medical model to be a subcategory of the rehabilitation model* (Bartollas, 1990:546). The aim of the treatment model is to set forth for offending juveniles conditional punishments that are closely related to treatment. Intake officers have the authority to refer certain youths to select community-based agencies and services, where they may receive the proper treatment. This treatment approach assumes that these intake officers have correctly diagnosed the "illness" and know best how to cure it. Of course, compliance with program requirements that are nonobligatory for juveniles is merely enhanced by the possibility that the intake officer may later file a delinquency petition with the juvenile court against uncooperative youths. This possibility is not lost on participating juveniles.

In San Diego County, California, for instance, an interagency agreement plan was instituted in December 1982 for the purpose of reducing delinquency through consistent, early intervention and graduated sanctions and to hold youths accountable for their acts (Pennell, Curtis, and Scheck, 1990). Specific guidelines were used by police and intake officers for determining the best disposition of a particular case following a juvenile's arrest. First-time nonserious offenders were to be handled informally, with an emphasis on diversion to and participation in various community-based services, and restitution for the purpose of establishing a youth's accountability. Recidivist youths would receive more in-depth counseling and referrals to formal probation, and eventually, formal petitions would be filed against them (Pennell, Curtis, and Scheck, 1990). The plan followed by San Diego intake officers appeared to have a favorable effect on reducing juvenile recidivism rates, where a pre- and posttest design was used over one- and two-year experimental periods.

One problem with the treatment model generally is that great variations exist among community agencies regarding the availability of certain services as remedies for particular kinds of juvenile problems (Kamerman and Kahn, 1990). Also, the intake officer may incorrectly diagnose one's "illness" and prescribe inappropriate therapy. Certain types of deep-seated personality maladjustments cannot be detected through superficial informal intake proceedings. Simply participating in some community-based service or treatment program may be insufficient to relieve particular juveniles of the original or "core" causes of their delinquent behaviors. Nevertheless, intake screenings may lead to community-based agency referrals that eventually may or may not be productive. In most jurisdictions, these are conditional sanctions that may be administered by intake officers without judicial approval or intervention.

The Noninterventionist Model

As the name implies, *the **noninterventionist model** means the absence of any direct intervention with certain juveniles who have been taken into custody. The noninterventionist model is best understood when considered in the context of labeling theory* (Lemert, 1967a). Labeling theory stresses that direct and frequent contact with the juvenile justice system will cause those having contact with it eventually to define themselves as delinquent. This definition will prompt self-definers to commit additional delinquent acts, since such behaviors are expected of those defined or stigmatized as such by others. Labeling theory advocates the removal of nonserious juveniles and status offenders from the juvenile justice system, or at least from the criminalizing influence and trappings of the juvenile courtroom. However, some experts question the validity of labeling theory as it is presently used to explain reductions in juvenile recidivism (Coumarelos and Weatherburn, 1995).

The noninterventionist model is strategically applied only to those juveniles who the intake officer believes are unlikely to reoffend if given a second chance or who are clearly status offenders without qualification (e.g., drug- or alcohol-dependent, chronic or persistent offenders) (Downs and Robertson, 1990). Intake officers who elect to act in a noninterventionist fashion with certain types of offenders may simply function as a possible resource person for juveniles and their parents. In cases involving runaways, truants, or curfew violators, it becomes a judgment call whether to refer youths and/or their parents to certain community services or counseling. The noninterventionist model would encourage no action by intake officers in nonserious or status offender cases, except under the most compelling circumstances. Since not all runaways are alike, certain runaways may be more in need of intervention than others, for instance (Miller, Eggertson-Tacon, and Quigg, 1990). Again, the aim of nonintervention is to assist youths in avoiding stigma and unfavorable labeling that might arise if they were to be involved more deeply within the juvenile justice system (Downs and Robertson, 1990). Even minor referrals by intake officers might prompt adverse reactions from offenders, so that future offending behavior would be regarded as a way of getting even with the system.

The noninterventionist model is popular today, particularly because it fits well with the deinstitutionalization of status offenses (DSO) movement that has occurred in most, if not all, jurisdictions. DSO was designed to divest juvenile courts of their jurisdiction over status offenders. Therefore, the primary intent of DSO was to minimize the potentially adverse influence of labeling that might occur should juveniles have to appear before juvenile court judges and have their cases adjudicated in a juvenile courtroom (Coumarelos and Weatherburn, 1995). Also, an intended function of DSO was to reduce the docket load for many juvenile court judges by transferring their jurisdiction over status offenders to community agencies and services. The noninterventionist strategy is significant here because it advocates doing nothing about certain juvenile dispositions. Siegel and Senna (1988:349) highlight the works of Lemert (1967a) and Schur (1973) as relevant for the noninterventionist perspective. These authors have promoted **judicious nonintervention** and **radical nonintervention** as terms that might be applied to noninterventionist "do nothing" policy.

At the same time that some experts promote judicious nonintervention, others favor *early intervention*, especially for first offenders and those who are 13 years old or younger at the time of their first police contact. An *Early Offender Program* (EOP) was established in 1985 in Oakland County, Michigan through the probate court (Howitt and Moore, 1991). The purpose of this program was to provide specialized, intensive, in-home interventions. Parents and youths would be visited in their homes by personnel working with the probate court. These personnel would assist the family through diverse and sometimes difficult interpersonal problems. Youths who were involved with drugs or had general chemical dependencies were assisted through community services as well as through home visits from counselors. Those youths with poor school adjustment received assistance from these counselors as well. This early in-home intervention proved quite valuable as a part of a general strategy to minimize recidivism among first offenders. Although there was some recidivism, it was slight. Those tending to recidivate most often were previously involved with drugs and had numerous adjustment problems in their schools (Howitt and Moore, 1991). Whether there is no intervention or early intervention, some experts believe that *all* youths should be expected to do *something*, such as restitution, so as to grasp and appreciate the harm or inconvenience they have caused others (Roy, 1995).

The Due-Process Model

The notion of due process is an integral feature of the criminal justice system. *Due process is the basic constitutional right to a fair trial, to have an opportunity to be heard, to be aware of matters that are pending, to a presumption of innocence until guilt is established beyond a reasonable doubt, to make an informed choice whether to acquiesce or contest, and to provide the reasons for such a choice before a judicial official* (Champion, 1990b:75). An important aspect of due process is that police officers must have probable cause to justify their arrests of suspected criminals. Therefore, one's constitutional rights are given considerable weight in comparison with any incriminating evidence obtained by police or others (Feld, 1989b, 1993a–c).

Intake officers who rely heavily on the **due-process model** in their dealings with juveniles are concerned that the juveniles' rights are fully protected at every stage of juvenile justice processing. Therefore, these officers would pay particular attention to how evidence was gathered by police against certain juveniles, and whether the juvenile's constitutional rights were protected and police officers advised the juvenile of the right to counsel at the time of the arrest and/or subsequent interrogation. The higher priority given to due process in recent years is considered by some researchers to be a significant juvenile justice reform (Blackmore, Brown, and Krisberg, 1988).

An intake officer's emphasis of due-process requirements in juvenile offender processing stems, in part, from several important U.S. Supreme Court decisions during the 1960s and 1970s, although professional associations and other interests have strongly advocated a concern for greater protection of juvenile rights in recent years (U.S. General Accounting Office, 1995a). In 1984, for instance, the Juvenile Justice Standards Project of the American Bar Association recommended that the rights of all minors can be best safeguarded by having legislatively created and narrowly defined doctrines dealing with specific problem areas, such as a juvenile's waiver of the right to counsel prior to interrogation by police, the search of juveniles, their premises, and seizures of their property, and the right against self-incrimination (Green, 1984). In this regard, some states have enacted statutes that render inadmissible any evidence police may have obtained as the result of a juvenile's waiver of one or more constitutional rights, without parental guidance or consent (Shaffner, 1985). Thus an intake officer's actions in certain states would be intended to comply with statutory requirements of juvenile case processing.

Because of the interest certain intake officers might take in one's right to due process, some intake hearings may be more formally conducted than others (Sellers, 1987; Shelden and Horvath, 1987). Legal variables, such as present offense, numbers of charges, and prior petitions, would be given greater weight in the context of due process. Shelden and Horvath (1987) have noted that legal variables such as these have accounted for or explained as much as 40 percent of the variance in intake processing in the jurisdictions they have investigated. Thus intake guidelines in these juris-dictions promote legal variables and downplay the significance of nonlegal factors. However, many offender dispositions seem to be affected by non-legal variables as well, including the youth's attitude, grades in school, and school status. While mildly related to dispositions, gender, race, and social class are only moderately related to offender dispositions (Shelden and Horvath, 1987).

The Just-Deserts/Justice Model

The juvenile justice system has strong rehabilitative roots, where the empha-sis in past years has been on serving the best interests of offending youths and the delivery of individualized services to them on the basis of their needs (Steinhart, 1988). *Parens patriae* explains much of the origin of this emphasis in the United States. However, the changing nature of juvenile offending dur-ing the last several decades and a gradual transformation of public sentiment toward more punitive measures have prompted certain juvenile justice reforms that are aimed at holding youths increasingly accountable for their actions and punishing them accordingly (Feld, 1995). Two proposed acts—the Model Delinquency Act and the Model Disobedient Children's Act—have been spawned through the federally funded Juvenile Justice Reform Project (Rossum, Koller, and Manfredi, 1987). These acts stress the importance of juvenile accountability to victims and society, as well as the responsibility of the system to punish these juveniles accordingly.

*The **just-deserts model** is punishment centered and seemingly revenge oriented, where the state's interest is to ensure that juveniles are* *punished in relation to the seriousness of the offenses they have committed. Further, those who commit identical offenses should be punished identically. This introduces the element of fairness into the punishment prescribed* (Schneider and Schram, 1986). The usefulness of this get-tough approach in disposing of various juvenile cases has both proponents and opponents and is clearly controversial (Stalans and Henry, 1994). It is significant that such an approach represents a major shift of emphasis away from juvenile offenders and their individualized needs and more toward the nature and seriousness of their actions. Just deserts as an orientation has frequently been combined with the justice model or orientation. The justice orientation is the idea that punishments should be gauged to fit the seriousness of offenses committed. Therefore, juveniles who commit more serious acts should receive harsher punishments, treatments, or sentences than those juveniles who commit less serious acts. Besides promoting punishment in proportion to offending behavior, the justice model includes certain victim considerations, such as provisions for restitution or victim compensation by offending juveniles.

Intake officers who seem to use the just-deserts/justice philosophy in their dealings with juveniles at the intake stage are concerned with ensuring that the intake disposition will be calculated to deliver *just* punishments. Punishment in this sense is regarded as a fair and equitable way of disposing of cases before they reach the juvenile court adjudication stage. Intake officers may suggest **consent decrees**, or formal agreements that involve children, their parents, and the juvenile court, where youths are placed under the court's supervision without an official finding of delinquency, with judicial approval (Rogers and Mays, 1987:565). Consent decrees often contain provisions for victim restitution and compensation by the juvenile or obligatory participation in some treatment program as possible conditions. These decrees may be entered into prior to any juvenile court appearance by juveniles. Intake officers may initiate these actions, again with court approval, provided that all parties are agreeable to their provisions and conditions.

Youths may appreciate the harm they have caused others, at least financially, through some form of restitution or compensation (Roy, 1995). Through their work and involvement in one or more assistance or treatment programs, they may acquire new values, outlooks, and self-concepts. But one important criticism of this approach is that intake officers who use it must make discretionary judgments and recommendations that involve punishments that may or may not be deserved. If certain juveniles had their cases adjudicated in a formal juvenile court proceeding, they might be more capably represented by attorneys who could introduce exculpatory evidence in their behalf. Juvenile court judges might be persuaded in these instances that the juvenile's guilt has not been sufficiently established beyond a reasonable doubt to warrant the imposition of one or more conditions as punishments. But similar to plea bargaining, some juveniles and their parents may believe that informally administered conditions as punishments offer relief from a formal court appearance, whether or not they are warranted by evidence and other circumstances.

The Crime Control Model

Perhaps the harshest of these orientations, the **crime control model** theorizes that one of the best ways of controlling juvenile delinquency is to incapacitate juvenile offenders, either through some secure incarceration or through an intensive supervision program operated by a community-based agency or organization. Perhaps consent decrees may include provisions for the electronic monitoring of certain juvenile offenders in selected jurisdictions. These juveniles might be required to wear plastic bracelets or anklets that are devised to emit electronic signals and notify juvenile probation officers of an offender's whereabouts. Or juvenile offenders may be incarcerated in secure facilities for short- or long-term periods, depending on the seriousness of their offenses (Jones and Krisberg, 1994; Mainprize, 1992).

The crime control perspective would influence intake officers to move certain chronic, persistent, and/or dangerous juvenile offenders further into the juvenile justice system. If they believe that certain juveniles pose serious risks to others or are considered dangerous, these intake officers might decide that certain juveniles should be held in secure confinement pending a subsequent detention hearing. If juveniles who are chronic or persistent offenders are incapacitated, they cannot reoffend. Treatment and rehabilitation are subordinate to simple control and incapacitation. Intake officers who favor the crime control view have few illusions that the system can change certain juvenile offenders (Gelber, 1988). Rather, the best course of action for them is secure incarceration for lengthy periods, considering the availability of space in existing juvenile secure confinement facilities. In this way, they are directly prevented from reoffending, since they are totally incapacitated. The cost-effectiveness of such incarceration of the most chronic and persistent juvenile offenders in relation to the monies lost resulting from thefts, burglaries, robberies, and other property crimes is difficult to calculate. Incarceration itself is costly, and immense overcrowding in existing juvenile secure confinement facilities already plagues most jurisdictions.

Often, traditional treatment and rehabilitation strategies do not work or are not particularly effective with certain hardcore, violent, or chronic offenders (Minnesota Criminal Justice Statistical Analysis Center, 1989; Stalans and Henry, 1994). However, if courts and other actors in the juvenile justice system, including intake officers, move toward more punitive measures against even the smaller numbers of these more dangerous offenders, including the widespread incarceration of them, we can expect to see a substantial increase in the need for additional facilities (U.S. General Accounting Office, 1995a).

Although many intake officers might not admit to being influenced by one particular orientation or another, it would be relatively easy to typify their general behaviors toward juveniles after observations of some duration. Also, much seems to depend on the different roles officers are assigned in the juvenile justice system. A survey of 772 juvenile justice

BOX 5.2   THE FBI AND JUVENILE GANGS

A Case of Federal Intervention in Gang Formation

The Villa Lobos are a gang of 8- to 13-year-olds in Fargo, North Dakota. Fargo, North Dakota, you say? Gangs are pervasive. They are *everywhere*. In the relatively small city of Fargo, North Dakota, a youth gang known as the Villa Lobos has been responsible for numerous drug transactions, beatings, shootings, extortion, and threats. The leader of the Villa Lobos is a 20-year-old youth, Sergio Granados. The ethnic composition of the gang is largely Hispanic, although membership is not restricted to Hispanics.

The Villa Lobos ("street wolves") began forming in early 1994. Sergio Granados came to Fargo with his family when they moved from Chicago. Granados persuaded some of his former Chicago boyhood friends to join him in Fargo, and together, they enticed numerous "wannabes" (nongang members who want to be in gangs) from among local youths to join their Villa Lobos gang.

When the gang first started, Granados got them involved in dealing drugs, especially heroin and cocaine. Drug trips between Fargo and Chicago became a routine, and many gang members helped in maintaining the constant drug trafficking between these two cities. As other gangs attempted to form, the Villa Lobos would intervene, threatening other youths with violence if they attempted to compete with the existing gang.

Youths attracted to the Villa Lobos included many youths who were unsuccessful in doing well in school or who had problems at home. They saw the gang as a way of "acting out," according to a police officer, David Miller, who had known of the activities of the Villa Lobos. The gang was so powerful that it controlled other, more organized aspects of drug trafficking in Fargo, even adult drug distribution organizations. Wannabes were easy for Granados to recruit, since they yearned for identity and power, and Granados could provide them with it.

The Villa Lobos escalated their gang activities to include drive-by shootings of rival gang members and even innocent pedestrians. The drive-by shootings were referred to as "sport" by some of the gang members when interviewed by police later. Besides drug involvement, the Villa Lobos became involved in major firearms dealing interstate. This is when the federal government became involved.

Ordinarily, the U.S. Department of Justice avoids involvement in juvenile matters, preferring that illegal activities involving juveniles be dealt with by state or local authorities. This is one reason why there is so little activity concerning juveniles in U.S. district courts. However, it became apparent to the U.S. Attorney's Office in Fargo that the Villa Lobos were clearly violating federal laws, and on a conspicuously large scale. Drug

Enforcement Agency and FBI investigations were conducted. These investigations focused on the Villa Lobos in general and on Granados and some of his close followers in particular.

The result of the federal investigation yielded numerous indictments against Granados and eight other gang members. These indictments included 11 federal gun and drug charges. In exchange for leniency through plea bargaining, some gang members offered incriminating testimony against Granados and his henchmen. By the time Sergio Granados was convicted, the full extent of drug and illegal gun activities of the Villa Lobos was exposed to the public. Fargo residents were shocked to learn that one gang had been the major conduit of illegal drugs and guns in the greater Fargo area for the past several years. The 8 to 13-year-old majority of gang members had escalated to this level of activity from less violent enterprises such as graffiti and car stereo thefts.

Granados was convicted on the 11 guns and drugs charges and sentenced to a lengthy prison term. Several other gang members were also given prison sentences. Some older gang members, John Byrd, 32, of Chicago, and Jesse Solis, 32, of Moorhead, Minnesota (a city adjacent to Fargo), received 6½-year sentences on drug-related charges. Eight other gang members entered guilty pleas to assorted drugs and weapons charges and received various sentences in exchange for their testimony against Granados. Some gang members were deported to Mexico following their federal convictions.

Prosecutors in the case claimed that Granados's conviction effectively terminated the Villa Lobos as a functioning Fargo gang. The convictions of the gang leadership destroyed the organizational strength necessary to keep the gang activities going, including terminating the Chicago–Fargo connection. Granados had done virtually everything to control gang activities, such as arranging for drug purchases and pickups, controlling drug distribution, purchasing illegal weapons, and receiving all the profits. "He saw a fragmented bunch of wannabes and he said, 'Sheesh, if I could get these guys organized,'" said Larry Costello, the sheriff of Clay County, Minnesota.

Should federal investigators become actively involved in gang activities in other cities? What can local officials do to deter youths from joining gangs? How much power should local authorities have to deal with gangs once formed?

Source: Associated Press, "Authorities Stop Fargo Area Gang," *Minot (ND) Daily News*, April 8, 1996:A3.

officials in Florida showed, for instance, that different degrees of commitment to either a rehabilitation philosophy or a just-deserts perspective were influenced by an officer's assignment (Farnworth, Frazier, and Neuberger, 1988). However, educational backgrounds and professional identifications of these officers appeared to modify somewhat these seemingly opposing commitments.

Even in those jurisdictions where intake officer behaviors are required to be more or less uniform and prescribed, we will not always see a perfect pattern of consistency among officers and how they manage intake screenings. For example, in San Diego County, California, where an interagency agreement plan was implemented as described above to handle informally all nonserious, first-offender juveniles in a standardized way, not all intake officers complied and followed consistent sets of program guidelines, even though there was a general agency commitment to do so. Individualized styles for juvenile offender dispositions and decision making were observed by investigators (Pennell, Curtis, and Scheck, 1990). But at least we can understand why many intake officers in most jurisdictions do not always resolve their common juvenile offender problems in the same ways. To some extent, these views enable us to appreciate the complexities of intake screening and decision-making behaviors. The various legal and extralegal criteria that operate to influence decisions made by these intake officers can now be examined.

LEGAL FACTORS: CRIME SERIOUSNESS, TYPE OF CRIME COMMITTED, EVIDENCE, AND PRIOR RECORD

A distinction is made between legal factors and extralegal factors that relate to intake decision making as well as at other stages of the juvenile justice process. *Legal factors relate to purely factual information about the offenses alleged, such as crime seriousness, the type of crime committed, any inculpatory (incriminating) or exculpatory (exonerating) evidence against offending juveniles, and the existence or absence of prior juvenile records or delinquency adjudications.* **Extralegal factors** *include, but are not limited to, juvenile offender attitudes, school grades and standing, gender, race or ethnicity, socioeconomic status, and age. (Note: Age functions also as a legal factor for certain types of offenses.)*

Both legal and extralegal factors influence an intake officer's screening decision during an intake hearing. While purely legal factors probably should be used exclusively in deciding whether to pursue any case, it is a fact that extralegal factors affect this decision, adversely for some offenders and favorably for others. Thus it is questionable whether equitable treatment can be received by juveniles from those intake officers who stress certain extralegal factors, such as gender or race, in their decision making. Each of these sets of factors is examined here.

Offense Seriousness

Offense or crime seriousness pertains to whether bodily harm was inflicted or death resulted from the youth's act (Stalans and Henry, 1994). Those offenses considered as "serious" include forcible rape, aggravated assault, robbery, and homicide. These are crimes against persons or violent crimes. By degree, they are more serious than the conglomerate of property offenses, including vehicular theft, larceny, and burglary. In recent years, drug use has escalated among youths and adults in the United States and is considered as one of the most serious of the nation's crime problems. One general deterrent in every jurisdiction has been the imposition of stiff sentences and fines on those who sell drugs to others, and lesser punishments imposed on those who possess drugs for personal use. All large cities in the United States today have numerous youth gangs, many of which are involved rather heavily in drug trafficking (Waldorf et al., 1990). One result of such widespread drug trafficking among youths is the provision in most juvenile courts for more stringent penalties to be imposed for drug sales and possession. Thus crimes don't always have to be violent in order to be considered serious.

Much ambiguity persists among the various actors in the juvenile justice system about how best to evaluate crime seriousness (Mahoney, 1989). For example, a survey of 32 prosecutors and six law clerks in a Union County, New Jersey, county prosecutor's office was conducted to determine how these professionals rated the seriousness of selected crimes when committed by offenders of different ages (Harris, 1988). Five hundred robbery and aggravated assault cases involving male offenders were selected from both juvenile and criminal court records and rated by these prosecutors and clerks according to their seriousness. Overall, the same robbery and aggravated assault behaviors committed by juveniles were considered as substantially less serious compared with the same offenses committed by adults. Not only does this finding suggest that more effort be made to give crime seriousness a more precise definition, it also suggests one important reason for why continuing allegations of lenient treatment of serious juvenile offenders by juvenile courts are made by diverse critics of the juvenile justice system (Kansas Juvenile Justice Task Force, 1995; U.S. General Accounting Office, 1995a).

Type of Crime Committed

Another key factor in screening cases for possible subsequent processing by the juvenile justice system is the type of crime or offense committed. Is the offense property related or violent? Was the act either a felony or a misdemeanor? Were there victims with apparent injuries? Did the youths act alone or in concert with others, and what was the nature of their role in the offense? Were they initiators or leaders, and did they encourage or incite others to offend?

Intake officers are more likely to refer cases to juvenile prosecutors where juveniles are older (i.e., 16 years of age and over) and where the offenses alleged are especially serious, compared with referring younger, petty, first offenders to prosecutors for additional processing (Schwartz and Barton, 1994). A study by McCarthy (1989) of numerous intake decisions suggests that at least in some jurisdictions, an overwhelming majority of juvenile cases are disposed of informally during intake. McCarthy studied data pertaining to 76,150 delinquent acts committed by 17,773 juveniles born between 1962 and 1965 in Maricopa County (Phoenix, Arizona). Gathered from juvenile court files, these data showed that the vast majority of first offenders under age 16, 89 percent, were handled informally at the intake level without the formal filing of delinquency petitions. Juveniles committing violent offenses such as robbery and aggravated assault and the property crime of burglary were more likely to be detained compared with other youthful offenders. Of particular interest is the fact that detainees and those who progressed further into the juvenile justice system had much higher recidivism rates compared with nondetainees. However, about half of all offenders became repeat offenders, with approximately 25 percent of these juveniles repeat offending at least three or more times.

One implication of these findings for juvenile justice policy is that generally, leniency with many offenders, particularly first offenders, is accompanied by less recidivism. However, this conclusion may be premature and misleading (Niarhos and Routh, 1992; U.S. General Accounting Office, 1995a). McCarthy has noted that greater intrusion into the juvenile justice system characterizes more serious offenders, probably meaning more chronic, persistent, dangerous, or habitual offenders—precisely the category of youthful offenders who are more likely to reoffend anyway. Perhaps the term *strategic leniency* would be appropriate here. Nagoshi (1986) found, for example, that among a sample of 93 Hawaiian juvenile delinquents, those who received special conditions of probation as punishments (e.g., restitution, community service) recidivated at a lower rate than those youths who were placed on probation without special conditions. The implication here is that at least some punishment, properly administered, appears to have therapeutic value for many juvenile offenders compared with no punishment (Kenney, Pate, and Hamilton, 1990).

BOX 5.3   TEENAGERS SIGN SUICIDE PACT

Frankie Avalon Songs Gone Awry

Teen suicide pacts are becoming increasingly frequent, and no one knows why. Are family values to blame? Are schools failing in their responsibility to educate and socialize? Can churches do more to instill the "right" values in children? What would possess teenagers to agree to a suicide pact and then carry it out? It happened in Brinkley, Arkansas in early April 1996. Kevin L. Hyde, 15, Joshua G. Rogers, 15, and a 12-year-old girlfriend were found in a stolen car after a high-speed chase. They vowed not to be taken alive. The two boys killed themselves with a stolen gun. The girl was rescued by police before she could reach the gun and complete the pact to kill herself. What happened? Is this a modern-day version of Bonnie and Clyde? Were these teenage felons on the run from police for committing heinous crimes? No.

Earlier that week, they got in trouble in school in Robbinsville, North Carolina. The "trouble" amounted to school rule infractions and possible suspension. The three youths stole a car and a pistol, fleeing from the town and vowing in a written suicide note not to be taken alive if caught by police. Hyde left a note for his father: "Dad. I'm sorry. I got into some trouble and had to leave. I've gone south." The other youths had similar notes on their person.

Both boys appeared to have been infatuated with the girl. During their spree through various states in the stolen car, state highway patrol officers spotted the stolen vehicle and pursued it. When the car stopped, each boy shot himself. The police approached the car and grabbed the girl before she had a chance to get the gun from the second dead boy's hand to complete the suicide pact. There was no reason given for the suicide pact. It is possible the girl will disclose later what happened and why. But what can account for two otherwise normal boys killing themselves in a senseless suicide pact? Two families are left to ponder what they could have done differently to change what happened to their sons. Will the girl someday join her dead friends when she is by herself? No one knows.

Are the school authorities responsible for these deaths? What school infraction was so humiliating that three youths agreed to suicide if they were caught? What prevention mechanisms could be incorporated into schools and homes to detect potential suicide-bound teenagers? Are there warning signs? If so, how should they be interpreted? What interventions are potentially workable, if any? What do these growing numbers of teenage suicides and suicide pacts say about our society?

Source: Associated Press, "Teens Carry Out Suicide Pact," *Minot (ND) Daily News*, April 7, 1996:A2.

Inculpatory or Exculpatory Evidence

While offense seriousness and type of crime are considered quite influential at intake hearings, some attention is also given by intake officers to the evidence that police officers and others have acquired to show offender guilt. Direct evidence, such as eyewitness accounts of the youth's behavior, tangible objects such as weapons, and the totality of circumstances give the intake officer a reasonably good idea of where the case would end eventually if it reached the adjudicatory stage in a juvenile court.

Also, intake officers can consider exculpatory evidence or materials and testimony from others informally that provide alibis for juveniles or mitigate the seriousness of their offenses. Evidentiary factors are important in establishing one's guilt or innocence, but referrals of juveniles by police officers to intake usually is indicative of the fact that the officers were persuaded to act in accordance with the situation they confronted. It is extraordinary for officers to pursue juvenile cases to the intake stage purely on the basis of whim, although some officers do so as a means of punishing certain juvenile offenders with poor attitudes.

Most intake officers screen the least serious cases quickly at intake or provide dispositions for juveniles other than formal ones. For instance, McCarthy (1987b) investigated the attrition rate of 620 juvenile cases in a metropolitan court in the United States during 1982. She found that charges were dropped against 23 percent of these juveniles at intake, that 11 percent received informal adjustments of their cases by intake officers, and that an additional 15 percent were granted consent decrees. About 50 percent of all youths were referred to prosecutors for judicial handling. These seem to be normal case attrition figures, considering investigations conducted by others of this process in other jurisdictions.

Another consideration made by the intake officer is what will probably happen to youths once they are brought before juvenile court judges, regardless of the amount of inculpatory evidence. In many jurisdictions, even violent juvenile offenders typically receive probation as a punishment (McCarthy, 1989). But for many intake officers, a juvenile court judge's punishment ideology has little or no bearing on their initial intake decisions (Hassenfeld and Cheung, 1985). Nevertheless, since leniency will probably be extended once an adjudicatory proceeding has been conducted, many intake officers may believe that they can reduce judicial caseloads by taking the initiative of exercising leniency themselves.

Prior Record

Intake officers in the state of Washington and other jurisdictions where guidelines are followed relating to intake dispositions use prior records of delinquency adjudications and factor these data into their decisions. In other jurisdictions, prior records strongly suggest that prior treatments and/or punishments were apparently ineffective at curbing offender recidivism. It would be logical to suspect that intake officers would deal more harshly with those having prior records of delinquency adjudications. In fact, some research has demonstrated that greater numbers of prior offenses tend to result in a youth's further involvement in the juvenile justice process beyond intake (Grisso, Tomkins, and Casey, 1988).

No doubt one's prior record of juvenile offenses would suggest persistence and chronicity, perhaps a rejection of and resistance to prior attempts at intervention and treatment. In some of these cases, harsher punishments and dispositions have been observed (Greenwood, 1986a). However, this is not a blanket generalization designed to cover all offense categories. Some offense categories have greater priority over others for many intake officers (Wordes, Bynum, and Corley, 1994).

Also, the previous disposition of a particular juvenile's case seems to be a good predictor of subsequent case dispositions for that same offender. For example, a study of the influence of prior records and prior adjudications on instant offense dispositions has shown that dispositions for prior offenses have a significant impact on current dispositions for those same offenses, regardless of the type or seriousness of the offense (Snyder, 1988; Snyder and Sickmund, 1995). Thus if a juvenile has formerly been adjudicated delinquent on a burglary charge and probation for six months was imposed as the punishment, a new burglary charge against that same juvenile will probably result in the same probationary punishment for six months. Only instant offense seriousness has a greater impact on one's current punishment than the influence of prior dispositions in many jurisdictions (Rhode Island Governor's Justice Commission Statistical Analysis Center, 1992).

We examine transfers or waivers more extensively in Chapter 6, but it is important to note here that often, repeat-offender appearances before the same juvenile court judge, regardless of the violent or nonviolent nature of such offending behaviors, may result in transfers of jurisdiction over that repeat offender to criminal courts. This is the judge's way of getting rid of particularly bothersome juveniles who are neither dangerous nor serious offenders (Champion and Mays, 1991).

EXTRALEGAL FACTORS: AGE, GENDER, RACE/ETHNICITY, AND SOCIOECONOMIC STATUS OF JUVENILE OFFENDERS

Most intake officers have vested interests in the decisions they make during screening hearings. They want to be fair to all juveniles, but at the same time, they are interested in individualizing their decision making according to each juvenile case. This means that they must balance their interests and objectives to achieve multiple goals, some of which may be in conflict. Furthermore, in recent years, greater pressure has been exerted on all juvenile justice components to implement those policies and procedures that will increase offender accountability at all stages of processing (Feld, 1995; U.S. General Accounting Office, 1995a).

A balanced approach has been suggested by Maloney, Romig, and Armstrong (1988). They envision three major goals of probation officers serving in various capacities in relation to their clients: (1) protecting the community, (2) imposing accountability for offenses, and (3) equipping juvenile offenders with competencies to live productively and responsibly in the community. This approach is also endorsed by the Ohio Experience, described by Wiebush (1990, 1993) elsewhere.

Ideally, each of these goals is equal. These researchers say that such balanced objectives have been used by probation officers in Deschutes County, Oregon; Austin, Texas; and the Menominee Indian Reservation in Wisconsin. Individuality in decision making, where all three goals can be assessed for each juvenile offender, is sought. However, these three goals may have variable importance to probation officers performing intake functions in other jurisdictions. Depending on their orientation, some intake officers may emphasize their community protection function, while others may emphasize juvenile offender accountability. Those officers with rehabilitative interests would tend to promote educational programs that would enable youths to operate productively in their respective communities.

In the context of attempting to achieve these three objectives and balance them, several extralegal characteristics of juvenile offenders have emerged to influence adversely the equality of treatment these youths may receive from probation officers at intake: (1) age, (2) gender, (3) race or ethnicity, and (4) socioeconomic status.

Age

As we have seen, age is both a legal and an extralegal factor in the juvenile justice system. Age is legally relevant in decisions about waivers to criminal court jurisdiction. Waivers of juveniles under the age of 16 to criminal courts are relatively rare, for example (Champion and Mays, 1991). Also, age has extralegal relevance. At least in some jurisdictions, such as Maricopa County (Phoenix), Arizona, intake officers seem to manage and dispose of informally large numbers of cases against youths under age 16 (McCarthy, 1989). Older youths perhaps are assumed to be more responsible for their actions compared with younger youths, and they are often treated accordingly. Also, older youths are more likely to have prior records as juvenile offenders, be more resistant to or unwilling to accept intervention, and manifest greater adultlike self-reliance (Grisso, Tomkins, and Casey, 1988). Further, arrest data show that the peak ages of criminality lie between the sixteenth and twentieth birthdays (Maguire and Pastore, 1996). Perhaps some intake officers believe that more aggressiveness in their decision making should be directed against older juveniles than against the younger ones.

The Case of 10-Year-Old Prozac Addict, Timmy Becton

Timmy Becton faced the judge in criminal court. Earlier, he had armed himself with a 12-gauge shotgun, pointed it at a sheriff's deputy, and used a 3-year-old child as a human shield to protect himself from officer gunfire. The judge sentenced Timmy to one year for aggravated assault, armed kidnapping, and criminal mischief. Sounds like a light sentence, doesn't it? But Timmy Becton is only 10 years old.

Becton was tried in criminal court and treated as an adult through the waiver or transfer process. In cases such as these, juvenile courts waive or transfer jurisdiction over such juveniles to criminal court judges. In effect, children are treated as adults for purposes of criminal prosecutions, where harsher sentences can be imposed for more serious types of offending.

In Timmy Becton's case, Timmy was truant from school. This is what caused sheriff's deputies to become involved in the first place. The visit to Timmy's home by police led to his grabbing the family shotgun and his 3-year-old niece and confronting police in a possible deadly situation.

Timmy's lawyer blamed Prozac, an antidepressant, for Timmy's behavior. Even Timmy himself seemingly cannot recall the events. "I can't remember much about this, but I'm sorry for everything I've done," said Timmy to the judge when the sentence was pronounced. The judge asked Timmy to write a letter of apology. The letter might persuade the judge to "lighten" the sentence of one year in a secure juvenile confinement facility. But Timmy told reporters after his trial, "I really don't want to write them letters." So much for acceptance of responsibility and remorse!

Should 10-year-olds be processed as adults in criminal courts? What should the minimum age be for such transfers or waivers of juvenile court jurisdiction? Is Prozac addiction a legitimate defense to criminal conduct? Should it be?

Source: Adapted from Associated Press, "Child Sentenced in 'Prozac' Case," *Minot (ND) Daily News,* June 1, 1996:A2.

However, research has shown that the earlier the onset of a juvenile's contact with the juvenile justice system and police, the more serious the problem (Pallone, 1994; U.S. General Accounting Office, 1995a). Thus *younger* offenders rather than *older* offenders are often treated with greater interest and attention. This is supported by the array of risk assessment instruments used by both juvenile and adult corrections departments throughout the United States today. Almost every one of these instruments uses age as an important component in arriving at one's degree of risk or dangerousness. The *younger* the offender, the *greater weight* is assigned. This means that if youths become involved with delinquent acts at earlier ages, greater weight is given and one's dangerousness score increases (Champion, 1994). This evidences the seriousness with which age is regarded as a predictor of chronic and persistent recidivism, whether property or violent offending is involved. Some studies also imply that the earlier the onset of delinquency, the more likely it will be that these youthful offenders will be arrested and incarcerated for crimes committed as adults (Florida House Committee on Criminal Justice, 1994; Kapp, Schwartz, and Epstein, 1994).

For many intake officers, the age factor appears to function in much the same fashion in influencing their intake decision making as it does when prosecutors assess the seriousness of identical offenses committed by both youths and adult offenders (Harris, 1988). For an assortment of nonrational reasons, armed robbery is not as serious for some prosecutors when committed by a 12-year-old as it is when it is committed by a 21-year-old. Applied to intake decision making, probation officers may regard certain serious offenses as less serious when committed by those 13 and under, while 14-year-olds and older youths may have those same offenses judged as more serious. There are no precise age divisions that separate younger from older youthful offenders when one's age is functioning as an extralegal factor.

Gender

Generally, traditional patterns of female delinquency have persisted over the years. Because there are so few female juvenile offenders compared with their male counterparts, the influence of gender on intake decision making and at other stages of the juvenile justice process has not been investigated extensively (Sommers and Baskin, 1994). Juvenile females make up approximately 10 percent or less of the juvenile incarcerative population in the United States annually (American Correctional Association, 1996). Females are only slightly more represented proportionately among those on probation or involved in assorted public and private aftercare services. Explanations for gender differences in their comparative rate of offending have ranged from different socialization experiences to different testosterone levels and genetic compositions (Brooks and Reddon, 1996; DeZolt, Schmidt, and Gilcher, 1996; Epps, 1996).

Differential treatment of males and females in both the juvenile and criminal justice systems is well documented (Heimer, 1996). However, some of the traditional reasons given for such differential treatment, especially about female juveniles and their delinquency patterns, appear to be largely mythical and misconceived (Rowe, Vazsonyi, and Flannery, 1995; Simpson and Elis, 1995). Contemporary assessments of the impact of gender on intake decision making show that it is only moderately related to dispositions, consistent with intake guidelines in selected jurisdictions such as Las Vegas, Nevada (Shelden and Horvath, 1987). Investigations of other jurisdictions as well as analyses of national figures show generally that female juveniles seem to be detained less often than male juveniles, and/or they are returned to the community at a greater rate than males, and/or they are committed to secure confinement at a much lower rate than males (Bottcher, 1993, 1995; Sommers and Baskin, 1994; Triplett and Myers, 1995).

Within the just-deserts, justice, or crime control frameworks, attention of interested actors in the juvenile justice system is focused on the act more than on the juveniles committing the act or their physical or social characteristics. Thus, gender differences leading to differential treatment of offenders who behave similarly would not be acceptable. However, the differential treatment of male and female juveniles in the United States and other countries persists (U.S. General Accounting Office, 1995a; Worling, 1995).

A strong contributing factor is the paternalistic view of juvenile court judges and others in the juvenile justice system that has persisted over time in the aftermath and influence of *parens patriae*. Differences between the arrest rates of female and male juveniles and the proportion of females to males who are subsequently adjudicated as delinquent suggests that the case attrition rate for females is significantly higher at intake than it is for male juveniles (Rowe, Vazsonyi, and Flannery, 1995). Specific studies of intake decision making have disclosed, however, that gender exerts only an indirect impact on such decision making by officers (McCarthy and Smith, 1986). Paradoxically, female juveniles with prior referrals to juvenile court seem to be treated more harshly than male offenders with prior referrals, especially for committing one of several index violent offenses. Based on his analysis of the juvenile court careers of 69,504 juvenile offenders in Arizona and Utah, Snyder (1988) calculated probabilities of being referred to juvenile court for an index violent offense, where both male and female juveniles had similar numbers of prior court referrals. He found that males with eight prior referrals were more than three times as likely to be referred to juvenile court for an index violent offense as a male with only one previous referral, and more than twice as likely as a male with two prior referrals.

However, females with eight prior referrals were six times as likely to be referred to juvenile court for an index violent offense as females who had only one prior referral, and three times as likely to be referred as females with two prior referrals (1988:44–45). There were negligible differences between male and female juvenile offenders relating to referrals for property crimes.

It would seem that first-offender females are more likely to experience favorable differential treatment from the juvenile justice system as those females with records of prior referrals (Triplett and Myers, 1995). In Howard Snyder's study, for instance, the great differential referral rate between male and female juveniles may have been the result of a backlash phenomenon, where females were being unduly penalized later for the greater leniency extended toward them earlier by juvenile justice authorities.

In some intervention projects designed to decrease or eliminate female gang delinquency, researchers have attempted to undermine the normative group functions served by gangs (DeZolt, Schmidt, and Gilcher, 1996). In one intervention project known as the *Tabula Rasa Intervention Project for Delinquent Gang-Involved Females* in Ohio, a sample of female gang members was targeted for intervention. The nature of the intervention consisted of several components: (1) an educational component, (2) a wellness component, and (3) a job skills and vocational component. Many female gang members lacked formal education and coping skills. Also, they lacked various skills that would make them employable. Each participant was obligated to develop specific goals within each of these components and strive to achieve them with interventionist assistance. The objective of the intervention was to interrupt the influence of gang membership and to divert these girls' interests in more productive directions. Early results of the intervention program for the participating females were regarded as successful (DeZolt, Schmidt, and Gilcher, 1996).

Race and Ethnicity

Considerably more important as predictors of decision making at virtually every stage of the juvenile justice process are *race* and *ethnicity*. An early investigation of the impact of race upon dispositional decision making at intake was conducted by Bell and Lang (1985). These researchers found that the relation between race and decision making was apparently indirect. Similarly, Shelden and Horvath (1987) found no direct influence of race on the nature of intake processing in 436 cases they analyzed for a Nevada county. Finally, McCarthy (1985) studied 649 juvenile delinquents who had been referred to family courts in 1982. Her preliminary impression was that at least at the adjudicatory stage, juvenile court judges did not seem to be influenced by racial or gender factors.

However, a subsequent analysis of the same data by McCarthy and Smith (1986) disclosed that some racial discrimination in handling existed, although it was unevenly distributed throughout various stages of the system. For example, these researchers discovered that at intake hearings, the racial factor did not appear significant in dispositions or adjustments made by intake officers. However, juvenile court adjudications and secure confinement decisions seemed influenced by racial factors. Specifically, greater proportions of blacks than whites were adjudicated delinquent and sentenced to secure confinement. Although this is not absolute proof of discrimination, it nevertheless implies that minority juveniles, particularly blacks, were disadvantaged by their race in judicial decision making. McCarthy and Smith (1986) suggest that a better understanding of the impact of race and other factors on decision making at various stages of the juvenile justice process can be gotten from considering several different stages of this process rather than focusing on a single stage such as intake exclusively or adjudicatory hearings exclusively.

Race and ethnicity appear prominent as predictor variables in arrest and detention discretion. For instance, Bishop and Frazier (1996) have found clear evidence of racial disparities in juvenile justice processing at the point of intake and at other stages. Generally, the effect of race was disadvantageous to those juveniles processed. They studied 161,369 youths processed by the Florida Department of Health and Rehabilitative Services in 1987. Further, they interviewed 34 juvenile justice officials. Most affected by racial factors were delinquent offenders rather than status offenders. Blacks, Hispanics, and other minorities tended to be advanced further into the juvenile justice system by intake officers. However, white status offenders were penalized more harshly than minority status offenders. In fact, white status offenders were more likely to be incarcerated more often than minority status offenders. Thus, at least for Florida during the year examined, racial factors were at work in different ways to influence how youths were processed, either as delinquents or as status offenders.

In another case study of a random sample of 228 cases involving juveniles referred by police officers and others to the juvenile probation intake and detention screening process in Travis County, Texas, it was determined that most juvenile referrals were between the ages of 13 and 15 and were disproportionately black (Arrigona and Fabelo, 1987). Although fewer than 50 percent of these referrals had subsequent referrals within a six-month period following their initial referrals, about 60 percent of all first referrals were diverted informally by intake officers. Thus disproportionate racial representations at the front end of intake help to explain subsequent racially disproportionate managements and dispositions of cases through the intake, detention hearing, and adjudicatory stages (Arrigona and Fabelo, 1987).

Minority overrepresentation throughout the juvenile justice process has been reported in a study of North Carolina juveniles. Data were obtained from case files of all juveniles processed through intake during 1993 in 10 North Carolina counties (Dean, Hirschel, and Brame, 1996). While black juveniles accounted for substantially less than half of the delinquency in these counties, half of the juveniles referred to intake were black. Interestingly, blacks comprised only about one-fourth of the entire juvenile population for these counties. Furthermore, half of those adjudicated delinquent were black, while two-thirds of those committed to secure confinement were black. The use of other control variables failed to reveal any other critical operating factor besides *race* in this disproportionate offender processing. Absent any other reason for such disparate treatment of these juveniles, we may conclude that at least in this study, *race* was a crucial intervening variable influencing juvenile case outcomes, even though it is an extralegal factor.

Socioeconomic Status

Closely related to racial and ethnic factors as extralegal considerations in intake decision making is the **socioeconomic status** (SES) of juvenile offenders. The U.S. General Accounting Office (1995a) has found that generally, the poor, as well as racial and ethnic minorities, are disenfranchised by the juvenile justice system at various stages. One immediate explanation for this alleged disenfranchisement is the more limited access to economic resources among the poor and minorities. More restricted economic resources reduce the quality of legal defenses that may be accessed by the socioeconomically disadvantaged. Greater reliance on public defenders is observed among the poor than among those who are financially advantaged. A greater proportion of the socioeconomically disadvantaged tend to acquiesce and quietly accept systemic sanctions that accompany charges of wrongdoing rather than acquire counsel and contest the charges formally in court. However, Feld (1995) observes that the presence of defense attorneys in juvenile proceedings aggravates rather than mitigates the harshness of dispositions and subsequent sentences imposed by judges. In any event, if we can elevate these generalizations to general principles that apply to the majority of cases involving socioeconomically disadvantaged youths and adults who are charged with crimes, one's SES becomes a powerful consideration in decision making at all stages throughout the juvenile justice system. However, not all investigators believe that the relation between SES and delinquency is necessarily strong or negative (Tittle and Meier, 1990).

A direct indicator of one's SES is **appearance**, although appearance is not always a totally reliable criterion (Rosenbaum and Chesney-Lind, 1994). A national sample of 1886 high school students was examined by interviewers and given self-administered questionnaires (Agnew, 1984). Interviewers were asked to make predictions about whether those interviewed "appeared" to be delinquents or nondelinquents. Also, youths acknowledged their involvement or noninvolvement in delinquent activities through individual self-reports on their questionnaires. One hypothesis tested in this study was that "unattractive people will be more delinquent than attractive people." Attractiveness and unattractiveness evaluations were made on the basis of interviewer judgments of one's appearance, demeanor, and general attire. Agnew (1984) found support for this hypothesis. At least some evaluators can make reasonably accurate judgments about youths strictly on the basis of their personal appearance, according to these findings. If interviewers can make such judgments, so can intake officers during intake hearings. Also, probation officers are further assisted by the personal appearances of parents or guardians and other personal information acquired during the intake interview and screening process. Studies supporting one's appearance as an adverse factor in selected instances of juvenile justice processing have been reported in other jurisdictions (Rosenbaum and Chesney-Lind, 1994; Williams and Cohen, 1993).

Although SES is believed to be an important consideration in virtually all stages of juvenile justice processing, there are inter- and intraregional inconsistencies reported. In Colorado, for example, studies of youths in Denver, Pueblo, Grand Junction, and the Thirteenth Judicial District were conducted (Hartstone, Slaughter, and Fagan, 1986). The official juvenile records of nearly 700 youths were examined in these jurisdictions. Minority and lower-SES youths tended to receive more severe sanctions at various decision points in the Denver jurisdiction, while harsher decisions were meted out to white and middle- and upper-SES youths in the Pueblo and Thirteenth Judicial District jurisdictions. However, the Grand Junction jurisdiction had mixed degrees of harshness in the handling of minorities and other youths.

It is difficult to operationalize all of the criteria that intake officers use in the screening process to prevent certain youthful offenders from being involved more deeply in the system. How does one describe accurately a youth's demeanor and attitude when arrested by the police or interviewed during intake? How do we translate into decision-making actions one's impressions of youths and their parents or guardians during interviews and the significance given answers to specific questions? Feelings cannot be calibrated to the extent that we can measure them on a scale and determine their influence on whether petitions are filed or not filed. Yet intake officers manifest complex decision-making styles. For some officers their behaviors may be perfunctory, particularly if they are involved in the processing of numerous youths daily. In less densely populated jurisdictions where lower caseloads are likely to be assigned, more individualized decision making can be applied, and the philosophical models discussed earlier in this chapter have increased significance for one's subsequent actions. It is evident that both legal and extralegal criteria are always operative, to varying degrees, as these intake officers perform their difficult tasks (U.S. General Accounting Office, 1995a).

PRELIMINARY DECISION MAKING: DIVERSION AND OTHER OPTIONS

Diverting Certain Juveniles from the System

A long-range interest of most, if not all, intake officers is minimizing recidivism among those diverted from the system at the time of an intake hearing (Fuller and Norton, 1993). **Recidivism** is also a commonly used measure of program effectiveness in both adult and juvenile offender treatment and sanctioning schemes (Champion, 1994). Intake officer interest in the type of offense committed is triggered not only by the seriousness of the act itself and what should be done about it, but by evidence from various jurisdictions which suggests that recidivism rates vary substantially for different types of juvenile offenders. For example, studies of violent and nonviolent and chronic and nonchronic juvenile recidivists suggest that greater proportions of chronic offenders repeat violent offenses than nonchronic offenders. However, chronic offenders also commit subsequent nonviolent acts as well as violent ones. Despite increasing juvenile violence, it remains the case that only a small proportion of youths accounts for a majority of the violent crimes committed. This has been a consistent finding across the years 1982–1992 (Jones and Krisberg, 1994).

How Should We Deal with Chronic Violent Offenders?

Closely associated with recidivism among chronic violent offenders in certain jurisdictions are predictor variables such as whether the delinquent has delinquent siblings and/or significant others as associates, whether the delinquent has school problems, and whether the acts committed were misdemeanors or felonies (U.S. General Accounting Office, 1995a). It is arguable whether juveniles escalate to more serious offenses over their careers as delinquents (Lockhart et al., 1991; Niarhos and Routh, 1992). The evidence seems to suggest that generally, career escalation does not occur with the frequency that some experts have implied in recent years.

Experimental policies in various jurisdictions, such as San Diego County, California, to divert and process nonserious and first offenders informally, called **interagency agreement plans**, seem to be modestly successful at reducing recidivism (Pennell, Curtis, and Scheck, 1990). For more serious offenders designated as chronic, violent, aggressive, or persistent, various types of mandatory group therapy have been regarded as successful interventions in past years (Ellsworth, Kinsella, and Massin, 1992; U.S. General Accounting Office, 1995a). However, there is strong sentiment and agreement among professionals that a combination of behavioral strategies or approaches is necessary to treat most aggressive teenagers effectively (Stalans and Henry, 1994; Williams and Cohen, 1993).

In some jurisdictions, such as Hawaii, chronic violent or serious offenders and other aggressive youths have been targeted for priority processing at intake and other stages (Hawaii Crime Commission, 1985; Hawaii Criminal Justice Commission, 1986). Harsher measures, including rapid identification of youths, expedited hearings, close monitoring of their cases, and their segregation from other, less serious offenders, have been employed by different Hawaiian juvenile justice units as a means of crime control. Continuous counseling, placement in long-term secure confinement facilities, extended court jurisdiction, and the revelation of these youths' identities to the public seem effective at curbing recidivism among these hard-core offenders (Bilchik, 1995). Of course, there are certain constitutional issues that must be resolved concerning identities of juvenile offenders and the publication of information about them made available to others (Bilchik, 1995).

The Inadequacy of Treatment and Community Services

Also, many jurisdictions are hard-pressed to provide adequate treatment facilities and interventions that contain the ingredients for effectiveness (Hamparian, 1987). Hamparian (1987) suggests that such programs might have security without a jail-like atmosphere, close coordination and cooperation between the community and the criminal justice system, paraprofessional staffs, and provisions for remedial education and job training for these youths. But existing limited budgets and other priorities in many jurisdictions prevent the development of such sophisticated interventions (Rapoport, 1987). Yet other experts believe that interventions should be aimed at modifying one's social and psychological environment that fostered such violence and chronicity originally (Kupfersmid and Monkman, 1987).

Intake officers are also influenced by existing services and programs, especially in their decisions about violent offenders. In Tucson, Arizona, for example, a **Stop Assaultive Children** (SAC) program was created in the late 1980s and designed especially for those youths who have committed family violence (Zazlow, 1989). In the SAC program, the child is usually detained or locked up in a juvenile detention center for one day, and release from detention is contingent on the youth's attendance at school, abiding by a curfew, refraining from committing future delinquent acts or violence, and an agreement by the youth to be interviewed by the intake officer. Children in the SAC program are ordered to reappear within two weeks, at which time their prosecution is deferred for three months, provided that they are accepted into SAC. Each SAC participant must sign a contract acknowledging responsibility for his or her acts, agreeing further to participate in counseling and/or volunteer work or to make a donation to a domestic violence service or agency. If the contract is unfulfilled for any reason, the juvenile is subsequently prosecuted.

Parents are also obligated to sign the contract and to enforce its conditions. The primary result of the successful completion of the SAC program is a dismissal of all charges against the juvenile (Zazlow, 1989). Zazlow (1989) reports favorably that the SAC program has had a recidivism rate of only 9.6 percent compared with a recidivism rate of 48.7 percent among a control group of assaultive delinquent nonprogram participants in the same jurisdiction. But while Tucson may be able to operate such programs successfully, other jurisdictions may not be as fortunate, or intake officers elsewhere may believe that their own plans for intervention are more effective.

Getting Tough with Persistent Offenders

For persistent offenders and otherwise hard-core violent recidivists, even for some violent first offenders, the strategy employed at intake may be a waiver of jurisdiction to criminal courts (Champion and Mays, 1991). Some jurisdictions, such as New York, Washington, and Illinois, have automatic transfer laws that compel juvenile authorities to send certain types of juvenile offenders in a particular age range (normally 16 or 17 years of age) directly to criminal court to be processed as adults. The manifest intent of such waivers to criminal court is for harsher punishments to be imposed on these youthful offenders beyond those that can ordinarily be administered within the power of juvenile court judges (Champion and Mays, 1991).

The get-tough movement clearly has incarceration in mind for those youths who have been adjudicated delinquent for violent offenses. Anything less than secure confinement for such youths adjudicated for aggravated assault, rape, robbery, or homicide is considered as too lenient.

However, some juvenile justice experts argue that there is presently too much incarceration, that incarceration is overdone, and that many youths can remain in their communities under close supervision, participating in productive self-improvement and rehabilitative programs.

Is There Too Much Juvenile Incarceration?

Brandau (1992) has investigated the use of alternatives to confinement in Delaware. In 1987 the Delaware Plan was established, whereby certain community programs were established as alternatives to incarcerating certain types of delinquent offenders. Brandau found that over time, a sample of 363 youths adjudicated for various serious delinquency offenses were assigned randomly to either reform school, placed on probation, or sent to the Delaware Bay Marine Institute (DBMI). The DBMI was a community-based program designed to equip certain youths with coping skills and other useful experiences. Legal, social, and demographic variables were controlled, and all youths were evaluated according to whether they were more likely to be assigned to the reform school following their delinquency adjudications. Subsequently, recidivism information was compiled for all youths to determine the influence of the different experiences on them. Youths in the DBMI program had recidivism rates similar to those placed on straight probation and those placed in reform schools. This finding is significant because it shows, in this instance, at least, that the DBMI program was about as effective as incarceration or probation for decreasing one's likelihood of recidivating. Since incarcerating juveniles is more expensive than placing them on probation or in the DBMI program, it is suggested that nonincarcerative community-based alternatives should be used more frequently, even for serious offenders.

Jones and Krisberg (1994) echo Brandau's assertion that secure confinement is overused in many instances where juveniles have been adjudicated. Jones and Krisberg examined general trends in juvenile justice and juvenile justice reform during the period 1982–1992 and found that many incarcerated youths did not need to be incarcerated. Over a third of those youths in state training schools (prisons for juveniles) belonged in less secure settings. Interestingly, Jones and Krisberg found that most incarcerated youths had committed nonviolent property offenses rather than violent offenses. This suggests strongly that in many jurisdictions, juvenile court judges are exercising a rather heavy hand when meting out punishments and disposing of cases through secure custody rather than imposing alternative community-based punishments. In many respects, this overuse of incarceration for juveniles mirrors what is happening in adult corrections, where chronic overcrowding is created by imprisoning many property offenders instead of using scarce prison space for more serious criminals (Koehler and Lindner, 1992).

ASSESSMENT OF GUARDIANSHIP

Although most cases that are furthered to the intake stage of the juvenile justice process involve some type of juvenile offending, criminal or otherwise, intake officers are often confronted with cases that require assessments of a youth's parents or guardians and the general sociocultural environment. Ordinarily, children in need of supervision (CHINS), including unruly or incorrigible youths, dependent and/or neglected youths, and abused children are diverted by police officers to the appropriate community agencies for special services and placement. Departments of health and human services, social welfare agencies, and family crisis or intervention centers are frequently contacted and receive youths for further processing. However, if some youths in need of supervision are eventually subject to intake screenings, probation officers must evaluate the nature of one's needs and the seriousness of the situation before a disposition of the case is made. Beyond the broad classification of CHINS, many youths may have chemical dependencies that precipitated their delinquent conduct and require medical attention rather than punishment.

Examples of such youths include youthful male and female prostitutes who originally may have been runaways and/or incorrigible alcohol- or drug-dependent youths who have turned to burglary and petty theft to support their dependencies, psychologically disturbed or mentally retarded juveniles, and sexually exploited children. If the facts disclosed at intake enable probation officers to make the strong presumption that certain youths should be diverted to human services shelters or community welfare agencies for treatment or temporary management, this conditional disposition can be made of the case. This decision is often predicated on the belief that a strong connection exists between the child's delinquency and physical, psychological, or sexual abuse received from adults or significant others (Krause and McShane, 1994; Pallone, 1994). However, evidence has also been presented showing a lack of a causal relation between child maltreatment seriousness and juvenile delinquency (Doerner, 1987).

It has also been found that parents who either maltreat their children or engage in substance abuse themselves often suffer multidimensional problems and may be disproportionately disposed to personality disorders, depression, criminality, and difficulty relating to peers and spouses (Famularo et al., 1988; Fields, 1994; Pallone, 1994; Rabinowitz, 1992). While testing for substance abuse among parents of those youths brought before juvenile courts is only a recommendation at this stage and not a requirement of any particular jurisdiction, it may be that such drug testing in the future could provide intake officers with mitigating factors that would modify their decision making and dispositions of certain juvenile cases (Kansas Juvenile Justice Task Force, 1995; Krause and McShane, 1994; Polan, 1994).

KEY TERMS

Appearance

Assessment centers

Consent decrees

Crime control model

Due process

Due-process model

Extralegal factors

Interagency agreement plan

Judicious nonintervention

Labeling

Labeling theory

Legal factors

Noninterventionist model

Radical nonintervention

Recidivism

Socioeconomic status (SES)

Stop Assaultive Children (SAC)

Strategic leniency

QUESTIONS FOR REVIEW

1. What are five philosophical views that may guide intake officers in their dispositions of juvenile cases? Do all officers subscribe to one view or another? Why or why not? What factors seem important that influence one's views about intake decision making?

2. Do intake hearings require that all constitutional safeguards be observed, including the same evidentiary standards that would apply in juvenile courts? Discuss your answer briefly.

3. Compare and contrast the intake process in the juvenile justice system with plea bargaining in the criminal justice system. Show the similarities and differences of each. What are the implications of intake for affected juveniles?

4. Of the various philosophies or models used by many intake officers in their decision-making activities at intake, which do you prefer, and why?

5. Which philosophy or model seems to fit the present get-tough movement that seems to be pervasive in both the criminal and juvenile justice systems? Write a short paragraph outlining your argument.

6. What legal factors are normally considered in an intake hearing? Describe each of the factors you list and cite research to show the relevance of each for intake decision making.

7. Differentiate between *inculpatory* and *exculpatory factors*. Why are they important and how might they influence an intake decision favorably or unfavorably?

8. Identify four major extralegal factors that may have an impact on an intake hearing. Are these factors easy to operationalize? Can we show direct connections between these factors and intake decision making? Why or why not?

9. How is one's appearance related to intake decision making? Cite some research pertaining to the attractiveness or unattractiveness of youths and whether they are treated harshly or leniently.

10. Do intake officers deal exclusively with criminal or status offenders? What are some exceptional cases?

SUGGESTED READINGS

Drowns, Robert W. and Karen M. Hess. *Juvenile Justice*, 2nd ed. St. Paul, MN: West Publishing Company, 1995.

Guarino-Ghezzi, Susan and Edward J. Loughran. *Balancing Juvenile Justice*. New Brunswick, NJ: Transaction, 1996.

Minnesota Office of the Legislative Auditor. *Guardians Ad Litem*. St. Paul, MN: Program Evaluation Division Minnesota Office of the Legislative Auditor, 1995.

Roberson, Cliff. *Exploring Juvenile Justice: Theory and Practice*. Placerville, CA: Copperhouse Publishing Company, 1996.

U.S. General Accounting Office. *Juvenile Justice: Juveniles Processed in Criminal Court and Case Dispositions*. Washington, DC: U.S. General Accounting Office, 1995.

U.S. General Accounting Office. *Juvenile Justice: Representation Rates Varied as Did Counsel's Impact on Court Outcomes*. Washington, DC: U.S. General Accounting Office, 1995.

CHAPTER 6

CLASSIFICATION AND PRELIMINARY TREATMENT: WAIVERS AND OTHER ALTERNATIVES

INTRODUCTION

Twenty-two year-old Brian Todd from Provo, Utah went to New York City with his family during the Labor Day weekend, 1990. He watched the New York Mets beat the San Francisco Giants 4–3 at Shea Stadium. Later that evening, he and his family had dinner at a nice restaurant. The following afternoon, he watched the U.S. Open tennis tournament. Later that evening after changing clothes in their New York Hilton Hotel room, the Todd family headed for Greenwich Village to have dinner at a well-known Moroccan restaurant. In less than an hour, Brian Todd would be dead after being attacked by muggers in a New York subway, a knife plunged deep into his chest by a youth gang member. The gang wanted fast money so they could attend a big disco party at Roseland Dance City, a local disco. Eight teenagers of the 10 who attacked the Todds were arrested the following day. They were members of Fuck That Shit (FTS), one of hundreds of gangs that roam New York City streets. They got $203 from Brian's father after cutting his wallet from his pocket with razor blades. Brian, weaponless, died trying to protect his mother, who was about to be mugged as well. The blood money gained admission to Roseland for several of these gang members, where they enjoyed music, drinks, and the rest of the evening. Showing no remorse in video-taped confessions, seven of the FTS gang members ratted on their buddy, 18-year-old Rocstar, the alleged stabber who always carried a "butterfly" knife (a double-edged device with 4-inch blades). For the Todds, it was the beginning of terrifying memories of a tragedy and a silent trip back to Provo accompanying the coffin of their son. For Rocstar and his friends, it was just another day in the city after a wild disco concert.

In 1993 in Washington, three youths murdered their parents and their 11-year-old brother. They committed these heinous acts in the middle of the night, bludgeoning to death the mother first, then the father, then their younger brother, while they slept. Two of the youths were brothers, age 18 and 16. The third youth was their cousin, age 17. All three were members of the Jehovah's Witness faith, and their parents tried to instill strong religious ideals in their children during their early years. Rebellion was apparent by the time these youths reached their early teen years. They began drinking and committing assorted acts, some of which were violent. One day, the older brother wrestled his mother to the floor and raised a hatchet over her head, intending to kill her. The mother said to him, "Let me stand up and face you. If you want to kill me then, I'll let you do it. But I want to look at you face to face when you kill me." The boy was stunned by these words, enough to permit his mother to stand up. She faced him. He dropped the hatchet and fled from the house. Later, his parents had him and his next younger brother placed in a mental hospital for a clinical examination and evaluation. The doctors recommended that they keep these boys under observation for a year. Following their observation, they were released into the custody of their parents. The parents, believing the boys were cured, bought them a car. The boys used the car to travel to other counties and eventually began associating with neo-Nazi groups and Skinheads. The boys began to plot the murder of their parents. A few months later, they killed them and the youngest brother while they slept. They were eventually apprehended and charged with murder. Subsequently, they were charged as adults in criminal court and sentenced to life-without-parole terms.

In 1993, a foreign motorist in Florida was shot to death by three youths. The shooters were 16 and 17, respectively, but the third youth was only 13 years old. While he only sat in the car while his brother and a friend murdered a tourist, he was eventually charged with first-degree murder. Florida decided to charge these youths in criminal court, treating them as though they were adults. This process is permissible under state law. The older brother and his friend were both eligible for the death penalty under existing Florida law, since they were 16 or older at the time they committed the premeditated murder. However, the 13-year-old could not receive the death penalty, because of his age. Subsequently, he entered a plea of "no contest" to aiding and abetting in the murder of the tourist, and he was given a sentence of probation for two years. In the aftermath at age 16, the youth was arrested again, this time for aggravated kidnapping and armed robbery. The criminal court convicted him of these crimes, and he was sentenced to life without parole.

These incidents involve only a few of the hundreds of thousands of arrests in the United States annually of youths aged 18 or younger. Juvenile arrest rates for violent crimes began to increase in the late 1980s. The juvenile violent crime rate soared between 1988 and 1994 after more than a decade of relative stability (Bilchik, 1996:1). By 1995, 2.2 million youths under age 18 had been arrested that year for various crimes. There were 47,094 youths arrested for rape, 379 for murder or nonnegligent manslaughter, 13,543 for robbery, and 23,190 for aggravated assault (Maguire and Pastore, 1996). If juvenile violence trends continue, it is estimated that by the year 2010, the number of juvenile arrests for violent crimes will have doubled (Bilchik, 1996:1).

What responses to these offenses should be made by the juvenile justice system? What are the limits of sanctions to be imposed by juvenile courts? Should some youths be held more accountable than others, in view of the crimes they commit? Are some youths more amenable to criminal punishments than others? Where should the line be drawn about who should receive criminal penalties and who should not receive them?

In this chapter we examine waiver decision making. Waivers, also known in different jurisdictions as transfers and certifications, are transferrals or shifts of jurisdiction over certain types of cases from juvenile courts to criminal courts. These terms are used throughout this and other chapters interchangeably. Youths who are subjected to waivers are not tried as juveniles in juvenile courts. Rather, they are redefined and classified as adults and eventually tried in criminal courts. Only a small proportion of juveniles are subject to criminal court transfers annually. Preliminary determinations are made of crime seriousness, the youth's characteristics, such as age and other factors associated with the type of crime committed, and the amount or degree of victim injuries inflicted. This process is described.

Several types of waivers may be exercised by either judges or juvenile prosecutors, depending on the jurisdiction. In some jurisdictions, provisions exist for the automatic transfer of certain juvenile offenders to criminal court. These variations in waiver procedures are outlined and discussed. Because of the potentially serious nature of penalties that criminal courts may impose if youths are eventually found guilty through bench or jury trials or plea bargaining, several implications of waivers for affected juveniles are examined. Waivers may be contested, and these occasions are known as waiver hearings. In those jurisdictions with statutory automatic transfer provisions, juveniles are entitled to reverse waiver hearings. Both options have strengths and weaknesses, benefits and disadvantages for youths charged with crimes. These are described. Because waivers of juveniles to criminal court may be made at several junctures in the juvenile justice process (e.g., automatically by statute, before or after intake, at the prosecution stage, or at adjudication in juvenile court), it was believed important to discuss this event now rather than in a later chapter. Subsequently, we can see how waivers function as options for various actors in the juvenile justice system, and we can understand and appreciate the significance of them as well as their several implications for affected juveniles.

An integral feature of the juvenile justice process is the adversarial relation between defense counsel and prosecutors. Both of these roles are examined as they relate to waiver decisions. Finally, a get-tough movement has been observed over the last few decades within both the criminal and juvenile justice systems. For criminals, *get tough* means stiffer sentences and heavier fines, fewer loopholes that may be used to elude convictions for crimes, and less prosecutorial and judicial discretion relating to minimizing charges filed and penalties assessed. For juveniles, *get tough* means moving away from the traditional rehabilitative orientation that characterized early juvenile court processes and decision making and toward more punitive sanctions; greater use of incarceration, especially for more serious youthful offenders, obligating more youths to be held accountable for their actions; and more liberal use of waivers to criminal courts for the most serious offenders. Waivers represent a hard line against selected juvenile offenders. Contemporary waiver patterns among the states will be illustrated and waiver trends described.

SERIOUSNESS OF THE OFFENSE, OFFENDER CHARACTERISTICS, AND WAIVER DECISION MAKING

Seriousness of the Offense

Investigations into the nature and degree of serious violent juvenile offending have been conducted by several researchers. In a comparison of mid-1990s juvenile offending with the nature and type of juvenile offending in 1980, for instance, Elliott (1994b) has found that about the same proportion of youths commit serious violent offenses today as they did in 1980. However, Elliott notes that the violent acts committed in the 1990s are more lethal, with larger proportions of these violent acts likely to result in either serious injury or death. Elliott has found that the peak years of committing violent acts among juveniles are ages 15 and 16. He also found that the major causes of juvenile violence were poor family relations, socioeconomically disadvantaged neighborhoods, poor school adjustments, peer pressure, greater availability of firearms, and greater dependence on alcohol or drugs.

Juvenile violence must be put in perspective. For instance, in 1994, juveniles accounted for 19 percent of all violent crime arrests (Snyder, Sickmund, and Poe-Yamagata, 1996). Thus fewer than one-fifth of all persons entering the justice system for a violent crime charge were juveniles. Also, fewer than one-half of 1 percent of juveniles in the United States were arrested for a violent offense in 1994. This is fewer than 1 in 200 juveniles, although these few violent juvenile offenders are driving national juvenile justice policy concerns (Bilchik, 1996:1). Therefore, while juvenile violence is on the increase, adults were responsible for 74 percent of the violent crime increase from 1985 to 1994 (Snyder, Sickmund, and Poe-Yamagata, 1996).

Causes of Juvenile Violence. The causes of juvenile violence cross both race/ethnic and gender lines. Studies of black adolescents show that many of them have dysfunctional families and poor school adjustment, are drug or alcohol dependent, and have low self-esteem (DuRant et al., 1994). Female juvenile violence is triggered by similar factors, including peer pressure, drug or alcohol dependencies, socioeconomically disadvantaged neighborhoods, and poor family relations (Sommers and Baskin, 1994). Many of those youths who have committed violent acts have been victims of violence. Kruttschnitt and Dornfeld (1993) found that often, family violence against children prompts these youths to act out their frustrations by committing violent acts against others in their neighborhoods or schools. Also, those youths who have suffered physical and sexual abuse in their homes have experienced an earlier onset of delinquent behaviors. Studies of youth violence in Canada and other countries have disclosed similar findings relative to violent youthful offenders (Awad and Saunders, 1991). Particularly for males and blacks, it has been found that childhood victimization increases overall risk for violent offending among affected juveniles (Rivera and Widom, 1990).

One explanation for greater juvenile violence has been the widespread availability of firearms to youths (Smith, 1996). In some areas, such as New York, Los Angeles, and Chicago, gang warfare has escalated to the point where more dominant gangs tend to possess more sophisticated weaponry than other gangs. Thus city streets or turfs have become major combat zones for rival groups of youths seeking territorial control (Thompson, Brownfield, and Sorenson, 1996).

In an effort to stem the rising tide of juvenile violence that typified much of the 1970s, various programs and policies were implemented legislatively that were intended as get-tough measures (Anonymous, 1996). Juvenile courts were viewed as too lenient in their dealings with youthful offenders. Rehabilitation of youths and various experimental treatment programs and helping strategies did not seem to work (Walker, 1989). Public sentiment seemed to favor more punitive measures and tactics that would incapacitate more serious or violent offenders.

Offense Seriousness: Separating Status from Delinquent Offenders. One of the first measures designed to separate juveniles into different offending categories was the widespread deinstitutionalization of status offenders (DSO). Also including divestiture, this major juvenile justice reform was calculated to remove the least serious and noncriminal offenders from the jurisdiction of juvenile courts in most jurisdictions. Presumably and ideally, after DSO, only those juveniles who were charged with felonies and/or misdemeanors, delinquents, would be brought into the juvenile justice process and formally adjudicated in juvenile courts. These courts would also retain supervisory control (in the *parens patriae* sense) over children in need of supervision, abused children, or neglected children. In reality, we have seen that events have not turned out as legislators had originally anticipated and that considerable improvement remains to be made in juvenile justice operations and functions. Many status offenders continue to filter into the juvenile justice system in various jurisdictions. Many of these offenders are the victims of net widening by police officers, who have haphazardly taken it upon themselves to redefine previously noncriminal behaviors as criminal ones.

When DSO originated on a large scale throughout the United States during the late 1970s, several jurisdictions, including West Virginia, made policy decisions that would have a different impact on how both nonserious and serious offenders would henceforth be treated by their juvenile justice systems. In West Virginia, for instance, the Supreme Court of Appeals ruled in 1977 that an adjudicated delinquent was constitutionally entitled to receive the *least restrictive alternative treatment consistent with his or her rehabilitative needs* [emphasis mine] (*State ex rel. Harris v. Calendine*, 1977). Although this decision did not eliminate incarcerating more serious or violent juveniles, it did encourage juvenile court judges to consider seriously various alternatives to incarceration as punishments for youthful offenders. Relating to DSO, the court also prohibited the commingling of adjudicated status offenders and adjudicated delinquent offenders in secure, prisonlike facilities (Mones, 1984). Again, the court did not necessarily rule out the secure confinement, long-term or otherwise, of status offenders as a possible sanction by juvenile court judges, despite encouragement by the court for judges first to attempt to apply nonincarcerative sanctions before imposing incarcerative penalties.

These mixed messages sent by the West Virginia Supreme Court of Appeals did little, if anything, to restrict the discretionary powers of juvenile court judges. The court's emphasis on rehabilitation and alternative treatments to be considered by juvenile court judges reinforced the court's traditional concept of juvenile courts as rehabilitative rather than punitive sanctioning bodies. However, the court's ruling led to a drastic overhaul of the West Virginia juvenile code as well as a substantial drop in the incarcerated juvenile offender population in state-operated correctional facilities.

Juvenile Court Dispositions for Status Offenders.   In other jurisdictions, DSO has reduced the volume of juvenile court cases over the years, but it has not prevented juvenile courts from continuing to adjudicate rather large numbers of status offenders annually. A comprehensive study of U.S. juvenile courts shows systematic increases in the absolute numbers of status offenders adjudicated across all status offense categories (Bilchik, 1996:34–36). Figure 6.1 illustrates the increase in sheer numbers of status offense cases adjudicated in juvenile courts. The number of status-offender petitioned cases increased between 1984 and 1993 from 69,707 to 111,200, a 60 percent increase (Bilchik, 1996:35). Figure 6.2 shows juvenile court processing of petitioned cases of status offenses within the offense categories of runaways, truants, ungovernable children, and liquor law violators.

Adjudicated Status Offender Cases.   In Figure 6.1 we see that there were 60,300 formal adjudications, representing about 54 percent of the total number of petitioned cases. Only 3 percent of these cases (1600) were dismissed. Sixty percent of these adjudicated status offenders were placed on

FIGURE 6.1 Juvenile Court Processing of Petitioned Status Offense Cases, 1993

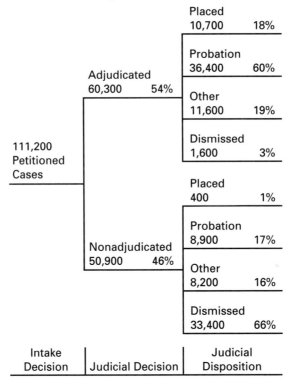

Note: Detail may not add to totals because of rounding.

Source: From Bilchik, 1996:35.

probation, while another 19 percent (11,600) were given other conditional dispositions, such as home confinement, electronic monitoring, or counseling. The remainder of the formally adjudicated cases, 10,700 (18 percent), were placed. **Placement** *refers to out-of-home placement, such as a group home or foster care.* Seldom does placement mean secure confinement for status offenders in a state industrial school or reform school.

Nonadjudicated Status Offender Cases. In Figure 6.1 the remaining 50,900 cases (46 percent) were nonadjudicated. Formal adjudications become an official part of a juvenile's record. For offenders who were nonadjudicated, a formal decision was not rendered; rather, an informal declaration was made by the judge to dispose of these cases with minimal intrusion into the families and lives of those affected by the court decision. Notice in Figure 6.1 that 66 percent of the nonadjudicated cases were simply dismissed. In short, the judges involved dismissed 33,400 status offenders from the juvenile

FIGURE 6.2 Juvenile Court Processing of Petitioned Status Offense Cases within Offense Categories, 1993

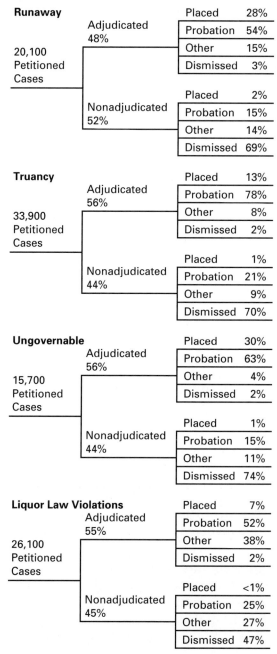

Note: Detail may not add to totals because of rounding.

Source: From Bilchik, 1996:35.

justice system without further court action. Probation or some other minimal intervention was used in another 33 percent of the cases (17,100). Only 1 percent of these nonadjudicated status offenders (400) were placed. **Placed** means that they were probably assigned to foster or group homes or placed under the supervision of social welfare agencies for short periods. It is highly unlikely that any of these placements were in secure custody facilities for juveniles.

Specific dispositions involving particular types of status offenders are illustrated in Figure 6.2. In Figure 6.2, the most petitioned cases are truants, with 33,900 cases. Liquor law violators account for the next most frequently represented petitioned offense category, with 26,100. These are followed by runaways (20,100 cases) and ungovernable children (15,700 cases). The most adjudications occur for truants and ungovernable children, with 56 percent of each of these types of cases formally adjudicated. The most nonadjudicated types of offenders are runaways, with about 52 percent of these cases nonadjudicated. Nearly 70 percent of these nonadjudicated cases result in dismissals. By far the largest number of dismissed cases occurs for nonadjudicated ungovernable children (CHINS), at 74 percent. Notice in Figure 6.2 that even among the adjudicated ungovernable cases, 63 percent received probation. However, 30 percent of these same types of offenders received placement in out-of-home settings.

Summarizing Status Offender Juvenile Court Actions. In 1993, 54 percent of all petitioned status offense cases handled by juvenile courts resulted in formal adjudications (Bilchik, 1996:35). Adjudication was most common for ungovernability and truancy cases. The majority of adjudicated status offense cases resulted in probation. Only 18 percent of all adjudicated status offense cases resulted in out-of-home placement. Formal probation was most likely involving adjudicated truancy cases (78 percent) and least likely in adjudicated liquor law violation cases (52 percent) (Bilchik, 1996:36–37). Between 1989 and 1993, the use of probation in all status offense adjudications increased by 13 percent. The greatest increase in probation use from 1989 to 1993 involved runaways (25 percent) and truants (19 percent).

Delinquent Offenders and Juvenile Court Dispositions. Assuming that for the majority of jurisdictions, juvenile courts have effectively weeded out the bulk of the nonserious, nondelinquent cases, the remainder should theoretically consist of those charged with delinquent offenses or acts that would be criminal if adults committed them. Figure 6.3 shows that in 1993, 1,489,700 cases came to the attention of the juvenile justice system (Bilchik, 1996:9). About half (53 percent) of these cases resulted in the filing of delinquency petitions. These petitions involved 789,300 juveniles.

Nonpetitioned cases made up the remainder, or 700,400 (47 percent). These nonpetitioned cases were informally resolved at the intake stage. Informal intake dispositions resulted in 27 percent of these nonpetitioned cases receiving probation, 23 percent social services, and 49 percent dismissed. Only 1 percent, or about 5800 of these youths, were placed.

Juvenile court judges heard 789,300 cases. Notice in Figure 6.3 that 58 percent of these cases, or 457,000, were adjudicated, with 56 percent receiving probation, 12 percent receiving social services, and 4 percent

FIGURE 6.3   Juvenile Court Processing of Delinquency Cases, 1993

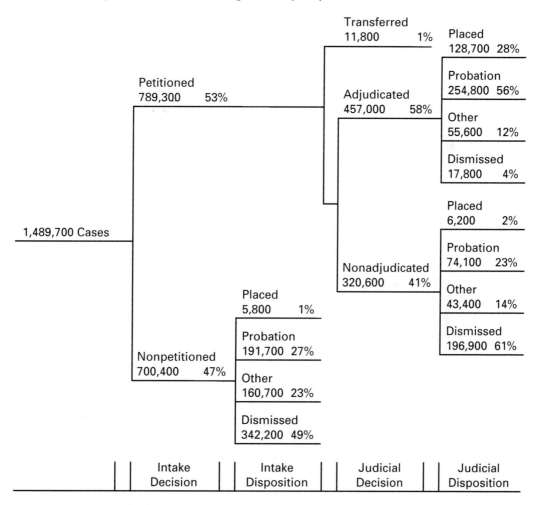

Note: Detail may not add to totals because of rounding.

Source: From Bilchik, 1996:9.

resulting in dismissals. Out-of-home placements involved 28 percent of these youths (128,700). Many of these out-of-home placements involved secure confinement in state industrial schools or reform schools. The rest included placements in foster care, group homes, or some type of supervision through community programming.

For the nonadjudicated cases, 61 percent resulted in dismissals, 23 percent resulted in probation, 14 percent resulted in social services, and 2 percent resulted in out-of-home placements or involvement in various community programs. *The critical figure in Figure 6.3 is the 1 percent, or 11,800 youths, who were transferred.*

Transfers, Waivers, or Certifications

What Are Transfers? **Transfers** refer to changing the jurisdiction over certain juvenile offenders to another jurisdiction, usually from juvenile court jurisdiction to criminal court jurisdiction. Transfers are also known as **waivers**, referring to a waiver or change of jurisdiction from the authority of juvenile court judges to criminal court judges. Prosecutors or juvenile court judges decide that in some cases, juveniles should be waived or transferred to the jurisdiction of criminal courts. Presumably, those cases that are waived or transferred are the most serious cases, involving violent or serious offenses, such as homicide, aggravated assault, forcible rape, robbery, or drug-dealing activities.

In some jurisdictions, such as Utah, juveniles are waived or transferred to criminal courts through a process known as certification. A **certification** is a formal procedure whereby the state declares the juvenile to be an adult for the purpose of a criminal prosecution in a criminal court (Sanborn, 1994a). The results of certifications are the same as for waivers or transfers. Thus certifications, waivers, and transfers result in juvenile offenders being subject to the jurisdiction of criminal courts, where they can be prosecuted as though they were adult offenders. A 14-year-old murderer, for instance, might be transferred to criminal court for a criminal prosecution on the murder charge. In criminal court, the juvenile, now being treated as though he were an adult, can be convicted of the murder and sentenced to a prison term for one or more years. If the juvenile is charged with capital murder, is 16 or older, and lives in a state where the death penalty is administered to those convicted of capital murder, he or she can potentially receive the death penalty as the maximum punishment for that offense, provided that there is a capital murder conviction. Or criminal court judges might impose life-without-parole sentences on these convicted 16- or 17-year-olds. Imposing life-without-parole sentences or the death penalty are *not* within the jurisdiction of juvenile court judges. Their jurisdiction ends when an offender becomes an adult. Thus a delinquency adjudication on capital murder charges in juvenile court might result in a juvenile being placed in the state industrial school until he is 18 or 21, depending on whichever is the age of majority or adulthood.

Between 1988 and 1992, the use of waivers by juvenile courts increased by 68 percent (Sickmund, 1994). An estimated 176,000 youths under age 18 were tried as adults in criminal courts in 1991. One reason for this large number of criminal cases involving youths under age 18 is that in various states, persons are considered adults at somewhat younger ages, such as 15, 16, or 17, for purposes of a criminal prosecution. Thus, in many of these cases, waivers, transfers, or certifications were not relevant to subsequent criminal court processing (Sickmund, 1994).

The Rationale Underlying the Use of Transfers, Waivers, or Certifications.
The basic rationale underlying the use of waivers is that the *most serious juvenile offenders* will be transferred to the jurisdiction of criminal courts, where the harshest punishments, including capital punishment, may be imposed as sanctions (Dawson, 1992). Since juvenile courts lack the jurisdiction and decision-making power to impose anything harsher than secure confinement dispositions of limited duration in industrial or reform schools, it would seem that the waiver would be an ideal way to impose the most severe punishments on those juveniles who commit the most violent acts.

A list of reasons for the use of transfers, waivers, or certifications include the following:

1. To make it possible for harsher punishments to be imposed
2. To provide just-deserts and proportionately severe punishments on those juveniles who deserve such punishments by their more violent actions
3. To foster fairness in administering punishments according to one's serious offending
4. To hold serious or violent offenders more accountable for what they have done
5. To show other juveniles who contemplate committing serious offenses that the system works and that harsh punishments can be expected if serious offenses are committed
6. To provide a deterrent to decrease juvenile violence
7. To overcome the traditional leniency of juvenile courts and provide more realistic sanctions
8. To make youths realize the seriousness of their offending and induce remorse and acceptance of responsibility

Ideal Offender Characteristics for Justifying Transfers to Criminal Courts.
Those designated for transfer or waiver by various participants in the juvenile justice process *should* exhibit certain consistent characteristics. *Age, offense seriousness*, and *prior record* (including previous referrals to juvenile court, intake proceedings and dispositions, or juvenile court delinquency adjudications) are some of these characteristics. For example, Grisso, Tomkins, and Casey (1988) indicate that several extralegal factors function to enhance the likelihood that a juvenile will be waived to criminal court. These researchers gathered data from 50 state juvenile codes. Using content analysis, they searched court records and read decisions involving transferred juveniles, appeals of these transfers to appellate courts, and various law review articles pertaining to transfers. They supplemented their analysis with interviews of 85 court personnel and a survey of 1423 representatives from 127 courts in 34 states. They concluded several things about the juveniles who were subjects of transfers. First, *those with extensive prior records* or involvement with the juvenile justice system were more frequently detained and subjected to transfer.

Second, many of these youths exhibited emotional disturbances of various kinds. Such emotional disturbance seemed to promote self-destructive behavior and poor school adjustment. These youths were most unwilling to accept interventions suggested by juvenile courts and intake officers. Thus *unwillingness to accept intervention* became an important extralegal factor that adversely influenced the transfer decision. Third, the researchers found that those transferred tended to lack self-discipline and failed to comply with rules or court orders and conditional sanctions imposed by juvenile court judges. Therefore, a youth's *unwillingness to comply with institutional rules* became another extralegal factor impinging on the waiver decision.

Actual Characteristics of Transferred Juveniles. In 1993, 11,800 youths were transferred to criminal court. Most juveniles transferred were male, with only 500 females (0.4 percent) being waived (Bilchik, 1996:24). About 6500 (55.5 percent) of all transferred juveniles were black or other minority, despite the fact that white juveniles comprised about 64.5 percent of all cases referred to juvenile court. Furthermore, those charged with person offenses and waived to criminal court made up only 42 percent of those transferred. About 46.6 percent of those charged with property or public order offenses were waived to criminal courts, while about 10 percent of those waived were charged with drug offenses (Bilchik, 1996:13). As we will see in a subsequent section of this chapter, the use of transfers is more extensive in recent years, although we have not necessarily been targeting the *most* serious offenders for waivers.

Youngest Ages at Which Juveniles Can Be Transferred to Criminal Court.
Table 6.1 shows the youngest ages at which juveniles could be transferred or waived to criminal courts in all U.S. jurisdictions in 1987. In 1987, 15 states and all federal districts indicated no specified age for transferring juveniles to criminal courts for processing. One state, Vermont, specified age 10 as the minimum age at which a juvenile could be waived. Montana established age 12 as the earliest age for a juvenile waiver. Fourteen states used age 14 as the youngest transfer age, while seven states and the District of Columbia set the minimum transfer age at 15, and seven states used the minimum transfer age of 16.

Some idea of the aggressiveness of state governments and public policies directed toward getting tough toward violent juvenile offending is provided by Table 6.2, which shows the various states that have modified or enacted changes in their transfer provisions for juveniles during the period 1992–1995. Inspecting the table, we can see that under judicial waiver modifications, 11 states lowered the age limit at which juveniles can be

TABLE 6.1

Youngest Age at Which Juvenile May Be Transferred to Criminal Court by Judicial Waiver[a]

Age	States
No specific age	Alaska, Arizona, Arkansas, Delaware, Florida, Indiana, Kentucky, Maine, Maryland, New Hampshire, New Jersey, Oklahoma, South Dakota, West Virginia, Wyoming, Federal districts
10	Vermont
12	Montana
13	Georgia, Illinois, Mississippi
14	Alabama, Colorado, Connecticut, Idaho, Iowa, Massachussets, Minnesota, Missouri, North Carolina, North Dakota, Pennsylvania, South Carolina, Tennessee, Utah
15	District of Columbia, Louisiana, Michigan, New Mexico, Ohio, Oregon, Texas, Virginia
16	California, Hawaii, Kansas, Nevada, Rhode Island, Washington, Wisconsin

[a]Many judicial waiver statutes also specify offenses that are waivable. This table lists the states by the youngest age for which judicial waiver may be sought without regard to offense.

Source: Linda A. Szymanski, *Waiver/Transfer/Certification of Juveniles to Criminal Court: Age Restrictions: Crime Restrictions* (Pittsburgh, PA: National Center for Juvenile Justice, February 1987)

transferred to criminal court. One example of a significant age modification is Missouri, where the minimum age for juvenile transfers was lowered from 14 to 12 for any felony. In the case of Texas, the minimum transfer age was lowered from 15 to 10. Virginia lowered the transfer age from 15 to 14. Table 6.2 also shows that other modifications were made to get tough toward juvenile offenders. Ten states added crimes to the list of those qualifying youths for transfer to criminal courts. In six states, the age of criminal accountability was lowered, while 24 states authorized additional crimes to be included that would automatically direct that the criminal court would have jurisdiction rather than the juvenile court.

Waiver Decision Making. Organizational and political factors are at work to influence the upward trend in the use of transfers. Politicians wish to present a get-tough facade to the public by citing waiver statistics and showing their increased use in the political response to the rise in serious youth crime. Despite political rhetoric, there has been an increase in the use of waivers. Between 1989 and 1993, for instance, the use of transfers increased by 41 percent (Bilchik, 1996:13). Many of those transferred have been charged with felonies (Minnesota Sentencing Guidelines Commission, 1994; Podkopacz, 1994).

As will be seen in the following section, several types of waivers can be used to negotiate transfers of jurisdiction from juvenile to criminal courts. One of these is the *automatic transfer* or *automatic waiver*, which several jurisdictions currently employ (Singer, 1993). This means that if youthful offenders are within a particular age range, usually ages 16 or 17, and are charged with specific types of offenses (usually murder, robbery, rape, aggravated assault, and other violent crimes), they will be transferred automatically to criminal courts. They may challenge this transfer to criminal court through a *reverse waiver hearing*. This is discussed in greater detail later in the chapter. The point is that these types of waivers, also known as legislative waivers because they were mandated by legislative bodies in various states and carry the weight of statutory authority, involve no discretionary action among prosecutors or judges (Bilchik, 1996; Sickmund, 1994). For other types of waivers, the decision-making process is largely discretionary (Butts and Poe, 1993; Frazier, 1991).

Because of the discretionary nature of the waiver process, large numbers of the wrong types of juveniles are transferred to criminal courts. The *wrong* types of juveniles are wrong because they are not those originally targeted by juvenile justice experts and reformers to be the primary candidates for transfers. The primary targets of waivers are intended to be the most serious, violent, and dangerous juveniles, who are also the most likely to deserve the most serious sanctions that criminal courts can impose. But

TABLE 6.2

States Modifying or Enacting Transfer Provisions, 1992–1995

Type of statute (period of change)	Action Taken (number of states)	States making changes	Examples
Judicial waiver (modifications, 1992–1995)	Added crimes (10)	AK, AR, CA, MO, NC, OH, OR, SC, TN, UT	*North Carolina* added Class A felonies to criteria.
	Lowered age limit (11)	ID, MO, NV, NC, OH, OR, TN, TX, VA, WV, WI	*Missouri* lowered age for certification of juvenile offenders from 14 to 12 for any felony.
	Added prior record provisions (2)	AK, CO	*Colorado* law allows consideration of two or more probation revocations based on acts that would be felonies.
Presumptive waiver (enactments since 1992)	Enacted provisions (9)	AK, CA, CO, DC, IL, MN, ND, SD, WI WI	In *Illinois*, under certain conditions and for certain serious violent crimes, there is rebuttable presumption that minor is not fit and proper to be dealt with by juvenile court.
Concurrent jurisdiction (modifications or enhancements, 1992–1995)	Enacted or modified (6)	AR, CO, FL, LA, UT[a], WY	In *Wyoming*, cases of children 14 or older charged with violent felonies can be commenced in juvenile or criminal court.
Statutory exclusion (modifications, 1992–1995)	Added crimes (24)	AL, CT, DE, GA, ID, IA, IL, IN, KS, KY, MD, MN, MS, NV, NH, NM, ND, OR, PA, RI, SC, UT, WA, WV	In *Idaho*, criminal court now has jurisdiction of juveniles accused of carrying concealed weapons on school property.
	Lowered age limit (6)	MS, NV, OK, OR, SC, WI	*Mississippi* lowered age of criminal accountability to 17 for felony offenses.
	Added lesser included offense (1)	ID	*Idaho* provides for continuation of criminal court jurisdiction with finding of guilt on offense other than original "excluding" offense.
	Changed language from "may" to "shall" (2)	ND, WV	*North Dakota* provides for mandatory transfer of juveniles to criminal court if: 14 or older; probable cause exists; and offense was murder, gross sexual imposition, or kidnapping.

Source: Bilchik, 1996:6.

[a]Utah's concurrent jurisdiction statute was repealed in 1995.

there is a wide credibility gap between the types of juveniles who are actually transferred each year and those who *should* be transferred. In 1993, for instance, we have already seen that nearly half (46.6 percent) of all youths transferred to criminal court were charged with property or public order

BOX 6.1   TEENAGER GETS LIFE FOR MURDER
OF MOTORIST

The Case of Barry Garcia

Barry Garcia, 17 years of age, lived in Moorhead, Minnesota. His mother had been murdered. His father went to prison. On July 2, 1996, Barry Garcia was sentenced to life without parole in prison for the murder of a motorist, Cherryl Tendeland. What happened?

Cherryl Tendeland and her husband were minding their own business, driving down a West Fargo, North Dakota, street one evening. Garcia and some other teenagers approached them with various weapons, including a shotgun. Suddenly, the shotgun discharged several times, killing Cherryl Tendeland instantly and seriously wounding her husband. The juveniles fled.

Police were able to capture all the juveniles involved in Cherryl's murder a few days later. They arrested Barry Garcia and charged him with her murder. A subsequent trial disclosed much about Garcia's childhood. The defense attorney argued that Garcia should be spared and given no more than a life-without-parole sentence. Actually, Garcia should at least have a chance at parole, said his attorney, Steve Mottinger. The possibility of parole would provide Garcia with at least *some* incentive to seek treatment and improve his life while imprisoned. However, the prosecutor had a different view. State's Attorney John Goff said that Barry Garcia is a sociopath, that he has been diagnosed as such by several state psychologists. Goff stated that Garcia had fired a shotgun at point-blank range at Mrs. Tendeland because she looked at him. That is no provocation, said Goff, who added that "It's the most senseless explanation for a murder I've ever heard of." The sentence Garcia received, life imprisonment without the possibility of parole, was the most severe under North Dakota law. Mr. Tendeland, husband of Cherryl, said: "I'm satisfied. It sends a message to other kids."

Should Garcia have received life instead of life without parole? Should juveniles be allowed to use their childhood as an excuse for murdering others? How would you punish Garcia?

Source: Adapted from Jeremiah Gardner, "Teen-Ager Sentenced to Life for West Fargo Slaying," *Minot (ND) Daily News*, July 3, 1996:B1, B7.

offenses. These types of offenses include theft, burglary, petty larceny, and disturbing the peace. Only 42 percent of those transferred in 1993 were charged with person offenses or violent crimes. If transfers, waivers, or certifications were applied as they *should* be applied, 100 percent of those transferred annually would be serious, violent offenders. Juvenile courts would handle all the other cases.

Why Do Property or Public Order Offenders Get Transferred to Criminal Court? An interested public wants to know why juvenile courts would send property offenders or public order offenders to criminal courts for processing. After all, these are the least serious offenders compared with those committing aggravated assault, attempted murder, homicide, forcible rape, and armed robbery. Studies of juvenile court judges disclose that often, persistent nonserious offenders are transferred from juvenile courts because juvenile court judges are tired of seeing these same offenders in their courts. They believe that if such persistent offenders are sent to criminal courts, this will be a better deterrent to their future offending (Champion and Mays, 1991). What these judges do not understand is that criminal court prosecutors and judges often tend to downplay the significance of these small-time offenders. At least half of these nonserious property offenders will have their cases dismissed, diverted, or downgraded (Jensen and Metsger, 1994; Virginia Commission on Youth, 1993). Another 40 percent will enter plea bargains and receive probation from criminal court judges. Most criminal court judges do not want to put 14-year-old property offenders or public order offenders in adult prisons, where chronic overcrowding and the potential for sexual exploitation are pervasive. Thus only about 10 percent of those nonserious offenders who are transferred annually will be placed in confinement for a term of months or years. About 90 percent will return to their neighborhoods and continue to reoffend (Champion and Mays, 1991).

A list of some of the factors cited by juvenile court judges that result in the transfer of nonserious property, public order, or drug offenders to criminal court are:

1. Although property offenders aren't especially serious or violent, their persistence in offending causes juvenile court judges to tire of their frequent appearances; transfers of these offenders to criminal court will "teach them a lesson."

2. Some jurisdictions mandate transfers to criminal court of those offenders who exceed some previously determined maximum of juvenile court adjudications; these may include property or public order offenders.

3. Individual differences among juvenile court judges will dictate which juveniles are transferred, despite the seriousness of their offense; if the judge doesn't like a particular youth's attitude, the youth will be transferred.

4. Any kind of drug offense should be dealt with by criminal courts; thus a simple "possession of a controlled substance" charge (e.g., prescription medicine) may be sufficient to qualify a juvenile for a criminal court transfer.

5. What is a serious or violent offense in one juvenile court jurisdiction may not be considered serious or violent in another jurisdiction; thus

different standards are applied to the same types of juveniles in different jurisdictions.

In 1997 there was a continuing pattern of transferring mostly property, public order, and drug offenders to criminal courts, despite major changes in state and federal transfer policies. Thus far, it is questionable whether waivers have functioned as effective deterrents to future juvenile offending. For example, a study of waived youths in Idaho between 1976 and 1986 found that numerous youths were transferred to criminal courts for processing. These youths ranged in age from 14 to 18. Once processed, a majority of these youths continued to reoffend in later years. This was attributed to prosecutorial leniency, whereby more serious offenses charged against juveniles were downgraded to less serious ones before being concluded with diversion or probation (Jensen and Metsger, 1994). Also cited were the facts that juveniles don't always know that when they commit certain acts, they will be transferred to criminal court; and one's youthfulness often functions as a mitigating factor, causing charge reductions or dismissals.

In some jurisdictions where gang presence is strong, local task forces have targeted gangs for harsher treatment, including the greater likelihood of being transferred to criminal court. A study of 38 state jurisdictions disclosed, however, that most prosecutors had no specific plans relating to dealing with gang members when they were transferred to criminal courts. Further, specialized gang prosecution units were rare (5 percent), even though it was believed that tougher juvenile laws would help combat the gang problem (Knox, Martin, and Tromanhauser, 1995). Most jurisdictions continue to experiment with various strategies that will target the most serious offenders for criminal prosecutions (Florida Advisory Council on Intergovernmental Relations, 1994; Schleuter et al., 1994; Virginia Commission on Youth, 1994b).

TYPES OF WAIVERS

There are four types of waiver actions: (1) prosecutorial waivers, (2) judicial or discretionary waivers, (3) legislative waivers or automatic transfers, and (4) demand waivers.

Prosecutorial Waivers

Whenever offenders are screened at intake and referred to the juvenile court for possible prosecution, prosecutors in various jurisdictions will conduct further screenings of these youths. They determine which cases merit further action and formal adjudication by judges. Not all cases sent to prosecutors by intake officers automatically result in subsequent formal juvenile court action. Prosecutors may decline to prosecute certain cases, particularly if there are problems with witnesses who are either missing or who refuse to testify, if there are evidentiary issues, or if there are over-loaded juvenile court dockets. A relatively small proportion of cases may merit waivers to criminal courts.

Prosecutorial waivers are also known as **direct file** or **concurrent jurisdiction**. Thus under direct file, the prosecutor has the sole authority to decide whether a particular juvenile case will be heard in criminal court or juvenile court. In Florida, one of the states where prosecutors have con-current jurisdiction, prosecutors may file extremely serious charges (e.g., murder, rape, aggravated assault, robbery) against youths in criminal courts and present cases to grand juries for indictment action. Or prosecutors may decide to file the same cases in the juvenile court.

Despite these prosecutorial options, all juveniles, as defined by their particular jurisdictions, are constitutionally entitled to a waiver hearing as one of their due process rights extended by the early landmark case of *Kent v. United States* (1966). Such hearings are particularly important if the juvenile wishes to contest the waiver action and remain within the juris-diction of the juvenile court.

Judicial or Discretionary Waivers

The largest numbers of waivers from juvenile to criminal court annually come about as the result of direct judicial action. *Judicial waivers give the juvenile court judge the authority to decide whether to waive jurisdiction and transfer the case to criminal court* (Bilchik, 1996:3). Known also as **dis-cretionary waivers**, judicial waivers typically involve a juvenile court judge's consideration of various criteria, including the juvenile's age, cur-rent offense, criminal history, and amenability to rehabilitation. This par-ticular type of transfer is invoked following a motion by the prosecutor (Bilchik, 1996:3).

Feld (1987b) and others have criticized judicial waivers largely because of their highly subjective qualities. Two different youths charged with identical offenses may appear at different times before the same judge. On the basis of impressions formed about the youths, the judge may decide to transfer one youth to criminal court and adjudicate the other youth in juvenile court. Obviously, the intrusion of extralegal factors into this important action generates a degree of unfairness and inequality. A youth's appearance and attitude emerge as significant factors that will either make or break the offender in the eyes of the judge. These socioeconomic and behavioral criteria often overshadow the seriousness or pettiness of offenses alleged. In the context of this particular type of transfer, it is easy to see how some persistent, nonviolent offenders may suffer waiver to criminal court. This is an easy way for the judge to get rid of them.

Although judges have this discretionary power in most jurisdictions, youths are still entitled to a hearing where they can protest the waiver action. While it is true that the criminal court poses risks to juveniles in terms of potentially harsher penalties, it is also true that being tried as an adult entitles youths to all of the adult constitutional safeguards, including the right to a trial by jury. In a later section of this chapter, we examine closely this and other options that may be of benefit to certain juveniles. Thus some juveniles may not want to fight waiver or transfer actions, largely because they may be treated more leniently by criminal courts.

Legislative Waivers or Automatic Transfers

Legislative waivers or *automatic transfers* *are statutorily prescribed actions that provide for a specified list of crimes to be excluded from the jurisdiction of juvenile courts, where offending juveniles are within a specified age range, and where the resulting action gives criminal courts immediate jurisdiction over these juveniles.* By the mid-1980s, 36 states excluded certain types of offenses from juvenile court jurisdiction. These excluded offenses were either very minor or very serious, ranging from traffic or fishing violations to rape or murder (U.S. Department of Justice, 1988:79). Also, many state jurisdictions have made provisions for automatic transfers of juveniles to criminal court. Among those states with automatic transfer provisions are Washington, New York, and Illinois (Bilchik, 1996).

Illinois's legislative waiver provisions were enacted in 1982 (Reed, 1983). While each state with automatic transfer provisions lists similar offenses as subjects of these waiver actions, some lists of offenses are longer than others. Usually, very serious crimes are listed, such as murder, rape, aggravated assault, and robbery. Certain types of theft, possessing cocaine, heroin, or other illicit substances for resale, and burglary may also be included. The typical age range for those subject to automatic transfers is 16 to 17. Thus if a 16-year-old youth has been charged with murder or rape and is in a state with an automatic transfer provision, the youth will be transferred to the jurisdiction of criminal court automatically. Again, such actions may be contested. In these instances, the contestations are conducted through reverse waiver hearings.

Legislative or automatic waivers are also known as statutory exclusion or mandatory transfer. *Statutory exclusion generally refers to provisions that automatically exclude certain juvenile offenders from the juvenile court's original jurisdiction* (Bilchik, 1996:3). An example of statutory exclusion is simply to lower the upper age of original juvenile court jurisdiction from 18 to 17 or 16. Thus juvenile court judges in these jurisdictions would not have power to decide cases involving 16- or 17-year-olds. Statutory exclusion may also involve specific offenses. For example, a state may exclude murder, rape, aggravated assault, and robbery from the jurisdiction of juvenile courts. Therefore, whenever a juvenile, regardless of his or her age, commits one of the listed offenses, the juvenile court is automatically barred from hearing and deciding these cases. Typically, states will make provisions for the statutory exclusion of offenders of particular ages who are alleged to have committed certain types of serious offenses. Thus a state may prohibit juvenile courts from hearing any case involving a 16-year-old rapist. The age and offense are combined to create the statutory exclusion.

Demand Waivers

Under certain conditions and in selected jurisdictions, juveniles may submit motions for demand waiver actions. **Demand waiver** *actions are requests or motions filed by juveniles and their attorneys to have their cases transferred from juvenile courts to criminal courts.* Why would juveniles want to have their cases transferred to criminal courts?

Most U.S. jurisdictions do not provide jury trials for juveniles in juvenile courts as a matter of right (*McKeiver v. Pennsylvania*, 1971). However, about a fifth of the states have established provisions for jury trials for juveniles at their request and depending on the nature of the charges against them. In the remainder of the states, jury trials for juveniles are granted only at the discretion of the juvenile court judge. Most juvenile court judges are not inclined to grant jury trials to juveniles. Thus if juveniles are (1) in a jurisdiction where they are not entitled to a jury trial even if they request one from the juvenile court judge, (2) face serious charges, and (3) believe that their cases would receive greater impartiality from a jury in a criminal courtroom, they may seek a demand waiver to have their cases transferred to criminal court. Florida permits demand waivers as one of several waiver options (Bilchik, 1996:3).

Other Waiver Variations

Thirteen states, including the District of Columbia, have established **presumptive waiver provisions**, *which require that certain offenders should be waived unless they can prove that they are suited for juvenile rehabilitation* (Bilchik, 1996:4). Essentially, a juvenile is considered waived to criminal court unless he or she can prove to be a suitable candidate for rehabilitation.

This rebuttable presumptive waiver, where the burden of proving one's rehabilitation potential rests with the juvenile and his or her attorney rather than the prosecutor, is used especially in those instances where juveniles have a history of frequent offending or where they have committed serious or violent offenses. It is difficult for any defense attorney to overcome this presumption if the juvenile client has committed an especially serious offense and has a prior record of violent offending.

The **reverse waiver** *is an action by the criminal court to transfer direct-filed or excluded cases from criminal court back to juvenile court, usually at the recommendation of the prosecutor* (Bilchik, 1996:4). Typically, juveniles who would be subject to these reverse waiver hearings would be those automatically sent to criminal court through a legislative waiver. Thus criminal court judges can act to remand at least some juveniles back to the jurisdiction of the juvenile court. Some juvenile offenders may be persistent property offenders who have committed new burglaries or larcenies or vehicular thefts. Such felonious offenses would fit certain automatic transfer criteria. However, a criminal court judge may wish to refer these types of cases back to juvenile courts for some type of formal action.

The **once waived/always waived provision** is perhaps the most serious and long-lasting for affected juvenile offenders. This provision means that *once juveniles at any age have been waived to the criminal court for processing, or once juveniles have been convicted and sentenced for one or more crimes by a criminal court, they are forever after considered adults for the purpose of criminal prosecutions.* Therefore, a 12-year-old who is transferred to criminal court in Vermont, for instance, and is subsequently convicted of a crime by that court will always be treated as an adult offender thereafter. At age 13, the same juvenile may commit vehicular theft. He would be subject to a criminal court prosecution. If at age 14 the same youth is arrested for disturbing the peace, a misdemeanor public order offense, his case would be prosecuted by the criminal court. At no time in the future would the juvenile court have jurisdiction over that juvenile. The same outcome would result from the *fact* of a transfer to criminal court, even though the criminal court declines to prosecute, reduces charges, or diverts the case. Once transferred, the youth remains within the exclusive jurisdiction of the criminal court. By 1996, 18 states, including the District of Columbia, had passed once waived/always waived laws (Bilchik, 1996:4–5).

Table 6.3 shows the different states and summarizes their juvenile transfer provisions as of 1995. By far the most popular type of waiver is the judicial waiver. Note that most states have statutory exclusions as well. Reverse waivers, which result from automatic or legislative waivers, are found in 44 percent of states. Eighteen states have enacted provisions for the once waived/always waived provision.

TABLE 6.3

Summary of Current Juvenile Transfer Provisions, 1995[a]

State	Judicial waiver	Prosecutor direct filing	Statutory exclusion	Presumptive waiver	Reverse waiver	Once waived/ always waived
Alabama	x		x			x
Alaska	x		x	x		
Arizona	x			x		
Arkansas	x	x			x	
California	x			x		
Colorado	x	x		x	x	
Connecticut	b		x		x	
Delaware	x		x		x	
District of Columbia	x	x	x	x		x
Florida	x	x	x			x
Georgia	x	x	x		x	
Hawaii	x		x			x
Idaho	x		x			x
Illinois	x		x	x		
Indiana	x		x			
Iowa	x		x			
Kansas	x		x			x
Kentucky	x		x		x	
Louisiana	x	x	x			
Maine	x					x
Maryland	x		x		x	
Massachusetts	x			x		
Michigan	x	x				
Minnesota	x		x	x		
Mississippi	x		x		x	x
Missouri	x					x
Montana	x		x			
Nebraska		x			x	
Nevada	x		x		x	x
New Hampshire	x	x		x	x	x
New Jersey	x					
New Mexico			x			
New York			x		x	
North Carolina	x		x			
North Dakota	x		x	x		
Ohio	x		x			x
Oklahoma	x		x		x	
Oregon	x		x			x
Pennsylvania	x		x		x	x
Rhode Island	x		x	x		
South Carolina	x		x		x	x
South Dakota	x			x		
Tennessee	x		x		x	
Texas	x		x		x	x
Utah	x	c	x		x	
Vermont	x	x	x			
Virginia	x				x	x
Washington	x		x			
West Virginia	x		x		x	
Wisconsin	x		x	x		
Wyoming	x	x				

[a]x indicates the provision(s) allowed by each state as of the end of the 1995 legislative session.
[b]Connecticut removed its judicial waiver provision in 1995.
[c]Utah's direct-file statute was repealed in 1995.

Source: Bilchik, 1996:5. Data source: Szymanski, Linda. *Special Analysis of the Automated Juvenile Law Archive* (Pittsburgh, PA: National Center for Juvenile Justice, 1996).

WAIVER AND REVERSE WAIVER HEARINGS

All juveniles who are waived to criminal court for processing are entitled to a hearing on the waiver if they request one (Bilchik, 1996). **Waiver hearings** are formal proceedings designed to determine whether the waiver action taken by the judge or prosecutor is the correct action and thus whether the juvenile should be transferred to criminal court. Waiver hearings are normally conducted before the juvenile court judge. These hearings are to some extent evidentiary, since a case must be made for why criminal courts should have jurisdiction in any specific instance. Usually, juveniles with lengthy prior records, several previous referrals, and/or one or more previous adjudications as delinquent are more susceptible to being transferred. While the offenses alleged are most often crimes, it is not always the case that the crimes are the most serious ones. Depending on the jurisdiction, the seriousness of crimes associated with transferred cases varies. As has been shown by previous research, large numbers of cases involving property crimes are transferred to criminal courts for processing. In some instances, chronic, persistent, or habitual status offenders have been transferred, particularly if they have violated specific court orders to attend school, participate in therapeutic programs, perform community service work, make restitution, or engage in some other constructive enterprise.

If waivers are to be fully effective, only those most serious offenders should be targeted for transfer. Transferring less serious and petty offenders accomplishes little in the way of enhanced punishments for these offenders. Criminal courts often regard transfers of such cases as nuisances, and it is not uncommon to see the widespread use of probation or diversion here. Criminal court prosecutors may *nolle prosequi* many of these cases before they reach the trial stage. In a significant number of other cases, plea-bargaining agreements are concluded that result in substantially more lenient penalties (Champion, 1989a; Jensen and Metsger, 1994).

Reverse Waiver Hearing

In those jurisdictions with automatic or legislative waiver provisions, juveniles and their attorneys may contest such waiver actions by using **reverse waiver hearings**. Such hearings are conducted before criminal court judges to determine whether to send the juvenile's case back to juvenile court. Reverse waiver hearings in those jurisdictions with automatic transfer provisions are also conducted in the presence of judges (Champion, 1989a; Poulos and Orchowsky, 1994; Virginia Commission on Youth, 1993). For both waiver and reverse waiver hearings, defense counsel and the prosecution attempt to make a case for their desired action. In many respects, these hearings are the equivalent of preliminary hearings or preliminary examinations conducted within the criminal justice framework. The main function of these examinations or hearings is to establish probable cause that one or more crimes were committed and that the accused probably committed those crimes. Some evidence and testimony are permitted, and arguments from both sides are heard. Once all arguments have been presented and each side has had a chance to rebut the opponents' arguments, judges decide the matter.

Time Standards Governing Waiver Decisions

Although less than 1 percent of all juveniles processed by the juvenile justice system annually are transferred to criminal courts for processing as adults, only eight states had time limits governing transfer provisions for juveniles as of 1993: Arizona, Indiana, Iowa, Maryland, Massachusetts, Michigan, Minnesota, New Mexico, and Virginia (Butts, 1996b:559). Table 6.4 shows the time limits that govern juvenile court handling of delinquency cases considered for transfer to criminal court. We can see from the table that in Maryland, for example, there is a 30-day maximum time limit between one's detention and the transfer hearing. If the transfer hearing results in a denial of the transfer, there is a 30-day maximum between the denial of the transfer and the juvenile court adjudication. In contrast, Minnesota provides only a one-day maximum between placing youths in adult jails and filing transfer motions by juvenile court prosecutors. New Mexico's provisions are similar to those of Maryland. The rest of the states not shown in this table did not have time limits for transfers or waivers by 1996.

IMPLICATIONS OF WAIVER HEARINGS FOR JUVENILES

Those juveniles who contest or fight their transfers to criminal courts or attempt to obtain a reverse waiver wish to remain within the juvenile justice system, be treated as juveniles, and be adjudicated by juvenile court judges. But not all juveniles who are the subject of transfer are eager to contest the transfer. There are several important implications for youths, depending on the nature of their offenses, their prior records, and the potential penalties the respective courts may impose. Under the right circumstances, having one's case transferred to criminal court may offer juvenile defendants considerable advantages not normally enjoyed if their cases were to remain in the juvenile court. In the following discussion, some of the major advantages and disadvantages of being transferred are examined.

TABLE 6.4

Time Limits on Juvenile Court Handling of Delinquency Cases Considered for Transfer to Criminal Court[a]

State	Limits
Arizona	• 30-day maximum between motion for transfer and transfer hearing • 30-day maximum between denial of transfer and juvenile court adjudication
Indiana	• 20-day maximum between case referral and transfer hearing if youth is detained (otherwise, 60 days maximum)
Iowa	• 40-day maximum between case referral and transfer hearing
Maryland	• 30-day maximum between time of detention and transfer hearing • 30-day maximum between denial of transfer and juvenile court adjudication
Massachusetts	• 30-day maximum between case referral and part A of transfer hearing • 45-day maximum between parts A and B of transfer hearing • 21-day maximum between denial of transfer and juvenile court adjudication if youth is detained (otherwise, 30 days maximum)
Michigan	• 28-day maximum between case referral and phase 1 of transfer hearing • 35-day maximum between case referral and phase 2 of transfer hearing • 28-day maximum between phases 1 and 2 of transfer hearing • 28-day maximum between denial of transfer and juvenile court adjudication if detained
Minnesota	• 1-day maximum between placement of youth in adult jail and filing of transfer motion
New Mexico	• 30-day maximum between motion of transfer and transfer hearing if youth is detained (otherwise, 90 days) • 30-day maximum between denial of transfer and juvenile court adjudication if youth is detained (otherwise, 90 days)
Virginia	• 21-day maximum between time of detention and *either* transfer hearing or adjudication • 30-day maximum between denial of transfer and juvenile court disposition if detained

[a]Forty-two states (and the District of Columbia) did not have time limits for transfer cases as of 1993.

Source: Butts, 1996b: 559–560. Data source: analysis by the National Center for Juvenile Justice.

Positive Benefits Resulting from Juvenile Court Adjudications

Among the positive benefits of having one's case heard in juvenile court are that:

1. Juvenile court proceedings are civil, not criminal; thus juveniles do not acquire criminal records.

2. Juveniles are less likely to receive sentences of incarceration.

3. Juvenile court judges have considerably more discretion than criminal court judges in influencing a youth's life chances prior to or at the time of adjudication.

4. Juvenile courts are traditionally more lenient than criminal courts.

5. There is considerably more public sympathy extended to those who are processed in the juvenile justice system, despite the general public advocacy for a greater get-tough policy.

6. Compared with criminal courts, juvenile courts do not have as elaborate an information-exchange apparatus to determine whether certain juveniles have been adjudicated delinquent by juvenile courts in other jurisdictions.

7. Life imprisonment and the death penalty lie beyond the jurisdiction of juvenile judges, and they cannot impose these harsh sentences.

First, since juvenile courts are civil bodies, records of juvenile adjudications are suppressed, expunged, or otherwise deleted when these adjudicated juveniles reach adulthood (Virginia Commission on Youth, 1993). Also, juvenile court judges often act compassionately, by sentencing youthful offenders to probation, or by issuing verbal warnings or reprimands, or by imposing nonincarcerative, nonfine alternatives as sanctions (Minnesota Sentencing Guidelines Commission, 1994; Podkopacz, 1994).

A fourth advantage is that juvenile courts are traditionally noted for their lenient treatment of juveniles (Rubin, 1988). This seems to be more a function of the influence of priorities in dealing with juvenile offenders rather than an immovable policy that might impose standard punishments of incarceration as penalties. For example, a national conference of juvenile justice experts in New Orleans recommended that juvenile courts emphasize three general goals in their adjudication decisions: (1) protection of the community, (2) imposing accountability, and (3) helping juveniles and equipping them to live productively and responsibly in the community (Maloney, Romig, and Armstrong, 1988). This balanced approach is largely constructive, in that it heavily emphasizes those skills that lead to the rehabilitation of youthful offenders. In the minds of many citizens, rehabilitation is equated with leniency. Increasingly used, however, are residential placement facilities in various jurisdictions, where the rate of recidivism among juveniles is relatively low compared with those offenders with more extensive histories of delinquent conduct (Feld, 1995; Florida Advisory Council on Intergovernmental Relations, 1994).

A fifth advantage of juvenile court processing is that sympathy for youths who commit offenses is easier to extend in sentencing. Many juveniles get into trouble because of sociocultural circumstances.

Individualized treatment may be necessary, perhaps administered through appropriate community-based facilities, to promote greater respect for the law as well as to provide needed services (Altschuler and Armstrong, 1992; Virginia Commission on Youth, 1994b). Mandatory diversion policies have received some public support in various jurisdictions, especially where less serious youthful offenders are involved and they are charged with nonviolent, petty crimes (Jensen and Metsger, 1994; Poulos and Orchowsky, 1994). Many of these juveniles may not require intensive supervised probation or incarceration, but rather, they require responsible supervision to guide them toward and assist them in various services and treatment-oriented agencies.

Juvenile courts do not ordinarily exchange information with most other juvenile courts in a massive national communication network. Local control over youthful offenders accomplishes only this limited objective— local control. Thus juveniles might migrate to other jurisdictions and offend repeatedly, where getting caught in those alternative jurisdictions would not be treated as recidivism in the original jurisdiction. This is beneficial for juveniles, who might seek to commit numerous offenses in a broad range of contiguous jurisdictions. The probability that their acts in one jurisdiction would come to the attention of juvenile officials in their own jurisdiction is often remote.

Furthermore, juveniles in certain jurisdictions may reappear before the same juvenile court judge frequently. Multiple adjudications for serious offenses do not mean automatically that these youths will be placed in juvenile detention or transferred to criminal court (Butts and Poe, 1993; Butts et al., 1996). Even those who reappear before the same juvenile court judge may be adjudicated repeatedly without significant effect. In one investigation it was found that a sample of serious juvenile offenders had been adjudicated in the same jurisdiction an average of 10 times (Snyder, 1988; Snyder, Sickmund and Poe-Yamagata, 1996). Thus juvenile court judges may give juveniles the "benefit of the doubt" and impose nondetention alternatives. Nondetention alternatives as sentences are influenced significantly by the degree of overcrowding in secure juvenile facilities. Thus leniency displayed by juvenile court judges may really be due to necessity rather than because of a personal belief that incarceration should be avoided.

Finally, it is beyond the jurisdiction of juvenile court judges to impose life imprisonment and/or the death penalty, despite the potential for jury trials in some juvenile court jurisdictions (Bilchik, 1996). Thus if offenders come before a juvenile court judge for processing and have committed especially aggravated violent or capital offenses, the juvenile court judge's options are limited. Incarceration in a juvenile facility, possibly for a prolonged period, is the most powerful sanction available to these judges.

However, if waiver actions are successful, the road is paved for the possible application of such punishments in criminal courts (Minnesota Sentencing Guidelines Commission, 1994; Singer, 1993).

Unfavorable Implications of Juvenile Court Adjudications

Juvenile courts are not perfect, however, and they may be disadvantageous to many youthful offenders. Some of their major limitations are that:

1. Juvenile court judges have the power to administer lengthy sentences of incarceration, not only for serious and dangerous offenders, but for status offenders as well.

2. In most states, juvenile courts are not required to provide juveniles with a trial by jury.

3. Because of their wide discretion in handling juveniles, judges may under-penalize a large number of those appearing before them on various charges.

4. Juveniles do not enjoy the same range of constitutional rights as adults in criminal courts.

On the negative side, juvenile court judges may impose on offenders as punishment, short- or long-term secure confinement in secure juvenile facilities, regardless of the nonseriousness or pettiness of their offenses. The case of *In re Gault* (1967) involved a 15-year-old, Gerald Gault, who was sentenced to nearly six years in the Arizona State Industrial School for making an obscene telephone call to a female neighbor. This sentence was arbitrarily imposed on Gault by the presiding juvenile court judge. For committing the same offense, an adult would have been fined $50 and may have served up to 30 days in a local jail. In Gault's case, the sentence was excessive and there were constitutional irregularities. This unusual incarcerative sentence was subsequently overturned by the U.S. Supreme Court on several important constitutional grounds. However, juvenile court judges continue to have broad discretionary powers and may impose similar sentences, provided that the constitutional guarantees assured by the *Gault* decision are present in any subsequent case.

The case of *Gault* is not an isolated instance of disposing of youths who have committed petty offenses with long periods of secure confinement. For instance, in Hennepin County, Minnesota, 330 transfer motions between 1986 and 1992 were studied by Podkopacz and Feld (1996). These researchers found that when juveniles were transferred to criminal courts for various crimes, those charged with violent offenses tended to serve longer prison terms than the periods of incarceration imposed on juveniles who committed the same types of offenses, but who had their cases adjudicated in juvenile courts. However, juvenile court judges typically imposed *longer* incarcerative sentences on property offenders compared with how criminal courts sentenced convicted juvenile property offenders who had been transferred to criminal court jurisdiction. Thus Podkopacz and Feld question existing juvenile court policies about the nature and types of dispositions imposed on adjudicated juvenile offenders. Presently, there is great diversity among juvenile court judges in different states about the nature and types of dispositions they impose on juveniles adjudicated for similar offenses.

Another disadvantage of juvenile courts is that granting any juvenile a jury trial is mostly the discretion of prosecutors and juvenile court judges (Table 6.5). If the judge approves, the juvenile may receive a jury trial in selected jurisdictions if a jury trial is requested. This practice typifies juvenile courts in 38 states. In the remaining states, juveniles may request and receive trials under certain circumstances. In other words, the state legislatures of at least 12 states have made it possible for juveniles to receive jury trials upon request, although the circumstances for such jury trial requests parallel closely the jury trial requests of defendants in criminal courts. Again, we must consider the civil–criminal distinction that adheres, respectively, to juvenile and criminal court proceedings. Jury trials in juvenile courts retain the civil connotation, without juveniles acquiring criminal records. However, jury trials in adult criminal courts, upon the defendant's conviction, result in the offender's acquisition of a criminal record.

A third limitation of juvenile proceedings is that the wide discretion enjoyed by most juvenile court judges is often abused (Florida Advisory Council on Intergovernmental Relations, 1994; Virginia Commission on Youth, 1994a). This abuse is largely in the form of excessive leniency, and it does not occur exclusively at the adjudicatory stage of juvenile processing. Earlier, during intake, many cases are resolved, diverted, or dismissed without a formal petition being filed for a subsequent adjudication. One investigator, Belinda McCarthy, has reported that in Maricopa County, Arizona near Phoenix, 17,773 juvenile delinquents who were born between 1962 and 1965 were tracked and determined to have committed over 76,000 delinquent acts (McCarthy, 1989). Nearly 90 percent of these juveniles under age 16 who were referred to juvenile court had their cases informally adjusted or dismissed at the intake stage. Furthermore, although more serious violent crime cases were more likely to result in incarceration than other offenses, the most frequent disposition was probation. A majority of those who had committed robbery, aggravated assault, and burglary recidivated within two years of their original adjudications for these offenses (McCarthy, 1989). Because of this leniency and wide discretion, real or imagined, many juvenile courts have drawn criticisms over the years from the public and professionals alike. A common criticism is that juvenile

TABLE 6.5

Interstate Variation in Jury Trials for Juveniles, 1988

Provision	States
Jury trial granted upon request by juvenile	Alaska, California, Kansas, Massachusetts, Michigan, Minnesota, New Mexico, Oklahoma, Texas, West Virginia, Wisconsin, Wyoming
Juvenile denied right to trial by jury	Alabama, Florida, Georgia, Hawaii, Indiana, Iowa, Louisiana, Maine, Maryland, Mississippi, Nebraska, Nevada, New Jersey, North Carolina, North Dakota, Ohio, Oregon, Pennsylvania, South Carolina, Tennessee, Utah, Vermont, Washington
No mention	Alaska, Arizona, California, Connecticut, Colorado, Idaho, Illinois, Missouri, New Hampshire, New Mexico, New York, Virginia
By court order	South Dakota

Source: Katherine M. Jamieson and Timothy J. Flanagan (eds.), *Source of Criminal Justice Statistics—1988* (Washington, DC: U.S. Department of Justice, 1989), pp. 156–157.

courts neglect the accountability issue through the excessive use of probation or diversion (Bilchik, 1996; Snyder and Sickmund, 1995).

Another major criticism of these courts is that juveniles do not enjoy the full range of constitutional rights that apply to their adult counterparts in criminal courts (Feld, 1993a,c, 1995; Sanborn, 1994a,b). In many jurisdictions, transcripts of proceedings are not made or retained for juveniles where serious charges are alleged unless special arrangements are made beforehand. Thus when juveniles in these jurisdictions appeal their adjudications to higher courts, they may or may not have the written record to rely on while attempting appellate authority to override the juvenile court judge's sentence.

DEFENSE AND PROSECUTORIAL CONSIDERATIONS RELATING TO WAIVERS

Juvenile Trial Options: Interstate Variations

As we have seen, juveniles are only infrequently given a jury trial if their cases are adjudicated by juvenile courts. In 1988, for instance, 12 states provided jury trials for juveniles in juvenile courts if juveniles made such requests and the allegations carried possible incarcerative penalties. Also, in 1988, in 23 other states, juveniles were denied the right to a jury trial. In the remaining states, with the exception of South Dakota, no mention was made of whether juveniles were entitled to jury trials. It is presumed that in these jurisdictions, at least, the sole authority granting jury trial privileges is the juvenile court judge. In South Dakota, a court order is required for a jury trial to be conducted in juvenile court (Maguire and Pastore, 1996). Table 6.5 shows the states that provided jury trials for juveniles in 1988.

Implications of Criminal Court Processing

When juveniles are transferred, waived, or certified to criminal court, all rules and constitutional guarantees attach for them as well as for adults. We have already examined the advantages of permitting or petitioning the juvenile court to retain jurisdiction in certain cases. An absence of a criminal record, limited punishments, extensive leniency, and a greater variety of discretionary options on the part of juvenile court judges make juvenile courts an attractive adjudicatory medium if the juvenile has a choice. Of course, even if the crimes alleged are serious, leniency may assume the form of a dismissal of charges, charge reductions, warnings, and other nonadjudicatory penalties.

The primary implications for juveniles of being processed through the criminal justice system are several, and they are quite important. First, depending on the seriousness of the offenses alleged, a jury trial may be a matter of right. Second, periods of lengthy incarceration in minimum, medium, and maximum security facilities with adults becomes a real possibility. Third, criminal courts in a majority of state jurisdictions may impose the death penalty in capital cases. A sensitive subject with most citizens is whether juveniles should receive the death penalty if convicted of capital crimes. In recent years, the U.S. Supreme Court has addressed this issue specifically and ruled that in those states where the death penalty is imposed, the death penalty may be imposed as a punishment on any juvenile who was age 16 or older at the time the capital offense was committed (*Stanford v. Kentucky*, 1989; *Wilkins v. Missouri*, 1989).

Jury Trials as a Matter of Right for Serious Offenses

A primary benefit of a transfer to criminal court is the absolute right to a jury trial. This is conditional, however, and depends on the minimum incarcerative period associated with one or more criminal charges filed against defendants. In only 12 state jurisdictions, juveniles have a jury trial right granted through legislative action (Mahoney, 1985). However, when juveniles reach criminal courts, certain constitutional provisions apply to them as well as to adults. First, anyone charged with a crime where the possible sentence is six months' incarceration or more, with exceptions, is entitled to a jury trial if one is requested (*Baldwin v. New York*, 1970). Therefore, jury trials are not discretionary matters for judges to decide. Any defendant who *may be* subject to six months or more in jail or prison on the basis of the prescribed statutory punishment associated with the criminal offenses alleged may request and receive a jury trial from any U.S. judge, in either state or federal courts.

Juveniles who are charged with particularly serious crimes where several aggravating circumstances are apparent stand a good chance of receiving unfavorable treatment from juries. Aggravating circumstances include a victim's death or the infliction of serious bodily injuries, committing an offense while on bail for another offense or on probation or parole, use of extreme

---

BOX 6.2   MAN INHERITS MILLIONS FROM PARENTS AFTER KILLING THEM

The Case of William Rouse

It happened in Waukegan, Illinois. On June 6, 1980, Bruce and Darlene Rouse were shot to death in the bedroom of their mansion in a fashionable part of Waukegan. Initially, police suspected that one or more unknown robbers had entered the Rouse home with the intent of burglarizing it. They theorized that the couple had interrupted the burglary and were killed to prevent them from identifying the robbers.

At the time of the murder, William Rouse was their 15-year-old son who was living on the premises with his younger sister and older brother. None of the children seemed to know what had happened. After an extensive investigation, the murders were classified as "unsolved." William Rouse and his siblings inherited the family fortune, which included several million dollars. The $2 million estate was established from the father's business chain of gas stations.

After Rouse had squandered his portion of the $2 million, he moved to Florida. He lived on a houseboat in Key West, where he committed robberies from time to time to maintain his lavish lifestyle. When Florida police officers apprehended Rouse for robbery, he also gave them a confession concerning his part in his parents' death in 1980. He described to police how he had argued with his parents over drugs and that he had become angry with them. After a violent confrontation with his parents over his suspected drug use, where his mother threatened to send him to military school, he got a gun and shot them. He gave a full videotaped confession and was extradited to Illinois, where he would be tried on the double-murder charges.

What is the statute of limitations on murder? What do you think William Rouse should receive as punishment for the double murder?

Source: Adapted from Associated Press, "Man Convicted of Killing Parents," *Minot (ND) Daily News*, August 11, 1996:A2.

cruelty in the commission of the crime, use of a dangerous weapon in the commission of a crime, a prior record, and leadership in the commission of offenses alleged. However, mitigating circumstances, those factors that tend to lessen the severity of sentencing, include duress or extreme provocation, mental incapacitation, motivation to provide necessities, youthfulness or old age, and no previous criminal record (Virginia Commission on Youth, 1993).

What criteria persuade juries to decide cases in particular ways? No one knows. Although some evidence exists to show the influence of race and gender on jury decision making, it is inconsistent and inconclusive (Leiber, 1995; U.S. General Accounting Office, 1995a). Impressions gleaned from various surveys of U.S. citizens suggest that very young or very old age might function favorably to reduce sentencing severity in jury trials, however. Thus youthfulness itself is an inherent mitigating factor in almost every criminal courtroom.

Among the several aggravating and mitigating circumstances listed above, having a prior record or not having one becomes an important consideration. Youths who are transferred to criminal courts sometimes do not have previous criminal records. This does not mean that they *have not* committed earlier crimes, but rather, that their records are **juvenile court records**. Juveniles may have **sustained petitions**, where the facts alleged against them have been determined to be true by the juvenile court judge. However, this adjudication hearing is a civil proceeding. As such, technically, these youths do not bring prior criminal records into the criminal courtroom. This is a favorable factor for juveniles to consider when deciding whether to challenge transfers or have their automatic waivers reversed. However, recent changes in state laws regarding the confidentiality of juvenile court records have been made so that greater access to such records is available to others, and for longer periods beyond one's adulthood (Bilchik, 1996). Increasingly, one's juvenile past may affect one's criminal court trial outcome and sentencing.

Another important factor relative to having access to a jury trial is that prosecutors often try to avoid them, opting for a simple plea bargain agreement instead (McDonald, 1985). Plea bargaining or plea negotiating is a preconviction bargain between the state and the defendant where the defendant enters a guilty plea in exchange for leniency in the form of reduced charges or less harsh treatment at the time of sentencing (Sanborn, 1993). Plea bargaining in the United States accounts for approximately 90 percent of all criminal convictions (Champion, 1988, 1989b).

Jury trials are costly and the results of jury deliberations are unpredictable. If prosecutors can obtain guilty pleas from transferred juveniles, they assist the state and themselves, both in terms of the costs of prosecution and avoidance of jury whims in youthful offender cases. Also, plea bargaining in transferred juvenile cases often results in convictions on lesser charges, specifically charges that would not have prompted the transfer or waiver from juvenile courts initially (Dougherty, 1988; Mershon, 1991; Sanborn, 1993). However, this is a bit ironic, since it suggests that the criminal justice system is inadvertently sabotaging the primary purpose of juvenile transfers through plea bargaining arrangements that are otherwise commonplace for adult criminals.

Furthermore, when prosecutors decide to file charges, sufficient evidence should exist to increase the chances of a successful prosecution. Also, the charges alleged should be serious. But many transferred juveniles are not necessarily the most serious youthful offenders, and the standard of evidence in juvenile courts is sometimes not as rigorous as it is in criminal courts. Thus, many transferred juvenile cases fail from the outset and are dismissed by the prosecutors themselves, often because of inadequate or poor evidence.

Closely associated with prosecutorial reluctance to prosecute many of these transferred juveniles is the fact that a majority of those transferred are charged with property crimes (Bilchik, 1996). Although these cases may stand out from other cases coming before juvenile court judges, prosecutors and criminal court judges might regard them as insignificant. Thus juveniles enter the adult system from juvenile courts, where their offenses set them apart from most other juvenile offenders. But alongside adults in criminal courts, they become one of many property offenders who face criminal processing. Their youthful age works in their behalf to improve the chances of having their cases dismissed or of being acquitted by juries. Most prosecutors wish to reserve jury trials for only the most serious offenders. Therefore, their general inclination is to treat youthful property offenders with greater leniency, unless they elect to *nolle prosequi* outright.

Incarceration

Arguing that it is cheaper to build more prisons than it is to tolerate a growing crime rate, van den Haag (1986) advocates blanket punishment of juveniles in criminal courts, where those juveniles have committed crimes, since it is cheaper in the long run to build more prisons than to tolerate a growing crime rate. Van den Haag advocates the abolition of parole. However, many experts believe that the confinement for juveniles is overused (Polhill et al., 1994; Virginia Commission on Youth, 1994b). Further, juveniles who are incarcerated in prisons together with adults are more frequently victimized by other prisoners than those juveniles who are remanded to secure juvenile facilities (Forst, Fagan, and Vivona, 1989).

There is strong public sentiment for keeping most juveniles away from adult prisons and jails, because such facilities are less well equipped to meet juvenile offender needs, and also because a greater range of community-based services exists for juveniles diverted or placed on probation in their respective communities (Forst, 1995; McCarthy and McCarthy, 1997). An offsetting argument is made for preserving incarceration as a punishment, in part because of the intensified fear of apprehension and punishment among juveniles that may tend to "suppress" their propensity to engage in juvenile crime (Fraser and Norman, 1988). This particular view lacks empirical support, however.

The number of incarcerated offenders under age 18 in state and federal prisons is relatively small, accounting for less than 1 percent of all inmates in 1995 (Maguire and Pastore, 1996). Thus the actual amount of incarceration in adult facilities imposed on juveniles processed by criminal courts is not particularly significant. At the same time, there has been a gradual increase in the numbers of juveniles detained for short- or long-term periods in secure juvenile facilities (American Correctional Association, 1996). This suggests a hydraulic effect, where juvenile populations are gradually being reduced within adult institutions, but also where increasing numbers of juveniles are being detained in secure facilities for youths. Thus the place, rather than the rate, of juvenile incarcerations is changing gradually. Regardless of how few youths are imprisoned in adult facilities, however, the *fact* of such incarcerations is troubling to more than a few citizens (Feld, 1995; Polhill et al., 1994).

For many juveniles who reach criminal courts, the possibility of incarceration is real. Many states currently employ presumptive or determinate sentencing guidelines that establish standard punishments for all criminal offenses (Champion, 1996; Feld, 1995). While judges in those jurisdictions have some latitude in varying the amount of incarceration, some incarceration must be imposed, especially for those convicted of serious crimes. Of course, age is a mitigating factor for convicted juveniles. Judges may tend to select the low end of the punishment range rather than the high end when sentencing convicted youths. With some exceptions, the average length of incarceration for juveniles convicted in adult courts is relatively short compared with their adult counterparts convicted of similar offenses (Maguire and Pastore, 1996). Furthermore, this average length of incarceration is no longer or greater than that which these affected juveniles would have received if adjudicated and sentenced to a secure juvenile facility by a juvenile court judge (Maguire and Pastore, 1996). These grounds alone are sufficient to challenge the get-tough policy of contemporary juvenile courts and the value of certifications or waivers to criminal courts.

The Potential for Capital Punishment

The most important implication for juveniles transferred to criminal courts is the potential imposition of the **death penalty** on their conviction for a capital crime. About two-thirds of the states use **capital punishment** for prescribed offenses that are especially aggravated. The methods of execution in those states that authorize the death penalty include lethal injection, electrocution, lethal gas, hanging, and firing squad (Camp and Camp, 1996:40). At the beginning of 1996, there were 3099 prisoners under sentence of death in U.S. prisons. Ninety-nine percent of these were males. There were 269 death row inmates age 19 or younger, which accounted for about 11 percent of all death row inmates (Stephan and Snell, 1996:8).

While the death penalty has long been accepted as a constitutional means to "redress grossly unacceptable antisocial behavior" (Smith, 1986), it was temporarily suspended (but not prohibited) in 1972 as the result of the *Furman v. Georgia* decision. This decision by the U.S. Supreme Court criticized the racially discriminatory and arbitrary nature of the death penalty as it was currently being applied in Georgia. For example, many blacks in Georgia were being executed for crimes of rape and robbery, whereas white offenders convicted of similar crimes received terms of 10 or 15 years rather than death. No provisions existed for Georgia juries to consider aggravating and mitigating circumstances associated with these capital offenses. Subsequently, Georgia statutes were changed to comply with the U.S. Supreme Court decision in the case of *Gregg v. Georgia* (1976). A major change in Georgia criminal procedure was the establishment of the bifurcated trial. A bifurcated trial is a two-stage proceeding, with guilt being decided in the trial phase and the punishment decided in the second phase. Currently, the two-phase nature of jury deliberations permits jurors to consider any especially aggravating or mitigating circumstances before deciding whether to impose the death penalty.

An alternative to the death penalty applied to juveniles is the life-without-parole option. In 1996, 40 states had **life-without-parole provisions** for capital murder statutes, including aggravated homicide, as well as for habitual or career offenders (Camp and Camp, 1996:42).

WAIVER PATTERNS AND TRENDS

Probably the most significant change in waiver patterns throughout the United States is that between 1992 and 1996, all but 10 states had adopted or modified laws making it *easier* to prosecute juveniles as adults in criminal courts (Bilchik, 1996:3). Some of the reasons suggested for this tougher stance toward juvenile offending are that (1) juvenile rehabilitation has not been particularly effective at deterring juveniles from further offending, and (2) that the juvenile justice system is simply not punitive enough to impose the nature and types of punishments deserved by an increasingly violent juvenile offender population (Bilchik, 1996:3). The major ways of making juveniles more amenable to criminal court punishment are (1) to lower the age at which they can be processed by criminal courts as adults, (2) to expand the number of crimes that qualify juvenile offenders as adults for criminal court action, and (3) to lower the age at which juveniles can be transferred to criminal courts for various offenses.

Increasing the frequency with which juveniles are waived to criminal courts means that transferred juveniles will be exposed to a broader range of punishments than could be imposed by juvenile courts. While the death penalty is the ultimate punishment for capital offenses in a majority of states in criminal courts, such a penalty is beyond the jurisdiction of juvenile courts. Once juveniles have been transferred, it does not mean that they will be prosecuted automatically. Furthermore, being transferred does

---

BOX 6.3   WHAT PRICE LIFE?

The Case of the Life-or-Death Locket

Dr. Haing S. Ngor was a 55-year-old Cambodian actor living in Los Angeles. Dr. Ngor had acted in the movie *The Killing Fields* and had won an Oscar for his performance. He was found dead in his driveway near his BMW on a Los Angeles street on February 25, 1996. His wallet, containing $3000 in cash, was untouched. However, his Rolex watch and gold chain were missing, sources said.

Suspected were members of an Asian gang known as the Oriental Lazyboys, a Chinatown-based gang specializing in home-invasion robberies and carjackings. The case was tentatively solved when an informant apprehended for another offense gave incriminating information to police about Dr. Ngor's death. It seemed that at least three gang members approached Dr. Ngor while he was about to enter his vehicle one evening and demanded that he turn over his gold chain and watch to them. He refused and one of the boys shot him at point-blank range.

The youths arrested included the suspected shooter, Tak Sun Tan, 19, and two other gang members, Jason Chan, 18, and Indra Lim, 19. The latter two youths were arrested earlier in connection with a robbery unrelated to Ngor's death. Their information provided to police led to the arrest of Tan. If convicted, Tan and his gang associates would face the death penalty.

How should the police deal with gangs? Is gang violence escalating? What sorts of punishments or interventions ought to be applied to deal most effectively with gang activities in cities such as Los Angeles?

Source: Adapted from Associated Press, "Was Ngor Slain over a Locket?" *Minot (ND) Daily News*, April 24, 1996:A2; Associated Press, "Men Charged with Killing Ngor," *Minot (ND) Daily News*, April 27, 1996:A2.

not mean that more severe punishments will be imposed, although this is the intended function of waivers.

Little is known about what happens to juveniles once they have been transferred to adult courts. A study of the final dispositions of transfers of juveniles in selected counties in four southern states for the years 1980–1988 is consistent with subsequent findings of other investigators (Champion, 1989a; Minnesota Sentencing Guidelines Commission, 1994; Virginia Commission on Youth, 1994b; Snyder, Sickmund, and Poe-Yamagata, 1996). For instance, out of 3424 transfer hearings during 1980–1988, 2818 (82 percent) resulted in waivers. However, the proportion of property offenders in these successful waiver hearings increased over the years from 19 percent to about 50 percent. In 1996 about 58 percent of all transferred juveniles involved property crimes, drug charges, or public order offenses. Only 42 percent of those transferred were charged with a serious or violent offense (Bilchik, 1996:13).

These findings suggest that at least in these jurisdictions, juveniles are not receiving harsher penalties, on the average, when transferred to criminal courts for a broad range of offenses. As Rubin (1985:26) suggests, these waivers appear to be cosmetic, primarily public-placating "escape valves" used to rid juvenile courts of chronic recidivists, largely property offenders. Automatic transfer laws in various states such as Florida, Illinois, and New York seem to be having the desired effect, however, although there is an inconsistent pattern that has developed.

Early research investigating the outcomes of juvenile transfers to criminal courts showed that in at least one jurisdiction, of 1817 successful waivers studied by year end 1983, 33 percent of these cases resulted in incarcerative terms no longer than would have been levied in family or juvenile courts had transfers not been initiated (Schack and Nessen, 1984). A study by Reed (1983) of 346 transfers from 1975 to 1981 also showed that while most of those transfers involved serious crimes (e.g., murder, rape, robbery), 66 percent were either dropped, led to acquittals, or were plea bargained to lesser charges. Singer's (1985) investigation of transfers in New York State also showed greater use of probation and shorter incarcerative sentences for those juveniles transferred to criminal court. Thus, these so-called tough new laws are not as tough as they appear.

In view of the types of cases that eventually reach criminal courts for disposition and how those cases are ultimately concluded, it would seem that juvenile court prosecutors and judges would be highly selective in the cases they designate for waiver. Ideally, those cases selected for waiver or transfer would be only the most serious cases, where the charges pending against juveniles would consist primarily of violent crimes such as homicide, rape, robbery, and aggravated assault. In at least a few jurisdictions, it seems to work this way. An early 1984 New Jersey survey of juvenile cases waived by the prosecutor to adult courts, for instance, showed that prosecutors' motions for waiver generally involved violent crimes (New Jersey Division of Criminal Justice, 1985). Of those cases waived, the majority resulted in guilty pleas through plea bargaining. Of those cases that went to trial, over 70 percent resulted in guilty verdicts, with 95 percent of these involving incarcerative terms (New Jersey Division of Criminal Justice, 1985). Unfortunately, these findings are exceptions rather than the rule.

Trend Toward Blended Sentencing Statutes

Barry Feld (1995) observes that in recent years, many states have legislatively redefined the juvenile court's purpose and role by diminishing the role of rehabilitation and heightening the importance of public safety, punishment, and accountability in the juvenile justice system. One of the most dramatic changes in the dispositional and sentencing options available to juvenile court judges is **blended sentencing**. *Blended sentencing refers to the imposition of juvenile and/or adult correctional sanctions to cases involving serious and violent juvenile offenders who have been adjudicated in juvenile court or convicted in criminal court. Blended sentencing options are usually based on age or on a combination of age and offense* (Bilchik, 1996:11). Figure 6.4 shows the five basic models of blended sentencing: (1) juvenile–exclusive, (2) juvenile–inclusive, (3) juvenile–contiguous, (4) criminal–exclusive, and (5) criminal–inclusive.

1. *The **juvenile–exclusive blend** involves a disposition by the juvenile court judge that is either a disposition to the juvenile correctional system or to the adult correctional system, but not both.* Thus a judge might order a juvenile adjudicated delinquent for aggravated assault to serve three years in a juvenile industrial school; or the judge may order the adjudicated delinquent to serve three years in a prison for adults. The judge cannot impose *both* types of punishment under this model, however. In 1996, only one state, New Mexico, provided such a sentencing option for its juvenile court judges.

2. *The **juvenile–inclusive blend** involves a disposition by the juvenile court judge that is both a juvenile correctional sanction and an adult correctional sanction.* In cases such as this, suppose that the judge had adjudicated a 15-year-old juvenile delinquent on a charge of vehicular theft. The judge might impose a disposition of two years in a juvenile industrial school or reform school. Further, the judge might impose a sentence of three additional years in an adult penitentiary. However, the second sentence to the adult prison would typically be suspended unless the juvenile violated one or more conditions of his or her original disposition and any conditions accompanying the disposition.

FIGURE 6.4 Models of Blended Sentencing

Court	Type of Sanction	Description	Examples
Juvenile Court → or → Juvenile / Adult		*Juvenile–Exclusive Blend:* The juvenile court has original jurisdiction and responsibility for adjudication of the case. The juvenile court has the authority to impose a sanction involving either the juvenile or adult correctional systems.	New Mexico
Juvenile Court → and → Juvenile / Adult		*Juvenile–Inclusive Blend:* The juvenile court has original jurisdiction and responsibility for adjudication of the case. The juvenile court has the authority to impose a sanction involving both the juvenile and adult correctional systems. In most instances, the adult sanction is suspended unless there is a violation, at which point it is invoked.	Connecticut Minnesota Montana
Juvenile Court — Juvenile △ Adult		*Juvenile–Contiguous:* The juvenile court has original jurisdiction and responsibility for adjudication of the case. The juvenile court has the authority to impose a sanction that would be in force beyond the age of its extended jurisdiction. At that point, various procedures are invoked to determine if the remainder of that sanction should be imposed in the adult correctional system.	Colorado (1) Massachusetts Rhode Island South Carolina Texas
Criminal Court → or → Juvenile / Adult		*Criminal–Exclusive Blend:* The criminal court tries the case. The criminal court has the authority to impose a sanction involving either the juvenile or adult correctional systems.	California Colorado (2) Florida Idaho Michigan Virginia
Criminal Court → and → Juvenile / Adult		*Criminal–Inclusive Blend:* The criminal court tries the case. The criminal court has the authority to impose a sanction involving both the juvenile and adult correctional systems. In most instances, the adult sanction is suspended unless there is a violation, at which point it is invoked.	Arkansas Missouri

©1996, National Center for Juvenile Justice, 710 Fifth Avenue, Pittsurgh, PA 15219.

Usually, this suspension period would run until the youth reaches age 18 or 21. If the offender were to commit a new offense or violate one or more program conditions, he or she would immediately be placed in the adult prison to serve the second sentence originally imposed.

3. The **juvenile–contiguous blend** *involves a disposition by a juvenile court judge that may extend beyond the jurisdictional age limit of the offender. When the age limit of the juvenile court jurisdiction is reached, various procedures may be invoked to transfer the case to the jurisdiction of adult corrections.* States with this juvenile–contiguous blend include Colorado, Massachusetts, Rhode Island, South Carolina, and Texas. In Texas, for example, a 15-year-old youth who has been adjudicated delinquent on a murder charge can be given an incarcerative term of from 1 to 30 years. At the time of the disposition in juvenile court, the youth is sent to the Texas Youth Commission and incarcerated in one of its facilities (similar to reform or industrial schools). By the time the youth reaches age 17½, the juvenile court must hold a transfer hearing to determine whether the youth should be sent to the Texas Department of Corrections. At this hearing, the youth may present evidence in his or her favor to show why he or she has become rehabilitated and no longer should be confined. However, evidence of institutional misconduct may be presented by the prosecutor to show why the youth should be incarcerated for more years in a Texas prison. This hearing functions as an incentive for the youth to behave and try to improve his or her behavior while confined in the juvenile facility. Some experts believe that this particular sentencing blend is the most effective at punishing serious and violent offenders while providing them with a final chance to access certain provided Texas rehabilitative programs (Dawson, 1995).

On February 16, 1997 a 12-year-old Austin, Texas girl was convicted and sentenced by a juvenile court judge to 25 years of imprisonment. She had beaten a 2½-year-old toddler, Jayla Belton, to death in her grandmother's unlicensed day care center. In May 1996 she had been found guilty of the toddler's murder and given a 40-year sentence. Her first conviction was thrown out, however, since the court found that she was not adequately defended. In her first conviction when she was 11, the girl could have been released by age 16 or transferred to an adult prison, where she would serve out the remaining years of her original sentence. Prosecutors said that the girl kicked and beat Jayla Belton because she was angry about being left to baby-sit the toddler. The child died of a ruptured liver. In the sentencing scheme used by the judge, the girl's case would be reviewed before she became an adult. If her conduct while confined as a juvenile is poor, there is a good likelihood that the results of a hearing will result in the girl being transferred to the Texas Department of Corrections to serve more time for her crime as an adult (Associated Press, 1997:A2).

4. The **criminal–exclusive blend** *involves a decision by a criminal court judge to impose either a juvenile court sanction or a criminal court sanction, but not both.* For example, a criminal court judge may hear the case of a 15-year-old youth who has been transferred to criminal court on a rape charge. The youth is convicted in a jury trial in criminal court. At this point, the judge has two options: The

judge can sentence the offender to a prison term in an adult correctional facility, or the judge can impose an incarcerative sentence for the youth to serve in a juvenile facility. The judge may believe that the 15-year-old would be better off in a juvenile industrial school rather than an adult prison. The judge may impose a sentence of adult incarceration, but he or she may be inclined to place the youth in a facility where there are other youths in the offender's age range.

5. The **criminal–inclusive blend** *involves a decision by the criminal court judge to impose both a juvenile penalty and a criminal sentence simultaneously.* Again, as in the juvenile court–inclusive blend model, the latter criminal sentence may be suspended depending on the good conduct of the juvenile during the juvenile punishment phase. For example, suppose that a 13-year-old boy has been convicted of attempted murder. The boy participated in a drive-by shooting and is a gang member. The criminal court judge sentences the youth to a term of five years in a juvenile facility, such as an industrial school. At the same time, the judge imposes a sentence of 20 years on the youth to be spent in an adult correctional facility following the five-year sentence in the juvenile facility. However, the adult portion of the sentence may be suspended, depending on whether the juvenile behaves or misbehaves during his five-year industrial school incarceration. There is an additional twist to this blend. If the juvenile violates one or more conditions of his confinement in the juvenile facility, the judge has the power to revoke that sentence and invoke the sentence of incarceration in an adult facility. Thus a powerful incentive is provided for the youth to show evidence that rehabilitation has occurred. It is to the youth's advantage to behave well while confined, since a more ominous sentence of confinement with adult offenders may be imposed at any time. Further, with good behavior, the youth can be free of the system following the period of juvenile confinement; the adult portion of the sentence is suspended if the youth deserves such leniency. One state that has the revocation power and ability to place youths in adult correctional facilities is Arkansas, although this power is rarely used by criminal court judges (Bilchik, 1996:14).

These statutes are intended to provide both juvenile and criminal court judges with a greater range of dispositional and/or sentencing options. In the 1980s and earlier, juvenile courts were notoriously lenient on juvenile offenders. Dispositions of juvenile court judges were mostly nominal or conditional, which usually meant verbal warnings and/or probation. While probation continues to be the sanction of choice in a majority of juvenile courts following delinquency adjudications, many states have armed their juvenile and criminal court judges with greater sanctioning powers. Thus, it is now possible in states such as Colorado, Arkansas, Missouri, and selected other jurisdictions for juvenile court judges to impose sanctions that extend well beyond their original jurisdictional authority. Juvenile court judges in New Mexico, for instance, can place certain juveniles in either adult or juvenile correctional facilities. Criminal court judges in Florida, Idaho, Michigan, or Missouri can place those convicted of crimes in either juvenile or adult correctional facilities, depending on the jurisdiction. These are broader and more powerful dispositional and sentencing options to hold youthful offenders more accountable for the serious offenses they commit.

Several important trends are indicative of the public's response to violent juvenile offending and the previous laxity demonstrated by juvenile and criminal courts in dealing with youthful offenders sent there for punishment. The absence of punishment was conspicuous, and it was widely known throughout the delinquent community that very little would happen to youths if they were caught by police for crimes they committed. But changing the statutes governing the confidentiality of juvenile records, making these records more accessible to the public and media, lowering the age of one's majority and the age at which transfers to criminal court or certifications can occur are all a part of a general get-tough movement designed to deter youthful offenders from committing serious offenses. However, the fact that only 42 percent of those transferred to criminal court in 1993 were violent or person offenders, coupled with the fact that only about 10 to 15 percent of those who are transferred will ever do time in either a juvenile or adult correctional facility, do little to promote fear and discourage juvenile violence. In later chapters we examine prosecutorial discretion and describe various alternative sanctions imposed on youthful offenders. We will also investigate the range of rights presently available to juveniles and the implications of these rights for their juvenile or criminal court chances.

KEY TERMS

Blended sentencing

Capital punishment

Certifications

Concurrent jurisdiction

Criminal–exclusive blend

Criminal–inclusive blend

Death penalty

Demand waivers

Direct file

Discretionary waivers

Judicial/discretionary waivers

Juvenile–contiguous blend

Juvenile court record

Juvenile–exclusive blend

Juvenile–inclusive blend

Legislative (automatic) waivers

Life-without-parole provisions

Nolle prosequi

Once waived/always waived provision

Placed

Placement

Presumptive waiver provisions

Statutory exclusion

Sustained petition

Waiver hearings

Waiver motion

QUESTIONS FOR REVIEW

1. What is a *waiver*? What other terms may be used interchangeably with this word? What is the purpose of a waiver?

2. What is a *waiver hearing*? Are all youths who are designated for waivers entitled to a hearing? What landmark case can you discuss briefly that pertains to waivers?

3. What is the nature of the mixed message sent to juvenile courts in West Virginia by its Supreme Court of Criminal Appeals?

4. What are *blended sentencing* statutes? Give four examples.

5. Distinguish among four kinds of waivers. In each case, describe the waiver action and who initiates it.

6. How does judicial discretion influence waiver actions? What appears to be the degree of subjectivity that is supposedly inherent in such waiver decisions by judges? What evidence is there that might support charges of bias in judicial discretion in certain judicial waiver actions?

7. What is a *reverse waiver hearing*, and what are its purposes?

8. Briefly compare and contrast the positive and negative effects for juveniles of having their cases adjudicated in juvenile courts.

9. Outline the favorable consequences possibly accruing to juveniles whenever their cases are heard in criminal courts rather than in juvenile courts.

10. Under what circumstances are youths entitled to a jury trial in juvenile courts, as a matter of right? What is criminal court policy relating to jury trials for criminals? What U.S. Supreme Court case is relevant here, and what did it prescribe?

SUGGESTED READINGS

Crippen, Gary. *Making the System Work: Courts as Agents of Accountability in Family and Juvenile Cases.* Philadelphia: Center for the Study of Youth Policy, University of Pennsylvania, 1993.

Forst, Martin L. (ed.). *The New Juvenile Justice.* Chicago: Nelson-Hall, 1995.

McGough, Lucy S. *Fragile Voices in the American Legal System.* New Haven, CT: Yale University Press, 1994.

Virginia Commission on Youth. *Report of the Virginia Commission on Youth on the Study of Serious Juvenile Offenders.* Richmond, VA: Virginia Commission on Youth, 1994.

Virginia Commission on Youth. *The Study of the Feasibility of Mandatory Monitoring of Juvenile Sex Offenders.* Richmond, VA: Virginia Commission on Youth, 1994.

CHAPTER 7

PROSECUTORIAL DECISION MAKING IN JUVENILE JUSTICE

INTRODUCTION

Although juvenile courts are primarily low-profile proceedings and civil in nature, they have become increasingly adversarial during the 1980s and 1990s. This means that the presence of defense attorneys and prosecuting attorneys is presently commonplace, and the differences between criminal courts and juvenile courts are rapidly diminishing (Feld, 1993a,b). Juvenile courts continue to retain many of their historical antecedents, however. Accordingly, much of what prosecutors and judges do is influenced by these antecedents, including the pervasive doctrine of *parens patriae*, although contemporary reforms have included many new and contrasting priorities. In this chapter we continue to examine the roles of prosecutors and defense attorneys and how these roles have taken on new significance in recent decades.

In the first section we review briefly some of the highlights of the historical evolution of the juvenile court and its original conception. The influence of tradition, of *parens patriae*, on juvenile justice procedures remains strong. However, both prosecutors and defense attorneys alike are having to adjust their thinking about how juveniles are presently treated in the aftermath of numerous juvenile justice reforms. New juvenile laws are being enacted in most jurisdictions, and assorted legal bodies, such as the American Bar Association and the American Law Institute, are undertaking the complicated tasks of formulating revised juvenile model procedural and penal codes.

The prosecutorial role is taking on greater significance commensurate with the more limited role and jurisdiction of juvenile court judges. As is the case in the criminal justice system in response to get tough criminal justice reforms, many of the juvenile reforms that have occurred in recent decades have shifted much of the discretionary power backward in the juvenile justice system, toward prosecutors, intake officers, and law enforcement officers. The deinstitutionalization of status offenders has removed from most juvenile court judges a substantial number of juveniles who may have appeared before them previously for lesser offenses and infractions. Prosecutors are confronted with more serious youthful offenders currently, and their tasks are made more complex because of the increased prominence given to defense attorneys in juvenile court proceedings by the U.S. Supreme Court. The nature of these changing roles is explored here.

Defense attorneys are increasingly important as negotiators in juvenile proceedings. Their presence has elevated the formality of these proceedings to new levels. Not everyone believes that such formality is desirable in the handling of juvenile offenders, although juveniles have been extended increasing numbers of constitutional guarantees by the U.S. Supreme Court. One important function performed by these defense counsels involves subjecting the juvenile justice system to frequent constitutional tests. It is largely through the appellate process that juveniles are able to acquire new rights and responsibilities. One consequence of the extensiveness of appeals of juvenile cases and the rate of success of such appeals is that many experts wonder whether we are heading toward a unified court system. While a unified court system refers to several innovative changes in general court reorganization, applied here it means greater centralization and unification of criminal and juvenile courts. This proposed reform is described and examined. Some of the more important implications of court unification for juveniles are also described.

THE JUVENILE COURT: A HISTORICAL FRAMEWORK

Juvenile courts are primarily an American creation. The first juvenile court was established in Illinois in 1899 under the *Illinois Juvenile Court Act*. The does not mean that other states were unconcerned about juveniles at the time or that other events had not occurred pertaining to youths, their conduct, and their welfare. In fact, numerous agencies and organizations had been established earlier in other jurisdictions, particularly during the latter half of the nineteenth century.

Reformatories

For example, the first public reformatory, the New York House of Refuge was established in New York City in 1825 by the Society for the Prevention of Pauperism (Cahalan, 1986:101). This house of refuge had several goals relating to juveniles, including providing food, clothing, and lodging for all poor, abused, or orphaned youths. However, the **Society for the Prevention of Pauperism** was comprised, in part, of many benefactors, philanthropists, and religionists, and these people sought to instill within the youths they serviced a commitment to hard work, strict discipline, and intensive study. These houses were established in various parts of New York and staffed largely by volunteers who knew little or nothing about individual counseling, group therapy techniques, or other useful interventions that might assist youths in surviving city hazards. Because the organization of these houses was decentralized, there were few, if any, external controls that could regulate the quality of care provided. Even today, historians are hard-pressed to decide whether these houses had any impact on the rate of delinquency in the areas where they were established or if they functioned positively to reduce delinquency among the youths they served (Cahalan, 1986; Rogers and Mays, 1987:426).

Other efforts were made in New York several years later to establish placement services for parentless youth. **Charles Loring Brace** created the

New York Children's Aid Society in 1853. This organization was of assistance in finding foster homes for displaced youths, orphaned youths, runaways, and others. This organization was especially effective following the Civil War, when large numbers of orphaned youths roamed city streets without any sort of parental supervision.

Childsavers

Although these organizations operated to service misplaced youths, there were numerous random efforts in many jurisdictions to perform similar tasks. These efforts led to the creation of various juvenile programs that were more or less interested in "saving children." *Childsavers* referred to no one in particular, because anyone who wished to be of assistance in helping children and intervening in their lives for constructive purposes could define themselves as childsavers. The precise nature of childsaving was not defined at the time, although houses of refuge and children's aid groups and societies could be included within this appellation.

During the mid-nineteenth century, a variety of juvenile behaviors was identified by different interests and targeted for differential treatment. A certain amount of specialization led to many of the distinctive terms we use today to describe different kinds of status offenders and delinquents. Generally, childsavers appeared to have humanitarian interests and seemed interested in helping youths avoid crime and pursue more normal lives. Unfortunately, the influence of charitable and private foundations and religious sponsorship created a coercive atmosphere where children often received punishment as therapy. The reform school atmosphere of the New York houses of refuge increasingly characterized many of the organizations and homes that purportedly catered to juvenile needs. Youths were compelled to learn crafts and other skills that might be of use in adulthood. This work was most often compulsory, in exchange for food and lodging provided by the childsavers.

Community-Based Private Agencies

There were exceptions. **Jane Addams** was instrumental in creating and operating Hull House in Chicago, Illinois, in 1889. Hull House was a settlement home used largely by children from immigrant families in the Chicago area. In those days, adults worked long hours, and many youths were otherwise unsupervised and wandered about their neighborhoods looking for something to do. Using money from various charities and philanthropists, Addams supplied many children with creative activities to alleviate their boredom and monotony. Addams integrated these activities with moral, ethical, and religious teachings. In her own way, she was hoping to deter these youths from lives of crime with her constructive activities and teaching. Thus her approach was consistent with the philosophy of **Cesare Beccaria**, the father of classical criminology. Beccaria wrote in 1764 that the purpose of punishment was deterrence and that punishment should be measured according to the seriousness of the criminal acts committed.

Truancy Statutes

Truants were established in Massachusetts in 1852, where the first compulsory school attendance statutes were passed. Many other states soon followed suit, until all jurisdictions had compulsory school attendance provisions by 1918. Colorado has been singled out by some historians as having drafted the first juvenile court provisions, although in reality, the Colorado legislature passed the Compulsory School Act in 1899, the same year that a juvenile court was established in Illinois. The Colorado action was aimed at preventing truancy, specifically mentioning those youths who were habitually absent from school, wandered about the streets during school hours, and had no obvious business or occupation. Colorado legislators labeled such youths "juvenile disorderly persons," but this action was not the juvenile court equivalent of what the Illinois legislature accomplished.

ORIGINAL INTERPRETATIONS OF JUVENILES AND JUVENILE DELINQUENCY

Illinois's Juvenile Court Act, enacted in 1899, says much about the times and how the legal status of juveniles was interpreted and applied. The full title of the act is revealing. On July 1, 1899, the Illinois legislature passed the **Act to Regulate the Treatment and Control of Dependent, Neglected, and Delinquent Children**. According to the act, it was applicable only to

> ...children under the age of sixteen (16) years not now or hereafter inmates of a State institution, or any training school for boys or industrial school for girls or some institution incorporated under the laws of this State, except as provided [in other sections].... "For purposes of this act the words dependent child and neglected child shall mean any child who for any reason is destitute or homeless or abandoned; or dependent upon the public for support; or has not proper parental care or guardianship; or who habitually begs or receives alms, or who is found living in any house of ill fame or with any vicious or disreputable person; or whose home, by reason of neglect, cruelty or depravity on the part of its parents, guardian or other person in whose care it may be, is an unfit place for such a child; and any child under the age of eight (8)

years who is found peddling or selling any article or singing or playing any musical instrument upon the streets or giving any public entertainment. The words delinquent child *shall include any child under the age of 16 years who violates any law of this State or any city or village ordinance. The word* child *or* children *may mean one or more children, and the word* parent *or* parents *may be held to mean one or both parents, when consistent with the intent of this act. The word* association *shall include any corporation which includes in its purposes the care or disposition of children coming within the meaning of this act.*

Even more insightful is what happens when such children are found. What are the limits of court sanctions? Illinois law authorized juvenile court judges to take the following actions in their dealings with dependent and neglected children:

When any child under the age of sixteen (16) years shall be found to be dependent or neglected within the meaning of this act, the court may make an order committing the child to the care of some suitable State institution, or to the care of some reputable citizen of good moral character, or to the care of some training school or an industrial school, as provided by law, or to the care of some association willing to receive it embracing in its objects the purpose of caring or obtaining homes for dependent or neglected children, which association shall have been accredited as hereinafter provided....

For juvenile delinquents, similar provisions were made. Judges were authorized to continue the hearing for any specific delinquent child "from time to time" and "may commit the child to the care and guardianship of a probation officer." The child might be permitted to remain in *its* own home, subject to the visitation of the probation officer. Judges were also authorized to commit children to state training or industrial schools until such time as they reach the age of their majority or adulthood.

Juveniles as Chattel

The curious word choice *it* used here in reference to children is indicative of how youths were viewed in those days. In early English times, children were considered chattel, lumped together with the cows, pigs, horses, and other farm property that one might lawfully possess. The act itself was sufficiently ambiguous so as to allow judges and others considerable latitude or discretion about how to interpret juvenile behaviors. For example, what is meant by "proper" parental care or guardianship? Who decides what is considered "habitual begging"? Would occasional begging be acceptable? Would children be subject to arrest and juvenile court sanctions for walking city streets playing a flute or other musical device? Who decides what homes and establishments are "unfit"? Where are the criteria that describe a home's fitness? Juvenile court judges know the answers to these questions in much the same way that courts generally have viewed and defined obscenity: They know it whenever they see it.

These statements are not intended to belittle the Illinois legislature and the intentions of the act "it" passed. Rather, they are intended to characterize the traditionalism that juvenile court judges have manifested over the years and the spirit of *parens patriae* that has dominated judicial decision making and adjudicatory outcomes. Taking dependent and neglected or abandoned children and placing them in training or industrial schools is the functional equivalent of adult incarceration in a prison or jail. By a stroke of the pen, the Illinois legislature gave juvenile court judges absolute control over the lives of all children under age 16 in the state of Illinois.

The Lack of Juvenile Court Uniformity

Currently, little uniformity exists among jurisdictions regarding juvenile court organization and operation (Butts, 1996b). Even within state jurisdictions, great variations exist among counties and cities relating to how juvenile offenders are processed. Historically, family or domestic courts have retained jurisdiction over most, if not all, juvenile matters. Not all jurisdictions have juvenile courts per se. Rather, some jurisdictions have courts that adjudicate juvenile offenders as well as decide child custody. Thus while it is true that all jurisdictions presently have juvenile courts, these courts are not always called juvenile courts.

The Shift from Gemeinschaft to Gesellschaft and a Gradual Reconceptualization of Juveniles

How were juveniles processed, adjudicated, and punished before the establishment of the specialized courts? How were dependent and neglected children treated? Social scientists would probably describe village and community life in the eighteenth and nineteenth centuries by referring to the dominant social and cultural values that existed then. The term *gemeinschaft* might be used here to describe the lifestyle that one might find in such settings. It is a term used to characterize social relations as being highly dependent on verbal agreements and understandings and informality. Ferdinand Tonnies, a social theorist, used *gemeinschaft* to convey the richness of tradition that would typify small communities where everyone was known to all others. In these settings, formal punishments, such as incarceration in prisons or jails, were seldom used. More effective than incarceration were punishments that heightened public humiliation through stocks and pillories and other corporal measures. Sufficient social pressure was exerted so that most people complied with the law. Thus, in gemeinschaft communities, people would probably fear social stigma, ostracism, and scorn more than their loss of freedom through incarceration.

In these communities, children would remain children through adolescence, eventually becoming adults as they began to perform trades or crafts and earned independent livings apart from their families. Children performed apprenticeships over lengthy periods under the tutorship of master craftsmen and others. Many of the terms we currently use to describe delinquent acts and status offenses were nonexistent then.

As the nation grew, urbanization and the increasing population density of large cities changed social relationships gradually but extensively. Tonnies described the nature of this gradual shift in social relationships from a gemeinschaft type of social network to a *gesellschaft* type of society. In the context of gesellschaft, social relationships are more formal, contractual, and impersonal. There is greater reliance on codified compilations of appropriate and lawful conduct as a means of regulating social relations.

During the advent of urbanization, children underwent a degree of reconceptualization. During the period of Reconstruction following the Civil War, there were no child labor laws, and children were exploited increasingly by industry and business. Children were thrust into employment in their early years, and they were paid meager wages in "sweatshops," usually manufacturing companies where long hours were required and persons worked at repetitive jobs on assembly lines. Thus, by the end of the nineteenth century, in part because of these widespread nonunionized and unregulated sweatshop operations and compulsory school attendance for youths in their early years, loitering youths became increasingly visible and attracted the attention of the general public as well as law enforcement.

Specialized Juvenile Courts

It became more convenient to establish special courts to adjudicate juvenile matters. The technical language describing inappropriate youthful conduct or misbehaviors was greatly expanded and refined. The courts were also vested with the authority to appoint probation officers and others deemed suitable to manage juvenile offenders and enforce new juvenile codes that most cities created. Today, most larger police departments have specialized juvenile sections or divisions, where only juvenile law violations or suspicious activities are investigated. In retrospect, Platt (1969) believes that the original aggregate of childsavers had much to do with inventing delinquency and its numerous, specialized subcategories as we now know them. At least they contributed to the formality of the present juvenile justice system by defining a range of impermissible juvenile behaviors that would require an operational legal apparatus to address. Once officialdom was properly armed with the right conceptual tools, it was a relatively easy step to enforce a fairly rigid set of juvenile behavioral standards and regulate most aspects of their conduct. Feld (1995) sees this as a part of a continuing pattern designed to criminalize the juvenile courts and hold juveniles accountable in the same way as adult offenders.

As juvenile court systems proliferated, it was quite apparent that these proceedings were decidedly different from criminal courts. Largely one-sided affairs, these proceedings typically involved the juvenile charged with some offense, a petitioner claiming the juvenile should be declared delinquent, or dependent, or neglected, and a judge who would weigh the evidence and decide things. Juveniles themselves were not provided with opportunities to solicit witnesses or give testimony themselves. Defense attorneys were largely unknown in juvenile courtrooms, since there were no issues to defend.

The Closed and Arbitrary Nature of Juvenile Court Proceedings

Juvenile court proceedings were closed to the general public, ostensibly to protect the identities of the youthful accused. While these proceedings were conducted behind closed doors for this manifest purpose, a latent function of the secrecy of juvenile courts was to obscure from view the high-handed and discriminatory decision making that characterized many juvenile court judges. In short, they didn't want the general public to know about the great subjectivity and arbitrary nature of their decisions. On the basis of allegations alone, together with uncorroborated statements and pronouncements from probation officers and others, juvenile court judges were free to declare any particular juvenile either delinquent or nondelinquent. The penalties that could be imposed were wide-ranging, from verbal reprimands and warnings to full-fledged incarceration in a secure juvenile facility. Virtually everything depended on the opinions and views of presiding juvenile court judges. And their decisions could never be appealed to higher courts.

For two-thirds of the twentieth century, juveniles had no real legal standing in American courts. Their constitutional rights were not at issue, since they did not enjoy any constitutional protections in the courtroom. No rules of evidence existed to govern the quality of evidence admitted or to challenge the reliability or integrity of testifying witnesses. They were not entitled to jury trials, unless the juvenile court judge permitted one. Comparatively few juvenile court judges have ever approved jury trials for any juveniles. Because these proceedings were exclusively civil proceedings, the rules of criminal procedure normally governing criminal courts were irrelevant. Juveniles did not acquire criminal records. Rather, they acquired civil adjudications of delinquency. Yet the incarceration dimension of the juvenile justice system has almost always paralleled that of the criminal justice system. Industrial or training schools, reform schools, and other types of secure confinement for juveniles have generally been nothing more than juvenile prisons. Thus, for many adjudicated juvenile offenders sentenced to one of these industrial schools, these sentences were the equivalent of imprisonment.

It is remarkable that such unchecked discretion among juvenile court judges continued for so many decades during the twentieth century. One explanation might be mass complacency or apathy among the general public about juvenile affairs. Juvenile matters were relatively unimportant and trivial. Another explanation might be a prevailing belief that juvenile courts knew what is best for adjudicated offenders and usually prescribed appropriate punishments, whatever they might be. Juvenile court judges and others often viewed juveniles as victims of their environment and peer associations. It might be easier to justify why new environments are required, including incarceration in the name of training, education, and rehabilitation, if the adverse effects of former environments can be illustrated (McDermott and Laub, 1987). However, in 1967, the U.S. Supreme Court decided the case of *In re Gault*, and it introduced for the first time the notion of juvenile court judge accountability to others.

Briefly, Gerald Gault was a 15-year-old Arizona youth who allegedly made an obscene telephone call to an adult female neighbor. The woman called police, suggested that the youth, Gault, was the guilty party, and Gault was summarily taken into custody and detained for nearly two days. The woman was never brought to court as a witness, and the only evidence she provided was her initial verbal accusation made to police on the day of Gault's arrest. Gault himself allegedly admitted that he dialed the woman's number, but he claimed that a boyfriend of his actually spoke to the woman and made the remarks she found offensive. Partly because Gault had been involved in an earlier petty offense and had a "record," the judge, together with the probation officer, decided that Gault was dangerous enough to commit to the Arizona State Industrial School, Arizona's main juvenile penitentiary, until he reached 21 years of age or until juvenile corrections authorities decided he that was rehabilitated and could be safely released. According to Arizona law, the sentence was unappealable. Any adult convicted of the same offense may have been fined $50 and/or sentenced to a 30-day jail term. Gault received six years in a juvenile prison, complete with correctional officers with firearms and barbed wire.

It is a sad commentary about juvenile courts and the justice dispensed by many of these judges prior to the *Gault* decision that numerous similar adjudications had been made against other juveniles in other jurisdictions. Appropriately, the U.S. Supreme Court referred to the court of the judge who originally sentenced Gault as a "kangaroo court." Gault's sentence was reversed and several important constitutional rights were conferred upon all juveniles as a result. Specifically, all of Gault's due process rights had been denied. He had been denied counsel, had not been protected against self-incrimination, had not been permitted to cross-examine his accuser, and had not been provided with specific notice of the charges against him. Now all juveniles enjoy these rights in every U.S. juvenile court.

The Increasing Bureaucratization and Criminalization of Juvenile Justice

For better or worse, the wheels were set in motion for major juvenile court reforms. After *Gault* and several other important Supreme Court decisions affecting juveniles directly, the nature of juvenile courts underwent a gradual transformation. But the transformation was anything but smooth. Even the U.S. Supreme Court continued to view juvenile courts as basically rehabilitative and treatment-centered apparatuses, thus reinforcing the traditional *parens patriae* doctrine within the context of various constitutional restraints. Nevertheless, annual changes in juvenile court procedures and the juvenile justice system generally suggested that it was becoming increasingly criminalized (Feld, 1993c; Hirschi and Gottfredson, 1993). Feld (1993a–c) observes that in Minnesota and other jurisdictions, the development of new rules of procedure for juvenile court and the current administrative assumptions and operations of these courts, with limited exceptions, often render them indistinguishable from criminal courts and the procedures these courts follow.

Generally, juvenile courts are currently viewed as *due process courts* rather than *traditional courts* (Feld, 1995). Due process juvenile courts are characterized by more formal case dispositions, a greater rate of intake dismissals, and greater importance attached to offense characteristics and seriousness. Traditional courts are characterized as less formal, with greater use made of secure confinement. Both defense and prosecuting attorneys play more important roles in due process juvenile courts compared with traditional ones (Butts, 1996b).

Currently, there continues to be widespread debate about the nature of and functions to be performed by juvenile courts (Butts, 1996a,b; Feld, 1993a–c). Should they be principally rehabilitative and treatment oriented, or should they be punishment-centered, just-deserts courts where juvenile offenders should get whatever they deserve? Feld (1988a) notes that today, juveniles suffer the "worst of both worlds," where they are presently subjected to harsh punishments in juvenile courts but lack the full range of constitutional guarantees extended to adults in criminal courts. Favoring the abolition of juvenile courts and the establishment of full procedural

The Case of the Kovalcins and Hate Crime

In Pompano Beach, Florida, two teenagers, 18-year-old Jason Kovalcin and 16-year-old Andrew Kovalcin, together with two other youths, Christian Heinsler and a minor, were driving around in their mother's Mercedes. They spotted a black person, 54-year-old Edward Chapman, who was riding a bicycle through the neighborhood. As the youths passed Chapman, they shot him in the back with 3-inch metal darts from blowguns. Chapman got their license number and telephoned police.

Subsequently, police officers arrested the youths for committing a hate crime and other charges, including felonious assault with a dangerous weapon. Under questioning by police, Andrew Kovalcin told police that they and their friends had left the Kovalcin's Fort Lauderdale home that afternoon to "go out and shoot some niggers." Kovalcin also admitted that they had attacked another black prior to the attack on Chapman. Apparently the earlier incident had not been reported.

Sandra King, spokesperson for the Pompano Beach authorities, said that this type of drive-by shooting is unusual inasmuch as metal darts were used instead of firearms. Nevertheless, the fact that blacks were targeted changes this assault charge to a hate crime with more serious potential penalties. If convicted of this crime, these brothers and their friends are in jeopardy of being jailed for a substantial time. "This is something a lot more than a childhood prank," said another source. "We hope this doesn't mean the beginning of a new fad in drive-by shootings."

What punishment should be imposed on these boys if they are convicted? What responsibilities do parents have for the actions of their children? How can such crimes be prevented?

Source: Adapted from Associated Press, "Brothers Charged with Hate Crime for Blowgun Dart Attacks on Blacks," *Minot (ND) Daily News*, April 3, 1996:A2.

parity as in criminal courts, Feld believes that this may end our fruitless attempts to bring all due process safeguards into the juvenile courtroom. Other experts report public attitudes and sentiments favoring a continuation of juvenile courts in their present form, with an emphasis on rehabilitation (Steinhart, 1988). However, an emerging sentiment is that all youths should be vested with a greater degree of responsibility and accountability to others. This has been one of the intended aims of juvenile justice reform in the state of Washington and other jurisdictions, where *both* rehabilitation and punishment may be combined to heighten offender accountability

(Challeen, 1986; Schneider and Schram, 1986; Springer, 1987).

One important result of the U.S. Supreme Court decision in *Gault* for youths to be represented by counsel in juvenile court was the immediate transition of juvenile proceedings from unilateral hearings into **adversarial proceedings**, with much higher levels of procedural formality (Feld, 1987c). The adversarial system has long been a feature of American courts for adults, where plaintiffs and defendants litigate cases civilly for damages and where prosecutors and defense attorneys attempt to convince judges or juries of the guilt or innocence of criminal defendants and seek either their incarceration or exoneration. This higher level of procedural formality associated with due process in juvenile justice has encouraged the development of new proposed juvenile codes that only further bureaucratize an already bureaucratized system (Ito, 1984).

The Rose Institute and the American Legislative Exchange Council have proposed a new model juvenile code. However, experts have criticized this model code as weakening current protections extended to dependent children, eliminating judicial discretion in disposition, requiring pretrial detention of juveniles accused of serious crimes, and permitting the incarceration of status offenders who violate court orders (Bilchik, 1996). The developers of such codes claim that their proposals will instill within juveniles a greater degree of accountability for their actions (U.S. General Accounting Office, 1995b).

Public Defenders for Juveniles

Greater procedural formality in the juvenile justice system has been observed relating to the appointment of public defenders for juvenile indigents. More than a few juvenile court jurisdictions, including Los Angeles County and Alameda County, California, now provide public defenders for juveniles and their families who cannot afford to appoint private counsel, especially in more serious cases where incarceration in secure confinement facilities is a strong possibility (Feeney, 1987; Hancock and Van Dusen, 1985). Formerly, defense counsels for juveniles often were the juvenile's probation officer or a social caseworker with a vested interest in the case. It is not entirely clear how these officers and workers were able to separate their law enforcement and defense functions to avoid allegations of conflicts of interest. But little interest in the quality of defense of juvenile cases was exhibited by the public in previous years anyway. While some experts believe that juveniles are now insulated to some extent from the whims of juvenile court prosecutors and judges, others suspect that defense attorneys have in some instances made it more difficult for juveniles to receive fair treatment.

During intake, it was found that the presence of attorneys who represented juveniles' interests and attempted to protect them so that their full range of constitutional rights are observed at each stage of the juvenile justice process actually detracted from the informal nature of intake. Intake officers would change such proceedings into formal ones, and recommendations for subsequent dispositions might be harsher than if attorneys had not been present. In fact, intake officers have openly discouraged juveniles and their parents from availing themselves of an attorneys' services at this stage, since their presence hampers informal adjustments of cases and limits a youth's informal compliance with informal probationary conditions. In some cases, intake officers consider themselves the primary source of a youth's understanding of legal rights, although a recommendation that these officers receive more training and preparation in law and juvenile rights suggests that their own understanding of the law merits improvement (Towberman, 1992). In a growing number of instances, many cases are being diverted to victim–offender mediation, where various nonprofit, private organizations receive referrals from juvenile courts. The intent of such victim–offender mediation is to reach a resolution of differences between victims and offenders without subjecting offenders to juvenile court and its adverse labeling impact. In those communities with mediation programs, there is support from community residents. Financial support in the form of grants is provided from local, state, and federal grants. Mediators may be interested citizens, retired judges, community leaders, or even intake officers who undertake these tasks during nonworking hours (Hughes and Schneider, 1989).

Despite these alternatives to juvenile court action, it *is* true that juvenile court proceedings have become increasingly formalized (Champion, 1992, 1996). Further, public access to these proceedings in most jurisdictions is increasing (Bilchik, 1996). Thus the presence of defense counsel, an adversarial scenario, a trial-like atmosphere where witnesses testify for and against juvenile defendants, and adherence to rules of procedure for juvenile courts are clear indicators of greater formalization, bureaucratization, and criminalization, as Feld (1987b) and others have suggested. We are only a few rights away from full-fledged criminal proceedings in many juvenile court jurisdictions (Feld, 1995).

THE CHANGING PROSECUTORIAL ROLE IN JUVENILE MATTERS

Juvenile court prosecutors have been forced to change and adapt to these new procedures as well. As juveniles acquire more legal rights, prosecutors must be increasingly cognizant of these rights and constitutional safeguards and ensure that they are not violated. Rights violations, particularly those involving constitutional issues, can and will be challenged in the event of unfavorable juvenile court adjudications and/or sentences.

It may be indicated here, for example, that the standard of proof in juvenile proceedings, as well as the introduction of evidence against youths, are currently different compared with pre-*Gault* times. Defense counsel may now challenge the quality of evidence against youths and how it was obtained, the accuracy of confessions or other incriminating utterances made by youths while in custody and under interrogation, the veracity of witnesses, and whether juveniles understand the rights they are asked to waive by law enforcement officers and others.

Modifying Prosecutorial Roles by Changing the Standard of Proof in Juvenile Proceedings

Regarding the standard of proof, it was traditionally the case that the standard of proof in determining delinquency and followed in juvenile courts (which were and still remain civil proceedings) was the **preponderance of the evidence** standard. In criminal proceedings, the standard of proof followed in determining a defendant's guilt is beyond a reasonable doubt. A juvenile case discussed elsewhere *In re Winship* (1970) resulted in the U.S. Supreme Court declaring that particularly where juveniles were in jeopardy of losing their freedom through placement in secure confinement for any period, they were entitled to the same standard of proof currently extended to adults in criminal proceedings—beyond a reasonable doubt. Although some jurisdictions retain the preponderance-of-evidence standard for certain juvenile proceedings, these jurisdictions are obligated to use the criminal standard of proof, beyond a reasonable doubt, whenever an adjudication of delinquency can result in confinement or a substantial loss of privileges.

Juveniles have benefited in at least one respect as the result of these new rights and standards of proof. These changed conditions have forced law enforcement officers, prosecutors, and judges to be more careful and discriminating when charging juveniles with certain offenses. However, changing the technical ground rules for proceeding against juveniles has not necessarily resulted in substantial changes in police officer discretion, prosecutorial discretion, or judicial discretion. Juveniles remain second-class citizens, in a sense, since they continue to be subject to street-level justice by police officers.

Prosecutors appear similarly unaffected by these juvenile justice changes. Studies of greater prosecutorial presence in juvenile courts suggest that their overall effect on juvenile adjudicatory proceedings has been minimal (Laub and MacMurray, 1987). Greater formality in the juvenile court proceedings of Middlesex County, Maryland has disclosed little change in the use and behaviors of *police prosecutors*, despite a substantially greater presence of assistant district attorneys in juvenile courts. Laub and MacMurray (1987) indicate that one explanation for this is the continued emphasis of the court on the youth's rehabilitation. Further, the organizational structure of these courts has remained unchanged.

It has long been a traditional feature of the juvenile justice system in more than a few jurisdictions for police officers to function in prosecutorial capacities in juvenile court proceedings. Thus they might arrest juveniles and retain the responsibility for their ultimate prosecution in juvenile courts. Interestingly, this would place police officers in the position of having to justify the probable cause leading to a juvenile's arrest at intake, to present the case against the juvenile in court, and to testify against the juvenile as a witness for the prosecution. The conflicts of interest inherent in this scenario are untenable in any criminal court today. Despite this conflict-of-interest situation, police prosecutors are still permitted in various jurisdictions.

The Laub–Macmurray study seems to typify much of what has happened in juvenile courts in recent years. Despite the increased bureaucratization of these courts, these courts seem to exhibit much of the traditionalism of the pre-*Gault* years. This means that little change has occurred in the nature of juvenile adjudications. Juvenile court judges, with the exception of those few jurisdictions that provide jury trials for serious juvenile cases, continue to make adjudicatory decisions as before. Regardless of new evidentiary standards and proof-of-guilt requirements, these judges continue to exercise their individual discretion and decide whether one's guilt or delinquency has been established "beyond a reasonable doubt." How are we ever to know whether these judges are continuing to use *old* proof standards (i.e., preponderance of the evidence) and merely saying that they are following *new* ones (i.e., beyond a reasonable doubt)?

Eliminating the Confidentiality of Juvenile Court Proceedings and Record Keeping

Enhancing the accountability of juvenile courts is greater public access to them under the provisions of the First Amendment. The Michigan Law Review (Anonymous, 1983) has argued editorially that such access would fulfill the First Amendment's structural role of ensuring a free flow of information necessary to effective self-government and of checking the abuse of official power. During the 1990s, considerable changes have occurred regarding the confidentiality of juvenile court matters as well as juvenile records. Table 7.1 is a summary of confidentiality provisions of the various states as of 1995. In 1995, for instance, 22 states had provisions for open

TABLE 7.1

Summary of Current Confidentiality Provisions Relating to Serious and Violent Juvenile Offenders, 1995[a]

State	Open hearing	Release of name	Release of court record[b]	Finger-printing	Photo-graphing	Offender regis-tration	State-wide repository[c]	Seal expunge records prohibited
Alabama			×	×	×		×	
Alaska		×	×	×		×	×	
Arizona	×	×	×	×	×	×		
Arkansas		×	×	×	×		×	
California	×	×	×	×	×	×	×	×
Colorado	×	×	×	×	×	×	×	×
Connecticut			×	×	×			
Delaware	×	×	×	×	×	×	×	×
District of Columbia			×	×	×			
Florida	×	×	×	×	×	×	×	
Georgia	×	×	×	×	×		×	×
Hawaii			×	×	×		×	
Idaho		×	×	×	×		×	
Illinois		×	×	×	×	×	×	
Indiana	×	×	×	×	×		×	
Iowa	×	×	×	×	×	×	×	
Kansas	×	×	×	×	×	×	×	
Kentucky				×	×		×	×
Louisiana	×	×	×	×	×		×	
Maine	×	×	×			×	×	
Maryland			×	×	×		×	
Massachusetts	×	×	×	×	×		×	
Michigan		×	×	×	×	×	×	×
Minnesota	×	×	×	×	×	×	×	×
Mississippi		×	×	×	×	×		
Missouri	×	×	×	×	×		×	
Montana	×	×	×	×	×	×	×	×
Nebraska		×	×	×			×	
Nevada	×	×		×	×		×	×
New Hampshire		×	×					
New Jersey		×	×	×	×	×	×	
New Mexico	×			×	×		×	
New York				×	×		×	
North Carolina			×	×	×			×
North Dakota		×	×	×	×		×	
Ohio				×	×	×	×	
Oklahoma	×	×	×	×	×		×	×
Oregon		×	×	×	×	×	×	×
Pennsylvania	×	×	×	×	×	×	×	

TABLE 7.1 (CONT'D)

State	Open hearing	Release of name	Release of court record[b]	Finger-printing	Photo-graphing	Offender regis-tration	State-wide repository[c]	Seal expunge records prohibited
Rhode Island		×	×			×	×	
South Carolina		×	×	×	×		×	×
South Dakota		×	×	×	×		×	×
Tennessee		×	×	×	×	×	×	
Texas	×		×	×	×	×	×	×
Utah	×	×	×	×	×	×	×	
Vermont				×	×		×	
Virginia		×	×	×	×	×	×	
Washington	×	×	×	×	×	×	×	×
West Virginia		×	×	×				×
Wisconsin		×	×			×	×	
Wyoming		×	×	×	×		×	×

[a] indicates the provision(s) allowed by each state as of the end of the 1995 legislative session.

[b] In this category, × indicates a provision for juvenile court records to be specifically released to at least one of the following parties: the public, the victim(s), the school(s), the prosecutor, law enforcement, or social agency; however, all states allow records to be released to any party who can show a legitimate interest, typically by court order.

[c] In this category, × indicates a provision for fingerprints to be part of a separate juvenile or adult criminal history repository.

Source: Linda Szymanski, *Special Analysis of the Automated Juvenile Law Archive* (Pittsburgh, PA: National Center for Juvenile Justice, 1996).

hearings in juvenile or family court proceedings. Only 11 states did *not* provide for the release of the names of juveniles charged with serious offenses. Only six states did not permit court record releases to interested parties. In fact, *all* states currently make available juvenile court records to any party showing a legitimate interest. In such cases, information is ordinarily obtained through a court order. Fingerprinting and photographing of juveniles is conducted routinely in most states. Half the states require registration of all juvenile offenders when they enter new jurisdictions. Also, most states presently have state repositories of juvenile records and other relevant information about juvenile offending. Seventeen states prohibited sealing or expunging juvenile court records after certain dates, such as one's age of majority or adulthood (Bilchik, 1996:37–38). Therefore, juveniles today are considerably more likely to have their offenses known to the public in one form or another. The protections previously enjoyed by juveniles are rapidly disappearing.

Open Juvenile Proceedings and Changing Judicial Conduct

The greater formality of juvenile proceedings as well as their openness to others may restrict the discretion of juvenile court judges, although this limitation is not particularly an undesirable one. Juvenile court judges have been known to make decisions that only incidentally related to one's alleged offense. For instance, Emerson (1969:88–89) reported that a juvenile court judge once ordered physical examinations for two 15-year-old girls who had been arrested for shoplifting [clothes] in a department store. Among other things, he wished to determine whether they had been sexually active. His motives were patently unclear, since knowing whether or not the girls had been sexually active is wholly unrelated to shoplifting. Nevertheless, the physicals were conducted, although it is unknown what the judge did with this information or how it was used in their adjudications and dispositions. Today, it is doubtful that many juvenile court judges would be able to get away with irrelevant and demeaning requests such as the one described by Emerson. The presence of a defense counsel representing the juvenile's interests and promoting due process would tend to deter judges from such conduct, although in 1969, *parens patriae* was still a strong feature of these courts, and juvenile females were particularly vulnerable to the overprotection of paternalistic juvenile court judges.

The Prosecution Decision in the 1990s

The juvenile justice system has been notoriously slow in its case processing of juvenile offenders. In fact, delays in filing charges against juveniles and the eventual adjudicatory hearing are chronic in many jurisdictions. Juveniles arrested for various types of offenses may wait a year or longer in some jurisdictions before their cases are heard by juvenile court judges. Juvenile court prosecutors may delay filing charges against particular juveniles for a variety of reasons. The most obvious reasons for delays—court caseload backlogs, crowded court dockets, insufficient prosecutorial staff, too much paperwork—are not always valid reasons. In many instances the actors themselves are at fault. In short, prosecutors and judges may simply be plodding along at a slow pace because of their own personal dispositions and work habits. It has been illustrated that in many jurisdictions where prosecutors and judges have aggressively tackled their caseload problems and forced functionaries to work faster, juvenile caseload processing has been greatly accelerated. Thus the time between a juvenile's arrest and disposition has been greatly shortened because of individual decision making and not because of organizational constraints or overwork (Butts and Halemba, 1996:73–91).

BOX 7.2 ON LIBERAL DISTRICT ATTORNEYS AND JUDGES

The Case of the Liberal DAs

The accusation has been made more than once. The district attorney was too lenient in this case or that one. Not enough was done to see the offender punished to the maximum degree. Whether the case involves a burglary, child molestation, rape, robbery, or murder, DAs are exposed to a persistent barrage of criticisms about their performance in prosecuting cases.

The primary culprit is plea bargaining. Plea bargaining has been practiced for at least a century. It is a preconviction agreement whereby guilty pleas are entered by defendants in exchange for some type of leniency from the prosecution. Usually, if cases are tried in court and defendants are convicted, their sentences are considerably more severe than if they were to accept a plea bargain arrangement from prosecutors.

Krista Absalon, from Gouverneur, New York, is a typical example of how prosecutors invite criticism through plea bargaining. One evening, Krista got into an argument with her ex-husband. She left her apartment and went to a bar/restaurant, where she became drunk and passed out in the restaurant rest room. When she regained consciousness, it was apparent to her that she had been sexually molested. In fact, she had been raped repeatedly while unconscious by five male bar customers, including the bartender. She filed charges of rape against these five men.

The district attorney of St. Lawrence County, where the alleged rapes occurred, interviewed the men and investigated the allegations. Subsequently, all five of the men were allowed to enter "guilty" pleas to "sexual misconduct," a misdemeanor, and they had to pay $750 and court costs. Krista learned of the plea bargain later and was stunned. She thought that there was going to be a trial and that the men would be tried and convicted of rape.

Eventually, Krista became a part of a larger organization known as the National Victim Center, operating from Ft. Worth, Texas. The National Victim Center is an advocate for any crime victim, male or female. It suggests the following questions to determine whether prosecutors in your community are doing a good job prosecuting criminal cases:

1. Is there consistent emphasis on prosecuting violent crimes? Or is the DA's office mobilized only for high-profile crimes?

2. How many and what kinds of felony arrests are dismissed or plea bargained for sentences of less than a year in jail? Why?

3. How are resources (money, staff) distributed?

4. Does the rhetoric match the reality? If the DA is touting a plea bargain as "proof" of "tough" policies, compare the maximum penalty to the date of parole eligibility.

However, in 30 states in 1997, juvenile court prosecutors were at liberty to file charges against juvenile offenders whenever they decided. No binding legislative provisions were applicable to these actors to force them to act promptly and bring a youth's case before the juvenile court. In the meantime, 20 states have established time limits that cannot be exceeded between the time of a juvenile's court referral and the filing of charges by prosecutors. Table 7.2 shows various time limits imposed by various states for juvenile court adjudication and disposition of cases. For instance, in Minnesota, juvenile court prosecutors must file charges against juveniles within 30 days of their referral to juvenile court by police if the juveniles are placed in secure confinement. These prosecutors must file charges against undetained juveniles within 60 days following the juvenile's referral to juvenile court by police. In Maryland, prosecutors have 60 days to file charges against either detained or undetained juveniles following their court referrals. In Georgia and Ohio, prosecutors must file charges within 10 days if juveniles are being detained. A failure to file charges against juveniles in these jurisdictions within the time periods specified results in a dismissal of their cases **with prejudice**, meaning that the prosecutors cannot refile charges again at a later date against the same offenders (Butts, 1996b:557–558).

Time Standards in Juvenile Court for Prosecutors and Other Actors

Establishing time standards for accomplishing various procedures within the juvenile justice process are not new. As early as 1971, various organizations were at work to encourage the juvenile justice system to process

TABLE 7.2

Time Limits (in Days) for Juvenile Court Adjudication and Disposition Hearings, in Cases *Not* Involving Proceedings for Transfer to Criminal Court[a]

State	Court referral	Start of adjudication deadline — Filing of charges (det/ not det)	Start of adjudication deadline — Preliminary hearing (det/ not det)	Detention admission	Detention hearing	Start of disposition deadline — Filing of charges (det/ not det)	Start of disposition deadline — Adjudication (det/not det)
Alaska							Immed. [b]
Arizona			30/60				30/45
Arkansas					14		14/—
California	30	30[b]		15			
Delaware				30[c]			
Florida		21/90[c]					15/—
Georgia		10/60					30/-
Illinois		120[b,c]		10[c]			
Iowa		60[b,d]					ASAP[b]
Louisiana			30/90				30[b]
Maryland		60[b]		30			30[b]
Massachusetts	60						
Michigan		180[b]		63			35/—
Minnesota		30/60					15[c]/45[c]
Mississippi		90/—		21			14/—
Montana							ASAP[b]
Nebraska		180/—				180[c]	
New Hampshire		21/30					21/30
New Jersey				30			30/60
New Mexico							20/—
New York			14/60				10/50
North Dakota		30[b]		14			
Ohio		10/—					Immed. [b]
Oregon	56			28			28[e]
Pennsylvania		10/—					20/—
Rhode Island				7			
South Carolina		40[b]					
Tennessee		—/90		30			15/90
Texas		10/—					
Vermont		15/—					30[b]
Virginia		—/120		21			30/—
Washington		30[b]/60[b]					14/21
Wisconsin			20[e]/30[e]			10[e]/30[e]	10/30
Wyoming					60		

[a]Twenty states did not have time limits for adjudication as of 1993: AL, AK, CO, CT, DC, HI, ID, IN, KS, KY, ME, MO, MT, NV, NM, NC, OK, SD, UT, and WV. Twenty-six states did not have time limits for dispositions: AL, CA, CO, CT, DE, DC, HI, ID, IL, IN, KS, KY, ME, MA, MO, NV, NC, ND, OK, RI, SC, SD, TX, UT, WV, and WY.
[b]Statute did not distinguish detention status.
[c]Extensions are possible.
[d]If statutory right to speedy trial is waived.
[e]Statute-specified time from "plea hearing."

Source: Butts, 1996b: 557–558. Data source: analysis by the National Center for Juvenile Justice.

cases more quickly. It was believed at the time that only legislatively created time standards would cause police, intake officers, prosecutors, and judges to take faster action in processing juvenile offenders.

Butts (1996b:544–547) notes, for instance, that the Joint Commission on Juvenile Justice Standards led the way in 1971 with early time standards for juvenile processing. A product of the Institute of Judicial Administration (IJA) and the American Bar Association (ABA), the IJA/ABA Project convened periodically over the next several years and issued 27 different volumes during the years 1977–1980. The standards promulgated by the IJA/ABA Project were intended as guidelines for juvenile courts and the juvenile justice system generally. The Commission formed through the IJA/ABA Project was guided by the principle that *juvenile court cases should always be processed without unnecessary delay* (Butts, 1996a:545).

The IJA/ABA standards relating to processing juveniles were as follows (Butts, 1996b:546):

TIME	ACTION
2 hours	Between police referral and the decision to detain
24 hours	Between detention and a petition justifying further detention
15 days	Between police referral and adjudication (if youth is detained)
30 days	Between police referral and adjudication (if youth is not detained)
15 days	Between adjudication and final disposition (if youth is detained)
30 days	Between adjudication and final disposition (if youth is not detained)

Notice in these time guidelines that law enforcement officers are not given much time to detain youths once they have been taken into custody. Once police officers have referred a youth to juvenile court, only *2 hours* is recommended for a decision to be made about detaining the youth. If a youth is detained, only *24 hours* is allowed between the start of one's detention and filing a petition to justify further detention. Depending on whether youths are detained or undetained, the time limits recommended are either 15 or 30 days, respectively, between detention and adjudication. These guidelines are rather rigorous compared with the traditional sluggishness of juvenile offender processing. Table 7.2 shows that only a handful of states thus far have adopted these or more rigorous standards for filing charges against juveniles (e.g., Georgia, Ohio, Pennsylvania, Texas, and Vermont).

Butts (1996b:547) also notes that similar time limits for juvenile processing were recommended contemporaneously by the National Advisory

Committee for Juvenile Justice and Delinquency Prevention in 1980. These limits are shown below (Butts, 1996b:546–547):

TIME	ACTION
24 hours	Between police referral and the report of intake decision (if youth is detained)
30 days	Between police referral and the report of intake decision (if youth is not detained)
24 hours	Between detention and detention hearing
2 days	Between intake report and the filing of a petition by the prosecutor (if detained)
5 days	Between intake report and the filing of a petition by the prosecutor (if not detained)
5 days	Between filing of the petition and the initial arraignment hearing
15 days	Between filing of the petition and adjudication (if detained)
30 days	Between filing of the petition and adjudication (if not detained)
15 days	Between adjudication and final disposition

Again, the National Advisory Committee gave little latitude to juvenile court prosecutors in dispatching juvenile cases. In this particular arrangement of scenarios, however, the intake stage was addressed, and rather strongly. Not only were prosecutors obligated to file petitions against specified juveniles more quickly following intake, but intake officers were required to make their assessments of juveniles and file reports of these assessments within a two-day period. One major difference in the National Advisory Committee recommendations and guidelines was the fact that if certain actors in the juvenile justice system did not comply with these time standards, cases against certain juveniles could be dismissed, but **without prejudice**. This meant that juvenile court prosecutors could resurrect the original charges and refile them with the juvenile court at a later date. Thus, no particularly compelling constraints were placed on either intake officers or prosecutors to act in a timely manner, according to this second set of standards. However, we must recognize that neither the IJA/ABA time guidelines nor the National Advisory Committee guidelines are binding on any state jurisdiction. They are set forth as *strongly recommended* guidelines for juvenile court officials to follow.

Why Should the Juvenile Justice Process Be Accelerated?

Several compelling arguments are made for why juvenile justice should be applied quickly. Butts (1996b:525–526) and others (McCarthy, 1989;

Towberman, 1992) make compelling arguments that adolescence is a critical period wherein youths undergo many changes. Maturational factors seem especially accelerated, while one's personality and response to peer pressures are modified and enhanced in diverse ways. A month may seem like a year to most adolescents. Secure confinement of 24 hours is a serious deprivation of one's freedom. When some juvenile cases undergo protracted delays of up to a year or longer, it is difficult for many youths to accept their subsequent punishment for something they did long ago. More than a few juveniles have grown out of delinquency by the time their cases come before the juvenile court, and they wonder why they are now being punished for something they did when they were younger.

Studies of juvenile justice system delays disclose that the *size* of a jurisdiction plays an important part in how fast juvenile cases are concluded. In 1985, for example, the median number of days it took to process juvenile cases in a large sample of U.S. county jurisdictions was about 44 days. By 1994, the median processing time in these same counties was 92 days (Butts and Halemba, 1996:131). For smaller jurisdictions with fewer and presumably less serious cases to process, case processing time ranged from 34 to 83 days in 1994, while larger counties took from 59 to 110 days to complete juvenile case processing.

These juvenile justice processing delays parallel criminal court processing of adult defendants. We might be inclined to accept these long juvenile justice delays if the cases processed were sufficiently serious to warrant more court time. However, only about 17 percent of all cases handled by both small and large county jurisdictions involved serious or person offenses in 1994 (Butts and Halemba, 1996:129).

Therefore, it has been recommended that juvenile justice case processing time should be decreased so as to move the disposition closer to the time when the offense was committed. Juveniles should be able to relate whatever happens to them in court later to the offense they committed earlier. In more than a few instances, juveniles awaiting trial on one charge have had subsequent opportunities to reoffend. When they are arrested for new offenses before being adjudicated for earlier offenses, their cognitive development may inhibit their understanding of the process and their disposition (Butts, 1996b:525).

Shine and Price (1992) have indicated that there are two primary reasons why juvenile cases should be processed quickly:

1. To maximize the realization by the juvenile that he or she has been caught in a criminal act, will be held accountable for what he or she has done, and that there will be consequences for this action, it is important that the case be resolved quickly. If the case continues too long, the impact of the message is diluted, either because the juvenile has been

subsequently arrested for other offenses and loses track of just what it is that he or she is being prosecuted for or because the juvenile has not engaged in further delinquent acts and feels that any consequences for the past offense are unfair.

2. If there are victims, unwarranted delays in juvenile case processing are unfair and damaging to victims (Shine and Price:1992, 101, 115). Many victims suffer some type of financial loss or physical injury. Expenses are incurred. Faster resolutions of juvenile court cases can lead to more rapid compensation and victim restitution plans imposed by the court. Such compensation of victim restitution can do much to alleviate any continued suffering that victims may endure.

THE SPEEDY TRIAL RIGHTS OF JUVENILES

Juveniles have no federal constitutional right to a speedy trial (Butts, 1996b:536). The U.S. Supreme Court has not decided any juvenile case that would entitle a juvenile to a speedy trial commensurate with adults in criminal courts. Criminal defendants are assured a speedy trial through the Sixth Amendment and the leading 1972 case of *Barker v. Wingo* (see Box 7.3). Each state and the federal government have established speedy trial procedures that establish time standards between different events, such as between the time of arrest and initial appearance, between one's initial appearance and arraignment, and between one's arraignment and trial. The federal government uses a 100-day standard. New Mexico is perhaps the most liberal, providing a 180-day period. Many states have adopted the federal standard.

For juveniles, there are no particular fixed standards between comparable stages of juvenile justice processing, such as between arrest and intake, between intake and prosecutorial decision making and case filing, between case filing and adjudication, and between adjudication and disposition. However, some state legislatures have provided time standards that proscribe different maximum time limits between each of these events. As of 1993, for instance, 30 states provided some form of time limit for adjudications following arrests. Twenty-six states did not have time limits between adjudications and dispositions of juveniles (Butts, 1996b:558). Only a handful of state courts have recognized some form of speedy trial rights for accused juveniles (Butts, 1996b:553).

Jeffrey Butts of the National Center for Juvenile Justice in Pittsburgh recommends that youths facing adjudication for delinquent offenses should be vested with the same speedy trial rights as adults. Thus a federal constitutional right to a speedy trial for juvenile defendants would send the message that efficient case processing is an essential element in the overall effectiveness of the juvenile justice system (1996b:554). Often, juvenile court actors themselves can greatly enhance juvenile case processing by their own behaviors. Juvenile court judges are particularly powerful entities, and their decision making can be far-reaching, extending back to the time of juvenile arrests and intake proceedings, as well as forward to prosecutorial filings, adjudicatory proceedings, and disposition hearings.

BOX 7.3   DO JUVENILES HAVE A RIGHT TO A SPEEDY TRIAL?

The Case of Barker v. Wingo

Barker and another person were alleged to have shot an elderly couple in July 1958. They were arrested later and a grand jury indicted them in September 1958. Kentucky prosecutors sought 16 continuances to prolong the trial of Barker. Barker's companion, Manning, was subjected to five different trials, where a hung jury was found except in the fifth trial, where Manning was convicted. Then Barker's trial was scheduled. During these five trials, Barker made no attempt to protest or to encourage a trial on his own behalf. After scheduling and postponing Barker's trial for various reasons, his trial was finally held in October 1963, when he was convicted. He appealed, alleging a violation of his right to a speedy trial. The U.S. Supreme Court heard the case and declared that since from every apparent factor, Barker did not want a speedy trial, he was not entitled to one. The case significance is that if you want a speedy trial, you must assert your privilege to have one. Defendants must assert their desire to have a speedy trial in order for the speedy trial provision to be invoked and for amendment rights to be enforceable. In Barker's case, the U.S. Supreme Court said that Barker was not deprived of his due process right to a speedy trial, largely because the defendant did not desire one (at 2195).

The present standard, known as the **Barker balancing test**, consists of four factors:

1. The length of the delay between charging the defendant and the defendant's trial
2. The reason for the delay
3. The defendant's assertion of his or her due process right to a speedy trial
4. The existence of prejudice to the defendant by prosecutorial and/or judicial actions

Source: Barker v. Wingo, 407 U.S. 514, 92 S.Ct. 2182 (1972).

The findings of researchers suggest that the longer juveniles remain within the juvenile justice system, the more adverse the consequences for their subsequent recidivism and seriousness of offending (Butts and Gable, 1992; Feld, 1989b; McCarthy, 1989; Towberman, 1992). One reason that juvenile case processing has been sluggish is that the doctrine of *parens patriae* has been pervasive, suggesting rehabilitation over other themes, such as punishment, crime control, or due process. According to the *parens patriae* concept, juvenile courts need a certain amount of time to provide for the needs of youths drawn into the system. If insufficient time is allocated for rehabilitation, rehabilitation will not occur. However, the U.S. Supreme Court has characterized the doctrine of *parens patriae* as "murky" and of "dubious historical relevance" in the case of *In re Gault* (1967). The U.S. Supreme Court also declared in *Gault* that juveniles do not need to give up their due process rights under the Fourteenth Amendment in order to derive juvenile justice system benefits because of their status as juvenile offenders, such as the greater concern for their well-being supposedly inherent in juvenile court proceedings (Butts, 1996b:538). Instead, the U.S. Supreme Court suggested the due process principles of fairness, impartiality, and orderliness were of paramount importance in contrast with the *parens patriae* philosophy.

Contemporary examinations of juvenile court prosecutorial opinions about the effectiveness of juvenile court processing indicate that in at least some jurisdictions, such as Illinois, prosecutors perceive juvenile courts to be relatively *ineffective* at rehabilitating juveniles (Ellsworth, Kinsella, and Massin, 1992). These prosecutors believe that probation services are most vital to a youth's rehabilitation and that specific community programs and services intended to prevent delinquency are either inadequate, nonexistent, or ineffective. Specific sectors of the community were targeted as most important by these prosecutors. They believe that greater juvenile court intervention should occur in school matters. All things considered, however, these prosecutors believe that their rehabilitative impact in specific juvenile cases becomes less effective as their involvement in such cases increases. Again, this suggests moving youths through the system more quickly, to minimize their exposure to the process.

THE ADVOCACY ROLE OF DEFENSE ATTORNEYS

For especially serious juvenile offender cases, defense attorneys are increasingly useful and necessary as a means of safeguarding juvenile rights and holding the juvenile justice system more accountable regarding its treatment of juvenile offenders. Widespread abuse of discretion by various actors throughout all stages of the juvenile justice process is well documented and has been described in this and previous chapters. The intrusion of defense attorneys into the juvenile justice process, under a new due process framework, is anticipated as a logical consequence of the rights juveniles have obtained from the U.S. Supreme Court in recent decades (Ito, 1984).

Attorneys for Juveniles as a Matter of Right

Although juveniles are entitled to the services of attorneys at all stages of juvenile proceedings, some investigators have shown that about half of all youths processed in the juvenile justice system are not represented by counsel (Feld, 1988b). Shortly after the *Gault* decision in 1967, the Minnesota legislature mandated the assistance of counsel for all juveniles in delinquency proceedings. It was believed that making provisions for defense counsel would maximize the equitable treatment of youths by Minnesota juvenile courts. However, Feld's (1988b) analysis of 17,195 cases involving adjudications of delinquency in 1986 found that only about half of all juveniles adjudicated delinquent in these Minnesota juvenile courts had attorneys to represent them.

Analyzing adjudication data from an earlier period in five other jurisdictions besides Minnesota, Feld (1988a, 1989b) discovered similar figures. Roughly half of all juveniles adjudicated delinquent in these state juvenile courts had legal representation at the time of their adjudications. It is unclear whether the juveniles who did not have defense counsel also did not request defense counsel. It would have been inconsistent with *Gault* as well as unconstitutional if these juveniles had requested defense counsel and been denied it in those jurisdictions. But Feld may have provided at least two plausible explanations for this finding. He found that juveniles who were represented by attorneys in each of these jurisdictions, and who were also adjudicated as delinquent, tended to receive harsher sentences and dispositions from juvenile court judges than did those juveniles who did not have defense counsel to represent them. Thus it would seem that the presence of defense counsel in juvenile courts, at least in those jurisdictions examined by Feld, actually aggravated the dispositional outcome rather than mitigated it. An alternative explanation is that the more serious offenders in those jurisdictions were more likely to acquire counsel. Thus they would logically receive harsher sentences than would less serious offenders if they were ultimately adjudicated as delinquents.

Defense Counsel and Ensuring Due Process Rights for Juveniles

The manifest function of defense attorneys in juvenile courts is to ensure that due process is fulfilled by all participants. Defense attorneys are the primary advocates of fairness for juveniles who are charged with crimes or

BOX 7.4 ON THE STATUTE OF LIMITATIONS FOR MURDER

The Case of Candace Rough Surface

The **statute of limitations** is a provision specifying a period of time lapsing between the time a crime was committed and during which one or more persons can be prosecuted for committing that crime. Some statutes of limitations are three years, while other statutes of limitations are six years. Once a statute of limitations has expired on a particular crime, persons cannot be prosecuted for it, even if they admit to it later in their lives. However, there is *no* statute of limitations for murder.

It happened in Mobridge, South Dakota on August 2, 1980. An 18-year-old Sioux woman, Candace Rough Surface, disappeared. The family reported her missing after three days, but her body was not found until nine months later, when the Missouri River receded. Her decaying skeleton was found by ranchers and her remains were identified. Foul play was obvious, since her skeleton revealed five gunshot wounds. No one knew who committed the crime or when.

In October, 1995, over 15 years since the murder occurred, police received a tip about the murder from someone who said she knew about it. The ex-wife of James E. Stroh II, an Eagle River, Wisconsin resident, told police that Stroh had admitted to Rough Surface's murder a long time ago when she and James were married. Allegedly, Stroh told his wife that he and another man had beaten, raped, and killed Rough Surface and dumped her body in the Missouri River near the Standing Rock Sioux Indian Reservation, where she had lived.

When Stroh was arrested by police officers, he grudgingly admitted to the crime, but he said that the killing was "masterminded" by his cousin, Nicholas A. Scherr of Mobridge. Stroh said that he and his family had been on vacation and had stopped for a few days in Mobridge. He was 15 years old then, and he was in the company of his 16-year-old cousin, Scherr. He said that Rough Surface approached them one evening and appeared to be drunk. They were outside a cafe after dark, and according to Stroh, Rough Surface appeared to be looking for sex. They went to a mobile home but had a dispute and decided to leave. When they were in Scherr's truck, Rough Surface allegedly slapped Scherr. That is when, according to Stroh, they decided to beat and rape her. Following the beating and rape, they shot her with a rifle. Scherr ordered Stroh to pull the trigger, too, to become implicated. Stroh remembered pulling the trigger of the rifle, but he wasn't sure whether he hit Rough Surface. Later, Stroh and Scherr wrapped a chain around Rough Surface's body and dragged her to the bank of the Missouri River, where they dumped her.

When Stroh gave his confession to police, the prosecutor agreed to allow Stroh to plead guilty to manslaughter in exchange for his testimony against Scherr, who faces the death penalty on first-degree murder charges. Interestingly, Stroh was held in jail without bail, while his cousin, Scherr, was permitted to post $200,000 bond and was freed pending a subsequent trial. This angered many Native Americans, who said that if a Native American had been charged with first-degree murder, there would have been no bail. Despite the racial overtones that this case has generated, the fact remains that justice was forthcoming in the woman's murder. There is no statute of limitations on murder.

Should Stroh have been allowed to plead guilty to manslaughter following his confession to police about the murder of Rough Surface? Should there be no statute of limitations for any crime?

Source: Adapted from Joe Kafka, "'Justice Should Be Done,'" *Minot (ND) Daily News*, April 9, 1996:A1, A6.

other types of offenses. Minors, particularly very young youths, are more susceptible to the persuasiveness of adults. Law enforcement officers, intake officers, and prosecutors might extract incriminating evidence from juveniles in much the same way as police officers and prosecutors might extract inculpatory information from suspects in criminal cases, provided that certain constitutional safeguards were not in place. For adults, a major constitutional safeguard is the *Miranda* warning, which, among other things, advises those arrested for crimes of their right to an attorney, their right to terminate police interrogations whenever they wish and remain silent, their right to have their attorneys present during questioning, and the right to have an attorney appointed for them if they cannot afford one. Normally, defense attorneys for adults charged with crimes are reluctant to have their clients say anything at all to police officers or others (Mershon, 1991).

When the *Miranda* warning became official policy for police officers and others to observe religiously, the warning and accompanying constitutional safeguards were not believed applicable to juveniles. Thus law enforcement officers continued to question youths about crimes during successive, post-*Miranda* years. Since it is generally accepted that a juvenile's understanding of the law is poor (Lawrence, 1984; Mershon, 1991; Peterson, 1988), it might be assumed further that juveniles might be more easily manipulated by law enforcement authorities. An attempt to protect juveniles from themselves in making incriminating Fifth Amendment–type statements was the U.S. Supreme Court case of *Fare v. Michael C.* (1979). This case involved a juvenile who waived his constitutional right to be questioned by police about his involvement in a crime. The Court ruled that the totality of circumstances test should govern whether juveniles intelligently and knowingly waive their right to be questioned by police about crimes and whether it is necessary first to obtain parental consent. Undoubtedly, this decision had led many states to enact statutes that specifically render inadmissible any admissions juveniles might make to police in the absence of parental guidance or consent (Shaffner, 1985).

Some experts believe that the U.S. Supreme Court has always supported the *parens patriae* nature of juvenile courts and that their purportedly liberal decisions about juvenile constitutional guarantees have been intended only to provide minimal procedural protections (Dale, 1987). Nevertheless, the possibilities of incarceration in secure juvenile incarcerative facilities and/or transfer to criminal court jurisdiction where harsher penalties may be administered are sufficient to warrant the intervention of defense counsel in many juvenile cases (Champion and Mays, 1991; Feld, 1993a–c). At the very least, defense counsel may prevent some youths from being railroaded into accepting unnecessary conditional interventions from intake officers or juvenile court judges. It is not the intention of defense attorneys to aggravate matters and cause their juvenile clients to receive harsher punishments than they would normally receive from the same judges if defense counsel were not present. But it is a curious paradox that those seeking justice and due process and who exercise their rights for these aims are often penalized for exercising these rights.

In many respects, this paradox is similar to the disparity in sentencing among those who have similar criminal histories and are convicted for the same offenses but who receive widely disparate sentences depending on whether their convictions are obtained through plea bargaining or a jury verdict in a criminal trial. There is no particular reason for judges to impose harsher punishments on convicted offenders who exercise their right to a jury trial than to those who enter into plea agreements and plead guilty, but differential punishments are frequently administered (Champion, 1988). One explanation, an extralegal or nonlegal one, is that the extra punishment is the penalty for obligating the state to prove its case against the defendant in open court. Knowing about this sentencing disparity, many defense attorneys counsel their clients, especially where there is strong inculpatory evidence, to plead guilty to lesser charges and accept a lesser penalty to avoid more severe punishments that judges almost certainly will impose upon conviction through a trial. It would appear from the available evidence that juvenile court judges are guilty of the same behavior when relating to juvenile clients who are represented by counsel and those who are not. For the present, anyway, being represented by counsel in juvenile court seems more of a liability than an asset.

BOX 7.5   PARENT–CHILD CONFIDENTIALITY PRIVILEGE?

The Case of the Parents Who Refused to Testify Against Their Son

In Williston, Vermont, Arthur and Geneva Yandrow went to jail. They had committed no crime, yet they were serving time. Their offense? Refusing to testify against their son, who was charged with rape. The Yandrows claimed **confidentiality privilege** *on the basis of the parent–child relationship.* Legal? No. At least that is what the judge concluded when citing them for contempt of court and placing them in jail for refusing to testify in the case against their son.

Craig Yandrow, 25 years old, lived with his parents. On February 14, 1996, a woman was raped, beaten, and left in the cold, unconscious and half-naked. The rapist had fled the scene, but he had left an incriminating jacket behind, a blue jacket with "Saint John's Bay" on the back. Craig's younger brother owned such a jacket. Further, the victim of the rape said that she had scratched and fought her attacker. When arrested, Craig had injuries consistent with those the victim said she inflicted.

Among other things, the prosecutor wants to know whether the parents can verify their son's whereabouts on Valentine's Day, 1996. Where was their son? If the parents can recall where he was, what was his condition, especially in the days following the rape? Was he injured? Did he have scratches? The parents won't say.

Paul Volk, attorney for the Yandrows, says that the Yandrows are claiming the "parent–child privilege" which, they believe, gives them the legal and moral authority to refuse to testify. Volk says, "My clients are absolutely adamant that they will not testify. They believe morally and based on their religious values they will not destroy their family and betray their son." Of course, the life of the rape victim has been destroyed in the process. What are her rights?

The Vermont Supreme Court ruled in March 1996 in a 5–0 vote that parents cannot claim parent–child privilege in instances where their son is a competent adult. Further, a lawyer for the Catholic Diocese of Burlington, Vermont, said that no church doctrine exists that allows the Yandrows to refuse to assist prosecutors in their case against the Yandrow's son, Craig. The judge can hold the parents in jail indefinitely for refusing to testify. Volk, the Yandrow's attorney, said that once the judge sees that the parents do not intend to testify, he will free them, however.

Should there be a parent–child privilege to be claimed by parents who might possess incriminating information about their children? Does refusing to testify against their son suggest that the Yandrows possess incriminating information? Can parents be compelled to testify against their children? What policies should govern this situation?

Source: Adapted from Associated Press, "Parents Jailed for Refusing to Testify against Their Son," *Minot (ND) Daily News*, April 6, 1996:A8.

Are Attorneys Being Used More Frequently by Juvenile Defendants?

Yes. At least a survey of five states during the 1980–1989 period (California, Montana, Nebraska, North Dakota, and Pennsylvania) found that attorney use by juvenile offenders increased systematically across these years (Champion, 1992). Attorney use varies by jurisdiction, however. In the late 1980s, about 90 percent of all California juvenile cases involved either private or publicly appointed defense counsel. However, in states such as Nebraska and North Dakota, attorney use by juveniles occurred in about 60 percent of cases.

It may seem that whenever youths invoke their right to an attorney, it would be under circumstances where the offenses alleged are serious or violent. Although it is true that attorney use was more prevalent in these states where serious and violent offenses were alleged, it is also true that attorney use increased during the 10-year period for status offenders and those charged with public order, property, and drug offenses as well (Champion, 1992). The primary implication of this research is that juvenile courts are experiencing greater defense attorney involvement each year. If these states are representative of all U.S. jurisdictions, the formalization of juvenile courtrooms is definitely increasing with greater involvement of defense counsel in juvenile cases.

Do Defense Counsel for Juveniles Make a Difference in Their Case Dispositions?

We know that the use of defense counsel by juveniles results in mixed outcomes. In some instances, because of the greater formality of the proceeding because defense counsel are present, outcomes occur that may be unfavorable to juvenile defendants. For instance, if an intake officer would be inclined to divert a particular case from the juvenile justice system because of his or her judgment that the youth will probably not reoffend, this diversion decision may not be chosen if an attorney is present to represent the juvenile's interests. The intake officer may feel that a higher authority should decide the case. The defense counsel may be intimidating. In an otherwise attorney-free environment, the intake officer would act differently. Thus different actions by different actors in the system may be anticipated, depending on the presence or absence of an attorney.

In cases adjudicated before juvenile court judges, a defense counsel's presence seems to work for the juvenile's benefit. Judicial discretion is affected to the extent that stricter or less strict adherence to juvenile laws is affected. There seems to be a tendency for juvenile court judges to be more lenient with juveniles who are represented by defense counsel than with those who are not represented by counsel. This leniency manifests itself in various ways. For instance, juvenile court judges may impose probation more often than incarceration where juveniles are represented by counsel. Represented juveniles who are disposed to a secure facility for a period of months may serve shorter incarcerative terms compared with those juveniles sent to these same secure facilities but who were not represented by counsel. More frequent granting of juvenile parole occurs among those youths represented by counsel compared with those youths not represented by counsel. Few data are available among the states concerning the frequency with which leniency is dispensed where attorneys are either present or absent in juvenile cases. However, the general impression from the literature is that defense counsel are of greater benefit to juvenile offenders than a total absence of counsel (Champion, 1988, 1992, 1994).

A study by the U.S. General Accounting Office (1995b) of juvenile proceedings in 15 states found results similar to those of previous research. State statutes guaranteeing a juvenile's right to counsel were exercised by juveniles in these states at the rate of from 91 to 97 percent of the time (California and Pennsylvania) to about 65 percent of the time (Nebraska). Dispositions of juvenile offenders varied according to whether juveniles were represented by counsel. Representation rates varied according to the type of offense. However, those not represented by defense counsel were least likely compared with the rest of the juveniles processed to receive out-of-home placement in an industrial school. One explanation is that their offenses were not serious enough to warrant counsel, and thus no secure confinement would be imposed anyway.

Comparative research studying the effects of counsel on juvenile court dispositions has been conducted in Australia and Canada. In Canada, for instance, an examination was made of 2000 juvenile delinquent cases during 1981 (Carrington and Moyer, 1990). Most juveniles had some type of legal representation at some point during their juvenile justice system processing. It was found that those accused juveniles with legal representation generally had lower rates of conviction, mainly because of the greater use of not-guilty pleas. Despite the lower rates of conviction, these researchers believed that the ultimate impact of legal representation on juvenile adjudication rates was rather small.

In Australia, it has been found that a considerable gap exists between the philosophical role *intended* for defense counsel in juvenile cases and what actually happens in practice. Sixteen lawyers were surveyed in 1989 to determine how they viewed their roles and effectiveness in juvenile matters. Most lawyers revealed that their impact on the legal process was that they facilitated plea bargaining for their youthful clients. In practice, they obtained for their clients the best possible deals in the short time provided for their interactions with juvenile courts and prosecutors. These informal agreements and legal shortcuts were neither contemplated nor intended by the Australian legislature. In fact, the intended function of greater attorney involvement in juvenile matters, according to the Australian legislature, was to ensure greater fundamental fairness in juvenile case processing. It would seem that more frequent plea bargaining and deal cutting were the more realistic outcomes of defense counsel involvement in the cases surveyed here (Naffine and Wundersitz, 1991).

Defense Counsel as *Guardians Ad Litem*

In some juvenile cases, child abuse has been alleged. Thus defense counsel perform additional responsibilities as they attempt to ensure that the best interests of their clients are served in ways that will protect children from parents who abuse them (Rodatus, 1994). *Guardians ad litem are special guardians appointed by the court in which a particular litigation is pending to represent a youth, ward, or unborn person in that particular litigation* (Black, 1990:706). Most juvenile court jurisdictions have *guardian ad litem* programs, where interested persons serve in this capacity. In some cases, defense counsel for youths perform the dual role of defense counsel and the youth's *guardian ad litem. Guardians ad litem* are supposed to work in ways that will benefit those they represent, and such guardians provide legal protection from others. Defense counsel working as *guardians ad litem* may act to further the child's best interests, despite a child's contrary requests or demands. Thus this is a different type of non-adversarial role performed by some defense counsel.

Juvenile Offender Plea Bargaining and the Role of Defense Counsel

Often, we tend to think that plea bargaining occurs only within the criminal justice system. The fact is that juveniles enter into plea agreements with juvenile court prosecutors with great frequency (Sanborn, 1993). Sanborn says that plea bargaining is an invaluable tool with which to eliminate case backlogs that might occur in some of the larger juvenile courts. Sanborn gathered data from 100 juvenile court officers in 1988. Specifically, Sanborn wanted to know whether plea bargaining was consistent with the guiding doctrine of *parens patriae* that characterized juvenile courts at that time. Most of those surveyed believed that plea bargaining was used solely to help those youths in need of social services or other forms of assistance. Defense counsel entering into plea agreements with juvenile court prosecutors wanted the least restrictive option imposed on their juvenile clients. Most frequently sought by defense counsel were charge reductions against their clients by prosecutors. Defense counsel were interested in reducing the stigma of a serious, negative juvenile court profile of their youthful clients by seeking reduced charges from prosecutors. Prosecutors would benefit in that plea agreements would speed up case processing and save them time from having to prove critical elements of crimes against juvenile defendants. Both actors, prosecutors and defense attorneys, sought personal goals instead of pursuing some type of *parens patriae* objective. The former were interested in concluding adjudications with sanctions, while the latter were interested in protecting their clients from more serious charges that could influence their future lives.

Sanborn (1994b) says that the degree to which *parens patriae* is alive and well depends on how much a particular court has accepted and furthered the due process renovation created by *Gault*. If fairness is to be realized in the adjudicatory hearing of juveniles, judges and defense attorneys should know the rules of criminal procedure and evidence, and they must be made aware that adjudications are serious for youths. Defense lawyers should also be reminded that appellate review is both a necessary and valuable weapon (Sanborn, 1994b).

Parental Intrusion in Juvenile Courts Is Often More Damaging Than Attorney Intrusion

Sanborn (1995) has studied the impact of the parents of juveniles who appear in juvenile courts. His research has investigated the attitudes and opinions of various juvenile justice actors, such as judges, prosecutors, defense attorneys, and probation officers. In more than a few instances, parents of processed juveniles tend to make matters for their children worse by their own actions. Some parents threaten intake officers, prosecutors, and/or judges. Many of those surveyed viewed the interventions of parents in juvenile proceedings as primarily negative. Some of their negative behaviors might be due to a basic misunderstanding of the due process rights of their children. Other parents may feel that the juvenile court is not a formally contrived proceeding with legal powers. As some parents attempt to intervene and circumvent procedural matters before the juvenile court, all actors, including defense counsel, become exasperated and tend to impose harsher sanctions than would otherwise be imposed if the parents were not there. However, parental involvement in juvenile matters is often required according to court or procedural rules (Sanborn, 1995).

It is clear from juvenile justice trends observed in most states thus far that defense counsel are increasingly present during all stages of juvenile processing. This increased involvement of defense counsel is intended to ensure that a juvenile's constitutional rights are observed. Another intention of counsel is to ensure the best deal for their youthful clients. This usually means some form of lenient treatment from the system. We have seen that attorney involvement *does* preserve one's rights at different processing stages; however, it is not yet clear whether a defense counsel's presence is totally beneficial to juvenile clients at all times. Too much formalization may cause various actors (e.g., intake officers, prosecutors, judges) to act differently when others are present who can monitor their actions. The traditional view of juvenile courts is that whatever is done to and for the juvenile will be in the youth's best interests. Sometimes, this means making one type of decision for one offender and a different type of decision for another offender, even when the offenders share similar background characteristics and have committed similar offenses.

Extralegal factors, such as race or ethnicity, socioeconomic status, gender, age, and a youth's demeanor, all contribute to decision making at different processing stages. Ideally, these criteria should *not* be considered when making decisions about juvenile offenders. But sometimes judges and others will respond and make decisions about some youths based on these and other variables. In many cases these decisions are favorable for the youths involved, but outsiders may perceive this differential treatment to be inherently unequal treatment. Thus questions arise about one's equal protection rights as set forth in the Fourteenth Amendment. In the name of equal protection, therefore, judges and others may tend to be harsher with some offenders, simply to preserve due process. This greater harshness is sometimes the result of a defense attorney's presence.

Consider the following scenario. Two 12-year-old youths have been taken into custody for theft. One boy stole some candy from a grocery store; the other boy stole some pencils from a convenience store. Both boys have no prior juvenile records. One boy is Hispanic, the other is Asian. The intake officer, who happens to be black, sees both boys and their families with no defense counsel present. The Hispanic boy utters various obscenities at the intake officer. The Asian boy sits calmly and responds politely to questions asked. The intake officer might be inclined to recommend further juvenile justice processing for the Hispanic juvenile, while he might be inclined to divert the Asian juvenile from the system. Is this decision motivated by prejudice? Or is the decision motivated by the *attitude* or *demeanor* displayed by each youth? If, in fact, these different decisions are made, the Hispanic boy is adversely affected by the intake officer's decision. But the Asian boy benefits from the informal handling of his case by the intake officer.

Now let's consider these same scenarios, but in each case we will place in the room defense counsel for both youths. Whether the defense counsel are privately retained or publicly appointed, they are interested in *justice* for their respective clients. Because of the presence of an attorney in each of the cases, the intake officer decides to apply standard decision-making criteria. Both of these boys have committed theft, at least a misdemeanor if an adult committed these acts. Thus the intake officer moves *both* boys further into the system, so that a juvenile court prosecutor can take over from there. In the Hispanic boy's case, the presence of his defense counsel merely gave credence to the intake officer's decision to move the boy further into the system. The boy's demeanor or attitude didn't help matters, but the intake officer is merely following the rules. The letter of the law is applied. In the Asian youth's situation, the intake officer moves the boy further into the system even though he believes that this decision is *not* in the boy's best interests. But the intake officer is treating both boys equally, thus ensuring their due process and equal protection rights under the Fourteenth Amendment. The presence of defense counsel explains the consistency of the intake officer's conduct in both cases.

Some get-tough observers may say, so what? The boys stole something of value and they must learn not to steal. If we send the Asian boy away from the system without punishing him, he will learn contempt for the system. Both boys need to be punished equally, because they have equal background characteristics and have committed commensurate offenses. Should they be punished equally? At the other end of the spectrum are those who wish to preserve the *parens patriae* concept of juvenile courts. Doing things that are in a youth's best interests may involve making decisions that may be inherently discriminatory. Should we punish one's demeanor or attitude, which varies greatly from youth to youth, or should we punish the same delinquent acts in the same ways? This hypothetical example shows both the good and bad stemming from greater attorney involvement in juvenile proceedings at any stage.

KEY TERMS

Act to Regulate the Treatment and Control of Dependent, Neglected, and Delinquent Children

Jane Addams

Adversarial proceeding

Barker balancing test

Cesare Beccaria

Charles Loring Brace

Confidentiality privilege

Guardians ad litem

New York Children's Aid Society

Preponderance of the evidence

Society for the Prevention of Pauperism

Statute of limitations

With prejudice

Without prejudice

QUESTIONS FOR REVIEW

1. What were some major provisions of the Illinois Juvenile Court Act of 1899? How were juvenile delinquents defined?

2. What were some of the punishments prescribed for dependent and neglected children under the Illinois Juvenile Court Act of 1899?

3. Did the Truancy Act in Colorado in 1899 provide for the establishment for a new juvenile court? What did this act accomplish? How did this event influence certain status offenders, and how they were treated?

4. What was the *New York House of Refuge*? When was it created, and what were some of its manifest goals? Was it successful at achieving its goals? Why or why not? Explain.

5. Who were the *childsavers*? What were their aims? How did they assist in the bureaucratization of juvenile courts? Give some examples.

6. What was *Hull House*? In what respect was it a community-based agency?

7. Briefly explain the difference between the terms *gemeinschaft* and *gesellschaft*. How do these terms relate to how juvenile offenders were originally treated in the small communities and villages of the American colonies?

8. Discuss the movement from gemeinschaft to gesellschaft. Compare this movement with the accompanying changes in social relations and modifications in how juveniles were eventually defined or conceptualized.

9. What are two significant landmark juvenile cases that did much to vest juveniles with specific constitutional rights? Describe briefly the rights conveyed and some of the changes these cases have caused in juvenile court operations.

10. Compare and contrast *due process courts* with *traditional courts*. Who are police prosecutors? How might these police prosecutors experience a conflict of interest in prosecuting juveniles?

SUGGESTED READINGS

American Prosecutors Research Institute. *Beyond Convictions: Prosecutors as Community Leaders in the War on Drugs*. Alexandria, VA: American Prosecutors Research Institute National Drug Prosecution Center, 1994.

Jones, Michael A. and Barry Krisberg. *Images and Reality: Juvenile Crime, Youth Violence and Public Policy*. San Francisco: National Council on Crime and Delinquency, 1994.

Minnesota Office of the Legislative Auditor. *Residential Facilities for Juvenile Offenders*. St. Paul, MN: Minnesota Office of the Legislative Auditor, Program Evaluation Division, 1995.

CHAPTER 8

THE ADJUDICATORY PROCESS: DISPOSITIONAL ALTERNATIVES

INTRODUCTION

THE NATURE OF THE OFFENSE

FIRST OFFENDER OR PRIOR OFFENDER?

AGGRAVATING AND MITIGATING CIRCUMSTANCES

JUVENILE RISK ASSESSMENTS AND PREDICTIONS OF DANGEROUSNESS

PREDISPOSITIONAL REPORTS

THE JUDICIAL DECISION

IMPLICATIONS OF THE JUDICIAL DECISION FOR JUVENILE OFFENDERS

KEY TERMS

QUESTIONS FOR REVIEW

SUGGESTED READINGS

INTRODUCTION

Ronnie was a 14-year-old runaway. She was found by police hiding in an alley of a large city. Subsequently, police confiscated a small quantity of heroin, a small .22 caliber pistol, and about two ounces of marijuana. Ronnie had numerous needle marks on her arms when she was subjected to a physical examination. She also tested positive for AIDS and had herpes symptoms in her genital area. According to others in the vicinity, Ronnie had been engaged in prostitution and drug use for about six months. No one knows where Ronnie came from, and she had a false ID showing her to be "Sally Jennings," age 22, 1621 Millford Lane, Davenport, Iowa. Communications with Davenport police revealed that there was no such address. Eventually she admitted that her first name was "Ronnie." While she was being transported to the hospital initially, she bit one of the officers on the hand as he attempted to handcuff her. She tried to escape the hospital at least twice during her physical examination. She also punched a nurse in the mouth, breaking one of the nurse's teeth. An intake officer has referred Ronnie to the juvenile court prosecutor to determine whether she should be sent to a hospital to undergo treatment for narcotics addiction. How should Ronnie be treated? What punishment, if any, should the juvenile court impose?

Erik is a 16-year-old. He is a gang member, belonging to a violent gang known as the Chicago Scorpions. Rumor has it that Erik has murdered other rival gang members on at least two occasions, and he has tattoos that are symbolic of one who has killed before. When Erik was arrested by police, he was burglarizing a closed convenience store. Police apprehended him after he climbed out of a back window, carrying several cartons of cigarettes and some beer. Erik's prior record shows he has been arrested 19 times for car theft, six times for assault, and four times for larceny. He has five delinquency adjudications. In each case, the juvenile court judge imposed probation for Erik, since the juvenile corrections in the Chicago area were overcrowded with presumably more serious offenders compared with Erik. The intake officer has completed her interview with Erik and she has now referred him to the prosecutor for further action. Should Erik be detained to await adjudication? Is he dangerous? What evidence suggests that Erik poses a danger to others or is a flight risk?

In the scenarios above, we have two totally different types of persons. We have a young runaway who has drifted into prostitution, drug use, and other illicit activities. We know that she will need treatment for her venereal disease, AIDS, and drug dependency. We don't know who her parents are or where they can be found. However, we have Ronnie in our custody and we have at least some resources that might help her.

In Erik's case we have a hard-core juvenile offender. Together with the rumor from others that Erik is truly a dangerous person who has killed in the past, his lengthy record of assault, car theft, and larceny do little to reassure us that there is much that can be done for him in the immediate future. We don't know whether Erik can be rehabilitated. He has been through the system nearly 30 times, with five delinquency adjudications. Now he is charged with burglary and larceny. He is a gang member. Thus far we know that the system has done little or nothing to change his behavior. Can we reasonably expect that one or more strategies exist that might cause Erik to change and to modify his present conduct? Should we send him to criminal court where more severe sanctions might be imposed? Does the juvenile court have the resources and expertise to make a difference in Erik's life?

These and millions of other similar scenarios have haunted juvenile court judges, prosecutors, intake officers, probation and parole officers, and other actors for many decades. How do we solve each of these problems? What resources can be energized to make a difference in the lives of these and other youths? Are either of these persons amenable to treatment and subsequent rehabilitation?

This chapter is about assessing juvenile offenders and making decisions about their prospects for treatment and/or rehabilitation. An important task performed by prosecutors and others at an early stage of the juvenile justice system is to select for prosecution those cases involving the most serious juveniles. Prosecutors must make assessments of probable case outcomes, weighing factors such as the dangerousness of certain youths and the probability of the effectiveness of various kinds of intervention that might be used in their control and management. Forecasts of dangerousness and risk are useful for anticipating the appropriate programs and interventions in diversion and/or probationary decisions with conditions and for making the proper recommendations to juvenile court judges for sanctions. Some of the fairly recent measures of risk assessment and dangerousness predictors are described. The effectiveness of these measures is also examined in light of prosecutorial and judicial decision making. Finally, an overview of judicial sentencing options is presented. Each of these options receives detailed coverage in later chapters.

THE NATURE OF THE OFFENSE

By year end 1995, there were 2,209,675 arrests of youths under age 18 (Maguire and Pastore, 1996:404). About 1,489,700 cases were sent to the juvenile justice system for processing (Bilchik, 1996:9). About half of these cases were processed formally. Of the 789,000 petitioned cases that were handled formally, 457,000 juveniles were adjudicated. Of these, about 128,700 were placed in secure institutions such as industrial schools. About 11,800 cases were transferred to criminal courts (Bilchik, 1996:9). Of all arrests of youths under age 18 in 1995, 519,898 were for violent or person offenses, such as aggravated assault, rape, and murder (Maguire and Pastore, 1996:404).

One investigation reveals a disturbing finding about youth who are transferred to criminal court. Juvenile court records in Boston, Detroit, Newark, and Phoenix during the period 1981–1984 showed that for 201 youths transferred from the jurisdiction of juvenile courts to criminal courts, *no* strong determinants of the judicial transfer decision were identifiable (Fagan and Deschenes, 1990). Fagan and Deschenes (1990) suggest that the absence of uniform criteria for juvenile transfers is an important finding, since it means that often, informal and inconsistent criteria and vague statutory language used to guide judges and prosecutors in making transfer decisions or recommendations are highly subjective and may invite disparity. Thus we are reminded that decisions about youths at various stages of the juvenile justice process are not fixed and perfectly objective, but rather, they are often diffuse and subjective. This underscores the importance of examining all relevant criteria that may be relevant in affecting a youth's life chances in the system.

Juveniles who remain in juvenile courts for disposition are subject to a limited range of penalties these courts can impose, from warnings or reprimands to secure confinement. Delinquent acts involving physical harm to others or the threat of physical harm are considered violent offenses, in contrast with the larger category of property offenses that encompasses vehicular theft, petty larceny, or burglary. Intake officers perform the initial screening function by sending forward only the more serious offenders or those who the intake officers believe should have their cases adjudicated by juvenile court judges.

Juvenile court prosecutors screen those cases further by deciding which cases have the most prosecutive merit. Prosecutors are influenced by numerous factors whether to prosecute juveniles formally. Age, offense seriousness, and one's previous record often convince prosecutors to move forward with selected cases, whereas they may be inclined to divert other cases to informal arbitration through alternative dispute resolution (Lattimore, Visher, and Linster, 1995). Despite the potential for recidivism, over 80 percent of the juvenile cases referred to juvenile courts annually are disposed of informally in many jurisdictions, without formal adjudication by juvenile court judges (Bilchik, 1996; Krisberg et al., 1993).

One important consideration is the willingness of juveniles to compensate victims for their monetary losses through a program of restitution (Bazemore, 1989). Juries comprised of one's peers may impose restitution as a condition of diversion, and a youth's satisfactory completion of such a diversion program will probably avoid the scars of a formal delinquency adjudication (North Carolina Administrative Office of the Courts, 1994). Juvenile courts continue to view their roles as largely rehabilitative, and judges seek to assist youths in avoiding any negative consequences of secure confinement (Bilchik, 1996). Various interventions are believed beneficial to juveniles in lieu of formal adjudicatory actions in juvenile courts (Champion, 1994). However, some evidence suggests that interventions involving intensive supervision of youthful offenders may not be particularly effective at reducing their rates of recidivism (Minor and Elrod, 1990).

Consideration is also given to whether juveniles are suffering from any psychiatric disorders, such as depression or anxiety, or whether they are drug or alcohol dependent (Murphy et al., 1991; Shichor and Bartollas, 1990). It is not unusual to observe severe psychiatric disorders among juvenile murderers (Malmquist, 1990). Private incarcerative facilities are often used to house youths suffering from various psychological ailments, whereas public facilities accommodate more traditional youthful offenders, or those who have more prior offenses, who are on probation, or who have had their probation revoked frequently (Shichor and Bartollas, 1990).

In many jurisdictions, secure confinement is a last resort of judges in their dealing with serious juvenile offenders (Pennell, Curtis, and Scheck, 1990). Nevertheless, growing rates of violence among juveniles, especially for offenses such as first-degree sexual assault, aggravated robbery, and homicide, and the increasing influence of the get-tough movement in juvenile courts, are causing juvenile court judges to impose harsher dispositions for those juveniles who commit more serious offenses (Krisberg et al., 1993; Towberman, 1992). Thus the nature of the offenses alleged, together with inculpatory evidence against youths charged, weighs heavily in favor of moving certain more chronic youths into the system toward formal adjudication. The rise of youth gangs in large U.S. cities, together with greater involvement in illicit drug trafficking, has done much to place more youths at risk regarding possible incarceration in secure facilities (Spergel, 1995).

FIRST OFFENDER OR PRIOR OFFENDER?

Are juveniles first offenders or do they have prior juvenile records? This is a key question raised by prosecutors when examining one's file to determine whether to prosecute the case in court. The overwhelming tendency among prosecutors is either to divert petty first offenders to a conditional program or to dismiss these cases outright (Bilchik, 1996). Many diversionary programs involve restitution or victim compensation in some form. Contracts are arranged between youths and their victims, whereby youths reimburse victims, either partially or completely, for their financial losses. These programs often involve mediators who are responsible for securing agreements between juvenile offenders and their victims. Known as alternative dispute resolution, these mediation programs are believed to be fairly

BOX 8.1   DRUGS AND DELINQUENCY

The Case of Jared Fe Benito, Honolulu

Drugs and delinquency don't mix. If they do, there are often disastrous results. On June 7, 1996, a teen gang member, Jared Fe Benito, of Honolulu stole a Honda automobile. When police officers located the automobile and gave chase, Benito tried to ram officers with the car. In self-defense, police officers opened fire, killing Benito.

A subsequent investigation revealed that Benito was a gang member. Further, evidence showed that he was implicated in a previous drive-by shooting resulting in the death of an innocent pedestrian on May 31, 1996. Another gang member, 19-year-old Michael Kahele, was being held on $70,000 bail awaiting trial on first-degree terrorism and threatening and firearms charges, as well as charges stemming from the May 31 drive-by shooting incident. Kahele had allegedly shot at rival gang members one day while they were outside a local Kalihi store.

When doctors performed an autopsy on Benito, they found significant amounts of crystal methamphetamine, an illegal drug. The drug was believed to be associated with his unusual conduct in attempting to elude police and ram them with the stolen automobile he was driving.

What drug prevention programs might be useful in deterring persons such as Benito from using drugs? Should drug use be considered a mitigating circumstance to excuse delinquent or criminal conduct among drug users? How would you charge an offender who committed a serious offense while on an illegal drug?

Source: Adapted from Associated Press, "Slain Teen Used Drugs Same Day," *The Honolulu Advertiser*, August 2, 1996:A3.

---

widespread and effective (Fuller and Norton, 1993; Rubin, 1988). Several diversionary programs are described in Chapter 10.

Evidence suggests that prior offenders, even chronic and violent offenders, stand good chances of receiving some nonincarcerative sanction if they are eventually adjudicated as delinquent (Torbet et al., 1996). However, chronic juvenile offenders compared with first offenders also have a greater chance of pursuing criminal careers as adults (Tremblay, 1992; Visher, Lattimore, and Linster, 1991). Currently, no uniform policies exist among jurisdictions about how chronic offenders should be identified. Because of poor record keeping and the lack of interjurisdictional record sharing, many youthful offenders are continually diverted from formal juvenile court processing, despite their chronic recidivism. Some jurisdictions measure whether formal action against juveniles should be taken on the basis of the number of times they have been arrested. After four arrests, youths in some jurisdictions may be considered serious enough to have petitions filed against them as delinquents. In the early to mid-1990s, however, the compilation and centralization of state delinquency figures has increased, as well as the openness and availability of this information to the public sector (Torbet et al., 1996).

Despite the relatively greater seriousness of violent offenses compared with property offenses, juvenile property offenders account for nearly two-thirds of all petitioned juveniles annually in most juvenile courts (Bilchik, 1996:9). Substantial numbers of status offenders continue to be processed by the juvenile justice system as well. Thus it is unclear who is being targeted by get-tough policies nationwide during the 1990s. Ideally, only most serious chronic and violent juveniles should be targeted for the harshest juvenile court penalties. However, an overwhelming majority of long-term detainees in public and private secure facilities are property offenders, again by a substantial margin of 2:1 (Maguire and Pastore, 1996).

One implication of this finding is that those most likely to be targeted for juvenile court action are chronic property offenders. They are considered the most troublesome in several respects. They clog juvenile court dockets again and again, and they sluggishly abandon their pattern of delinquent conduct. They cost taxpayers considerable money.

Relatively few juveniles are violent offenders. Often, however, many of these juveniles are placed in residential facilities for individual or group therapy or given psychiatric examinations and treatment. In Tennessee, for example, a 13-year-old boy plotted the murder of his 11-year-old sister for several months. One Sunday morning, he took his mother's .38 caliber revolver and shot his sister point blank in the face, killing her. He propped her up in her bed to make the deed look like suicide. He forged a suicide note. Later, he was confronted by overwhelming incriminating evidence and confessed. He was placed in a psychiatric facility, where he was held for observation and treatment for several years. During his time spent in this facility, he openly boasted to others about his sister's murder. Further, he frequently used a video-game pistol to "shoot" other patients in the dayroom of the mental hospital. He was released from the psychiatric institution in 1994 and left the state. He was freed because the juvenile court lost its control or jurisdiction over him. Several hospital attendants believe he will kill as an adult. There is little or nothing the system could do to keep him from reentering society. If the same act were to be committed today, Tennessee has revised its juvenile code so that boy could be subjected to prolonged confinement and treatment. Thus if authorities had serious questions about whether such persons should be freed in the near or distant future, this information could be used to extend their confinement.

The strong rehabilitative and reintegrative principles upon which the juvenile courts have operated for most of the twentieth century continue to influence how violent juvenile offenders are treated. For instance, Fagan (1990) has described various reintegrative programs designed especially for violent juvenile offenders [**violent juvenile offender programs**] (VJOPs) that provide several positive interventions and treatments. Instead of long-term incarceration in secure confinement, many violent juvenile offenders are placed in community-based secure facilities, where they remain for short periods before being reintegrated into their communities. Transitional residential programs include sustained intensive supervision as youths are gradually given freedoms and responsibilities (Fagan, 1990:238–239).

The VJOP described by Fagan is based on a theoretical model integrating strain, control, and learning theories (Fagan, 1990:239). Four program dimensions include (Fagan, 1990:240):

1. *Social networking:* the strengthening of personal bonds (attitudes, commitments, and beliefs) through positive experiences with family members, schools, the workplace, or nondelinquent peers

2. *Provision of opportunities for youths:* the strengthening of social bonds (attachment and involvement) through achievement and successful participation in school, workplace, and family activities

3. *Social learning:* the process by which personal and social bonds are strengthened and reinforced; strategies include rewards and sanctions for attainment of goals or for contingent behaviors

4. *Goal-oriented behaviors:* the linking of specific behaviors to each client's needs and abilities, including problem behaviors and special intervention needs (e.g., substance abuse treatment or psychotherapy)

Fagan reports that violent juvenile offenders who have participated in these programs seem less inclined to recidivate. He believes that "carefully implemented and well-managed intervention programs," those that involve "early reintegration activities preceding release from secure care and intensive supervision in the community, with emphasis on gradual reentry and development of social skills to avoid criminal behavior," do much to "avert the abrupt return to criminality after release from the program" of these youths. Those youths exposed to more conventional and longer secure confinement and treatment appear to recidivate at greater rates and to persist in their delinquent behaviors (Fagan, 1990:258). Fagan's view is shared by others (Knight and Tripodi, 1996).

Therefore, it is difficult to formulate specific guidelines about how violent juvenile offenders ought to be handled in their juvenile court processing.

BOX 8.2 GANGSTA RAP LEADS TO GANGSTA TREATMENT

The Case of Tupac Shakur, Rapper and Movie Star

Tupac Shakur was a black movie star and singer. He was best known for his rap music and singing about "gangsta rap." Gangsta rap contains violent lyrics and messages for those who are most likely to listen to it—teenagers. The pulsing beat of rap, coupled with lyrics advocating death to cops and other forms of violence, is wildly popular with a large segment of the youthful population. Many persons believe that he was a role model for today's children, whether certain citizens like it or not.

Shakur, 25-year-old son of a former Black Panther leader, had many scrapes with the law. Sporting a "Thug Life" tattoo across his chest and stomach, Shakur had been arrested at least half a dozen times in the past. One incident involved a sex-abuse conviction that caused him to be jailed for eight months. Another involved a shooting where Shakur was shot five times in the lobby of a Manhattan recording studio, where he was robbed. In September 1996, Shakur was in Las Vegas, Nevada, attending a Mike Tyson fight. Following the fight, he rode in a car down a Las Vegas street with some of his friends. Suddenly, some Las Vegas gang members pulled alongside and shot at Shakur's car several times. Shakur was hit four times by bullets. He died a few days later.

Some experts believe that Shakur invited such violence into his life by composing and singing the types of songs that have come to be his trademark. Others say that he was "touched by an angel" to have been shot so many times and survived, although in the latest Las Vegas incident, he wasn't as fortunate. Before Shakur died, those closest to him took his survival as a sign that Shakur was a symbol to American youth and that he should change his lifestyle to a more favorable role image. Yet others say that actors, such as Robert De Niro, Al Pacino, and Joe Pesci, can play gangster roles on the screen and not go out on the streets and act like gangsters. In short, Shakur had a choice about the way he behaved. Now he has no choices.

How much of a role model do you think persons such as Shakur are to the youth of today? Should rap music be censored? At what point does our constitutional right to free speech jeopardize the lives of youths who are attracted to songs with lyrics advocating physical violence and death to pigs (police officers)? What do you think?

Source: Adapted from Associated Press, "Thug Life Catches Up with Rapper Shakur," *Minot (ND) Daily News*, September 11, 1996:A7.

Currently, competing philosophies of rehabilitation and just deserts recommend polarities in treatments, ranging from total diversion to total secure confinement. According to the Minnesota Criminal Justice Statistical Analysis Center (1989), if courts or legislatures move to punish and incarcerate serious juveniles, we can expect to see a substantial increase in the need for additional secure facilities. It is doubtful that the services provided by these facilities will be effective at reducing recidivism among these types of serious offenders. However, if the traditional treatment and rehabilitation approach of juvenile courts is used, there are strong indications that such treatments are equally ineffective.

Certain objective criteria might be applied to decision making at various points throughout the juvenile justice system. These criteria are prevalent in most state criminal codes and describe an assortment of conditions or circumstances that are more or less influential regarding juvenile offender dispositions, regardless of their seriousness. These objective criteria are *aggravating* and *mitigating circumstances.*

AGGRAVATING AND MITIGATING CIRCUMSTANCES

Playing an important part in determining how far any particular juvenile moves into the juvenile justice system are various aggravating and mitigating circumstances accompanying their acts. In the early stages of intake and prosecutorial decision making, aggravating and mitigating circumstances are often informally considered, and much depends on the amount of detail furnished by police officers about the delinquent events. ***Aggravating circumstances** are usually those actions on the part of juveniles that tend to intensify the seriousness of their acts. Accordingly, where aggravating circumstances exist, one's subsequent punishment might be intensified. At the other end of the spectrum are **mitigating circumstances**, those factors that might weigh in the juvenile's favor. These circumstances might lessen the seriousness of the act as well as the severity of punishment imposed by juvenile court judges.* Lists of aggravating and mitigating circumstances are presented below.

Aggravating Circumstances

Aggravating circumstances applicable both to juveniles and adults include:

1. *Death or serious bodily injury to one or more victims.* The most serious juvenile offenders are those who cause death or serious bodily injury to their victims. Homicide and aggravated assault are those offenses that most directly involve death or serious physical harm to others, although it is possible to inflict serious bodily injury or inflict deep emotional scars through armed robbery and even some property crimes, including burglary. In the event that death or serious

bodily injury occurs as the result of one's delinquent acts, this weighs heavily against offenders as a strong aggravating circumstance. However, as we have seen in some jurisdictions, even death to victims may be insufficient to warrant committal of juveniles to secure confinement. Instead, they may be hospitalized and treated for mental illness or psychological problems. The harshest option available to juvenile court judges is direct commitment to secure confinement, such as an industrial school or reform school.

One judicial consideration is whether the youth contemplated the act and its consequences in advance. Was the bodily injury or death premeditated or accidental or unintentional? Some authorities argue that if one or more deaths follow armed robbery or any other serious crime, these deaths were premeditated to the extent that the offenders knew the risks they were taking and the potential for death or serious bodily injury to their victims. Nevertheless, judges must determine for themselves whether the youthful offenders involved calculated the consequences. This consideration would cause some offenders to receive treatment rather than incarcerative punishment. Some studies of juvenile murderers disclose, for example, that homicidal adolescents are also likely to have criminally violent family members, participate in gangs, abuse alcohol and drugs, and suffer severe educational difficulties, including mental retardation, perceptual deficiencies, and lowered intellectual, perceptual, and achievement test performance (Busch et al., 1990; Ewing, 1990). With these social and psychological antecedents, many youths appear disadvantaged at the outset by extralegal factors. Judges may consider these environmental and psychological inputs in determining whether particularly serious offenders should have enhanced sentences or more lenient, treatment alternatives (Visher, Lattimore, and Linster, 1991).

2. *An offense committed while the offender is awaiting other delinquency charges.* Are juveniles awaiting an intake hearing after being arrested for previous offenses? Many juveniles commit new delinquent acts between the time they are arrested for other offenses and the date of their intake hearing. These offenders are probably good candidates for temporary confinement in secure holding facilities until their cases can be heard by intake officers and delinquency petitions can be filed. Recommendations from intake officers will probably include information about the new charges filed against them. This is an aggravating circumstance that might serve to intensify the harshness and severity of punishments imposed later by juvenile court judges (Harada and Suzuki, 1994; Krisberg et al., 1993).

3. *An offense committed while the offender is on probation, parole, or work release.* Offenders with prior adjudications and who are currently serving their sentences may reoffend during these conditional periods. Usually, a condition of diversionary and probationary programs is that youths refrain from further delinquent activity. Thus they may be in violation of a program condition. Probation, parole, and work release program violations are separate offenses that are accompanied by harsher penalties. In effect, these are incidents of *contempt of court*, since they involve violations of direct court-ordered conditional activities. The probation, parole, or work release conditional programs have usually been granted to certain offenders because they have been deemed trustworthy

by officials. Therefore, violations of the court's trust are especially serious, and it becomes less likely that these juveniles will be extended such privileges in the future. But again, jurisdictional variations in this regard suggest that some juveniles continue to receive the same types of punishments imposed in previous adjudications (Doob and Beaulieu, 1992; Podkopacz, 1994).

4. *Previous offenses for which the offender has been punished.* Possessing a prior record is a strong indicator of one's chronicity and potential for future offending behavior. Juvenile court judges may be less inclined to be lenient in sentencing those with prior records, especially where serious delinquent acts have been committed. Incarcerative punishments are imposed frequently by these judges, although as we have seen, property offenders are incarcerated more frequently than violent juvenile offenders by a margin of at least 2:1. Because the juvenile justice system continues to endorse rehabilitation as one of its primary aims, it is disturbing when recidivists reappear before judges facing new charges. This suggests that previous treatments and probationary programs have been less effective than anticipated, or even completely ineffective. Harsher handling of these offenders is indicated in future sentencing decisions (Bilchik, 1996; Doob and Beaulieu, 1992; Snyder and Sickmund, 1995).

5. *Leadership in the commission of the delinquent act involving two or more offenders.* Especially in gang-related activities, one's leadership role is an aggravating circumstance. Are certain youths gang leaders? Do they incite others to commit delinquent acts? Gang leaders are often targeted for the harshest punishments, since they are most visible to their peers and serve as examples of how the system deals with juvenile offenders. Those playing minor roles in gang-related activity might be treated more leniently by judges (Rosenbaum, 1996; Sorrentino and Whittaker, 1994).

6. *A violent offense involving more than one victim.* As the number of victims increases as the result of any delinquent conduct, the potential for physical harm and death rapidly escalates. Robberies of convenience stores and other places where large numbers of customers might be are likely to involve multiple victims. The number of victims or potential victims aggravates the initial delinquent conduct.

7. *Extreme cruelty during the commission of the offense.* Maiming victims or torturing them during the commission of delinquent acts is considered extreme cruelty and worthy of enhanced punishments by juvenile court judges. The murder of Gregg Smart, a 24-year-old salesman from Derry, New Hampshire, in May 1990 is indicative of such extreme cruelty that might be considered as an aggravating circumstance. Smart had married Pamela Wojas, a college girlfriend, in May 1989. While he took on the responsibilities of married life and attempted to provide for his wife and family, his wife rapidly became disenchanted with the boredom of her new life. She yearned for the rock and roll of the younger set and sought the companionship of teenagers, including 16-year-old William Flynn, who became her secret lover. Later, Flynn allegedly conspired with two other teenagers to kill Gregg Smart. Smart begged for his life while being held by one of Flynn's teenaged associates. Flynn allegedly shot

Smart in the head with a .38 caliber revolver. Pamela Smart and her lover, Flynn, were arrested later and charged with first-degree murder. Flynn was to be tried as an adult in criminal court. Flynn's act was considered especially serious and aggravated, since extreme cruelty would have been inflicted on Gregg Smart before he was killed. He was allegedly made to beg for his life by Flynn and his associates. Flynn ultimately was sentenced to 30 years in exchange for his testimony against Pamela Smart. Smart was subsequently convicted of arranging her husband's murder and sentenced to life imprisonment.

8. *Use of a dangerous weapon in the commission of the offense, with high risk to human life.* The second and third leading causes of death among juveniles under age 21 are homicides and suicides, and most of these events include the use of firearms (University of Hawaii at Manoa, 1990). The rise in the number of youth gangs in the United States, together with a rise in drug trafficking among youths, suggests a new level of juvenile violence emerging (Spergel, 1995). Using firearms to commit delinquent acts increases greatly the potential harm to victims of such acts. Thus, possessing dangerous weapons, such as knives, firearms, or other instruments, will probably enhance the severity of sentence judges might impose in adjudicatory proceedings. Many states currently have mandatory flat time associated with using firearms during the commission of felonies. For example, felony offenders who use firearms and are subsequently apprehended and convicted stand a good chance of receiving an additional two years beyond the sentences imposed by judges. These are mandatory two-year incarcerative terms that cannot be reduced through parole or the accumulation of good-time credits. For juveniles, the use of dangerous weapons is considered as an aggravating circumstance. While mandatory penalties do not accompany firearms use by youths, their sentences will probably be harsher where firearms are involved compared with the sentences meted out to youths who commit the same offenses but without the use of firearms.

Mitigating Circumstances

Mitigating circumstances include the following:

1. *No serious bodily injury resulting from the offense.* Petty property offenders who do not endanger lives or injure others may have their sentences mitigated as a result. Interestingly, however, property offenders account for a majority of long-term juvenile detainees in industrial schools or secure juvenile facilities.

2. *No attempt to inflict serious bodily injury on anyone.* Those juveniles who commit theft or burglary usually wish to avoid confrontations with their victims. While some juveniles prepare for such contingencies and therefore pose bodily threats to others, most youthful offenders committing such acts run away from the crime scene if discovered. This is evidence of their desire to avoid inflicting serious bodily harm on their victims.

3. *Duress or extreme provocation.* A compelling defense used in criminal court cases is that offenders were under duress at the time they committed their crimes. They

may have been forced to act certain ways by others. Under certain circumstances, youths may plead that they were coerced or were acting under duress when committing delinquent acts in concert with others. Gang membership and gang violence may be precipitated to a degree because of duress. Youths may join gangs for self-protection and to avoid being assaulted by other gang members. Juvenile court judges must decide whether duress actually existed or whether the youths acted voluntarily. Also, if youths were provoked by others into fighting, their illegal behaviors might be mitigated by this finding by the court.

4. *Circumstances that justify the conduct.* Any circumstance that might serve to justify one's conduct can be a mitigating factor. If youths act to protect themselves or others, judges may find these circumstances strong enough to justify whatever conduct was exhibited. Youths may intervene in a spousal assault, in an effort to protect one spouse from killing or seriously injuring the other spouse. Later, one or both spouses may bring assault charges against these youths. Judges would probably agree that their intervention was justified, since they believed one spouse to be in danger from the actions of the other spouse.

This particular mitigating factor usually refers to some act of necessity, such as breaking and entering to prevent a neighbor's house from burning. An automobile might be stolen, but later it is found that an emergency existed requiring the participating youths to bring their family members or friends to hospitals for treatment. These factors are most often subjectively determined and are raised by families, defense attorneys, or the youths themselves at the time they are adjudicated. Intake officers may make their own observations and recommendations about these circumstances and pass these along to prosecutors and judges. This particular mitigating factor has been written in such diffuse language that it is subject to broad interpretation by judges.

5. *Mental incapacitation or physical condition that significantly reduced the offender's culpability in the offense.* This factor specifies conditions that relate to drug or alcohol dependencies or to mental retardation or mental illness. If youths are suffering from some form of mental illness or are retarded, or if they are alcohol or drug dependent, this may limit their capacity to understand the law and interfere with their ability to comply with it. Investigations of the childhoods of numerous delinquent youths have revealed that many have antisocial behaviors that formed during their interactions with childhood peers (Tremblay, 1992). Antisocial behavior, characterized in part by high novelty seeking, low harm avoidance, and low reward dependence characterized the childhood experiences of a majority of 1033 Canadian delinquents studied (Tremblay, 1992). Other studies have found similar personality characteristics and childhood experiences related to subsequent delinquent behaviors (Patterson, Crosby, and Vuchinich, 1992). Many youths have had childhood experiences with considerable family violence (Lattimore, Visher, and Linster, 1995).

6. *Cooperation with authorities in apprehending other participants in the act of making restitution to the victims for losses they suffered.* Those youths who assist police in apprehending others involved in delinquent acts are credited with these positive deeds. Also, juveniles who make restitution to victims or

compensate them in part or in whole for their financial losses stand a good chance of having their cases mitigated through such restitution and good works.

7. *No previous record of delinquent activity.* First-offender juveniles, particular those under age 16, are especially targeted for the most lenient treatment. These youths are frequently diverted from the system at the point of intake. Even first-offender youths who have committed violent acts are often given a second chance through participation in a diversion program (Polan, 1994; Rabinowitz, 1992).

These aggravating and mitigating circumstances are not exhaustive. Other factors may exist that affect the judicial decision. At each stage of the juvenile justice process, interested officials want to know with some certainty whether certain offenders will recidivate if treated leniently. No one knows for sure whether certain offenders will recidivate more frequently than other offenders, although certain factors appear to be correlated closely with recidivism. Below, we examine several ways of assessing a juvenile's dangerousness or risk to the community. Such assessments are crucial in many jurisdictions in influencing prosecutorial and judicial decision making.

JUVENILE RISK ASSESSMENTS AND PREDICTIONS OF DANGEROUSNESS

Risk assessment *is an element of a classification system and traditionally means the process of determining the probability that a person will repeat unlawful or destructive behavior* (Champion, 1994). Risk prediction takes several forms, including the prediction of violent behavior, predictions of new offenses (recidivism), and the prediction of technical program violations associated with probation and parole (Baird, 1985:34).

Dangerousness and Risk. The concepts of *dangerousness* and *risk* are often used interchangeably. Dangerousness and risk both convey propensities to cause harm to others or oneself. What is the likelihood that any particular offender will be violent toward others? Does an offender pose any risk to public safety? What is the likelihood that any particular offender will commit suicide or attempt it? ***Risk (or dangerousness) instruments*** *are screening devices intended to distinguish between different types of offenders for purposes of determining initial institutional classification, security placement and inmate management, early release eligibility, and the level of supervision required under conditions of probation or parole.* Most state jurisdictions and the federal government refer to these measures as *risk instruments*. There is considerable variability among states regarding the format and content of such measures.

BOX 8.3 WOMEN ON DEATH ROW

The Case of Guinevere Garcia

In 1996, there weren't many women on death rows throughout the United States. In Illinois, a convicted offender, Guinevere Garcia, 36, was awaiting a date with the executioner for the murder of her husband, George Garcia, 60, in 1991. Guinevere Garcia was only 30 when she married George. George was one of her customers. Guinevere was a prostitute. In a taped statement to police following the murder, Guinevere admitted she did it and said: "He deserved to die. I killed George Garcia, and only I know why." What was her life like before she met George Garcia?

When Guinevere was 6 years of age, she had already been orphaned and sexually abused. She was an alcoholic by age 11 and pregnant at age 16. She became a prostitute to make ends meet. She married an Iranian student to keep him in the United States and conceived a daughter. Before her daughter's first birthday, Guinevere suffocated the baby to death with a plastic bag. For years, the baby's death was treated as an accident. However, an arson investigator later obtained a confession from Guinevere admitting that she killed her daughter and set fires near the anniversaries of her daughter's birth and death. She was convicted for that crime and served 10 years. While she was in prison, Guinevere married George Garcia, one of her former "johns," or customers. She was paroled in March 1991 and lived with George. Records indicate that George Garcia was physically and sexually abusive to Guinevere, and that after a few weeks, they separated. Guinevere said that she and George argued one evening outside his apartment in Bensenville, Illinois, and that she shot him in a rage after he told her that he gave her money and attention only in exchange for sex.

Guinevere showed no remorse for George's death. In fact, she proclaimed that she, too, deserved to die for her crimes. Death penalty opponents engaged in aggressive attempts to influence the governor to commute her death sentence by lethal injection scheduled for midnight, January 16, 1996. "She's not a heinous criminal. She's a person who was a victim herself, and some of these forces she probably couldn't control," said Janet Kittlaus of the Illinois Coalition Against the Death Penalty. Guinevere wanted to get it over with. "This is not a suicide," she said. "I am not taking my own life. I committed these crimes. I am responsible for these crimes." If executed, Garcia would be only the second woman to be executed in the United States since the U.S. Supreme Court approved the bifurcated trial procedure for capital offenses in *Gregg v. Georgia* in 1976. On January 15, the day before her scheduled execution, Illinois Governor Jim Edgar commuted Guinevere Garcia's sentence to life without parole.

Are life-without-parole sentences "just" in view of the crimes Garcia admitted? Should we differentiate between capital offenders according to gender? What should we do when convicted offenders such as Guinevere Garcia ask the state to execute them?

Sources: Adapted from Associated Press, "'Let Me Die,'" *Minot (ND) Daily News*, January 15, 1996:A3; personal communication with Public Information Officer, Illinois Department of Corrections, May 9, 1996.

Needs Assessment and Its Measurement. *Needs assessment devices are instruments that measure an offender's personal/social skills, health, well-being and emotional stability, educational level and vocational strengths and weaknesses, alcohol/drug dependencies, mental ability, and other relevant life factors, and which highlight those areas for which services are available and could or should be provided.* Risk and need assessments may also be referred to jointly and contained in longer inventories or measures, labeled **risk/needs assessment instruments**.

Attempts to forecast juvenile dangerousness/risk and needs are important, because many actors in the juvenile justice system use these predictions or forecasts as the basis for their decision making. Intake officers who initially screen youthful offenders try to decide which offenders are most deserving of leniency and which should be pushed further into the system for formal processing. Prosecutors want to know which juveniles are most receptive to diversion and amenable to change. Thus they can ensure that only the most serious and chronic offenders will be processed, while the remaining youths will have another chance to live reasonably normal lives in their communities without juvenile justice system supervision. Judges want to know which youths will probably reoffend if returned to their communities through probation or some other nonincarcerative option. Some juvenile offenders may be penalized purely on the basis of their likelihood of future offending. Some offenders may receive leniency because they are considered good probation or parole risks and unlikely to reoffend. Thus some juveniles are selectively incapacitated, that is, confined because they are predicted to pose a risk to others, usually on the basis of their prior record and/or risk score on a risk instrument.

Selective Incapacitation

False Positives and False Negatives. There are at least two major dangers inherent in risk or dangerousness predictions. First, youths who are identified as probable recidivists may receive harsher treatment compared with those who are considered unlikely to reoffend. In fact, many of those youths considered as good risks for probation or diversion may eventually turn out to be dangerous, although predictions of their future conduct gave assurances to the contrary. Second, those youths who receive harsher punishment and longer confinement because they are believed to be dangerous may not, in fact, be dangerous. Therefore, we risk *overpenalizing* those who will not be dangerous in the future, although our forecasts suggest that they will be dangerous. We also risk *underpenalizing* those believed by our forecasts not to be dangerous, although a portion will eventually turn out to be dangerous and kill or seriously injure others.

These two scenarios identify false positives and false negatives. ***False positives*** *are those persons predicted to be dangerous in the future but who turn out not to be dangerous.* ***False negatives*** *are those persons predicted not to be dangerous in the future but turn out to be dangerous anyway. False positives are those who are unduly punished because of our predictions, while false negatives are those who do not receive needed punishment or future supervision.* For adult criminals, attempts to forecast criminal behaviors have led to recommendations for selective incapacitation in many jurisdictions. ***Selective incapacitation*** *involves incarcerating or detaining those persons believed to be likely recidivists on the basis of various behavioral and attitudinal criteria* (Greenwood, 1982; Van Dine et al., 1977; Wolfgang, Figlio, and Sellin, 1972). The theory behind selective incapacitation is that if high-risk offenders can be targeted and controlled through long-term confinement, their circulation will be limited as well as the potential crimes they might commit (Struckhoff, 1987:30).

Selective incapacitation is controversial (Champion, 1994). Walker (1989) raises five general questions about the usefulness and desirability of selective incapacitation in dealing with offenders in general. They are:

1. Can we correctly estimate the amount of crime reduction?
2. Can we accurately identify chronic offenders and predict their future behavior?
3. Can we afford the monetary costs of implementing selective incapacitation should it involve massive new detention center construction?
4. Can we implement a policy of consistent selective incapacitation without violating constitutional rights?
5. What will be the side effects?

Basically, incapacitation is a strategy for crime control involving the physical isolation of offenders from their communities, usually through incarceration, to prevent them from committing future crimes (Gottfredson and Gottfredson, 1990). But Walker's questions are quite important, since there are some important implications of selective incapacitation for youthful offenders. The major harm is penalizing certain youths for acts they have not yet committed. Can we legitimately punish anyone in the United States for suspected future criminality or delinquency? Whatever one's personal feelings in this regard, the answer is that such punishments *are* imposed each time parole boards deny parole requests or probation recommendations are rejected in favor of incarceration.

Visher (1987:514–515) describes two types of incapacitation: collective and selective. Under *collective incapacitation*, crime reduction would be accomplished through traditional offense-based sentencing and incarcerative policies, such as mandatory minimum sentences. Under *selective incapacitation*, however, those offenders predicted to pose the greatest risk of future crimes would become prime candidates for incarceration and for longer prison sentences (Visher, 1987:515). A major problem throughout both the criminal justice system and the juvenile justice system is that no universally acceptable implementation policies have been adopted in most jurisdictions supporting the use of such incapacitation strategies.

The quality of risk assessment devices is such at present that we cannot depend on them as absolutely perfect indicators of one's future conduct (Champion, 1994). Baird (1985:34) says that some of the problems associated with scales that purportedly predict risk are that they are too new to have generated much data concerning their accuracy and that many scales used to forecast delinquency have been adapted from adult offender versions. Thus they have questionable validity when applied to youthful offender aggregates. Also, follow-up periods have been relatively short, thus preventing researchers from validating the predictive utility of these scales over time. Despite the continuing controversy surrounding the application of risk prediction measures and the criticisms by some researchers that such predictions are either impossible or inappropriate, such predictions continue to be made (Gottfredson and Gottfredson, 1990). However, Jesness (1987:156–157) suggests that while our predictive tools are not perfect, they exhibit sufficient accuracy to be taken seriously and used in practice.

Generally, risk assessment measures are one of three types: (1) anamnestic prediction devices, (2) actuarial prediction devices, and (3) clinical prediction devices.

1. *Anamnestic prediction devices.* **Anamnestic prediction** involves the use of past sets of circumstances to predict future behaviors. If the current circumstances are similar to past circumstances, where previous offense behaviors were observed, it is probable that youths will exhibit future offending.

2. *Actuarial prediction devices.* **Actuarial prediction** is an aggregate predictive tool. Those youthful offenders who are being considered for diversion, probation, or parole are compared with former offenders who have similar characteristics. Performances and records of previous conduct in view of diversion, probation, or parole decisions serve as the basis for profiling the high-risk recidivist. Certain youths may exhibit characteristics similar to previous juveniles who became recidivists. The expectation is that current youths will probably recidivate as well.

3. *Clinical prediction devices.* **Clinical prediction** involves professional assessments of diagnostic examinations and test results. The professional training of probation officers, prosecutors, and judges, as they experience working with youthful offenders directly, enables them to forecast probable behaviors of their present clients. Clinical prediction involves administration of psychological tools and personality assessment devices. Certain background and behavioral characteristics are assessed as well.

Common Elements of Risk Assessment Instruments

Most risk assessment measures, for both adult and juvenile offenders, contain several common elements. Adapting these common elements to youthful offender scenarios, the following elements seem prevalent:

1. Age at first adjudication
2. Prior criminal behavior (a combined measure of the number and severity of priors)
3. Number of prior commitments to juvenile facilities
4. Drug or chemical abuse
5. Alcohol abuse
6. Family relationships (parental control)
7. School problems
8. Peer relationships

For each of the elements above, some evidence has been found to establish a definite association between these and a youth's recidivism potential. These associations are not always strong, but in an actuarial prediction sense, they provide a basis for assuming that each of these elements has some causal value. The earlier the age of first adjudication and/or contact with the juvenile justice system, the greater the risk of recidivism (Jesness, 1987:154). Poor school performance, family problems and a lack of parental control, drug and/or alcohol dependencies, prior commitments to juvenile facilities, and a prior history of juvenile offending are individually and collectively linked with recidivism.

For example, the California Youth Authority includes the following variables and response weights as a means of assessing one's risk level (adapted from California Youth Authority, 1990):

1. Age at first police contact:
   - 9 = score 6 points
   - 10 = score 5 points
   - 11 = score 4 points
   - 12 = score 3 points
   - 13 = score 2 points
   - 14 = score 1 point
   - 15 = score 0 points

2. Number of prior police contacts (number): (score actual number)

3. Aggression and/or purse snatching: score "yes" = 1, "no" = 0

4. Petty theft: score "yes" = 1, "no" = 0

5. Use of alcohol or glue: score "yes" = 1, "no" = 0

6. Usually three or more others involved in delinquent act: score "yes" = 1, "no" = 0

7. Family on welfare: score "yes" = 1, "no" = 0

8. Father main support in family: score "no" = 1, "yes" = 0

9. Intact family: score "no" = 1, "yes" = 0

10. Number of siblings:
    - 3 = score 1 point
    - 4 = score 2 points
    - 5+ = score 3 points

11. Father has criminal record: score "yes" = 1, "no" = 0

12. Mother has criminal record: score "yes" = 1, "no" = 0

13. Low family supervision: score "yes" = 1, "no" = 0

14. Mother rejects: score "yes" = 1, "no" = 0

15. Father rejects: score "yes" = 1, "no" = 0

16. Parents wanted youth committed:
score "no" = 1, "yes" = 0

17. Verbal IQ:
equal to or less than 69 = 4
70 - 79 = 3
80 - 8 = 2
90 - 99 = 1
100+ = 0

18. Grade level:
at grade level = 1
1 year retarded = 2
2 years retarded = 3
3 years retarded = 4
4+ years retarded = 5

19. Negative school attitude:
score 0–3

20. School disciplinary problems:
score "yes" = 1, "no" = 0

On the basis of the score obtained, youths might be assigned the following risk levels:

RISK-LEVEL SCORE	DEGREE OF RISK
0–22	Low
21–31	Medium
32+	High

Youths who receive scores of 0 to 22 are considered low risks, while those with scores of 32 or higher are considered high risks. California Youth Authority officials believe that while these scores do not necessarily indicate that all youths with higher scores will be recidivists and all those with lower scores will be nonrecidivists, there does appear to be some indication that these categorizations are generally valid ones. Thus these classifications might be used to segregate more serious offenders from less serious ones in secure confinement facilities. Or such scores might be useful in forecasts of future performance in diversion or probationary programs. A similar instrument has been devised for adult parolees and has been used by the U.S. Parole Commission in its early-release decision making relating to federal prisoners. Figure 8.1 shows the **Salient Factor Score Index** (SFS 81), developed by Hoffman (1983).

When measures or indices such as these are examined critically, it is interesting to note how such important life-influencing decisions are reduced to six or seven predictive criteria. In the case of the instrumentation

FIGURE 8.1   Hoffman's SFS 81 Salient Factor Score Index

The Federal Parole Board's Salient Factor Score Index

Register Number _____Name_____

Item A: Prior Convictions/Adjudications (Adult or Juvenile)   ❏
None   = 3
One   = 2
Two or three   = 1
Four or more   = 0

Item B: Prior Commitment(s) of More than Thirty Days (Adult or Juvenile)   ❏
None   = 2
One or two   = 1
Three or more   = 0

Item C: Age at Current Offense/Prior Commitments   ❏
Age at commencement of the current offense:
   26 years of age or more   = 2***
   20–25 years of age   = 1***
   19 years of age or less   = 0
***Exceptions: If five or more prior commitments of
more than thirty days (adult or juvenile), place an "x"
here and score this item   = 0

Item D: Recent Commitment Free Prior (Three Years)   ❏
No prior commitment of more than thirty days
(adult or juvenile) or released to the community
from last such commitment at least three years
prior to the commencement of the current offense   = 1
Otherwise   = 0

Item E: Probation/Parole/Confinement/Escape Status Violator This Time   ❏
Neither on probation, parole, confinement, or escape
status at the time of the current offense; nor committed
as a probation, parole, confinement, or escape status
violator this time   = 1
Otherwise   = 0

Item F: Heroin/Opiate Dependence   ❏
No history of heroin/opiate dependence   = 1
Otherwise   = 0
   Total Score   ❏
Note: For purposes of the Salient Factor Score, an instance of criminal behavior resulting in a judicial
determination of guilt or an admission of guilt before a judicial body shall be treated as a conviction,
even if a conviction is not formally entered.

Scores on the SFS 81 can range from 0 to 10 and receive the following interpretation:

Score Range	Parole Prognosis	Score Range	Parole Prognosis
0–3	Poor	5–7	Good
4–5	Fair	8–10	Very Good

devised by the California Youth Authority, decisions about youths made by this organization are supplemented with several other important **classification** criteria, such as personality assessment tools, youth interviews, and professional impressions.

The Functions of Classification

1. Classification systems enable authorities to make decisions about appropriate offender program placements.

2. Classification systems help to identify one's needs and the provision of effective services in specialized treatment programs.

3. Classification assists in determining one's custody level if confined in either prisons or jails.

4. Classification helps to adjust one's custody level during confinement, considering behavioral improvement and evidence of rehabilitation.

5. While confined, inmates may be targeted for particular services and/or programs to meet their needs.

6. Classification may be used for offender management and deterrence relative to program or prison rules and requirements.

7. Classification schemes are useful for policy decision making and administrative planning relevant for jail and prison construction, the nature and number of facilities required, and the types of services to be made available within such facilities.

8. Classification systems enable parole boards to make better early-release decisions about eligible offenders.

9. Community corrections agencies can utilize classification schemes to determine those parolees who qualify for participation and those who do not qualify.

10. Classification systems enable assessments of risk and dangerousness to be made generally in anticipation of the type of supervision best suited for particular offenders.

11. Classification schemes assist in decision making relevant for community crime control, the nature of penalties to be imposed, and the determination of punishment.

12. Classification may enable authorities to determine whether selective incapacitation is desirable for particular offenders or offender groupings.

For most states, the following general applications are made of risk assessment instruments at different client-processing stages:

1. To promote better program planning through optimum budgeting and deployment of resources

2. To target high-risk and high-need offenders for particular custody levels, programs, and services without endangering the safety of others

3. To apply the fair and appropriate sanctions to particular classes of offenders and raise their level of accountability

4. To provide mechanisms for evaluating services and programs as well as service and program improvements over time

5. To maximize public safety as well as public understanding of the diverse functions of corrections by making decision making more open and comprehensible to both citizens and offender-clients

Several important and desirable characteristics of such predictive models are (Rans, 1984:50):

1. The model should be predictively valid.
2. The model should reflect reality.
3. The model should be designed for a dynamic system and not remain fixed over time.
4. The model should serve practical purposes.
5. The model should not be a substitute for good thinking and responsible judgment.
6. The model should be both qualitative and quantitative.

Risk Prediction from Missouri, Texas, and North Dakota

Figures 8.1, 8.2, and 8.3 are three risk prediction instruments devised by Missouri, Texas, and North Dakota. As a simple exercise, read the following scenarios involving several hypothetical delinquents. Next, read through the particular risk prediction instruments, paying attention to their instructions for score determinations. Then complete each instrument and determine the total score for each juvenile. It will be apparent that this task is easier for some instruments than for others. You will need to do several things when you compute scores for each of these juvenile offenders. You will need to keep track of their ages, how many formal and informal delinquency or status offender adjudications they have acquired, and whether they have escaped or attempted escape from a secure juvenile facility. In some of the instruments, you will need to determine whether they are drug or alcohol dependent. A brief solution is provided at the end of these three scenarios.

Scenario 1: Missouri. John lives in Independence, Missouri. For the first 15 years of John's life, he has been a good boy. He has attended school regularly, church attendance has been good, and he has lots of friends who are straight-A students. One day John brought a .45 automatic, his dad's Desert Storm service pistol, with him to school, and shot and wounded six students and his gym teacher. Police arrested John immediately, after some football players tackled him in class and disarmed him. They referred him to juvenile court. John went before the juvenile court judge and the judge ordered a psychiatric evaluation. The psychologist said that John apparently has been drinking alcohol occasionally and that he has sometimes smoked marijuana. In fact, the day he shot the teacher and students, he was high on crack cocaine. This was based on a drug test administered to John immediately following his arrest. The juvenile court judge ordered John placed in a group home temporarily while being evaluated. John escaped from the group home for a few hours, but he was caught a while later. The juvenile court judge adjudicated John delinquent on the assault charge, a felony, and John's disposition was secure confinement in the Missouri State Industrial School for one year. What is John's risk score on the Missouri Division of Youth Services Risk Assessment Form? (See Figure 8.2.)

Scenario 2: Texas. Jeffrey is 14 years old. When Jeffrey was 10, he stole a car and was subsequently arrested by police. The intake officer sent him to juvenile court through a petition where he was adjudicated delinquent on car theft charges. He was given probation. When he was 11, he began drinking vodka and smoking marijuana as well as shooting up with heroin. He did this for a year, during which time he was brought before an intake officer six times and informally placed back into the custody of his parents. When he turned 13, he mugged a drunk in an alleyway, and he was arrested shortly thereafter when an eyewitness saw him and reported him to police. Based on a petition filed with the juvenile court, the juvenile court judge adjudicated Jeffrey delinquent on an "assault" charge, a felony in Texas, and placed him in a secure facility for 31 days. During his stay in the secure facility, he was diagnosed by doctors and psychologists as having chronic substance abuse and dependency, which definitely interfered with his functioning normally. Further, authorities conceded that his parents had no control over Jeffrey whatsoever and that Jeffrey had been absent from school at least 30 percent of the time. School reports suggested that he was a "problem student" also, giving teachers headaches every day. He was expelled from school twice during the past two years for short periods. Authorities also found out recently that Jeffrey is the leader of a violent gang called "The Losers," which has been engaging in narcotics trafficking for several months. What is Jeffrey's risk score according to the Texas assessment of risk? (See Figure 8.3.)

Scenario 3: North Dakota. Lucy is 17 years old. When she was 11 years old, she set fire to the family barn, killing livestock. At the time the authorities took her into custody and an intake officer informally made a record of her arson activity but placed her back in the custody of her parents. When

FIGURE 8.2   Missouri Division of Youth Services Risk Assessment Form

Missouri Risk Assessment Form

Source: Missouri Division of Youth Services, 1993

Name: _____No.: _____Region:_____Date: _____

1. Age at first juvenile court referral (excluding CA/N)   _____
   (consider both sustained and unsustained)

12 and under	5
13–14	3
15	2
16 and over	0

2. Most serious juvenile court referral   _____
   (consider only sustained referrals)

Highest	6
High	3
Moderate	3
Low	1

3. Number of juvenile court referrals (excluding CA/N)   _____
   (consider both sustained and unsustained)

8 or more	6
5–7	4
3–4	2
2 or fewer	0

4. Most serious assaultive behavior   _____

Assault leading to sustained court referral	6
Assault on authority figure, no conviction	5
Fighting resulting in injury or school suspension	4
None	0

5. Most serious escapes/runaways (within past 12 months)   _____

Escape from detention/institution/custody	6
Run from group care/foster care	4
Run or attempt from home	2
None	0

6. Drug/chemical/alcohol abuse   _____

Chronic abuse	5
Abuse resulting in some disruption	3
No known use/use with no interference	0

FIGURE 8.2   Missouri Division of Youth Services Risk Assessment Form (cont'd)

7. Most recent public school adjustment   _____
   (prior to commitment)
Not attending/expelled	5
Severe truancy, behavior problems	3
Problems handled at school level	I
Attending/graduated/GED	0

8. Peer relationships at time of commitment   _____
Gang member	4
Negatively influenced, companions involved in delinquency	2
Good support, positively influenced	0

   TOTAL SCORE _____

"Highest" means those offenses that involve aggressiveness and are crimes against people. Examples are: homicide, rape, assault, armed robbery, sodomy.

"High" means those offenses that are serious property offenses. Examples are: burglary, stealing, arson, property damage, fraud.

"Moderate" means those offenses that do not involve aggressive behavior. These crimes may be either felonies or misdemeanors. Examples are: peace disturbance, weapon possession, possession of drugs, public drunkenness, trespass, petty theft.

"Low" means status offenses or very minor law violations. In-violation-of-court-order commitments are included in this category.

Source: From the Missouri Division of Youth Services, 1993.

she was 12, she set fire to her house one day while her parents were away. The house burned down and she was again taken into custody. This time, the juvenile court judge adjudicated her delinquent on an arson charge. He placed her in a secure facility for 90 days. While there, Lucy escaped, only to be apprehended a few days later. Also, during her stay in the secure facility, she assaulted a guard, breaking the guard's arm. She was charged with aggravated assault and again brought before the juvenile court judge, where she was adjudicated delinquent on that charge. She was given an additional 180 days in the secure facility. She remained delinquency-free for the next five years. Last week, however, she stole a .357 magnum pistol from a gun shop and held up the owner, robbing him of $3000. She was quickly apprehended and charged with armed robbery. She has just been adjudicated delinquent on the robbery charge. What is her risk score on the North Dakota classification/risk assessment instrument? (See Figure 8.4.)

FIGURE 8.3   Texas Assessment of Risk Instrument

Texas Juvenile Probation and Aftercare Assessment of Risk

Select the *highest* point total applicable for each category.

Age at First Referral
    0 = 16 or older
    3 = 14 or 15
    5 = 13 or younger   ____

Age at First Adjudication
    0 = 16 or older
    3 = 14 or 15
    5 = 13 or younger   ____

Prior Criminal Behavior
    0 = No prior arrests
    2 = Prior arrest record, no formal sanctions
    3 = Informal adjustment/continuance
    4 = Prior delinquency petition sustained; no assaultive
        offenses on petition
    5 = Prior delinquency petitions sustained;
        at least one assaultive offense on petition   ____

Institutional Commitments or Placements of 30 Days or More
    0 = None
    2 = One
    4 = Two or more   ____

Drug/Chemical Abuse
    0 = No known use or no interference with functioning
    2 = Some disruption of functioning
    5 = Chronic abuse or dependency   ____

Alcohol Abuse
    0 = No known use or no interference with functioning
    1 = Occasional abuse, some disruption of functioning
    3 = Chronic abuse, serious disruption of functioning   ____

Parental Control
    0 = Generally effective
    2 = Inconsistent and/or ineffective
    4 = Little or none   ____

FIGURE 8.3 Texas Assessment of Risk Instrument (cont'd)

School Disciplinary Problems

    0 = Attending, graduated, GED equivalence

    1 = Problems handled at school level

    3 = Severe truancy or severe behavioral problems

    5 = No attending/expelled   ____

Peer Relationships

    0 = Good support and influence

    2 = Negative influence

    3 = Several friends involved in delinquent-type behavior

    4 = Gang member   ____

    TOTAL ____

Source: From the Texas Department of Corrections, Youth Division, 1994.

Calculating the Missouri Score for John. Notice that the Missouri risk assessment form consists of eight parts. Part 1 is determined by John's age *at his first juvenile court referral.* This is important. We aren't interested in his present age, only the age at his first juvenile referral. Inspecting the scenario, John was first referred to juvenile court when he was 15, after shooting and wounding several students and his gym teacher at school with his dad's .45 automatic pistol. He receives a "2" for being 15 at his first age of referral to juvenile court. Question 2 pertains to his most serious juvenile court referral. We must be careful here to include only the most serious referral where an adjudication was made which sustained the referral. In other words, what is the most serious juvenile court referral for John? This referral was for the assault charge. Although John was subjected to a psychiatric examination following the assault and committed several other offenses, such as running away from the group home where he was being held temporarily, the assault charge clearly qualifies as one of those at the "highest" level. We must read the instructive footnotes at the end of this instrument to determine what is meant by each of the words "highest," "high," "moderate," and "low." Since *assault* is included in the "highest" category, we give John a "6" for this part.

    The third item is the number of juvenile court referrals John has had, whether they have been sustained by a delinquency adjudication or unsustained. John has had only one referral. Therefore, his score for the third part of this instrument is "0" for "2 or fewer." The fourth part of the measure asks about John's most serious assaultive behavior. Again, John's case involved "assault leading to a sustained court referral," which earns him a "6" on this part. The fifth question pertains to whether John has escaped from certain places during the past year. We know that John escaped from a

FIGURE 8.4 North Dakota Classification/Risk Assessment Form

North Dakota Division of Juvenile Services
Classification/Risk Assessment

NAME: _____ DOB: _____
Last   First   Mi

Score

1. Severity of Current Offense (adjudications/informals)   _____
   See offense list   (10)
   See offense list   (5)
   See offense list   (1)
   See offense list   (0)

2. Severity of Prior Adjudications (adjudications/informals)   _____
   See offense list   (5)
   See offense list   (3)
   See offense list   (1)
   See offense list   (0)

3. Number of Prior Adjudications and/or Informals   _____
   2 or more felonies   (5)
   Less than 2   (0)

4. Age at First Adjudication   _____
   12–13 years old*   (2)
   14+ years old   (0)

5. Prior Runaway Behavior While Under Supervision   _____
   Secure facility   (2)
   Community placement   (1)
   Parents' home   (0)

*Any youth who is younger than 12 is placed in this category.

Placement Scale:

   10 and above   Consider for secure placement
   4–9   Short-term placement
   0–4   Community placement/services

Mitigating/Aggravating Factors—Review for Placement: Yes____   No____

OFFENSE CODES
F = Felony; M = Misdemeanor

TYPE PERSON	CURRENT OFFENSE	OFFENSE	F/M	PRIOR OFFENSE
	10	Murder, homicide	F	5
	5	Manslaughter	F	3
	3	Negligent manslaughter	F	1
	10	Gross sexual imposition	F	5
	5	Sexual imposition	F	3
	3	Sexual assault	F	2
	5	Robbery	F	3
	10	Armed robbery	F	5

FIGURE 8.4 North Dakota Classification/Risk Assessment Form

	10	Aggravated assault	F	5
	3	Assault	M	2
	1	Simple assault	M	1
	10	Kidnapping	F	5
	5	Terrorizing, reckless endangerment	F	3
	3	Menacing	F	2
	5	Vehicular manslaughter (alcohol related)	F	3
PROPERTY	5	Arson	F	3
	5	Burglary	F	3
	3	Theft	F	2
	1	Theft	M	1
	3	Criminal trespass	F	2
	1	Trespassing, tampering, and mischief	M	1
	3	Forgery	F	2
	1	Forgery	M	1
	3	Fraud	F	2
	1	Obscenity	M	1
PUBLIC ORDER	1	Prostitution	M	1
	1	Public indecency	M	1
	1	Obstruction	F/M	1
	1	Contraband	M	1
	1	Public peace and order, disorderly conduct, loitering	M	1
	1	Cruelty to animals	M	1
	1	Gambling	F/M	1
	3	Firearms and weapons	F	2
	1	Firearms and weapons	M	1
DRUGS and ALCOHOL	5	(Sales) Controlled substances and marijuana	F	3
	1	(Sales) Controlled substances and marijuana	M	1
	1	Drug paraphernalia	M	1
		Criminal attempt (1 pt less than offense attempted) (1 pt minimum)	F/M	
		Criminal conspiracy (1 pt less than offense attempting) (1 pt minimum)	F/M	

POINTS FOR OFFENSES NOT LISTED ABOVE

Class A felony	10
Class B felony	5
Class C felony	3
Misdemeanor	1
Status offenses	0

Source: From the North Dakota Division of Juvenile Services, 1997.

group home while he was undergoing a psychiatric evaluation. Therefore, he should receive the score of "4" for the choice "run from group care/foster care." Part 6 has to do with his chemical/alcohol abuse. Does John appear to have either a drug or alcohol problem? If so, to what extent does this problem interfere with John's functioning? We determine from the scenario that John had been caught several times drinking alcohol, and that he has smoked marijuana. When he attacked the students and teacher, he had taken crack cocaine. We are led to believe from the scenario that John's use of drugs and alcohol has started only recently, after he has lived a life of conformity to society's rules for 15 years. We cannot infer from the scenario that his use of alcohol or drugs is *chronic*, however. Therefore, we will give him the score of "3" associated with "abuse resulting in some disruption."

The seventh item has to do with his most recent public school adjustment prior to commitment for the assault. John had not been truant. He did not exhibit problems with his school work. Thus we give John the score of "0" because he had been attending school, as that response suggests. The eighth item refers to his peer relations. John was not a gang member and he was well liked by others, having "lots of friends." Thus we will give him a "0" for "good support, positively influenced." Adding these scores, we have 2 + 6 + 0 + 6 + 4 + 3 + 0 + 0 = 21. (These scores for each item were item 1 = 2; item 2 = 6; item 3 = 0; item 4 = 6; item 5 = 4; item 6 = 3; item 7 = 0; and item 8 = 0.) The *maximum* score for the Missouri risk assessment form is 43. John's score is about half of the largest score attainable.

We do not have the guidebooks and other interpretive materials needed to determine where John should be placed or for how long. Usually, this information is provided in handbooks accompanying these instruments. The important thing here is to make a determination of one's risk score based on the behaviors they exhibit. Administrators, prosecutors, and juvenile court judges will use this information to assist them in determining what is best for John, under the particular circumstances of his case. *No risk score is binding on any personnel.* Usually, these instruments have **overrides**, where certain officials can either upgrade or downgrade the seriousness of the behaviors as suggested by the scores obtained. For instance, if a "21" in John's case called for commitment to the Missouri Industrial School for one year for serious and violent juvenile offenders, an administrator could override this recommendation and perhaps suggest mental evaluations and hospitalization, treatment, and psychological therapy for John as an alterative to incarcerating him. Judicial approval would be required in most cases for such overrides and recommendations.

Calculating the Texas Score for Jeffrey. The Texas Juvenile Probation and Aftercare Assessment of Risk is somewhat different from the Missouri instrument, although several features are shared by the two instruments. One's age, peer relations, school adjustment, and alcohol/drug/chemical dependency are common elements. There are several differences, however. We will see these differences as we calculate Jeffrey's risk score. Also note that the Texas instrument says to use the *highest* point value whenever applicable for each category. Let's calculate Jeffrey's score for this Texas instrument.

The first item, "age at first referral," is easy. Jeffrey was 10 when he stole a car and was referred to juvenile court. Thus we give Jeffrey a "5" for item 1. Item 2 deals with Jeffrey's "age at first adjudication." Remember that just because a juvenile is referred to juvenile court, this doesn't mean that he or she will be adjudicated delinquent or a status offender. But in Jeffrey's case, he was adjudicated delinquent on the car theft charge when he was 10. Again, he receives a score of "5" since he was "13 or younger," when he was adjudicated for that offense. Item 3 asks us to assess Jeffrey's "prior criminal behavior." We will give Jeffrey a "5" for this item, since he had a prior delinquency petition sustained where an assaultive offense was on the petition. Remember that Jeffrey had mugged a drunk in an alleyway when he was 13 and that this resulted in a delinquency adjudication. The assault charge was considered a felony according to Texas law.

Item 4 asks us how many institutional commitments Jeffrey has had of 30 days or longer. Jeffrey has had only one commitment in a secure facility for 31 days. Therefore, he receives a "2" for this item. Item 5 asks us about Jeffrey's drug/chemical abuse. We know from the scenario that examining physicians and psychiatrists have determined that Jeffrey has "chronic substance abuse and dependency," and therefore we assign a "5" to this item. Item 6 asks about Jeffrey's alcohol abuse. Although we are not given especially current information about Jeffrey's alcohol abuse, we know that in previous years, Jeffrey consumed vodka on a regular basis. We might infer from the psychiatric examination that alcohol abuse has continued in his case. Thus we will give Jeffrey a "3" for "chronic abuse, serious disruption of functioning." (Bear in mind that the Texas instrument wants us to assign the highest possible value applicable for each category, based on an objective assessment of the facts in this particular scenario.)

Item 7 has to do with parental control over Jeffrey. It is clear from the facts in the scenario that Jeffrey's parents have no control over him; thus he should receive a "4" for this item. Item 8 concerns school disciplinary problems. For Jeffrey, his school behavior was especially problematic. Because Jeffrey has been expelled several times, we *could* assign him a "5" for this item, although we will give him a "3" in this case since he is still in school, although he has been expelled in the past and has had severe truancy or severe behavioral problems with other students and teachers. For item 9, *peer relationships*, we must give Jeffrey a "4" since it has been determined that he is a gang member, even the leader of a gang known as "The Losers." Totaling Jeffrey's scores, we have $5 + 5 + 5 + 2 + 5 + 5 + 4 + 3 + 4 = 38$. Respectively, these scores have been derived as follows: item $1 = 5$; item $2 = 5$; item $3 = 5$; item $4 = 2$; item $5 = 5$; item $6 = 5$; item $7 = 4$; item $8 = 3$; item $9 = 4$. Summing these item scores gives us 38 for Jeffrey's risk score on the Texas assessment of risk. The maximum score attainable is 40. Thus Jeffrey's score is near the highest risk score on this instrument. In all likelihood, Jeffrey would be a good candidate for secure placement in some Texas industrial school for juveniles.

Again, we lack the interpretive information that would ordinarily be provided in a booklet or scoring manual. There are no specific recommendations made on this form for which type of disposition would be recommended for any offender. Again, the use of an override might be used to lower Jeffrey's score, although whenever overrides are used, explanations for these overrides must be provided in writing. Judges and others can consider this risk assessment information in determining the best disposition for Jeffrey and other delinquents.

Calculating the North Dakota Score for Lucy. The North Dakota classification/risk assessment instrument consists of five items. Age, prior runaway behavior and prior adjudications are similarly included compared with the previously discussed Missouri and Texas instruments. One major difference in the North Dakota instrument is the "offense list" at the end of the instrument. Take a moment to look over the offense list. Two columns are observed: "current offense/prior offense." Thus whenever we are referring to a prior offense, we would look in the "prior offense" column on the right. If we were interested in point values for the current or instant offense in the most recent juvenile court adjudication, we would look at the "current offense" listing on the left side. These point values would be used to determine individual item scores. Also, letter designations are provided. "F" is for a felony, "M" is for a misdemeanor.

Scoring delinquent Lucy, we first look at item 1, which asks us to determine the severity of the current offense. In this case the current offense is either an adjudication offense, which is arrived at through the formal adjudicatory hearing for Lucy, or an *informal*, which refers to an informal and unofficial resolution of the case. For example, the judge may simply give the juvenile a verbal reprimand and not officially adjudicate as delinquent or status offender. About half of all adjudicatory proceedings result in informal handling of juvenile cases in the United States annually (Bilchik, 1996).

For Lucy, her current offense is "armed robbery." She stole $3000 from a store owner at gunpoint. Armed robbery has a score of "10." Thus Lucy earns a "10" for the first item. The second item is the "severity of prior adjudications." We are asked to select the most serious offense, where Lucy has either been formally or informally treated by the juvenile court. Her past acts include arson and aggravated assault. Using the right side of the page for "prior offense," we find that Lucy should receive a "5" for the aggravated assault charge. For item 3, "number of prior adjudications and/or informals," Lucy has at least three prior adjudications or informals. She was informally treated on the arson charge by an intake officer; she was adjudicated delinquent on a subsequent arson charge and placed in a secure facility; and she assaulted a guard and was adjudicated delinquent on that charge. Examining the offense listing, arson and aggravated assault are both felonies. This qualifies Lucy for "2 or more felonies" and a score of "5" for item 3. For item 4, "age at first adjudication," Lucy was 12 when she was first adjudicated in juvenile court. The intake proceeding a year earlier when she was 11 doesn't count, because it was not an official adjudication. We will give Lucy a "2" for being 12 at the time of her first adjudication.

For item 5, we are asked whether Lucy has had any prior runaway behavior while under supervision. Yes, she has. When she was placed in a secure facility for the arson charge when she was 12, she escaped, although she was apprehended a few days later. This counts as running away or escaping from a secure facility. This earns Lucy a score of "2" on item 5. Adding Lucy's scores, we have 10 + 5 + 2 + 2 + 2 = 21. The maximum possible score earned by anyone on this instrument is 24. Summing the individual items on the North Dakota instrument to yield Lucy's score of 21, we have item 1 = 10; item 2 = 5; item 3 = 2; item 4 = 2; and item 5 = 2. Summing these gives us 21. According to the guidelines suggested at the end of this scale, "10 and above" is sufficient to consider Lucy for secure placement.

Notice that the North Dakota instrument contains a section for persons to include any mitigating or aggravating factors. An official reviews this instrument and any accompanying information about Lucy and determines whether Lucy should be confined or placed on probation. Judicial approval is required no matter what the recommendation by the official conducting Lucy's evaluation and determining her risk. This instrument component should not be underestimated. Sometimes juveniles get especially high scores, indicating that they should be placed in an industrial school, a secure facility. Other times, juveniles may get especially low scores, indicating that they are suitable for community placement and services. Overrides may be required at times if these scores do not accurately reflect the seriousness posed by any specific offender.

Two examples from actual North Dakota juvenile files can be cited. In one instance, an 8-year-old girl committed sodomy against her 5-year-old brother. In North Dakota, sodomy is placed under the heading "gross sexual imposition." Other sex offenses, such as rape, are also included under this same designation. If this girl were given a "10" according to the "gross sexual imposition" score, she would be placed in a secure facility. But administrators and test experts at the North Dakota industrial school where this girl was evaluated overrode her high score and recommended her for some type of community treatment instead of confinement. In this instance they believed that the circumstances warranted the downgrading of her charges.

In another case, a young boy, age 14, had engaged in numerous crimes. Every crime committed was a misdemeanor, however. Thus he was a chronic, persistent offender. But his score on the North Dakota instrument was only a "4." Ordinarily, officials would place this youth in a community treatment program. But authorities decided that his offending was so persistent and serious that they decided to override his low score and cause him to be confined in the North Dakota industrial school, with judicial approval. Thus overrides can work both ways for juveniles, depending on the nature and persistence of their offending and other factors.

Needs Assessments

Besides measuring a juvenile's potential risk or dangerousness, it is important for juvenile justice practitioners to know what types of problems afflict particular youths. Many youths enter the juvenile justice system who are drug or alcohol dependent, or who have psychological problems, suffer from maladjustments in their homes or schools, or who are impaired physically in some respect. Therefore, practitioners must assess juveniles who are processed to determine their respective needs. Sometimes scales are combined to obtain information about *both* risk and needs. These risk/needs assessment instruments enable those conducting such assessments to obtain both types of information from youths in one test administration. Figure 8.5 shows a risk/needs assessment coding form used by the Kansas Department of Corrections for its prospective parolees.

Not all juveniles need to be subjected to the same community services. There are diverse community resources available to meet a wide variety of needs exhibited by the youth who enter the juvenile justice system. Some juveniles require minimal intervention, other youths need extensive treatments and services. Whether youths are confined in secure facilities or allowed to attend their schools and remain with their families in their communities, different provisions often must be made to individualize their needs. Needs assessment instruments are used to determine which specific services and treatments ought to be provided each youth. In Alaska, for instance, a needs assessment instrument is administered to all youths who are adjudicated delinquent or status offenders by the juvenile court. Figure 8.6 illustrates the Alaska needs assessment instrument currently applied and administered to various types of juvenile offenders.

FIGURE 8.5 Kansas Parolee Risk/Needs Assessment Form

KANSAS DEPARTMENT OF CORRECTIONS
PAROLEE RISK AND NEEDS ASSESSMENT CODING FORM

NAME _____NUMBER _____

ASSESSMENT DATE _____ _____ _____   TYPE OF ASSESSMENT _____
                  MO   DA   YR

ACTION CODE: [ ]   DISTRICT [ ]   PO NO. _____

Risk Assessment			Needs Assessment		
Pts.	Item	Code	Pts.	Item	Code
[ ] 1.	Severity level I offense	[ ]	[ ] 17.	Academic/vocational	[ ]
[ ] 2.	No. prior periods problems/par sup.	[ ]	[ ] 18.	Employment	[ ]
[ ] 3.	Attitude	[ ]	[ ] 19.	Financial management	[ ]
[ ] 4.	Age first felony conviction	[ ]	[ ] 20.	Marital family	[ ]
[ ] 5.	No. prior felony convictions	[ ]	[ ] 21.	Companions	[ ]
[ ] 6.	Convictions certain offenses	[ ]	[ ] 22.	Emotional stability	[ ]
[ ] 7.	No. prior probles/par revocations	[ ]	[ ] 23.	Alcohol usage	[ ]
[ ] 8.	Alcohol usage problems	[ ]	[ ] 24.	Other drug usage	[ ]
[ ] 9.	Other drug usage	[ ]	[ ] 25.	Mental ability	[ ]
[ ] 10.	No. address changes	[ ]	[ ] 26.	Health	[ ]
[ ] 11.	% Time employed	[ ]	[ ] 27.	Sexual behavior	[ ]
[ ] 12.	Social identification	[ ]	[ ] 28.	Officer impression	[ ]
[ ] 13.	Problem interpersonal relations	[ ]	[ ] 29.	Needs total	[ ]
[ ] 14.	Use of community resources	[ ]	[ ]		
[ ] 15.	Response to supervision	[ ]	[ ]		
[ ] 16.	Risk total	[ ]			

Decision
30. Supervision determination   [ ]
31. Override   [ ]
32. Supervision level assigned   [ ]
33. Next assessment date _____
                            MO   YR

ASSESSMENT COMPLETED BY: Signature

Distribution
   Original   Data entry
   Copy   PO file
   Copy   Deputy secretary if override required

Source: From the Kansas Department of Corrections, 1996.

The contexts of this risk assessment device highlight particular types of deficiencies or needs that juveniles might have. For example, if some youths have drug/chemical abuse problems, this needs instrument assesses in a crude way the extent of the problem and how such drug or chemical

FIGURE 8.6   Alaska Needs Assessment Instrument

ALASKA NEEDS ASSESSMENT INSTRUMENT

For each item below, select the single appropriate answer and enter the associated number in the adjacent blank. Where appropriate, concretely describe the present situation/need.

SPECIFY
DRUG/CHEMICAL ABUSE

0 No interference with functioning	I Occasional abuse, some disruption of functioning, unwilling to participate in treatment program	2 Frequent abuse, serious disruption, needs immediate treatment _____

SPECIFY
ALCOHOL ABUSE

0 No known use	I Occasional abuse, some disruption of functioning, unwilling to participate in treatment program	2 Frequent abuse, serious disruption, needs immediate treatment _____

SPECIFY
PRIMARY FAMILY RELATIONSHIPS

0 Relatively stable relationships or not applicable	I Some disorganization or stress but potential for improvement	2 Major disorganization or stress _____

SPECIFY
ALTERNATIVE FAMILY RELATIONSHIPS

0 Relatively stable relationships or not applicable	I Some disorganization or stress but potential for improvement	2 Major disorganization or stress _____

SPECIFY
EMOTIONAL STABILITY

0 Appropriate adolescent responses	I Exaggerated periodic or sporadic responses (e.g. aggressive acting out or depressive withdrawal)	2 Excessive responses; prohibits or limits adequate functioning _____

SPECIFY
INTELLECTUAL ABILITY

0 Able to function independently	I Some need for assistance potential for adequate adjustment; mild retardation	2 Deficiencies severely limit independent functioning, moderate retardation _____

SPECIFY
LEARNING DISABILITY

0 None	I Mild disability, able to function in a classroom	2 Serious disability, interferes with social functioning _____

SPECIFY
EMPLOYMENT (Where applicable)

0 Not needed or currently employed	I Currently employed but poor work habits	2 Needs employment _____

FIGURE 8.6   Alaska Needs Assessment Instrument (cont'd)

SPECIFY
VOCATIONAL/TECHNICAL SKILLS

| 0 | Currently developing marketable skill | 1 | Needs to develop marketable skill | _____ |

If appropriate, enter the value 1 for each characteristic which applies to this case.

Educational Adjustment	Not working to potential	_____
	Poor attendance	_____
	Program not appropriate for needs, age, and/or ability	_____
	Disruptive school behavior	_____
	TOTAL	_____
Peer Relationships	Socially inept	_____
	Loner behavior	_____
	Receives basically negative influence from peers	_____
	Dependent on others	_____
	Exploits and/or victimizes others (especially in placement)	_____
	TOTAL	_____
Health, Mental Health, and Hygiene	Medical or dental referral needed	_____
	Needs health or hygiene education	_____
	Handicap or illness limits functioning	_____
	Need for mental health intervention (specify)	_____
	TOTAL	_____
Sexual Adjustment	Lacks knowledge (sex education)	_____
	Avoidance of the opposite sex	_____
	Promiscuity (not prostitution)	_____
	Sexual deviant (not prostitution)	_____
	Unwed parent	_____
	Prostitution	_____
	TOTAL	_____

Range: low (0–12); medium (13–23); high (24–36)   TOTAL NEEDS SCORE _____

Source: From the Alaska Department of Corrections, Youth Division, 1996.

abuse interferes with how these youths function around others. The needs instrument also examines one's family relationships, emotional stability, intellectual abilities, learning disabilities (if any), employment problems (if any), vocational or technical skills, peer relations, educational attainment and adjustment, health, mental health and hygiene, and sexual adjustment.

If we making an assessment of a 16-year-old female unwed parent, for instance, we might wish to place this youth with the specific social services that provide information about child care and parenting. If the girl were engaged in prostitution as well, we might wish to place her into some form of counseling and physical health course, where she could learn about sexually transmitted diseases. The idea is to associate each juvenile with the types of services that he or she might need, depending on the types of problems indicated by the instrument.

It should be emphasized that juvenile justice officials do not depend exclusively on instruments for their information about youth needs. Interviews with youths and their families are often conducted. Intake officers acquire extensive information about a youth's background. If certain youths are recidivists and have extensive juvenile records, some indication of their needs will already be on file. Thus we will know what interventions have been applied in the past and whether these interventions have helped in any way. If not, we might try alternative interventions and programs. Another source of information about youths and their needs comes from juvenile probation officers. These court officials compile information about a youth's background and furnish this material to juvenile court judges. Subsequently, dispositions are individualized according to the probation officer's report. This is known as a predispositional report.

PREDISPOSITIONAL REPORTS

Assisting juvenile court judges in their decision making relating to sentencing juvenile offenders during adjudicatory proceedings are predispositional reports that are often filed by juvenile probation officers, especially in serious cases. *Predispositional reports contain background information about juveniles, the facts relating to their delinquent acts, and possibly probation officer recommendations for particular dispositions. They serve the function of assisting judges make more informed sentencing decisions.* They also serve as needs assessment devices, where probation officers and other juvenile authorities can determine high-need areas for certain youths and channel them to specific community-based organizations and agencies for particular treatments and services.

The Predisposition Report and Its Preparation

Juvenile court judges in many jurisdictions order the preparation of predisposition reports, which are the functional equivalent of presentence investigation reports for adults. Predisposition reports are intended to furnish judges with background information about juveniles to make a more informed sentencing decision (Rogers and Williams, 1995). They also function to assist probation officers and others to target high-need areas for youths and specific services or agencies for individualized referrals. This information is often channeled to information agencies such as the

National Center for Juvenile Justice in Pittsburgh, Pennsylvania, so that researchers may benefit in the juvenile justice investigations. They may analyze the information compiled from various jurisdictions for their own research investigations (Osgood, 1983; Polk, 1984).

Trester (1981:89–90) has summarized four important reasons for why predisposition reports should be prepared:

1. These reports provide juvenile court judges with a more complete picture of juvenile offenders and their offenses, including the existence of any aggravating or mitigating circumstances.

2. These reports can assist the court in tailoring the disposition of the case to an offender's needs.

3. These reports may lead to the identification of positive factors that would indicate the likelihood of rehabilitation.

4. These reports provide judges with the offender's treatment history, which might indicate the effectiveness or ineffectiveness of previous dispositions and suggest the need for alternative dispositions.

It is important to recognize that predispositional reports are not required by judges in all jurisdictions. By the same token, legislative mandates obligate officials in other jurisdictions to prepare them for all juveniles to be adjudicated. Also, there are no specific formats universally acceptable in these report preparations. Figure 8.7 is an example of a predisposition report. Rogers (1990:44) indicates that predisposition reports contain insightful information about youths that can be helpful to juvenile court judges prior to sentencing. Six social aspects of a person's life are crucial for investigations, analysis, and treatment: (1) personal health, physical and emotional; (2) family and home situation; (3) recreational activities and use of leisure time; (4) peer-group relationships (types of companions); (5) education; and (6) work experience (Rogers, 1990:44). According to the National Advisory Commission on Criminal Justice Standards and Goals as outlined in 1973, predisposition reports have been recommended in all cases where the offenders are minors. In actual practice, however, predisposition reports are prepared only at the request of juvenile court judges. No systematic pattern typifies such report preparation in most U.S. jurisdictions. Table 8.1 shows the type of information reported in a sample of 162 predisposition reports.

Rogers (1990:46) notes that the following characteristics were included in 100 percent of all the cases: (1) gender; (2) ethnic status; (3) age at first juvenile court appearance; (4) source of first referral to juvenile court; (5) reason(s) for referral; (6) formal court disposition; (7) youth's initial placement by court; (8) miscellaneous court orders and conditions; (9) type of counsel retained; (10) initial plea; (11) number of prior offenses; (12) age and time of initial

FIGURE 8.7 Predisposition Report

THE PREDISPOSITION REPORT

A Model Set of Field Notes to Guide Preparation of Juvenile Court Predisposition Reports

COURT REPORT OUTLINE

Case No.:_____Hearing Date:_____

Address:_____Phone:_____

I.	Reason for Hearing:	Petition No.:	Petition Date:	W&I	SUB:
	Name: (AKA):			Age:	
	Allegation and Reference to P.D. Report or Complaint:				

2.	Present Situation:	First Court	Referral Date and Agency:	
		Ward		
	Place and Date of Detention or Custody:		Released to:	Date:

3.	Citation	Served	To:		
		Mailed			
	Served by:		Location:		Date:

4.	Legal Residence:	Determining Parent:	Arrived in San Diego County:
	Verification:		Residence of Child:

5.	Previous History:

6.	Statement of Child (Description, attitude, and statements re: allegation and home):

Race:	Hair:	Eyes:	HT:	WT:	Marks:

FIGURE 8.7 Predisposition Report (cont'd)

7.	Statement of Parents (Description, attitude, and statement re: allegation and child):
8.	Statement of Victim, Witnesses, Relatives or Others (Name, Address, Date and Relation to Case):

9.	Family History:	Marriage or Natural Parents, Date and Place:

Children and Order of Birth:

Age, Educational Level and Background of Natural Parents:

Date, Place, Reason and Effects of Separation, Divorce, Remarriage (Custody):

Previous Residence; Employment; Date Arrived S. D. CO., Present Family Unit:

Description of Home and Furnishings:	Owned	$
	Rented	$

Community Relationship and Environmental Factors: Police Record of Parent and/or Siblings:

Diseases in History of Either Parent: Handicaps, Mental Disorders, Alcoholism, Suicide; Health Insurance and Hospital Eligibility:

Religion and Attendance:

Parent–Child Relationship:

FIGURE 8.7   Predisposition Report (cont'd)

| 10. | Economic Situation: | Parent(s) Employed: | | Type Job: | | Employer: |

10. Economic Situation:	Parent(s) Employed:	Type Job:	Employer:
Hours of Employment:		Weekly/Monthly Income:	
Other Sources of Income:		Hardships (Financial Statement):	

11. Child's History:	Date and Place of Birth:	Hospital	Full Term
		Home	Other

Normal Delivery		Weight:	Birth Injuries:	
Cesarean or Other				

Mother's Health and Attitude of Parents:	Weaned:	Talked:
	Walked:	Toilet:

Dates and After Effects of Childhood Diseases:

Diptheria:	Scarlet Fever:
Chicken Pox:	Whooping Cough:
Measles:	Mumps or Other:

Developmental History:	Injuries or Operations:		
Handicaps:	Speech:	Hearing:	Sight:
Enuresis:	Temper Tantrums:	Stealing:	
Lying:	Runaway:	Other:	

Relationship with Siblings and Peers:

Discipline Methods:

Child's Room:	Allowance:	Hobbies, Sports:	
Child's Employer:	Hours of Employment:		Wages:

Sex Education:

12. School Records:	Previous School(s):	Present School and Grade:
Subjects and Grade Average:		
Truancy:		Behavior:
Refer to School or Guidance Bureau Reports:		

13.	Psychological, Psychiatric, and Medical Findings (Reports):
14.	Other Agencies (Central Index Clearance):
15.	Summary and Plan:
16.	Recommendation:

Source: From Joseph W. Rogers, "The Predisposition Report: Maintaining the Promise of Individual and Juvenile Justice," *Federal Probation* **54**:51–52 (1990), pp. 51–52.

TABLE 8.1

Percentage of Juvenile Case Records in Which Line Item Information Was Located

Variable Identification	IBM Col.	N–162
Case code number	1–3	100
Sex	4	100
Ethnic status	5	100
Age at first juvenile court appearance	6	100
Source of first referral	7	100
Reason for first referral/court hearing	8–9	100
Recoding of prior item	10	100
Formal court disposition	11	100
Youth's initial placement by court	12	100
Miscellaneous court orders	13	100
Detention prior to first hearing	14	100
Type of counsel retained	15	100
Initial plea	16	100
Presiding, initial court hearing	17	99
Number of prior offenses	18	100
Age at time of initial offense	19	100
Number of offenses after first hearing	20	100
Youth's total offense number	21	100
Number companions, first offense	22	100
Usual companionship portrait	23	92
Living arrangements first court hearing	24	99
Parents' marital status	25	99
Youth's age at divorce/death	26	93
Household economic status	27	95
Public assistance recipient?	28	88
Income dependence number	29	96
Type of neighborhood	30	60
Home assessment	31	85
Parental work situation	32	94
Parental education background	33	19
Father's health	34	78
Mother's health	35	85
Youth's school academic standing	36	94
Youth's school attendance	37	94
Youth's attitude/perception: school	38	83
Parents' attitude toward youth's education	39	59
Child's birth	40	72

TABLE 8.1 (CONT'D)

Variable Identification	IBM Col.	N–162
Organic/emotional dysfunctions	41	85
Other educational problems	42	80
Youth's church attendance	43	28
Youth's job record	44	73
Leisure-time interests	45	64
Youth's mental health portrait	46	86
Highest IQ recorded	47	45
Psychological intervention	48	85
Community outpatient care	49	35
Residential inpatient care	50	43
Statement of juvenile	51	92
Statement of mother	52	83
Statement of father	53	56
Youth's generalized explanation	54	95
Parents' generalized explanation	55	88
JPO's generalized explanation	56	93
Alienation	57	96
Childhood rejection	58	88
Childhood concept of self	59	90
Dominant manifest personality	60	97
Personality direction	61	93
Usual peer group relationship	62	89
Achievement orientation	63	77
Sibling relationships	64	74
Mother–child relationship	65	93
Father–child relationship	66	84
Principal discipline source	67	85
Quality of discipline	68	77
Family difficulty with police	69	76
Last known offense	70–71	99
Decoding of prior item	72	99
Time under JPO supervision	73	93
Number of detentions	74	100
Number of out-of-home placements	75	100
Dominant form of JPO contact	76	83
JPO home visit frequency	77	67
Overall frequency of contact	78	78
Final status of case	79	95
Judge, last court hearing	80	99

Source: Joseph W. Rogers, "The Predisposition Report," *Federal Probation* 54:48 (1990).

offense; (13) number of offenses after first hearing; (14) youth's total offense number; (15) number of companions, first offense; (16) number of detentions; and (17) number of out-of-home placements.

Not all juvenile courts require the preparation of predispositional reports. They take much time to prepare, and their diagnostic information is often limited, since juvenile justice system budgets in many jurisdictions are restricted. In many respects these reports are comparable to **presentence investigation reports** (PSIs) filed by probation officers in criminal courts for various convicted adult offenders. Unfortunately, there is no consistent pattern regarding the use of such predispositional reports and their preparation among jurisdictions.

In recent years, various juvenile justice reforms have been implemented in many juvenile courts. Some of these reforms have been mandated by U.S. Supreme Court decisions regarding more extensive rights of juvenile offenders. Greater uniformity in handling and less disparity in sentencing are desirable outcomes in the aftermath of extensive informal juvenile processing that characterized the juvenile courts of previous decades (Rogers, 1990). Nevertheless, there continues to exist a great deal of individualism exhibited among juvenile court judges in different jurisdictions and how the various laws and decisions pertaining to juveniles should be interpreted (Farnworth, Frazier, and Neuberger, 1988; Krisberg, 1988).

Victim-Impact Statements in Predisposition Reports

Predisposition reports may or may not contain victim impact statements. Presentence investigation reports (PSIs) that are prepared for adults who are convicted of crimes in criminal courts are the adult equivalents to predisposition reports. It is more common to see such victim impact statements in PSI reports, although some predisposition reports contain them in certain jurisdictions. These statements are often prepared by victims themselves and appended to the report before the judge sees it. They are intended to provide judges with a sense of the physical harm and monetary damage victims have sustained, and thus they are often aggravating factors that weigh heavily against the juvenile to be sentenced.

Since 1992, however, there has been a trend among state legislatures to increase the rights of victims of juvenile crime (Torbet et al., 1996:48). By 1996, 22 state legislatures had enacted legislation addressing the victims of juvenile crime. This state legislation addresses the role of victims in various ways, including (Torbet et al., 1996:48):

1. Including victims of juvenile crime in the victim's bill of rights.
2. Notifying the victim upon release of the offender from custody.

3. Increasing opportunities for victims to be heard in juvenile court proceedings.

4. Expanding victim services to victims of juvenile crime.

5. Establishing the authority for victims to be notified of significant hearings (e.g., bail disposition).

6. Providing for release of the name and address of the offender and the offender's parents to the victim upon request.

7. Enhancing sentences if the victim is elderly or handicapped. States enacting such legislation include Alabama, Alaska, Arizona, California, Connecticut, Florida, Georgia, Idaho, Iowa, Louisiana, Minnesota, Montana, New Mexico, North Dakota, Pennsylvania, South Dakota, Texas, Utah, Virginia, and Wyoming.

A strong consideration when enacting this legislation is the matter of restitution to victims. Restitution is increasingly regarded as an essential component of fairness in meting out dispositions for juvenile offenders. Offender accountability is heightened as restitution is incorporated into the disposition, especially if there was some type of property loss, damage, physical injury, or death. In reality, however, many states continue to haggle over how reparations will be imposed on either the youths or families or both. Some states have incorporated into their juvenile statutes high dollar limits relating to parental liability whenever their children destroy the property of others or cause serious physical injuries. The theory is that if parents are held accountable, they will hold their own children accountable. Thus reparations assessed against parents for the wrongdoing of their children are an indirect way of preventing delinquency, or so some state legislatures have contemplated. Some experts question the wisdom of punishing the parents, however (Torbet et al., 1996:50–51).

THE JUDICIAL DECISION

In most jurisdictions, juvenile court judges may exercise several options when deciding specific cases. These judges may adjudicate youths as delinquent and do no more other than to record the event. If the juvenile reappears before the same judge in the future, a harsh disposition may be imposed. In some cases, juvenile court judges might divert juveniles to community-based services or agencies for special treatment. Those youths with psychological problems or who are emotionally disturbed, sex offenders, or those with drug and/or alcohol dependencies may be targeted for special community treatments. Various conditions as punishments, such as fines, restitution, or some form of community service, may also be imposed by judges. The more drastic alternatives are varying degrees of custodial sentences, ranging from the placement of juveniles in foster homes, camp ranches, reform schools, or industrial schools. These nonsecure and secure forms of placement and/or confinement are usually reserved for the most serious offenders. Below is a summary of judicial options. These are explored in greater detail in subsequent chapters. One or more of the following 11 options may be exercised in any delinquency adjudication:

1. A stern reprimand may be given.
2. A verbal warning may be issued.
3. An order may be given to make restitution to victims.
4. An order may be given to pay a fine.
5. An order may be given to perform some public service.
6. An order may be given to submit to the supervisory control of some community-based corrections agency on a probationary basis.
7. A sentence may be imposed, but the sentence may be suspended for a fixed term of probation.
8. An order may be issued for the placement of the juvenile in a foster home.
9. An order may be issued for the placement of the juvenile in a residential center.
10. An order may be given to participate under supervision at a camp ranch or special school (either nonsecure or secure confinement).
11. An order may be given to be confined in a secure facility for a specified period.

The verbal warnings and reprimands are classified as *nominal punishments*, while making restitution to victims, payment of fines, performance of community service, community-supervised probation, and suspended sentences with conditional probationary alternatives are considered *conditional punishments*. Finally, placement in foster or group homes, at camp ranches or schools, or confinement in secure facilities, such as industrial schools, are considered *custodial punishments* (Coumarelos and Weatherburn, 1995; Roy, 1995).

As we have seen in earlier chapters, the juvenile court is becoming increasingly an adversarial adjudicatory proceeding. Although not all juvenile offenders are defended by attorneys, many youths and their families exercise their right to due process and retain a defense attorney's services (Feeney, 1987; Feld, 1988b; Ito, 1984). This formalizes juvenile court dispositions and to some extent reduces the latitude in sentencing a juvenile court judge may exercise. In some jurisdictions at least, sentences imposed by judges have been harsher in those instances where juveniles have been represented by attorneys. Of course, if the greater seriousness of the offense prompted the retention of an attorney initially, this would explain the harsher sentences imposed on such juveniles. Regardless, juvenile proceedings have been characterized more formally in recent years compared with earlier traditional court conduct. The use of nominal reprimands has perhaps declined with greater formality, since juvenile court judges are less inclined to moralize in the presence of defense counsels.

IMPLICATIONS OF THE JUDICIAL DECISION FOR JUVENILE OFFENDERS

In recent years, a considerable amount of the authority of juvenile court judges has been undermined by various reforms, including the deinstitutionalization of status offenses and automatic transfers of certain youths to criminal courts for processing. New York's *Juvenile Offender Law* (JO Law), for example, mandates the transfer to criminal court of certain youths who commit particular types of crime (Singer and McDowall, 1988). However, it is doubtful whether such reforms have accomplished their desired objectives. As we have seen in previous chapters, transferring or waiving juveniles to criminal court has not always resulted in the most violent or serious juveniles being transferred. As recently as 1995, nearly 60 percent of those youths transferred to criminal courts nationwide were property offenders. Person offenders accounted for only 42 percent of those transferred (Butts et al., 1996; Maguire and Pastore, 1996).

Many juvenile court judges have expressed the view that the juvenile justice system is superior to the criminal justice system regarding how juveniles are treated and how public safety is protected (Rubin, 1983). Rubin says that many judges do not consider either serious or repetitive minor juvenile offenders to be an overwhelming problem. They believe that juveniles should receive the rehabilitative protection that juvenile courts can provide. Finally, they reportedly stress the importance of relying on community-based services as the major means of meeting a youth's needs. Although they do not rule out secure confinement, they believe it should be reserved only for the most serious and persistent offenders.

Some judges believe that the shock value of exposing juveniles to the prison environment might be sufficient to scare them into becoming more law abiding. In some jurisdictions in Colorado, for instance, judges direct certain juveniles to participate in a program known as **SHAPE-UP**, an aversion program involving two visits to the Colorado State Penitentiary and discussions with some of the prisoners confined there (Berry, 1985). Despite this exposure to prison life for certain youths, recidivism rates seem to be comparable for program participants in contrast with those not exposed to the SHAPE-UP program.

The implications of judicial decision making for youthful offenders are several. Depending on a judge's philosophical stance, certain juveniles may receive more lenient treatment compared with other juveniles charged with the same offenses (Hassenfeld and Cheung, 1985). There are obvious pressures exerted on judges from various sectors within communities. These pressures encourage them to impose more severe sanctions on juvenile offenders, although some of these sectors continue to promote reintegrative and rehabilitative sanctions. The recent influence of the get-tough movement on juvenile court judges is apparent (Torbet et al., 1996). Juvenile codes are constantly being revised in favor of sanctions that hold youths increasingly accountable for their actions (Jones and Krisberg, 1994). Some evidence suggests that our changing conceptions of adolescence have helped to shift the perspectives of certain judges from viewing juveniles as societal victims in need of treatment to responsible offenders deserving of punishment (Torbet et al., 1996).

Judges are seemingly caught in the middle of the punishment dilemma. If they impose sanctions considered by juveniles themselves to be too light, judges may inadvertently cause youths to acquire cynicism about the system and the meaningfulness of sanctions. They may push the system to the limit through chronic recidivism, knowing that the system will not act against them and restrain their movements through long-term confinement until other, more lenient, measures have been exhausted. Leniency may breed greater amounts of recidivism among those treated leniently by the juvenile justice system (McCarthy, 1989). But by placing juveniles in secure confinement, some degree of criminalization is likely to occur, where juveniles are socialized by their peers and emerge as more hard-core delinquents than when they initially entered those secure facilities.

Judicial decision making and sentencing decisions depend, in part, on available programs for juveniles in their respective communities. If diversion programs or extensive community-based services are nonexistent or limited, this fact limits their sentencing options. Not all juvenile court jurisdictions have alternative dispute resolution mechanisms, for instance (National College of Juvenile and Family Law, 1989). Even where judges are inclined to favor secure confinement of juvenile offenders, chronic overcrowding of secure juvenile facilities may prevent them from imposing incarcerative sanctions for all juveniles who merit them (Krisberg et al., 1993). In those communities with extensive community-based services and resources, there is a fear among the public and even among judges that some net widening may occur, simply because of the availability and prevalence of such services (Ashford and LeCroy, 1990; Towberman, 1992). Simultaneously, a heavy reliance on community-based services by juvenile court judges means that more juveniles will remain free to move about in their communities. Thus there is the continuing question of whether community residents are sufficiently insulated and protected from the more dangerous youthful offenders who are selected for community-based treatments rather than for secure confinement (Murphy et al., 1991; National Council on Crime and Delinquency, 1990).

KEY TERMS

Actuarial prediction

Aggravating circumstances

Anamnestic prediction

Classification

Clinical prediction

Dangerousness

False negatives

False positives

Flat time

Mitigating circumstances

Overrides

Prediction

Predictors of dangerousness and risk

Predisposition reports

Presentence investigation reports (PSIs)

Risk

Risk/needs assessment instruments

Salient Factor Score Index (SFS 81)

Selective incapacitation

SHAPE-UP

Violent juvenile offender program

QUESTIONS FOR REVIEW

1. What are *aggravating circumstances*? At what stages of juvenile justice system proceedings are they considered? What are some examples of aggravating factors?

2. What are *mitigating circumstances*? Give five examples. How are mitigating factors used by juvenile court judges in their sentencing of juveniles? How much subjectivity is there is considering any given factor as either mitigating or aggravating? Explain.

3. What are three types of prediction devices? Define each and give an example. Which types of measures do you feel are most valid, and why?

4. What is the basic nature of the role conflict experienced by juvenile court judges in sentencing youthful offenders? Describe this conflict and how it has occurred in view of certain juvenile justice reforms.

5. What is a *violent juvenile offender program* and what is it designed to do? What are some of its key dimensions? Is it effective? Discuss.

6. Differentiate between *collective* and *selective incapacitation*. What are the goals of each? How does each type of incapacitation achieve its goals?

7. What are *risk assessment instruments* or *predictors of dangerousness*? Give two examples.

8. What are some common criteria associated with these measures? What relation do these criteria have with delinquent conduct? Explain.

9. Differentiate between *false positives* and *false negatives*. What relevance does each have for predicting dangerousness and controlling delinquent conduct? How does each conceivably overpenalize and underpenalize juveniles? Explain.

10. What is a *predispositional report*? What functions does it serve? Do all juvenile court jurisdictions use predispositional reports?

SUGGESTED READINGS

Costin, Lela B., Howard Jacob Karger, and David Stoesz. *The Politics of Child Abuse in America*. New York: Oxford University Press, 1996.

Hoffman, Allan M. (ed.). *Schools, Violence and Society*. Westport, CT: Praeger, 1996.

U.S. General Accounting Office. *At-Risk and Delinquent Youth: Multiple Federal Programs Raise Efficiency Questions*. Washington, DC: U.S. General Accounting Office, 1996.

CHAPTER 9

THE LEGAL RIGHTS OF JUVENILES

INTRODUCTION

In Harvey, Louisiana, near New Orleans, two teenage girls, ages 14 and 15, mixed up a deadly poison and planned to line the family's coffeemaker with it. Their goal was to poison their mother. They wrote detailed letters to one another about how they would go about perpetrating this crime. One of the girls wrote to her boyfriend about how her mother wouldn't let her telephone him late at night. She even told her boyfriend about the poison concoction she had prepared and wondered whether it would be potent enough. Luckily, the mother detected a white paste smeared around the inside of the coffeemaker and contacted police when she learned of her daughters' plans. The girls were taken into custody and charged with attempted murder. (Adapted from Associated Press, "Teens Accused of Plotting Mom's Death," Minot (ND) Daily News, January 10, 1996:A2)

It happens all the time in Detroit, New York, Chicago, Los Angeles, Miami, Newark, and Boston. Armed robbery among teenagers is increasing at an alarming rate. Who is being robbed? An 18-year-old was shot to death by a band of teenagers who wanted his Triple F.A.T Goose parka and $70 Nike sneakers in Chicago. Another four Chicago youths were killed for their leather jackets. One youth was stabbed to death when he failed to turn his Cincinnati Bengals jacket over to teenage gang members in Newark. Certain athletic sportswear, such as British Knights sneakers, have been adopted by city street gangs, notably the Los Angeles gang known as the Crips, because the initials "B.K." can also stand for "Blood Killers" (The Bloods are a rival gang of the Crips). When you leave home on any given day, you might get killed because of what you are wearing. (Adapted from Nina Darnton, "Street Crimes of Fashion," Newsweek, March 5, 1990:58).

Escalating juvenile violence and increasingly bizarre incidents involving juveniles have caused many experts to question whether existing juvenile laws are adequate to deal with these offenders. For some persons, the get-tough approach seems the most feasible alternative in dealing with youths who commit more serious offenses (Elliott, 1994b). If they commit the crime, they should do the time, or so some experts reason. There is little question that (1) youths are committing more serious offenses, especially during the 1990s; and (2) the onset of delinquency is occurring at earlier ages. More youths involved in drive-by shootings are under 10 years of age. Capital offenses are being committed by younger children annually. Many experts are perplexed about this state of affairs and what to do about it. One solution that is gaining in popularity is to hold juveniles more accountable for their actions and to exact harsher penalties whenever juveniles commit more serious crimes. As their accountability increases in juvenile courts, the law has vested juveniles with rights more commensurate with those of adults in criminal courts. In this chapter we describe the rights of juvenile offenders as well as some of the implications of these rights for their life chances.

Prior to the mid-1960s, almost every juvenile court in the nation made important, life-altering decisions affecting juveniles according to what the courts believed to be in the youths' best interests. These best interests were almost always subject to court definition and interpretation. This was and continues to be the fundamental doctrine of *parens patriae*. Since the mid-1960s, juveniles have achieved several significant legal milestones, including, but not limited to, the right to be represented by counsel, the right to cross-examine their accusers, and the right against self-incrimination. In this chapter we examine the contemporary range of legal rights extended to juveniles. Several landmark cases are described where significant rights have been established through U.S. Supreme Court decisions. Some of the more important implications of these decisions for juvenile offenders are discussed.

Juvenile rights are best understood in the context of the traditional *parens patriae* doctrine and how it has gradually been transformed by social and institutional changes. As one consequence of greater urbanization, Americans have enjoyed the advantages of greater professional and geographical mobility. Furthermore, the educational level of citizens has gradually increased. Today, citizens are more sophisticated than in previous times, and their legal understanding and interest has greatly improved. In past chapters we have described the gradual shift from *gemeinschaft* to *gesellschaft* community life and some of the changes that this shift has made in modifying the nature of social relationships. The dominant *parens patriae* doctrine remained unchallenged for decades. However, a growing wave of appeals of juvenile court decisions has resulted in an extensive erosion of the *parens patriae* doctrine by the U.S. Supreme Court.

The issue of capital punishment for juveniles will also be treated briefly. This is especially important since the U.S. Supreme Court determined in 1988 that the death penalty may not be administered to any juvenile under the age of 16 at the time a capital crime was committed (*Thompson v. Oklahoma*, 1988) and the following year upheld the executions of two other youths, aged 16 and 17. The application of the death penalty to juveniles is likely to generate large numbers of appeals in future years.

ORIGINAL JUVENILE JURISDICTION: *PARENS PATRIAE*

Until the mid-1960s, juvenile courts had considerable latitude in regulating the affairs of minors. This freedom to act in a child's behalf was rooted in the largely unchallenged doctrine of *parens patriae*. Whenever juveniles were apprehended by police officers for alleged infractions of the law, they were eventually turned over to juvenile authorities or taken to a juvenile hall for further processing. They were not advised of their right to an attorney, to have an attorney present during any interrogation, or to remain silent. They could be questioned by police at length, without parental notification or legal contact. In short, they had little, if any, protection against adult constitutional rights violations on the part of law enforcement officers and others. They had no access to due process because of their status or standing as juveniles.

When juveniles were caused to appear before juvenile court judges, they seldom had an opportunity to rebut evidence presented against them or to test the reliability of witnesses through cross-examination. This was rationalized at the time by asserting that juveniles did not understand the law and had to have it interpreted for them by others, principally juvenile court judges. Subsequent investigations of the knowledge that youths have of their rights seems to confirm this assertion (Lawrence, 1984). Sanborn (1994a) has characterized these early adjudicatory proceedings as informal cliniclike sessions. Despite the many recent reforms in juvenile court procedures, Sanborn believes that unfairness continues to be prevalent throughout contemporary adjudicatory hearings.

Prosecutors were seldom present in juvenile proceedings since they were nonadversarial, and juvenile court judges handled most cases informally, independently, and subjectively, depending on the youth's needs and offense seriousness. If judges decided that secure confinement would best serve the interests of justice and the welfare of the juvenile, the youth would be placed for an indeterminate period in a secure confinement facility in many ways similar to adult prisons or jails. These decisions were seldom questioned or challenged.

A primary reason for this silent acceptance of juvenile court judges' decisions was that the U.S. Supreme Court had repeatedly demonstrated its reluctance to intervene in juvenile matters or question decisions made by juvenile court judges. In the case of *In re Gault* (1967), Justice Stewart typified the traditional orientation of former Supreme Courts by declaring:

> The Court today uses an obscure Arizona case as a vehicle to impose upon thousands of juvenile courts throughout the Nation restrictions that the Constitution made applicable to adversary criminal trials. I believe the Court's decision is *wholly unsound* [emphasis mine] as a matter of constitutional law, and sadly unwise as a matter of judicial policy.... The inflexible restrictions that the Constitution so wisely made applicable to adversary criminal trials have no inevitable place in the proceedings of those public social agencies known as juvenile or family courts. (387 U.S. at 78–79)

The *parens patriae* doctrine received formal recognition in U.S. courts in 1839 in the case of *Ex parte Crouse* (1839). A youth, Mary Ann Crouse, was committed to the Philadelphia House of Refuge by her mother, because, as her mother alleged, Mary Ann was "incorrigible." Mary Ann's father opposed the commitment to the House of Refuge, and he filed a petition for her release. The petition cited the facts that she had been denied a jury trial and that the state action to incarcerate her was unconstitutional. The courts denied his petition, arguing instead that Mary Ann was being confined in a school, not a prison, and that reform, not punishment, was the objective. Weisheit and Alexander (1988:56) believe that the *Crouse* case was the first to spell out the legal justification for applying the *parens patriae* principle to children in the United States.

Thus juvenile courts or public social agencies were given almost complete autonomy and authority to act in a juvenile's behalf, taking whatever action was deemed necessary. Usually, the action deemed necessary was closely aligned with some form of rehabilitation or had rehabilitation as a primary objective. However, Weisheit and Alexander (1988:56–57) note that the original meaning of *parens patriae* was connected with the need to support or care for children, not necessarily to rehabilitate or reform them. In some respects, this **hands-off doctrine** was similar to the hands-off policy of the U.S. Supreme Court in relation to adult corrections policies and practices. The high court elected not to intervene in correctional matters, since they believed that prison wardens and superintendents knew what was best for their inmates and could be trusted to act responsibly in their behalf. This was the *parens patriae* doctrine applied to state and federal prisoners and exercised by prison administrators.

The hands-off policy of the U.S. Supreme Court toward corrections lasted from 1871 until 1941, exactly 70 years. In the case of *Ruffin v. Commonwealth* (1871), a Virginia judge declared that "prisoners have no more rights than slaves." During the next 70 years, prisoners were used as guinea pigs in various biological and chemical experiments, particularly in the testing of gases used on the front lines in Europe during World War I. Such tests of chemical agents on prisoners were conducted at the Michigan State Prison at Jackson. Some prisons mandated inmate sterilization, because it was believed that criminal behavior was hereditary. No committees for the protection of human subjects existed to protest these inmate treatments. Additionally, prisoners were subject to extensive corporal punishment. For example, the Arkansas State Prison Farm in Tucker, Arkansas used the Tucker Telephone to torture nonconforming prisoners. Electrodes from an old crank-type telephone were connected to an inmate's testicles, penis, and toes, and shocks were administered that left many prisoners crippled for life. Long-distance calls were made on the Tucker Telephone for especially unruly prisoners. Inmates had absolutely no rights, including mail privacy, visitation, or other privileges, other than those rights dispensed or withheld by prison authorities.

The U.S. Supreme Court began to change this unfortunate inmate condition in 1941 in the case of *Ex parte Hull* (1941). This case involved attempts by prisoners to petition the courts to hear various grievances or complaints. Prison superintendents and staff would routinely trash these petitions, contending that they were improperly prepared and hence legally unacceptable. In the *Hull* decision, the Court held that no state or its officers could abridge inmates of their right to access the federal or state courts through their petitions. This decision opened the floodgates of prison reform, and in successive years, inmate rights expanded considerably.

In many respects, juveniles were like adult inmates in prisons. Youths had no legal standing and virtually no rights other than those extended by the courts. The right to a trial by jury, a basic right provided any defendant who might be incarcerated for six months or more by a criminal court conviction, did not exist for juveniles unless juvenile court judges permitted such trials. Most juvenile court judges abhor jury trials for their juveniles and refuse to permit them. Even today, juveniles do not have an absolute right to a trial by jury, with few exceptions through state statutes. Thus juveniles may be deprived of their freedom for many years on the basis of a personal judicial decision.

Because of the informality of juvenile proceedings in most jurisdictions, there were frequent and obvious abuses of judicial discretion. These abuses occurred because of the absence of consistent guidelines whereby cases could be adjudicated. Juvenile probation officers might casually recommend to judges that particular juveniles "ought to do a few months" in an industrial school or other secure confinement facility, and the judge might be persuaded to adjudicate these cases accordingly.

However, several forces were at work simultaneously during the 1950s and 1960s that would eventually have the conjoint consequence of making juvenile courts more accountable for specific adjudications of youthful offenders. One of these forces was increased parental and general public recognition of and concern for the liberal license taken by juvenile courts in administering the affairs of juveniles. The abuse of judicial discretion was becoming increasingly apparent. Additionally, there was a growing disenchantment with and apathy for the rehabilitation ideal, although this disenchantment was not directed solely at juvenile courts. Rogers and Mays (1987:383) note that "disaffection during the 1960s and 1970s with the juvenile court was typical of the disenchantment then with many of society's institutions."

Feld (1995) observes that the juvenile court as originally envisioned by progressives was procedurally informal, characterized by individualized, offender-oriented dispositional practices. However, the contemporary juvenile court departs markedly from this progressive ideal. Today, juvenile courts are increasingly criminalized, featuring an adversarial system and greater procedural formality. This formality effectively inhibits any individualized treatment these courts might contemplate, and it has increased the perfunctory nature of sentencing juveniles adjudicated as delinquent.

Sanborn (1993) and Sutton (1985) describe the transformation of juvenile courts into more formal proceedings as part of the national trend toward bureaucratization and as an institutional compromise between law and social welfare. Bureaucracy stresses a fixed hierarchy of authority, task specialization, individualized spheres of competence, impersonal social relationships between organizational actors, and impartial enforcement of abstract rules. Thus, in the context of bureaucracy, decision making is routinized rather than arbitrary. Personalities and social characteristics are irrelevant.

Applied to juvenile court proceedings, juvenile court decision making would most likely be a function of the nature and seriousness of offenses committed and the factual delinquent history of juvenile defendants (Leiber, 1995). Emotional considerations in bureaucratic structures are nonexistent. The bureaucratic approach would be that juveniles should be held to a high standard of accountability for their actions. Furthermore, an individualized, treatment-oriented sanctioning system would be inconsistent with bureaucracy and violative of its general principles of impartiality. This type of system for juvenile justice seems consistent with the sentiments of a large portion of U.S. citizens and their belief that juvenile courts should get tough with juvenile offenders (Feld, 1993a,b). Despite this due-process and bureaucratic emphasis, juvenile courts have continued to retain many of their seemingly haphazard characteristics (Feld, 1989a). Good policies have been established, but their implementation has remained inconsistent and problematic for many juvenile courts (Feld, 1989a; Jensen and Metsger, 1994.

The primary elements of *parens patriae* that have contributed to its persistence as a dominant philosophical perspective in the juvenile justice system are summarized as follows:

1. *Parens patriae* encourages informal handling of juvenile matters as opposed to more formal and criminalizing procedures.
2. *Parens patriae* vests juvenile courts with absolute authority to provide what is best for youthful offenders (e.g., support services and other forms of care).
3. *Parens patriae* strongly encourages benevolent and rehabilitative treatments to assist youths in overcoming their personal and social problems.

4. *Parens patriae* avoids the adverse labeling effects that formal court proceedings might create.

5. *Parens patriae* means state control over juvenile life chances.

A major change from *parens patriae* state-based interests to a due-process juvenile justice model means an abandonment of most of these elements, or at least giving them less priority in decision making (U.S. General Accounting Office, 1995a). Decision making relative to youthful offenders is increasingly rationalized, and the principle of just deserts is operative. This means that less discretionary authority will be manifested by juvenile court judges, as they decide each case more on the basis of offense seriousness and prescribed punishments rather than according to individual factors or circumstances. Table 9.1 provides a general chronology of events relating to juvenile rights during the last 200 years.

During the mid-1960s and for the next 30 years, significant achievements were made in the area of juvenile rights. Although the *parens patriae* philosophy continues to be somewhat influential in juvenile proceedings, the U.S. Supreme Court has vested youths with certain constitutional rights. These rights do not encompass all the rights extended to adults who are charged with crimes. But those rights conveyed to juveniles thus far have had far-reaching implications for how juveniles are processed. In the following section, several landmark cases involving juvenile rights are described.

LANDMARK CASES IN JUVENILE JUSTICE

Regardless of the causes, several significant changes have been made in the juvenile justice system and how youths are processed in recent decades. In this section we examine several important rights bestowed upon juveniles by the U.S. Supreme Court during the past several decades. Describing these rights will make clear those rights that juveniles did not have until the landmark cases associated with them were concluded. Then a comparison will be made of juvenile rights and those rights that may be exercised by adults charged with crimes. However, despite sweeping juvenile reforms and major legal gains, there remain substantial differences between the current rights of juveniles and adults when charged with offenses.

Currently, juvenile courts are largely punishment centered, with the justice and just-deserts models influencing court decision making. Interests of youths are secondary, whereas community interests are seemingly served by juvenile court actions. Juveniles are being given greater responsibility for their actions, and they are increasingly expected to be held accountable for their wrongdoing.

TABLE 9.1

Chronological Summary of Major Events in Juvenile Justice

Year	Event
1791	Bill of Rights passed by U.S. Congress
1825	New York House of Refuge established
1839	*Ex parte Crouse*, established right of juvenile court to intervene in parent–child matters
1841	John Augustus initiates probation in Boston
1853	New York Children's Aid Society established
1855	Death penalty imposed on 10-year-old, James Arcene, in Arkansas for robbery and murder; earliest juvenile execution was Thomas Graunger, 16-year-old, for sodomizing a horse and cow in 1642
1866	Massachusetts statute passed giving juvenile court power to intervene and take custody where parents are unfit
1868	Fourteenth Amendment passed by U.S. Congress, establishing right to due process and equal protection under the law
1874	Massachusetts established first Children's Tribunal to deal with youthful offenders
1889	Indiana established children's guardians to have jurisdiction over neglected and dependent children
1889	Hull House established in Chicago by Jane Addams to assist unsupervised children of immigrant parents
1899	Compulsory School Act, Colorado; statutory regulation of truants
1899	Illinois Act to Regulate the Treatment and Control of Dependent, Neglected, and Delinquent Children; first juvenile court established in United States
1901	Juvenile court established in Denver, Colorado
1907	Separate juvenile court with original jurisdiction in juvenile matters established in Denver, Colorado
1912	Creation of U.S. Children's Bureau, charged with compiling statistical information about juvenile offenders; existed from 1912 to 1940
1918	Chicago slums studied by Shaw and McKay; delinquency related to urban environment and transitional neighborhoods
1938	Federal Juvenile Delinquency Act
1966	*Kent v. United States* case established juvenile's right to hearing before transfer to criminal court, right to assistance of counsel during police interrogations, right to reports and records relating to transfer decision, and right to reasons given by judge for transfer
1967	*In re Gault* case established juvenile's right to an attorney, the right to notice of charges, the right to confront and cross-examine witnesses, and the right against self-incrimination
1970	*In re Winship* case established juvenile's right to criminal court standard of "beyond a reasonable doubt" where loss of freedom is a possible penalty
1971	*McKeiver v. Pennsylvania* case established that juvenile's right to a trial by jury is not absolute

TABLE 9.1 (CONT'D)

Year	Event
1974	Juvenile Justice and Delinquency Prevention Act
1974	Office of Juvenile Justice and Delinquency Prevention, instrumental in promoting deinstitutionalization of status offenses
1975	*Breed v. Jones* case established that double jeopardy exists if juvenile is adjudicated as delinquent in juvenile court and tried for same offense later in criminal court; prohibits double jeopardy
1982	*Eddings v. Oklahoma* case established that death penalty applied to juveniles was not "cruel and unusual punishment" per se
1984	*Schall v. Martin* case established the constitutionality of the preventive detention of juveniles
1985	*New Jersey v. T.L.O.* case established lesser standard of search and seizure on school property; searches and seizures permissible without probable cause or warrant
1988	*Thompson v. Oklahoma* case established that death penalty applied to juveniles convicted of murder who were under age 16 at time of murder is cruel and unusual punishment
1989	*Stanford v. Kentucky* and *Wilkins v. Missouri* cases that established that death penalty is not cruel and unusual punishment applied to juveniles convicted of murder and who were aged 16 or 17 at the time the murder was committed

Each of the cases presented below represents attempts by juveniles to secure rights ordinarily extended to adults. Given these cases, juveniles have fared well with the U.S. Supreme Court in past years. While juveniles still do not enjoy the full range of rights extended to adult offenders who are tried in criminal courts, juveniles have acquired due-process privileges that were not available to them prior to the 1960s (Feld, 1993a). The first three cases presented, *Kent v. United States, In re Gault,* and *In re Winship,* make up the "big three" of juvenile cases involving their legal rights. The remaining cases address specific rights issues, such as the right against double jeopardy, jury trials as a matter of right in juvenile courts, preventive detention, and the standards that should govern searches of students and seizures of contraband on school property.

Kent v. United States (1966)

Regarded as the first major juvenile rights case to preface further juvenile court reforms, *Kent v. United States* (1966) established the universal precedents of (1) requiring waiver hearings before juveniles can be transferred to the jurisdiction of a criminal court (excepting legislative automatic waivers as discussed in this and other chapters, although reverse waiver hearings must be conducted at the juvenile's request), and (2) juveniles are entitled to consult with counsel prior to and during such hearings.

The facts in the case are that in 1959, Morris A. Kent, Jr., a 14-year-old in the District of Columbia, was apprehended as the result of several housebreakings and attempted purse snatchings. He was placed on probation in the custody of his mother. In 1961, an intruder entered the apartment of a woman, took her wallet, and raped her. Fingerprints at the crime scene were later identified as those of Morris Kent, who was fingerprinted when apprehended for housebreaking in 1959. On September 5, 1961, Kent, 16, was taken into custody by police, interrogated for seven hours, and admitted the offense as well as volunteering information about other housebreakings, robberies, and rapes. Although the records are unclear about when Kent's mother became aware of Kent's arrest, she did obtain counsel for Kent shortly after 2:00 P.M. the following day. She and her attorney conferred with the social service director of the juvenile court and learned that there was a possibility that Kent would be waived to criminal court. Kent's attorney advised the director of his intention to oppose the waiver.

Kent was detained in a receiving home for one week. During that period there was no arraignment and no determination by a judicial officer of probable cause for Kent's arrest. His attorney filed a motion with the juvenile court opposing the waiver as well as a request to inspect records relating to Kent's previous offenses. Also, a psychiatric examination of Kent was arranged by Kent's attorney. Kent's attorney argued that because his client was "a victim of severe psychopathology," it would be in Kent's best interests to remain within juvenile court jurisdiction, where he could receive adequate treatment in a hospital and would be a suitable subject for rehabilitation.

Typical of juvenile court judges at the time, the juvenile court judge failed to rule on any of Kent's attorney's motions. He also failed to confer with Kent's attorney and/or parents. In a somewhat arrogant manner, the juvenile court judge declared that "after full investigation, I do hereby waive" jurisdiction of Kent and direct that he be "held for trial for [the alleged] offenses under the regular procedure of the U.S. District Court for the District of Columbia." He offered no findings, nor did he recite any reason for the waiver or make mention of Kent's attorney's motions. Kent was later found guilty of six counts of housebreaking by a federal jury, although the jury found him "not guilty by reason of insanity" on the rape charge. Because of District of Columbia law, it was mandatory that Kent be transferred to a mental institution until such time as his sanity is restored. On each of the housebreaking counts, Kent's sentence was 5 to 15 years, or a total of 30 to 90 years in prison. His mental institution commitment would be counted as time served against the 30- to 90-year sentence.

Kent's conviction was reversed by a vote of 5–4. This is significant, because it signified a subtle shift in Supreme Court sentiment relating to juvenile rights. The majority held that Kent's rights to due process and to the effective assistance of counsel were violated when he was denied a formal hearing on the waiver and his attorneys' motions were ignored. It is also significant that the Supreme Court stressed the phrase "critically important" when referring to the absence of counsel and waiver hearing. In adult cases, critical stages are those that relate to the defendant's potential loss of freedoms (i.e., incarceration). Because of the *Kent* decision, waiver hearings are now critical stages. Regarding the effective assistance of counsel, this was also regarded by the Court as a "critically important" decision. They observed that "the right to representation by counsel is not a formality. It is not a grudging gesture to a ritualistic requirement. It is of the essence of justice.... Appointment of counsel without affording an opportunity for a hearing on a 'critically important' decision is tantamount to a denial of counsel" (383 U.S. at 561).

In re Gault (1967)

The case of *In re Gault* (1967) is perhaps the most noteworthy of all landmark juvenile rights cases. Certainly, it is considered the most ambitious. In a 7–2 vote, the U.S. Supreme Court articulated the following rights for all juveniles: (1) *the right to a notice of charges*, (2) *the right to counsel*, (3) *the right to confront and cross-examine witnesses*, and (4) *the right to invoke the privilege against self-incrimination*. The petitioner, Gault, requested the Court to rule favorably on two additional rights sought: (1) *the right to a transcript of the proceedings*, and (2) *the right to appellate review*. The Court elected *not* to rule on either of these rights.

The facts in the case are that Gerald Francis Gault, a 15-year-old, and a friend, Ronald Lewis, were taken into custody by the sheriff of Gila County, Arizona, on the morning of June 8, 1964. At the time, Gault was on probation as the result of "being in the company of another, who had stolen a wallet from a lady's purse," a judgment entered February 25, 1964. A verbal complaint had been filed by a neighbor of Gault, Mrs. Cook, alleging that Gault had called her and made lewd and indecent remarks. [With some levity, the Supreme Court said that "It will suffice for purposes of this opinion to say that the remarks or questions put to her were of the irritatingly offensive, adolescent, sex variety" (387 U.S. at 4).] When Gault was picked up, his mother and father were at work. Indeed, they did not learn where their son was until much later that evening. Gault was being held at the children's detention home.

Gault's parents proceeded to the home. Officer Flagg, the deputy probation officer and superintendent of the children's detention home where

Gault was being detained, advised Gault's parents that a hearing would be held in juvenile court at 3:00 P.M. the following day. Flagg filed a petition with the court on the hearing day, June 9. This petition was entirely formal, stating only that "said minor is under the age of 18 years, and is in need of the protection of this Honorable Court; [and that] said minor is a delinquent minor." It prayed for a hearing and an order regarding the "care and custody of said minor." No factual basis was provided for the petition, and Gault's parents were not provided with a copy of it in advance of the hearing.

On June 9, the hearing was held, with only Gault, his mother and older brother, probation officers Flagg and Henderson, and the juvenile court judge present. The original complainant, Mrs. Cook, was not there. No one was sworn at the hearing, no transcript was made of it, and no memorandum of the substance of the proceedings was prepared. The testimony consisted largely of allegations by Officer Flagg about Gault's behavior and prior juvenile record. A subsequent hearing was scheduled for June 15. On June 15, another hearing was held, with all above present, including Ronald Lewis and his father, and Gerald's father. What actually transpired is unknown, although there are conflicting recollections from all parties who were there. Mrs. Gault asked why Mrs. Cook was not present. Judge McGhee said "she didn't have to be present at that hearing." Furthermore, the judge did not speak to Mrs. Cook or communicate with her at any time. Flagg spoke with her once by telephone on June 9. Officially, the charge against Gault was "lewd telephone calls." When the hearing was concluded, the judge committed Gault as a juvenile delinquent to the Arizona State Industrial School "for a period of his minority" (until age 21). (Parenthetically, if an adult had made an obscene telephone call, he would have received a $50 fine and no more than 60 days in jail. In Gerald Gault's case, he was facing nearly six years in a juvenile prison for the same offense).

A **habeas corpus** hearing was held on August 17, and Judge McGhee was cross-examined regarding his actions. After "hemming and hawing," the judge declared that Gault had "disturbed the peace" and was "habitually involved in immoral matters." Regarding the judge's reference to Gault's alleged "habitual immorality," the judge made vague references to an incident two years earlier when Gault had been accused of stealing someone's baseball glove and had lied to police by denying that he had taken it. The judge also recalled, again vaguely, that Gault had testified some months earlier about making "silly calls, or funny calls, or something like that."

After exhausting their appeals in Arizona state courts, the Gaults appealed to the U.S. Supreme Court. Needless to say, the Court was appalled that Gault's case had been handled in such a cavalier and unconstitutional manner. They reversed the Arizona Supreme Court, holding that Gault did, indeed, have the right to an attorney, the right to confront his accuser (Mrs.

Cook) and to cross-examine her, the right against self-incrimination, and the right to have notice of the charges filed against him. Perhaps Justice Black summed up the current juvenile court situation in the United States when he said: "This holding strikes a well-nigh fatal blow to much that is *unique* [emphasis mine] about the juvenile courts in this Nation."

In re Winship (1970)

Winship was a less complex case compared with *Gault*. But it established an important precedent in juvenile courts relating to the *standard of proof* used in established defendant guilt. The U.S. Supreme Court held that "beyond a reasonable doubt," a standard ordinarily used in adult criminal courts, was henceforth to be used by juvenile court judges and others in establishing a youth's delinquency. Formerly, the standard used was the civil application of "preponderance of the evidence."

The facts in the *Winship* case are that Samuel Winship was a 12-year-old charged with larceny in New York City. He purportedly entered a locker and stole $112 from a woman's pocketbook. Under Section 712 of the New York Family Court Act, a juvenile delinquent was defined as "a person over 7 and less than 16 years of age who does any act, which, if done by an adult, would constitute a crime." Interestingly, the juvenile court judge in the case acknowledged that the proof to be presented by the prosecution might be insufficient to establish the guilt of Winship beyond a reasonable doubt, although he did indicate that the New York Family Court Act provided that "any determination at the conclusion of [an adjudicatory hearing] that a [juvenile] did an act or acts must be based on a preponderance of the evidence" standard (397 U.S. at 360). Winship was adjudicated as a delinquent and ordered to a training school for 18 months, subject to annual extensions of his commitment until his eighteenth birthday. Appeals to New York courts were unsuccessful.

The U.S. Supreme Court heard Winship's case and, in a 6–3 vote, reversed the New York Family Court ruling. A statement by Justice Brennan succinctly states the case for the "beyond a reasonable doubt" standard:

> In sum, the constitutional safeguard of proof beyond a reasonable doubt is as much required during the adjudicatory stage of a delinquency proceeding as are those constitutional safeguards applied in Gault—notice of charges, right to counsel, the rights of confrontation and examination, and the privilege of self-incrimination. We therefore hold, in agreement with Chief Justice Fuld in dissent in the Court of Appeals, that where a 12-year-old child is charged with an act of stealing which renders him liable to confinement for as long as six years, then, as a matter of due process...the case against him must be proved beyond a reasonable doubt. (397 U.S. at 368)

McKeiver v. Pennsylvania (1971)

The *McKeiver* case was important because the U.S. Supreme Court held that juveniles are not entitled to a jury trial as a matter of right. [It should be noted that as of 1990, 12 states legislatively mandated jury trials for juveniles in juvenile courts if they so requested such trials, depending on the seriousness of the offense(s) alleged.] The facts are that in May 1968, Joseph McKeiver, age 16, was charged with robbery, larceny, and receiving stolen goods. Although he was represented by counsel at his adjudicatory hearing and requested a trial by jury to ascertain his guilt or innocence, Judge Theodore S. Gutowicz of the Court of Common Pleas, Family Division, Juvenile Branch, of Philadelphia, Pennsylvania denied the request. McKeiver was subsequently adjudicated delinquent. On subsequent appeal to the U.S. Supreme Court, McKeiver's adjudication was upheld. Again, of interest to criminal justice analysts, the remarks of a U.S. Supreme Court Justice are insightful. Justice Blackmun indicated: "If the formalities of the criminal adjudicative process are to be superimposed upon the juvenile court system, there is little need for its separate existence. Perhaps that ultimate disillusionment will come one day, but for the moment, we are disinclined to give impetus to it" (403 U.S. at 551).

Throughout the opinion delivered in the McKeiver case, it is apparent that the Supreme Court was sensitive to the problems associated with juvenile court procedure. Since criminal courts were already bogged down with formalities and lengthy protocol that frequently led to excessive court delays, it was not unreasonable for the Court to rule against perpetuating such formalities in juvenile courts. But we must recognize that in this instance, the Court merely ruled that it is not the constitutional right of juveniles to have the right to a jury trial upon their request. This proclamation had no effect on individual states that wished to enact or preserve such a method of adjudicating juveniles as delinquent or not delinquent. Therefore, about a fourth of the states today have legislative provisions for jury trials in juvenile courts. See the discussion below on the 1997 status of jury trials for juveniles.

Breed v. Jones (1975)

This case raised the significant constitutional issue of **double jeopardy**. The U.S. Supreme Court concluded that after a juvenile has been adjudicated as delinquent on specific charges, those same charges may not be alleged against those juveniles subsequently in criminal courts through transfers or waivers.

The facts of the case are that on February 8, 1971 in Los Angeles, California, Gary Steven Jones was 17 years old, was armed with a deadly weapon, and allegedly committed robbery. Jones was subsequently apprehended and an adjudicatory hearing was held on March 1. A petition was filed against Jones. After testimony was taken from Jones and witnesses, the juvenile court found that the allegations in the petition were true and sustained the petition. A dispositional hearing date was set for March 15. At that time, Jones was declared "not...amenable to the care, treatment and training program available through the facilities of the juvenile court" under a California statute. Jones was then transferred by judicial waiver to a California criminal court where he could be tried as an adult. In a later criminal trial, Jones was convicted of robbery and committed for an indeterminate period to the California Youth Authority. The California Supreme Court upheld the conviction.

When Jones appealed the decision in 1971, the U.S. Supreme Court reversed the robbery conviction. Chief Justice Warren Burger delivered the Court opinion: "We hold that the prosecution of [Jones] in Superior Court, after an adjudicatory proceeding in Juvenile Court, violated the Double Jeopardy Clause of the Fifth Amendment, as applied to the States through the Fourteenth Amendment." The Court ordered Jones' release outright or a remand to juvenile court for disposition. In a lengthy opinion, Justice Burger targeted double jeopardy as (1) being adjudicated as delinquent on specific charges in a juvenile court, and (2) subsequently being tried and convicted on those same charges in criminal court. Within the context of "fundamental fairness," such action could not be tolerated.

Schall v. Martin (1984)

In this case the U.S. Supreme Court issued juveniles a minor setback regarding the state's right to hold them in preventive detention pending a subsequent adjudication. The Court said that the preventive detention of juveniles by states is constitutional if judges perceive these youths to pose a danger to the community or an otherwise serious risk if released short of an adjudicatory hearing. This decision was significant, in part, because many experts advocated the separation of juveniles and adults in jails, those facilities most often used for preventive detention. Also, the preventive detention of adults was not ordinarily practiced at that time. [Since then, the preventive detention of adults who are deemed to pose societal risks has been upheld by the U.S. Supreme Court (*United States v. Salerno*, 1987).]

The facts are that 14-year-old Gregory Martin was arrested at 11:30 P.M. on December 13, 1977 in New York City. He was charged with first-degree robbery, second-degree assault, and criminal possession of a weapon. Martin lied to police at the time, giving a false name and address. Between the time of his arrest and December 29 when a fact-finding hearing was held, Martin was detained (a total of 15 days). His confinement was based largely on the false information he had supplied to police and the seriousness of the charges pending against him. Subsequently, he was adjudicated a delinquent and placed on two years' probation. Later, his attorney filed an appeal, contesting his preventive detention as violative of the "due process" clause of the Fourteenth Amendment. The U.S. Supreme Court eventually heard the case and upheld the detention as constitutional. Table 9.2 summarizes some of the major rights available to juveniles and compares these rights with selected rights enjoyed by adults in criminal proceedings.

IMPLICATIONS FOR JUVENILES

Some of the major implications of greater juvenile court formalization for youths include (1) more equitable treatment through less disparity in dispositions among juveniles judges; (2) greater certainty of punishment through the new justice orientation; (3) less informality in dispositions and less individualized rehabilitative treatments; (4) greater likelihood of acquiring a juvenile offender record, since procedures from intake through adjudication are increasingly codified; and (5) greater likelihood of being transferred to criminal courts through waivers, since the most serious cases will move forward more frequently to juvenile courts.

At present, most juvenile courts in the United States are civil courts. That is, those juveniles adjudicated as delinquent do not acquire criminal records as a result of these adjudications. Once youths reach the age of majority or adulthood, their juvenile records are forgotten or sealed. They begin a new slate as adults. This works to their advantage. However, the jurisdiction of juvenile courts in various states is changing. As we have seen earlier, there are blended sentencing statutes in increasing numbers of states where the jurisdiction of juvenile court judges is being extended. Thus it is possible in some states to impose *both* juvenile and adult sanctions on youthful offenders in juvenile courts. Furthermore, for those youths who have been transferred to criminal courts, some jurisdictions currently permit these judges to impose juvenile and adult correctional sanctions (Bilchik, 1996).

However, for the majority of jurisdictions as of 1996, while juveniles remain within juvenile court jurisdiction, they are subject to conceivably harsher penalties as juveniles than might otherwise be the case if they were treated as adults. For instance, the case of *Gault* reported earlier in this chapter saw a boy disposed to nearly *six years* in a state industrial school for allegedly making an obscene telephone call. Adults would not be subject to such a heavy penalty. Currently, juvenile court judges have considerable power to control a juvenile's liberty to the limits of one's infant status. Even now in most jurisdictions, if juvenile court judges

TABLE 9.2

Comparison of Juvenile and Adult Rights Relating to Delinquency and Crime

Right	Adults	Juveniles
1. "Beyond a reasonable doubt" standard used in court.	Yes	Yes
2. Right against double jeopardy	Yes	Yes
3. Right to assistance of counsel	Yes	Yes
4. Right to notice of charges	Yes	Yes
5. Right to a transcript of court proceedings	Yes	No
6. Right against self-incrimination	Yes	Yes
7. Right to trial by jury	Yes	No in most states
8. Right to defense counsel in court proceedings	Yes	No
9. Right to due process	Yes	No[a]
10. Right to bail	Yes	No, with exceptions
11. Right to cross-examine witnesses	Yes	Yes
12. Right of confrontation	Yes	Yes

13. Standards relating to searches and seizures:
  a. "Probable cause" and warrants required for searches and seizures
  b. "Reasonable suspicion" required for searches and seizures without warrant
	
	Yes, with exceptions
	
	No
		
		No
		
		Yes

14. Right to hearing prior to transfer to criminal court or to a reverse waiver hearing in states with automatic transfer provisions	N/A	Yes
15. Right to a speedy trial	Yes	No
16. Right to *habeas corpus* relief in correctional settings	Yes	No
17. Right to rehabilitation	No	No
18. Criminal evidentiary standards	Yes	Yes
19. Right to hearing for parole or probation revocation	Yes	No
20. Bifurcated trial, death penalty cases	Yes	Yes
21. Right to discovery	Yes	Limited
22. Fingerprinting, photographing at booking	Yes	No, with exceptions
23. Right to appeal	Yes	Limited

24. Waivers of rights:
  a. Adults
  b. Juveniles
	Knowingly, intelligently
	Totality of circumstances	

25. Right to hearing for parole or probation revocation	Yes	No, with exceptions
26. "Equal protection" clause of 14th Amendment applicable	Yes	No, with exceptions
27. Right to court-appointed attorney if indigent	Yes	No, with exceptions
28. Transcript required of criminal/delinquency trial proceedings	Yes	No, with exceptions
29. Pretrial detention permitted	Yes	Yes

Right	Adults	Juveniles
TABLE 9.2 (CONT'D)		
30. Plea bargaining	Yes, with exceptions	No, with exceptions
31. Burden of proof borne by prosecution	Yes	No, with exceptions[b]
32. Public access to trials	Yes	Limited
33. Conviction/adjudication results in criminal record	Yes	No

[a]Minimal, not full, due-process safeguards assured.
[b]Burden of proof is borne by prosecutor in 23 state juvenile courts; the remainder make no provision or mention of who bears the burden of proof.

wish, they may dispose youths to long-term secure confinement far beyond those incarcerative terms normally imposed on adults who have been convicted of similar offenses. This unfairness is a carryover from the *parens patriae* years of juvenile courts.

The Juvenile's Right to Waive Rights

With all of the legal rights extended to juveniles since 1966, there are more than a few occasions when juveniles may waive various rights, such as the right to counsel, at one or more critical stages of their juvenile justice system processing. For instance, a 1968 case decided following the *In re Gault* decision was *West v. United States*. In the *West* case, a juvenile had waived his right to counsel, as well as several other important rights that had been extended to juveniles through the *Gault* case. A nine-point standard for analysis was established by the Fifth Circuit Court of Appeals when the *West* disposition was imposed and an appeal followed. The nine-point standard was devised in order for judges to determine whether *any* juvenile is capable of understanding and waiving one or more of their constitutional rights. These nine points are:

1. Age
2. Education
3. Knowledge of the substance of the charge and the nature of the right to remain silent and the right to an attorney
4. Whether the accused is allowed contact with parents, guardian, attorney, or other interested adult
5. Whether the interrogation occurred before or after the indictment
6. Methods used in interrogation
7. Length of interrogation

8. Whether the accused refused to voluntarily give statements on prior occasions

9. Whether the accused had repudiated an extrajudicial statement at a later date

While these nine points are interesting and relevant, the fact that they were decreed by the Fifth Circuit Court of Appeals meant that they were not binding on federal district courts in other circuits. For that matter, since these were rights conveyed through a federal circuit, they were not binding on any particular state jurisdiction, even a state within the territory of the Fifth Circuit Court of Appeals.

However, 11 years later in 1979, the U.S. Supreme Court decided a case that did make these points relevant considerations for *all* juvenile courts in the case of *Fare v. Michael C.* Michael C. was a juvenile charged with murder. During a preliminary interrogation, Michael C. was alone with police officers and detectives. Neither his parents nor an attorney were present. Michael C. asked to see his probation officer, but the interrogating detectives denied this request, since a probation officer is not an attorney and cannot be permitted to function as defense counsel under these circumstances. Subsequently, Michael C. waived his right to counsel and answered police questions. He was convicted of murder and appealed, alleging that his right to counsel was violated when he asked to see his probation officer and his request had been denied by the investigating officers. The court considered Michael C.'s case and determined that Michael C. had, indeed, made an intelligent, understanding and voluntary waiver of his rights. The standard devised by the U.S. Supreme Court was the totality of circumstances test, which was essentially a standard they had adopted earlier in a criminal case involving an adult offender. Thus the U.S. Supreme Court said that juvenile rights waivers should not be based on one sole characteristic or procedure, but rather, on all the relevant circumstances of the case (Caeti, Hemmens, and Burton, 1996:618–619).

In subsequent cases, the totality of circumstances test has resulted in mixed decisions by appellate courts. For instance, in *Woods v. Clusen* (1986), the Seventh Circuit Court of Appeals ruled that a 16½-year-old's confession was inadmissible because the juvenile had been taken from his home at 7:30 A.M., handcuffed, stripped, forced to wear institutional clothing but no shoes or socks, showed pictures of the crime scene, and intimidated and interrogated for many hours. These police tactics were criticized by the court and the investigators were reprimanded for their failure to uphold and respect the offender's constitutional rights and provide fundamental fairness. But in the case of *United States v. Bernard S.* (1986), the Ninth Circuit Court of Appeals determined that although the youth was 17 and had difficulty with the

English language, the totality of circumstances justified including a confession against the youth later in court (Caeti, Hemmens, and Burton, 1996:619).

Early research by Grisso (1980), for instance, shows that juveniles have had little grasp of their constitutional rights. Grisso studied a large sample of juveniles and found that only 10 percent of them chose not to waive their rights where serious charges were alleged. Grisso found that they (1) demonstrated less comprehension than adults of their *Miranda* rights; (2) had less understanding of the wording of the **Miranda warning**; (3) misunderstood their right to counsel; and (4) did not understand their right to remain silent, believing that they could later be punished if they failed to tell about their criminal activities. A later study by Caeti, Hemmens, and Burton (1996) was conducted to determine the degree of compliance of state juvenile codes with the actual rights juveniles have been extended by U.S. Supreme Court decisions. In this study a content analysis was made of all state statutes pertaining to legal counsel for juveniles. Caeti, Hemmens, and Burton wanted to determine, among other things, whether there were statutory guarantees of a juvenile defendant's right to counsel, whether judicial discretion is permitted in the actual appointment of counsel for indigent juveniles, whether strict rights waivers were included, and whether defense counsel was mandated for all critical stages of juvenile justice processing.

First, these researchers found that all states, with the exception of Hawaii, Massachusetts, Michigan, Mississippi, Missouri, New Hampshire, North Carolina, North Dakota, Rhode Island, South Carolina, South Dakota, and West Virginia, had a specific juvenile statute identifying the juvenile's right to legal counsel. Table 9.3 shows a distribution of the states according to this and other legal rights of juveniles regarding defense counsel appointments and waivers of the right to counsel. Only about half of all states have vested juvenile court judges with the discretion to appoint counsel for juveniles; even fewer states provide strict rights waiver requirements and mandatory defense counsel appointments.

Subsequently, Caeti, Hemmens, and Burton divided the states according to which were least and most protective of juveniles. They divided all states according to five categories. These are shown in Table 9.4. The first category in Table 9.4 shows six states where no specific statute exists guaranteeing juveniles the right to counsel. Caeti, Hemmens, and Burton correctly indicate that despite the fact that these states are absent such statutes, the case of *In re Gault* is applicable to *all* states and ensures a juvenile's right to counsel at critical stages of processing. Thus there may not be a need to articulate this right as a legislated statute. The second category contains those states where minimal statements exist concerning a child's right to counsel at specific stages. They use Indiana as such a state where a

TABLE 9.3

Conditions under Which the Right to Counsel Is Invoked[a]

State	Specific Juvenile Statute	Discretionary Appointment	Strict Waiver Requirements	Mandatory Appointment
Alabama	×	×		
Alaska	×			
Arizona	×	×		
Arkansas	×	×	×	
California	×	×		×
Colorado	×	×	×	
Connecticut	×	×	×	
Delaware				
Florida	×			
Georgia	×	×		
Hawaii				
Idaho	×	×		
Illinois	×	×		×
Indiana	×	×		
Iowa	×	×	×	
Kansas	×	×		×
Kentucky	×			
Louisiana	×		×	×
Maine	×			
Maryland	×	×	×	
Massachusetts		×	×	×
Michigan				
Minnesota	×			
Mississippi				
Missouri				
Montana	×	×	×	
Nebraska	×			
Nevada	×			
New Hampshire				
New Jersey	×		×	
New Mexico	×	×	×	×
New York	×			
North Carolina		×		×
North Dakota		×		
Ohio	×	×	×	

State	Specific Juvenile Statute	Discretionary Appointment	Strict Waiver Requirements	Mandatory Appointment
Oklahoma	×	×	×	
Oregon	×	×		
Pennsylvania	×	×	×	
Rhode Island		×		
South Carolina		×		
South Dakota		×	×	
Tennessee	×	×		
Texas	×	×	×	×
Utah	×	×		
Vermont	×	×		
Virginia	×	×	×	
Washington	×			
West Virginia		×		
Wisconsin	×	×		
Wyoming	×			

[a]Six states—Delaware, Hawaii, Michigan, Missouri, Mississippi, and New Hampshire—do not have statutory references to a juvenile's right to legal counsel in their state legal codes.

Source: Caeti, Hemmens, and Burton, 1996:622–623.

statute says that "a child charged with a delinquent act is also entitled to be represented by counsel" (p. 627). The third category contains states where statutory language extends the right to counsel to all juveniles at all stages or every stage of proceedings against them. The fourth category contains those states that provide counsel for juveniles beyond the stages articulated by *Gault*. These researchers cite Arkansas as a state where strict criteria are applicable in the event that a juvenile wishes to waive certain constitutional rights. In the fifth and final category, states are shown where the right to counsel is extended, even to juveniles who do not face the prospect of secure confinement or any loss of freedom. Table 9.4 is actually a continuum of the degree of statutory protection provided juveniles by various states, ranging from least protective to most protective.

TABLE 9.4

Degree of Statutory Protection[a]

Category 1	Category 2	Category 3	Category 4	Category 5
Delaware	Alaska	Arizona	Alabama	California
Hawaii	District of Columbia	Colorado	Arkansas	Illinois
Michigan	Florida	District of Columbia	Connecticut	Kansas
Mississippi	Indiana	Georgia	Georgia	Louisiana
Missouri	Kenucky	Idaho	Iowa	New Mexico
New Hampshire	Maine	Maryland	Montana	North Carolina
	Minnesota	Massachusetts	Ohio	Texas
	Missouri	New Jersey	Oklahoma	
	Nebraska	North Dakota	Pennsylvania	
	Nevada	Ohio	Virginia	
	New York	Oregon	Wisconsin	
	North Dakota	Pennsylvania	Wyoming	
	Rhode Island	South Dakota		
	South Carolina	Tennessee		
	South Dakota	Utah		
	Tennessee	Vermont		
	Washington	Virginia		
	West Virginia	Washington		
		Wisconson		

[a]Category 1 is least protective; category 5 is most protective.

Source: Caeti, Hemmens, and Burton, 1996:626.

The matter of juvenile rights waivers continues to generate considerable research interest. As juvenile violence escalates and more drastic procedural measures are contemplated by state legislatures and the federal government, greater consideration will be given to the constitutional guarantees extended to juveniles. At the same time, more than a few experts believe that the juvenile courts can continue to dispense justice on an individualized basis, thus preserving the notion of *parens patriae*. We have already noted the inherent inequity of the *parens patriae* doctrine, although it continues to be pervasive in juvenile courts.

The Continued Leniency of Juvenile Court Adjudications and Dispositions

Juvenile court actions continue to be fairly lenient. The sanction of choice among juvenile court judges is probation. Even those offenders who appear multiple times before the same judge are likely to continue to receive probation for their persistent offending. However, the many juvenile justice reforms that have occurred during the 1980s and 1990s have caused some experts to see little difference between how adults are processed by criminal courts and how juveniles are processed by juvenile courts (Feld, 1993a). However, despite the increased criminalization of juvenile courts, there are significant differences that serve to differentiate criminal courts and criminal processing from how youths are treated or processed by the juvenile justice system.

Perhaps the most important implication for juveniles is that in most cases, juvenile court adjudications do not result in criminal records. These courts continue to exercise civil authority. Once juveniles reach adulthood, their juvenile records are routinely expunged and forgotten, with some exceptions. But having one's case adjudicated by a juvenile court operates to a youth's disadvantage in some respects. For instance, the rules governing the admissibility of evidence or testimony are relaxed considerably compared with the rules governing similar admissions in criminal courts. Thus it is easier in juvenile courts to admit inculpatory evidence and testimony than in criminal courtrooms. Further, cases against juveniles do not need to be as convincing as cases against criminal defendants. Lower standards of proof are operative relative to search and seizure and the degree of probable cause required. Schoolchildren are particularly vulnerable in this regard, in view of *New Jersey v. T.L.O.* discussed in an earlier section of this chapter.

On the negative side, juveniles do not always receive jury trials if they request them. Less than a fourth of all states permit jury trials for juveniles by statute. In all other states, jury trials are available to juveniles only if judges permit them. In most cases, therefore, the judgment of the juvenile court is final, for all practical purposes. Appeals of decisions by juvenile court judges are relatively rare. Long-term dispositions of incarceration may be imposed by juvenile court judges at will, without serious challenge. Current profiles of long-term detainees in secure juvenile facilities suggest that judges impose dispositions of secure confinement frequently. Further, a majority of these long-term detainees are less serious property offenders with some chronicity in their rate of reoffending.

An Update on Jury Trials for Juvenile Delinquents

In 1997 the National Center for Juvenile Justice investigated various state jurisdictions to determine their present status concerning jury trials and other formal procedures for juveniles. The categories created by this investigation included the following: (1) states providing no right to a jury trial for juvenile delinquents under any circumstances; (2) states providing a right to a jury trial for juveniles delinquents under any circumstances; (3) states not providing a jury trial for juvenile delinquents except under specified circumstances; (4) states providing the right to a jury trial for juvenile delinquents under specified circumstances; and (5) states with statutes allowing juvenile delinquents with a right to jury trial to waive that right.[*]

1. *States not providing jury trials for juvenile delinquents under any circumstances*
   a. Alabama (12-15-65)
   b. Arizona (Juvenile Court Rule 7)
   c. Arkansas (9-27-325)
   d. California (Welfare and Institutions Code, section 702.3)
   e. District of Columbia (16-2316)
   f. Georgia (15-11-28)
   g. Hawaii (571-41)
   h. Indiana (31-6-7-10)
   i. Kentucky (610.070)
   j. Louisiana (Children's Code, sections 808 and 882)
   k. Maryland (Courts and Judicial Proceedings, section 812)
   l. Mississippi (42-21-203)
   m. Nevada (62.193)
   n. New Jersey (2a:4a-40)
   o. North Dakota (27-20-24)
   p. Ohio (2151.35)
   q. Oregon (419C.400)
   r. Pennsylvania (Title 42, section 6336)
   s. South Carolina (20-7-755)
   t. Tennessee (37-1-124)
   u. Utah (78-3a-511)

---

[*]The following summary is reprinted with permission from the National Center for Juvenile Justice. Adapted from Linda A. Szymanski, *Juvenile's Right to a Jury Trial in a Delinquency Hearing* (*1996 Update*) (Pittsburgh, PA: National Center for Juvenile Justice, 1997).

v. Vermont (Title 33, section 5523)

w. Washington (13.04.021).

2. *States providing jury trials for juvenile delinquents under any circumstance*

   a. Alaska (47.12.110)

   b. Massachusetts (Chapter 119, section 55-A)

   c. Michigan (712A.17)

   d. West Virginia (49-5-6 and 49-5-9)

3. *States not providing jury trials for juvenile delinquents, except under specified circumstances*

   a. Colorado (19-1-105 and 19-22-401): all hearings, including adjudicatory hearings shall be heard without a jury; (19-2-501): juvenile not entitled to a trial by jury when petition alleges a delinquent act which is a class 2 or class 3 misdemeanor, a petty offense, a violation of a municipal or county ordinance, or a violation of a court order if, prior to the trial and with the approval of the court, the district attorney has waived in writing the right to seek a commitment to the department of human services or a sentence to the county jail.

   b. District of Columbia (16-2327): probation revocation hearings heard without a jury.

   c. Florida (39.052): adjudicatory hearings heard without a jury.

   d. Louisiana (Children's Code, Article 882): adjudication hearings heard without a jury.

   e. Maine (Title 15, section 3310): adjudicatory hearing heard without a jury.

   f. Montana (41-5-206): hearing on whether juvenile should be transferred to adult criminal court heard without a jury; (41-5-533): probation revocation proceeding heard without a jury.

   g. Nebraska (43-279): adjudicatory hearing heard without a jury.

   h. New Mexico (32A-2-24): probation revocation proceedings heard without a jury.

   i. North Carolina (7A-631): adjudicatory hearing heard without a jury.

   j. Texas (Family Code, section 54.01): detention hearing heard without a jury; (Family Code, section 54.02): hearing to consider transfer of child for criminal proceedings and hearing to consider waiver of jurisdiction held without a jury; (Family Code, section 54.04): disposition hearing heard without a jury, unless child in jeopardy of a determinate sentence; (Family Code, section 54.05): hearing to modify a disposition heard without a jury, unless child in jeopardy of a sentence for a determinate term.

   k. Wisconsin (938.18): no right to a jury trial in a waiver hearing.

   l. Wyoming (14-6-232): probation revocation hearing heard without a jury; (14-6-237): Transfer hearing heard without a jury.

4. *States where juvenile delinquent has a right to a jury trial under specified circumstances*

    a. Arkansas (9-27-331): if amount of restitution ordered by the court exceeds $10,000, juvenile has right to jury trial on all issues of liability and damages.

    b. Colorado (19-1-105): no right to a jury trial unless otherwise provided by this title; (19-2-501): juvenile may demand a jury trial, unless the petition alleges a delinquent act which is a class 2 or class 3 misdemeanor, a petty offense, a violation of a municipal or county ordinance, or a violation of a court order if, prior to the trial and with the approval of the court, the district attorney has waived in writing the right to seek a commitment to the department of human services or a sentence to the county jail; (19-2-804): any juvenile alleged to be an aggravated juvenile offender (defined in statute) has the right to a jury trial.

    c. Idaho (20-509): any juvenile age fourteen to eighteen alleged to have committed a violent offense (defined in statute) or a controlled substance offense has the right to a jury trial.

    d. Illinois (Chapter 705), section 405/5-35): any Habitual Juvenile Offender (defined in statute) has the right to a jury trial.

    e. Kansas (38-1656): any juvenile alleged to have committed an act which would be a felony if committed by an adult has the right to a jury trial.

    f. Minnesota (260.155): child who is prosecuted as an extended jurisdiction juvenile has the right to a jury trial on the issue of guilt.

    g. Montana (41-5-521): any juvenile who contests the offenses alleged in the petition has the right to a jury trial.

    h. New Mexico (32A-2-16): jury trial on issues of alleged delinquent acts may be demanded when the offenses alleged would be triable by a jury if committed by an adult.

    i. Oklahoma (Title 10, section 7003-4.1): child has right to a jury trial in adjudicatory hearing.

    j. Rhode Island (14-1-7.3): child has right to jury when court finds child is subject to certification to adult court.

    k. Texas (Family Code, section 54.03): child has right to jury trial at adjudicatory hearing; (Family Code, section 54.04): child has right to a jury trial at disposition hearing only if child is in jeopardy of a determinate sentence; (Family Code, section 54.05): child has right to a jury trial at a hearing to modify the disposition only if the child is in jeopardy of a determinate sentence on the issues of the violation of the court's orders and the sentence.

    l. Virginia (16.1-272): if juvenile indicted, juvenile has the right to a jury trial; if found guilty of capital murder, court fixes sentence with intervention of a jury; (16.1-296): where appeal is taken by child on a finding that he or she is delinquent and the alleged delinquent act would be a felony if done by adult, the child is entitled to a jury.

 m. Wyoming (14-6-209 and 14-6-223): juvenile has right to jury trial at adjudicatory hearing.

5. *States providing right to a jury trial for juvenile delinquents where juvenile delinquents can waive their right to a jury trial*

 a. Colorado (19-2-501): unless a jury is demanded, it shall be deemed waived.

 b. Illinois (Chapter 705, section 405/5-35): minor can demand in open court and with advice of counsel, a trial by the court without a jury.

 c. Massachusetts (Chapter 119, section 55-A): child can file written waiver and consent to be tried by the court without a jury; this waiver cannot be received unless the child is represented by counsel or has filed, through his parent or guardian, a written waiver of counsel.

 d. Montana (41-5-521): in the absence of a demand, a jury trial is waived.

 e. Oklahoma (Title 10, section 7003-4.1): child has right to waive jury trial.

 f. Texas (Family Code, sections 51.09 and 54.03): trial shall be by jury unless jury is waived.

 g. Wyoming (14-6-223): failure of party to demand a jury no later than 10 days after the party is advised of his right, is a waiver of this right.

Gelber (1990) has attempted to envision the juvenile court as it might exist in the twenty-first century. He sees a court, conceivably renamed the *Juvenile Services Consortium*, with two tiers. The first tier will be devoted to adjudicating offenders under age 14. These offenders will always receive rehabilitative sanctions, such as probation or placement in conditional, community-based correctional programs. The second tier consists of those aged 14 to 18. For these juveniles, jury trials will be available and these offenders will be subject to the same incarcerative sanctions that can be imposed by criminal courts.

Gelber's two-tiered juvenile court projection for the twenty-first century may not be far off the mark in relation to societal expectations for such courts in future years. The public mood seems to be in favor of deserts-based sentencing and toward due process for juvenile offenders. The two-tiered nature of Gelber's projected court organization would seemingly achieve this get-tough result, although provisions would remain for treatment-centered rehabilitative sanctions for younger offenders. In a sense, this two-tiered court projection seems to be nothing more than lowering the age jurisdiction of criminal courts from 18 to 14. However, Gelber's intent is to preserve the jurisdictional integrity of the juvenile justice system in relation to the criminal justice system. In any case, this would be an effective compromise between those favoring the traditional rehabilitative posture of juvenile courts and those favoring a shift to more punitive court policies and practices.

THE DEATH PENALTY FOR JUVENILES

By 1996, there were 3099 prisoners on death row awaiting the penalty of death (Stephan and Snell, 1996:8). There were 269 death row inmates age 19 or younger, which accounted for about 11 percent of all death row inmates (Camp and Camp, 1996). Between 1642 and 1996 there were nearly 300 executions of youths in the United States when they were under age 18 when committing capital crimes. The first execution in 1642 was Thomas Graunger, a 16-year-old who was convicted of bestiality. He was caught sodomizing a horse and a cow. The youngest age where the death penalty was imposed was 10. A poorly documented case of a 10-year-old convicted murderer in Louisiana occurred in 1855. A more celebrated case, that of 10-year-old James Arcene, occurred in Arkansas in 1885. Arcene was 10 years old when he robbed and murdered his victim. He was eventually arrested at age 23 before being executed (Streib, 1987:57).

Arguments for or against the death penalty for adults pertain to juveniles as well. Those favoring the death penalty say that it is "just" punishment and a societal revenge for the life taken or harm inflicted by the offender. It is an economical way of dealing with those who will never be released from confinement. It may be administered "humanely," through lethal injection. It functions as a deterrent to others to refrain from committing capital crimes. Opponents say that it is cruel and unusual punishment. They claim that the death penalty does not deter those who intend to take another's life. It is barbaric and uncivilized. Other countries do not impose it for any type of offense, regardless of its seriousness. It makes no sense to kill as a means of sending messages to others not to kill.

For juveniles, the argument is supplemented by the fact that age functions as a mitigating factor. In any capital conviction, the convicted offender is entitled to a bifurcated trial where guilt is established first, and then the punishment is imposed in view of any prevailing mitigating or aggravating circumstances. Was the crime especially brutal? Did the victim suffer? Was the murderer senile or mentally ill? Or was the murderer a juvenile? Since age acts as a mitigating factor in cases where the death penalty is considered for adults, there are those who say that the death penalty should not be applied to juveniles under any condition. Early English precedent and common law assumed that those under age 7 were incapable of formulating criminal intent and thus they were absolved from any wrongdoing. Between ages 7 and 12, a presumption exists that the child is capable of formulating

BOX 9.1   CONFESSION FROM SON WHO KILLED
MOTHER 18 YEARS AGO

The Case of David D'Autremont

It happened in June 1978 in Morton Grove, Illinois. A man entered his mother's bedroom and suffocated her to death with a pillow. The 59-year-old widow didn't have a chance. At the time, police suspected burglars. The case went nowhere because of an absence of leads.

However, 18 years later, in August 1996, a man came forward to police in Skokie, Illinois and said, "I know who killed Mrs. D'Autremont of Morton Grove 18 years ago. Her son." With that information, police quickly moved to apprehend David D'Autremont, now 38 years old, and questioned him about the murder. D'Autremont had moved to Denver, Colorado, where police eventually found him. He gave them his full cooperation, saying that "he wanted to get it over with." He was being held on $1 million bail.

D'Autremont's friends said that David had admitted to them that he planned to kill his mother. He did not give them any particular reason. However, police say that D'Autremont inherited $70,000 from his mother's death. Thus this money could have been his motive. There is no statute of limitations on murder.

What should be David D'Autremont's punishment? Should he receive the death penalty? Should his exemplary life in Colorado have any bearing on the outcome of his subsequent murder trial?

Source: Adapted from Associated Press, "Son Charged with Suffocating Mother 18 Years Ago," *Minot (ND) Daily News*, August 16, 1996:A2.

criminal intent, and in every jurisdiction, the burden is borne by the prosecution for establishing beyond a reasonable doubt that the youth was capable of formulating criminal intent.

Although each case is judged on its own merits, there are always at least two sides in an issue involving the murder of one by another. The survivors of the victim demand justice, and the justice they usually seek is the death of the one who brought about the death of their own. This is a manifestation of "an eye for an eye." In many respects it is an accurate portrayal of why the death penalty is imposed for both juveniles and adults. It is supposed to be a penalty that fits the crime committed. But attorneys and family members of those convicted of capital crimes cannot help but feel compassion for their doomed relatives. Someone they love is about to lose his or her life. But hadn't they taken someone's life in the process? Does taking another life bring back the dead victim? Does taking the life of the murderer fulfill some lofty societal purpose? The arguments about this issue are endless.

In 1977 in Fort Jackson, South Carolina, a 17-year-old mentally retarded youth and a 16-year-old companion were living with a 22-year-old soldier in a rented, run-down house. (The following account has been adapted from Streib, 1987:125–127.) Alcohol, THC, PCP, marijuana, and other drugs were readily available. On a warm Saturday, October 29, after heavy drinking and consuming drugs, the three decided to look for a girl to rape. They drove to a baseball park in nearby Columbia. They parked next to a young couple, a 17-year-old boy and his 14-year-old girlfriend. On orders from the soldier, they shot the boy three times with a high-powered rifle, killing him instantly. Then they drove off with the girl to a secluded area where each raped her repeatedly. Finally, they finished her off by shooting her and mutilating her body.

The three were soon arrested by police. The youngest youth agreed to testify against the soldier and the 17-year-old in exchange for a lighter punishment. Both the soldier and the 17-year-old eventually entered guilty pleas and were sentenced to death. After lengthy appeals, the soldier was executed by South Carolina authorities on January 11, 1985. Finally, on January 10, 1986, James Terry Roach, the 17-year-old who killed the boy and girl and mutilated the girl's body, was executed in the South Carolina electric chair. Justice was served. Or was it? A crowd cheered outside the prison walls as the execution of Roach occurred. Roach wrote his last letter, and as he was strapped into the electric chair, he read it with shaky hands: "To the families of the victims, my heart is still with you in your sorrow. May you forgive me just as I know that my Lord has done." Two one-minute surges of electricity hit him and he was pronounced dead at 5:16 A.M. (Streib, 1987:125–127). The minimum offender age for the death penalty in those states where the death penalty is imposed for capital crimes is given in Table 9.5.

Until recently, the U.S. Supreme Court has consistently refused to become embroiled in the capital-punishment-for-juveniles issue, although it has heard several juvenile death penalty cases in past years. One frequently cited case is *Eddings v. Oklahoma* (1982). The case raised the question of whether the death penalty as applied to juveniles was "cruel and unusual" punishment under the Eighth Amendment of the U.S. Constitution. The U.S. Supreme Court avoided the issue. The justices did not say that it was cruel and unusual punishment, but they also did not say that it wasn't. What they said was that *the youthfulness of the offender is a mitigating factor of great weight that must be considered.* Thus many jurisdictions were left to make their own interpretations of the high court's opinion.

TABLE 9.5

Minimum Age for Death Penalty in Selected States in 1997

Age	States
16	Alabama, Arkansas, Idaho, Indiana, Kentucky, Louisiana, Mississippi, Missouri, Montana, Nevada, North Carolina, Utah, Virginia
17	Georgia, New Hampshire, Texas
18	California, Colorado, Connecticut, Illinois, Nebraska, New Jersey, New Mexico, Ohio, Oregon, Tennessee
No minimum	Arizona, Delaware, Florida, Maryland, Oklahoma, Pennsylvania, South Carolina, South Dakota, Washington, Wyoming

Reasons for Applying the Death Penalty

The primary reasons for applying the death penalty in certain capital cases are threefold: (1) retribution, (2) deterrence, and (3) just deserts.

1. *The death penalty is retribution.* Retribution is defended largely on the basis of the philosophical just-deserts rationale (Bohm, 1992). Offenders should be executed because they did not respect the lives of others. Death is the just desert for someone who inflicted death on someone else. Retribution is regarded by some experts as the primary purpose of the death penalty (Bohm, Clark, and Aventi, 1990, 1991; Haas, 1994).

2. *The death penalty deters others from committing murder.* The deterrence function of the death penalty is frequently questioned as well. An examination of homicide rates in Illinois during a 48-year period (1933–1980) was conducted. It revealed that average homicide rates did not fluctuate noticeably for three different periods: (1) times when the death penalty was allowed, (2) years when the death penalty was allowed but no executions were performed, and (3) years when the death penalty was abolished (Decker and Kohfeld, 1990). Persons favoring the abolition of the death penalty argue that *no* criminal act ever justifies capital punishment (Bedau, 1992; Forst, 1995; Grasmick, Bursick, and Blackwell, 1993).

3. *The death penalty is a just desert for commission of a capital offense.* The just-deserts philosophy would argue that the death penalty is just punishment for someone who has committed murder (Sandys and McGarrell, 1995; Seis and Elbe, 1991). The U.S. Supreme Court has indirectly validated this reasoning by refusing to declare the death penalty cruel and unusual punishment (Haas, 1994).

Reasons for Opposing the Death Penalty

Some of the reasons that persons use to oppose the death penalty are that (1) it is barbaric; (2) it may be applied in error to someone who is not actually guilty of a capital offense; (3) it is nothing more than sheer revenge; (4) it is more costly than life imprisonment; (5) it is applied arbitrarily; (6) it does not deter others from committing murder; and (7) most persons in the United States are opposed to the death penalty.

1. *The death penalty is barbaric.* Hugo Bedau (1992) says that the death penalty is barbaric. There are other avenues whereby convicted capital offenders can be punished. The United States is one of the few civilized countries of the modern world that still uses the death penalty. Portraits of persons condemned to death include accounts of their past lives by close friends and family members who oppose capital punishment in their cases (Dicks, 1991). Even statements from various family members of victims express opposition to the death penalty because of its alleged barbarism.

2. *The death penalty is unfair and may be applied erroneously.* Some convicted offenders are wrongly convicted. Evidence subsequently discovered has led to freeing several persons who were formerly on death row awaiting execution. Bedau (1992) and the American Civil Liberties Union are strong death penalty opponents. This reason is one of their strongest arguments against its application. Thus this view proposes an outright ban on the death penalty because of the mere possibility that some persons sentenced to death are actually innocent and should not be executed. A study by Radelet, Bedau, and Putnam (1992) showed, for instance, that over 400 persons have been wrongly convicted of capital crimes and sentenced to death as miscarriages of justice in the United States. Evidence eventually discovered and used to free these persons included the confessions of the real perpetrators, reversals on appeal, and unofficial judgments when crimes were found not to have occurred (e.g., missing bodies eventually discovered and found not to have been murdered).

3. *The death penalty is nothing more than revenge.* Haas (1994) and others argue that by condoning the death penalty, the U.S. Supreme Court has sanctioned vengeance, which is an unacceptable justification for imposing capital punishment. For persons who are retarded or intellectually disabled, it is likely that they cannot reach the level of culpability necessary to trigger the need for the death penalty. They cannot engage in "cold calculus" to weigh committing the crime against the potential death penalty used to punish it (Miller, 1990).

4. *The death penalty is more costly than life-without-parole sentences.* Many opponents of capital punishment grasp the cost factor to show that executing prisoners under death sentences is more costly over time than imprisoning them for life (Bedau, 1992; Bohm, 1992; Simmons et al., 1995). However, a key reason for the high cost of executing prisoners is that they have been entitled to file endless appeals and delay the imposition of their death sentences (Costanzo and White, 1994). In 1996, Congress acted to limit the number of appeals inmates on death rows could file. Thus it is expected in future years that the length of time between conviction and imposition of the death penalty will be greatly abbreviated. This shorter period of time will decrease the expense of death penalty appeals and undermine this particular argument.

5. *The death penalty is still applied arbitrarily despite efforts by legislatures and Congress to make its application more equitable.* Evidence suggests that although bifurcated trials have decreased the racial bias in death penalty applications, disproportionality of death sentences according to race and ethnicity have not been eliminated (Bohm and Vogel, 1994; Simmons et al., 1995). Although some experts argue that some races and ethnic categories have higher rates of capital murder and thus are disproportionately represented on death row, other experts say that the death penalty continues to be applied in a discriminatory manner in many jurisdictions (Baird and Rosenbaum, 1995; Costanzo and White, 1994; Simmons et al., 1995).

6. *The death penalty does not deter others from committing murder.* The literature strongly supports the idea that the death penalty apparently has no discernible deterrent effect. Persons will commit murder anyway, even knowing that there is a chance they may be caught eventually and executed for the crime (Decker and Kohfeld, 1990). An examination of crime statistics and comparisons of those jurisdictions where the death penalty is applied and jurisdictions where it isn't applied show few, if any, differences in capital murder cases (Cheatwood, 1993; Godfrey and Schiraldi, 1995). Thus, the argument goes, if capital punishment fails to deter capital murder, it should be abolished (Bedau, 1992; Cochran, Chamlin, and Seth, 1994).

7. *Most persons in the United States are against the death penalty.* Bedau (1992) has suggested that there is growing lack of public support for the death penalty in the United States. However, several national surveys show that over 75 percent of those interviewed support the death penalty and its application (Haas, 1994; Simmons et al., 1995). Certainly, a knowledge of the death penalty and its deterrent and retributive effects makes a difference in whether persons support or oppose its use (Bohm, 1992; Bohm, Clark, and Aventi, 1990; Bohm and Vogel, 1994). Growing violent street crimes, especially violent street crimes resulting in the deaths of innocent victims, do nothing but trigger pro-capital punishment reactions from an increasingly frightened public. The debate continues (Baird and Rosenbaum, 1995).

All the arguments that function as either pros or cons relative to the death penalty also apply directly to the issue of juvenile executions. However, the nature of juvenile justice reforms is such that a strong belief persists that substantial efforts must be made by juvenile courts and corrections to rehabilitate juveniles rather than incarcerate or execute them. For example, a study conducted by Amnesty International examined public attitudes toward the death penalty among a sample of 1400 Florida residents (Cambridge Survey Research, 1986). While the survey disclosed overwhelming support for the death penalty, at least among those surveyed, it was also disclosed that most respondents considered the death penalty inappropriate as the ultimate punishment for juvenile offenders convicted of capital crimes. In those states where executions are conducted, where should the line be drawn concerning the minimum age at which someone becomes liable, accountable, and subject to the death penalty (Robinson and Stephens, 1992)?

It is difficult to dissuade some persons from the view that certain violent juvenile offenders should be executed for their crimes (Finkel et al., 1994). It is a fact that about the same proportion of youths today commit serious violent offenses as they did in 1980 (Elliott, 1994b). However, today's violent acts are more lethal. A larger proportion of violent acts today result in either serious injuries or deaths to innocent victims (Elliott, 1994a). In Denver, Colorado in 1994, for example, two youths in their mid-teens approached a couple who were returning from an athletic event at about 1:00 A.M. As the couple drove into their parking space near their apartment complex, the two teens walked out of the shadows and shot the man to death. His wife, an attractive woman in her mid-20s, was punched by the other teen and shoved in the back seat of her car. The boys drove to a dark alley in their own neighborhood. They beat and raped the woman repeatedly. When they were through, they left her for dead, bleeding and naked, sprawled in the back seat of her car. A police car happened to see the car in the alleyway and approached. Emergency surgery and a long recovery period saved the woman's life. She was able to survive and identify her attackers in court. She required extensive and painful reconstructive surgery on her face, jaw, scalp, and upper torso. Her front upper and lower teeth had to be replaced with extensive dental surgery. Her attackers scoffed at her in court. They made gang signs to their friends, who were often hustled from court by sheriff's deputies. Considerable incriminating evidence placed them at the scene. While the prosecutor could have sought the death penalty because of the death of the woman's husband, he decided to seek life-without-parole sentences for these boys instead. One reason was that although the evidence was persuasive, the prosecutor believed that he stood a better chance of convicting the boys on a lesser murder charge. They were convicted by a Denver, Colorado court and given life-without-parole sentences for their roles in these terrible crimes. Many viewers who watched these trial proceedings were incensed that the prosecutor did not go for the death penalty.

Several U.S. Supreme Court cases have been decided in recent years involving questions of executions of juveniles. These cases have been especially significant in providing a legal foundation for such executions. These include *Eddings v. Oklahoma* (1982), *Thompson v. Oklahoma* (1988), *Stanford v. Kentucky* (1989), and *Wilkins v. Missouri* (1989). As a prelude to discussing these cases, it should be noted that until 1988, 16 states had minimum-age provisions for juvenile executions (under age 18), where the range in minimum age was from 10 (Indiana) to 17 (Georgia, New

The Case of Rashaad Staggie

Rashaad Staggie was the leader of the gang. The gang was called the "Hard Living Kids." The gang was not nice. On more than one occasion, Staggie and his gang dealt drugs, put prostitutes on the street, and generally made life unpleasant for the neighbors nearby.

Local authorities convened weekly town meetings to see what could be done about Staggie and his gang. The talks went on and on, with nothing ever getting resolved. Putting more police on the streets didn't slow down Staggie or his gang or their illegal activities. The neighborhood was a pretty dangerous place to be.

Then one evening as Staggie sat in his car, he was approached by some masked persons. They pointed guns at him and told him to raise his hands. He complied. Next, they shot Staggie through the ear, killing him instantly. Next, they poured gasoline over his body and set it up beside his car. Someone lit a match and ignited Staggie. Police and the fire department looked on helplessly, as 200 unknown and masked persons burned Staggie's body. One of the masked persons said, "Yes, we can rid our society of scum." While Staggie burned, other masked persons shot his body full of holes. The final statement came from one of the masked assailants, who said: "What has happened tonight shows what happens when you put your trust in Allah."

Where did this happen? New York City? South Central Los Angeles? Miami, Florida? No. It happened in Cape Town, South Africa. The good people of Cape Town had had enough of Staggie and his gang. They sent a message to both Staggie and his gang—Stay out of our neighborhood! No arrests were made by the police, who had no idea who participated in Staggie's death.

Should anyone be punished for Staggie's death? If so, what should be the punishment? Did Staggie deserve to die? Was the community justified in doing something about Staggie when it was apparent that police were not prepared to do anything? Under what circumstances should vigilantism be condoned, if at all?

Source: Adapted from Alexandra Zavis, "A Savage Attack in South Africa: Vigilantes Slay Gang Leader on the Streets," *USA Today*, August 6, 1996:6A.

Hampshire, and Texas). When the *Thompson v. Oklahoma* case was decided in 1988, the minimum age for juvenile executions in all states was raised to 16. The following year, the U.S. Supreme Court upheld death sentences of a 16-year-old and a 17-year-old as well.

1. *Eddings v. Oklahoma* (1982). On April 4, 1977, Monty Lee Eddings and several other companions ran away from their Missouri homes. In a car owned by Eddings' older brother, they drove, without direction or purpose, eventually reaching the Oklahoma Turnpike. Eddings had several firearms in the car, including several rifles that he had stolen from his father. At one point, Eddings lost control of the car and was stopped by an Oklahoma State Highway Patrol officer. When the officer approached the car, Eddings stuck a shotgun out of the window and killed the officer outright. When Eddings was subsequently apprehended, he was waived to criminal court on a prosecutorial motion. Efforts by Eddings and his attorney to oppose the waiver failed.

   In a subsequent bifurcated trial, several aggravating circumstances were introduced and alleged, while several mitigating circumstances, including Eddings' youthfulness, mental state, and potential for treatment, were considered by the trial judge. However, the judge did not consider Eddings' "unhappy upbringing and emotional disturbance" as significant mitigating factors to offset the aggravating ones. Eddings' attorney filed an appeal that eventually reached the U.S. Supreme Court. Although the Oklahoma Court of Criminal Appeals reversed the trial judge's ruling, the U.S. Supreme Court reversed the Oklahoma Court of Criminal Appeals. The reversal pivoted on whether the trial judge erred by refusing to consider the "unhappy upbringing and emotionally disturbed state" of Eddings. The trial judge had previously acknowledged the youthfulness of Eddings as a mitigating factor. The *fact* of Eddings' age, 16, was significant, precisely because the majority of justices did not consider it as significant. Rather, they focused on the issue of introduction of mitigating circumstances specifically outlined in Eddings' appeal. Oklahoma was now in the position of lawfully imposing the death penalty on a juvenile who was 16 years old at the time he committed murder.

2. *Thompson v. Oklahoma* (1988). In the case of William Wayne Thompson, he was convicted of murdering his former brother-in-law, Charles Keene. Keene had been suspected of abusing Thompson's sister. In the evening hours of January 22–23, 1983, Thompson and three older companions left his mother's house, saying "We're going to kill Charles." Facts disclose that later that early morning, Charles Keene was beaten to death by Thompson and his associates with fists and hand-held weapons, including a length of pipe. Thompson later told others: "We killed him. I shot him in the head and cut his throat in the river." Thompson's accomplices told police shortly after their arrest that Thompson had shot Keene twice in the head and then cut his body in several places (e.g., throat, chest, and abdomen), so that, according to Thompson, "the fish could eat his body." When Keene's body was recovered on February 18, 1983, the medical examiner indicated that Keene had been shot twice in the head, had been beaten, and that his throat, chest, and abdomen had been cut.

   Since Thompson was 15 years old at the time of the murder, juvenile officials transferred his case to criminal court. This transfer was supported, in part, by an Oklahoma statutory provision indicating that there was "prosecutive merit" in pursuing the case against Thompson. Again, the subject of the defendant's youthfulness was introduced as a mitigating factor (among other factors), together with aggravating factors such as the "especially heinous, atrocious, and cruel" manner in which Keene had been murdered. Thompson was convicted of first-degree murder and sentenced to death.

Thompson filed an appeal that eventually reached the U.S. Supreme Court. The Court examined Thompson's case at length, and in a vigorously debated opinion, it overturned Thompson's death sentence, indicated in its conclusory dicta that "petitioner's counsel and various *amici curiae* have asked us to 'draw the line' that would prohibit the execution of any person who was under the age of 18 at the time of the offense. Our task, today, however, is to decide the case before us; we do so by concluding that the Eighth and Fourteenth Amendments prohibit the execution of a person who was under 16 years of age at the time of his or her offense" (108 S.Ct. at 2700). Accordingly, Thompson's death penalty was reversed. Officially, this Supreme Court action effectively drew a temporary line of 16 years of age as a minimum for exacting the death penalty in capital cases. This "line" awaited subsequent challenges, however.

3. *Stanford v. Kentucky* (1989). Kevin Stanford was 17 when, on January 17, 1981, he an accomplice repeatedly raped and sodomized and eventually shot to death 20-year-old Baerbel Poore in Jefferson County, Kentucky. This occurred during a robbery of a gas station where Poore worked as an attendant. Stanford later told police, "I had to shoot her [since] she lived next door to me and she would recognize me.... I guess we could have tied her up or something or beat [her up]...and tell her if she tells, we would kill her...." A corrections officer who interviewed Stanford said that after Stanford made that disclosure, "he [Stanford] started laughing." The jury in Stanford's case found him guilty of first-degree murder and the judge sentenced him to death. The U.S. Supreme Court eventually heard his appeal, and in an opinion that addressed the "minimum age for the death penalty" issue, decided both this case and the case of Heath Wilkins in the paragraphs to follow.

4. *Wilkins v. Missouri* (1989). Heath Wilkins, a 16-year-old at the time of the crime, stabbed to death Nancy Allen Moore, a 26-year-old mother of two who was working behind the counter of a convenience store in Avondale, Missouri. On July 27, 1985, Wilkins and his accomplice, Patrick Stevens, entered the convenience store to rob it, agreeing that with Wilkins' plan that they would kill "whoever was behind the counter" because "a dead person can't talk." When they entered the store, they stabbed Moore, who fell to the floor. When Stevens had difficulty opening the cash register, Moore, mortally wounded, offered to help him. Wilkins stabbed her three more times in the chest, two of the knife wounds penetrating Moore's heart. Moore began to beg for her life, whereupon Wilkins stabbed her four more times in the neck, opening up her carotid artery. She died shortly thereafter. Stevens and Wilkins netted $450 in cash and checks, some liquor, cigarettes, and rolling papers from the robbery and murder. Wilkins was convicted of first-degree murder and the judge sentenced him to death.

The U.S. Supreme Court heard the *Stanford* and *Wilkins* cases simultaneously, since the singular issue was whether the death penalty was considered cruel and inhumane as it pertained to 16- and 17-year-olds. At that time, not all states had achieved consensus about applying the death penalty to persons under the age of 18 as a punishment for capital crimes. Although several justices dissented from the majority view, the U.S. Supreme Court upheld the death sentences of Stanford and Wilkins, concluding that "we discern neither a historical nor a modern societal consensus forbidding the imposition of capital punishment on any person who murders at 16 or 17 years of age. Accordingly, we conclude that such punishment does not offend the Eighth Amendment's prohibition against cruel and unusual punishment" (109 S.Ct. at 2980). Thus this crucial opinion underscored age 16 as the minimum age at which the death penalty may be administered.

Considerable debate has been generated among professionals concerning the juvenile death penalty issue (Baird and Rosenbaum, 1995). Apart from the question of whether the death penalty should be administered at all to anyone, there is no apparent consensus concerning the application of the death penalty to juveniles convicted of capital crimes. Arguments favoring the death penalty stress the accountability of these youthful offenders and the justice of capital punishment where capital crimes have been committed. Arguments opposing the death penalty for juveniles are often emotionally laden or address issues related only remotely to the death penalty issue (Bedau, 1992). For instance, it is argued that juveniles are more amenable to treatment and rehabilitation, and thus provisions should be made for this rehabilitation and treatment to occur (Bohm, 1992). Whatever the appeal of such an argument, the U.S. Supreme Court has, at least for the time being, resolved the age/death penalty issue with some degree of finality. Other factors will have to be cited as mitigating in a youth's defense if a capital crime is alleged.

Currently, there are only a small number of juveniles on death rows in U.S. state prisons. Because of the declining frequency with which juveniles have been executed in recent years, the death penalty issue as it applies to juveniles does not seem as strong as it once was. There will always be many persons in society who will oppose the death penalty for any reason. But it is doubtful that major changes will be made about the death penalty policy applied to capital juvenile offenders, unless the present composition of the U.S. Supreme Court changes significantly. Although public sentiment is not always easy to measure, there seems to be strong sentiment for harsher penalties meted out to juveniles. This does not necessarily mean the death penalty or life imprisonment, but it does mean tighter laws and enforcement of those laws where juveniles are concerned.

Public Sentiment about the Death Penalty for Juveniles

Views of professionals in criminal justice and criminology are not that different from the views held by the general public about juvenile delinquency and what should be done to prevent or punish it (Amnesty International, 1991; Reddington, 1992). Victor Streib (1987:189) has summarized succinctly a commonly expressed, though nebulous, solution that "our society must be willing to devote enormous resources to a search for the causes and cures of violent juvenile crime, just as we have done in the search for the causes and cures of such killer diseases as cancer. And we must not demand a complete cure in a short time, since no one knows how long it will take." Obviously, we have not cured cancer. We are even further away from discovering the etiology of delinquent behavior in all its diverse forms and finding one or more satisfactory cures for it.

One intervention proposed by professionals is the early identification of chronic or hard-core delinquents in a multiple-gating technique (Loeber and Dishion, 1987). This technique purportedly identifies extreme cases in terms of frequency, variety, seriousness, age of onset, and the number of settings in which the behavior tends to occur. Thus antisocial and delinquency-prone youths may be identified early in their delinquent careers, and appropriate intervention programs may be applied to certain youths selectively. This selectivity is more cost-effective in the long run than are more costly programs that are generally applicable to youths in general, regardless of their offense behaviors or personal characteristics (Loeber and Dishion, 1987). However, a social experiment covering a two-year period and involving a small number of hard-core juvenile offenders was not particularly optimistic about intensive, specialized treatment and intervention as delinquency prevention forms (Gelber, 1988). Even where high-quality staff are made available to youths on a 24-hour-a-day, seven-day-a-week basis, without limitation on time or cost, and where the family's needs (e.g., jobs, food, health care, housing, schooling) were met, a majority of these assisted youths reverted to criminal conduct, were convicted, and sent to prison (Gelber, 1988).

Early identification of at-risk youths who have suffered some type of child abuse from their parents has been linked with subsequent youthful violence (Kruttschnitt and Dornfeld, 1993; Sommers and Baskin, 1994). Family dysfunction has been linked with assault behavior manifested by a sample of male juveniles in a Toronto, Canada study (Awad and Saunders, 1991). Explanations for youth violence are varied and complex (Elliott, 1994a). So far, we do not have a good grasp of the specific factors that produce violent behavior among adolescents. We can say, for instance, that in certain instances, childhood victimization has increased the overall risk of violent offending among affected juveniles (Rivera and Widom, 1990). But we are not yet in a position to say *which* juveniles will commit specific violent types of offenses in their future years.

However, our failure to identify background factors that can be manipulated experimentally to cause law-abiding behavior among samples of youths has not deterred us from investigating juvenile violence (DuRant et al., 1994; Kruttschnitt and Dornfeld, 1993). Much of this research has been productive, in that some juveniles appear to have been assisted by suggested interventions. In 1985, for example, an *early offender program* (EOP) was established in Oakland County, California (Howitt and Moore, 1991). An experimental group of 145 youths was studied and compared with a control group of 61 juveniles. The Oakland County Probate Court provided specialized, intensive in-home interventions for those youths aged 13 or younger at the time of their first contact with the court. Data about these youths were gathered from case files, interviews, and court records. Over time, the EOP cases exhibited lower career recidivism rates compared with the control group who did not receive any type of intervention. Both parents and youths involved in the EOP reported positive changes in family situations, peer relations, school performance, and general conduct as a result of participating in EOP (Howitt and Moore, 1991).

Nevertheless, the general public has inconsistent views toward those juveniles who commit violent acts. Results from a survey of 681 householders were mixed when they were asked about different hypothetical scenarios involving juveniles who committed different kinds of violent offenses, including murder. About half of those surveyed recommended that the juveniles be processed by juvenile court. Other respondents believed that criminal court was the best option for repeat offenders. Most respondents actually preferred criminal court for those offenders charged with murder who had no history of child abuse (Stalans and Henry, 1994).

UNIFICATION OF CRIMINAL AND JUVENILE COURTS

Presently, there are several different types courts in every U.S. jurisdiction. Usually, these courts have general, original, and concurrent jurisdiction, meaning that some courts share adjudicatory responsibilities involving the same subject matter. In Arkansas, for example, chancery courts have jurisdiction over juvenile delinquency cases, although separate county courts may also hear cases involving juveniles. In Colorado, district courts have general jurisdiction over criminal and civil matters, probate matters, and juvenile cases. However, there are specific juvenile courts in Colorado that hear juvenile cases as well. Tennessee county courts, circuit courts, and juvenile courts have concurrent jurisdiction over delinquency and other types of juvenile cases (e.g., children in need of supervision, child custody cases).

Court unification is a general proposal that seeks to centralize and integrate the diverse functions of all courts of general, concurrent, and exclusive jurisdiction into a more simplified and uncomplicated scheme. One way of viewing court unification is that it is ultimately intended to abolish concurrent jurisdiction wherever it is currently shared among various courts in a common jurisdiction, although no presently advocated court unification model has been shown to be superior to others proposed (Flango, 1994a). Thus there are different ways of achieving unification, although not everyone agrees about which method is best. One example of court unification is Pennsylvania.

Prior to 1969, Pennsylvania had two appellate courts and numerous local courts that functioned independent of one another (Yeager, Herb, and Lemmon, 1989). Even the Pennsylvania Supreme Court lacked full and explicit administrative and supervisory authority over the entire judicial system. As the result of the Pennsylvania Constitutional Convention of 1967–1968, a new Judiciary Article, Article V of the Pennsylvania Constitution, was framed. Vast changes were made in court organization and operations. A family division was established to deal exclusively with all juvenile matters. A 10-year follow-up evaluation of Pennsylvania's court unification concluded that the present court organization is vastly superior to the pre-1969 court organization (Yeager, Herb, and Lemmon, 1989). Efficiency and economy were two objectives sought by these court changes. Both aims were achieved.

Earlier studies of jurisdictions representing various degrees of unification have been conducted to assess whether there is necessarily greater economy, coordination, and speed associated with maintaining records and processing cases (Henderson et al., 1984). Georgia, Iowa, Colorado, New Jersey, and Connecticut were examined. Data were collected from records maintained by state administrative officials and local trial courts, and interviews were conducted with key court personnel. A total of 103 courts were selected for analysis, including 20 courts of general jurisdiction, 69 courts of limited jurisdiction, and 15 juvenile courts. More centralized organizational schemes fulfilled the expectations of these researchers only partially. Henderson et al. (1984) report that under centralization, poorer areas were likely to do better financially, although courts in well-off areas faced tighter budget restrictions. Greater uniformity of operations was observed in most jurisdictions. Further, centralization of court organization tended to highlight problems in previously neglected areas, including family and juvenile services. Their findings relating to differences in the effectiveness and efficiency of case process-ing in trial courts in both decentralized and centralized systems were inconclusive, however.

Presently, few states have adopted the high degree of court central-ization exhibited by Pennsylvania. One explanation for the general reluctance of various jurisdictions to commit to substantial court reform is that such change threatens vested interests and has the potential for blunting judicial and political power. This phenomenon was observed, for example, in the state of Washington during the period of divestiture of status offenses from the jurisdiction of juvenile courts. The intended goals of divestiture in Washington included ridding juvenile courts of nonserious status offenders. Divestiture was inconsistently received among Washington's juvenile court judiciary (Schneider, 1984a). If such reactions to divestiture, one specific court reform, occur among juvenile court judges, what may we contemplate the reception of court unifica-tion to be among judges at large in any jurisdiction?

Implications of Court Unification for Juveniles

For juveniles, court unification poses potentially threatening conse-quences. For example, in those jurisdictions where considerable frag-mentation exists in the processing of juvenile cases or where concurrent jurisdiction distributes juvenile matters among several different courts, juveniles, especially habitual offenders, may be able to benefit because of a general lack of centralization in record keeping. Thus juveniles may be adjudicated delinquent in one juvenile court jurisdiction, but this record of adjudication may not be transmitted to other courts in adjacent juris-dictions. In time, it is likely that a national record-keeping network will exist, where all juvenile courts may access information from other juris-dictions. Currently, however, the confidentiality of record keeping is a structural constraint that inhibits the development of such extensive record sharing. However, as has been reported in earlier chapters, one major change in juvenile justice record keeping has been the creation of various state repositories of juvenile information that can be shared among interested agencies. This is considered a part of the get-tough movement and is intended to hold juveniles more accountable for their offending by giving authorities in different jurisdictions greater access to their prior offense records (Torbet et al., 1996).

Those who favor a separate and distinct juvenile justice system apart from the criminal justice system contend that the primary goal of juvenile courts should be individualized treatment, with therapy and rehabilitation as dominant factors (Dwyer and McNally, 1987). However, other voices encourage perpetuating a separate juvenile justice system that not only is designed to treat and prevent delinquency but is also designed to hold juveniles strictly accountable for their actions (Torbet et al., 1996). Thus it is suggested that less use be made of secure confinement, and greater use be made of probation and parole, with the primary objectives of offering restitution to victims, compensating communities and courts for the time taken to process cases, and performing community services to learn valuable lessons (Maloney, Romig and Armstrong, 1988; Rubin, 1988).

Getting Tough and Court Unification

There is no question that the get-tough movement is still in force and is pervasive throughout the juvenile justice system. One indication of this is the increased use of waivers or transfers, as more juveniles are shifted to the jurisdiction of criminal courts. We have seen certain implications of juveniles as they enter criminal courts for processing, although some of these implications are not entirely unfavorable. Increasing numbers of juvenile court judges are soliciting the involvement of members of the community in voluntary capacities to assist in monitoring adjudicated youths. Greater responsibilities are shifting toward parents in many jurisdictions, particularly when their children commit crimes against property and do extensive damage monetarily (National Council of Juvenile and Family Court Judges, 1986).

Public policy currently favors protecting juveniles as much as possible from the stigmatization of courts and criminal labeling, including the large-scale removal of youths from jails and prisons (Flango, 1994a). Accordingly, recommendations from the public include greater use of nonsecure facilities and programs as opposed to confinement in secure facilities. Especially manifest is the concern for very young offenders. More children under age 10 are entering the juvenile justice system annually (Sametz, 1984). Clearly, effective programs and procedures for processing such youths need to be in place and operative. Encouragement for greater use of community-based services and treatment programs, special education services, and school-based early-intervention programs is apparent (Steinhart, 1988).

There is increasing bureaucratization of juvenile courts, indicated in part by greater formality of juvenile case processing. Juvenile proceedings are increasingly adversarial proceedings similar to criminal courts. Almost all of the criminal court trappings are found in juvenile courts, with some significant exceptions that have been noted above (Feld, 1993a, 1995). Most juvenile courts are not courts of record, and much informality exists regarding calling witnesses and offering testimony. Federal and state rules of evidence are relaxed considerably and do not attach directly to juvenile civil proceedings. However, in some jurisdictions where prosecutorial presence has been increased greatly (as one indication of greater bureaucratization of juvenile courts), little perceptible impact on juvenile processing was observed (Laub and MacMurray, 1987).

Juvenile courts are sometimes classified according to a **traditional model** or **family model** and due process distinction (Watkins, 1987). The traditional courts tend to perpetuate the doctrine of *parens patriae*, and juvenile court judges retain a good deal of discretion in adjudicating offenders. They rely more heavily on confinement as a punishment. The due-process juvenile courtroom relies more heavily on preadjudicatory interactions between defense counsels and prosecutors, and nonjudicial handling of cases is more the rule rather than the exception. More frequently used in such courts are nonsecure facilities, community-based programs, probation, and diversion with conditions.

Politicizing Juvenile Punishments

The political approach to punishing juveniles is to rely heavily on the sentiments expressed by voting constituencies. State legislators are at the helm of juvenile justice reforms currently, and several organizations are in strategic positions to offer their guidance and assistance in formulating new juvenile policies. The American Bar Association, the American Legislative Exchange Council, and the Institute of Judicial Administration have provided legislators with model penal codes and proposed juvenile court revisions to introduce consistency throughout an inconsistent juvenile justice system (Treanor and Volenik, 1987). The federally funded Juvenile Justice Reform Project, which has reviewed existing juvenile codes and statutes in all 50 states, has conducted an extensive national opinion survey of child-serving professionals (Rossum, Koller, and Manfredi, 1987). Two model juvenile justice acts have been proposed: the Model Delinquency Act and the Model Disobedient Children's Act. Among other things, these acts, respectively, distinguish between delinquent and status offenders and make provisions for their alternative care, treatment, and punishment. Both acts are designed to hold juveniles responsible for their acts and to hold the system accountable for its treatment of these youths as well (Rossum, Koller, and Manfredi, 1987).

It is debatable whether these codes are functional and in the best interests of those youths served. Some experts say that these codes will weaken the current protection extended to dependent children or children in need of supervision. Furthermore, a serious erosion of judicial discretion may occur, accompanied by increased use of pretrial detention for juveniles where serious crimes are alleged. Also, status offenders may be jailed for violating court orders (Orlando, Breed, and Smith, 1987). Indeed, it is difficult to devise a code of accountability founded on the principle of just deserts that nevertheless performs certain traditional treatment functions in the old context of *parens patriae* (Treanor and Volenik, 1987). Additionally, codes of any kind promote a degree of blind conformity or compliance with rules for the sake of compliance. With greater codification of juvenile procedures, less latitude exists for judges and others to make concessions and impose individualized dispositions where appropriate. The very idea of individualized dispositions, while appealing to just-deserts interests, invites abuse through discriminatory treatment on racial, ethnic, gender, and socioeconomic grounds.

KEY TERMS

Court unification	*Hands-off doctrine*
Double jeopardy	*Miranda warning*
Family model	*Traditional model*
Habeas corpus	

QUESTIONS FOR REVIEW

1. What elements of *parens patriae* seemed to dominate juvenile courts for many decades prior to the reforms of the 1970s and 1980s? Discuss each.

2. Write a short essay contrasting the *parens patriae* doctrine with offender accountability and due process.

3. What is *court unification*? How is court unification beneficial to court operations and organizations generally?

4. How is court unification potentially threatening to juvenile recidivists? Explain.

5. In what respects can juvenile court judicial discretion act both for and against juvenile offenders at the time of their adjudication as delinquents?

6. Briefly describe the hands-off policy of the U.S. Supreme Court in relation to juvenile courts. How does this policy compare with the U.S. Supreme Court's early position toward correctional institutions and inmate problems? Compare and contrast the Court's policies relating to juvenile courts and correctional institutions.

7. Discuss briefly the significance of *Kent v. United States*. At the time, why was this considered a landmark case?

8. How did the case of *In re Gault* expand the case for juvenile rights beyond the *Kent* case? Explain briefly.

9. Can juvenile offenders be adjudicated as delinquent in juvenile courts on certain charges, and then can they be tried as adults in criminal court on those same charges? Why or why not? Cite the facts of a relevant case.

10. What standard is used in juvenile courts for determining whether a juvenile is delinquent?

SUGGESTED READINGS

Altschuler, David M. and Troy L. Armstrong. *Intensive Aftercare for High-Risk Juveniles: An Assessment.* Washington, DC: U.S. Office of Juvenile Justice and Delinquency Prevention, 1994.

Miller, Neal. *State Laws on Prosecutors' and Judges' Use of Juvenile Records.* Washington, DC: U.S. National Institute of Justice, 1995.

Reinharz, Peter. *Killer Kids, Bad Law: Tales of the Juvenile Court System.* New York: Barricade Books, 1996.

Schwartz, Ira M. and William H. Barton (eds.). *Reforming Juvenile Detention: No More Hidden Closets.* Columbus, OH: Ohio State University Press, 1994.

Strange, Carolyn. *Toronto's Girl Problem: The Perils and Pleasures of the City.* Toronto, Ontario, Canada: University of Toronto Press, 1995.

CHAPTER 10

NOMINAL SANCTIONS: WARNINGS, DIVERSION, AND STANDARD PROBATION

INTRODUCTION

A status offender, Daniel W., was originally placed in the custody of the Children at Risk Education program because of his uncontrollable behavior. Eventually, a probation officer completed a detention authorization finding against Daniel W., finding him uncontrollable. Further, the officer believed that Daniel W.'s behavior posed a danger both to himself and to others. Subsequently, he was placed in Boy's Town for a period of time. He appealed his placement in the Boy's Town facility, arguing that his "status" as a status offender entitled him to less restrictive treatment. The court disagreed and upheld the original juvenile court decision to maintain him for a period of time in secure confinement. [In re Interest of Daniel W. (529 N.W. 2d 548) (Neb. App. Apr. 1995)]

A female juvenile, Joie Dawn R., was placed in a limited secure facility in New York following her delinquency adjudication for possessing a dangerous weapon and aggravated assault. Joie Dawn R. appealed her 18-month confinement in the secure facility, but an appellate court upheld the juvenile court disposition as proper. No less restrictive alternative was available to Joie Dawn R. under the circumstances of her prior delinquency record and the instant adjudication offense leading to her incarceration. [In re Joie Dawn R. (631 N.Y.S. 2d 678) (N.Y. Sup. App. Div. Sept. 1995)]

In this chapter we examine the least punitive and restrictive options imposed as punishments by juvenile court judges or recommended by intake officers and/or prosecutors. These options include nominal reprimands, such as *verbal warnings* and *diversion*, as well as the least punitive conditional option, *standard probation*. Both diversion and standard probation are programs that may require offenders to perform various acts, such as victim restitution or compensation, community services and other good works, and pay fines or other monetary penalties. Several diversionary programs currently used in various U.S. jurisdictions are described. Their effectiveness will also be assessed.

Because standard probation means that juveniles may be required to perform certain services, make restitution, or comply with other program requirements, several probation programs will be described. The role of juvenile probation officers is also examined. These officers are important in part because they are direct links between juveniles and juvenile courts.

In many jurisdictions, high labor turnover characterizes the probation officer role. Individual probation officers report various reasons for this turnover, including dissatisfaction with caseloads and other work pressures. Other officers find their work rewarding and challenging. The activities of juvenile probation officers are described and their role in the juvenile justice system is illustrated. Some attention is given to how these officers are recruited initially. Finally, the overall success of the programs presented here is described.

NOMINAL DISPOSITIONS DEFINED

Nominal dispositions are verbal and/or written warnings issued to low-risk juvenile offenders, often first offenders, for the purpose of alerting them to the seriousness of their acts and their potential for receiving severe conditional punishments if they ever should reoffend. These sanctions are the least punitive alternatives. Nominal dispositions may be imposed by police officers in their encounters with juveniles. These verbal warnings or reprimands are often in the form of station "adjustments," where youths are taken into custody and released to their parents later, without a record being made of the incident.

Juvenile court judges are encouraged in most states to utilize the least restrictive sanctions after adjudicating juveniles as delinquents, status offenders, or CHINS. The use of incarceration as a sanction is within the judicial powers of juvenile courts, although these courts are obliged and encouraged to seek other options as sanctions (Koehler and Lindner, 1992). Some experts believe that secure confinement as a disposition is overused and that public safety is better served to the extent that most juveniles can remain at home within their communities, where a more therapeutic milieu exists for them to become rehabilitated (Jones and Krisberg, 1994). Indeed, states such as Delaware have attempted to downsize their juvenile correctional institutions as one means of discouraging juvenile court judges from exercising this option (Brandau, 1992). One community-based option in Delaware is the Delaware Bay Marine Institute (DBMI), a program that emphasizes sea-related activities and underwater skills. Although the results of this research were inconclusive, the fact remains that there are feasible alternatives to incarcerating juveniles that may work as well or better than simply incarcerating them (Brandau, 1992). For some experts, even better alternatives include doing little or nothing other than issuing certain juveniles verbal warnings or reprimands.

For example, intake officers may also use nominal dispositions against certain juveniles if it is perceived that they merit only verbal warnings instead of more punitive sanctions. If petitions against certain juveniles are filed, depending on the circumstances, judges may find them to be delinquent as alleged in these petitions. However, these adjudications do not automatically bind judges to implement conditional or custodial sanctions. Thus judges may simply issue warnings to adjudicated juveniles. These warnings are serious, especially after a finding that the juvenile is delinquent. Juveniles with prior records face tougher sentencing options later if they reoffend in the same juvenile court jurisdiction and reappear before the same judges. Actually, various juvenile court actors engage in the process of attempting to forecast a youth's behavior if certain actions are taken or not taken. Some persons have created decision trees to operationalize this process. Rogers (1990:51) suggests the decision tree shown in Figure 10.1.

This **juvenile aftercare decision tree** begins with the question of whether the youth is violent. Depending on the answer to this question, either "yes" or "no," the tree branches two different ways, where other questions are posed. Notice that if the answers to successive questions are "yes," the degree of restrictiveness recommended to the juvenile court increases. The more "no" answers suggest less restrictiveness. This tree merely conceptualizes court thinking, particularly following an adjudication. However, actors may utilize similar decision trees much earlier in the system. For instance, intake officers and prosecutors may contemplate seriously the use of **diversion** for some youths.

DIVERSION

The Juvenile Justice and Delinquency Prevention Act of 1974 and its subsequent amendments was intended, in part, to deinstitutionalize status offenders and remove them from the jurisdiction of juvenile courts. Another provision of this act was to ensure that all other adjudicated delinquent offenders would receive the least punitive sentencing options from juvenile court judges in relation to their adjudication offenses. In fact, the National Advisory Committee for Juvenile Justice and Delinquency Prevention declared in 1980 that juvenile court judges should select the least restrictive sentencing alternatives, given the nature of the offense, the age, interests, and needs of the juvenile offender, and the circumstances of the conduct (National Advisory Committee for Juvenile Justice and Delinquency Prevention, 1980). Therefore, judicial actions that appear too lenient are the result of either federal mandates or national recommendations.

In one jurisdiction, particularly as the result of labeling theory, juvenile justice policy has emphasized the importance of diverting young offenders away from court. The emphasis has been reinforced by claims that community-based restorative sanctions, such as community aid panels (CAPs) and family group conferences (FGCs), are more effective at reducing juvenile recidivism than sending youths to court (Coumarelos and Weatherburn, 1995). Experts say that those who benefit the most from juvenile court experiences are those with lengthy records of recidivism, especially those who are chronic, serious, violent offenders.

According to some experts, a primary, intended consequence of diversion is to remove large numbers of relatively minor offenders from juvenile

FIGURE 10.1   Juvenile Aftercare Decision Tree

INSTRUCTIONS: Starting at the left, circle yes or no for each question.
Refer to decision criteria for clarification of each question. When the
degree of restrictiveness is reached, place an X in the box.

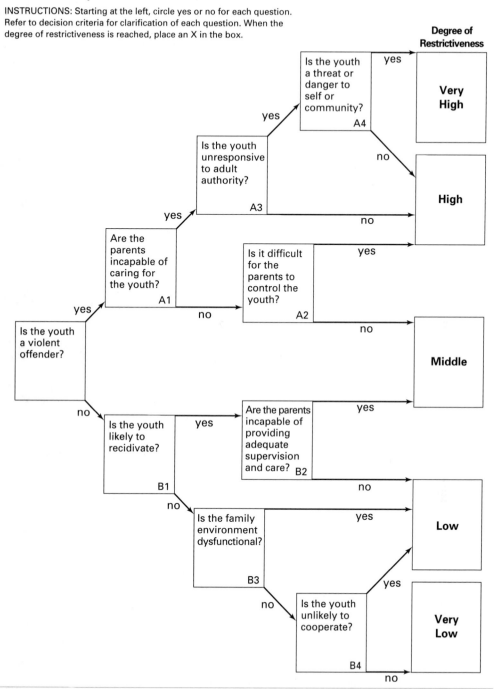

Source: From Jose B. Ashford and Craig Winston Le Croy, "Decision-Making for Juvenile Offenders in Aftercare," *Juvenile and Family Court Journal* **39**:49 (1988).

court processing as quickly as possible (Schwartz, 1989). However, other professionals caution that one unintended consequence of diversion is the development of wider, stronger, and different nets (Austin and Krisberg, 1982). This means in the simplest terms that those youngsters diverted from the formal juvenile justice system are captured in "nets" formed by the community-based agencies (Binder, 1989). Thus if we view social control in its broadest terms, this means that more, not fewer, children will fall under some form of social control through diversionary programs. Some experts believe that children who are delabeled as delinquents through diversion may become relabeled as the result of being placed in community mental health centers and private psychiatric care facilities or treatment programs (Chesney-Lind and Matsuo, 1995; Hepburn et al., 1992).

It is claimed by some authorities that diversion of offenders should be aimed at the client population that would otherwise have received formal dispositions if diversion had not occurred (Krause and McShane, 1994; Pallone, 1994). This client population consists of youths who have committed delinquent acts and not simply status offenses. However, some critics say that status offenders may escalate to more serious offenses if left untreated by the system. Therefore, intervention of some sort is necessary to prevent this escalation of offense seriousness (Harada and Suzuki, 1994; Krause and McShane, 1994). Status offenders do not necessarily progress to more serious offenses. Sometimes, their apparent involvement in more serious offenses is a function of relabeling of the same acts differently by police (Coumarelos and Weatherburn, 1995; Fuller and Norton, 1993; Rabinowitz, 1992). On other occasions, status offenders may be upgraded to misdemeanants by juvenile court judges if they fail to obey valid court orders. If a status offender is ordered to attend school and does not, this provides the judicial grounds for issuing a contempt of court citation, a misdemeanor (Beger, 1994a). Not everyone favors this particular use of juvenile court contempt power, especially against status offenders. Regardless of whether they are status offenders or have committed serious delinquent acts, divertees often exhibit some recidivism. Therefore, it is true that at least some of these divertees do progress to more serious offenses as some critics allege (Benda, 1987; Jones and Krisberg, 1994).

Functions and Dysfunctions of Diversion

Diversion has certain logistical benefits and functions. First, it decreases the caseload of juvenile court prosecutors by shuffling less serious cases to probation departments. Of course, this increases the supervisory responsibilities of probation departments who must manage larger numbers of

BOX 10.1   TEEN PROSTITUTION IN JAPAN

On the Seamy Side of Tokyo

Several girls ranging in age from 14 to 19 hung around the corner telephone on a busy street corner. The telephone rang frequently, and each girl would answer it, speak briefly, and then leave the area. More girls would arrive and the telephone would ring again. This would go on all day long and well into the evening hours.

What is transpiring is sex by telephone, one instance of a growing number of telephone clubs. Telephone clubs offer teen sex in exchange for money or gifts. Middle-aged businessmen call to these locations and arrange sexual interludes with these girls. The arrangements may include only a peep show in a secluded, private location. Or the arrangement may be for sex all night long, again in a private room in some obscure motel.

New York? Chicago? Miami? No. Tokyo, Japan. In a country once known for its virtuous and reverent treatment of women, a growing problem is teenage prostitution. Many Japanese citizens are quite upset about it, but an immediate solution is not apparent.

Tokyo police say that growing numbers of schoolgirls are becoming involved in telephone clubs, where many of them are under age 15. Free-spending men, both Caucasians and Orientals, are attracted to these women through televised "specials" and news segments, where matter-of-fact reports are given about liaisons and lurid interludes. These older men, known to the girls as "papas," pay up to a thousand dollars or more for an evening of sex.

The girls themselves are attracted to prostitution because of the easy money it brings and the material goods it can buy. One girl, Sana, says she meets her dates simply by walking around the Shinjuku, dressed as a student with a pleated skirt and blue school sweater. For $20, Sana accompanies men to bars, where she drinks with them. Sometimes sex follows, but for several hundred dollars, depending on what is requested.

Another girl, Junko Kobayashi, 18, and a friend of hers met a lawyer who paid her $720 for spending the night with him. Junko said that the money made it possible for her to buy some expensive sunglasses and a Louis Vuitton bag. For other girls, customers may pay from $10 to $50 to view them through a window in a video porn shop. The customer sits on one side of the glass and the girl on the other. The girl removes her clothes and fondles herself, while the customer may do the same. In 1993, 3946 girls were picked up by police and held temporarily on prostitution charges in the Shinjuku district. In 1995, 5481 girls were picked up in the same area on similar charges. This is a 40 percent increase and it does not appear to be abating. Some experts say that Japan's rapid rise in affluence has undermined traditional family values of home and family with an all-out pursuit of high-status luxury goods.

Is this type of teenage problem any different from what is happening in many of the larger cities in the United States? To what extent is a country's affluence connected to teenage prostitution? What are some preventive measures authorities might take to either curtail or decrease the extent of rising teenage prostitution? Can diversion work for these female juveniles?

Source: Adapted from Associated Press, "Japanese Angry over Rising Teen Prostitution," *Minot (ND) Daily News*, October 4, 1996:A4.

divertees in addition to juvenile probationers. Another function of diversion is that it seems to reduce recidivism in those jurisdictions where it has been used (Fields, 1994; Polan, 1994). Another intended consequence of diversion is to reduce the degree of juvenile institutionalization or placement in either secure or nonsecure incarcerative facilities. A fourth function is that diversion is potentially useful as a long-range crime prevention measure. Finally, diversion reduces certain youth risks, such as suicide attempts as the result of being confined in adult jails or lockups for short periods. At the 1991 Congress of Corrections, Peter Reinharz, chief of the Family Court Division of the New York City Law Department, indicated that the increasingly disturbed and violent nature of incarcerated youths and the need for corrections professionals to examine the ways in which these cases are handled are currently key correctional priorities (American Correctional Association, 1992). Rowan (1989:218) and Smith (1991) have described the stress and anxiety generated as the result of even short-term confinement for certain juveniles and their propensity to commit suicide. At least for some youths, diversion assists in avoiding the stresses of confinement or prosecution.

One of the dysfunctional consequences is that diversion may widen the net by including some youths who otherwise would have received station adjustments by police or warnings from juvenile court judges (Chesney-Lind and Matsuo, 1995; Koehler and Lindner, 1992). Much of this net widening occurs through changes in police discretion and relabeling of juvenile behaviors as more serious, however (Schneider, 1984a; Klein, 1979). Another dysfunction is that some affected youths may acquire beliefs about the juvenile justice system that it is lenient and will tolerate relatively minor lawbreaking. The fact that many juvenile offenders are not disposed to secure confinement until their fourth or fifth delinquency adjudications would provide support for these beliefs.

DIVERSION PROGRAMS FOR JUVENILES

Youth Service Bureaus. Diversion programs have operated in the United States for many years. In the early 1960s, **youth service bureaus** (YSBs) were established in numerous jurisdictions to accomplish diversions' several objectives. Although we still cannot identify precisely those youths considered delinquency-prone (rather, we refer to certain youths as at risk), YSBs were created, in part, as places within communities where delinquent-prone youths could be referred by parents, schools, and law enforcement agencies (Norman, 1970). Actually, YSBs were forerunners of our contemporary community-based correctional programs, since they were intended to solicit volunteers from among community residents and to mobilize a variety of resources that could assist in a youth's treatment. The nature of treatments for youths, within the YSB concept, originally included referrals to a variety of community services, educational experiences, and individual or group counseling. YSB organizers attempted to compile lists of existing community services, agencies, organizations, and sponsors who could cooperatively coordinate these resources in the most productive ways to benefit affected juveniles (Norman, 1970; Romig, 1978).

Norman (1970:15–19) has described five types of model YSB programs in the general case:

1. *The cooperating agencies model.* This model consists of several different community-based agencies and organizations. Each organization or agency furnishes at least one paid full-time worker to the YSB program. As a team, these workers attempt to involve citizens and youth by bringing in interested professionals and others to work with juveniles who might have poor self-concepts or social adjustment problems.

2. *The community organization model.* This particular model utilizes community citizens who work on a strictly voluntary basis. They are encouraged to form a board of directors who will assist them in coordinating diverse community services in ways that can benefit those juveniles serviced. Such organizations would provide temporary shelter for runaways or those youths who are experiencing family difficulties or school problems. Thus these agencies would function to accommodate those who need emergency treatment or assistance.

3. *The citizen action model.* As the name implies, citizen involvement in the citizen action model is intensified. Community volunteers are attracted from various types of youth services. Each youth referred to these organizations is regarded as a case, and case conferences are held to determine the best treatment approaches to assist youths in solving their problems. A YSB patterned after this model was implemented in Wise County, Virginia, in 1979. By the mid-1980s, 22 locally operated programs had been established in Virginia, costing the state about $36,000 per program. In Wise County, from 1979 to 1984, groups of interested

citizens formed a youth commission that began intensive assistance programs for troubled juveniles. During that period, the number of teenage pregnancies in the county dropped from 185 to 116, while the school dropout rate declined from 8 percent to 5.6 percent. Further, the total number of juvenile arrests in that county has decreased systematically. Virginia officials have been excited about what they consider to be the successes of their YSB programs.

4. *The street outreach model.* This model provides for the establishment of neighborhood centers in business areas, where group and individual therapy may be administered to troubled youths. The accessibility of such centers in business districts is an attractive feature, since it caters to assisting juvenile transients who are roaming those same streets constantly.

5. *The systems modification model.* This type of model has led to the establishment of community-based facilities that function in relation with other agencies, schools, churches, and institutions to help these other organizations become more effective in supplying the needed youth services.

Interestingly, YSBs have been accused of contributing to the net-widening problem, since they draw in numerous youths who might otherwise have avoided prolonged contact with the juvenile justice system. Nevertheless, they have established common patterns that many community-based organizations have found useful as program guides over the years. Generally, diversion programs operate in pretty much the same ways for juveniles as they operate for adult offenders. Diversion in the juvenile justice system has the primary objective of avoiding labeling and the stigma associated with involvement in juvenile court (Polan, 1994). Diversion may be either *unconditional* or *conditional*. **Unconditional diversion** *simply means that the divertee will attend school, behave, and not reappear before the juvenile court for a specified period.* **Conditional diversion** *may require juveniles to attend lectures, individual or group psychotherapy, drug or alcohol treatment centers, police department–conducted DUI classes, and/or vocational or educational classes or programs.* Successful completion of the diversion program means dismissal of the case. These programs are of variable lengths, but most run for periods of six months to a year.

The Youth Services/Diversion and Community Service Programs, Inc.

In Orange County, California, the **Youth Services/Diversion** (YS/D) and **Community Service Programs, Inc.** (CSP, Inc.) were established in the early 1990s to fulfill two goals. These goals are to teach client responsibility and reduce family dysfunction (Polan, 1994). Samples of youths from Orange County were selected and subjected to several experimental interventions. Family counseling sessions were established on a regular basis for youths diverted from juvenile court. Youths themselves participated in several self-help programs designed to enhance their self-esteem and confidence. Not all youths and their families completed the project. Those who dropped out were compared with those who finished the program requirements. Evidence suggests that most of those who completed their programs successfully fared better over time by exhibiting reduced recidivism compared with those who dropped out. Experts suggest that the program is cost-effective and can conceivably be implemented on a large scale in other jurisdictions. One of the most positive benefits of this program accrued to juveniles whose self-concepts and general psychological well-being were improved (Polan, 1994).

The Juvenile Diversion/Noncustody Intake Program

In another experiment in Orange County, California, investigators implemented in 1982 a diversionary program called the **Juvenile Diversion/Noncustody Intake** (JD/NCI) **Program**. Diversionary efforts in previous years by Orange County officials had been ineffective. The JD/NCI Program was designed to target more serious juvenile offenders by giving them more concentrated attention by police, probation, community agencies, schools, and families (Binder et al., 1985). The JD/NCI Program was a type of conditional diversion, because juvenile clients were required to pay restitution to their victims. In addition, the more traditional elements were required, such as school attendance, employment, and school counseling. Of those juveniles entering the program, 71 percent had prior felony arrests. Binder et al. reported that the program successfully diverted a large proportion of intake cases ordinarily referred to the district attorney for formal processing. Besides easing the juvenile court caseload, the JD/NCI Program clients tended to have lower recidivism rates than those of more traditional programs, although these differences were not substantial.

The PINS Diversion Program

In New York City, the **PINS Diversion Program** for persons alleged to be in need of supervision (PINS) was instituted in February 1987. Data collected from juvenile records during 1989–1990 yielded questionnaire information for a 1986 prediversion group of 693 youths as well as a 1988 postdiversion group of 728 youths. Using out-of-home placements and increased access to community-based services, New York youth counselors worked with numerous PINS cases diverted from New York juvenile courts. Ultimately, the program proved successful at diverting numerous PINS cases from otherwise proceeding to the family court, the numbers of youths subsequently placed in either secure or nonsecure confinement, and the use of court-mandated services. The percentage of cases at intake where formal sanctions were received was reduced from 10 percent to only 4 percent, while the placement rate decreased from 6.8 percent to 4.1 percent (Rabinowitz, 1992).

The Youth at Risk Program

Significant success rates (i.e., lower recidivism) have been reported by another California program known as the **Youth at Risk Program**, which was operated in Los Angeles and Contra Costa Counties during the 1982–1984 period for youths age 13 to 19. The program consisted of a 10-day rural training course comprising classes, outdoor sites for running and other physical activities, and emphasis on self-reliance, peer resistance, peer and staff support, and individual responsibility (MetaMetrics, Inc., 1984). A community follow-up program was implemented as a continuation of these experiences. Of the 155 youths participating in the program during the period 1982–1983, 49 were studied over a 15-month period and compared with a matched group of probationers with similar characteristics and delinquency histories. Youth at Risk Program participants had incident recidivism rates of 34.7 percent compared with 55.1 percent for the comparison group, and a serious offense recidivism rate of only 18.4 percent contrasted with 40.8 percent for the comparison group. These figures led program officials to conclude that their program had profound positive impact on their juvenile clients (MetaMetrics, Inc., 1984).

The See Our Side (SOS) Program

In Prince George's County, Maryland, a program was established in 1983 called the **See Our Side** (SOS) **Program** (Mitchell and Williams, 1986:70). SOS is referred to by its directors as a "juvenile aversion" program, and dissociates itself from "scare" programs such as Scared Straight. Basically, SOS seeks to educate juveniles about the realities of life in prison through discussions and hands-on experience and attempts to show them the types of behaviors that can lead to incarceration (Mitchell and Williams, 1986:70). Clients coming to SOS are referrals from various sources, including juvenile court, public and private schools, churches, professional counseling agencies, and police and fire departments. Youths served by SOS range in age from 12 to 18, and they do not have be adjudicated as delinquent to be eligible for participation. SOS helps *any* youth who might benefit from such participation. SOS consists of four three-hour phases.

- *Phase I:* Staff orientation and group counseling session where staff attempt to facilitate discussion and ease tension among the youthful clients; characteristics of jails are discussed, including age and gender breakdowns, race, and types of juvenile behavior that might result in jailing for short periods.

- *Phase II:* A tour of a prison facility.
- *Phase III:* Three inmates discuss with youths what life is like behind bars; inmates who assist in the program are selected on the basis of their emotional maturity, communications skills, and warden recommendations.
- *Phase IV:* Two evaluations are made—the first is an evaluation of SOS sessions by the juveniles; a recidivism evaluation is also conducted for each youth after a one-year lapse from the time they participated in SOS; relative program successfulness can therefore be gauged.

SOS officials conducted an evaluation of the program in September 1985. It was found that SOS served 327 youths during the first year of operation and that a total of 38 sessions were held. Recidivism of program participants was about 22 percent. Again, this low recidivism rate is favorable. Subsequent evaluations of the SOS program showed that the average rate of client recidivism dropped to only 16 percent. The cost of the program was negligible. During the first year, the program cost was only $280, or about 86 cents per youth served.

The Community Board Program

One innovation introduced by the San Francisco juvenile courts is the **Community Board Program**, which is a civil mediation mechanism. This program involves first- and second-time juvenile offenders who have been charged with minor offenses, often property offenses, where damage to or loss of property was sustained by one or more victims. The Community Board Program uses volunteers to meet with both offenders and their victims as an alternative to a full juvenile court adjudicatory hearing. Mediation is conducted wherein a mutually satisfactory solution is arranged by the mediator.

One of the positive aspects of this program is that victims can meet and confront their attackers. Victims may become involved and empowered. Their face-to-face encounters with youths who victimized them enable victims to tell them of the harm they caused. In a selective way, the mediation program was successful. That is, some types of juveniles directly benefited from their confrontation experience. In a comparative investigation of program evaluation, 113 juveniles who completed mediation were compared with 157 controls. Younger juveniles were the least responsive to mediation, however. Interestingly, in younger-offender cases, recidivism rates were much higher for them than for youths of similar ages in the control group. Simply put, this mediation program did not seem to work with particularly youthful offenders. However, older juveniles seemed favorably affected by the confrontation and mediation. Their recidivism rates were much lower than those of comparable controls (URSA Institute, 1993).

IMPLICATIONS OF DIVERSION PROGRAMS FOR JUVENILES

One result of the Juvenile Justice and Delinquency Prevention Act of 1974 was to deinstitutionalize status offenders and remove them from the jurisdiction of juvenile courts (McNally, 1984:30). This has been done in some jurisdictions but not in all. One result is that there is much variation among jurisdictions about how juvenile offenders are processed and treated. In recent years, however, an increasing number of juvenile courts have imposed dispositions according to offender needs as well as according to what is *just* and deserved (O'Neil, 1987). Better classifications of offenders need to be devised. More needs to be discovered about offender characteristics, their backgrounds, and specific circumstances in order that proper punishments and treatments can be meted out by juvenile court judges. For diversion programs to be successful, they must be targeted at the most successful juvenile candidates. Most frequently, these are low-risk first offenders or juveniles who are quite young.

Some diversion programs include some rather stringent conditions and may even involve participation in intervention projects designed to remedy certain manifested problems. For example, a sample of 39 juvenile sex offenders was assigned to the Behavioral Studies Program of the Pines Treatment Center in Portsmouth, Virginia (Hunter and Goodwin, 1992). All participants received a minimum of six months of verbal satiation, in addition to individual, group, and family counseling and other therapies. Youths were also exposed to psychophysiological assessments of changes in their penile circumference by various testing procedures. The result was that deviant sexual arousal was decreased significantly and that the youths had favorably responded to therapy designed to treat their deviant conduct. However, not all divertees are subjected to these or similar experiences.

Juvenile courts have come under attack in recent years as the result of what the public considers excessive judicial leniency in dealing with youthful offenders (Kansas Juvenile Justice Task Force, 1995; U.S. General Accounting Office, 1995a,b). Often, juvenile cases are dismissed. This occurs not only during formal adjudicatory proceedings by juvenile court judges, but also by intake officers in earlier screenings of offenders. Thus it is unreasonable to identify any specific part of the juvenile justice process as unusually lenient in juvenile case processing. All phases of the system seem to be influenced by the rehabilitative philosophy. For many people, rehabilitation is equated with leniency.

The degree of case attrition through diversions dismissals has been investigated by several researchers (Bilchik, 1996; Snyder, Sickmund, and Poe-Yamagata, 1996; U.S. General Accounting Office, 1995a,b). In the mid-1970s, for example, a study by the National Assessment of Juvenile Corrections reported that about two-thirds of all juvenile referrals were dismissed at either intake or at the judicial hearing (Sarri and Hansenfeld, 1976). Studies of juvenile case dismissal rates in later years disclosed similar results, although attrition figures were somewhat lower, ranging from 30 to 54 percent (Ito, 1984; McCarthy, 1987b:239). McCarthy (1987b:240) says that dismissal rates are influenced by the same kinds of factors that impinge on prosecutors and judges in adult criminal cases: crowded court dockets, too many cases to handle adequately, overcrowding in juvenile secure confinement facilities, and greater concern for the due-process rights of offenders.

McCarthy (1987b:248–251) found that often, case dismissals occurred at the request of the petitioner, failure of the petitioner/victim/witness to appear, and the trivial nature of the case. However, dismissals are not always trivial. She also found that 35 percent of all dismissals involved violent offenses, and 44 percent of all petitions filed for violent felonies were dismissed as well. McCarthy is certainly not alone when she expresses concern that the attrition of juvenile cases involving serious crime represents a major juvenile justice problem (McCarthy, 1987a:251).

In addition to charges of being too lenient with offenders and dismissing or diverting their cases, the juvenile court has been targeted for other criticisms. Critics say that the juvenile court has failed to distinguish adequately between less serious and more serious offenders; it has often ignored the victims of juvenile violence; it has often failed to correct or rehabilitate juveniles in a manner consistent with its manifest purposes; it has been unconcerned or complacent about juvenile offenders and how they should be punished; it has confined children at times in adult jails; it has failed often to protect juveniles' rights; its services have been too thinly spread; and it has been too resistant to self-examination and suggestions for improvement (O'Neil, 1987:189). But one criticism of these criticisms is that collectively, they do not especially apply to any single juvenile court at a particular point in time. Rather, they are loosely distributed and shared by many juvenile courts. By the same token, there are many juvenile courts operating with few serious flaws.

TEEN COURTS

The Use of Teen Courts, Day Treatment, and Alternative Dispute Resolution

First-offender cases, where status offenses or misdemeanors have been committed, are given priority in a different type of court setting involving one's peers as judges. Increasing numbers of jurisdictions are using teen courts as an alternative to juvenile court for determining one's guilt and punishment (Schiff and Wexler, 1996). Judges may divert minor cases to the teen courts (North Carolina Administrative Office of the Courts, 1994).

Teen courts *are informal jury proceedings, where jurors consist of teenagers who hear and decide minor cases.* Adults function only as presiding judges, and these persons are often retired judges or lawyers who perform such services voluntarily and in their spare time. The focus of teen courts is on therapeutic jurisprudence, with a strong emphasis on rehabilitation. One objective of such courts is to teach empathy to offenders. Victims are encouraged to take an active role in these courts. Youths become actively involved as advisory juries (Schiff and Wexler, 1996).

Among the first cities to establish teen courts were Seattle, Washington, and Denver, Colorado (Rothstein, 1985:18). Subsequently, teen courts have been established in many other jurisdictions, including Odessa, Texas. In Odessa, for instance, juveniles are referred to teen courts for class C misdemeanors and minor traffic violations. Defendants range in age from 10 to 16. Traffic citation cases result in teen court referrals by municipal judges, who give youths the option of paying their fines or having their cases heard by the teen court. If youths select the teen court for adjudication, they do not acquire a juvenile record. The teen court listens to all evidence and decides the matter.

Teen court dispositions are always related closely to community service as well as jury service. Thus juveniles who are found *guilty* by teen courts may, in fact, serve on such juries in the future, as one of their conditional punishments. Or they may be required to perform up to 22 hours' of community service, such as working at the animal shelter, library, or nursing home; picking up trash in parks or ballfields; or working with various community agencies (Rothstein, 1985:22). The teen court program in Odessa has been very successful. Prior to using teen courts, the recidivism rate for all juvenile offenders in the city was between 50 and 60 percent. However, teen court adjudications all but eliminated this recidivism figure. Interestingly, juveniles who are tried by the teen court often develop an interest in the legal system. Rothstein (1985:22) says that teen courts place a high priority on educating young people about their responsibilities as individuals, family members, and citizens. As a part of one's diversion, conditional options such as restitution, fines, or community service may be imposed in those cases where property damage was incurred as the result of the juvenile's behavior. Juvenile court judges must exercise considerable discretion and impose dispositions that best meet the juvenile's needs and circumstances.

Constructive dispositions are the objective of teen courts in northern Kentucky. In September, October, and November 1992, teen jurors in a Kentucky teen court heard case details in nine different cases (Williamson, Chalk, and Knepper, 1993). Referrals to teen court were made from the regular juvenile court, a division of the state's district court. If juveniles are found guilty by the teen court, the court imposes constructive dispositions involving community service hours. It should be noted that these teen courts do not determine one's guilt or innocence—rather, they convene and recommend appropriate dispositions. Teenagers act as prosecutors, defense attorneys, clerks, bailiffs, jury forepersons, and jurors as they carry out roles similar to their counterparts in criminal courts. The Kentucky teen court variety is interesting because accused and judged teens are themselves recruited subsequently to serve as teen jurors. Thus all defendants are assigned to jury duty following their teen court appearances. When this study was conducted, no youth had been returned to the teen court for non-compliance. Perhaps seeing how the process works from the other side, as jurors, made these teenagers understand the seriousness of what they had done themselves as victimizers in the past.

DAY TREATMENT CENTERS

Some jurisdictions have *day treatment program* centers. **Day reporting centers** were established first in England in 1974 to provide intensive supervision for offenders who would otherwise be incarcerated (Larivee, 1990). Offenders in England day treatment centers typically lived at home while remaining under the supervision of a correctional administrator. Inmates would either work or attend school, regularly participate in treatment programming, devote at least four hours a week to community service, and observe a strict curfew. A variation on day treatment programs in England has been attempted in the United States for juvenile offenders.

The Bluegrass County, Kentucky Program

In Bluegrass County, Kentucky, the day treatment program is one of 13 community-based day treatment programs throughout the state operated by the Department of Social Services (Bowling, 1987:104). *Day treatment programs are community-based treatments, operated either publicly or privately, that combine counseling, education, and regular school attendance with vocational assistance and job placement* (Larivee, 1990). The average cost of these programs is about $30 per day. These programs bridge the gap "for some troubled youths between parental control and round-the-clock juvenile justice supervision" (Bowling, 1987:104). Client involvement is either voluntary or results from court or school referrals. Day treatment programs have indicated a 75 percent success rate, which is translated into a recidivism rate of about 25 percent. This is well under the amount of recidivism normally observed as the result of standard probation.

BOX 10.2   ON THE GET-TOUGH MOVEMENT

The Case of Getting Tough with Juvenile Offenders

What is the get-tough movement? You can't find it in most dictionaries. If you look in the criminal justice literature, you will see references to it, but almost nowhere will you find a definition of it. Rather, the get-tough movement is more of a generalized set of policies directed toward toughening criminal laws and the way we view juvenile offenders.

For decades, the public and certain lawmakers have believed that the criminal justice system is coddling criminals and juveniles. Coddling takes the form of lenient dispositions following criminal convictions or delinquency adjudications. When murderers, rapists, and armed robbers get probation or early release through parole, some people, especially crime victims, get very upset with the system.

The get-tough movement is more of an *idea* of creating greater accountability for those who offend, whether they are adults or juveniles. Indiana is a good example of a state that exemplifies the get-tough movement. Indiana has passed many laws against youthful offenders in recent years. Indiana has lowered the age at which juveniles can be prosecuted as adults for serious crimes they commit. Indiana has made the names of juvenile suspects public. Indiana has opened formerly confidential hearings to the public, and it has made juvenile records available to public scrutiny. In past years these kinds of things would be regarded as a violation of a juvenile's privacy. But Indiana is fed up with juvenile crime and wants to eliminate it. Although it is unlikely that Indiana will eliminate juvenile delinquency, no matter how tough it gets toward juvenile offending, there is no question that its policies are getting the attention of juveniles in the state.

Just ask Donna Ratliff of Indianapolis. Donna was 13 when she sprinkled her mother's house with kerosene and set it on fire. The arson committed by Donna resulted in the deaths of her mother, Glissie Ratliff, 37, and her older sister, Jamie, 16. Donna was tried as an adult for her crime of arson and convicted. She was placed in an adult prison in December 1996—a maximum-security prison, no less. Donna doesn't like it.

Donna says that already, she has been threatened with assault by other female inmates. During her group therapy sessions at the prison, she has been asked by prison authorities *not* to talk about her crimes among the other women, because the other inmates would find the crimes too upsetting. Donna claims to have been sexually abused by her father when she was 7. She said that she set the fire to escape an abusive home environment. She said she had no intention of killing her mother and sister.

Donna Ratliff, 14, is not unlike many other youthful offenders who want to pass the blame for their offending on to others, or to an abstraction such as "society" or "an abusive home environment." They quickly learn the key phrases and psychobabble enabling them to create elaborate and convincing scenarios for themselves to explain away why they have done what they have done. But in Indiana, it doesn't work. Perhaps other states will adopt Indiana's posture toward juvenile offenders who kill or cause serious bodily injury.

The get-tough movement is characterized in the following way, especially for juvenile offenders. The age has been lowered where juveniles can be considered adults and be prosecuted for criminal offenses they have committed. Juvenile records are made public and juveniles are named in newspapers. Teenage criminals are confined in adult prisons together with the general offender population. If they become sexual targets of adult offenders while confined, this is part of the price they pay for committing adult crimes. No special treatment will be extended to them by prison officials. They are simply another "con" or "fish."

In 1996, it was found that:

- Twenty-four states have expanded the crimes for which juveniles can be prosecuted as adults.
- Six states have lowered the minimum age for offenders.
- Ten states have opened formerly confidential hearings to the public.
- Eleven states have made the names of juvenile suspects public.
- Twenty-one states have made juveniles' court records public.

What do you think of the get-tough movement? Should *all* states have this get-tough movement? Why or why not? Do you think the get-tough movement will deter juvenile offending?

Source: Adapted from Associated Press, "Teen Firestarter: Imprisonment of Teen on Arson Charges Raises Issues of Justice for Juveniles," *Minot (ND) Daily News*, December 6, 1996:A4.

ALTERNATIVE DISPUTE RESOLUTION

In New Mexico, many youths are subject to **alternative dispute resolution** (ADR) or mediation to resolve school problems. Melinda Smith (1990:112) says that the mediation process allows people to resolve conflicts in a nonthreatening and nonpunitive atmosphere. Mediators are third-party neutrals who help people in a dispute to express their points of view, identify their needs, clarify issues, explore solutions, and negotiate satisfactory agreements.

The New Mexico Center for Dispute Resolution operates a school mediation program that trains students in grades 5 through 12 as mediators to intervene in school-based disputes among students (Smith, 1990:112). Smith describes the program as consisting of three components: (1) a conflict resolution curriculum that can be taught in either academic or residential settings,

(2) a mediation program that trains residents and staff to help resolve conflicts among themselves, and (3) a reintegration component involving parents and residents developing terms of daily living for when the residents return home. She further indicates that the program's rationale is that by giving students a model for positive expression and conflict resolution, it can teach them alternatives to violent and self-destructive behavior. By using these skills within the institutional setting, students can be assisted to interact successfully with their peers and adults. A voluntary program, this mediation effort has seemingly reduced juvenile deviance in the jurisdiction. Thus it may be viewed as an early intervention for preventing juvenile delinquency.

The prevailing correctional philosophy applied to juvenile corrections today as well as to programs for adults is punishment/control rather than treatment/rehabilitation. But like adults, not all juvenile offenders are the same according to their emotional needs, offense seriousness, educational levels, vocational skills, and honesty. Therefore, it is difficult for judges to prescribe meaningful, categorical punishments for aggregates of youthful offenders facing similar charges (Baird, 1985:32). Even if specific predictor variables could be identified, they are not always foolproof for effective program placement decision making (Simone, 1984:110–112).

THE FUTURE OF DIVERSION PROGRAMS

In the long run, diversion programs will tend to vary in their successfulness, depending on how they are established and operated. For instance, a study of 213 juvenile offenders in a midwestern city was conducted during 1976–1980 (Davidson et al., 1987). The program provided four interventions, including behavioral contracting, advocacy and behavioral contracting only with family members, court intervention, and development of interpersonal relationships. Self-reported delinquency and recidivism were measures of program effectiveness. Recidivism rates of program participants were compared with another group exposed to traditional supervisory and monitoring methods. Although no significant differences were reported between the two groups where delinquency self-reports were used, recidivism rates among program members were slightly lower than those of the control group (Davidson et al., 1987). Generally, diversion efforts have been favorable in other jurisdictions, where lower recidivism has been reported (Koehler and Lindner, 1992; U.S General Accounting Office, 1995a,b).

KEY TERMS

Alternative dispute resolution (ADR)

Citizen action model

Community Board Program

Community organization model

Community Services Program, Inc.
  (CSP, Inc.)

Cooperating agencies model

Day reporting centers

Diversion

Juvenile Diversion/Noncustody
  Intake Program

PINS Diversion Program

See Our Side (SOS) Program

Street outreach model

Systems modification model

Teen courts

Youth at Risk Program

Youth service bureaus

Youth Services/Diversion (CYS/D)
  Program

QUESTIONS FOR REVIEW

1. What are two types of nominal sanctions that juvenile court judges may impose? What are some of the factors that seem to contribute to the use of nominal sanctions as opposed to conditional ones? Explain.

2. What are some important functions of diversion? What are some dysfunctions of diversion? In what sense may youths acquire a cynicism for the juvenile justice system where diversion is used as a sanction?

3. What are *youth service bureaus* and what are their functions? What are five general models that are used as patterns by youth service bureaus? What evidence is there that YSBs are effective?

4. Differentiate between conditional and unconditional diversion. What are two types of conditional diversion programs? Describe each briefly.

5. What is the *See Our Side Program*? Describe it briefly.

6. What is a teen court? How are teen courts effective in sanctioning low-risk juvenile offenders?

7. What are *day treatment programs*? Compare these with alternative dispute resolution programs. Evaluate the effectiveness of each for reducing recidivism of delinquent offenders.

8. What are two types of standard probation? Describe each.

9. What are several of the special conditions of probation ordinarily imposed by juvenile court judges?

10. What is the *Highfields Project*? Describe the program format briefly. How does it rate regarding its influence on delinquency recidivism?

SUGGESTED READINGS

Cowles, Ernest L., Thomas C. Castellano, and Laura A. Gransky. *"Boot Camp" Drug Treatment and Aftercare Intervention: An Evaluation Review.* Washington, DC: U.S. Government Printing Office, 1995.

Glick, Barry and Arnold P. Goldstein (eds.). *Managing Delinquency: Programs That Work.* Laurel, MD: American Correctional Association, 1995.

Gold, Martin and D. Wayne Osgood. *Personality and Peer Influence in Juvenile Corrections.* Westport, CT: Greenwood Press, 1992.

Welsh, Lesley A. et al. *Running for Their Lives: Physical and Sexual Abuse of Runaway Adolescents.* New York: Garland, 1995.

CHAPTER 11

JUVENILE PROBATION AND COMMUNITY-BASED CORRECTIONS

INTRODUCTION

K.W. is an Ohio juvenile who was taken into custody by police for possessing a weapon and committing various other offenses. When he was initially referred to juvenile court, he was placed in detention following a detention hearing. During the time that he was in detention, he escaped. Subsequently, he was apprehended. His subsequent apprehension by police was for new offenses, including receiving stolen property and carrying another weapon. Both offenses are felonies in Ohio when adults commit them. During the adjudicatory hearing, the juvenile court judge addressed the matter of K.W.'s amenability to treatment. The judge ordered a complete mental and physical examination of K.W. Later, the judge declared that "the court finds after a fully investigation...and after a full consideration of the child's prior juvenile record, efforts previously made to treat and rehabilitate the child, the child's family environment, the child's school record, and other matters of evidence, that there are reasonable grounds to believe that the child...is not amenable to care or rehabilitation in any facility designed for the care, supervision, and rehabilitation of delinquent children, and that the safety of the community may require that the child be placed under legal restraint for a period extending beyond his majority." [In re K.W., 657 N.E. 2d 611 (Ohio Common Pleas, Oct. 1995)]

Rivera was a juvenile who had been adjudicated in a New York juvenile court for aggravated assault. Both a clinical psychologist and the probation department recommended that Rivera be placed in a long-term, highly structured secure facility. Rivera protested and appealed, arguing that he should be placed in the "least restrictive alternative" according to New York State Juvenile Offender Law guidelines. The appeals court considered the placement decision of the original New York juvenile court judge. Rivera had had a prior juvenile record of escalating serious offenses. His most recent adjudication offense involved an assault involving serious physical injuries on a slightly built, 12-year-old victim. The clinical psychologist believed that Rivera would continue his predatory ways in the future, particularly in light of strong gang involvement and his absolute lack of remorse. His secure placement was affirmed on appeal. [In re Rivera, 636 N.Y.S. 2d 780 (N.Y. Sup. App. Div. Jan. 1996)]

It has been the traditional view toward juvenile offenders that they should be exposed to the least restrictive confinement conditions if adjudicated delinquent. Further, every attempt should be made to rehabilitate them. The two cases above illustrate that (1) not all youths are considered by juvenile courts to be capable of becoming rehabilitated; and (2) the least restrictive alternative is not always the best choice for a juvenile, especially a juvenile with a long record of serious violent offending.

At the other end of the continuum is a majority of youths who are capable of becoming rehabilitated and who should be granted the least restrictive conditions upon their adjudication for various offenses. There is a particular class of youths who should not be diverted from the juvenile justice system. Neither should their cases be thrown out or downgraded by prosecutors. Rather, these youths should be subjected to minimal supervisory conditions and community controls for various periods of duration. In this chapter we describe several more intensive, conditional sanctions that juvenile court judges may impose, including an array of intermediate punishment programs for juveniles. According to McCarthy and McCarthy (1997), *intermediate punishment programs* are sanctions that exist somewhere between incarceration and [standard] probation on the continuum of criminal penalties. Intermediate punishments described here include intensive supervised probation (ISP), community-based juvenile corrections, electronic monitoring, home confinement, and shock probation.

The significance of intermediate punishment programs is that they are characterized as having a higher degree of supervisory control over juvenile offenders. They are generally considered to be delinquency deterrents and repressive, in the sense that they are intended to promote a strong degree of crime or delinquency control through offender monitoring. Therefore, they deter by controlling offender behaviors and by making it increasingly difficult for individual offenders to deviate from program conditions. Offenders who are closely supervised or monitored have fewer opportunities to reoffend than do offenders on traditional probationary or diversionary programs. Collectively, intermediate punishment programs are generally intended for more serious, habitual or chronic, juvenile offenders, although it is not unusual to place certain first offenders in an intermediate punishment program if the first offense is a particularly serious one.

It is not uncommon for juvenile court judges to impose fines and restitution orders in addition to other program requirements if intermediate punishments are imposed. The use of fines and victim reparations for juvenile offenders is discussed briefly. Each intermediate punishment program presented will also be assessed in terms of its effectiveness at reducing recidivism.

STANDARD PROBATION FOR JUVENILES

Standard juvenile probation is a fairly simple and often routine for most juvenile courts. Of all sentencing options available to juvenile court judges, standard probation is the one used most frequently. The first probation law was enacted in Massachusetts in 1878, although probation was used much earlier. John Augustus is credited with inventing probation in Boston in 1841. *Standard probation is either a conditional or unconditional nonincarcerative disposition of a specified period following an adjudication of delinquency.* An assessment of the organization and administration of juvenile probation services suggests that there is now greater coordination of efforts between various community agencies and juvenile courts, leading to more effective services delivery to juveniles (Hurst and Torbet, 1993).

There are several types of standard probation programs. Like their diversion program counterparts, probation programs for juveniles are either unconditional probation or conditional probation. Again, there are many similarities between probation programs devised for adults and those structured for juvenile offenders. *Unconditional standard probation basically involves complete freedom of movement for juveniles within their communities, perhaps accompanied by periodic reports by telephone or mail with a* probation officer *(PO) or the probation department.* Because a PO's caseload is often high, with several hundred juvenile clients who must be managed, individualized attention cannot be given to most juveniles on standard probation. The period of unsupervised probation varies among jurisdictions depending upon offense seriousness and other circumstances.

Conditional probation programs may include optional conditions and program requirements, such as performing a certain number of hours of public or community service, providing restitution to victims, payment of fines, employment, and/or participation in specific vocational, educational, or therapeutic programs. It is crucial to any probation program that an effective classification system is in place so that juvenile court judges can dispose offenders accordingly. Baird (1985:32–34) suggests that a variation of the National Institute of Corrections' (NIC) Model Classification Project scheme be used for juvenile classifications, where both risk and needs are assessed.

The terms of standard probation are outlined in Figure 11.1. Although these terms may be accompanied by special conditions, known as *special conditions of probation*, more often than not, no special conditions are attached. The basic terms are:

1. To obey one's parents or guardians
2. To obey all laws of the community, including curfew and school laws

3. To follow the school or work program approved by the probation officer

4. To follow the instructions of the probation officer

5. To report in person to the probation officer or court at such times designated by the probation officer

6. To comply with any special conditions of probation

7. To consult with the probation officer when in need of further advice

INSTRUCTIONS:
1. Original to Probation Files
2. Pink to Parents
3. Blue to Minor
4. Goldenrod to Division Officer

ORANGE COUNTY PROBATION DEPARTMENT
INFORMAL PROBATION AGREEMENT

The authority for undertaking a plan of informal probation which may include the use of a crisis resolution home or shelter-care facility is contained in Section 654 of the Welfare and Institutions Code, which is printed in full on the reverse side of this form. Before signing this agreement, please read it and resolve any questions about it with the deputy probation officer.

Minor's Initials   **GENERAL RULES AND REQUIREMENTS**

_____ 1. You are to report in person and submit written reports to your probation officer as directed.

_____ 2. You are to obey all laws, including traffic rules and regulations. You are not to operate a motor vehicle in any street or highway until properly licensed and insured. You are to report to your probation officer any arrests or law violations immediately.

_____ 3. You are to obey the curfew law of the city or county in which you live or any special curfew imposed by the Court or the probation officer, specifically: _____

_____ 4. You are not to leave the State of California or change your residence without first getting permission from your probation officer. Prior to change of residence, you are to nofity your probation officer of the new address. You are not to live with anyone except your parents or approved guardian without specific permission of your probation officer.

_____ 5. You are to attend school every day, every class, as prescribed by law, and obey all school regulations. Suspension from school and/or truancies/tardiness could result in action being taken by the Probation Department. You are to notify your probation officer by 10:00 a.m. on any school day that you are absent from school. If you are home from school because of illness or suspension, you are not to leave your home that day or night except to keep a doctor's appointment.

_____ 6. You are not to use or possess any intoxicants, alcohol, narcotics, other controlled substances, related paraphernalia, poisons, or illegal drugs; including marijuana. You are not to be with anyone who is using or possessing any illegal intoxicants, narcotics or drugs. Do not inhale or attempt to inhale or consume any substance of any type or nature, such as paint, glue, plant material or any aerosol product. You are not to inject anything into your body uness directed so by a medical doctor.

_____ 7. You are not to frequent any places of business disapproved by your probation officer, parents or guardians, specifically:
_____

_____ 8. You are not to associate with individuals disapproved by your probation officer, parents or guardians, specifically: _____
_____

_____ 9. You may be required to participate in any program outlined in Section 654 W&I Code.

_____ 10. You are to seek and maintain counseling if and as directed by the probation officer.

_____ 11. You are not to have any weapons of any description, including firearms, numchucks or martial arts weaponry, and knives of any kind, in your possession while you are on probation, or involve self in activities in which weapons are used, i.e., hunting, target shooting.

_____ 12. You are ordered to obey the following additional terms of probation:
_____
_____

Probation supervision will expire on _____ unless you fail to abide by the above terms and conditions of your probation resulting in court action.

I have personally initialed, read and understand the above rules and requirements of informal probation that apply in my particular case as explained to me by the probation officer. I understand that my failure to comply with the initialed items could result in the petition, that is pending in my case, being filed with the District Attorney.

SIGNED: _____   DATE: _____
                        (minor)

SIGNED: _____   DATE: _____
                        (parent)

SIGNED: _____   DATE: _____
                        (parent)

MICHAEL SHUMACHER
Chief Probation Officer

BY: _____   DATE: _____
              (Deputy Probation Officer)

Thus youths disposed to standard probation experience little change in their social routines. Whenever special conditions of probation are attached, they usually mean additional work for probation officers. Some of these conditions might include medical treatments for drug or alcohol dependencies, individual or group therapy or counseling, or participation in a driver's safety course. In some instances involving theft, burglary, or vandalism, restitution provisions may be included, where youths must repay victims for their financial losses. Most standard probation programs in the United States require little, if any, direct contact with the probation office. Logistically, this works out well for probation officers, who are frequently overworked and have enormous client caseloads of 300 or more youths. However, greater caseloads means less individualized attention devoted to youths by POs, and some of these youths require more supervision than others while on standard probation. Item 12 of the juvenile probation form used by Orange County, California, shown in Figure 11.1, specifies which, if any, special conditions apply for particular juveniles.

Community service orders are increasingly used, although in some states, juvenile probation departments have found it difficult to find personnel to supervise youthful probationers. For instance, a North Dakota delinquent was ordered to perform 200 hours of community service. The community had about 500 residents, and the work ordered involved park maintenance and general cleanup duties. However, the youth never performed any of this community service, since the probation department did not have the money to pay a juvenile probation officer to monitor the youth for the full 200 hours.

In view of the fact that little or no monitoring of juvenile conduct exists in many state probation agencies, standard probation has fairly high rates of recidivism, ranging from 40 to 75 percent. Even certain youth camps operated in various California counties, where some degree of supervision over youths exists, have reported recidivism rates as high as 76 percent among their youthful clientele (Palmer, 1994; Palmer and Wedge, 1994). Therefore, it is often difficult to forecast which juveniles will have the greatest likelihood of reoffending, regardless of the program we are examining.

Early studies by Wolfgang, Figlio, and Sellin (1972) and later investigations by Tracy, Wolfgang, and Figlio (1985) have shown that only a small proportion of juvenile delinquents account for a large proportion of violent crimes. In fact, references are increasingly made to the **chronic 6 percent**, the 6 percent of all juveniles studied by Marvin Wolfgang and his associates from different birth cohorts in 1945 and 1958 that account for over 50 percent of all delinquent acts. In fact, more recent research has been directed at targeting small cores of juvenile offenders who have disproportionately high rates of reoffending. Kurz and Moore (1994) studied 3000 juvenile offenders during 1985 and 1987. These were two cohorts of juveniles who entered the juvenile justice system for the first time during the first six months of these two years. They were both tracked for a three-year period. As it turned out, about 8 percent of each cohort accounted for over half of all subsequent delinquent offenses committed by each cohort. Kurz and Moore used various risk assessment techniques to profile these youths and to suggest subsequent intervention strategies that might be targeted selectively at other youths considered to be high risks to reoffend.

One factor associated with significant reductions in recidivism is restitution. Programs that use restitution and enforce it seem to have lower recidivism rates associated with their youthful clientele (Jacobs and Moore, 1994). In Lincoln, Nebraska, for example, a study evaluated the effectiveness of the **Youth-to-Victim Restitution Project**, a program operated through the Lincoln Juvenile Court. Juveniles are ordered to pay restitution as a condition of probation. To assure their compliance, the juvenile court arranges for and supplies their employment at various jobs. Between 1984 and 1993, 183 youths had participated in the restitution project. Jacobs and Moore found that successful compliance with the court restitution orders was the most significant predictor of recidivism. Specifically, these researchers determined that among the youths ordered to pay restitution, certain variables existed, such as the restitution goal, time given to pay, amount ordered to be paid, and subsequent offenses charged. Youths could be arranged according to a continuum in terms of which youths paid the greatest proportion of restitution. The least amount of recidivism was observed among those who paid the greatest proportion of restitution. Those paying the least amount of restitution or not paying it at all had high rates of delinquency recidivism. Thus it has been found that the use of simple risk instruments alone is ineffective at distinguishing between those who recidivate at different rates (Ashford and LeCroy, 1990). Restitution is a powerful deterrent to further offending. At least a financial connection is made between what the youthful offenders did and how much it cost to compensate victims for their losses (Roy, 1994, 1995). These tangible punishments were considered most effective, therefore, as delinquency deterrents.

Another program described by Leiber and Mawhorr (1995) is the **Second Chance Program**. This was a program established in an Iowa county during the early 1990s. The Juvenile Court in Iowa placed several samples of adjudicated youths into a program, Second Chance, which included social skills training, preemployment training, and job placement opportunities as means of reducing recidivism and delinquency. A one-year follow-up showed that while Second Chance youth had recidivism rates similar to those of a control group not participating in the Second Chance program, the Second Chance participants tended to engage in far less serious offenses.

Four characteristics tended to be associated with program success and long-term recidivism-free behavior: family involvement, treatment integrity, cultural sensitivity, and follow-up care and monitoring (Leiber and Mawhorr, 1995).

California's Juvenile Probation Camps

In the early 1980s, California experimented with several types of **juvenile probation camps** (JPCs) (Palmer and Wedge, 1994). These camps were county-operated and included physical activities, community contacts, and academic training. These nonincarcerative camps were designed as dispositional alternatives to secure custody for youthful offenders. Eligibility requirements included first-offender status and nonviolent behaviors. Counselors worked with youth who were carefully screened before entering the program. Groups of youths were deliberately small to maximize individualized attention for each youth. Older juveniles who participated in these probation camps had lower rates of recidivism than those of younger youths. Overall, the camps were viewed as successful in minimizing recidivism and maximizing rehabilitation of participants.

The Philadelphia Juvenile Probation Department's Intensive Aftercare Probation (IAP) Program

Between 1988 and 1990, the **Intensive Aftercare Program** (IAP) was designed in Philadelphia and targeted serious youthful offenders (Sontheimer and Goodstein, 1993). A sample of 46 youths committed to the Bensalem Youth Development Center was compared with a control group of 46 youths who received traditional aftercare probation services. While the IAP participants exhibited lower rates of recidivism than did those subject to conventional aftercare probation, the differences were not significant. It was reported, however, that IAP officers believed that their interventions with IAP youth were both rapid and positive. Thus some officials believed that they were able to assist some of these IAP participants from incurring subsequent rearrests (Sontheimer and Goodstein, 1993).

On Ineffective Specialized Treatment Programs for Juvenile Probationers

Not all specialized programs involving juvenile probationers are successful. For example, an assessment was made of the **Sexual Offender Treatment** (SOT) **Program** established by a juvenile probation department of a large midwestern U.S. metropolitan county in January 1988 (Lab, Shields, and Schondel, 1993). The program consisted of 20 peer-group meetings with psychosocioeducational intervention focus, supplemented by individual family counseling sessions with youths who had been adjudicated delinquent for assorted sex offenses. Subsequently, an experimental program was conducted for 46 youths referred to the SOT program and compared with a control group of 109 youths assigned to nonsexually specific interventions during the same period. Data sources included juvenile court and program records. Essentially, youths handled by the SOT program fared no better than youths processed through normal, nonoffense-specific programming. Thus these researchers concluded that simply knowing one's symptoms and problems and designing specific interventions for those problems are not always workable. Additional study is needed to identify appropriate treatment factors that might make a difference in reducing their recidivism rates for sexual offending (Lab, Shields, and Schondel, 1993).

Critical Elements Associated with Juvenile Recidivism

Baird (1985:36) cites the following elements that appear to be predictive of future criminal activity and reoffending by juveniles: (1) one's age at first adjudication, (2) a prior criminal record (a combined measure of the number and severity of priors), (3) the number of prior commitments to juvenile facilities, (4) drug or chemical abuse, (5) alcohol abuse, (6) family relationships (parental control), (7) school problems, and (8) peer relationships.

Baird recommends that needs assessments should be individualized, based on the juvenile's past record and other pertinent characteristics, including the present adjudication offense. The level of supervision should vary according to the degree of risk posed to the public by the juvenile. Although Baird furnishes no weighting procedure for the risk factors listed above so that judges can use these criteria effectively at the sentencing stage, he does describe a supervisory scheme that acts as a guide for juvenile probation and aftercare. This scheme would be applied based on the perceived risk of each juvenile offender. His scheme would include the following:

Regular Supervision

1. Four face-to-face contacts per month with youth
2. Two face-to-face contacts per month with parents
3. One face-to-face contact per month with placement staff
4. One contact with school officials

Intensive Supervision

1. Six face-to-face contacts per month with youth
2. Three face-to-face contacts per month with parents

3. One face-to-face contact per month with placement staff

4. Two contacts with school officials

Alternative Care Cases

1. One face-to-face contact per month with youth

2. Four contacts with agency staff (one must be face-to-face)

3. One contact every two months with parents

An assignment to any of these supervision levels should be based on both risk and needs assessments. Baird says that often, agencies make categorical assignments of juveniles to one level of supervision or another, primarily by referring to the highest level of supervision suggested by two or more scales used (Baird, 1985:38). Each juvenile probation agency prefers specific predictive devices, and some agencies use a combination of them. Again, no scale is foolproof, and the matter of false positives and false negatives arises, as some juveniles receive more supervision than they really require, whereas others receive less than they need.

Near the beginning of the twentieth century, when probation began to be used for juvenile supervision, a report was issued entitled *Juvenile Courts and Probation* (Flexner and Baldwin, 1914). Writing seven years following the establishment of the National Probation Association in 1907, Flexner and Baldwin described three important aspects of probation as it applied to juvenile offenders (Hurst, 1990a:17):

1. The period of probation should always be indeterminate because judges cannot possibly fix the period of treatment in advance.

2. To be effective, probation work must be performed by full-time, professionally trained probation officers.

3. Probation is not a judicial function.

It is interesting to see how Flexner and Baldwin openly discounted the value of the judiciary in fixing one's term of probation and performing supervisory functions. They are adamant in the belief that only professional probation officers should engage in such supervisory tasks, and that the judicial function should be minimal. The strong treatment orientation of probation is apparent as well, suggesting their belief that probationer treatment programs should be tailored to fit the probationer's needs. Further, they underscore the power originally assigned to probation officers and the leverage that probation officers could exert on their clients, including possible probation revocation action if program infractions occurred.

An effective probation program is one where probation officers (POs) have an awareness of the juvenile offender's needs and weaknesses. One problem in many existing probation programs is that POs find it hard to establish rapport between themselves and their juvenile clients. A high degree of mistrust exists, in large part because of the age differential between the PO and offender.

Some POs have suggested an approach normally practiced by psychological counselors in developing rapport between themselves and their clients. Sweet (1985:90) suggests, for instance, that each PO should (1) thoroughly review the youth's case, including family and juvenile interviews and other background information; (2) engage in introspection and attempt to discover his or her own reactions to adolescents and responses to verbal exchanges; (3) attempt to cultivate a relationship of acceptance rather than rejection and punitiveness; (4) react favorably to a "critical incident," where the juvenile may "screw up" and expect reprimand or punishment but where acceptance and understanding are reflected instead; and (5) follow-through with continued support, which bolsters juvenile confidence in the PO.

Some juveniles are unreachable through any kind of effective exchange. Chronic offenders, hard-core offenders, or psychologically disturbed juveniles frequently reject any attempts by authorities to understand them or assist them in any task. However, sometimes it is the PO who has lost a "clear sense of what their mission is and how it is a part of the larger juvenile justice system" (Breed and Krisberg, 1986:15). This is possibly one consequence of the current trend toward a more punitive approach to juvenile crime (Byrne, Lurigio, and Petersilia, 1992; Woodward and English, 1993).

THE SUCCESS OF STANDARD JUVENILE PROBATION

The successfulness of standard juvenile probation as well as other probation and parole programs is measured according to the **recidivism rate** accompanying these program alternatives. **Recidivism** is measured in various ways, including rearrests, reconvictions, new adjudications, return to secure confinement, movement from standard probation to intensive supervised probation, and simple probation program condition violations, such as drug use or alcohol and curfew violation. One of the best discussions of recidivism and its numerous definitions is *Recidivism,* by Michael Maltz (1984).

The most popular meaning of *recidivism* is a new adjudication as delinquent for reoffending. It is generally the case that, with exceptions, intensive supervision programs have less associated recidivism than does standard probation. Over the years, a recidivism standard of 30 percent has been established among researchers as the cutting point between a successful probation program and an unsuccessful one. Programs with recidivism rates of 30 percent or less are considered successful, whereas those programs with more than 30 percent recidivism are not particularly successful.

This figure is arbitrary, although it is most often used as a success standard. Those programs with more than 30 percent recidivism are not particularly successful, while those with 30 percent or less recidivism are considered more successful. No program presently has zero percent recidivism.

Standard probation, which means little or no direct and regular supervision of offenders by probation officers, has a fairly high rate of recidivism among the various state jurisdictions. Recidivism rates for juveniles on standard probation range from 30 to 70 percent, depending on the nature of their offenses and prior records. Not all intensive supervision programs have low rates of recidivism, however. Clarke and Craddock (1987) report, for instance, that for samples of North Carolina probationers exposed to two types of probation programs, **intensive supervised probation** (ISP) and standard probation, intensive probation juveniles had a recidivism rate of 64 percent. This is compared with a recidivism rate of 34 percent for standard probationers. Clarke and Craddock suggested that one reason for this unusual difference was that the intensive probationer sample consisted of high-risk juveniles with a greater likelihood of reoffending. Thus some amount of natural selection occurred, where the more hard-core offenders received closer probation supervision. For some juvenile clients, it matters little whether they are intensively supervised or placed under standard probation, since they will probably reoffend later anyway. Recidivism rates for adults on probation are very similar to those of juvenile offenders. Recidivism rates for both adult probationers and parolees range from 60 to 70 percent during one- to two-year follow-up studies of these adult clientele (Maguire and Pastore, 1996).

INTERMEDIATE PUNISHMENTS FOR JUVENILE OFFENDERS

Intermediate punishments are community-based sanctions that range from intensive probation supervision to nonsecure custodial programs. These programs include more intensive monitoring or management of juvenile behaviors through more intensive supervision (Jackson, deKeijser, and Michon, 1995). They may include home confinement, electronic monitoring, or both. Other community-based services are included, where the goal is to maintain fairly close supervision over youthful offenders (Gowdy, 1993; Petersilia and Turner, 1990).

Intermediate punishment programs are operated in every state for both juvenile and adult offenders. They are sometimes referred to as **creative sentencing**, since they are somewhere between standard probationary dispositions and traditional incarcerative terms that might be imposed by judges (Brandau, 1992; Koehler and Lindner, 1992). These alternatives to incarceration are regarded as positive interventions for a majority of today's youth who are brought to the attention of the juvenile justice system (Hepburn et al., 1992; Jones and Krisberg, 1994).

Some General Goals of Intermediate Punishment Programs

There is considerable variation among intermediate punishment programs, although they tend to exhibit similar goals or objectives. These include, but are not limited to:

1. Provision of less expensive sanctions compared with secure confinement
2. Achievement of lower rates of recidivism than with standard probation
3. Greater emphasis on reintegration into communities as the primary correctional goal
4. Provision of greater range of community services and organizations in a cooperative effort to assist youthful offenders
5. Minimization of adverse influence of labeling that might stem from secure confinement
6. Improvement in personal educational and vocational skills of individual offenders, together with acquisition of better self-concepts and greater acceptance of responsibility for one's actions

In Colorado, for example, an ISP program has been established to divert prison-bound youthful offenders (English, Chadwick, and Pullen, 1994). Colorado juvenile agency records were obtained for 2782 offenders who were sentenced to prison; 933 to community corrections; and 3214 to probation, including 200 sentences to ISP. A 12-month follow-up of 247 ISP cases matched with comparable samples of offenders sentenced to probation and community corrections was conducted. ISP was successful in diverting offenders from prison while adequately protecting the public, and at a lower cost than community corrections or prison. The program diverted offenders with rather lengthy juvenile records and adult arrests for violent crimes. ISP offenders were six times as likely to be terminated from the program because of technical violations than for a new crime, which suggests that increased surveillance of these offenders directly detects more technical program infractions. Most of the time, these infractions are not particularly serious (e.g., violating curfew, minor use of alcohol). The cost savings of the Colorado ISP program was substantial. It was estimated by English and her associates that the average daily cost of supervising ISP clients was about $6, while community corrections average daily costs were $33 and prison was $53. These researchers have recommended that their ISP program should be replicated elsewhere to see if similar results are obtained with ISP clients in other jurisdictions. Related research by Woodward and English (1993) has yielded similar findings about ISP programs.

Earlier in 1989, several ISP programs were assessed by Krisberg et al. (1989). These included:

1. The Key Program, Inc. (Massachusetts)
2. The Associated Marine Institutes, Inc. Program (Florida)
3. The Youth Advocate Programs, Inc. (Pennsylvania)
4. The Kentfields Rehabilitation Program (Michigan)
5. The Firestone Community Day Center (California)
6. The Pennsylvania Intensive Probation Supervision Program (Pennsylvania)
7. The Specialized Gang Supervision Program (California)
8. The Hennepin County Surveillance Program (Minnesota)
9. The Ramsey County Juvenile Intensive Supervision Project (Minnesota)
10. The Lucas County Intensive Supervision Unit (Ohio)
11. The Wayne County Intensive Probation Program (Michigan)

Subsequent follow-ups of these programs indicated that whereas recidivism of participating youths was not entirely eliminated, most of these programs exhibited reasonably low rates of recidivism among participating juveniles. Some experts refer to these and similar programs under the general category of creative sentencing or **smart sentencing**, inasmuch as they do not require secure confinement and offer meaningful and rehabilitative alternatives to youths who would otherwise be incarcerated (Byrne, Lurigio, and Petersilia, 1992).

Classification Criteria for Placement in ISP Programs

One problem for juvenile court judges is deciding which juveniles should be assigned to which programs (Hale et al., 1991). This is a classification problem, and the level of accuracy associated with juvenile risk prediction instruments is about as poor as adult risk-prediction devices (Baird, 1985). This problem is considered one of correction's greatest challenges (Joyce, 1985:86). Nevertheless, judges attempt to make secure or nonsecure confinement decisions on the basis of the following elements (Baird, 1985:34):

1. Classification based on risk of continued criminal activity and the offender's need for services
2. A case management classification system designed to help probation and parole officers develop effective case plans and select appropriate casework strategies

3. A management information system designed to enhance planning, monitoring, evaluation, and accountability

4. A workload deployment system that allows agencies to allocate their limited resources effectively and efficiently

Chronic recidivists and serious offenders are prime candidates for secure confinement. However, an increasing number of community-based programs are being designed to supervise such offenders closely and offer them needed services and treatments. It is helpful to review briefly some of the issues relating to the effectiveness of such instrumentation (Jacobs and Moore, 1994).

Classification of any offender is made difficult by the fact that the state of the art is such in predictions of risk and dangerousness that little future behavior can be forecasted accurately. This holds for juveniles as well as adults. We know that status offenders may or may not escalate to more serious offenses, with the prevailing sentiment favoring or implying nonescalation (Datesman and Aickin, 1985; Nagoshi, 1986). Effective classification schemes have not been devised, although we know that on the basis of descriptions of existing offender aggregates, gender, age, nature of offense, seriousness of offense, race or ethnicity, and socioeconomic status are more or less correlated.

The flaws of various classification schemes are made more apparent when program "failures" are detected in large numbers. Juvenile court judges make the wrong judgments and decisions about juvenile placements. Intake officers make similar errors of classification when conducting initial screenings of juveniles. The issue of false positives and false negatives is relevant here, because some youths may be unfairly overpenalized for what authorities believe are valid predictive criteria of their future dangerousness. Also, some youths are wrongfully underpenalized, because it is believed that they will not pose risks or commit serious offenses in the future, and they do (Gottfredson and Tonry, 1987; Gottfredson and Gottfredson, 1988). Two classification instruments used for determining community-based agency and program placements are the *Delaware Initial Security Placement Instrument* and the *Florida Dangerousness Instrument.* Figures 11.2 and 11.3 show the contents of these instruments and the points assigned for various offenses and prior adjudications.

Depending on the scores received by various juvenile clients when classified, they may or may not be entitled to assignment to intensive supervised probation or to a community-based program. Theoretically, those youthful offenders who are considered dangerous and violent are poor candidates for inclusion, because it is predicted that they might harm themselves or others, including agency staff or probation officers. Also, those considered not dangerous would be predicted to be good candidates as program

FIGURE 11.2   Delaware Initial Security Placement Instrument

Initial Security Placement Instrument

Date:_____

File no.:_____

Score:_____

1. Name

2. D.O.B.

3. Date of current commitment

4. Current most serious instant offense which resulted in adjudication and present commitment

5. Most serious prior adjudicated offense
   (against person)

6. Number of prior felony adjudications

7. Open felony charges   Yes____ No_____ Specify_____

8. History of in-patient psychiatric hospitalization

                                            Yes____   No____

   I. Severity of current offense

      Class A felony (10 pts)   _____

      Class B felony (7 pts)   _____

   II. Most serious prior adjudication

      Class A felony (5 pts)   _____

      Class B felony (3 pts) (exclude escape)   _____

   III. Number of prior adjudications for felonies—three
        or more in last two years (pts)   _____

   IV. Prior out-of-home court ordered placement
       as a result of adjudication for delinquent act

                                            Yes (1 pt) _____

                                            No (0 pt) _____ _____

                                            TOTAL   _____

Source: Naneen Karraker et al., *Public Safety with Care: A Model System for Juvenile Justice in Hawaii.* San Francisco, CA: National Center on Institutions and Alternatives, 1988:84).

clients. However, the flaws of our instrumentation do not always discriminate effectively. Ironically, Karraker, Macallair, and Schiraldi (1988:88) report that in some jurisdictions, such as Massachusetts, secure confinement has been used unsuccessfully with violent juveniles, and they appear most responsive when assigned to nonsecure programs, including ISP and community-based projects.

FIGURE 11.3   Florida Dangerousness Instrument

DANGEROUSNESS

1. Present alleged offense is:

   _____First-degree felony   THE CHARGE IS_____

   Score 6 points for first-degree. SCORE = _____

   _____Second-degree felony THE CHARGE IS _____

   _____Third-degree felony THE CHARGE IS _____

2. The alleged offense required the victim to receive medical attention.
   YES   NO   If yes, explain _____

   _____

   Score 1 point for yes, and "0" for no. SCORE = _____

3. The alleged offense involved an overt THREAT of physical harm to another person.
   YES   NO   If yes, explain _____

   _____

   Score 1 point for a yes answer and "0" for no. SCORE = _____

4. How many adjudicated felonies does the alleged perpetrator have during the last 2 years?

   _____

   Score 1 point for two (2) or more and "0" for less than 2. SCORE = ____

5. How many adjudicated violent felonies does the alleged perpetrator have during the last 2 years?

   _____

   Score 1 point for 2 or more and "0" for less than 2. SCORE = _____

   TOTAL SCORE FOR DANGEROUSNESS = _____

   Six (6) or above = high dangerousness
   3–5 = moderate dangerousness
   Below 3 = low dangerousness

Source: Karraker, Macallair, and Schiraldi, 1988:84.

Butts and DeMuro (1989) have reached similar conclusions, and they caution that risk assessment instruments may suggest institutionalization for some youths who might be better accommodated by alternative, nonsecure programs that are a part of ISP. In their investigations of risk assessments and placements of samples of Massachusetts youths under the supervision of the Division for Children and Youth Services (DCYS), they found that most youths have had prior delinquency adjudications, records of drug or alcohol abuse, and families that were dependent on public assistance in the recent past. They support juvenile court actions that involve a graduated series of sanctions to handle nonviolent youths who violate their probationary conditions. They also favor the development of strong, nonresidential, alternative schools/attention centers in lieu of traditional incarceration in state facilities. However, they recognize a continuing problem that causes many juvenile court jurisdictions to incarcerate large numbers of youths who actually should receive some ISP nonincarcerative alternative. The problem is that inadequate resources in many of these jurisdictions have inhibited the development of ISP programs that would, ironically, lower the cost of institutionalization.

INTENSIVE SUPERVISED PROBATION FOR JUVENILES

Intensive supervised probation (ISP) programs, also known as **intensive probation supervision** (*IPS*), have become increasingly popular for managing nonincarcerated offender populations (Snyder and Marshall, 1990). ("ISP" is used here to describe the programs developed in different jurisdictions, regardless of whether the ISP or IPS designation is used by individual programs.) Since the mid-1960s, these programs have been aimed primarily at supervising adult offenders closely, and in recent years, ISP programs have been designed for juvenile offenders as well (Armstrong, 1988:342). *Intensive supervised probation is a highly structured and conditional supervision program for either adult or juvenile offenders that serves as an alternative to incarceration and provides for an acceptable level of public safety* (Armstrong, 1988:343). For administrators of secure facilities for juveniles, community-based options such as ISP are desirable, since overcrowding is reduced (Koehler and Lindner, 1992).

Characteristics of ISP Programs

ISP programs for juveniles have been developed and are currently operating in about half of all U.S. jurisdictions (Armstrong, 1988; Wiebush, 1990). Two popular adult ISP programs that have been copied and applied to juveniles in certain jurisdictions are the **New Jersey ISP Model** (Pearson and Bibel, 1986) and the **Georgia ISP Model** (Erwin, 1986). Typically, both of these programs are intended for prison-bound offenders and are perceived as one means of alleviating jail and prison overcrowding.

1. *The Georgia ISP Model.* The Georgia ISP model, considered by some experts to be the toughest probation program for adults in the United States, is a three-phase enterprise and includes five face-to-face contacts per week with offenders; 132 hours of mandatory community service; mandatory curfew; mandatory employment; weekly checks of local arrest records; routine alcohol and drug screenings; a 25-client caseload for POs; PO-determined counseling, vocational/educational offender training; and regular court reports on offender progress. Offenders are in the Georgia program for an indeterminate period, usually from 6 to 12 months.

2. *The New Jersey ISP Model.* The New Jersey ISP model is an 18-month program, featuring 20 PO–client contacts during the first 14 months (with at least 12 of these visits being face to face during the first six months); regular curfew checks; employment checks; payment of fines; victim restitution; and program maintenance costs; drug and alcohol screenings; community service work; maintenance by clients of a daily diary of their progress and improvement; and a PO caseload of 25.

Both the Georgia and New Jersey ISP programs have exhibited low rates of recidivism among adult clients, or recidivism rates of less than 30 percent. However, they have been criticized because their clients are hand-picked and "creamed" from the most eligible offenders, and thus they are among the least likely candidates to reoffend anyway.

Similar to their adult ISP program counterparts, juvenile ISP (JISP) programs are ideally designed for secure incarceration-bound youths and are considered as acceptable alternatives to incarceration. According to Armstrong (1988:342), this is what JISP programs were always meant to be. Armstrong differentiates JISP programs from other forms of standard probation by citing obvious differences in the amount of officer–client contact during the course of the probationary period. For example, standard probation is considered no more than two face-to-face officer–client contacts per month. He says that JISP programs might differ from standard probation according to the following face-to-face criteria: (1) two or three times per week versus once per month, (2) once per week versus twice per month, or (3) four times per week versus once per week (the latter figure being unusually high for standard probation contact) (Armstrong, 1988:346).

The brokerage nature of probation officer dispositions toward their work is evident in the different types of services provided by the different JISP programs investigated by Armstrong. For example, of the 55 programs he examined (92 percent of his total program sample), he found that the following range of services, skills, and resources were mentioned as being brokered by POs in different jurisdictions:

1. Mental health counseling
2. Drug and alcohol counseling
3. Academic achievement and aptitude testing
4. Vocational and employment training
5. Individual, group, and family counseling
6. Job search and placement programs
7. Alternative education programs
8. Foster grandparents programs
9. Big Brother/Big Sister programs

Wiebush (1990:26) cautions that not all ISP programs are alike. Nevertheless, many juvenile ISP programs share similarities, including the following (Armstrong, 1991):

1. The shortcomings of traditional responses to serious and/or chronic offenders (e.g., incarceration or out-of-home placement) are recognized.

2. There are severe resource constraints within jurisdictions that compel many probation departments to adopt agencywide classification and workload deployment systems for targeting a disproportionate share of resources for the most problematic juvenile offenders.

3. Programs are intended to reduce the incidence of incarceration in juvenile secure confinement facilities and reduce overcrowding

4. Programs tend to include aggressive supervision and control elements as a part of the get-tough movement.

5. All programs have a vested interest in rehabilitation of youthful offenders.

From these analyses of ISP program content generally, we can glean the following as basic characteristics of ISP programs (Clear, 1991; Fagan and Reinarman, 1991; Feinberg, 1991):

1. Low officer–client caseloads (i.e., 30 or fewer probationers)

2. High levels of offender accountability (e.g., victim restitution, community service, payment of fines, partial defrayment of program expenses)

3. High levels of offender responsibility

4. High levels of offender control (home confinement, electronic monitoring, frequent face-to-face visits by POs)

5. Frequent checks for arrests, drug and/or alcohol use, and employment or school attendance (drug or alcohol screening, coordination with police departments and juvenile halls, teachers, family).

An excellent illustration of the value of JISP has been described as the **Ohio experience** by Richard G. Wiebush (1990). Wiebush has compared three different Ohio counties that have used different ISP programs for their juvenile offenders, as well as the Ohio Department of Youth Services (ODYS). The different counties include Delaware County (predominantly rural), Lucas County (Toledo), and Cuyahoga County (Cleveland). The ODYS is state operated and manages the most serious offenders, since these are exclusively felony offenders on parole from secure confinement. In each of the county jurisdictions, most of the offenders are incarceration bound, with the exception of the Lucas County juveniles, who are disposed to ISP after having their original dispositions of secure confinement reversed by juvenile court judges. Tables 11.1 and

11.2 show the basic parameters of the different Ohio programs as well as the program sizes and staffing patterns.

An inspection of Table 11.1 shows the different types of agencies involved, the particular program models used by each, and the types of juvenile offender-clients served. Each of the programs uses risk scores for client inclusion, with the exception of the Lucas County program. Table 11.2 shows that all four programs follow a four-phase plan, where the intensity of supervision and surveillance over offenders is gradually reduced after particular time intervals. The ODYS program elects to reevaluate juveniles at three-, five-, and seven-month intervals, through the use of a risk assessment device, rather than to graduate them to new phases automatically.

The Delaware JISP program targets those juveniles with a high propensity to recidivate as well as more serious felony offenders who are incarceration-bound. Youths begin the program with a five-day incarceration, followed by two weeks of house arrest. Later, they must observe cur-

TABLE 11.1

Basic Parameters of the Ohio Programs: Models, Goals, and Client Selection

| Characteristic | Jurisdiction | | | |
	Delaware	Lucas	Cuyahoga	ODYS
Agency type	County probation	County probation	County probation	State parole
Program model	Progation enhancement and alternative incarceration	Alternative to incarceration	Probation enhancement	Probation enhancement
Program goals	Reduced recidivism Reduced commitments	Reduced commitments Reduced commitments	Reduced recidivism	Reduced recidivism Reduced recommitment
	Reduced overhead placement		Reduced overhead placement	
Primary client selection criterion	High-risk schore	Postcommitment status	High-risk score	High-risk score
Additional criteria	Chronic felony offenders; high	Excluded offenses = use of weapon, victim injury, drug trafficking	Status offenders excluded	Metro area resident; 2 + violent offenders included auto matically
Philosophy, supervision emphasis	All stress "balanced" approach—relatively equal emphasis on public safety and rehabilitation.			

Source: Richard G. Wiebush, "Programmatic Variations in Intensive Supervision for Juveniles: The Ohio Experience," *Perspectives* **14**:28 (1990).

TABLE 11.2

ISP Program Size and Staffing Patterns

Characteristic	Jurisdiction			
	Delaware	Lucas	Cuyahoga	ODYS
Total agency caseload[a]	225	500	1500	1500
ISP caseload	17	60	360[b]	525
ISP staff/youth ratio (probation/parole officers)	1:17	1:15	1:30	1:13
Surveillance staff/youth ratio	2:17	2.5:60	3:60	2:39
Team configuration	Court administrator	1 unit supervisor	1 team leader	3 ISP Pos
	1 ISP PO	4 ISP Pos	2 ISP Pos	2 surveillance staff (part-time)
	2 surveillance staff (part-time)	2 surveillance staff (full-time)	3 surveillance staff (full-time)	
	Student interns	2 surveillance staff (part-time)		
	Family advocates	3 comm. service staff (part-time)		
Number of teams	1	1	6	1–3 per region, 14 total
Coverage	7 days; 14 hours/day	7 days; 14 hours/day	7 days; 24 hours/day	7 days; 14 hours/day

[a]Caseload = cases under supervision at any one time.
[b]Projected figure for summer 1989.

Source: Richard G. Wiebush, "Programmatic Variations in Intensive Supervision for Juveniles: The Ohio Experience," *Perspectives* **14:**29 (1990).

fews, attend school and complete school work satisfactorily, report daily to the probation office, and submit to periodic urinalysis. Each youth's progress is monitored by intensive counselors and surveillance staff 16 hours a day, seven days a week. Wiebush says that although the Delaware program has a rather strict approach, it embodies rehabilitation as a primary program objective. The Delaware program has about a 40 percent recidivism rate, which is high, although it is better than the 75 percent rate of recidivism among the general juvenile court population of high-risk offenders elsewhere in Ohio jurisdictions.

In Lucas County, program officials select clients from those already serving incarcerative terms and who are considered high-risk offenders. Lucas County officials wished to use this particular selection method, since they wanted to avoid any appearance of net widening that their JISP program might reflect. Drawing from those already incarcerated seemed the best strategy in this case. The Lucas program is similar to the Delaware program in its treatment and control approaches. However, the Lucas program obligates offenders to perform up to 100 hours of community service as a program condition. House arrest, curfew, and other Delaware program requirements are also found in the Lucas program. The successfulness of the Lucas program has not been evaluated fully, although it reduced institutional commitments by about 110 percent between 1986 and 1987.

The Cuyahoga County program (Cleveland) was one of the first of several ISP programs in Ohio's metropolitan jurisdictions. It is perhaps the largest county program, with 1500 clients at any given time, as well as six juvenile court judges and 72 supervisory personnel. One innovation of the Cuyahoga program was the development of a team approach to client surveillance and management. Like the other county programs, this program performs certain broker functions by referring its clients to an assortment of community-based services and treatments during the program duration. Currently, there are six teams of surveillance officers, who each serve about 60 youths. These teams are comprised of a team leader, two counselors, and three surveillance staff. The nature of contact standards for this and the other three programs are shown in Table 11.3. In 1989, an interim evaluation of the Cuyahoga program was made by Hamparian and Sametz (1989). This evaluation showed that the rate of recidivism among Cuyahoga clients was about 31 percent during a nine-month follow-up. Additional evaluations of the program were being made at the time of this writing.

The ODYS program operates the state's nine training schools in addition to supervising the 3000 youths each year who are released on parole. The ODYS has 93 youth counselors to staff seven regional offices. The ODYS began JISP in February 1988 and supervised those high-risk offenders with a predicted future recidivism rate of 75 percent or higher. Since these clients were all prior felony offenders with lengthy adjudication records, they were considered the most serious group to be supervised. Accordingly, the ODYS supervision and surveillance structure exhibited the greatest degree of offender monitoring. The team approach has been used by the ODYS, with teams consisting of three youth counselors and two surveillance staff. Because of geographical considerations, some variations have been observed among teams regarding the numbers of offenders supervised as well as the intensity of their supervision or surveillance. Basically, the ODYS program incorporated many of the program conditions that were included in the various county programs. These conditions or components have been divided into *control* components and *treatment* components and are shown in Tables 11.4 and 11.5, respectively.

TABLE 11.3

Contact Standards by Type and Phase

Type of Contact[a]	Jurisdiction[b]			
	Delaware	Lucas	Cuyahoga	ODYS[c]
Phase I				
PO, direct with youth	5/week	2/week	1/week	6.5/month
Family, direct	n.s.	4/month	n.s.	2/month
Surveillance	11/week	14/week	17/week	4/week
Duration (minimum)	21 days	30 days	30 days	90 days
Phase II				
PO, direct with youth	5/week	2/week	1/week	4–6/month
Family, direct	n.s.	2/month	n.s.	2/month
Surveillance	11/week	10/week	8/week	4/week
Duration	28 days	50 days	75 days	60 days
Phase III				
PO, direct with youth	3/week	1/week	1/week	2–6/month
Family, direct	n.s.	2/month	n.s.	1/month
Surveillance	0–11/week	7/week	5/week	2–4/week
Duration	70 days	50 days	75 days	60 days
Phase IV				
PO, direct with youth	1–3/week	2/month	As needed	2–6/month
Family, direct	n.s.	1/month	n.s.	1/month
Surveillance	None	5/week	3/week	2–4/week
Duration	By contract	26 days	75 days	60 days

[a]Surveillance includes direct and telephone contacts.
[b]n.s., not specified.
[c] Ohio Department of Youth Services does not use phase sytem to govern youth movement through the program. Youths are classified at three, five, and seven months, based on reassessment of risk.

Source: Richard G. Wiebush, "Programmatic Variations in Intensive Supervision for Juveniles: The Ohio Experience," *Perspectives* **14**:30 (1990).

Since its creation, the JISP program operated by the ODYS has exhibited a drop in its recidivism rate. On the basis of a comparison of the first year of its operation with recidivism figures for its clients from the preceding year, the ODYS program had a 34 percent reduction in its rate of recidivism. Further, a 39 percent reduction in parole revocations occurred. This is significant, considering the high-risk nature of the offender population being managed.

Wiebush notes that all these programs have required enormous investments of time and energy by high-quality staff. Further, each program has illustrated how best to utilize existing community resources to further its objectives and best serve juvenile clients in need. However, Wiebush says that what is good for Ohio probationers and parolees may not necessarily

TABLE 11.4

Program Components: Control Elements[a]

Component	Jurisdiction			
	Delaware	Lucas	Cuyahoga	ODYS
Surveillance	×	×	×	×
Curfew	×	×	×	×
Front-end detention	×	—[b]	—	—
House arrest	×	×	×	o
Prior permission	×	—	—	—
Electronic surveillance	—	—	o	—
Urinalysis	o	×	o	o
Daily sanctioning (phase system)	×	×	×	—
Hourly school reports	×	×	×	—
Formal graduated sanction schedule	—	×	—	×

Source: Richard G. Wiebush, "Programmatic Variations in Intensive Supervision for Juveniles," *Perspectives* **14**:31 (1990).

[a]× = Mandatory component; — = component not available; o = component optional, varies by youth.
[b]Most Lucas ISP youth do have front-end detention, but it is not mandated.

be suitable for those offenders of other jurisdictions. Nevertheless, these programs function as potential models after which programs in other jurisdictions may be patterned.

Mardon (1991) has described other programs designed for both male and female juvenile offenders. The Youth Center in Beloit, Kansas, is the state's only institutional facility for female juvenile offenders. The emphasis of treatment programs at the Youth Center is assisting these female youths to deal with problems of sexual abuse, which many of these offenders have experienced. Besides treatment, the females are exposed to vocational and educational experiences designed to prepare them for useful lives once they are released. Another program described by Mardon is the Fort Smallwood Marine Institute near Baltimore, Maryland. This program was established in 1988. Between 1988 and 1991, approximately 225 delinquent youths have been treated successfully.

Similar programs described by Mardon include the Eckerd Youth Challenge Program, which is a community-based alternative to placing adjudicated youths in training schools. Youths are housed in residences at this site, and they participate in programs designed to improve their

TABLE 11.5

Program Components: Treatment Elements[a]

Component	Jurisdiction			
	Delaware	Lucas	Cuyahoga	ODYS
Individualized contracts	×	×	×	×
Individual counseling (non-PO)	o	o	o	o
Family counseling or family conferences	o	×	o	o
Group counseling	×	×	o	o
In-home family services	×	—	×	—
Community sponsors, advocates	—	—	—	–
Alternative education	o	o	o	o
Job training	o	o	o	o
Substance abuse counseling	o	o	o	o
School attendance (or work)	×	×	×	×
Community service	o	×	o	o
Restitution	o	o	o	o

Source: Richard G. Wiebush, "Programmatic Variations in Intensive Supervision for Juveniles," *Perspectives* **14**:32 (1990).

[a]× = Mandatory component; — = component not available; o = component optional, varies by youth.

interpersonal and living skills. Experiential and action-oriented phases of this program include activities such as hikes, canoe trips, and community service projects.

WEAKNESSES AND STRENGTHS OF ISP PROGRAMS

An underlying weakness of most JISP programs is that local demands and needs vary to such an extent among jurisdictions that after 25 years we have yet to devise a standard definition of what is meant by *intensive supervised probation* (Ellsworth, 1988:28). Thus the dominant themes of current ISP programs appear to be (1) those which are designed as "front-end" alternatives to secure confinement, (2) those which combine incarceration with some degree of community supervision (shock probation), and (3) those that follow secure confinement.

Ellsworth's insightful analysis of the progress of developing ISP programs in the United States since the early 1960s highlights certain problems that JISP programs are currently facing. One of the first strategies employed by probation departments was the "numbers-game" reshuffling of caseloads, where reduced caseloads for POs were ordered to improve officer–client interpersonal contact. It was argued that reduced caseloads would necessarily intensify the supervision as well as the supervisory quality of client–offenders. Several recent studies have experimented with varying degrees of officer–client contact and recidivism rates [see Sontheimer, Goodstein, and Kovacevic (1990) for a review of some of these studies]. PO caseload reductions were mandated by one of the recommendations of the Task Force on Corrections appointed by the President's Commission on Law Enforcement and the Administration of Justice in 1967.

However, a project investigating the differential recidivism rates of probationers supervised more or less intensively and conducted subsequently in San Francisco, known as the **San Francisco Project**, did much to undermine the nation's confidence in manipulating sheer caseload numbers (Banks, Siler, and Rardin, 1977). The San Francisco Project compared recidivism rates of probationers supervised by POs with caseloads of 20 and 40, respectively, with the former caseloads defined by probation departments as "intensive" and the latter caseloads defined as "ideal." No significant differences in recidivism rates of probationers were reported between intensive and ideal caseload scenarios. In fact, those POs with caseloads of 20 probationers reported more technical program violations (e.g., curfew violations, traveling violations, drug or alcohol violations) than did those POs with caseloads of 40 probationers. Greater offender monitoring simply made it possible for POs to spot more program violators.

Despite the methodological and theoretical flaws cited by various critics of the San Francisco Project, the study suggested that something beyond sheer numbers of cases assigned POs should be an integral part of the officer–client relation. Ellsworth (1988:28–29) says that the next step to be taken by probation departments was the construction of risk/needs assessment instruments and classification systems that would enable probation departments to plan their case assignments more effectively. One of these instruments was the Wisconsin Case Classification System, which introduced the idea of *case supervision planning* through the Client Management Classification interview. This interview purportedly enabled POs to proactively supervise their clients more effectively, since they could identify in advance certain problems that otherwise would interfere with productive officer–client relationships. Therefore, instead of reacting to client problems whenever they surfaced, POs could anticipate certain client problems and take steps to deal with them in advance of their occurrence (Ellsworth, 1988:28).

Subsequently, various probation departments implemented case assignment policies according to a finer degree of specialization than case allocation procedures formerly used. Those offenders with drug abuse problems would be grouped according to this problem and assigned to POs who acquired a drug abuse specialty. Ideally, probation departments would benefit because officers would be assigned cases they enjoyed working with and where their particular skills could be maximized. They would be in a better position to understand client problems and to be better enablers and brokers for their clients, arranging contacts between them and existing community services.

Unfortunately, there have been unanticipated consequences arising from such case supervision planning. Intradepartmental jealousies and a lack of POs with specific competencies have made it either impossible or impractical for certain probation departments to implement case supervision planning fully. Further, specialized case allocations have at times undermined the officer–client relation, since the enforcement nature of PO work has sometimes collapsed through changing interpersonal relationships. In short, some officers have become too close (emotionally) to their offender–clients to the extent that they are no longer effective enforcers of other program requirements. Ellsworth (1988:29) indicates that currently, a basic incompatibility exists between POs who favor a law-and-order approach to PO work (consistent with the get-tough philosophy) and those who favor a rehabilitation or treatment approach that is closely associated with the case planning process. Case supervision planning, therefore, is considered irrelevant by some POs, since in their view, the primary function of POs is to conduct surveillance activities, control the behaviors of their clients, ensure offender accountability, and ensure offender compliance with program conditions.

Case supervision planning makes more sense if we consider several alternative case assignment strategies that are presently used by different probation departments. The most popular model is the **conventional model**, the random assignment of probationers to POs on the basis of one's present caseload in relation to others. This is much like the **numbers game model**, where total probationers are divided by the total POs in a given department and each PO is allocated an equal share of the supervisory task. Thus POs may supervise both very dangerous and nondangerous probationers. Another model is the **conventional model with geographic considerations**. Simply, this is assigning probationers to POs who live in a common geographic area. The intent is to shorten PO travel between clients. Again, little or no consideration is given to an offender's needs or dangerousness in relation to PO skills. The **specialized caseloads model** is the model used for case supervision planning, where offender assignments are made on the basis of client risks and needs and PO skills and interests in dealing with those offender risks and needs (Carlson and Parks, 1979).

Some of the problems of JISP have been attributable to different case-load assignment models or to other organizational peculiarities and conflicting organizational goals that interfere with the performance of juvenile PO roles. One solution is referred to as the *balanced approach*, and it has been described by Virginia Department of Youth and Family Services (1995). *The **balanced approach** to juvenile probation is neither a wholly punitive nor rehabilitative formulation, but rather is a more broad-based, constructive approach. It operates on the assumption that decision making must take into consideration the converging interests of all involved parties in the juvenile justice process, including offenders, victims, the community at large, and the system itself. No party to the decision making should benefit at the expense of another party; rather, a balancing of interests should be sought. The balanced approach, therefore, simultaneously emphasizes community protection, offender accountability, individualization of treatments, and competency assessment and development.*

The balanced approach obligates community leaders and juvenile justice system actors to consider their individual juvenile codes and determine whether a balance exists between offender needs and community interests. Punitive provisions of these codes should address victim needs as well as the needs of juvenile offenders, to the extent that restitution and victim compensation are a part of improving an offender's accountability and acceptance of responsibility. The fairness of the juvenile justice system should be assessed by key community leaders, and a mission statement should be drafted that has the broad support of diverse community organizations. Training programs can be created through the close coordination of chief probation officers in different jurisdictions, where offender needs may be targeted and addressed. All facets of the community and the juvenile justice process should be involved, including juvenile court judges. The high level of community involvement will help to ensure a positive juvenile probation program that will maximize a youth's rehabilitative benefits (Armstrong, Maloney, and Romig, 1990:12).

Ellsworth contends that ISP programs fail because they often neglect to address many of the problems, including those suggested by Armstrong, Maloney, and Romig in their balanced approach. Ellsworths' (1988:29–30) reasons for why case supervision planning is often unsuccessful are as follows:

1. *Purpose.* The purposes of case supervision planning have not been thought out carefully.

2. *Perceptual differences.* Offenders often change only when they find it necessary to change, not because we want them to change.

3. *Resistance.* We don't always recognize that resistance to change is normal; sometimes we prematurely shift emphasis to an enforcement orientation and rules of probation; case planning starts to look more like the probation order whenever this occurs.

4. *Expectation.* Desired change is sought too quickly; we sometimes expect too much from offenders or expect unrealistic changes to be made.

5. *Focus. There is a tendency to focus on lesser problems in order to gain "success."*

6. *Involvement.* We often fail to involve offenders in the case planning process.

7. *Stereotyping.* Case supervision planning is equated with treatment and rehabilitation, and thus it is often rejected without an adequate consideration of its strengths.

8. *Getting too close.* Sometimes POs are perceived as getting too close to offenders.

9. *Perceptions of accountability.* Nonspecific case plans cannot be criticized by supervisors.

10. *Use of resources.* There is tendency to "burn out" community resources by referring involuntary offenders, those who are not ready to work on their problems.

11. *Measurement.* Probation successes or failures are not measured according to some case plan, but rather, according to arrests, convictions, or numbers of technical violations; how should success be evaluated or measured?

12. *Management.* There is a general lack of understanding or support for case supervision planning by management; POs are considered exclusively officers of the court, and judges don't particularly expect offenders to change because of officer "treatments," only that someone shares the blame or accountability whenever offenders commit new crimes or violate one or more of their probationary conditions.

13. *Training.* Staff members have not been adequately trained in the development, implementation, and evaluation of case plans.

The principles of JISP programs are sound. Basically, implementation problems of one type or another have hindered their successfulness in various jurisdictions (Jones, 1990). It is apparent that to maximize goal attainment, juvenile probation services will need to coordinate their activities and align their departmental and individual PO performance objectives with those of community-based agencies that are a part of the referral network of services and treatments. Consistent with the balanced approach to managing offenders, Klein (1989:6) recommends that for ISP programs to maximize their effectiveness, they should be individualized to a high degree, so that a proper balance of punishment/deterrence and rehabilitation/community protection may be attained. Public safety remains a key goal of any community-based program responsible for serious and violent juvenile offenders (Kansas Legislative Division, 1994). An offender's constitutional rights should be recognized, but at the same time, accountability to victims and the community must be ensured. In the next section we examine several specific ISP programs that are considered community-based alternatives, in contrast with state or locally operated public programs.

COMMUNITY-BASED ALTERNATIVES

Community-based corrections agencies and organizations are not new. An early community-based corrections program for adult offenders, known as the Probation Subsidy Program, was created in California in 1965 (Lawrence, 1985). Originally, these programs were intended to alleviate prison and jail overcrowding by establishing community-based organizations that could accommodate some of the overflow of prison-bound offenders. However, corrections officials soon realized that the potential of such programs was great for offender rehabilitation and reintegration, and that juveniles as well as adult offenders could profit from involvement in them. Many states subsequently passed *community corrections acts* that were aimed at funding local government units to create community facilities that could provide services and other resources to juveniles. Huskey (1984) says that the overall objective of community corrections agencies is to develop and deliver front-end solutions and alternative sanctions in lieu of state incarceration.

The American Correctional Association (ACA) Task Force on Community Corrections Legislation has recommended that these community corrections acts should not be directed at especially violent offenders. Rather, the states should be selective about who fits program requirements. General ACA recommendations are that (1) states should continue to house violent juvenile offenders in secure facilities, (2) judges and prosecutors should continue to explore various punishment options in lieu of incarceration, and (3) local communities should develop programs with additional funding from state appropriations (Huskey, 1984:45). The ACA Task Force identified the following elements as essential to the success of any community corrections act:

1. There should be restrictions on funding high-cost capital projects as well as conventional probation services.
2. Local communities should participate on a voluntary basis and may withdraw at any time.

3. Advisory boards should submit annual criminal justice plans to local governments.

4. There should be a logical formula in place for allocating community corrections funds.

5. Incarceration-bound juveniles should be targeted rather than adding additional punishments for those who otherwise would remain in their communities (in short, avoid "net widening").

6. Financial subsidies should be provided to local government and community-based corrections agencies.

7. Local advisory boards in each community should function to assess program needs and effectiveness and to propose improvements in the local juvenile justice system and educate the general public about the benefits of intermediate punishments.

8. A performance factor should be implemented to ensure that funds are used to achieve specific goals of the act.

Community-based corrections agencies often utilize volunteers from the community to lower their operating costs. Besides using volunteers, community-based agencies should attempt to employ only the most qualified support personnel, to enhance community acceptance of such programs. Local advisory boards, consisting of community residents and business persons, do much to promote community acceptance of such community-based programs. They function as liaison and help to dispel certain myths that are associated with these agencies and programs. A good example of a community-based corrections agency is the Allegheny Academy in Pennsylvania.

The Allegheny Academy

In February 1982, the **Allegheny Academy** was opened and operated by the Community Specialists Corporation, a private, nonprofit corporation headquartered in Pittsburgh, Pennsylvania and specializing in the community-based treatment of young offenders (Costanzo, 1990:114). The program's general aim is to change the negative behavior of offenders. The targets of the Allegheny Academy are those juvenile offenders who have failed in other, traditional probation programs in Pennsylvania. Thus the youthful clients are recidivists who, Allegheny officials believe, would not particularly benefit from further institutionalization through secure confinement.

The Allegheny Academy was originally designed as a facility that could provide meaningful aftercare to adjudicated offenders. Clients are referred to the academy by juvenile court judges in lieu of incarceration. The program may be completed by clients in about six months. Youths live at home, but they must attend the academy each day after school and also on weekends. They receive two full-course meals a day and arrive at their homes around 8:00 or 9:00 P.M. each evening. Follow-up calls are made to these youths' homes by supervisors, who monitor the program-imposed curfew of 10:30 P.M. The academy offers instruction and other forms of assistance enable participants to acquire greater responsibilities. Buses carrying 15 passengers each pick clients up daily and return them to their homes in the evenings. After they have complied successfully with program requirements for 28 days in a row, they are gradually allowed community days at home on weekends. Student failure to attend classes or observe curfews may result in sending them to the county juvenile secure incarceration facility for 2 to 14 days (Costanzo, 1990:116).

Student activities at Allegheny Academy include woodworking, carpentry, masonry, painting, electrical and structural repair, food services, vehicle maintenance, graphic arts, and computer skills. They also receive individual or group counseling as well as some family counseling. They are encouraged to learn about substance abuse and behaving well in their schools and homes. Between 1982 and 1990, the cost of operating Allegheny Academy has been only a fraction of what it would have required to impose long-term confinement on all the juveniles served. Further, clients have paid out over $100,000 in restitution to various victims through earnings from summer work programs. Two other programs that have become popular as rehabilitative strategies for dealing with youthful offenders are the Boston Offender Project and Project New Pride.

The Boston Offender Project

Sometimes it is prudent to seek a compromise relating to the custody imposed in various juvenile probation programs, where a degree of secure custody over juveniles is necessary for a short time but where nonsecure supervision would also be permitted and desirable. One of the most frustrating aggregates of juvenile offenders is that small minority who commit violent offenses (Murphy, 1985:26). Judges and probation officers are often at a loss for strategies to deal effectively with such offenders. Often, the options are secure custody in a reform school or a waiver to criminal courts, presumably for more stringent punishments and longer dispositions of confinement. Some professionals in juvenile corrections have continued to believe, however, that other options are available, provided that the time and resources could be allocated properly.

In 1981, an experimental program was begun in Boston to give some of these professionals their chance to put into practice what they believed could be done in theory. The Massachusetts Department of Youth Services was awarded a grant to implement what eventually became known as the **Boston Offender Project** (BOP). BOP was one of five demonstration sites selected. Its target was violent juveniles, and the program goals included reducing recidivism among them, enhancing public protection by increasing accountability for major violators and improving the likelihood of successful reintegration of juveniles into society by focusing on these offenders' academic and vocational skills (Murphy, 1985:26).

BOP sought to improve the typical handling of a violent juvenile case in the following ways (Murphy, 1985:26):

1. By developing three coordinated phases of treatment that include initial placement in a small, locked, secure-treatment program, followed by planned transition into a halfway house, and finally, a gradual return to the juvenile's home community.

2. By assuring the delivery of comprehensive services by assigning particularly experienced caseworkers responsible for working intensively with a caseload of not more than eight violent offenders and their families.

3. By providing services focused on increasing the educational level of offenders and tying educational programs to the marketplace, significantly increasing the prospects of meaningful employment.

BOP was similar to shock probation, in that violent juvenile offenders would experience some confinement in a secure facility, but after a short time, they would be released to less secure surroundings. Thus a shock element was included, at least implicitly, in the BOP structure. The BOP has several important features compared with the treatment received by those juveniles in the control group. First, diagnostic assessments of juveniles in BOP went well beyond standard psychological assessments, and these measures were administered on an ongoing basis to chart developments in psychological, vocational, and medical areas. Second, caseworkers in the BOP program were three times more experienced (in numbers of years) than standard program caseworkers. A third important difference was that BOP caseworker loads were limited to seven, whereas caseloads for workers in the standard program were as high as 25.

A fourth feature was that BOP caseworkers were actively involved in the treatment phase, whereas the standard program caseworker involvement was passive. A fifth feature of BOP was that caseworker visits to juveniles were eight times as frequent per month as standard program visits. A sixth BOP feature was an automatic assignment to nonsecure residential facilities once the first secure phase of the program was completed. For standard program participants, this was not necessarily an option. Furthermore, in the BOP program, continued violence would subject a participant to regression, so that the offender could be placed back in secure confinement. In the standard program, there was only limited flexibility to make this program shift. Finally, the standard program was terminated for youths when they reached 18 years of age, whereas the BOP could be discontinued or continued before or after age 18, depending on caseworker judgment.

Some important differences between the two groups emerged over the next several years. For instance, 79 percent of BOP clients found unsubsidized employment compared with only 29 percent of the control group. Also, only about a third of the BOP clients had been rearrested. This was about half the rearrest rate exhibited by the control group. Thus while the BOP may not be the most perfect solution to the problem of violent juvenile offenders, it does offer a feasible, middle-ground alternative that has demonstrable success, at least with some offenders. For the chronic, hardcore, and most dangerous offenders, secure confinement is one of the last resorts as a judicial option.

BOX 11.3   JUVENILE JUSTICE IN NORWAY

Parens Patriae and Norwegian Youth

What was it like for juveniles accused of crimes in the United States before *In re Gault*, the *Miranda* warning, and minimum due-process provisions? Look at how juveniles are processed by the Norwegian juvenile justice system for a possible answer.

An expert on Norwegian juvenile justice, Dr. Katherine van Wormer has conducted an in-depth investigation of the Norwegian system for dealing with juvenile offenders. Her work as a social worker during the course of her investigations enabled her to see many facets of the Norwegian system of juvenile justice that the general public might not see. Her observations are of interest here. Her general opinion is that while Norway leads the world in health care, social equality, and child care, much of the world leads Norway when it comes to juvenile justice. Frankly, no mechanism exists for controlling youthful lawbreaking behavior.

A brief foundation for understanding the Norwegian juvenile justice system is in order. First, Norwegians learn to trust others at an early age. Little pressure is exerted on youths, who only begin to learn about reading by age 7. They have the same teacher until they are 12. Until the seventh grade, they receive no marks or grades to indicate their educational progress. Corporal punishment or spanking has been prohibited both at home and at school. There are no private schools in Norway; thus all children receive a public education, consistent with Norway's egalatarian philosophy.

In this context it is quite understandable that the doctrine of *parens patriae* is strong throughout a youth's life. There are no punishments prescribed for youthful offenders under age 15. There are no special courts with the jurisdiction to adjudicate juvenile offenders. Teenagers age 15 or older are subject to criminal punishments and may be sent to prison. However, sentencing in Norway for most crimes is lenient: Most offenders receive probation, a suspended sentence, or incarceration for a limited period in an "open" prison.

How are juveniles sanctioned then? Ordinarily, public prosecutors representing the police will transfer most juvenile cases to a division of the *barnevern* or "social office," which oversees and ensures child protection. Older youths might be sent to the *barnevern* for processing following a criminal trial. Any police evidence is turned over to the *barnevern* and to social workers, who will treat offenders, not punish them. The first step taken by the *barnevern* is an emergency measure, where youths are placed in the custody of the *ungdomshjem* or youth home. Parental consent for this action is largely irrelevant, since a *barnevernsnemnd* or child welfare committee may convene and determine the most appropriate treatment for the juvenile. These are five-member boards elected by the municipal council to serve for periods of four years. Most board members are women and nonprofessionals whose membership is largely prestigeful rather than functionally relevant to a child's needs. However, this board has almost absolute control over a youth's life chances.

Many cases before the *barnevern* are child abuse and neglect, and the board has power to place children in foster homes or youth homes. The burden of proof is on parents to retain custody of their children, and this burden is often an impossible one to bear. Thus it is easy for the board to remove children from homes, but there is an absence of provisions for parental retrieval of those children taken away. For those youths who break the law, the *barnevern* imposes appropriate treatment conditions, including foster home placements. If police officers are not satisfied with these arrangements, van Wormer says that these officers may reopen a case and have it disposed of through the criminal courts. The *barnevern*'s jurisdiction pertains to all youths under age 18.

Typically, the *barnevernsemnd* receives a report from the child welfare office, which has examined the case during the period of the emergency foster home placement of children. A judge presides at a hearing of the *barnevernsnemnd*, although this role is strictly one of protocol. Van Wormer indicates that the social welfare office presents its one-sided evidence in the matter and the board decides the child's disposition in advance of the hearing. Thus any arguments raised by parents or the parents' attorney regarding child custody are largely irrelevant, since the disposition of the case has already been decided. The hearing is largely for show, or, as van Wormer indicates, a "mere formality after the fact."

At such hearings, no transcript of the hearing is made, and proof of a juvenile's guilt consists of a copy of the original police report. *Barnevern*-appointed psychologists and social workers also submit their reports, although these reports have been rubber-stamped in advance by the *barnevernsnemnd*. Any institutional placement is for an indeterminate period. The press is barred from any knowledge of the proceedings, thus insulating both the board and the child from public scrutiny. Interestingly, van Wormer says that the punishment for children is often more severe than for adults charged with the same offense. Adults will ordinarily receive a suspended sentence, whereas children may "languish away in an institution for years." Even if children request to be tried as adults (similar to a request by an American juvenile to be transferred to the jurisdiction of criminal courts), the Norwegian criminal court will turn the cases of convicted youthful offenders over to the *barnevernsnemnd* anyway.

Van Wormer cites the *Lom om Barnevern* or Law on Children's Protection, which provides for the protection of all children under age 18.

One phrase of this law is particularly unclear and has led to abuses by these boards. The law says, in part, that special measures are required (for children) "because of misdemeanors or *other behavior* shows such poor adjustment to the surroundings or community" [emphasis mine]. This "other behavior" may be broadly interpreted to include poor motivation, little cooperation, a tendency to idealize and trivialize, and a lack of maturity among school-children. Thus this vague phraseology entitles the board to make institutional placements of children for any behaviors considered "other behaviors," whatever those behaviors might be. This is a dangerous amount of power to be wielded in the hands of a nonprofessional board.

Van Wormer's observations of youth homes or *undomshjems* indicates that they can accommodate up to 10 children, and they have staffs up to 10 persons. Children are placed in these youth homes for the remainder of their childhood for a variety of offenses, including truancy, theft, and drug use. There are no structured treatment programs or recreational activity. Children from these youth homes attend the local schools for their education, but there is widespread evidence that they are labeled as "reform school" kids. The staff is minimally trained in therapy methods, although the children receive little meaningful therapy. Rather, they receive generous amounts of clothing and other material items, including bicycles, cameras, and skis. Van Wormer says that one boy mentioned that they get a lot of expensive things, but they get no love "as in a family."

Van Wormer recommends that to avoid the abuses of power and secrecy that currently characterize Norwegian juvenile justice, the following kinds of changes should be contemplated:

1. Children's rights should begin at the police station, through being informed in the parent's presence of their right to an attorney and their right to refuse to answer questions.

2. There must be no punishment for crimes without a trial.

3. Children should not be punished in the name of treatment.

4. Children should be kept at home, under supervision, whenever possible.

5. Children should not be subject to two legal systems simultaneously.

6. Children should be entitled to full constitutional rights, including the right to hear testimony against them, the right of cross-examining witnesses, and the subjection of evidence to a legal finding of guilty or not guilty.

7. Children should have access to an attorney's services at all critical stages.

8. Roles of social workers should be related to treatment, not to the prosecution of cases.

9. The *barnevernsnemnd* should be abolished altogether; it serves no useful purpose and does more harm than good.

Norwegian delinquency is not extensive, and in view of how juveniles are processed, it is unlikely that completely reliable figures of the amount of juvenile offending can ever be produced. There are several interest groups at work currently attempting to provide youths in Norway with at least some of the legal rights commensurate with those enjoyed by U.S. youths. However, strong traditional elements persist throughout the Norwegian juvenile justice system to make such progress slow. For the present, at least, *parens patriae* is still alive and well in Norway.

Sources: Adapted with permission from Katherine van Wormer, "The Hidden Juvenile Justice System in Norway: A Journal Back in Time," *Federal Probation* **54**:57–61, 1990; and Katherine van Wormer, "Norway's Juvenile Justice System: A Journey Back in Time," *Corrections Today* **52**:106–116, 1990.

Project New Pride

One of the most popular probation programs is **Project New Pride**, which was established in Denver, Colorado, in 1973. It has been used widely as a model for probation programs in other jurisdictions in subsequent years (Laurence and West, 1985). New Pride is a blend of education, counseling, employment, and cultural education directed at those more serious offenders between the ages of 14 and 17. Juveniles eligible for the New Pride program must have at least two prior convictions for serious misdemeanors and/or felonies, and they must be formally charged or adjudicated for another offense when referred to New Pride. There are very few females in New Pride, only about 10 or 15 percent. This is not deliberate exclusion, but rather, females tend to have lower rates of recidivism and commit less serious offenses than those of their male delinquent counterparts. Those who are deliberately excluded are offenders previously diagnosed as severely psychotic or who have committed forcible rape.

Project New Pride's goals include (1) reintegrating participants into their communities through school participation or employment, and (2) reducing recidivism rates among offenders. The project emphasizes schooling, employment, and closeness with families. It is a community-based project and utilizes professional probation officers as well as volunteers. The project staff offers employment counseling services and job placement, tutoring for school assignments and projects, and vocational training. Project New Pride personnel will help juveniles fill out job application forms and answer other questions relevant for effective job hunting and success in school.

Some of the areas where New Pride programs have been established have led to juveniles developing small businesses such as bakeries, janitorial services, and lawn and gardening services to help defray the costs of their program expenses. Taxpayer dollars finance New Pride projects in various jurisdictions. It is estimated that the cost for each juvenile serviced by Project New Pride is $4500, compared with $28,000, the cost of incarcerating the same offender in a reform or industrial school (Project New Pride, 1985). The goals of Project New Pride seem obtainable. Over the years, recidivism rates have been low, less than 20 percent. Furthermore, nearly half the juveniles who have participated in various New Pride projects through the United States have returned to finish their high school education or have completed the GED. Almost three-fourths of all participants hold full-time jobs successfully (McCarthy and McCarthy, 1997).

Community-based programs are particularly advantageous for youths because they provide opportunities for them to remain integrated into their communities. At the same time, youths receive assistance from agency referrals to available services and treatments. Altschuler and Armstrong (1990a:170) suggest that community-based correctional programs and other intensive probation supervision programs can maximize their effectiveness and assistance to youthful clients if they attempt to realize five important principles. These include:

1. Preparing youths for gradually increased responsibility and freedom in the community
2. Helping youths become involved in the community and getting the community to interact with them
3. Working with youths and their families, peers, schools and employers to identify the qualities necessary for success
4. Developing new resources and supports where needed
5. Monitoring and testing youths and the community on their abilities to interact

In the next section we examine three increasingly important intermediate punishments that seem to be working well with adult and juvenile offenders alike: (1) electronic monitoring, (2) home confinement, and (3) shock probation.

ELECTRONIC MONITORING

Electronic monitoring is the use of telemetry devices to verify that an offender is at a specified location during specified times (Raider, 1994; Roy, 1994). Electronic monitoring devices were first used in 1964 as an alternative to incarcerating certain mental patients and parolees (Gable, 1986). Subsequently, electronic monitoring was extended to include monitoring office work, employee testing for security clearances, and many other applications (Kenosha County Department of Social Services, 1990; Roy, 1994). Other countries are currently experimenting with electronic monitoring. In British Columbia, Canada, for instance, the Corrections Branch's Electronic Monitoring System was pilot-tested in 1988 and was being used on a broad scale in 1992 (Mainprize, 1992).

The Second Judicial District Judge Jack Love of New Mexico is credited with implementing a pilot electronic monitoring project in 1983 for persons convicted of drunk driving and certain white collar offenses, such as embezzlement (Houk, 1984). Subsequent to its use for probationers, the New Mexico State Supreme Court approved the program, since it required the voluntariness and consent of probationers as a condition of their probation programs. Judge Love directed that certain probationers should wear either anklets or bracelets that emitted electronic signals that could be intercepted by their probation officers who conducted surveillance operations. After a short period of such judicial experimentation, other jurisdictions decided to conduct their own experiments for offender monitoring with electronic devices. Eventually, experiments were under way not only for probationers, but for parolees and inmates of jails and prisons (Clarkson and Weakland, 1991; U.S. General Accounting Office, 1995a). By year end 1995, there were over 28,300 offenders on electronic monitoring programs in at least 45 states (Camp and Camp, 1995d, 1996). This represents a 368 percent increase in the use of electronic monitoring since 1993 (Boone, 1996:18). Over 5000 youths were involved in electronic monitoring programs by 1996 (American Correctional Association, 1996:xxxvii).

There are at least four types of electronic monitoring signaling devices. First, a *continuous-signal device* consists of a miniature transmitter that is strapped to the probationer's wrist. The transmitter broadcasts an encoded signal that is received by a receiver–dialer in the offender's home. The signal is relayed to a central receiver over the telephone lines. A second type of monitor is the *programmed contact device*, which is similar to the continuous-signal device. However, in this case, a central computer from the probation office is programmed to call the offender's home at random hours to verify the probationer's whereabouts. Offenders must answer their telephones, insert the wristlet transmitter into the telephone device, and their voices and signal emissions are verified by computer (Papy, 1994).

A third monitor is a *cellular device*. This is a transmitter worn by offenders and emits a radio signal that may be received by a local area monitoring system. Up to 25 probationers may be monitored at once with such a system. The fourth type of monitor is the *continuous signaling transmitter*, which is also worn by the offender. These also send out continuous signals which may be intercepted by portable receiving units in the possession of probation officers. These are quite popular, since POs may conduct "drive-bys" and verify whether offenders are at home during curfew hours when they are supposed to be.

These wristlet–anklet transmitters are certainly not tamperproof. They are similar in plastic construction to the wristlet ID tags given patients at the time of hospital admissions. However, these electronic devices are somewhat more sturdy. Nevertheless, the plastic is such that it is easy to remove. It is easily seen whether the device has been tampered with (e.g., stretched, burned, mutilated), since it is impossible to reattach without special equipment in the possession of the probation department. If tampering has occurred and probationers have attempted to defeat the intent of the device, they may be subject to probation revocation. This offense may be punished by incarceration.

Gradually, the use of electronic monitoring devices was extended to include both low- and high-risk juvenile offenders. In Knoxville, Tennessee, for example, electronic monitoring is used to a limited degree with juvenile probationers, but only as a last resort. Thus juvenile offenders who have failed in other types of probation programs or community-based agencies are placed in an electronic monitoring program prior to being placed in secure confinement. If they do not comply with their electronic monitoring program conditions, they will be sent to secure confinement at one of the state's several public and private secure confinement facilities.

Charles (1989a,b) describes the implementation of an electronic monitoring program for juvenile offenders in Allen County, Indiana. Known as the *Allen County, Indiana, Juvenile Electronic Monitoring Program Pilot Project* (EMP), this program was begun as an experimental study in October 1987 and was conducted for nine months, through May 1988. At the time the study started, the probation department had 25 POs who were appointed by the court and certified by the Indiana Judicial Conference. During 1987, 2404 juveniles were referred to the probation department by the court. About 34 percent of these were female offenders. During that year, 167 youths were incarcerated in secure facilities for delinquents at a total cost of $1.5 million.

Charles (1989b:152–153) indicates that because of fiscal constraints, Allen County agreed to place only six juveniles in the electronic monitoring program. However, two of these youths recidivated and were dropped from it shortly after it started. The remaining four youths remained in the program. The juvenile court judge in these cases disposes each youth to a six-month probationary period with electronic monitoring. Each youth wore a conspicuous wristlet, which eventually became a symbol of court sanctions. Like the proverbial string tied around one's finger, the wristlet was a constant reminder that these juveniles were "on probation." Further, others who became aware of these electronic devices became of assistance in helping these youths to avoid activities that might be considered in violation of probation program conditions.

Despite the small number of participants in Charles' research, his findings are of interest and suggest similar successful applications on larger offender aggregates. Each juvenile was interviewed at the conclusion of the program. They reported that their wristlets were continuous reminders of their involvement in the probation program. However, they didn't feel as though program officials were spying on them. In fact, one of the youths compared his experience with electronic monitoring with his previous experience of being supervised by a probation officer. He remarked that whenever he was under the supervision of the probation officer, he could do whatever he wished, and there was little likelihood that his PO would ever find out about it. However, he was always under the threat of being discovered by the computer or by the surveillance officer.

Another interesting phenomenon was the fact that the wristlet enabled certain offenders to avoid peer pressure and interacting with their friends. Since they had wristlets, they had good excuses to return home and not violate their curfews. Also, the families of these juveniles took a greater interest in them and their program. In short, at least for these four youths, the program was viewed very favorably and considered successful. Parents who were also interviewed at the conclusion of the program agreed that the program and monitoring system had been quite beneficial for their sons. While electronic monitoring for juveniles is still in its early stages of experimentation in various jurisdictions, Charles (1989c) believes that it is a cost-effective alternative to incarceration.

Some jurisdictions, such as the Dane County, Wisconsin, Sheriff's Office, have implemented a SpeakerID program (Listug, 1996:85). *SpeakerID is a voice verification monitoring system allowing law enforcement and criminal justice agencies to monitor low-risk offenders under probation or house arrest.* Implemented in October 1994, the SpeakerID program is a completely automated system that calls clients at their authorized locations at random times. Prior to using SpeakerID, the Dade County Sheriff's Office used traditional ankle bracelets and wristlets as described earlier. The SpeakerID system started out with only 8 to 12 offenders. In 1996 there were between 30 and 35 offenders participating in this system. When offenders answer their telephones, they are asked specific questions. Voice matches are verified perfectly; thus there is little likelihood that any particular offender can fool the system with a previously recorded tape or some other device. Because of the automated nature of the system, SpeakerID is cost-effective. Apart from initial startup costs, the SpeakerID system costs about $3 per day per monitored offender. This compares very favorably with jail and prison costs of $40 and $49 per prisoner per day in Wisconsin jails and prisons.

Some Criticisms of Electronic Monitoring

Some limitations of electronic monitoring programs are that they are quite expensive to implement initially (Boone, 1996; Evans, 1996). The direct costs associated with their purchase or lease are seemingly prohibitive to local jurisdictions that are used to incarcerating juveniles and defraying their maintenance costs over an extended period. However, once a given jurisdiction has installed such equipment, it eventually pays for itself and functions to reduce overall incarcerative expenses that otherwise would have been incurred had these youths been placed in secure confinement.

Also, electronic monitoring programs require some training on the part of the users (Papy, 1994). While those using such systems do not need to be computer geniuses, some computer training is helpful. Electronic monitoring is a delinquency deterrent for many offenders. However, it is not foolproof. Despite the fact that they may easily be tampered with, electronic wristlets and anklets only help to verify an offender's whereabouts. They do not provide television images of these persons and whatever they may be doing. One federal probation officer has reported that one of his federal probationers on electronic monitoring was running a successful stolen property business out of his own home. Thus he was able to continue his criminal activity unabated, despite the home confinement constraints imposed by electronics.

Electronic monitoring has also been criticized as possibly violative of the Fourth Amendment search-and-seizure provision, where, it is alleged by some critics, electronic eavesdropping might be conducted within one's home or bedroom. This argument is without serious constitutional merit, since the primary function of such monitoring is to verify an offender's whereabouts. Some sophisticated types of monitoring systems are equipped with closed-circuit television transmissions, such as those advertised by the Bell Telephone Company as viewer phones of the future. But even if such monitoring were so equipped, this additional feature would only intrude where offenders wished it to intrude, such as their living rooms or kitchens.

The fact is that many offenders may be inexpensively tracked through these monitoring systems and their whereabouts can be verified without time-consuming face-to-face checks (Gowan, 1995). For instance, a single juvenile probation officer may conduct drive-bys of client residences during evening hours and receive their transmitted signals with a portable unit. This silent means of detection is intended only to enforce one program element: observance of curfews. Other checks, such as those conducted for illegal drug or alcohol use, must be verified directly, through proper testing and expert confirmation. As we will see, electronic monitoring is increasingly used in tandem with another sentencing option—home confinement (Boone, 1996).

HOME CONFINEMENT OR HOUSE ARREST

The use of one's home as the principal place of confinement is not new. In biblical times, St. Paul was sentenced in Rome to house arrest for two years, where he performed tentmaker services for others (Lilly and Ball, 1987:359). *Home confinement is a program of intermediate punishment involving the use of the offender's residence for mandatory incarceration during evening hours after a curfew and on weekends* (Ball and Lilly, 1987).

Most experts agree that Florida pioneered the contemporary use of home confinement in 1983 (Boone, 1996; Papy, 1994). At that time, corrections officials considered the use of homes as incarcerative facilities as acceptable alternatives to defray the high cost of traditional incarceration in prisons or jails. When Florida implemented its home confinement program, it was established under the Correctional Reform Act of 1983. This act provided that the home could be used as a form of intensive supervised custody in the community (Boone, 1996). This highly individualized program is intended primarily to restrict offender movement within the community, home, or nonresidential placement, together with specific sanctions such as curfew, payment of fines, community service, and other requirements. When Florida implemented it, prison costs ran almost $30 per inmate per day, while home confinement required an expenditure of about $3.00 per offender per day.

Although Florida officials consider **home incarceration** or **house arrest** punitive, some persons disagree. They believe that incarceration should be in a jail or prison if it is meaningful incarceration. But Petersilia (1986) reports that home confinement may be even worse as a punishment than prison. Her interviews with probation officers in San Diego, California yielded a statement from one probationer to the effect that while on home confinement, his kids would beg him to take them to the corner store to buy them ice cream cones. It was punishment to have to refuse their requests.

In many jurisdictions, home confinement is supplemented with electronic monitoring (Boone, 1996; Roy, 1994). Relatively little is known about the extent to which home confinement is used as a sentencing alternative for juvenile offenders. Since probation is so widely used as the sanction of choice except for the most chronic recidivists, home confinement is most often applied as an accompanying condition of electronic monitoring. However, this type of sentencing may be redundant, since curfew for juvenile offenders means home confinement anyway, especially during evening hours. As a day disposition, home confinement for juveniles would probably be counter-productive, since juveniles are often obligated to finish their schooling as a probation program condition. Again, since school hours are during the day-time, it would not make sense to deprive juveniles of school opportunities through some type of home confinement.

A survey of several home detention and electronic monitoring programs was conducted and reported in 1993 by Baumer, Maxfield, and Mendelsohn. Three separate programs were established in Marion County, Indiana in 1986 to electronically supervise both adults and juveniles in (1) postconviction; (2) pretrial; and (3) juvenile burglary.

The postconviction program was designed for adult offenders convicted of nonviolent offenses that can be suspended as an alternative to incarceration. Actually, Indiana law provides that convicted offenders must be sentenced to a term of incarceration. After this sentence is imposed, it is suspended and offenders are placed on electronic monitoring and house arrest. The pretrial program involves defendants charged with nonviolent crimes who are screened according to their criminal history, living arrangements, and length of stay at the jail before their trials. Persons who qualify are placed into a programmed contact system identical to that furnished for convicted offenders.

The juvenile burglary program was begun in June 1989 by the Juvenile Division of the Marion County Superior Court. All juveniles initially charged with burglary and convicted of either burglary or theft are targeted. Participating juveniles must be eligible for either probation or a suspended sentence; thus more violent and serious juvenile offenders are excluded automatically. Juveniles assigned to home confinement can also receive a blend of treatments, including electronically programmed contact, manual monitoring, and random home visits by police officers (Baumer, Maxfield, and Mendelsohn, 1993:125–126). Table 11.6 shows a summary of the three programs. These researchers report favorable results with all three programs, especially with the juvenile burglary program. The participating youths had low rates of absconding and recidivism compared with adult offenders. Thus public safety as a program goal was reasonably achieved. Although these investigators suggest further study concerning the feasibility of applying home confinement and programmed electronic monitoring systems with juveniles, Marion County's efforts thus far have been very favorable.

TABLE 11.6

Summary of Programs

	Adult	Pretrial	Juvenile
Criminal justice processing stage	Postconviction	Pretrial	Postconviction
Implementing agency	Community corrections	Community corrections	Juvenile court, police
Monitoring methods	Manua (N = 76) Electronic (N = 78)	Electronic (N = 224)	Manual (N = 39) Electronic (N = 43) Police visits (N = 44) Electronic and police (N = 44)
Assignment method (groups)	Random (2)	Nonrandom (1)	Random (4)
Evaluation data	Prior record Intake and program delivery Electronic call records New arrests Intake, exit interview Follow-up criminal history	Prior record Intake and program delivery Electronic call records New arrests	Prior record Intake and program delivery Electronic call records New arrests Intake, exit interview Follow-up criminal history

Source: Baumer, Maxfield, and Mendelsohn, 1993:127.

SHOCK PROBATION

Shock probation is an intermediate punishment where offenders are initially disposed to incarcerative terms; after a period of time, between 90 and 180 days, youths are removed from secure confinement and obligated to serve the remainder of their disposition on probation (Vito, 1984). The actual term *shock probation* was coined by Ohio authorities in 1964 (Vito, 1984:22). Shock probation is also known as **shock parole**, because it technically involves a release from jail or prison after serving some amount of time in incarceration.

Sometimes, shock probation is used synonymously with **combination sentences** or **split sentences**. Other terms, such as **intermittent sentences**, **mixed sentences**, or **jail as a condition of probation**, are also used interchangeably with shock probation, although they have somewhat different meanings. Combination sentences or split sentences occur whenever judges sentence offenders to a term a portion of which includes incarceration and a portion of which includes probation. Mixed sentences occur whenever offenders have been convicted of two or more offenses and judges sentence them to separate sentences for each conviction offense. Intermittent sentences occur whenever judges sentence offenders to terms such as weekend confinement only. Jail as a condition of probation is a sentence that prescribes a specified amount of jail incarceration prior to serving the remainder of the sentence on probation.

Technically, shock probation is none of these. Youths disposed to shock probation don't know they have received such dispositions. The judge disposes them to incarceration. The youths have no way of knowing that within three or four months, they will be yanked out of incarceration, brought before the same judge, and disposed to probation. This new probationary disposition is contingent on their good behavior while they are incarcerated. Thus they are shocked or traumatized by their incarceration. When they are redisposed to probation later, they should be sufficiently shocked to avoid further offending. But recidivism figures suggest that it doesn't always work that way.

Yurkanin (1989:87) indicates that shock probation, at least for adult offenders, is escalating in its use among state jurisdictions. She reports that in mid-1988, nearly 1100 offenders were participating in at least nine shock probation programs in different states, including Georgia, Oklahoma, Mississippi, Louisiana, South Carolina, New York, and Florida. At least five additional states were planning to implement shock probation programs during the next few years.

Shock probation is a misnomer in a sense. If we recall that probation is a disposition in lieu of incarceration, it doesn't make much sense to incarcerate offenders first, then release them later and call them probationers. Technically, it might be more accurate to refer to this type of intermediate punishment as shock parole, since these are previously incarcerated offenders who are redisposed to a supervised release program. In any case, the intended effect of incarceration is to scare offenders sufficiently so that they refrain from reoffending. Simply, their incarcerative experiences are so shocking that they don't want to face further incarceration.

Shock probation has sometimes been compared erroneously with **Scared Straight**, a New Jersey program implemented in the late 1970s. Scared Straight sought to frighten samples of hard-core delinquent youths by having them confront inmates in a Rahway, New Jersey prison. Inmates would yell at and belittle them, calling them names, cursing, and yelling. Inmates would tell them about sexual assaults and other prison unpleasantries in an attempt to get them to refrain from reoffending. However, the program was unsuccessful. Despite early favorable reports of recidivism rates of less than 20 percent, the actual rate of recidivism among these participating youths was considerably higher. Furthermore, another control group not exposed to Scared Straight had a lower recidivism rate (Lundman, 1984). The Scared Straight program is perhaps closer in principle to the SHAPE-UP program implemented in Colorado and discussed as a diversionary measure earlier. However, SHAPE-UP program authorities deny any program similarities other than prisoner–client interaction for brief periods (Mitchell and Shiller, 1988).

BOOT CAMPS

The juvenile version of shock probation or shock incarceration is perhaps best exemplified by juvenile boot camps (Bourque et al., 1996). Also known as the Army model, boot camp programs are patterned after basic training for new military recruits. Juvenile offenders are given a taste of hard military life, and such regimented activities and structure for up to 180 days are often sufficient to "shock" them into giving up their lives of delinquency or crime and staying out of jail (Ratliff, 1988:98). Boot camp programs in various states have been established, including the regimented inmate discipline program in Mississippi, the **About Face** program in Louisiana, and the shock incarceration program in Georgia. These are paramilitary-type programs that emphasize strict military discipline and physical training (Ratliff, 1988:98).

What Are Boot Camps?

Boot camps are highly regimented, militarylike, short-term correctional programs (90 to 180 days) where offenders are provided with strict discipline, physical training, and hard labor resembling some aspects of military basic training; when completed successfully, boot camps provide for transfers of participants to community-based facilities for nonsecure supervision. By 1993, boot camps had been formally established in over half the states (Florida Office of Program Policy Analysis, 1995; Virginia State Crime Commission, 1993). In 1995, there were 35 federal and state boot camps being operated, with a total of 9304 inmate-clients. Of these, there were 626 females. Of the 9304 inmate-clients, 455 were juvenile offenders distributed throughout nine locally operated programs (Bourque, Han, and Hill, 1996:3). Some experts regard boot camps as the latest correctional reform (Florida Advisory Council on Intergovernmental Relations, 1994). Other professionals are skeptical about their success potential (Lieb, Fish, and Crosby, 1994). Much depends on how particular boot camps are operated and for how long. Boot camp programs are operated for as short a time as 30 days or as long as 180 days (Camp and Camp, 1995c:47). While boot camps were officially established in 1983 by the Georgia Department of Corrections Special Alternative Incarceration (SAI), the general idea for boot camps originated some time earlier in late 1970s, also in Georgia (Parent, 1989b).

The Rationale for Boot Camps

Boot camps, also known as *shock incarceration*, have been established as an alternative to long-term traditional incarceration. Austin, Jones, and Bolyard (1993:1)outline a brief rationale for boot camps:

1. A substantial number of youthful first-time offenders now incarcerated will respond to a short but intensive period of confinement followed by a longer period of intensive community supervision.

2. These youthful offenders will benefit from a military-type atmosphere that instills a sense of self-discipline and physical conditioning that was lacking in their lives.

3. These same youths need exposure to relevant educational, vocational training, drug treatment, and general counseling services to develop more positive and law-abiding values and become better prepared to secure legitimate future employment.

4. The costs involved will be less than a traditional criminal justice sanction that imprisons the offender for a substantially longer period of time.

Boot Camp Goals

Boot camps have several general goals: (1) rehabilitation/reintegration; (2) discipline; (3) deterrence; (4) ease prison/jail overcrowding; and (5) vocational, educational, and rehabilitative services.

1. *To provide rehabilitation and reintegration.* In 1986, the Orleans (Louisiana) Parish Prison System established a boot camp program called *About Face* (Caldas, 1990). This program sought to improve one's sense of purpose, self-discipline, self-control, and self-confidence through physical conditioning, educational programs, and social skills training, all within the framework of strict military discipline (Caldas, 1990). One early criticism of this Louisiana program was the amount of inexperience among boot camp staff. Over time, however, this criticism was minimized (Caldas, 1990; MacKenzie and Shaw, 1993:463–466).

2. *To provide discipline.* Boot camps are designed to improve one's discipline. Certain boot camps, especially those aimed at younger offenders, must deal with adjudicated juvenile offenders who usually resist authority and refuse to listen or learn in traditional classroom or treatment environments (Taylor, 1992:122). Physical conditioning and structure are most frequently stressed in these programs. But most boot camp programs also include educational elements pertaining to literacy, academic and vocational education, intensive value clarification, and resocialization (MacKenzie and Shaw, 1993).

3. *To promote deterrence.* The sudden immersion of convicted offenders into a militarylike atmosphere is a frightening experience for many participants. The rigorous approach to formal rules and authority was a challenging dimension of boot camp programs for most participants (Shaw and MacKenzie, 1991, 1992). Latessa and Vito (1988) observe that offenders who are released early from prisons or jails will be deterred from returning to crime. They cite low recidivism rates among clients as evidence of the deterrent value of such programs. Other experts concur that boot camps and shock incarceration have positive impacts on crime deterrence. Mack (1992:63–65) reports that of the many clients who have participated in the *Rikers Boot Camp High Impact Incarceration Program* (HIIP), only 23 percent have recidivated compared with 28 percent of those released from traditional incarceration. While these recidivism rate differences are not substantial, the direction of the difference says something about the potential deterrent value of boot camp programs.

4. *To ease prison and jail overcrowding.* Boot camps are believed to have a long-term impact on jail and prison overcrowding. Theoretically, this is possible because of the low recidivism rates among boot camp participants (MacKenzie and Souryal, 1994). The short-term nature of confinement in boot camp programs with the participant's subsequent return to the community helps to ease the overcrowding problem in correctional settings. It is believed that boot camp experiences are significant in creating more positive attitudes among participants (Florida Department of Corrections, 1990; Klein-Saffran and Lutze, 1991).

5. *To provide vocational and rehabilitative services.* An integral feature of *most* boot camp programs is the inclusion of some form of educational and/or vocational training (MacKenzie, Shaw, and Gowdy, 1993; Parent, 1989b). A New York Shock Incarceration program makes it possible for participants to work on GED diplomas and provides elementary educational instruction (New York State Department of Correctional Services, 1989, 1990, 1991, 1992). Educational training is also a key feature of **IMPACT** (Intensive Motivational Program of Alternative Correctional Treatment) in Louisiana jurisdictions (Piquero and MacKenzie, 1993). As an alternative to traditional incarceration, boot camps do much to promote greater social and educational adjustment for clients reentering their communities (Osler, 1991).

Profiling Boot Camp Participants

Who can participate in boot camps or shock incarceration programs? Participants may or may not be able to enter or withdraw from boot camps voluntarily. It depends on the particular program. Most boot camp participants are prison-bound youthful offenders convicted of less serious, nonviolent crimes, and who have never been previously incarcerated (Bottcher and Isorena, 1994). Depending on the program, there are some exceptions (MacKenzie, Shaw, and Gowdy, 1993:1–3).

Participants may either be referred to these programs by judges or corrections departments or they may volunteer. They may or may not be accepted, and if they complete their programs successfully, they may or may not be released under supervision into their communities. Screening of boot camp participants is extremely important. For instance, a boot camp program in California, LEAD, sponsored by the California Youth Authority, conducted screenings for 365 eligible juveniles during 1992–1993. Only 180 were admitted into the LEAD program, while only 107 graduated successfully and were granted parole after four months (Bottcher and Isorena, 1994).

Representative Boot Camps

1. *The Camp Monterey Shock Incarceration Facility (New York State Department of Correctional Services).* New York State has a major boot camp project with the following features:

   a. Accommodates 250 participants in minimum-security institution.

   b. Has 131 staff (83 custody positions).

   c. Participants are screened and must meet statutory criteria; three-fourths volunteer; one-third of applicants rejected.

   d. Inmates form platoons and live in open dormitories.

   e. Successful program completion leads to parole board releases to an intensive probation supervision program called "aftershock."

   f. Physical training, drill, eight hours daily of hard labor.

   g. Inmates must participate in therapeutic community meetings, compulsory adult basic education courses, mandatory individual counseling, and mandatory recreation;

   h. All must attend alcohol and substance abuse treatment.

   i. Job-seeking skills training and reentry planning.

2. *The Oklahoma Regimented Inmate Discipline Program.* Oklahoma has a **regimented inmate discipline** (RID) **program** with the following features:

   a. A 145-bed facility at the Lexington Assessment and Reception Center; also houses 600 long-term general population inmates as medium security.

   b. Offenders screened according to statutory criteria and may volunteer.

   c. Inmates live in single or double-bunk cells.

   d. Strict discipline, drill, physical training; housekeeping and institutional maintenance.

   e. Six hours daily in educational and vocational programs.

f.   Drug abuse programs, individual and group counseling.

g.   Subsequently, participants are resentenced by judges to intensive supervised probation or "community custody," perhaps beginning at a halfway house.

3.   *The Georgia Special Alternative Program.* This program includes the following characteristics (MacKenzie, Shaw, and Gowdy, 1993):

a.   Program for male offenders.

b.   Judges control selection process, and SAI is a "condition of probation"; if successful, boot camp graduates are released, since judges do not ordinarily resentence them to probation.

c.   Program includes physical training, drill, hard work; two exercise and drill periods daily, with eight-hour hard labor periods in between.

d.   Participants perform limited community services.

e.   *Little emphasis* on counseling or treatment.

f.   Inmates *do* receive drug abuse education and information about sexually transmitted diseases.

g.   Inmates are double-bunked in two 25-cell units at Dodge, and at Burris, 100 inmates are single-bunked in four 25-cell units.

Because many of these boot camp programs have been established since about the late 1980s and early 1990s, extensive evaluation research about general boot camp program effectiveness has not been abundant (Florida Office of Program Policy Analysis, 1995). However, indications from available research are that boot camps generally are effective at reducing recidivism among participants. Currently, some states, such as Georgia, report relatively high rates of recidivism among boot camp clientele, whereas New York and Oklahoma have much lower recidivism rates. Besides reducing recidivism, boot camps might also be effective at saving taxpayers' money over time. For various states, operating boot camps is considerably cheaper than using traditional incarceration for particular offenders. In some instances the cost savings is considerable.

OTHER ISP PROGRAM CONDITIONS

Judicial dispositional options, at one end of the sentencing spectrum, may adjudicate youths as delinquent, impose nominal sanctions, and take no further action other than to record the event. Therefore, if the same juveniles reappear before the same judge in the future, sterner measures may be taken in imposing new dispositions. Or the judge may divert juveniles to particular community agencies for special treatment. Juveniles with psychological problems or who are emotionally disturbed, sex offenders, or those with drug and/or alcohol dependencies may be targeted for special community treatment. At the other end of the spectrum of punishment are the most drastic alternatives of custodial sanctions, ranging from the placement of juveniles in nonsecure foster homes and camp ranches, or in secure facilities such as reform schools and industrial schools (Chamberlain, 1994). These nonsecure and secure forms of placement and/or incarceration are usually reserved for the most serious offenders (Montgomery and Torbet, 1994).

Probation is the most commonly used sentencing option. Probation is either unconditional or conditional. In this chapter we have examined several conditional intermediate punishments, including intensive probation supervision and community-based programs. A youth's assignment to any of these programs may or may not include conditions. Apart from the more intensive monitoring and supervision by POs, juveniles may be expected to comply with one or more conditions, including restitution, if financial loss was suffered by one or more victims in cases of vandalism, property damage, or physical injury. Also, fines may be imposed. Or the judge may specify some form of community service. All of these conditions may be an integral part of a juvenile's probation program. Violation of or failure to comply with one or more of these conditions may result in a probation revocation action. Probation officers function as the link between juvenile offenders and the courts regarding a youth's compliance with these program conditions.

Restitution, Fines, and Victim Compensation

An increasingly important feature of probation programs is **restitution** (Roy, 1994, 1995). Several models of restitution have been described (Schneider and Schneider, 1985):

1. *The financial–community service model:* stresses the offender's financial accountability and community service to pay for damages.
2. *The victim–offender mediation model:* focuses on victim–offender reconciliation.
3. *The victim–reparations model:* juveniles compensate their victims directly for their offenses.

The potential significance of restitution, coupled with probation, is that it suggests a reduction in recidivism among juvenile offenders. In a restitution program in Atlanta, Georgia, for example, 258 juvenile offenders participated in several experimental treatment programs, where one of the programs included restitution. The restitution offender group had a 26 percent reduction in recidivism compared with other juveniles where restitution was not included as a condition (Schneider and Schneider, 1985). But other experts caution that if restitution is not properly implemented by the court or carefully supervised, it serves little deterrent purpose (Roy, 1994, 1995).

Beyond reductions in recidivism, restitution, payment of **fines**, and **victim compensation** also increase offender accountability. Given the present philosophical direction of juvenile courts, this condition is consistent with enhancing a youth's acceptance of responsibility for wrongful actions committed against others and the financial harm it has caused. Rubin (1988:38) suggests that an important part of the mission of probation is to increase a youth's personal accountability. He notes, for example, that in the Santa Clara County (San Jose), California, Probation Department "offenders will be held responsible to the community and to themselves through personal accountability and restitution as a part of any sanction whether or not it involves custody" (Rubin, 1988:38).

Many of the programs we have already discussed include restitution as a part of their program requirements (Schwartz and Hsieh, 1994). Restitution orders may be imposed by juvenile court judges with or without accompanying dispositions of secure confinement. The Lucas County, Ohio, Juvenile Court, highlighted earlier in this chapter because of its intensive supervision program, utilizes about $90,000 of its state monies to pay restitution-owing juveniles to perform community service for repayment to victims (Rubin, 1988:39).

However, Rubin (1988) cautions that imposing restitution as a program condition may at times be difficult to enforce. In part because the juvenile court continues to have an informal quality, it is difficult to ensure that restitution orders have been met by youthful offenders. Youths themselves may feel that the level of restitution set by judges is excessive. If they fail to comply with court-ordered restitution, they face a contempt-of-court charge, which is a new, more serious, offense. In some instances, juveniles are ordered to repay insurance companies that have reimbursed victims for their medical expenses and other losses. Juvenile court judges attempt to impose restitution, in part, according to the amount of a victim's loss and, in part, according to a youth's ability to pay. Rubin (1988:42) recommends that the burden of ensuring a youth's compliance with a restitution order should be upon the supervising agency or placement facility. These institutions are in the best position of monitoring a youth's performance and can measure fairly accurately one's earnings and restitution contributions. Restitution does seem to improve offender accountability and responsibility.

Community Service

Often connected with restitution orders is **community service**. Community service may be performed in diverse ways, from cutting courthouse lawns and cleaning up public parks to painting homes for the elderly or repairing fences on private farms. Youths typically earn wages for this service, and these wages are usually donated to a victim compensation fund. The different types of community-service activities are limited only by the imagination of the juvenile court and community leaders. Similar to restitution, community-service orders are intended to increase offender accountability and individual responsibility. Evidence suggests that community service achieves such objectives, although offender accountability is enhanced if they participate in community-service programs with clear goals and guidelines (Roy, 1995).

JUVENILE PROBATION OFFICERS

Many probation and parole officers (POs) who work with juvenile **probationers** report that their work is satisfying. Many of them see themselves as playing an important part in shaping a youth's future by the nature of the relationship they can establish between themselves and the juveniles with whom they work (Sluder and Reddington, 1993). Some juvenile **probation officers** have cynical attitudes toward their work, believing that their intervention and assistance are of limited value to the juveniles they supervise (Rush, 1992).

In a technical sense, POs are also **corrections officers**, *because probation and parole departments are under the correctional umbrella of the criminal justice system. However, corrections or correctional officers are traditionally associated with supervisory functions in relation to inmates of prisons and jails.* Prison and jail correctional officers receive a basically different type of training compared with POs, although there are certain aspects of their training which are commonly shared (e.g., legal liabilities in relation to inmates and clients, firearms training, and report preparation). For clarity, we will use the PO designation rather than the correctional officer designation in our discussions of probation and parole officers here.

In many jurisdictions, POs supervise both types of offenders, probationers and parolees. Further, POs in many jurisdictions supervise both juvenile and adult offenders. Depending on how their caseloads are assigned, these POs may be more or less specialized, and they may deal with clients with certain types of problems. Table 11.7 shows a distribution of the personnel in adult and juvenile probation and parole systems in the United States during 1996. Table 11.8 shows both adult and juvenile state administrations of probation and parole programs during 1996. It is apparent from an inspection of this table that considerable variation exists among the states about which agencies supervise juvenile offenders. It also shows complex divisions of labor in these jurisdictions. Various directories exist to show precisely which state agencies process certain types of juvenile offenders and where such offenders are housed. For instance, the American Correctional Association publishes the *National Juvenile Detention Directory*. This directory contains

BOX 11.4   FOCUS ON JUVENILE PROBATION OFFICER WORK

Some Experiences of Former Probation Officer James R. Davis

James R. Davis, a former probation officer with the Department of Probation in New York City for 22 years, has supervised both adults and juvenile offenders. Usually, the juveniles he supervises are those age 16 and over who have been transferred to criminal courts because of more serious offenses they have committed. He shares his experiences by noting:

Generally, I supervise adults from the age of 16 and over who are placed on probation by the court. Sometimes, I have supervised juveniles under age 16 who are tried in adult courts under the New York State Juvenile Laws. Although I have had only a few cases of juveniles who are tried as adults, they present the worst cases to me, and I am sure, to other probation officers. This is logical, since they are accused of violent crimes. Now there is a special worker who handles these [kinds of] cases.

I remember a case of a juvenile who was 15 and tried as an adult. He was charged with felonious assault. He was hostile and non-cooperative when supervised by me. For example, he didn't report on time, he was verbally abusive to me, and loud and hostile. He was arrested while on probation for another felony assault charge. He was known to have beaten up his grandmother. When I initiated a violation of probation for the new arrest, he became quite hostile and wanted to know why I did this. He even followed me one night into the street and I had to get into a cab to escape him. He beat up another probationer in the waiting area of the office and was finally transferred to an intensive probation caseload.

I was supervising another juvenile who was placed on adult probation at the age of 15 for robbery. He had an arrest prior to being placed on probation for robbery and was arrested again during supervision for another robbery. He always tried to work, and at first he was cooperative. However, during supervision he became hostile, non-cooperative, failing to keep appointments, and failing to wait for his turn in the office. He was black and insisted that he wanted a black probation officer, since I was white. However, the judge incarcerated him for a few weeks because of this new robbery charge. He is now awaiting the disposition of his new robbery case. Although I am still supervising him, the relationship between him and me is tense and fragile; he is still nervous and impatient, and he doesn't keep appointments on time. He minimizes his arrest record. He claims that blacks do not receive justice with white agents of the criminal justice system.

His mother absconded from the home, and he is now supervised by his grandmother.

Although I [now] supervise [primarily] adults, anyone from the age of 16 to 19 is given a youthful offender status except for a few violent offenders. However, I believe that juveniles under 16 who are tried as adults present some special problems and do need supervision in a special caseload by experienced probation officers who are trained for this type of experience.

Davis recalls on another occasion:

This probationer was a young, white, 19-year-old male. I was supervising him on a misdemeanor charge of possession of drugs. This entails three years of probation. He expected special privileges, I believe, because he was white. Ninety percent or more of our probationers were either black or Hispanic. He worked sporadically at low-paying jobs, but he failed to keep them. He was a roofer's assistant and did odd jobs for a construction company.

He failed to keep many of his appointments with me. Warnings did very little to correct this. He refused to be drug tested, and this could have resulted in a violation of his probation. He seemed to have an attitude that because he was white and unlike the other minority offenders, he didn't have to comply with probation orders.

He never completed his high school education, but he appeared very bright to me, and he planned to continue his education. He lived with an older, sick father who was noncooperative with me, and he was always screaming at me and at the offender. His mother was not in the house, and he had an older sister who was also out of the house. The offender was single. I hadn't initiated a violation of probation because of my very heavy work schedule and the possibility that violations based on a lack of cooperation and a failure to report were not taken seriously by most judges. I used admonitions instead.

Finally, he failed to appear for several visits. I issued a violation of probation. I eventually received a call from the probationer that he was in Minnesota in a drug program. He had left the jurisdiction of the state (without permission) and had entered a drug program in another state without informing me of all this. His father was angry at me and accused me of picking on him. He was very protective of his son. When the probationer finally went to court, the judge remanded him. The father again blamed me for his remand and threatened to pursue this further.

It turned out that the judge was lenient and terminated his probation after the offender had served two days in remand. The offender had completed two years of his three years on probation. This case is significant because it represents the possible divergent techniques we might have to use on different types of offenders. It also represents the techniques we have to use with hostile family members. Should we give white offenders differential treatment compared with minority offenders? Probationers do not represent a homogeneous group. Are race and ethnicity cues to differential treatment? We need more research on this.

In another case, Davis reports:

This 16-year-old immigrant from Equador was on probation for attempted murder as the original charge, but felonious assault, a felony, as the final charge. Although he kept most of his appointments with me, he was rearrested several times while on probation. His rearrests included trespassing, drugs, sexual abuse, and attempted burglary. He had no prior record here.

His original charge involved firing a gun at a school kid and assaulting him. The victim suffered injury. The probationer showed no remorse for these offenses, instead tending to rationalize his behavior. He did cooperate with me by keeping his appointments. However, he eventually failed to attend school. He failed to report regularly. He seemed to be involved with a number of petty and semi-serious crimes. He seemed always to elude jail. This might have been because of his age. He was eligible for the present offense under probation.

I finally issued a violation of probation. However, since I retired from my job in 1993, I wasn't able to find out what subsequently happened to the probationer. I did suggest, however, that the new probation officer should recommend jail. I also recommended that a special punitive officer be assigned to this case.

This case is interesting because it illustrates the techniques we should use to supervise dangerous offenders. Should we be strict with them immediately? Should we be patient to see if probation works? Will judges take our recommendations seriously? Perhaps these cases need special matching probation officers. More research is needed on this.

Source: Interviews with James R. Davis, January 1991; November, 1996; Chicago.

much valuable information about juvenile detention facilities and their populations; number of detention facilities and dates opened; and juvenile detention populations by gender, race, age, and other types of classification. The American Correctional Association is located at 8025 Laurel Court, Laurel, Maryland 20707. The ACA distributes this and much more information about both juvenile and adult corrections and probation/parole programs.

TABLE 11.7

Personnel in Adult and Juvenile Corrections[a]

State	Adult — Employees total	Adult White M	Adult White F	Adult Black M	Adult Black F	Adult Hispanic M	Adult Hispanic F	Adult All others M	Adult All others F	Juvenile — Employees total	Juv White M	Juv White F	Juv Black M	Juv Black F	Juv Hispanic M	Juv Hispanic F	Juv All others M	Juv All others F
AL	3,478	1,289	380	1,140	640	13	4	26	3	703	154	107	317	125				
AK	790[b]	480	99	51	10			98	35	582	260[c]	322[c]						10
AZ	6,604	3,347	1,478	239	121	927	353	89	50	740	284	197	72	40	92	40	5	10
AR	2,367	1,034	330	729	271	1		2		210[d]	52	47	77	34				
CA	34,510	13,401	6,159	3,179	2,205	4,745	2,300	1,697	824	5,325	1,613	1,006	708	474	742	398	229	155
CO	3,430	1,870	790	149	52	366	122	65	16	544[e]	226	150	43	22	65	26	7	5
CT	6,204	3,105	1,225	950	385	395	96	30	18	425	139	116	78	36	32	20	3	1
DE	1,516	725	270					371	150	229[e]	55	46	77	48	2	1		
FL	23,105	10,813	5,735	2,553	2,619	696	327	248	114	4,500	4,500[c]							
GA	13,821	5,773	2,781	3,437	1,659	90	15	54	12	2,482	470	515	816	663	6	4	7	1
HI	1,514[e]	209	88	57	18	25	6	821	290	76	5	4	3		2		42	20
ID	1,083	718	289	14	4	31	13	10	4	167	90	68		3	1	4	1	
IL†	12,381	7,846	2,463	1,230	556	151	45	64	26									
IN†	7,134	4,136	1,785	636	468	50	10	34	15	304	234	70	69	19			3	
IA	2,010	1,410	494	35	15	29	6	12	9	443[e]	159	172	65	31	16			
KS	2,901	1,906	677	154	56	62	10	25	11	775	388	291						
KY	3,052	1,975	845	121	94	4	2	10	1									
LA†	4,898[f]	2,020	410	954	433	5		5										
ME†	1,232	926	288	7		2		6	3									
MD	6,242	2,962	657	1,541	1,058	20	4	27	4	1,033	312	226	202	276	1	2	6	8
MA	4,894	3,386	997	244	110	110	16	27	4	594	301	129	87	19	37	14	4	3
MI	14,930	8,514	3,366	1,265	1,209	164	75	247	90	958	958[c]							
MN†	2,992	1,812	955	77	30	23	11	54	30									
MS	2,710	560	364	939	823	4	2	6	12	421	83	114	125	99				
MO	6,180	3,971	1,807	199	154	16	4	15	14	330[e]	128	102	63	33	8	3	12	6
MT	483	387	92	1				2	1	181	94	58					1	
NE†	1,570	920	486	74	33	33	11	8	5	150[e]	99	39	1					
NV	1,716	1,051	395	93	48	64	20	36	9	262[e]	158	100	3		4	1	6	
NH	815	652	148	1		9		3	1									
NJ†	8,839[g]	4,163	1,215	2,107	846	347	89	48	24									
NM	1,184	324	41	39	2	682	52	33	11	484	42	15	4	5	226	185	6	1
NY	30,749[h]	21,122	5,207	1,951	1,041	768	246	265	149	3,295	1,145	793	778	367	134	47	27	4
NC	13,589	6,842	2,331	2,926	1,203	45	8	179	55	882	223	204	291	155	3		1	5
ND	403	247	150			5		5	1	122	66	55	1					
OH	9,795	5,834	1,965	1,140	693	64	18	61	20	2,071	583	503	549	364	9	5	52	6
OK	4,325	2,375	1,124	250	201	35	13	226	101	567	208	174	95	61	3	3	16	7
OR	2,088	1,294	561	45	20	61	21	60	26	522	328	131	21	3	19	6	8	6

TABLE 11.7 (CONT'D)

	Adult Corrections									Juvenile Corrections								
	Employees total	White M	White F	Black M	Black F	Hispanic M	Hispanic F	All others M	All others F	Employees total	White M	White F	Black M	Black F	Hispanic M	Hispanic F	All others M	All others F
State																		
PA	9,427	6,758	1,696	632	242	65	10	18	6	917	431	156	220	102	2	4		1
RI	1,535	1,127	262	78	21	29	8	7	3	208	208[c]							
SC	5,925	1,800	994	1,922	1,112			76	21	972	142	274	282	270		1	3	
SD†	670	469	174	7	2	3	1	10[i]	4[i]									
TN	5,541	3,055	1,360	586	480	19	8	25	8	1,227	489	404	185	141		2	3	2
TX	31,821	14,107	7,735	3,484	2,774	2,554	913	170	84	2,152	620	506	366	256	245	140	12	7
UT	1,810	1,139	556	19	8	32	29	16	11	649[e]	320	223	31	6	28	13	25	3
VT	857	608[c]	249[c]							33[e]	22	9	1		1		1	
VA	9,551	3,845	1,814	2,362	1,431	45	20	26	8	1,729	445	546	397	322	6	9	2	2
WA	5,924	3,195	1,865	296	98	134	61	158	117	819[j]	405	321	39	19	12	6	12	5
WV†	867	620	229	12	5	1												
WI	3,664[k]	1,849	371	59	24	43	7	35	7	662	330	246	37	25	4	4	11	5
WY	281	191	43	2		31	9	5		124	59	63		1		1		
Total	323,407	168,162	65,795	37,986	23,275	12,993	4,965	5,448	2,403	38,869	16,828	8,502	6,103	4,015	1,706	929	507	269
Other entities																		
FBP	25,515	13,324	4,462	3,062	1,616	1,876	497	555	123									
Cook	3,164	692	159	1,255	860	130	43	25										
DC	3,925	275	68	2,182	1,299	31	8	45	17	507	3	18	340	140	3	3		
NYC	13,639[e]	13,639[e]								266	7		152	82	19	3	2	1
PHL	1,851	429	117	698	498	80	17	9	3									
PRᵇ	5,318					5,067	251											
CSC	11,426	7,383[c]	4,043[c]															
ABᵇ	1,935	1,935[c]																
MB†,ˡ	550	550[c]																
FN	227	221						6										
PEI†	93	85	8															

[a] Entities noted with a dagger reported figures for combined adult and juvenile departments. M, male; F, female.
[b] Data as of 6/30/92.
[c] Ethnic and/or sex breakdown unavailable at time of publication.
[d] Fewer personnel due to closing of one institution.
[e] Data as of 6/30/93.
[f] Includes 1,071 juvenile services staff without ethnic/sex breakdown.
[g] Fewer personnel due to reorganization.
[h] Temporary and summer school employees not included.
[i] Native Americans.
[j] Data as of 6/30/91.
[k] Includes 1,269 probation and parole staff without ethnic/gender breakdown.
[l] Data as of 3/31/94.

Source: American Correctional Association, 1996:xlii–xliii.

TABLE 11.8

Probation/Parole/Aftercare Service Providers as of June 30, 1994

State[a]	Number of board members	Adult paroling authorities	Adult parole services	Adult probation services	Juvenile parole/aftercare services	Juvenile probation services
AL	3	Bd Pardons & Paroles	Bd Pardons & Paroles	Bd Pardons & Paroles	Co Courts	Dept Youth Svcs ($ only) & Co. Cts
AK	5 (PT)	Bd Parole	Dept Corrections	Dept Corrections	No parole/aftercare	DHSS/Div Family & Youth Svcs[c]
AZ	7	Bd of Exec Clemency	Bd of Exec Clemency	States Courts	DYTR/Parole Admin	State Courts
AR	7 (PT)[d]	Post-Prison Transfer Board	Bd C&Cmty Pun/Dept Cmty Pun[c]	Bd C & Cmty Pun/Dept Cmty Pun[c]	Courts/HDS/Youth Svc Bd	Courts/DHS/Youth Svcs Bd
CA	9	Bd Prison Terms	YAC/DOC/Par & Cmty Svcs Div	YAC/DOC/Par & Cmty Svcs Div	YAC/DYA/Parole Svcs & Cmty Corr	Co Courts
CO	7	Bd Parole	DOC/Div Adult Parole Supv	Judicial Dept	DHS/Div Youth Svcs	Judicial Dept
CT	11 (PT)[e]	Bd Parole	DOC/Div Op/Cmty Svcs	Office Adult Prob	Dept Children & Families	Superior Court Juv Matters/Family Div
DE	5 (PT)[e]	Bd Parole	DOC/Div Cmty Svcs	DOC/Div Cmty Svcs	DSCYF/Div Youth Rehab/Cmty Svcs[c]	DSCYF/Div. Youth Rehab/Cmty Svcs[c]
DC	5	Bd Parole	Bd Parole	DC Superior Ct/Social Svcs Div	DHS/YS Admin/Bu of Ct & Cmty Svcs	DC Superior Ct/Social Svcs Div
FL	7	Parole Cmsn	DOC/Prob & Parole Svcs[c]	DOC/Prob & Parole Svcs[c]	DHRS/Juvenile Justice	DHRS/Juvenile Justice
GA	5	Bd Pardons & Paroles	Bd Pardons & Paroles[c]	DOC/Cmty Corr Div	DHR/Dept CH Youth Svcs & Co Court	DHR/Dept Ch Youth Svcs & Co Courts
HI	3 (PT)[e]	Paroling Authority	Paroling Authority/Field Svcs	State Judiciary/Prob Ofc	DHS/OYS/Yth Corr Facil/Cmty Svcs	State Judiciary/Family Courts
ID	5 (PT)	Cmsn for Pardons & Parole	DOC/Div Field & Cmty Svcs	DOC/Div Field & Cmty Svcs	DHW/Bur of Juv Justice	DHW/Bur of Juv Justice/Co Courts
IL	12	Prisoner Review Bd	DOC/Cmty Svcs Div[c]	Judicial Circuits/Prob Div	DOC/Div Div/Juv Fields Svcs	Judicial Circuits/Prob Div
IN	5	Parole Bd	DOC/Parole Svcs Section	Judicia/County Courts	DOC/Parole Svcs Section	Judicial/County Courts
IA	5 (PT)[e]	Bd Parole	DOC/Div Cmty Corr Svcs	DOC/Div Cmty Corr Svcs	DHS/Div Adult, Children & Family Svcs	Judicial Districts
KS	5	Parole Bd	DOC/Cmty Field Svcs[c]	Judicial Districts/Ct Svcs Div	DSRS/Youth & Adult Svcs	Judicial Districts/Ct Svcs Div
KY	7	Parole Bd	DOC/Cmty Svcs & Facil/Div PP	DOC/Cmty Svcs & Facil/Div PP	CHR/DSS/Div Family Svcs	CHR/DSS/Div Family Svcs
LA	7	Bd Parole	DPSC/Div Prob & Parole[c]	DPSC/Div Prob & Parole[c]	DPSC/Ofc Youth Development	DPSC/Ofc Youth Development
ME	5 (PT)	Parole Bd[f]	DOC/Div Prob & Parole	DOC/Div Prob & Parole	DOC/Div Prob & Parole	DOC/Div Prob & Parole
MD	7	Parole Cmsn	DPSCS/Div Parole & Prob	DPSCS/Div Parole & Prob	Dept Juv Svcs	Dept Juv Svcs
MA	8	Parole Bd	Parole Bd	Office of Cmsnr Prob/Courts	DYS/Bur Cmty Svcs	Office of Cmsnr of Prob/Courts
MI	10	Parole Bd	DOC/Field Op Admin	DOC/Field Op Admin & Dist Cts	DSS/Office Delinq Svcs/Co Cts	DSS/Office Deling Svcs/Co Cts
MN	4 (PT)[g]	DOC/Office Adult Release[c] Co Cts or CCA	DOC/Prob Par Supv Rel[c] Co Cts or CCA	DOC/Prob Par Supv Rel[c] Co Cts or CCA	DOC/Prob Par Supv Rel[c] Co Cts or CCA	DOC/Prob Par Supv Rel[c] Co Cts or CCA
MS	5	Parole Bd	DOC/Cmty Svcs Div	DOC/Cmty Svcs Div	DHS/DYS/Cmty Svcs Div	DHS/DYS/Cmty Svcs Div
MO	5	Bd Prob & Parole	DOC/Bd Prob & Parole	DOC/Bd Prob & Parole	DSS/Div Youth Svcs & Jud Circuits	Judicial Circuits
MT	3 (PT)	Bd Pardons	DCHS/CD/Prob & Parole Bureau	DCHS/CD/Prob & Parole Bureau	Dept Family Svcs/Corr Div	Judicial Districts
NE	5	Bd Parole[e]	DCS/Adult Paorle Admin[c]	NE Prob System	DJS/Juv Parole Admin[c]	NE Prob System
NV	6	Bd Parole Cmsnrs	DMV/Div Parole & Prob	DMV/Div Parole & Prob	DHR/YCS/Youth Parole Bureau	District Courts
NH	5 (PT)	Bd Parole	DOC/Div Field Svcs[c]	DOC/Div Field Svcs[c]	DHHS/DCYS/Bur Children	DHHS/DCYS/Bu Children
NJ	9	Parole Bd	DOC/Bureau Parole	The Judiciary/Prob Div	DOC/Bureau Parole	The Judiciary/Prob Div
NM	4	Adult Parole Bd	CD/Prob & Parole Div	CD/Prob & Parole Div	CYFD/Cmty Svcs Div	CYFD/Cmty Svcs Div

TABLE 11.8 (CONT'D)

State[a]	Number of board members	Adult paroling authorities	Adult parole services	Adult probation services	Juvenile parole/aftercare services	Juvenile probation services
NY	19	Bd Parole	Div Parole	Div Prob & Corr Alt/Co Courts	Exec Dept/Div for Youth/Div Parole[c]	Exec Dept/Div Prob & Corr Alt/Courts
NC	5	Parole Cmsn	DOC/Div Adult Prob & Parole	DOC/Div Adult Prob & Parole	Admin Office Courts/Juv Svcs Div	Admin Office Courts/Juv Svcs Div
ND	3 (PT)	Parole Bd	DCR/Div Parole & Prob	DCR/Div Parole & Prob	DCR/Div Juv Svcs[c]	DCR/Div Juv Svcs[c]/Supr Cts
OH	11[h]	DRC/Div Parole & Cmty Svcs/Ad Parole Auth & Parole Bd	DRC/Div Parole & Cmty Svcs	DRC/Div Parole & Cmty Svcs & Co Courts	DYS/Div Courts, Par. & Cmty Svcs[c]	Co Courts
OK	5 (PT)	Pardon & Parole Bd	DOC[c]	DOC[c]	DHS/OJJ/Juvenile Svcs Unit[c]	DHS/OJJ/Juvenile Svcs Unit[c]
OR	4	Bd Parole & Post Prison Supv	DOC/Cmty Corrections	DOC/Cmty Corrections	DHR/CSD/Juv Corr Svcs	Co Courts
PA	5	Bd Parob & Parole[c] & Co Cts[h]	Bd Prob & Parole[c] & Co Cts	Bd of Prob & Parole[c] & Co Cts	Co Courts	Co Courts
RI	6 (PT)	Parole Bd	DOC/Div Rehab Svcs	DOC/Div Rehab Svcs	DCYF/Div Juv Corr Svcs	DCYF/Div Juv Corr Svcs
SC	7 (PT)	Bd Prob, Parole, & Pardon Svcs	Dept Prob, Parole, & Prob Svcs	Dept Prob, Parole, & Pdn Svcs	Dept Juv Justice/Cmty Div	Dept Juv Justice/Cmty Div
SD	6 (PT)	Bd Pardons & Parole	DOC	Unified Judicial Sys/Ct Svcs Dept	Unified Judicial Sys/Ct Svcs Dept	Unified Judicial Sys/Ct Svcs Dept
TN	7	Bd Paroles	BP/Parole Field Svcs[c]	DOC/Div Field Svcs[c]	DYD/Div Prob[c]	DYD/Div Prob[c]
TX	18	Bd Pardons & Paroles	TDCJ/PPD/Parole Supv	TDCJ/Cmty Jus Asist Div/Dist Cts	TYC/Cmty Svcs Div/Ofc Par Supv[c]	Co Courts
UT	5	Bd Pardons	DOC/Div Field Operations	DOC/Div Field Operations	DHS/Div Youth Corr	Juv Courts
VT	5 (PT)	Bd Parole	AHS/DOC	AHS/DOC	AHS/DSRSi	DSRS/Div Social Svcs
VA	5	Parole Bd	DOC/Div Cmty Corr	DOC/Cmty Corr	Dept Youth & Fam Svcs[c]	Dept Youth & Fam Svcs[c]
WA	3	Indeterminate Sent Review Bd	DOC/Div Cmty Corr	DOC/Div Cmty Corr & Co Cts	DSHS/Juv Rehab Admin	Co Courts
WV	3	Parole Bd	DPS/Div Corrections	DPS/DOC & Judicial Circuits	DPS/DOC (Compact) and courts	DPS/DOC (Compact), Jud Circuits[k]
WI	5	Parole Cmsn	DOC/Div Prob & Parole	DOC/Div Prob & Parole	DHSS/Div Yth Svcs/Co Soc Svcs Depts	Co Social Svcs Depts
WY	7 (PT)	Bd Parole	DOC/Div Field Services	DOC/Div Field Services	Dept Family Svcs	Dept Family Svcs/Co Munic Depts
US	9	Parole Cmsn[c]	Admin Ofc of US Courts	Admin Ofc of US Courts/Dept of Prob		

[a]The following states have one or more independent county, municipal, or city departments: CO, GA, IN, KS, KY, LA, MO, NE, NY, OK, TN, WY. All boards are independent except MD, MI, MN, OH, and TX.

[b]All members serve full-time unless coded PT.

[c]Accredited by Commission on Accreditation for Corrections.

[d]Three full-time, four part-time.

[e]Chairman serves full-time; members part-time.

[f]Parole Board hears pre-1976 cases of parole. Flat sentences.

[g]Executive Officer & three Deputy Executive Officers (CCA Cmty Corr Act).

[h]Plus 15 hearing officers.

[i]The Board of Probation and Parole administers adult services when sentence is over two years; county courts when sentence is two years or less.

[j]No functional juvenile parole system. Children in custody go into placement and eventually return to community under supervision of caseworker.

[k]Under state statute, juv. release is judicially, rather than administratively, determined and is considered probation.Source: American Correctional Association, 1996:xii–xiii.

Source: American Correctional Association, 1996:xii–xiii.

Probation Work and Professionalism

There is a keen sense of professionalism among most POs. The *American Correctional Association* and the *American Probation and Parole Association* are two of the most important professional organizations today that disseminate information, programs, and workshops for various forms of professional training for both juvenile and adult corrections and probation/parole services. Many POs attend the meetings of these and other professional organizations to learn about the latest innovations and probation programs.

Sweet (1985) views probation work with juveniles as a timely opportunity to intervene and make a difference in their lives. Thus he sees probation for juveniles as therapeutic. He divides the therapy function that probation officers can perform into five simple steps (Sweet, 1985:90):

1. *Case review.* Probation counselors need skills to read the behaviors of the youths they supervise and their probable antecedents.

2. *Self-awareness.* Probation counselors need to inspect their own reactions to youths; are they too impatient or overly sensitive? Traditional transference and countertransference issues must be addressed.

3. *Development of a relationship.* Great patience is required; children are often rejected, and probation officers must learn to accept them and demonstrate a faith in their ability to achieve personal goals.

4. *The critical incident.* This is the testing phase of the relationship, where juveniles may deliberately act up to test honesty and sincerity of PO.

5. *Following through.* Successive tests will be made by juveniles as they continue to verify the PO's honesty and sincerity; POs do much of the parenting that their clients' parents failed to do. Sweet considers these stages integral features of action therapy that can often be more effective than insight-oriented therapy.

Because of their diverse training, POs often orient themselves toward juvenile clients in particular ways that may be more or less effective. Because many juvenile offenders are considered manipulators who might take advantage of a PO's sympathies, some POs have devised interpersonal barriers between themselves and their youthful clients. Other POs have adopted more productive interpersonal strategies. Strong (1981) has identified several different types of PO orientations toward youthful offenders that might have different implications, depending on how these orientations influence the nature of the PO–client relation. These orientations include (1) the **enforcer**, where POs perceive themselves as enforcement officers who must regulate juvenile behaviors; (2) the **detector**, where the PO attempts to identify troublesome juvenile clients in advance on the basis of probation program rule infractions; (3) the **broker**, where POs try to refer youths to appropriate community services and treatments; and (4) the **educator**, **mediator** and **enabler**, where POs seek to instruct and assist offenders to deal with their personal and social problems to fit better into their community environments.

If POs check up on their youthful clients continuously or regard them with suspicion, they inhibit the growth of productive interpersonal relations that might be helpful in facilitating a youth's reentry into society. Enforcement-oriented officers and those who attempt to detect rule infractions almost always create a hostile working relationship with their clients, and communication barriers are often erected that inhibit a PO's effectiveness. Educators, enablers, and mediators are perhaps most helpful to youths, although broker-oriented POs are instrumental in helping juveniles receive the treatments and services they need.

Entry-Level Requirements for Probation/Parole Officers

There were 57,530 POs and staff in 1996 (Camp and Camp, 1996:134). There were 20,660 persons who were limited exclusively to probation work, about 9983 officers and staff limited to exclusively parole work, and 26,887 officers and staff who were assigned to *both* probation and parole work (Camp and Camp, 1996:128–129). About two-thirds (72.2 percent) were white and 53.4 percent of all probation and probation/parole agency staff were women. Between 15 and 20 percent of all persons employed in these probation and parole services were support staff, while the rest were officers or supervisors who managed probationers and parolees.

The average number of preservice training hours required of state POs was 135 hours, with an average of 31 in-service hours required (Camp and Camp, 1995d:11). States such as Wisconsin, Nebraska, New Jersey, and North Carolina required no preservice hours, while Utah and Nevada required 440 and 460 preservice hours, respectively. The District of Columbia and Wisconsin required no in-service hours or training, while most other jurisdictions required between 20 and 40 hours of such training (Camp and Camp, 1995d:11). Educational requirements vary according to the jurisdiction, with most requiring a high school diploma or GED. A few departments and agencies require bachelor's degrees for entry-level positions. Those with either bachelor's or master's degrees in some law enforcement or criminal justice program are at a definite advantage for obtaining probation or parole work. Many states and universities work collaboratively to create internships, where prospective job applicants can work directly with clients in probation and parole agencies for 300 to 400 hours. Following their training, they receive priority whenever job openings become available.

Salaries

The average starting salary for probation officers in the United States in 1996 was $26,126, while starting salaries for parole officers were slightly higher, at $26,829. High salaries for probation officers averaged $44,879, while the average high parole officer salary was $44,294 (Camp and Camp, 1996:134). Tennessee had the distinction of having the lowest starting salary of all states at $15,948 (for either beginning probation or parole officers), while California and New York had the highest starting salaries for both types of officers at about $39,200. Overall high salaries were in New Jersey and California, at approximately $58,000 (Camp and Camp, 1996:134). Probation and parole administrators had average salaries of $73,785 and $67,892 per year, respectively (Camp and Camp, 1996:135).

POs for the federal government and attached to the U.S. Probation Office are perhaps the highest-paid POs in the nation. Their fringe benefits and pay rates make their jobs especially attractive. Often, federal POs are recruited from those who have performed PO work in different states. Thus they enter their federal positions with considerable experience. Labor turnover among POs with the U.S. Probation Office is extremely low. Many officers retire from the U.S. Probation Office because of the many rewards, both financial and psychological, that it offers. Rosalind Andrews, Chief Probation Officer of the U.S. Probation Office in Knoxville, Tennessee, has remarked: "Nobody quits around here. They're here for the duration. We simply pay better than most states, and our work is interesting. There is never a dull moment around here" (excerpts from personal interview, May 1990). Although the U.S. Probation Office performs supervised release functions mostly for adult probationers and parolees, they also supervise a small proportion of juvenile offenders who have violated federal laws.

PO Labor Turnover

Largely because of the relatively high labor turnover among POs in state probation and parole agencies, recruitment of new POs is brisk. In 1995 there was a 19 percent turnover among state and federal probation/parole officers. Entry requirements in many states are not particularly demanding. Although the sample of POs surveyed by the American Correctional Association tended to have bachelor's degrees, most states require only a high school diploma or GED as the minimum educational level for PO work. In 12 percent of the state jurisdictions, there are no specific educational requirements for PO work (American Correctional Association, 1996).

Probation Officer Functions and Responsibilities

The functions of POs are diverse, and they include such tasks as report preparation, home and school visits, and a variety of other client contacts. They often arrange contacts between their clients and various community-based corrections agencies who provide services and specific types of psychological and social treatments. POs themselves perform counseling tasks with their clients. They must also enforce laws associated with probation or parole program conditions. Thus if offenders have been ordered to comply with a specific curfew and/or reimburse victims for their financial losses, POs must monitor them to ensure that these program conditions have been fulfilled.

A detailed analysis of PO responsibilities was conducted for all states by Burton, Latessa, and Barker (1992). Many of these responsibilities are statutory or legislatively mandated. These functions and responsibilities are diverse and include the following (Burton, Latessa, and Barker, 1992:277):

1. Supervision
2. Surveillance
3. Investigate cases
4. Assist in rehabilitation
5. Develop/discuss probation conditions
6. Counsel
7. Visit home/work
8. Arrest
9. Make referrals
10. Write PSI reports
11. Keep records
12. Perform other court duties
13. Collect restitution
14. Serve warrants
15. Make contact with court and recommend sentences/dispositions
16. Develop community service programs
17. Assist law enforcement agencies
18. Assist court in transferring cases
19. Enforce criminal laws
20. Locate employment
21. Initiate revocations

It is clear from this list of duties and responsibilities for probation officers that they cover a wide range of functions. There are both recordkeeping and law enforcement functions. These officers also act as liaison between the various courts and convicted/adjudicated offenders. They also have counseling functions, make referrals to various community services for clients with special needs, and they even collect restitution payments in some jurisdictions.

Assessment Centers

The writing chores of PO work cannot be overemphasized. Report preparation accounts for over half of a PO's time on the job. Therefore, writing skills are not only useful, they are necessary. Dade County, Florida, operates an *assessment center* that is used to train its correctional officers, including many POs in the state. Assessment centers perform screening functions and administer tests and other devices to recruit new POs and train them. Law enforcement agencies in various jurisdictions utilize assessment centers similar to those existing in various Florida jurisdictions.

Assessment centers help administrators of juvenile probation programs identify various skills of prospective officers, including (1) the ability to understand and implement policies and procedures, (2) the ability to be aware of all elements in a given situation and to use sensitivity to others and good judgment in dealing with various situations, and (3) the ability to communicate effectively. Personal and social skills are highly prized among POs, and those who appear most qualified are further subjected to a series of tests and interviews. The testing pertains to the preparation of written reports, role-playing, and acting out problem situations, and some videotaping is used to present those trained with a variety of client scenarios. Three-person teams of evaluators conduct final screenings of applicants and attempt to select those who will minimize agency liabilities arising from client lawsuits (Florida House Committee on Criminal Justice, 1994).

Some of the major PO dimensions that are deemed most important are:

1. *Problem solving:* problem analysis—the ability to grasp the source, nature, and key elements of problems; judgment—recognition of the significant factors to arrive at sound and practical decisions

2. *Communication:* dialogue skills—effectiveness of one-on-one contacts with youthful clients, small group interactions; writing skills—expression of ideas clearly and concisely

3. *Emotional and motivational:* reactions to reassure—functioning in a controlled, effective manner under conditions of stress; keeping one's head; drive—the amount of directed and sustained energy to accomplish one's objectives

4. *Interpersonal:* insight into others—the ability to proceed, giving due consideration to the needs and feelings of others; leadership—the direction of behavior of others toward the achievement of goals

5. *Administrative:* planning—forward thinking, anticipating situations and problems, and preparation in advance to cope with these problems; commitment to excellence—determination that the task will be well done

Probation Officer Stress and Burnout

Stress and burnout are two primary factors that may interfere with one's work and impair a PO's performance. **Stress** *is a nonspecific response to a perceived threat to a person's well-being* (Whitehead and Lindquist, 1985). Reactions to stress might be somatic complaints of aches and pains; irritability, loss of attention span, and fatigue are other stress concomitants. **Burnout** *is a result of stress. Burnout conveys work alienation, depersonalization, depression, and other job-related complaints.* Various definitions of burnout suggest emotional, mental, and physical exhaustion that might debilitate and weaken a PO's ability to work effectively with others (Whitehead and Lindquist, 1985). As more dangerous juvenile offenders are placed in probation programs, it might be anticipated that PO stress and burnout will increase. While firearms training is often required as a part of a PO's recruitment program, in past years POs have not typically carried firearms. However, there are indications that this situation is changing, particularly with growing **caseloads** of more serious, violent offenders to supervise (Brown, 1990:25).

In 1995 it was estimated that there were 102,582 juveniles in most U.S. correctional systems (Camp and Camp, 1995c:1). There were 45,274 employees in state juvenile agencies who processed about 1.5 million juveniles. This processing included the preparation of predisposition reports for over 600,000 cases, and over 500,000 cases were processed for supervision (American Correctional Association, 1996). These cases are not distributed evenly throughout the various juvenile probation departments in the United States. Thus caseloads for some POs are considerably larger than they are for others. A high caseload is defined arbitrarily as 50 or more juvenile clients, although caseloads as high as 400 or more have been reported in some jurisdictions, such as California. Hurst (1990a:19) says that a standard probation caseload recommendation of 35 has been made by the President's Crime Commission, although this figure is rarely achieved in most probation agencies today. When caseloads are particularly high, this places an even greater burden on the shoulders of POs who must often prepare predisposition reports for youths at the juvenile court judge's direction.

RECRUITMENT AND CASELOADS: EFFECTIVENESS EVALUATED

Juvenile probation officers have been guided since 1900 by their belief in the probation mission—*protecting society and acting in the best interests of children* (Hurst, 1990a:19). Although a general lack of a strong professional membership has hampered the influence of juvenile probation officers in most U.S. jurisdictions, the U.S. Supreme Court rulings of the 1960s and 1970s in favor of juvenile rights has further undermined their powers. Today, the following issues have been identified that continue to be debated (Hurst, 1990b:19; Torbet, 1987):

1. *Organizational sponsorship.* Should probation services be administered by executive branches of government or by judiciary branches?

2. *Local versus state administration.* Should probation services be operated by the state or by local government?

3. *Client caseload.* The National Probation Association standard of a maximum caseload of 50 cases was recommended in 1923, but this figure was reduced to 35 at the recommendation of the President's Crime Commission in 1967; however, such numbers are seldom achieved in actual practice.

4. *Method of supervision.* Should probation officers suppress offenders and conduct extensive surveillance on them, or should they assess their needs and bring services to bear to meet these needs?

5. *Diagnosis and classification.* Are empirical classification approaches superior to qualitative assessments of client needs?

6. *Private versus public administration of probation services.* What should be the limits of privatization in juvenile probation?

7. *Performance measurement.* How can juvenile probation officers be evaluated and compensated effectively?

KEY TERMS

About Face

Allegheny Academy

Army model

Balanced approach

Boot camps

Boston Offender Project

Broker

Burnout

Caseloads

Chronic 6 percent

Client Management Classification

Combination sentences

Community service

Conventional model

Conventional model with geographic considerations

Corrections officers
Creative sentencing
Detector
Electronic monitoring
Enabler, educator, mediator
Enforcer
Fines
Georgia ISP model
Home confinement
Home incarceration
House arrest
IMPACT (Intensive Motivational Program of Alternative Correctional Treatment)
Intensive Aftercare Program (IAP)
Intensive probation supervision (IPS)
Intensive supervised probation (ISP)
Intermediate punishments
Intermittent sentences
Jail as a condition of probation
Juvenile intensive supervised probation (JISP)
Juvenile probation camps (JPCs)
Mediator
Mixed sentences
New Jersey ISP model
Numbers game model

Ohio experience
Probationer
Probation officer
Project New Pride
Recidivism
Recidivism rate
Regimented inmate discipline (RID) program
Restitution
San Francisco Project
Scared Straight
Second Chance Program
See Our Side (SOS) Program
Sexual Offender Treatment (SOT) Program
Shock parole
Shock probation
Smart sentencing
SpeakerID
Specialized caseloads model
Split sentences
Standard probation
Stress
Unconditional probation
Victim compensation
Youth-to-Victim Restitution Project

QUESTIONS FOR REVIEW

1. What is an *intermediate punishment program*? Give some examples of intermediate punishments.

2. Describe *community service, payment of fines, restitution*, and *victim compensation* as four conditions judges might impose, together with probationary dispositions. Write a short essay evaluating these conditions.

3. What is *creative sentencing*? In what respect is an intermediate punishment a creative disposition?

4. What is the *Ohio experience*? Discuss the four types of Ohio programs and their major differences.

5. Describe four different programs for assigning PO caseloads. Which ones do you feel best meet the needs of offenders? Why? Explain.

6. What is the *balanced approach to probation work*?

7. What is *electronic monitoring*? Describe four types of electronic monitoring systems.

8. How is the work of POs enhanced by electronic monitoring? What are *drive-bys*?

9. What is *home confinement*? Briefly give a history of its use in the United States. What are some accompanying punishments that might be imposed together with home confinement?

10. What are *boot camps*? Describe the characteristics of boot camp experiences. What are the goals of boot camps? Do they appear to be successful? Why or why not?

SUGGESTED READINGS

Mortimer, Allyn M. *Consultation on After-School Programs.* New York: Carnegie Corporation, 1994.

Poole, Carol and Peggy Slavick. *Boot Camps: A Washington State Update and Overview of National Findings.* Olympia, WA: Washington State Institute for Public Policy, 1995.

Sakumoto, Raymond E. *Report of a Statistical Study and Evaluation of the Juvenile Intensive Supervision Program.* Honolulu, HI: University of Hawaii at Manoa, 1995.

Whitfield, Dick and David Scott (eds.). *Paying Back: Twenty Years of Community Service.* Winchester, UK: Waterside Press, 1993.

CHAPTER 12

JUVENILE CORRECTIONS: CUSTODIAL SANCTIONS AND PAROLE

INTRODUCTION

A juvenile, M.C., was placed in a Texas juvenile detention center which appeared crowded. M.C. filed a motion with the court to be released from detention, alleging that the overcrowded detention facility was (1) not certified, and (2) overcrowded to the extent that M.C.'s discharge from that institution should be ordered. An appeals court examined the juvenile detention center and determined that it was properly certified. Further, even though there was some overcrowding, the overcrowding in and of itself did not entitle M.C. to immediate release from the facility. The court also cited recognized professional standards, such as those articulated by the American Correctional Association, in determining whether the facility was overcrowded to the extent that it created conditions of cruel and unusual punishment. In this instance, there was no such finding and M.C. was required to continue his detention in the facility. [Matter of M.C., 915 S.W. 2d 118 (Tex. App. Jan. 1996)]

Paul C. was a juvenile with a history of truancy, behavioral problems, and assaultive behavior. An evaluating psychologist examined Paul C., spent time examining Paul C.'s home environment, and eventually recommended to the juvenile court judge that Paul C. should be incarcerated for his most recent offense. This offense was robbing (mugging) a woman on a subway, where serious physical injuries were inflicted. The family court placed Paul C. in a minimum secure facility. Paul C. objected and appealed, arguing that he did not deserve to be confined in a secure facility. Rather, the judge should have imposed the "least restrictive alternative" instead. An appeals court upheld the family court secure placement decision. Paul C. remained confined for a period of time. [In re Application of Paul C. (619 N.Y.S.2d 564) (N.Y. Sup. App. Div. Dec. 1994)]

A 10-year-old child, Doe, was adjudicated delinquent and committed to the Reception Evaluation Center in South Carolina for a period of time to undergo examination and evaluation. During the detention of Doe in the evaluation center, Doe's parents and attorney appealed his detention, alleging that he was "too young to be detained." Doe had originally been taken into custody by police when he committed assault and disturbed a school. The South Carolina appellate court convened and determined that according to South Carolina juvenile statutes, a child after his twelfth birthday and before his seventeenth birthday may be committed to the custody of the Division of Juvenile Justice. Therefore, they held that the 10-year-old's detention in the evaluation center, which was the equivalent of institutional confinement, was improper and should be discontinued. However, by the time of the court ruling, Doe had been released to the custody of his parents and the ruling was moot. [In Interest of Doe (458 S.E.2d 556) (S.C. App.June 1995)]

By year end 1995, there were 102,582 juveniles under some form of correctional supervision in 51 jurisdictions in the United States (Camp and Camp, 1995c:1). There were approximately 2 million admissions and discharges of juveniles from secure confinement facilities during 1995 (Maguire and Pastore, 1996). Minority youths made up 65 percent of those confined (Camp and Camp, 1995c:9). Sheer admission rates of juveniles to confinement of any kind, even for a few hours, are staggering. In 1990 there were 690,000 admissions of juveniles to detention centers and other facilities (Parent, 1993). In 1996, nearly 1 million youths were admitted to detention centers for a few hours or longer (Maguire and Pastore, 1996).

One of the most important components of the juvenile justice system is *juvenile corrections. Juvenile corrections encompasses all personnel, agencies, and institutions that supervise youthful offenders.* We have previously examined various nominal and conditional options that related to supervising juveniles who are placed on diversion or disposed to probation or intermediate punishment programs. In this chapter we describe several custodial sentencing options, the most severe sanctions that juvenile court judges may impose. These sanctions are usually administered to youthful offenders who have been adjudicated as delinquent and considered sufficiently serious or dangerous to merit close supervision or secure confinement.

First, a brief history of juvenile corrections in the United States is presented. Some of the more important goals of juvenile corrections are described. Next, an overview of several custodial sentencing options is provided. This overview is followed by a description of some of the more popular nonsecure and secure custodial alternatives. Because some juvenile offenders require greater discipline and harsher treatment than others, secure confinement facilities vary in their degree of supervision and control exerted over juvenile inmates. These facilities and programs are described and assessed.

Juveniles released from nonsecure or secure confinement are often placed on parole for limited periods. Those juveniles placed on parole are ordinarily expected to abide by various parole conditions in order to fulfill their parole programs successfully. Some of these conditions and parole programs are described. If juveniles violate one or more parole conditions, their parole may be revoked. Parole revocation may mean that juveniles will be returned to their original custodial institutions. This revocation process is described. Finally, several key issues in juvenile corrections are presented. These issues include the privatization of juvenile corrections, housing juveniles in adult lockups or jail facilities, classifying offenders for their subsequent placement, and offender recidivism.

THE HISTORY OF JUVENILE CORRECTIONS

Our definition of **juvenile delinquency** *is any act committed by a juvenile which, if committed by an adult, would be a crime* (Rogers and Mays, 1987:566). In the United States, especially during the nineteenth century and early twentieth century, juvenile matters were handled by a variety of civil courts and nonlegal institutions such as welfare agencies. The doctrine under which juveniles were managed and processed was called *parens patriae*, which means "parent of the country" (Black, 1990:1114). Historically, this term was a part of English common law during the medieval period, and it meant that juvenile matters were within the purview of the sovereign and his or her agents, usually chancellors and other officials in various regions. Figuratively, the sovereign, as "parent," assumed responsibility for all juveniles. Through the centuries this term was accepted by most jurisdictions. Subsequently, the United States adopted the *parens patriae* doctrine as an effective way of dealing with juvenile matters.

Arguably, one of the first correctional facilities to recognize juveniles as a status different from adult males and females was the Walnut Street Jail in Philadelphia, Pennsylvania. The Walnut Street Jail was constructed in 1776 to house the overflow of inmates from the High Street Jail. When the Walnut Street Jail was constructed, little or no thought was given to whether males, females, and minors would be housed in separate areas. Usually, inmates of all ages and genders were housed in common rooms with straw strewn on floors for sleeping. No attempt was made to segregate prisoners. In 1790, new policies were implemented within the Walnut Street Jail to provide for the separate confinement of prisoners according to gender and youthfulness. Further, the jail provided for segregating more dangerous prisoners from less dangerous ones through an innovation known as *solitary confinement*. Ironically, more than a few jails in the United States today house juveniles with adult inmates for various durations, despite certain regulations to the contrary. Thus at least some jails continue to exhibit some of congregate accommodations that typified the original Walnut Street Jail constructed in 1776. This particular problem is addressed later in the chapter.

The first public reformatory for juvenile offenders was the New York House of Refuge, organized in New York City in 1825 by the Society for the Prevention of Pauperism (Cahalan, 1986:101). Since there was little centralized organization to these houses of refuge, it is difficult to determine the impact of these facilities on delinquency (Rogers and Mays, 1987:426). The manifest goals of these houses of refuge were to provide poor, abused, or orphaned youths with food, clothing, and lodging, although in return, hard work, discipline and study were expected.

Charles Loring Brace established the New York Children's Aid Society in 1853, which functioned primarily as a placement service for parentless children (Mennel, 1983:199). The term *juvenile delinquency* was seldom used during the early nineteenth century, because public authorities stressed parental control of children and regarded youthful misbehaviors as lack of discipline rather than something that should be dealt with more formally (Mennel, 1983:198). Many early institutions designed to care for and reform juveniles were operated under private, charitable, and religious sponsorship.

Subsequently, the Civil War, followed by the reconstruction period and vast industrialization, left many families fatherless. In the subsequent years, many of these families moved to urban areas, such as Chicago, Boston, and New York, where they sought jobs in shops and factories. Many children were exploited as cheap labor by "sweatshops" in the absence of child labor laws. Also, large numbers of youths roamed the streets unsupervised while their parents worked at jobs for long hours. Eventually, *children's tribunals* were established in various states, including Massachusetts and New York, to punish youths charged with various offenses. The first statute authorizing such a tribunal to deal with juvenile matters was passed in Massachusetts in 1874 (Hahn, 1984). A similar statute was passed in 1892 in New York.

Jane Addams established and operated Hull House in 1889, a settlement home for children of immigrant families in Chicago. Financing for this home came largely from charitable organizations and philanthropists, and it existed to provide children with activities to alleviate boredom and monotony while their parents were at work. Many children without parents were accommodated by Addams. Teaching children morality, ethics, and certain religious precepts were important components of juvenile treatment programs in Addams's day (Hahn, 1984).

The *Compulsory School Act* was passed by the Colorado State Legislature in 1899. Its goal was preventing truancy among juveniles. This act targeted youths who were habitually absent from school, wandered about the streets during school hours, and had no obvious business or occupation. These youths were labeled "juvenile disorderly persons." Since the act was aimed primarily at truancy, it is not considered a juvenile court act in a technical sense. The Illinois legislature created the first juvenile court act on July 1, 1899. It was called *An Act to Regulate the Treatment and Control of Dependent, Neglected, and Delinquent Children*. Between 1899 and 1909, 20 states had passed similar legislation for the establishment of juvenile courts. By 1945, all states had juvenile court systems. However, these systems varied greatly among jurisdictions, and the responsibility for deciding juvenile dispositions rested with different types of court systems.

In 1880 the first census of juvenile offenders in public institutions was conducted by the U.S. Bureau of Census. This report indicated that there were over 11,000 juvenile offenders in U.S. institutions. That figure doubled by 1904, and by 1980, there were over 59,000 juveniles in various U.S. secure and nonsecure facilities (Cahalan, 1986:104). By year end 1995 there were 102,582 youths under some form of residential or nonresidential supervision, nearly double the 1980 numbers (Camp and Camp, 1995c:1).

GOALS OF JUVENILE CORRECTIONS

Various goals of juvenile corrections include (1) deterrence, (2) rehabilitation and reintegration, (3) prevention, (4) punishment and retribution, and (5) isolation and control. These goals may at times appear to be in conflict (Thornton, Voigt, and Doerner, 1987:350–351). For instance, some experts stress delinquency prevention through keeping juveniles away from the juvenile justice system through diversion and warnings. However, other critics say that the juvenile justice system is too lenient with offenders and must get tough with them through more certain and stringent penalties for the offenses they commit (Garrett, 1985). A middle ground stresses both discipline and reform.

Deterrence

According to correctional critic Robert Martinson, who has said "nothing works" in American corrections, no program has been shown to be 100 percent effective in deterring juveniles from committing delinquent acts or recidivating (Martinson, 1974). However, other researchers suggest that significant deterrent elements of juvenile correctional programs include clearly stated rules and formal sanctions, anticriminal modeling and reinforcement, and a high degree of empathy and trust between the juvenile client and staff (Butts and Gable, 1992). Traditional counseling, institutionalization, and diversion are considered largely ineffective, according to other investigators (Wordes, Bynum, and Corley, 1994). Also, it may be that a natural intervention occurs apart from any particular program designed to deter, simply as the result of aging. As youths grow older, their offending appears to reach a plateau and then declines. Thus many youths may grow out of the delinquency mode as they become older.

Rehabilitation and Reintegration

Surveys of public opinion conducted by independent polling agencies suggest that despite media reports to the contrary, much of the public continues to favor rehabilitative programs for juvenile offenders (Krisberg, Schwartz, and McGarrell, 1993). Community-based publicly and privately operated correctional programs for juveniles often have a strong rehabilitative orientation (Virginia Department of Youth and Family Services, 1995).

Some rehabilitative and reintegrative programs stress internalizing responsibilities for one's actions, while other programs attempt to inculcate youths with social and motor skills (Palmer and Wedge, 1994; Roy, 1994, 1995). Other programs are aimed at diagnosing and treating youths who are emotionally disturbed. Alternative medical and social therapies are often used. For instance, Weber and Burke (1986) describe a Teaching-Family Treatment Model that has been used in 125 group homes throughout the United States. It currently contains elements such as (1) teaching delinquent youths communication skills, daily living skills, survival skills, educational advancement and study skills, and career skills; (2) breaking such skills into specific behaviorally defined components; (3) assuring that the delinquents practice the skills in the problem setting; (4) assessing each youth's skill needs; (5) developing individualized teaching plans; and (6) teaching to the individual skill deficits.

Group homes are becoming increasingly popular as alternatives to incarceration, since a broader array of services can be extended to juveniles with special needs (Haghighi and Lopez, 1993). Failure/success rates of 152 youths assigned to group homes between 1988 and 1990 were examined to determine whether group homes had any positive impact on reducing recidivism. Recidivism rates were modest, ranging from 29 percent for female participants to 39.7 percent for males. Group homes were especially valuable for first offenders. Those with prior juvenile records tended not to fare as well in these homes. Further, those youths who were placed in secure confinement during this same investigative period tended to have higher recidivism rates than those of group home clientele. Haghighi and Lopez believe that group homes, at least in the jurisdictions they studied, have been valuable interventions for reducing recidivism among a broad class of juvenile offenders.

A valuable part of any rehabilitative program is a strong educational component (Rhode Island State Council on Vocational Education, 1995). Many of the successful delinquency prevention programs described by Glick and Goldstein (1995) have strong educational components. Cox, Davidson, and Bynum (1995) note that although in many instances, education programs by themselves do not automatically rehabilitate youthful offenders, they *do* tend to make a small difference when coupled with other specific program goals, such as building one's self-esteem and self-confidence. Delinquents considered at-risk or low achievers have been especially amenable to educational programs to assist them in various skill improvements.

Prevention

Delinquency prevention seems to be a function of many factors. One factor is early preschool intervention. Early preschool intervention programs seem to be modestly successful. In 1962 the Perry Preschool Project was implemented in Ypsilanti, Michigan (Berrueta-Clement et al., 1984). Nearly 70 percent of the children who participated in the program had no future reported offenses as juveniles and only 16 percent were ever arrested for delinquent acts. However, about half of the nonparticipants in the same school had future reported offenses as juveniles, and 25 percent were subsequently arrested for delinquency.

A delinquency prevention program was established in 1953 by the Oakland County Probate Court and known as the Youth Assistance Program. The program has subsequently expanded to include 26 service locations in 27 school districts. Secondary prevention services follow a casework model in which the Youth Assistance Child Welfare Worker meets with families to assess home, school, and community problems and to develop an intervention plan. Emphasis is on short-term supportive counseling, augmented by intensive individual or group therapy, summer camps, parent education, youth restitution, volunteer work, and other program options (Howitt and Moore, 1993). Over the years, youthful participants have had a 92 percent success rate and have remained free of further juvenile court contact. As we have seen with other programs, younger participants have not had the same amount of success as older participants, suggesting that the earlier the onset of delinquency, the harder it is to prevent on any long-term basis. Certain types of offenders, including runaways, truants, and alcohol or drug abusers, seem more responsive than other youths to these types of interventions (Greenwood and Turner, 1993; Northrup, 1993).

Punishment and Retribution

Some people want to see youths, especially violent ones, punished rather than rehabilitated. Early juvenile corrections clearly emphasized this punishment orientation. In Hell's Kitchen, a New York ethnic enclave with a large proportion of street children, apprehended youths spent a lot of their time in brutal correctional facilities where sadistic guards assaulted and taunted them (Carcaterra, 1995). The "wilding" incident involving the near-death of a female jogger by a gang of youths in New York City's Central Park involves a much later incident where a punishment philosophy was promoted by community leaders. Anthony P. Travisono, former Executive Director of the American Correctional Association (ACA), has indicated that he has been plagued by questions from the media about the official policy of the ACA toward how juveniles should be treated. Travisono says that "judging from the questions [from reporters about the juvenile violence in the jogger incident], without a doubt, they wanted to see [these] teenagers treated as adults and sent straight to prison; most seemed to feel that a trial would be an unnecessary bother" (Travisono, 1989:4). However, Travisono added that currently, there is no clear correctional policy about how these and other violent youths should be processed or punished.

One major impact of the get-tough-on-crime policy adopted by many jurisdictions is that the juvenile justice system seems to be diverting a larger portion of its serious offenders to criminal courts, where they may conceivably receive harsher punishments. This may be one reaction to widespread allegations that the juvenile courts are too lenient in their sentencing of violent offenders, or that the punishment options available to juvenile court judges are not sufficiently severe. For those juveniles who remain within the juvenile justice system for processing, secure confinement for longer periods seems to be the court's primary response to citizen allegations of excessive leniency.

Isolation and Control

Apprehension and incarceration of juvenile offenders, especially chronic recidivists, is believed important to isolating them and limiting their opportunities to reoffend. In principle, this philosophy is similar to selective incapacitation. However, the average length of juvenile incarcerative terms in public facilities in the United States is less than 10 months (Maguire and Pastore, 1996). Thus incarceration by itself may be of limited value in controlling the amount of juvenile delinquency. Greenwood (1990) says that control for the sake of control may be self-defeating as a long-range delinquency prevention strategy. Further, whenever youths are placed in custodial settings, the emphasis of the facility is more often on control rather than on rehabilitation.

CURRENT JUVENILE CUSTODIAL ALTERNATIVES

The custodial options available to juvenile court judges are of two general types: (1) nonsecure, and (2) secure. **Nonsecure custodial facilities** are those that permit youths freedom of movement within the community. Youths are generally free to leave the premises of their facilities, although they are compelled to observe various rules, such as curfew, avoidance of alcoholic beverages and drugs, and participation in specific programs that are tailored to their particular needs. These types of nonsecure facilities include *foster homes, group homes and halfway houses,* and *camps, ranches, experience programs,* and *wilderness projects* (Harris et al., 1993).

Secure custodial facilities are the juvenile counterpart to adult prisons or penitentiaries. Such institutions are known by various names among the states. For example, secure, long-term secure confinement facilities might be called *youth centers* or *youth facilities* (Alaska, California, Colorado, District of Columbia, Illinois, Kansas, Maine, Missouri), *juvenile institutions* (Arkansas), *schools* (California, Connecticut, New Mexico), *schools for boys* (Delaware), *training schools or centers* (Florida, Indiana, Iowa, Oregon), *youth development centers* (Georgia, Nebraska), *youth services centers* (Idaho), *secure centers* (New York), *industry schools* (New York), and *youth development centers* (Tennessee). This list is not intended to be comprehensive, but it illustrates the variety of designations states use to refer to their long-term, secure confinement facilities.

In earlier years, these facilities would have been known as "reform schools," reflecting the influence of *houses of reformation* in the United States established during the early 1850s. However, an inspection of the most recent ACA Directory listing all juvenile confinement facilities in the United States shows a conspicuous absence of the term *reform school*. Interestingly, these contemporary designations imply "helping," "treatment," "rehabilitative," or "reintegrative" milieus. Despite this Machiavellian-like name-changing designed to lend dignity to these settings and their functions, they remain principally custodial, strict, and punitive, as well as questionably rehabilitative or reintegrative. The distribution of juveniles under various forms of supervision among state systems in 1996 is shown in Table 12.1.

NONSECURE CONFINEMENT

Nonsecure confinement involves placing certain youths in (1) foster homes, (2) group homes and halfway houses, or (3) camps, ranches, experience programs, and wilderness projects.

Foster Homes

If the juvenile's natural parents are considered unfit, or if the juvenile is abandoned or orphaned, **foster homes** are often used for temporary placement. Those youths placed in foster homes are not necessarily law violators. They may be *children in need of supervision* (CHINS). Foster home placement provides youths with a substitute family. A stable family environment is believed by the courts to be beneficial in many cases where youths have no consistent adult supervision or are unmanageable or unruly in their own households. In 1996, approximately 4000 youths were under the supervision of foster homes in state-operated public placement programs (American Correctional Association, 1996). Rogers and Mays (1987:429) indicate that

TABLE 12.1

Juveniles Under Supervision

State	Total	Institutions Training Schools Total	M	F	Detention M	F	Diagnostic M	F	Other M	F	Community Residential M	F	Med/Drg Men Hlth Res M/F	Splty Facilities M/F	Group/Foster Homes M	F	Detention M/F	Other M	F	(Avg) Entering Offender M&F	Under 16 Ttl	16 up to 18 Ttl	18 & over Ttl
AL	721	496	448	48					25					117/	63	20				15.70	—	—	—
AK	220	146	132	14	63	11															723	1,311	—
AZ	1,683	500	472	28			41	3			105	16	24/4	49/	88	14		772	116	15.50	117	76	
AR	193	90	75	15							44	10								15.30			
CA	9,219	8,281	8,016	265	256	8	121	4			36	1	9/	404/				96	3	17.50	456	2,411	6,352
CO[1]	1,005	372	361	11	337	62	29				119	13	37/	36/						15.90	282	552	171
CT	253	253	218	35																14.30	193	60	
DE[1]	193	63	63		34	3														16.05	36	134	23
FL	5,595	253	253*		1,601*				126*	6	20		39/9	155*	132*	4	1,129*	423*		15.30	2,796[2]	1,700[2]	
GA	2,660	737	685	52	945	145					1,756*		480[2]/184[2]	86[2]/12[2]	31					15.44	14		20[2]
HI	76	41	34	7					3		40	1	3/1		14	3	3/			16.60		50	12
ID	125	110	105	5	13	2					5									16.60			
IL	1,530	1,530	1,445	85																15.50	402	963	165
IN	976	800	605	195							176									16.00			
IA	223	193	193																30	16.10			
KS[1]	1,827	459	343	116			5	5			68*		19*	10/	339*		95*	827*	187	15.80	171	220	58
KY	1,280	323	273	50										128/	104	32		506	78	15.67	896	371	13
LA	2,400	983	907	76	319	10	50		34	6	290	34	64/9		110	73	4/4 /1	338	1	15.60	855	1,197	348
ME	341	211	181	30	25	4					78	8	78/8					7		16.00	143[3]	194[3]	18[3]
MD	1,734	279	249	30	380	52	3	6	63	8	415		19/2	16/3	331	33		64	14	16.00	563[3]		
MA	1,158	185	173	12	229	7	44		41		90		17		331	35	30/7	106	13	15.30		1,415[4]	71[4]
MI	821	630	590	40	98	24						52								15.40	85[5]	128[5]	
MN	263	213	204	9																17.00	309	309	
MS	620	595	539	56											96					15.00	261	230	2
MO	491	184[6]	171	13					25		22			160/51						15.10	36[5]	88[5]	
MT	152	130	100	30			19	12						11/2	32	24		26	3	16.90	195	345	6[5]
NE	582	212	168	44							199	28	13/1							16.20	195	345	42
NV[1]	250	250	201	49									19/	46/	423		28/17	45		15.74	95	152	3
NH[1]	670	75	66	9	14	3			30											15.90			
NJ	639	609	597	12			25	5			95	11				72		122	16	16.90	85	364	190
NM	547	411	382	29	25						1,406	248		44/	260					16.80	230	274	43
NY	3,419	1,251	1,129	122							42									15.00	2,250	1,118	51
NC	1,078	760	671	89	276		7	4	3		104	23	6/		28	19		215	58	14.90	616[5]	144[5]	
ND	540	72	57	15																15.00	295	219	26
OH	2,300	2,300	2,153	147																15.78	631	1,295	374
OK	193	178	166	12																15.70	65	116	12
OR	840	493	442	51	15		15		39	8			109/		132	23		29	7	15.70	209	456	175

TABLE 12.1 (CONT'D)

Juveniles Under Supervision

State	Total	Institutions Training Schools Total	M	F	Detention M	Detention F	Diagnostic M	Diagnostic F	Other M	Other F	Community Residential M	Community Residential F	Med/Drg Men Hlth Res M/F	Spltly Facilities M/F	Group/Foster Homes M	Group/Foster Homes F	Detention M/F	Other M	Other F	(Avg) Entering Offender M&F	Entering Under 16 Ttl	Entering 16 to 18 Ttl	18 & over Ttl
PA	741	462	442	20							259	20			45					16.60	—	—	207
RI	222	155[8]	143[8]	12[8]		5					12	10								15.00	35[5]	70[5]	50[5]
SC	1,355	769	708	61	38		221	59						154/16	55	32		3	3	15.06	58	107	16
SD	181	108	96	12										/20				53	3	16.40			16
TN	1,413	532	511	21			14				653[9]	66[9]			109	31				16.00	58	870	74
TX	2,653	1,382	1,323	59	145	19	105	9			172	17	57/7	178/8	97	27	86/8	283	32	15.70	469	1,600	168
UT	856	79	78	1	50	1	59	3			337	26		21/	186	38		50	6	16.00	885	469	82
VT[1]	269	12	12						193	35			4/	10/						15.50	305	183	
VA	963	779	729	50			138	7			39									15.60	86	541	13
WA	1,230	836	767	69							264	21			109					15.30	409	592	295
WV	135	65	56	9			21	4						45/						17.00	342	125	10
WI[10]	1,196[10]	855	786	51							69				48	8		186	19	16.00	349	720	106
WY	144	144	70	74																15.00	64	69	11
Total	58,175	30,846	28,588	2,240	4,835	357	917	121	611	53	6,967	578	891/225	1,829/112	3,178	488	1,381/37	4,159	587	15.70 Median	16,012	21,238	9,207
*		30,846			5,192		1,038		664		7,545		1,116	1,941	3,666		1,418	4,746					
DC	693	58	58		115	13					86	18			80			230	47				
NYC	392				271	21							6/0	20/20						16.90	51[5]	98[5]	37
VI[1]	570				104	3					12	2	2/0		88	12		416	31	15.00	341	51	
MB	403	403	385	19																16.00	182	370	18
NF[1]	142	71	61	10																	—	—	—
PEI[1]	42	42	38	4																	—	—	—

Frequency of Ages for Classification as Juvenile Offender

Lower Limit No. States	Age	Upper Limit No. States	Age
9	0	2	15
2	7	4	16
2	8	9	17
14	10	22	18
3	11	4	19
18	12	8	21
2	13	13	25

Average length of stay:
Secure 8.02 months
Nonsecure 6.45 months

— Data unavailable at time of publication
* Combined male/female total
1. Data as of 6/30/93
2. Data as of 4/1/94
3. Data for 9/2/94
4. Includes population living at home
5. Secure population only
6. Youth Center population
7. Community residential population transferred to Department of Human Services 7/1/93
8. Includes detention and diagnostic/evaluation
9. Includes mental health, drug Rx, and medical
10. Includes 21 without sex/ethnic breakdown

Secure "Other": AL, Max security; DE, Out-of-state; FL, Boot camps, etc; HI, Escapees; LA, Absent offenders; MA, Adult corrections; MD, Psychiatric; ME, Escapees; MS, Maximum Security; ND, Time out; NJ, County back-up; OR, Hospital, jail; TX, 208 Mental Health/20 Marine; UT, Jail.

Nonsecure "Other": FL, Non-residential; HI, AWOL, IA, Toledo subcampus; KS, Home and other; KY, Day treatment; LA, Jail/Day, AWOL; MA, AWOL; MD, Structured shelters; ND, Home/Job corps, NE, Abscon/arrest; NH, Shelter care/etc; NY, Day placement; OR, AWOL; SC, Runaway shelter; SD, Forestry camp; TN, Peabody TRC; TX, 259 Escape/59 Furlough; UT, AWOL/hospital; WI, Aftercare; DC, Home detention; VI, off-island home.

many of those assigned to foster homes are dependent, neglected, or abused, and youths typically are younger, in the age range 10 to 14.

A survey of 266 specialist foster family care programs was conducted in the early 1990s to determine how well these programs were assisting juveniles (Galaway et al., 1995). While foster care programs are not designed directly to cater to hard-core delinquents, about half of all foster home placements involve adjudicated delinquent youths. Delinquent youths tend to be slightly older on average than the nondelinquent youths who participated in these foster care programs. Furthermore, delinquent youths spent less time in foster care before being released. Recidivism rates among delinquent youths tended to be much lower than those of other delinquent youths placed either on probation or in secure confinement (Galaway et al., 1995).

Foster home placements are useful in many cases where youths have been apprehended for status offenses. Most families who accept youths into their homes have been investigated in advance by state or local authorities to determine their fitness as foster parents. Socioeconomic factors and home stability are considered important for child placements. Foster parents often typify middle-aged, middle-class citizens with above-average educational backgrounds. Despite these positive features, it is unlikely that foster homes are able to provide the high intensity of adult supervision required by more hard-core juvenile offenders. Further, it is unlikely that these parents can furnish the quality of special treatments that might prove effective in the youth's possible rehabilitation or societal reintegration. Most foster parents simply are not trained as counselors, social workers, or psychologists. For many nonserious youths, however, a home environment, particularly a stable one, has certain therapeutic benefits.

Group Homes and Halfway Houses

Another nonsecure option for juvenile court judges is the assignment of juveniles to **group homes** and **halfway houses**. Placing youths in group homes is considered an intermediate option available to juvenile court judges. Group homes or halfway houses are community-based operations that may be either publicly or privately administered (Mutchnick and Fawcett, 1991). The notion of a halfway house is frequently that of a community home used by adult parolees recently released from prison. Such halfway houses provide a temporary base of operations for parolees as they seek employment and readjustment within their communities. Therefore, they are perceived as transitional residences halfway between incarceration and full freedom of life "on the outside." To many ex-inmates, exposure to unregulated community life is a traumatic transition from the rigidity of prison culture. Many ex-inmates need time to readjust. The rules of halfway houses provide limited structure as well as freedom of access to the outside during the transitory stage.

Usually, group homes will have counselors or residents to act as parental figures for youths in groups of 10 to 20. Certain group homes, referred to as *family group homes*, are actually family operated and thus in a sense are an extension of foster homes for larger numbers of youths. In group homes, nonsecure supervision of juvenile clients is practiced. About 4000 youths were in group homes during 1996 (American Correctional Association, 1996:xxxvi–xxxvii). The number of youths in group homes has remained fairly constant since 1990.

No model or ideal group home exists in the nation to be emulated by all jurisdictions, and what works well for youths in some communities may not be effective in other jurisdictions (Kapp, Schwartz, and Epstein, 1994; Sametz, Ahren, and Yuan, 1994). However, most successful group homes have strong structural components, where all residents are obligated to participate in relevant program components, where predictable consequences for rule violations are rigorously enforced, and where constant monitoring by staff workers occurs. Thus juveniles have the best of both worlds—they can live in a homelike environment and visit with family and friends in a home setting. Yet they must comply with strict rules governing curfew, program participation, and other court-imposed conditions (Mutchnick and Fawcett, 1991). In an examination of nine facilities located in five counties in southwestern Pennsylvania, for example, all the facilities operated under the principles of community-based treatment and relied on behavior modification as the major program. Little victimization occurred, especially where supervision was fairly intensive.

Privately or publicly operated, group homes require juvenile clients to observe the rights of others, participate in various vocational or educational training programs, attend school, participate in therapy or receive prescribed medical treatment, and observe curfew. Urinalyses or other tests may be conducted randomly as checks to see whether juveniles are taking drugs or consuming alcohol, contrary to group home policy. If one or more program violations occur, group home officials may report these infractions to juvenile court judges, who retain dispositional control over the youths. Assignment to a group home or any other type of confinement is usually for a determinate period.

Positively, group homes provide youths with the companionship of other juveniles. Problem sharing often occurs through planned group discussions, where the subjects might include peer relations in school to suicide prevention (Miller, 1994). Staff are available to assist youths to secure employment, work certain difficult school problems, and absorb emotional burdens arising from difficult interpersonal relationships. However, these homes are sometimes staffed by community volunteers with little training or experience with a youth's problems. There are certain risks and legal liabilities that may be incurred as the result of well-intentioned but bad advice or inadequate assistance. Currently, there are limited regulations among states for how group homes are established and operated. Training programs for group home staff are scarce in most jurisdictions, and few standards exist relating to staff preparation and qualifications. Therefore, considerable variation exists among group homes relating to the quality of services they can extend to the juveniles they serve.

One way that group homes can improve their effectiveness is for staff workers and home administrators to develop associations with various community interests. Kearon (1990) has made several recommendations, including the following:

1. Develop a network in every community of voluntary service delivery systems, such as day treatment, nonsecure shelter and group homes, and small, nonsecure institutional care centers.

2. Increase staffing levels in these systems.

3. For the most disturbed and abused youth, who will inevitably escape from a nonsecure setting, establish perimeter-secure facilities.

4. Ensure that authorities intervene with youths at crucial entry points such as bus and railway terminals.

5. Educate youths in facilities about AIDS and at-risk behavior and make voluntary testing available, and provide these services as outreach centers to youths still on the streets.

Depending on how youths are screened, some youths are more suited than others for placement under conditions where supervision may be minimal (Tolan and Guerra, 1994; U.S. General Accounting Office, 1994a,b). For instance, the Texas Youth Commission operated *Independent Living*, where selected youths were placed away from home, such as in an apartment, and possibly received some temporary financial support from the Commission (Texas Youth Commission, 1990). Some Independent Living youths engaged in new delinquent offenses, but their recidivism rate was low (9 percent). Rearrests where no charges were subsequently placed against youths also yielded a successful result for Independent Living participants. Compared with standard juvenile parolees who had a 52 percent rearrest rate, Independent Living participants had a rearrest rate of only 33 percent. One factor cited by Texas authorities was the additional trust and confidence in these youths by the Texas Youth Commission, as well as the living and financial support while these youths attended school or looked for work.

Sometimes the simple fact that youths are the subject of an experiment can have a halo effect for them. That is, they may behave well because they know they are being studied. The Intensive Aftercare Probation Program of the Philadelphia Family Court was investigated by Sontheimer, Goodstein, and Kovacevic in 1990. Between December 1988 and January 1990, 90 juveniles were released into this aftercare program and assigned to probation officers with maximum caseloads of 12 youths each. These youths were compared with a control group of juveniles whose probation officers had average caseloads of 90 clients each. While the overall results were not impressive, the more intensively supervised Aftercare Probation Program youths had a rearrest rate of 50 percent compared with a 64 percent rearrest rate of conventionally supervised youthful probationers. The risk-management component was cited as the major factor leading to lower rates of rearrest. Similar successful experiences with intensive supervision of juvenile parolees have been reported elsewhere (Altschuler, 1991; Springer, 1991).

Camps, Ranches, Experience Programs, and Wilderness Projects

Camps, ranches, or camp ranches are nonsecure facilities that are sometimes referred to as **wilderness projects** or *experience programs*. A less expensive alternative to the incarceration of juvenile offenders, even those considered chronic, is participation in *experience programs*. Experience programs include a wide array of outdoor programs designed to improve a juvenile's self-worth, self-concept, pride, and trust in others (McCarthy and McCarthy, 1997).

Three Springs Wilderness School. In Trenton, Alabama, a wilderness-based residential treatment program was established in the late 1980s (McCord, 1995). Screening juveniles was accomplished through interviews with residential counselors and administration of the Minnesota Multiphasic Personality Inventory (MMPI), a widely used personality assessment device. The MMPI results helped to profile and select 46 juvenile participants. These juveniles were clustered into three groups, according to their MMPI scores. One group was labeled *nonconformist.* Those in this group exhibited the following characteristics: anger, resentment, passivity-aggressivity, immaturity, and narcissism. A second group, labeled *party animal,* tended to exhibit hedonism, extroversion, rule avoidance, and defiance toward authority. The third group, *emotionally disturbed,* were primarily distressed. According to the different characteristics exhibited by the three groups, specialized treatments were configured to fit those with particular needs. The results of the treatment experiences were considered positive by staff researchers, indicating that the MMPI might be a useful tool as a means of differentiating between juveniles and their individual needs in subsequent wilderness experiments. These data have received independent support from other research under different treatment conditions (Swenson and Kennedy, 1995). In the latter research, scales were used for youth selection, including the Child Behavior Checklist, the Multidimensional Measure of Children's Perceptions of Control, the Perceived Contingency Behavioral Domain Scale, and the Piers–Harris Self-Concept Scale.

Hope Center Wilderness Camp. Another wilderness experiment that appears successful is the **Hope Center Wilderness Camp** in Houston, Texas (Clagett, 1989). This camp has an organized network of four interdependent living groups of 12 teenagers each. The camp's goals are to provide quality care and treatment in a nonpunitive environment, with specific emphases on health, safety, education, and therapy. Emotionally disturbed youths whose offenses range from truancy to murder are selected for program participation. Informal techniques are used, including "aftertalk" (informal discussing during meals), "huddle up" (a group discussion technique), and "pow wow" (a nightly fire gathering). Special nondenominational religious services are conducted. Participants are involved in various special events and learn to cook meals outdoors, camp, and other survival skills. Follow-ups by camp officials show that camp participants exhibit recidivism rates of only about 15 percent (Clagett, 1989).

APPEL Program. In Williamson County, Texas, a wilderness challenge program was created in 1988 (Harris et al., 1993). This program involved weekly two-hour meetings, two one-day sessions, and two half-day sessions held over a 12-week period. Unlike many of the programs designed for juveniles, the **APPEL** program was designed to complement other correctional services, particularly those offered by various community supervision agencies. The challenge curriculum has an articulated mission that addresses the documented, underlying problems of a large proportion of youthful community corrections clients. These wilderness treatments are relative low in cost and can be adopted easily by community corrections agencies (Harris et al., 1993).

Project Outward Bound. Another wilderness project, Project Outward Bound, is one of more than 200 programs of its type in the United States today. **Outward Bound** was introduced in Colorado in 1962 with objectives emphasizing personal survival in the wilderness. Youths participated in various outdoor activities, including rock climbing, solo survival, camping, and long-range hiking during a three-week period (McCarthy and McCarthy, 1997). Program officials were not concerned with equipping these juveniles with survival skills per se, but rather, they wanted to instill within the participants a feeling of self-confidence and self-assurance to cope with other types of problems in their communities.

Spectrum Wilderness Program.   Similar to the Outward Bound Program, the **Spectrum Wilderness Program** was established in a large northern Illinois county in 1987. The program consisted of 30-day wilderness courses and was offered to youths being supervised by local probation departments. The program was designed to provide youths with self-confidence and self-reliance. Recidivism was targeted by attempting to provide youths with internal incentives to succeed and achieve vocational and educational goals. A one-year follow-up disclosed disappointing results, however, as 75 percent of the participants were rearrested for various offenses. Thus, at least in the Spectrum Wilderness case, the experiences were not promising for reducing a youth's recidivism (Castellano and Soderstrom, 1990).

Homeward Bound.   A program known as **Homeward Bound** was established in Massachusetts in 1970. Homeward Bound was designed to provide juveniles with mature responsibilities through the acquisition of survival skills and wilderness experiences. A six-week training program subjected 32 youths to endurance training, physical fitness, and performing community service (McCarthy and McCarthy, 1997). Additionally, officials of the program worked with the boys to develop a release program when they completed the project requirements successfully. During the evenings, the juveniles were given instruction in ecology, search and rescue, and overnight treks.

Toward the end of the program, the boys were subjected to a test—surviving a three-day, three-night trip in the wilderness to prove that each boy had acquired the necessary survival skills. Recidivism rates among these boys were lower than for boys who had been institutionalized in industrial or reform schools (Willman and Chun, 1974). Although these programs serve limited numbers of juveniles and some authorities question their value in deterring further delinquency, some evidence suggests that these wilderness experiences generate less recidivism among participants than that for youths institutionalized in industrial schools under conditions of close custody and monitoring (McCarthy and McCarthy, 1997).

VisionQuest.   A well-established wilderness program is **VisionQuest**, a private, for-profit enterprise operated from Tucson, Arizona. Currently, VisionQuest operates in about 15 states, serves about 500 juveniles annually, and is about half of the cost of secure institutionalization (Gavzer, 1986:10). Among the various jurisdictions that have used VisionQuest for its juvenile probationers is San Diego County, California (Greenwood and Turner, 1987). Juvenile offenders selected for participation in the VisionQuest program in

San Diego were secure incarceration-bound offenders with several prior arrests and placements with the California Youth Authority. VisionQuest staff members conducted interviews with certain juveniles who were tentatively selected for inclusion in the program. On the basis of VisionQuest staff recommendations, juvenile court judges would assign these juveniles to VisionQuest, where they would be under an indeterminate disposition of from six months to a year or more (Greenwood, 1990).

Greenwood (1990:20) describes the VisionQuest experiences of youths as follows. They are placed immediately in a rustic type of boot camp environment, where they live in an Indian tepee with six to 10 other youths and two junior staff. They sleep on the ground and engage in a strenuous physical fitness program. They complete regular schoolwork. Failure to perform their daily chores adequately results in an immediate confrontation between them and senior staff. They participate in an orientation and outdoor training program, which takes several months to complete. Eventually, they take a wagon train on the back roads of the Western states to Canada, averaging about 24 miles a day, for four to six months. All the while, they are given increased responsibilities, including breaking horses that VisionQuest acquires annually. Eventually, they attend the VisionQuest group home in Arizona, where it is determined whether they can be reintegrated into their communities (Greenwood, 1990:20–21).

Greenwood and Turner (1987) have evaluated the effectiveness of VisionQuest by comparing a sample of 89 male juvenile offenders with a sample of 177 juveniles assigned to San Diego County Probation. Both the San Diego County probationers and the VisionQuest youths were tracked for one year following the completion of their respective programs. VisionQuest participants had a recidivism rate of 55 percent, compared with 71 percent for the regular probationers. Although this rate of recidivism is high compared with many other intensive-supervision probation programs, the sizable difference in recidivism is viewed favorably as moderately successful. Other researchers in different jurisdictions where VisionQuest has been used report that average recidivism figures are about 33 percent for VisionQuest participants (Gavzer, 1986).

SECURE CONFINEMENT: VARIATIONS

Persistent Problems

As noted earlier, secure juvenile incarcerative facilities in the United States are known by various names. Further, not all of these secure confinement facilities are alike. While many institutions provide only custodial services for chronic or more serious juvenile offenders, other incarcerative facilities offer an array of services and treatments, depending on the diverse needs of the juveniles confined. Breed and Krisberg (1986:14) contend, for instance, that "the history of juvenile corrections has been governed by a repetitive cycle of institutional abuses and scandals, public exposure to these problems, and spurts of reformist activity." A major contributing factor for these problems, they argue, is the fact that "juvenile corrections has not evolved from a set of rational or planned responses to explicit goals" (p. 14). Clarifying the mission and goals of corrections agencies also helps staff to do a better job of supervising youthful clientele. Institutional rules tend to be couched in a more meaningful context, and incarcerated youth are able to cope more effectively with their confinement (Bazemore and West, 1990; Clarkson and Weakland, 1991; Polhill et al., 1994).

Architectural Improvements and Officer Training Reforms

In recent years, however, numerous improvements have been made generally in the overall quality of juvenile secure confinement facilities throughout the United States (U.S. General Accounting Office, 1995a). Evidence of improvement in juvenile corrections is the massive effort made by authorities in numerous jurisdictions to design and build more adequately equipped juvenile facilities that minimize youthful inmate problems of idle time and overcrowding (Davis, 1993; Maine Juvenile Corrections Task Force, 1993). Examples of modern facility designs and creative architectural structures that offer dormitorylike settings rather than penal ones are the Young Adult Offenders Program facility in Draper, Utah, and the Denver, Colorado, Mount View School (Sullivan, 1988). Private interests, including the Corrections Corporation of America, have assisted as well in providing more modern designs and plant operations for secure juvenile facilities in various states, including California and Tennessee.

Besides constructing more attractive physical plants in which to house hard-core offenders, juvenile corrections planners have also made efforts to improve the quality of all levels of the staff who administer and supervise juvenile inmates (Parent, 1993). Entering juveniles exhibit a myriad of personal and social problems. Some youths are psychologically disturbed and suicidal. Others are distinctly antisocial and violent. Correctional officers at these facilities must be prepared for virtually any behavior that might arise. At the Taft Youth Development Center in Pikeville, Tennessee, which is a facility that houses felons and misdemeanants from 15 to 21, a male correctional officer was attacked by a 15-year-old. The youth lunged at the officer and bit into the officer's crotch area. Six officers were required to pull the youth away from the officer. The officer's pants had been ripped apart, and his scrotum had been bitten off by the youth. Such incidents are not limited to violent juvenile males. A 16-year-old female juvenile at the same facility attacked her female teacher during a history lesson, and portions of the teacher's blouse and breast were bitten off by the youth, who apparently didn't like the grade she received on an exam.

Admittedly, these incidents are bizarre, but they do occur. Textbook instruction cannot be extensive enough to cover all situations and what to do whenever these and similar incidents arise. In an effort to prepare correctional officers to cope with various types of inmate problems, several local and national organizations have established training courses to heighten an officer's awareness of problems and skills to deal with them. Santa Clara County (San Jose), California, has one of the largest direct-supervision jails in the nation. It has over 4500 bookings per month, as well as at least 600 psychiatric referrals. A portion of these bookings and referrals are juveniles. Recognizing that staff training should be a major priority, administrators from the Custody and Mental Health services established a training experience for officers, including classes in suicide identification and intervention, psychiatric illnesses, management of assaultive behavior, and communication skills (Quinlan and Motte, 1990:22–23).

In Tacoma, Washington, Pierce County Sheriff Raymond A. Fjetland has developed a program, the Master Correctional Officer Program, which is designed to increase the performance of staff correctional officers for future roles within the corrections division (Tess and Bogue, 1988:66). The program has three stages: the entry level, the senior level, and the master level. Officers must accumulate points in various educational and on-the-job training areas, including weapons qualification, comprehensive written examinations, and frequent performance evaluations. Thus Sheriff Fjetland has help in developing a program that provides officer incentives to advance as well as to acquire more effective skills to deal with offenders of all types and ages. Greater professionalism, expertise, and productivity are the outcomes of this innovative "continuous motivator" program (Tess and Bogue, 1988:67).

Both male and female correctional officers are targeted for additional training to cope with inmate problems. Formerly, it has been alleged by some critics that female correctional officers tend to lack the degree of authority of their male officer counterparts when dealing with inmates. However, programs such as on-the-job training and self-improvement courses sponsored and conducted by the American Correctional Association have done much to improve correctional officer credibility and performance (Lonardi, 1987:142). According to ACA standards, correctional officers should have at least 160 hours of orientation and training during their first year of employment. Certification is awarded after satisfactorily completing the ACA training course. An analysis of female correctional officer effectiveness in relation to male officers has been made by Simon and Simon (1988). They indicate that

BOX 12.1   FEMALE DELINQUENCY ON THE RISE?

The Case of 14-Year-Old Donna Ratliff, Arsonist

Donna Ratliff, 14, wasn't born an arsonist. She became one when she was 13 years of age. One afternoon she set fire to her home by sprinkling kerosene throughout the house. Her mother and older sister were inside and perished in the resulting blaze. Donna was charged with arson and murder. She was convicted and sentenced to 25 years in a maximum-security Indiana penitentiary for women. Donna claims that when she was 7, she was sexually and physically abused by her uncle, mother, and father. Her father denies that she was ever abused. Donna claims that to escape this abusive environment, she set the fire and torched the house. She says she didn't want to kill anyone when she set the fire.

Indiana is one of a growing number of states practicing a get-tough policy toward its juvenile offenders. Donna is no exception. Indiana authorities ordered Donna placed in an adult prison when she was convicted. The American Civil Liberties Union and other interested groups protested, saying that Donna deserved to be placed in a juvenile facility instead. Indiana ignored these protestations, saying simply that Donna's treatment would be uninterrupted if she were placed in the adult facility. If she had been placed in a juvenile facility, she would have had to have been transferred to an adult facility when she turned 21 anyway. Furthermore, Indiana Prisons Commissioner Christopher DeBruyn said that "sexual abuse and neglect of our children is too often a fact of life for too many kids. It should not be a function of a state prison system to respond to such neglect."

The Indiana Women's Prison in Indianapolis is not a particularly nice place. It was never intended to be a nice place. It is a place for punishment for those who have been convicted of serious crimes. Murder and arson are serious crimes. Those who commit murder and arson deserve punishment. Donna Ratliff is being punished like everyone else. She did the crime and now she must do the time.

This view is not shared by everyone. There is a prevalent belief among many criminal justice professionals that juveniles do not have the emotional maturity of adults; thus it is not correct to treat them in the same ways that adults would be treated for the same types of crimes. According to the non-interventionist philosophy espoused by such experts, juveniles are entitled to be rehabilitated, not punished. We should treat their immaturity as an illness that can be cured. However, many victims and other experts counter by saying that there are far too many juveniles who "survive" their childhoods and who don't commit serious crimes.

at least for the samples they studied of 45 female officers and 115 male officers of a large state institution, gender made no difference when it came to upholding the legitimacy of sanctions imposed by these officers. Other research supports the view that female correctional officers exhibit performance levels equal to those of their male officer counterparts (Zimmer, 1986).

Juvenile Detention Resource Centers

The U.S. Department of Justice's Office of Juvenile Justice and Delinquency Prevention (OJJDP) promulgated specific guidelines for all juvenile detention facilities in the early 1980s. These guidelines were published as *Guidelines for the Development of Policies and Procedures for Juvenile Detention Facilities.* The goal of the OJJDP was to establish *national juvenile detention resource centers* around the United States in various jurisdictions that would provide information, technical assistance, and training to juvenile detention professionals who wished to participate (Criswell, 1987:22). The ultimate aim of these juvenile detention centers was to provide juveniles with better and more adequate services and assistance. These model centers would act as prototypes for other centers to be established in different jurisdictions. In 1985, the Southwest Florida Juvenile Detention Center at Fort Myers was established as the state-operated resource center. In subsequent years, numerous regional detention resource centers were created throughout Florida to provide juvenile inmates with a broader array and quality of services and personnel.

Such **detention centers** have done much to improve juvenile incarceration standards throughout the nation. The ACA has been actively involved in assisting various jurisdictions in their efforts to establish juvenile detention resource centers and operate them successfully. Rousch (1987:33) notes that "the most striking factor is that each resource center is a model of how secure confinement should be operated. Each center has specific strengths and different priorities regarding the use of resources....[The strengths of these centers include] comprehensive intake screening, a wide range of effective alternatives to incarceration, a variety of effective programs, excellent staff, volunteer involvement, staff training, and medical and health care services." The educational dimension of such centers can assist in transmitting knowledge about communicable diseases such as AIDS, and inform adolescents about the risks of sexual misconduct (Slonim-Nevo et al., 1996). Other positive contributions of these centers might be to assist youths in managing their anger and providing them with opportunities to improve their general mental health (Hardwick and Rowton-Lee, 1996).

Short- and Long-Term Facilities

Secure juvenile confinement facilities in the United States are either short-term or long-term. **Short-term confinement** facilities are designed to accommodate juveniles on a temporary basis. These juveniles are awaiting either a later juvenile court adjudication, subsequent foster home or group home placement, or a transfer to criminal court (Minnesota Department of Corrections, 1993). Whether a juvenile is held for a period of time in detention depends on the outcome of a **detention hearing**, where the appropriateness of the detention is determined.

Sometimes youths will be placed in short-term confinement because their identity is unknown and it is desirable that they should not be confined in adult lockups or jails. Other youths are violent and must be detained temporarily until more appropriate placements may be made (Hurst and Torbet, 1993; Krisberg and DeComo, 1993). The designations *short term* and *long term* may range from a few days to several years, although the average duration of juvenile incarceration across all offender categories nationally is about six to seven months (Maguire and Pastore, 1996). The average short-term incarceration in public facilities for juveniles is about 30 days (Camp and Camp, 1995c).

Some short-term confinement is *preventive detention* or *pretrial detention*, where juveniles are awaiting formal adjudicatory proceedings (Minnesota Department of Corrections, 1993). While some authorities question the legality of jailing juveniles or holding them in detention centers prior to their cases being heard by juvenile court judges, the U.S. Supreme Court has upheld the constitutionality of pretrial or preventive detention of juveniles, especially dangerous ones, in the case of *Schall v. Martin* (1984). One objective of pretrial detention is to prevent certain dangerous juveniles from committing new pretrial crimes. Juvenile court judges must make a determination as to whether certain juveniles should be held in pretrial detention or released into the custody of parents or guardians. Although their discretion is not perfect, many juvenile court judges exercise good judgment in determining which juveniles should be temporarily detained.

A study was conducted by Fagan and Guggenheim (1996) of juvenile court judge discretion with two groups of juveniles: one group consisting of a cohort of 69 juveniles predicted to be dangerous, who required custody but were released, and a control group of 64 other juveniles. A sample of juvenile court judges was asked to predict which juveniles from the two groups would have the greatest likelihood of being rearrested prior to their trials. Judges predicted with 40 percent accuracy which juveniles would be rearrested and who were actually rearrested. However, they had a high rate of false-positive predictions. Sixty percent of those determined to be dangerous by these judges and who were predicted to reoffend did not commit new offenses prior to their trials. Eighty-five percent of the control group did not reoffend either. Thus the study showed that some ambiguity existed about the criteria that should be used for dangerousness forecasts made by juvenile court judges.

Although no national policy is in place currently about the temporary jailing of juveniles together with adult offenders, various organizations and agencies have issued statements urging legislative action to formally prohibit such practices and establish separate juvenile secure confinement facilities in affected jurisdictions (Bilchik, 1996). In Massachusetts and several other states, juveniles may post bail for their offenses to avoid pretrial detention (Parent, 1991; Wordes, Bynum and Corley, 1994). In some states, including Pennsylvania, legislative mandates have prohibited the jailing of juveniles altogether (U.S. General Accounting Office, 1995a).

Because of space limitations in certain jurisdictions or the general lack of proper juvenile secure confinement facilities, juveniles are sometimes housed in special areas in jails. However, a movement away from confining juveniles in jails has gained momentum in recent years under the federally funded Jail Removal Initiative. Started in 1981, this program has assisted over 20 jurisdictions in 12 states to provide alternatives to juvenile confinement in jails or other adult lockups (Brown, 1985). New laws enacted in various state jurisdictions, including Illinois, currently mandate that no juveniles may be placed in adult jails for periods longer than six hours. Further, no child under the age of 10 may be held in an adult jail, and no juvenile can be disposed to spend time in an adult jail. However, by year end 1995, 7888 juveniles were being held in adult jails in various U.S. jurisdictions (Gilliard and Beck, 1996:10). This figure has declined considerably from the more than 50,000 juveniles held in jails in 1989.

Some Criticisms of Incarcerating Juveniles

There are numerous proponents and opponents of juvenile secure confinement of any kind. Those favoring incarceration cite the disruption of one's lifestyle and separation from other delinquent youths as a positive dimension (Altschuler and Armstrong, 1994). For example, youths who have been involved with delinquent gangs or friends who engage in frequent law-breaking would probably benefit from incarceration, since these unfavorable associations would be interrupted or terminated (Cronin, 1994; Henggeler et al., 1994; Pallone, 1994). Of course, juveniles can always return to their old ways when released from incarceration. There is nothing the juvenile justice system can do to prevent these reunions. But at least the pattern of interaction that contributed to the delinquent behavior initially is interrupted temporarily (Glick and Goldstein, 1995).

Another argument favoring incarceration of juveniles is that long-term secure confinement is a deserved punishment for their actions. This is consistent with the just-deserts philosophy that seems to typify contemporary thinking about juvenile punishment. There is a noticeable trend away from thinking about the best interests of youths and toward thinking about ways to make them more accountable for their actions (Feld, 1995). Feld says that this shift has prompted debate among juvenile justice scholars about the true functions of juvenile courts and the ultimate aims of the sanctions they impose.

For some critics, the question of whether juvenile incarceration is rehabilitative is irrelevant. The fact is, juvenile incarceration restricts a juvenile's mobility and is seen as a deterrent to delinquent conduct. We don't know for sure how much of a deterrent effect is achieved through incarcerating juveniles. But incarceration does suffice as a punishment. If juveniles break the law, they should be punished. Thus incarceration may be viewed as a form of retribution. Some types of screening mechanisms seem fruitful for targeting particular youths for special treatment. The Juvenile Justice Assessment Instrument (JJAI) has been used successfully in selected jurisdictions to determine the best treatment and interventions while youths are confined (Stein, Lewis, and Yeager, 1993). Areas measured by the JJAI include the offense; aggressive acts; use of weapons; chronology of living situations; school history; family medical, psychiatric, and behavioral history; social history; sexual abuse; physical abuse and witnessing family violence; psychiatric history; psychomotor/dissociative symptoms; medical/neurological history; and scars (Stein, Lewis, and Yeager, 1993).

Maloney (1989) summarizes the opinions of many juvenile justice experts who believe that incarceration can serve multiple ends. He says that currently, many rules of supervision in secure confinement facilities and other supervision programs are negatively oriented. Youths are told which rules to follow and which behaviors are prohibited. He believes that dispositions imposed by juvenile courts and implemented by the juvenile correctional system should be geared toward improving a youth's ability to perform in society. Dispositions "should be action-oriented and skill-based, supported by counseling and therapy only when necessary to help youths reach their competency goals." He recommends that "the nature of services provided at each level of the system should be consistent, and that there should be an element of accountability, a competency-building element, and a public protection element" (Maloney, 1989:34).

Opponents to long-term secure confinement of juveniles believe, among other things, that there are possibly adverse labeling effects from confinement with other offenders. Thus juveniles might acquire labels of themselves as juvenile delinquents and persist in reoffending when released from incarceration later. However, it might be maintained that if they are incarcerated, they know they are delinquents anyway. Will they necessarily acquire stronger self-definitions of delinquents beyond those they already possess? In some respects it is status enhancing for youthful offenders to have been confined in a "joint" or juvenile secure confinement facility, so that they may brag to others later about their experiences. No doubt, confinement of any kind will add at least one dimension to one's reputation as a delinquent offender among other offenders in the community.

Most successful incarcerative programs for juveniles have built-in educational and vocational components, many of which are voluntary. It seems to make a difference whether confined juveniles are forced to take vocational or educational courses or whether they can enroll in such programs on a voluntary basis. For example, a literacy program in the South Carolina Department of Youth Services was investigated in 1990–1991. The sample consisted of 415 participants enrolled in the General Educational Development (GED) program. Although few differences were exhibited between those forced to enroll in this program and those who entered it voluntarily, the volunteers seemed to make a better adjustment in a subsequent follow-up program evaluation (Ryan and McCabe, 1993; U.S. General Accounting Office, 1996). Providing needed psychological and medical services also seems to make a difference in those institutions managing hard-core offenders (Thompson and Farrow, 1993). Some evidence also supports efforts to intervene in offense-specific matters such as sex crimes for qualified juveniles (Burnett and Rathbun, 1993).

Other arguments suggest that the effects of imprisonment on a juvenile's self-image and propensity to commit new offenses are negligible (U.S. General Accounting Office, 1995a). Thus incarceration as a punishment may be the primary result, without any tangible, long-range benefits such as self-improvement or reduction in recidivism (Altschuler and Armstrong, 1994). At least there does not appear to be any consistent or reliable evidence that detaining juveniles causes them automatically to escalate to more serious offenses or to become adult criminals. According to some analysts, the peak ages of juvenile criminality fall between the sixteenth and twentieth birthdays, with participation rates falling off rapidly (Cavender and Knepper, 1992). Thus, incarceration for a fixed period may naturally ease the delinquency rate, at least for some of the more chronic offenders (Bazemore, 1993a; New Jersey Juvenile Delinquency Commission, 1993). Some opponents note that racial, ethnic, and gender factors are more operative than legal factors in secure confinement decisions (Ashford and LeCroy, 1993; DeComo, 1993; Johnson and Secret, 1990; Wooldredge et al., 1994).

Despite how many youths are incarcerated, however, there is little disagreement that more juveniles are incarcerated than need to be incarcerated (Parent et al., 1994). Experts estimate that at least half of all youths currently incarcerated could be released with little fear for community safety or further recidivism (U.S. General Accounting Office, 1996; Wiebush, 1993). One program that appears to have promise as a deterrent to further delinquency has been pioneered in Missouri. It is called the Missouri Intensive Case Monitoring System (Onek, 1994). In 1994 there were five programs in various Department of Youth Services regions throughout Missouri. In 1991, 215 youths were tracked by researchers at Southeastern Missouri State University. Each delinquent youth was paired with a college student to act as an intensive case monitor. Participating youths benefited in various ways from the closeness of the monitoring, together with the valuable assistance, frequent contact, and mentoring of older college students. At the same time, criminal justice students who participated as mentors benefited from the real-world experience of assisting juvenile delinquents. Thus a very cost-effective alternative was created and proved successful as an alternative to out-of-home placements (Onek, 1994).

Example of Residential Failure

Not all residential programs for juveniles are successful. One such program was operated for a brief period in Kane County, Illinois, under the direction of the Court Services Department. The Kane County Youth Home was established and designed to house up to nine male delinquents, aged 13 to 17, who had previously been adjudicated delinquent and deemed in need of intensive services that could not be provided otherwise on an outpatient basis (Kearney, 1994). The program failed because the essential balance between safety and trust could not be achieved. Staff workers could not be hired, trained, or evaluated primarily as residential treatment workers. The program director, court service hierarchy, and child care workers' theory and philosophy of change contrasted dramatically with the therapists' philosophy. Thus the program philosophy itself was self-contradictory. Through no fault of their own, the youths served by the program were destined to "fail," simply because the administrators and practitioners could not agree on which philosophy should govern the youths' treatment. Kearney has observed that to be successful, such programs should have the following three essential components: (1) they must have a consistent philosophy of management shared by all participants; (2) staff should be hired and trained according to that philosophy; and (3) administration of the program should be consonant with the program philosophy, including any changes introduced into program operations. Thus the program itself was probably workable. However, staff disagreements about how best to implement the program led to its demise.

Example of Program Success

Kent State University's Department of Criminal Justice established a Juvenile Justice Assistants Program in December 1990 (Babb and Kratcoski, 1994). The goals of the program were to maximize the community-based treatment potential for unruly, delinquent, or victimized youths. To ensure the effectiveness of this program, program coordinators screened prospective employees in recruitment, training, and placement over a one-year period. About 45 juvenile justice assistants were hired and devoted a minimum of 200 hours to juvenile courts and justice agencies in a five-county area.

During the first 18 months of the program, 69 assistants were assigned to placement agencies for further training, together with service to the agency and its clients. Ultimately, more than 11,400 hours of training and service were completed in approximately 25 agencies. Students involved in the program were able to assist numerous clientele during this period. Thus a successful internship/field experience was converted into a meaningful assistance program with juvenile justice *assistants*. A director oversaw the project and ensured that all program goals were consistent and implemented evenly. Any staff–client problems were dealt with immediately. Equitable solutions were found. The study yielded little recidivism among participating clientele during a follow-up period.

JUVENILE PAROLE

Parole for juveniles is similar to parole for adult offenders (Vogel and Champion, 1993). Those juveniles who have been detained in various institutions for long periods may be released prior to serving their full sentences. *Generally,* **parole** *is a conditional supervised release from incarceration granted to youths who have served a portion of their original sentences* (Altschuler and Armstrong, 1993). They become known as **parolees**.

Purposes of Parole for Juveniles

The general purposes of parole are:

1. To reward good behavior during detention
2. To alleviate overcrowding
3. To permit youths to become reintegrated back into their communities and enhance their rehabilitation potential
4. To deter youths from future offending by ensuring their continued supervision under juvenile parole officers

Some authorities also believe that *the prospect of earning parole might induce greater compliance to institutional rules among incarcerated youths* (Cavender and Knepper, 1992). Also, parole is seen by some experts as a *continuation of the juvenile's punishment*, since parole programs are most often conditional in nature (e.g., observance of curfew, school attendance, staying out of trouble, periodic drug and alcohol urinalyses, participation in counseling programs, and vocational and educational training). Experts agree that early-release decision making should not necessarily be automatic. Rather, releases should be based on a well-defined mission, strategy, and a matching continuum of care, which might include assorted aftercare enhancements (Glick and Goldstein, 1995; Goldsmith, 1995).

A standard parole agreement from the Minnesota Department of Corrections for juveniles is shown in Figure 12.1. Notice that this agreement specifies that the particular juvenile must remain in the legal custody and control of the commissioner of corrections "subject to the rules, regulations, and conditions of this parole as set forth on the reverse side of this agreement." The reverse side of this agreement (not shown here) provides sufficient space for the juvenile parole board to specify one or more program conditions, such as mandatory attendance at vocational/educational training schools, therapy or counseling, community service, restitution orders, or fine payments and maintenance fees. The parole plan is actually a *continuation* of the youth's punishment.

Often, the public thinks that if a youth is free from custody, he or she is completely unrestricted. This is not true. Both probation and parole are considered *punishments*. The behavioral conditions specified under either parole or probation may be very restrictive. Also, it is ordinarily the case that juvenile probation/parole officers have unlimited access to the premises where the youth is located. This intrusion by parole officers is unrestricted, so that if youths are using drugs or are in possession of illegal contraband, it can be detected by surprise, through an unannounced visit from an officer at any time of the day or night.

FIGURE 12.1   Juvenile Parole Agreement

Minnesota Department of Corrections

JUVENILE PAROLE AGREEMENT

WHEREAS, it appears to the Commissioner of Corrections that

_____
(NAME)

❑ presently in custody at _____, and

❑ presently on parole, and

WHEREAS, the said Commissioner, after careful consideration, believes that parole at

this time is in the best interests of this said individual and the public.

Now, THEREFORE, be it known that the Commissioner of Corrections, under authority

vested by law,   ❑ grants parole to,   _____
                  ❑ continues parole for,   (NAME)

and does authorize his/her release from the institution with the parole plan which has been

approved. Upon being paroled and released he/she shall be and remain in legal custody and

under the control of the Commissioner of Corrections subject to the rules, regulations, and

conditions of this parole as set forth on the reverse side of this agreement.

Signed this_____day of_____19_____.

**COMMISSIONER OF CORRECTIONS
BY:**

_____
(HEARING OFFICER)

DISTRIBUTION:
Original—Central Office
2nd Copy—Parolee
3rd Copy—Agent
4th Copy—Inst. File
CR-00100-03

❑ New Parole Agreement

❑ Restructured Parole Agreement

How Many Juveniles Are on Parole?

The American Correctional Association (1996:xxxvi–xxxvii) has reported that over 20,400 juveniles were in nonsecure, state-operated halfway houses and other community-based facilities in 1996. Also, there were over 60,000 youths in secure institutions and training schools in 1996. Another 5000 youths were under other forms of state-controlled supervision as parolees.

Characteristics of Juvenile Parolees

Selected studies of juvenile parolees indicate that a majority is male, black, and between 17 and 19 years of age (Maguire and Pastore, 1996). Some jurisdictions, including New York, have **juvenile offender laws**. These laws define 13-, 14-, 15-, and 16-year-olds as adults when they are charged with committing specified felonies. They may be tried as adults and convicted. When they are subsequently released from institutionalization, they are placed under adult parole supervision. Many other jurisdictions do not have such juvenile offender laws but have waiver or transfer provisions for particularly serious juvenile offenders.

Juvenile parolees share many of the programs used to supervise youthful probationers. Intensive supervised probation programs are used for both probationers and parolees in many jurisdictions. Further, juvenile probation officers often perform dual roles as juvenile parole officers and supervise both types of offenders.

In 1990 the Office of Juvenile Justice and Delinquency Prevention (OJJDP) conducted a research project designed to formulate guidelines for and to identify favorable features of successful intensive parole supervision programs for juveniles (Altschuler and Armstrong, 1990a,b). Their research interests were targeted at identifying those youths who might benefit most from a parole program as well as the most useful methods for supervising offenders. Among their concerns was the reduction and potential elimination of recidivism among youthful parolees. Although it is unrealistic to expect that any program will ever eliminate recidivism, it is possible to target certain program features that might serve to reduce it among specific populations, including juvenile parolees. It is hopeful that the efforts of the OJJDP will eventually yield more successful strategies for managing an especially troublesome offender aggregate.

Juvenile Parole Policy

Between November 1987 and November 1988, Ashford and LeCroy (1993:186) undertook an investigation of the various state juvenile parole programs and provisions. They sent letters and questionnaires to all state juvenile jurisdictions, soliciting information on their juvenile paroling policies. Their response rate was 94 percent, with 47 of the 50 states responding. One interesting result of their survey was the development of a typology of juvenile parole. Ashford and LeCroy (1993:187–191) discovered eight different kinds of juvenile parole used more or less frequently among the states.

1. *Determinate parole:* the length of parole is linked closely with the period of commitment specified by the court; paroling authorities cannot extend the confinement period of a juvenile beyond the original commitment length prescribed by the judge; a juvenile can be released short of serving the full sentence.

2. *Determinate parole set by administrative agency:* the parole release date is set immediately following the youth's arrival at a secure facility.

3. *Presumptive minimum with limits on the extension of the supervision period for a fixed or determinate length of time:* the minimum confinement period is specified, and the youth must be paroled after that date unless there is a showing of bad conduct.

4. *Presumptive minimum with limits on the extension of supervision for an indeterminate period:* parole should terminate after a fixed period of time; the parole period is indeterminate, with the parole officer having discretion to extend the parole period with justification; parole length can extend until the youth reaches the age of majority and leaves juvenile court jurisdiction.

5. *Presumptive minimum with discretionary extension of supervision for an indeterminate period:* same as type 4 except PO has discretion to extend parole length of juvenile with no explicit upper age limit; lacks explicit standards limiting the extension of parole.

6. *Indeterminate parole with a specified maximum and a discretionary minimum length of supervision:* follows the Model Juvenile Court Act of 1968, providing limits for confinement but allows a parole board authority to specify the length of confinement and the period of supervised release within these limits.

7. *Indeterminate parole with legal minimum and maximum periods of supervision:* a parole board is vested with vast power to parole youths at any time with minimum and maximum confinement periods; more liberal than types 1 and 2.

8. *Indeterminate or purely discretionary parole:* the length of parole unspecified; may maintain youths on parole until they reach the age of majority; at this time, parole is discontinued; may release youths from parole at any time during this period. The most popular parole type is 8; the least popular is 1.

Deciding Who Should Be Paroled

The decision to parole particular juveniles is left to different agencies and bodies depending on the jurisdiction. Studies of juvenile delinquent dispositions indicate that in 45 state jurisdictions, the dispositions imposed are indeterminate (Cavender and Knepper, 1992; Greenwood, Deschenes, and Adams, 1993). In 32 states, early-release decisions are left up to the particular juvenile correction agency; six states use parole boards exclusively; and five states depend on the original sentencing judge's decision. Only a few states had determinate sentencing schemes for youthful offenders, so their early release would be established by statute in much the same way as it is for adult offenders.

In New Jersey, for instance, a seven-member parole board appointed by the governor grants early release to both adult and juvenile inmates. In Utah, the Youth Parole Authority is a part-time board consisting of three citizens and four staff members from the Utah Division of Youth Corrections (Norman, 1986). Ideally, the Utah Youth Parole Authority utilizes objective decision-making criteria in determining which youths should be released short of serving their full incarcerative terms. Norman (1986) observes, however, that often, discrepancies exist between what the authority actually does and what it is supposed to do. Some criticisms have been to the effect that the primary early-release criteria are related to one's former institutional behavior rather than to other factors, such as one's prospects for successful adaptation to community life, employment, and participation in educational or vocational programs. Norman investigated approximately 300 juvenile parole hearings over 37 days as the basis for his observations.

The Utah Youth Parole Authority is not alone as the recipient of criticism from others about the fairness of parole decision making. Many parole boards for both adults and juveniles are comprised of persons who make subjective judgments about inmates on the basis of many factors beyond so-called objective criteria. Predispositional reports prepared by juvenile probation officers, records of institutional behavior, a youth's appearance and demeanor during the parole hearing, and the presence of witnesses or victims may have unknown effects upon individual parole board members. Parole decision making is not an exact science. Where elements of subjectivity intrude into the decision-making process, a juvenile's rights are seemingly undermined. Thus parole board decision-making profiles in various jurisdictions may exhibit evidence of early-release disparities attributable to racial, ethnic, gender, or socioeconomic factors.

RECIDIVISM AND PAROLE REVOCATION

Parole revocation is the termination of one's parole program, usually for one or more program violations. When one's parole is terminated, regardless of who does the terminating, there are several possible outcomes. One is that the offender will be returned to secure confinement. This is the most severe result. A less harsh alternative is that offenders will be shifted to a different kind of parole program. For instance, if a juvenile is assigned to a halfway house as a part of the parole program, the rules of the halfway house must be observed. If one or more rules are violated, such as failing to observe curfew, failing drug or alcohol urinalyses, or committing new offenses, a report is filed with the court or the juvenile corrections authority for possible revocation action. If it is decided later that one's parole should be terminated, the result may be to place the offender under house arrest or home confinement, coupled with electronic monitoring. Thus, the juvenile would be required to wear an electronic wristlet or anklet and remain on the premises for specified periods. Other program conditions would be applied as well. The fact is that one is not automatically returned to incarceration following a parole revocation.

Usually, if a return to incarceration is not indicated, the options available to judges, parole boards, or others are limited only by the array of supervisory resources in the given jurisdiction. These options ordinarily involve more intensive supervision or monitoring of offender behaviors. Severe overcrowding in many juvenile incarcerative facilities discourages revocation action that would return large numbers of offenders to industrial schools or youth centers. Intermediate punishments, therefore, function well to accommodate larger numbers of serious offenders, including those who have their parole revoked.

Recidivism is measured many different ways. Maltz (1984) describes at least 10 different ways that it can be defined. However, the more common meanings of recidivism pertain to committing new offenses, being arrested for suspicion of committing new offenses (rearrests), being convicted of new offenses (reconvictions), violating parole or probation program rules, or being returned to secure confinement (reincarceration). As we have seen in earlier chapters, recidivism is often used as the gauge of program success or failure. An arbitrary figure of 30 percent recidivism is considered by many professionals to be a "cutting point," where amounts of recidivism in excess of 30 percent are indicative of program failure, and amounts of recidivism below 30 percent are considered as evidence of program successes. Like juvenile probationers, juvenile parolees exhibit differing degrees of recidivism, depending on the types of supervision programs to which they are assigned. Usually, though not always, the more intensive supervision programs yield lower recidivism rates. Average recidivism figures for juveniles nationally are misleading, since each jurisdiction uses different programs and assigns juvenile parole officers different caseloads. But recidivism rates among juvenile parolees seem to range from 25 to 40 percent, in view of various studies that have examined this phenomenon (Chambers, 1983; Palmer and Wedge, 1989; Wiederanders, 1983; Wylen, 1984). Regardless of how recidivism is measured, when it occurs while juveniles are on probation or parole, this constitutes grounds for parole or probation revocation actions.

The process of parole revocation for juveniles is not as clear-cut as it is for adult offenders. The U.S. Supreme Court has not ruled thus far concerning how juvenile parole revocation actions should be completed. Prior to several significant U.S. Supreme Court decisions, either parole or probation revocation could be accomplished for adult offenders on the basis of reports filed by probation or parole officers that offenders were in violation of one or more conditions of their programs. Criminal court judges, those ordinarily in charge of determining whether to terminate one's probationary status, could decide this issue on the basis of available evidence against offenders. For adult parolees, former decision making relative to terminating their parole could be made by parole boards without much fanfare from offenders. In short, parole officers and others might simply present evidence that one or more infractions or violations of probation or parole conditions had been committed. These infractions, then, could form the basis for revoking probation or parole as well as a justification for these decisions.

A probationer's or parolee's right to due process in any probation or parole revocation action was largely ignored prior to 1967. Thus, technical violations, such as failing to submit monthly reports, violating curfew, filing a falsified report, or drinking alcoholic beverages "to excess," might result in an unfavorable recommendation from one's PO that the probation or parole program should be terminated. Popular television shows sometimes portray parole officers as threatening their clients with parole revocation: "Do this or else I'll have you back in the joint!", meaning a return to prison for adult offenders. Currently, it is not so easy to accomplish either type of revocation.

For adult parolees as well as for adult probationers, revocations for either probation or parole are currently two-stage proceedings. The landmark cases that have directly affected parolees and probationers and their rights are (1) *Mempa v. Rhay* (1967), (2) *Morrissey v. Brewer* (1972), and (3) *Gagnon v. Scarpelli* (1973). Although these landmark cases pertain to adult probationers and parolees, they have significance for juvenile probationers and parolees. The significance is that juvenile justice policies are often formulated or influenced on the basis of U.S. Supreme Court decisions about the rights of inmates, parolees, or probationers and the procedures involved in their processing throughout the criminal justice system. Thus, these cases are not binding on juvenile court judges or juvenile paroling authorities. But they provide a legal basis for specific actions in pertinent juvenile cases if the juvenile justice system chooses to recognize them as precedent setting.

Mempa v. Rhay (1967). Jerry Mempa was convicted in criminal court of "joyriding" in a stolen vehicle on June 17, 1959, in Spokane, Washington. The judge placed him on probation for two years. A few months later, Mempa was involved in a burglary on September 15, 1959. The county prosecutor in Spokane requested that Mempa's probation be revoked. Mempa admitted that he committed the burglary to police. At a *probation revocation hearing* conducted later, the sole testimony about his involvement in the burglary came from his probation officer, who obtained his factual information largely from police reports. Mempa, an indigent, was not permitted to offer statements in his own behalf, nor was he provided counsel, nor was he asked if he wanted counsel, nor was he permitted to cross-examine the probation officer about the officer's incriminating statements. The judge revoked Mempa's probation and sentenced him to 10 years in the Washington State Penitentiary.

A short time later, Mempa filed a writ of *habeas corpus*, which essentially challenges the *fact of his confinement and its nature.* He alleged that he had been denied the right to counsel in his probation revocation hearing, and thus he claimed that his due process rights had been violated in part. The Washington Supreme Court denied his petition, but the U.S. Supreme Court elected to hear it on appeal. The U.S. Supreme Court overturned the Washington Supreme Court and ruled in Mempa's favor. Specifically, the U.S. Supreme Court said that Mempa was entitled to an attorney but was denied one. Furthermore, and perhaps most important, the Court declared that a *probation revocation hearing is a "critical stage" that falls within the due process provisions of the Fourteenth Amendment. Critical stages refer to any stages of the criminal justice process where a defendant is in jeopardy.* If defendants are accused of crimes, or arraigned, or prosecuted, their due process rights "attach" or become relevant. Thus they are entitled to attorneys at any of these critical stages, since they are in jeopardy of losing their freedom. This ruling did not mean that Mempa would be entirely free from further court action. However, it did provide for a rehearing, and his 10-year sentence in the Washington State Penitentiary was set aside.

Morrissey v. Brewer (1972). In 1967, John Morrissey was convicted in an Iowa court for falsely drawing checks. He was sentenced to "not more than seven years" in the Iowa State Prison. He was paroled in June 1968. Seven months later, his parole officer learned that Morrissey had bought an automobile under an assumed name and operated it without permission, had obtained credit cards giving false information, and had given false information to an insurance company when he became involved in an automobile accident. Further, Morrissey had given his parole officer a false address for his residence. After interviewing Morrissey, Morrissey's parole officer filed a report recommending that Morrissey's parole be revoked. The parole violations involved all of the infractions and false information noted above. In his own defense, Morrissey claimed to be "sick" and had been prevented from maintaining continuous contact with his parole officer during the car-buying, credit-card accumulating, and automobile accident period. The parole officer countered by alleging that Morrissey was "continually violating the rules." The Iowa Parole Board revoked Morrissey's parole and he was returned to Iowa State Prison to serve the remainder of his sentence.

During his parole revocation hearing, he was not represented by counsel, nor was he permitted to testify in his own behalf, nor was he permitted to cross-examine witnesses against him, nor was he advised in writing of the charges against him, nor was there any disclosure of the evidence against him. Further, the Iowa Parole Board gave no reasons to Morrissey for their revocation action. Morrissey appealed to the Iowa Supreme Court, which rejected his appeal. The U.S. Supreme Court decided to hear his appeal, however, and overturned the Iowa Supreme Court and Iowa Parole Board actions. The Court did not specifically address the issue of whether Morrissey should have been represented by counsel, but it did establish the foundation for a *two-stage parole revocation proceeding*. The first or preliminary stage or hearing would be conducted at the time of arrest or confinement, and its purpose would be to determine whether probable cause exists that the parolee actually committed the alleged parole violations. The second stage or hearing would be more involved and designed to establish the parolee's guilt or innocence concerning the alleged violations. Currently, all parolees in all states must be extended the following rights relating to **minimum due-process rights**:

1. The right to have written notice of the alleged violations of parole conditions
2. The right to have disclosed to the parolee any evidence of the alleged violation
3. The right of the parolee to be heard in person and to present exculpatory evidence as well as witnesses in his behalf
4. The right to confront and cross-examine adverse witnesses, unless cause exists why they should not be cross-examined
5. The right to a judgment by a neutral and detached body, such as the parole board itself
6. The right to a written statement of the reasons for the parole revocation

Thus the primary significance of the Morrissey case was that *it established minimum due process rights for all parolees and created a two-stage proceeding where alleged infractions of parole conditions could be examined objectively and where a full hearing could be conducted to determine the most appropriate offender disposition.*

Gagnon v. Scarpelli (1973). Because the matter of representation by counsel was not specifically addressed in the Morrissey case, the U.S. Supreme Court heard yet another parolee's case concerning a parole revocation action where court-appointed counsel had not been provided. Gerald Scarpelli was convicted of robbery in July 1965 in a Wisconsin court. At his sentencing on August 5, 1965, Scarpelli was sentenced to 15 years in prison, but the judge suspended the sentence and placed him on probation for seven years. Believe it or not, the following day, August 6, 1965, Gerald Scarpelli was arrested and charged with burglary. The judge immediately revoked his probation and ordered Scarpelli placed in the Wisconsin State Reformatory for a 15-year term.

At this point, Scarpelli's case becomes a little complicated. During his early stay in prison, Scarpelli filed a *habeas corpus* petition with the court, alleging that his due process rights were violated when his probation was revoked. He was not represented by counsel and he was not permitted a hearing. However, Scarpelli was paroled from prison in 1968. Nevertheless, the U.S. Supreme Court acted on his original *habeas corpus* petition filed earlier and ruled in his favor. The U.S. Supreme Court held that Scarpelli was indeed denied the right to counsel and had not been given a hearing in the probation revocation action. Although this might seem to be a hollow victory since Scarpelli was already free on parole, the case had profound significance on both subsequent parole and probation revocation actions. The U.S. Supreme Court, referring to the Morrissey case that it had heard the previous year (1972), said that "a probation revocation, like parole revocation, is not a stage of a criminal prosecution, but does result in loss of liberty.... We hold that *a probationer, like a parolee, is entitled to a preliminary hearing and a final revocation hearing in the conditions specified in Morrissey v. Brewer.*"

The significance of the Scarpelli case is that it equated probation with parole regarding revocation hearings. Although the Court *did not say* that all probationers and parolees have a right to be represented by counsel in all probation and parole revocation hearings, it *did* say that counsel *should be provided in cases where the parolee or probationer makes a timely claim contesting the allegations.* This U.S. Supreme Court decision has been liberally interpreted by the courts and parole boards in all jurisdictions. Thus, while no constitutional basis currently exists for providing counsel in *all* probation or parole revocation proceedings, most of these proceedings usually involve defense counsel if legitimate requests are made in advance by probationers or parolees.

Some persons are understandably perplexed by the seemingly excessive time interval that lapses between when questioned events occur, such as probation revocation actions which may be conducted unconstitutionally, and when the U.S. Supreme Court gets around to hearing such petitions or claims and deciding cases. It is not unusual for these time intervals to be five or six years, or even longer. The wheels of justice move slowly, especially the wheels of U.S. Supreme Court actions. Interestingly, of the more than 3500 cases that are presented to the U.S. Supreme Court annually for hearing, only about 150 to 175 cases are heard where decisions are written. Four or more justices must agree to hear any specific case, and even then, their convening time may expire before certain cases are heard. It is beyond the scope of this book to discuss the process by which U.S. Supreme Court cases are initiated and processed, but this short discussion serves to explain the apparent slowness in rendering significant opinions in landmark cases.

For juveniles, these three cases are important because they provide juvenile courts and juvenile paroling authorities within juvenile corrections with certain guidelines to follow. These guidelines are not mandatory or binding, since these U.S. Supreme Court rulings pertain to adults rather than to juveniles. However, the law is not always abundantly clear regarding its application in a wide variety of different cases. Although it may be anticipated that the U.S. Supreme Court will eventually address probation and parole revocation issues that pertain to juvenile offenders, we can only use adult guidelines for the present.

Currently, probation and parole revocation proceedings for juveniles differ widely among jurisdictions. Knepper and Cavender (1990), for instance, indicate that in a western state they examined, informal hearings were conducted by a juvenile parole board outside the presence of juveniles. In such informal settings, decisions about parole revocations were made. Subsequently, juveniles were brought before the board and advised in a more formal hearing of the rightness of the board's decision about the revocation action taken. This is strongly indicative of the continuation of *parens patriae* in juvenile matters. In other jurisdictions, explicit criteria exist for determining court or parole board actions relating to juvenile parolees who violate program rules or commit new offenses. Statutory constraints may or may not be in place to regulate judicial or parole board decision making in these situations. Again, the cases of *Morrissey, Scarpelli*, and *Mempa* have not yet been interpreted as binding on juvenile procedures.

EXAMPLES OF PROBATION AND PAROLE REVOCATION FOR JUVENILES

Since there is no federal law governing juvenile probation or parole revocation, we must examine state statutes and decisions to determine the types of situations and circumstances where the probation or parole programs of juveniles have been revoked. This will give us some indication of what practices are prevalent among the states, as well as the grounds used in such revocation actions.

Juvenile Probation Revocation Cases

Several cases have been reported involving revocations of juvenile probation. These are reported below.

Can a probation program be revoked when juveniles do not attend treatment programs assigned by the court as a part of their probation? Yes.

In re William H. (664 N.E.2d 1361) (Ohio App. Aug. 1995). William H. was a juvenile placed on probation in Ohio. One of the conditions of his probation was that he attend a treatment center periodically to receive therapy and other forms of assistance designed to rehabilitate him. On one occasion, William H. ran away from the treatment center, and center authorities reported his behavior to the juvenile court. Subsequently, the juvenile court revoked William H.'s probation because his runaway behavior violated one of the conditions of his probation. When asked about the charges of running away from the center, William H. confessed and the judge revoked his probation. William H. appealed, alleging that he was not bound to *comply strictly* with the original court order requiring his attendance on a regular basis at the treatment center. However, the appellate court affirmed the juvenile court judge's action and upheld William H.'s probation revocation.

Can a youth's probation be revoked because of the juvenile's failure to follow a judge's verbal (rather than written) order to attend vocational school training? No.

Matter of Appeal in Maricopa County (915 P.2d 1250) (Ariz. App. Apr. 1996). A juvenile was verbally ordered by a judge to attend Valley Vocational School in Arizona as a condition of his probation. No written order requiring such attendance was provided, however. Later, evidence was presented to the juvenile court that the juvenile had failed to attend the Valley Vocational School. The judge brought the youth before him and revoked his probation.

The youth appealed, contending that there had been no written order requiring his attendance at the vocational school. In this case, the appellate court in Arizona reversed the juvenile court judge's revocation order. They concluded that probation revocation for juveniles is an area where the adult criminal requirement regarding written notice of the terms of probation upon which revocation is based must appropriately be applied in juvenile cases as a matter of due process and general fairness. The appeals court noted that although there had been a verbal order from the judge to require the youth's attendance at the vocational school, it was not sufficiently important, since a written order was issued to revoke one's probation. The court said, "If an order is important enough to warrant a revocation petition, the order first must be reduced to writing and given to [the] probationer."

Can judges combine fines and restitution from different delinquency petitions against the same juvenile offender? Yes. Can the total of all fines and restitution be such that the jurisdiction of the judge to impose such fines is exceeded? Yes. Can probation programs for juveniles be revoked because of failure to pay excessive fines? No.

In re Paul R. (50 Cal. Rptr. 2d 421) (Cal. App. Feb. 1996). Two petitions were filed against a California juvenile, although the presiding juvenile court judge combined both dispositions into a single proceeding. The judge entered an order of restitution in both cases as a condition of Paul R.'s probation. The first case involved a fine as restitution in the amount of $250, while the other fine/restitution order was for $750. Paul R., the juvenile, could not pay these fines. Thus the judge ordered Paul R.'s probation revoked. Paul R. appealed and the appellate court determined that because the total victim restitution equaled $1000, a restitution fine could not be imposed by the judge. The probation revocation order was reversed.

Can juvenile court judges wait until after the expiration of one's probation period to impose new penalties and extended probation terms for old program violations? No.

State v. May (911 P.2d 399) (Wash. App. Feb. 1996). A juvenile was adjudicated delinquent and placed on probation with community supervision. Subsequently, the period of community supervision expired; however, May, the juvenile, had violated one or more probation conditions during the community supervision period. The juvenile court ordered May's probation revoked *after* the community supervision period. May appealed and the appellate court reversed the judge's revocation order, saying that a timely hearing was required to revoke someone's probation program. Simply put, May could not have his probation program revoked after having fulfilled it, where the time limit had expired (despite program infractions occurring earlier during his program).

Can juveniles have their probation programs revoked if they possess illegal chemical substances? Yes.

In re Manzy W. (48 Cal. Rptr. 2d 403) (Cal. App. Dec. 1995). Manzy W. was a 17-year-old juvenile who was placed on probation following being expelled from school for selling drugs, receiving stolen property, and battery. The juvenile court placed him on probation and required that he attend school, remain drug-free, and try to earn good grades. However, he was chronically truant, engaged in purse snatching, used marijuana, and continued to sell drugs. Police arrested him for possession of methamphetamine, which he admitted. The juvenile court revoked his probation and sent him to the California Youth Authority, a secure confinement facility, for a period of time. Manzy W. appealed. The appellate court reviewed Manzy W.'s case and determined that all the facts about Manzy W.'s drug involvement and other crimes were true. The only fact remaining to be determined was whether Manzy W. had committed a felony or a misdemeanor because of the possession of illegal drugs. Manzy W.'s placement in the California Youth Authority was proper.

Are probation revocation hearings required at a youth's request before probation revocation orders are issued by juvenile court judges? Yes.

State v. Tony G. (909 P.2d 746) (N.M. App. Nov. 1995). Tony G. was a juvenile placed on probation in New Mexico. While on probation he violated one or more express terms of his program. He demanded and received a hearing before his probation was revoked. He was permitted to confront and cross-examine witnesses against him, and he was allowed to present his own witnesses to speak on his behalf. At certain points, some hearsay evidence was introduced to support the government's claim that Tony G. had indeed violated his probation conditions. Nevertheless, the revocation orders were issued properly following the hearing, which was designed to verify the facts alleged.

Are adult probation/parole revocation guidelines and U.S. Supreme Court decisions binding on juvenile courts and boards that revoke juvenile probation/parole? No.

People v. Dennison (618 N.Y.S.2d 289) (N.Y. Sup. App. Div. Nov. 1994). Dennison was a juvenile confined to a New York State secure institution for a delinquency adjudication. Subsequently, he was granted parole. While on parole, Dennison violated one or more parole conditions.

His parole was revoked and he appealed, arguing that his revocation proceeding did not involve the full range of due process rights of adult parole revocation proceedings. The appellate court upheld the revocation against Dennison. However, it noted that there is no question that due process considerations apply in juvenile proceedings. However, whether any particular revocation hearing for juveniles passes constitutional muster must be determined on a case-by-case basis. Further, due process does not require the sentencing court to consider alternatives to incarceration before revoking probation or parole. Dennison's argument that the parole revocation proceeding for juveniles should mirror similar proceedings for adults neglects the reality of the special relationship to and responsibilities concerning adult prisoners as markedly disparate from its position and duty with respect to delinquent children. Thus children on conditional release remain the responsibility of the state for the period of the order of placement. Dennison was given a notice of charges against him, a right to counsel at a fact-finding hearing, the opportunity to present evidence in his own behalf, and the right to confront and cross-examine witnesses against him. All of these factors fully comply with the essence of due process. Dennison's revocation order was upheld.

Can time spent on parole be counted against actual hard time served in an institution for a juvenile found guilty of violating one or more parole conditions? No.

Charry v. State of California (13 F.2d 1386) (U.S. 9th Cir. Jan. 1994).
Charry was a juvenile adjudicated delinquent for various serious offenses. He was sent to the California Youth Authority for a period of time, after which he was paroled. While on parole, Charry violated one or more of his parole program conditions and his parole was revoked following a revocation hearing. He was placed back into the California Youth Authority to complete the remainder of his incarcerative term. He appealed, alleging that the time he spent while on parole should be deducted from his actual time served in the California Youth Authority. The appeals court turned down Charry's request to have the parole time deducted from his full sentence. In this case, the court noted that juveniles cannot be held for any period longer than for adults found guilty of the same offense. In other words, the punishment for a juvenile cannot be more severe than the punishment imposed on an adult offender for the same offense. In Charry's case, the parole time was considered a part of his total sentence to be served, and it was held that it would not be proper to deduct some amount of parole time from his original sentence length.

SELECTED ISSUES IN JUVENILE CORRECTIONS

Investigations of the rate of secure confinement of juveniles during the past two centuries have disclosed that the rate of juvenile institutionalization has increased, especially during the most recent decades (Sherraden and Downs, 1984). Many of those youths detained for fairly long periods (30 days or longer) are less serious misdemeanants and status offenders (U.S. General Accounting Office, 1983). For this and other reasons, juvenile corrections has been under attack from various sectors for years (Dwyer and McNally, 1987:47; McNally, 1984). This attack comes from many quarters, and it coincides with a general attack on the criminal justice system for its apparent failure to stem the increasing wave of crime in the United States. Sentencing reforms, correctional reforms, experiments with probation and parole alternatives, and a host of other options have been attempted in an apparent effort to cure or control delinquents and criminals.

In 1985, the United Nations and National Council of Juvenile and Family Court Judges adopted policy statements about the juvenile justice system that bear directly on juvenile corrections. The issues to be discussed in this final section may be better understood in the context of these statements. Several recommendations have been made by Dwyer and McNally (1987:50–51):

1. Primary dispositions of juvenile courts should be to have a flexible range for restricting freedom, with the primary goal focused on the restoration to full liberty rather than let the punishment fit the crime; that no case dispositions should be of a mandatory nature, but rather, they should be left to the discretion of the judge based on predetermined dispositional guidelines; that in no case should a juvenile under 18 years of age be subject to capital punishment.

2. Individualized treatment of juveniles should be continued, including the development of medical, psychiatric, and educational programs that range from least to most restrictive, according to individual need.

3. While being held accountable, chronic, serious juvenile offenders should be retained within the jurisdiction of the juvenile court. As a resource, specialized programs and facilities need to be developed that focus on restorations rather than punishment.

4. Policymakers, reformers, and researchers should continue to strive for greater understanding as to the causes and most desired response to juvenile crime; that research should be broad-based rather than limited to management, control, and punishment strategies.

5. Where the juvenile court judge believes that the juvenile under consideration is nonamenable to the services of the court and based on the youth's present charges, past record in court, and his or her age and mental status, the judge may waive jurisdiction; that in all juvenile cases the court of original jurisdiction be that of the juvenile court; that the discretion to

waive be left to the juvenile court judge; that the proportionality of punishment would be appropriate with these cases, but the highest-risk offenders should be treated in small, but secure facilities.

Each of the issues discussed below is affected directly by these recommendations and policy statements. Although these statements are not obligatory for any jurisdiction, they do suggest opinions and positions of a relevant segment of concerned citizens: juvenile court judges and juvenile corrections personnel. These issues include (1) the privatization of juvenile corrections, (2) the classification of juvenile offenders, (3) juveniles held in adult jails and lock-ups, and (4) recidivism among juvenile offenders.

The Privatization of Juvenile Corrections

Juvenile corrections has many of the same problems as adult corrections. Chronic overcrowding in secure confinement facilities is extensive among jurisdictions (California Department of Youth Authority, 1984). Furthermore, sexual assaults of juvenile inmates by others, including administrative staff and guards, are not uncommon. Existing facilities in many states are deteriorating rapidly. Furthermore, there are disproportionate representations of black, Hispanic, and Native American youths (Breed and Krisberg, 1986:14–15). With the current emphasis on more punitive juvenile sentencing policies, it is unlikely that significant improvements in the quality of juvenile incarcerative facilities will be implemented in the near future. Some experts are quite pessimistic about whether the current political environment is flexible enough or willing to support a more humanistic and rational approach to juvenile corrections (Breed and Krisberg, 1986:20). **Privatization** is believed by some authorities to be one solution to overcrowded publicly operated facilities.

Nonsecure and secure facilities are both publicly and privately operated (Keating, 1984). However, private operations have been criticized because of the comparatively low accountability of administrators to citizens in contrast with publicly operated facilities (del Carmen, 1985). Florida is one of several states experimenting with various forms of private juvenile secure confinement. Historically, Florida sought to rehabilitate youths through incarceration, including placement of serious offenders in reform or training schools (Pingree, 1984:60). The first school for male juveniles opened in Florida in 1900, and by 1972, four schools were operating in various jurisdictions throughout the state. But because of serious institutional overcrowding and the ineffectiveness of program treatments, Florida officials decided to shift their incarcerative priorities to the development of less secure, community-based facilities (Pingree, 1984:60).

Some Florida community-based facilities are currently privately operated, although some of these are not-for-profit organizations such as the Jack and Ruth Eckerd Foundation. This foundation sponsors various wilderness projects, seeking to provide juveniles with opportunities to develop certain skills and acquire more positive self-images (Pingree, 1984:61). Florida's objectives are to (1) reduce the number of juveniles actually placed in secure confinement facilities, and (2) to provide juveniles with a broader base of community options that will be instrumental in helping them to acquire vocational training and education. Much emphasis is placed on assisting youths with psychological problems as well. Thus trained counselors work closely with Florida juvenile offenders to meet their psychological and social needs more effectively. The Florida model has served as an example for other jurisdictions in later years (Criswell, 1987).

Robbins (1986:29) has outlined several important issues relating to the privatization of corrections, for both adult and juvenile offenders. He raises the following questions:

1. What standards will govern the operation of the institution?
2. Who will monitor implementation of the standards?
3. Will the public still have access to the facility?
4. What recourse will members of the public have if they do not approve of how an institution is operated?
5. Who will be responsible for maintaining security and using force at an institution?
6. Who will be responsible for maintaining security if the private personnel go on strike?
7. Where will the responsibility for [incarcerative] disciplinary procedures lie?
8. Will the company be able to refuse to accept certain inmates, such as those with AIDS?
9. What options will be available to the government if the corporation raises its fees substantially?
10. What safeguards will prevent a private contractor from making a low initial bid to obtain a contract and then raising the price after the government is no longer immediately able to reassume the task of operating the facility?
11. What will happen if the company declares bankruptcy?
12. After private vendors have gained a foothold in the corrections field, what safeguards will prevent them from lobbying for philosophical changes for their greater profit?
13. What options will the public have if they do not approve of how an institution is operated?

These are important questions that often impede the progress of the private sector as it insinuates itself into the correctional field. Currently, juvenile corrections seems to have the lion's share of the privatization business. The Corrections Corporation of America, headquartered in Nashville, Tennessee, currently operates numerous facilities for both adults and juveniles throughout the United States. Increasingly, other private interests are entering these correctional areas to provide services and supervisory tasks, often at less cost to taxpayers than that of government-operated facilities.

On the positive side, Turner (1988) and others suggest that private interests can often cut the red tape associated with secure confinement operations. He and other professionals promote the idea that the private sector can work cooperatively with the public sector in providing the best of both worlds for offenders (Longmire, 1985; Ring, 1987; Springer, 1976, 1988). Turner notes that private-sector operations can reward employees more quickly for excellent service performed and that new operational ideas may be implemented more quickly in private operations compared with government organizations. Further, many of those involved in private corrections operations have formerly been employed in administrative and staff capacities in public corrections agencies and institutions. Thus they possess experience to do the job and do it well.

Turner says that the "profit" motive is an issue often raised by opponents of privatization of corrections. In turn, this may inspire private interests to keep inmates confined for longer periods to maximize profits. However, it is apparent that the current state of chronic overcrowding in public incarceration facilities with no relief in sight will maintain consistently high inmate populations in both juvenile and adult incarcerative facilities, regardless of whether they are operated privately or publicly. Also, if private interests can make a profit while providing good-quality services to inmates at less cost to government, this seems to be a compelling argument in favor of greater privatization.

The Classification of Juvenile Offenders

Classification of any offender is made difficult by the fact that the state of the art is such in predictions of risk and dangerousness that little future behavior can be accurately forecasted. This holds for juveniles as well as adults. We know that status offenders may or may not escalate to more serious offenses, with the prevailing sentiment favoring or implying nonescalation (Datesman and Aickin, 1985; McCarthy and Smith, 1986; Nagoshi, 1986). Fully effective classification schemes have not yet been devised, although we know that on the basis of descriptions of existing aggregates of offenders, factors such as gender, age, nature of offense, seriousness of offense, race or ethnicity, and socioeconomic status are more or less correlated.

The flaws of various classification schemes are made more apparent when program "failures" are detected in large numbers. Juvenile court judges make the wrong judgments and decisions about juvenile placements. Intake officers make similar errors of classification when conducting initial screenings of juveniles. The issue of "false positives" and "false negatives" is raised here because some youths may be unfairly penalized for what authorities believe are valid predictive criteria of future dangerousness. By the same token, some youths are underpenalized, because it is believed, wrongly, that they will not pose risks or commit serious offenses in the future, and they do (Gottfredson and Tonry, 1987; Gottfredson and Gottfredson, 1988).

Guarino-Ghezzi (1989) has suggested that a systematic classification model can be devised by incorporating objective predictors of an offender's risk of recidivism into the intake assessment (p. 112). She believes that an objective risk classification procedure can accomplish the following objectives (Guarino-Ghezzi, 1989:112–114):

1. Increase control over juvenile offenders who are placed in community settings
2. Increase agency accountability for placement decisions
3. Increase consistency in decision making
4. Direct allocation of scarce resources
5. Increase support for budget requests

Table 12.2 shows an overview of possible risk, need, and control factors that might comprise a risk–need classification instrument that might be used by juvenile custodial institution officials. Guarino-Ghezzi (1989:116) says that with few exceptions, administrative control factors are often given low priority whenever classification models are designed. But she encourages their adoption, since they are crucial in influencing how private vendors will react toward youths (in a privatization context, for instance), how youths will adjust to their programs, in determining which youths are most likely to cause behavioral problems and assault staff, and in determining whether gang involvement is indicated (possibly requiring a youth's separation from other gang members upon arrival at a new facility). Some results of more effective classification schemes include greater staff accountability, greater staff and inmate safety, and more effective programming relative to individual offenders and their needs.

TABLE 12.2

An Overview of Possible Risk, Need, and Control Factors

Factors	Risk	Need	Control
Total offense record	×		
Recent offense record	×		
History of assaultive behavior	×		×
Commitment history (if applicable)	×		×
Family relationships		×	
Intellectual ability		×	
Learning disability		×	
Employment	×	×	
Voc/tech skills		×	
Health and hygiene		×	
Sexual adjustment		×	
AWOL record	×		×
Behavior in previous programs			×
Public perception of offender			×
Age			×
Drug/alcohol	×	×	
Educational adjustment	×	×	×
Peer relationships	×	×	×
Emotional response/attitude	×	×	×
Placement record	×		×
Parental control	×	×	×

Source: Susan Guarino-Ghezzi, "Classifying Juveniles: A Formula for Case-by-Case Assessment," *Corrections Today* 51 (1989), p. 114.

Juveniles Held in Adult Jails or Lock-Ups

Estimates vary about the number of juveniles who are currently detained in adult jails or lockups. Figures from Bessette (1990:2) suggest that the number of juveniles admitted into and released from adult jails during 1989 was 54,000. Other professionals claim that these figures are actually much higher. For instance, Dale (1988:46) indicates that approximately 479,000 juveniles are locked up in adult jails annually in the United States on either a pretrial detainee or postadjudication basis. Whichever figure is more accurate, the fact remains that large numbers of juveniles are incarcerated in adult jails and lockups annually.

Police officers frequently make arrests of juvenile suspects who may not appear to be juveniles and who do not provide police with proper identification. Later, investigations reveal the juveniles' true ages, and they are placed in juvenile incarceration or some other juvenile facility for further processing. Some jurisdictions simply lack the facilities to accommodate juvenile offenders in areas separate from adults. Thus there are occasions where juveniles continue to be celled with adult inmates, although these occurrences are decreasing.

The most apparent problems with celling juveniles in adult lockups or jails are that (1) youths are subject to potential sexual assault from older inmates and (2) youths are often traumatized by the jailing experience. The latter problem leads to another problem that is even more serious—jail suicides. Rowan (1989) and others indicate that juveniles are especially suicide-prone during the first 24 hours of their incarceration in jails. Thus it is little consolation that states such as Illinois pass laws prohibiting a juvenile's confinement in adult jails for periods longer than six hours (Huskey, 1990). Dale (1988:46) says that a juvenile's potential sexual exploitation does not always involve other, older inmates. In Ironton, Ohio, for example, Dale reports a case of sexual assault against a detained juvenile status offender by a corrections officer. Although a $40,000 judgment was subsequently awarded the youth, no amount of money can buy away the trauma to a juvenile resulting from such a violent sexual incident (*Doe v. Burwell*, 1981).

Currently, there are organized movements in many jurisdictions to mandate the permanent removal of juveniles from adult jails, even on temporary bases. Civil rights suits as well as class action claims are being filed by and on behalf of many juveniles currently detained in adult facilities. Dale (1988:46) cites the Iowa case of *Hendrickson v. Griggs* (1987) as a step in this direction. A federal district judge, Donald E. O'Brien, ruled that the Juvenile Justice and Delinquency Prevention Act could be used as the basis for a lawsuit seeking the permanent removal of juveniles from adult jails. Presently, no nationwide precedents have been established to prevent juvenile incarcerations in adult lockups or jails in any absolute sense. Clearly, much remains to be done to rectify a situation that seems more within the purview of the juvenile justice system than within the criminal justice system.

Recidivism Among Juvenile Offenders

Because a broad range of intermediate punishments is not available to juvenile court judges in certain jurisdictions, dispositions are often imposed to detain youths in secure facilities for prolonged periods. These decisions frequently involve youths believed to pose threats to their communities. But some juveniles are detained for their own protection or because no other form of care is available (McCarthy, 1985). One problem with detaining less serious offenders in secure facilities is that unfavorable changes in juvenile self-images have been known to occur (Anson and Eason, 1986). These perceived adverse changes in juveniles' self-images are believed by some to contribute to greater recidivism among youthful offenders.

BOX 12.2   CHILDREN SOUND THE ALARM

The Case of the Watchful Shepherd

The Watchful Shepherd is alive and well in Pittsburgh, Pennsylvania. The Watchful Shepherd proposes to end child abuse or at least decrease its incidence. It will sound an alarm and issue a cry for help. It will assist children and protect them from abusive guardians or parents. The Watchful Shepherd isn't human. It is a machine.

Sponsored by Allegheny County's Children and Youth Services Agency, the Watchful Shepherd is an electronic emergency device. Children will be equipped with it and can use the device, about the size of a yo-yo, to sound an alarm if they are in trouble or are being abused. In 1996, plans were implemented to place the Watchful Shepherd system in various homes in the city's low-income North Side.

Not everyone shares the optimism that this system will deter child abuse. Irwin Hyman, a psychology professor at Temple University in Philadelphia, says that the system is like "putting a cop in the house rather than training the parents not to abuse their kids. If it works, fine. But there a million things that come down the pike, like lie detectors, and they don't work."

Children may engage the device merely by pressing a button on the portable unit or on a wedge-shaped unit by a telephone. The button also activates a siren within the home. Hospital officials or police departments are alerted and can conduct investigations to determine whether child abuse is happening.

Allegheny County officials responsible for implementing the Watchful Shepherd program say that the plan is *not* to put parents in jail. Rather, the intent is to bring families closer together by stressing more positive outlets for anger and frustration. The program is especially useful for social workers if they are counseling families where child abuse is suspected.

Is this another Big Brother watching device? What about false alarms? What are some potential abuses of the Watchful Shepherd?

Source: Adapted from Associated Press, "Alarm May Deter Abuse at Home," *Minot (ND) Daily News,* June 14, 1996:A3.

Like adult incarceration, juvenile secure confinement frequently fails to rehabilitate offenders, and they emerge more hardened, better-schooled delinquents than when they entered. Although some highly regimented programs in certain states seem to work, many of the secure facilities for juveniles throughout the United States fail miserably in their rehabilitative ambitions. One problem encountered by many juvenile corrections authorities is how to deal effectively with aggressive youths. Sources of aggressiveness have often been traced to ineffective or undeveloped interpersonal skills.

One New York jurisdiction implemented an *aggression replacement training* (ART) program in 1983 to assist aggressive youths in developing more acceptable social skills. The ART program introduced juveniles to beginning social skills such as starting conversation and listening, advanced social skills such as apologizing and asking for help, and skills for dealing with aggression and one's feelings (Goldstein and Glick, 1987). Thus far, evaluations of the ART program have been promising; participants have been less likely to engage in physical violence or aggression than have nonparticipant controls. Thus these officials have concluded tentatively that aggression replacement training appears to have considerable potency as an intervention strategy (Goldstein and Glick, 1987).

The emphasis currently seems to be on minimizing the maximum-security nature of juvenile secure confinement and permitting juveniles greater freedom through the establishment of minimum-security facilities (McMillen, 1987:44). Although public support for minimum-security facilities for dangerous juvenile offenders is not particularly strong at present, there are signs of increasing receptivity to the idea. This is especially true when the costs of maximum-security incarceration of juveniles are compared with the costs of minimum-security secure confinement. Furthermore, juvenile self-concepts seem to be affected positively (McMillen, 1987:48).

KEY TERMS

Detention centers	*Parolee*
Foster home	*Parole revocation hearing*
Group homes	*Privatization*
Halfway houses	*Probation revocation hearing*
Homeward Bound	*Short-term confinement*
Minimum due process rights	*VisionQuest*
Outward Bound	*Walnut Street Jail*
Parole	*Wilderness projects*

QUESTIONS FOR REVIEW

1. What is meant by *juvenile corrections*? Discuss several important parts or components of juvenile corrections.
2. What are four major aims or objectives of juvenile corrections? Discuss each briefly.

3. Describe briefly the early efforts of corrections officials in the United States to accommodate juvenile offenders in secure confinement. What was the role of the Walnut Street Jail in this regard?

4. Describe VisionQuest and some of its major strengths that might relate to juvenile rehabilitation.

5. Differentiate between short- and long-term secure confinement facilities for juveniles. What are the purposes of each?

6. What are some of the pros and cons of long-term confinement for juvenile offenders?

7. Identify three important landmark cases pertaining to adult probation and parole revocation hearings. Discuss the significance of each case as it might relate to juvenile corrections and juvenile parole.

8. What are some of the major problems confronted by officials who attempt to classify juvenile offenders? What factors seem to be most predictive of one's risk?

9. About how many juveniles move through adult lockups and jails annually? What legal provisions are in place to limit such incarcerations and admissions? Discuss some of the problems of holding juveniles in adult facilities, even for short periods.

10. What do we know about the rights of juvenile parolees? Are they the same as the rights of juveniles probationers? What are some examples of juvenile parole and the conditions under which it has been revoked?

SUGGESTED READINGS

Bourque, Blair B. et al. *Boot Camps for Juvenile Offenders: An Implementation Evaluation of Three Demonstration Programs*. Washington, DC: U.S. National Institute of Justice, 1996.

Galaway, Burt and Joe Hudson (eds.). *Criminal Justice, Restitution, and Reconciliation*. Monsey, NY: Criminal Justice Press, 1991.

Sheleff, Leon Shaskolsky. *Ultimate Penalties: Capital Punishment, Life Imprisonment, and Physical Torture*. Columbus, OH: Ohio State University Press, 1991.

Shichor, David. *Punishment for Profit: Private Prisons/Public Concerns*. Thousand Oaks, CA: Sage, 1995.

BIBLIOGRAPHY

AGNEW, ROBERT (1984). "Appearance and Delinquency." *Criminology* **22**:421–440.

AGOPIAN, MICHAEL W. (1989). "Targeting Juvenile Gang Offenders for Community Service." *Community Alternatives: International Journal of Family Care* **1**:99–108.

ALASKA DEPARTMENT OF HEALTH AND SOCIAL SERVICES DIVISION OF FAMILY AND YOUTH SERVICES (1992). *Children in Crisis: A Report on Runaway and Homeless Youth in Alaska.* Juneau, AK: Alaska Department of Health and Social Services Division of Family and Youth Services.

ALEXANDER, RUDOLPH JR. (1995). "Incarcerated Juvenile Offenders' Right to Rehabilitation." *Criminal Justice Policy Review* **7**:202–213.

ALTSCHULER, DAVID M. (1991). *The Supervision of Juvenile Offenders in Maryland: Policy and Practice Implications of the Workload Study.* Baltimore, MD: Institute for Policy Studies, Johns Hopkins University.

ALTSCHULER, DAVID M. and TROY L. ARMSTRONG (1990a). "Designing an Intensive Aftercare Program for High-Risk Juveniles." *Corrections Today* **52**:170–171.

ALTSCHULER, DAVID M. and TROY L. ARMSTRONG (1990b). "Intensive Parole for High-Risk Juvenile Offenders: A Framework for Action." Unpublished paper presented at the American Society of Criminology meetings, Baltimore, MD (November).

ALTSCHULER, DAVID M. and TROY L. ARMSTRONG (1992). *Intensive Aftercare for High-Risk Juvenile Parolees: A Model Program Design.* Baltimore, MD: Institute for Policy Studies, Johns Hopkins University.

ALTSCHULER, DAVID M. and TROY L. ARMSTRONG (1993). "Intensive Aftercare for High-Risk Juvenile Parolees: Program Development and Implementation in Eight Pilot Sites." Unpublished paper presented at the annual meeting of the American Society of Criminology, Phoenix, AZ (October).

ALTSCHULER, DAVID M. and TROY L. ARMSTRONG (1994). *Intensive Aftercare for High-Risk Juveniles: An Assessment.* Washington, DC: U.S. Office of Juvenile Justice and Delinquency Prevention.

ALTSCHULER, DAVID M. and WILLIAM V. LUNEBURG (1992). "The Juvenile Justice and Delinquency Prevention Formula Grant Program: Federal–State Relationships in a Quasi-regulatory Context." *Criminal Justice Policy Review* **6**:136–158.

AMANDES, RICHARD B. (1979). "Hire a Gang Leader: A Delinquency Prevention Program That Works." *Juvenile and Family Court Journal* **30**:37–40.

AMERICAN CORRECTIONAL ASSOCIATION (1983). *The American Prison: From the Beginning...A Pictorial History.* Laurel, MD: American Correctional Association.

AMERICAN CORRECTIONAL ASSOCIATION (1992). *Juvenile Caseworker: Resource Guide.* Laurel, MD: American Correctional Association.

AMERICAN CORRECTIONAL ASSOCIATION (1996). *1996 Directory.* Laurel, MD: American Correctional Association.

AMNESTY INTERNATIONAL (1991). *United States of America: The Death Penalty and Juvenile Offenders.* New York: Amnesty International.

ANGENENT, HUUB and ANTON DE MAN (1996). *Background Factors of Juvenile Delinquency.* New York: Peter Lang.

ANONYMOUS (1983). "Access to Juvenile Delinquency Hearings." *Michigan Law Review* **81:**1540–1565.

ANONYMOUS (1988). "Juvenile Justice." *Criminal Justice Newsletter* **19:**1–8.

ANONYMOUS (1991). "Teenagers Victims of Violent Crime More Often Than Adults." *Corrections Compendium* **16**.

ANONYMOUS *(1992a)* "R.O.C.K.: Reach Out, Convicts and Kids." *Corrections Compendium* **17**.

ANONYMOUS (1992b). "Runaways Flee Severe Problems." *Corrections Compendium* **17**.

ANONYMOUS (1996). "Research Note: What Kind of 'Report Card' Do American Criminal Justice Agencies Give the Department of Justice in Dealing with the Gang Problem?" *Journal of Gang Research* **3:**44.

ANSON, RICHARD H. and CAROL S. EASON (1986). "The Effects of Confinement on Delinquent Self-Image." *Juvenile and Family Court Journal* **37:**39–47.

ANTI-DEFAMATION LEAGUE OF B'NAI-B'RITH (1995). *The Skinhead International: A Worldwide Survey of Neo-Nazi Skinheads.* New York: Anti-Defamation League of B'Nai-B'Rith.

APPIER, JANIS (1990). "Juvenile Crime Control: Los Angeles Law Enforcement and the Zoot-Suit Riots." In *Criminal Justice History: An International Annual*, Vol. 11, Louis A. Knafla (ed.). Westport, CT: Meckler.

ARIZONA CRIMINAL JUSTICE COMMISSION (1994). *Street Gangs in Arizona 1993.* Phoenix, AZ: Arizona Statistical Analysis Center.

ARMOR, JERRY C. and VINCENT KEITH JACKSON (1995). "Juvenile Gang Activity in Alabama." *Journal of Gang Research* **2:**29–35.

ARMSTRONG, TROY L. (1988). "National Survey of Juvenile Intensive Probation Supervision, Part I." *Criminal Justice Abstracts* **20:**342–348.

ARMSTRONG, TROY L. (ed.) (1991). *Intensive Interventions with High-Risk Youths: Promising Approaches in Juvenile Probation and Parole.* Monsey, NY: Criminal Justice Press.

ARMSTRONG, TROY L., DENNIS MALONEY and DENNIS ROMIG (1990). "The Balanced Approach in Juvenile Probation: Principles, Issues, and Application." *APPA Perspectives* **14:**8–13.

ARRIGONA, NANCY and TONY FABELO (1987). *Case Study of Juvenile Probation in Texas.* Austin, TX: Criminal Justice Policy Council.

ASHFORD, JOSE B. and CRAIG WINSTON LECROY (1990). "Juvenile Recidivism: A Comparison of Three Prediction Instruments." *Adolescence* **25:**33–41.

ASHFORD, JOSE B. and CRAIG WINSTON LECROY (1993). "Juvenile Parole Policy in the United States: Determinate versus Indeterminate Models." *Justice Quarterly* **10:**179–195.

ASSOCIATED PRESS (1997). "Girl Found Guilty in Toddler's Death." *Minot (ND) Daily News*, February 18, 1997:A2.

AUSTIN, JAMES, MICHAEL JONES, and MELISSA BOLYARD (1993). *Assessing the Impact of a County Operated Boot Camp: Evaluation of the Los Angeles County Regimented Inmate Diversion Program.* San Francisco: National Council on Crime and Delinquency.

AUSTIN, JAMES and BARRY KRISBERG (1982). "The Unmet Promise of Alternatives to Incarceration." *Crime and Delinquency* **29:**374–409.

AWAD, GEORGE A. and ELISABETH B. SAUNDERS (1991). "Male Adolescent Sexual Assaulters: Clinical Observations." *Journal of Interpersonal Violence* **6**:446–460.

BABB, SUSAN and PETER C. KRATCOSKI (1994). "The Juvenile Justice Assistants Program." *Juvenile and Family Court Journal* **45**:483–499.

BACH, KATHLEEN K. (1986). "The Exclusionary Rule in the Public School Administrative Disciplinary Proceeding: Answering the Question after *New Jersey v. T.L.O.*" *Hastings Law Journal* **37**:1133–1170.

BAIRD, S. CHRISTOPHER (1984). *Classification of Juveniles in Corrections: Model Systems Approach.* Washington, DC: Arthur D. Little.

BAIRD, S. CHRISTOPHER (1985). "Classifying Juveniles: Making the Most of an Important Management Tool." *Corrections Today* **47**:32–38.

BAIRD, CHRISTOPHER and DEBORAH NEUENFELDT (1990). *Improving Correctional Performance through Better Classification.* San Francisco: National Council on Crime and Delinquency.

BAIRD, ROBERT M. and STUART E. ROSENBAUM (1995). *Punishment and the Death Penalty: The Current Debate.* Amherst, NY: Prometheus Books.

BALL, RICHARD A. and J. ROBERT LILLY (1987). "The Phenomenology of Privacy and the Power of the State: Home Incarceration with Electronic Monitoring." In *Critical Issues in Criminology and Criminal Justice*, J. E. Scott and J. Hirschi (eds.). Thousand Oaks, CA: Sage.

BANKS, J., T. R. SILER, and R. L. RARDIN (1977). "Past and Present Findings in Intensive Adult Probation." *Federal Probation* **41**:20–25.

BANKSTON, CARL L., III and STEPHEN J. CALDAS (1996). "Adolescents and Deviance in a Vietnamese American Community: A Theoretical Synthesis." *Deviant Behavior* **17**:159–181.

BARON, STEPHEN W. and TIMOTHY F. HARTNAGEL (1996). "'Lock 'Em Up': Attitudes toward Punishing Juvenile Offenders." *Canadian Journal of Criminology* **39**:191–212.

BARTEK, SOPHIE E., DENNIS L. KREBS, and MICHAEL C. TAYLOR (1993). "Coping, Defending, and the Relations between Moral Judgment and Moral Behavior in Prostitutes and Other Female Delinquents." *Journal of Abnormal Psychology* **102**:66–73.

BARTOLLAS, CLEMENS (1990). *Juvenile Delinquency,* 2nd ed. New York: Macmillan.

BAUMER, ERIC (1994). "Poverty, Crack and Crime: A Cross-City Analysis." *Journal of Research in Crime and Delinquency* **31**:311–327.

BAUMER, TERRY L., MICHAEL G. MAXFIELD, and ROBERT MENDELSOHN (1993). "A Comparative Analysis of Three Electronically Monitored Home Detention Programs." *Justice Quarterly* **10**:121–142.

BAZEMORE, S. GORDON (1989). *The Restitution Experience in Youth Employment: A Monograph and Training Guide to Job Components.* Washington, DC: U.S. Department of Justice.

BAZEMORE, S. GORDON (1993a). "Designed Work Experience as an Alternative Intervention for Juvenile Offenders." *Justice Professional* **7**:47–67.

BAZEMORE, S. GORDON (1993b). "Formal Policy and Informal Process in the Implementation of Juvenile Justice Reform." *Criminal Justice Review* **18**:26–45.

BAZEMORE, S. GORDON (1994). "Understanding the Response to Reforms Limiting Discretion: Judges' Views of Restrictions on Detention Intake." *Justice Quarterly* **11**:429–452.

Bazemore, S. Gordon and Barbara R. West (1990). "Conflict and Change in a State Correctional System: A Case Study in Program Implementation." *Criminal Justice Policy Review* **3**:133–148.

Bedau, Hugo Adam (1992). *The Case against the Death Penalty.* Washington, DC: American Civil Liberties Union, Capital Punishment Project.

Beger, Randall R. (1994a). "The Consistently Inconsistent Application of Contempt Power in Juvenile Courts." *Journal of Crime and Justice* **17**:93–106.

Beger, Randall R. (1994b). "Illinois Juvenile Justice: An Emerging Dual System." *Crime and Delinquency* **40**:54–68.

Bell, D. and K. Lang (1985). "The Intake Dispositions of Juvenile Offenders." *Journal of Research on Crime and Delinquency* **22**:309–328.

Benda, Brent B. (1987). "Comparison of Rates of Recidivism among Status Offenders and Delinquents." *Adolescence* **22**:445–458.

Benda, Brent B. and Leanne Whiteside (1995). "Testing an Integrated Model of Delinquency Using LISREL." *Journal of Social Science Research* **21**:1–32.

Berger, Randall R. (1994). "The Consistently Inconsistent Application of Contempt Power in Juvenile Courts." *Journal of Crime and Justice* **17**:93–106.

Bergsmann, Ilene R. (1988). *State Juvenile Justice Education Survey.* Washington, DC: Council of Chief State School Offenders.

Bergsmann, Ilene R. (1989). "The Forgotten Few: Juvenile Female Offenders." *Federal Probation* **53**:73–78.

Berrueta-Clement, John R. et al. (1984). "Preschool's Effects on Social Responsibility." In *Changed Lives: The Effects of the Perry Preschool Program on Youths through Age 19.* Ypsilanti, MI: High/Scope Press.

Berry, Richard L. (1985). Shape-Up: *The Effects of a Prison Aversion Program on Recidivism and Family Dynamics.* Ann Arbor, MI: University Microfilms International.

Bessette, Joseph M. (1990). *Jail Inmates, 1989.* Washington, DC: U.S. Department of Justice.

Bilchik, Shay (1995). *Unlocking the Doors for Status Offenders: The State of the States.* Washington, DC: Office of Juvenile Justice and Delinquency Prevention.

Bilchik, Shay (1996). *State Responses to Serious and Violent Juvenile Crime.* Pittsburgh, PA: National Center for Juvenile Justice.

Binder, Arnold (1989). "Juvenile Diversion." In *Juvenile Justice: Policies, Programs and Services,* Albert R. Roberts (ed.). Chicago: Dorsey Press.

Binder, Arnold et al. (1985). "A Diversionary Approach for the 1980s." *Federal Probation* **49**:4–12.

Bishop, Donna M. and Charles E. Frazier (1992). "Gender Bias in Juvenile Justice Processing: Implications of the JJDP Act." *Journal of Criminal Law and Criminology* **82**:1162–1186.

Bishop, Donna M. and Charles E. Frazier (1996). "Race Effects in Juvenile Justice Decision Making: Findings of a Statewide Analysis." *Journal of Criminal Law and Criminology* **86**:392–414.

Bishop, Donna M., Charles E. Frazier, and John C. Henretta (1989). "Prosecutorial Waiver: Case Study of a Questionable Reform." *Crime and Delinquency* **35**:179–201.

Black, Henry Campbell (1990). *Black's Law Dictionary.* St. Paul, MN: West Publishing Company.

BLACKMORE, JOHN, MARCI BROWN and BARRY KRISBERG (1988). *Juvenile Justice Reform: The Bellwether States.* Ann Arbor, MI: University of Michigan.

BLUSTEIN, JEFFREY (1983). "On the Doctrine of *Parens Patriae*: Fiduciary Obligations and State Power." *Criminal Justice Ethics* 2:39–47.

BOHM, ROBERT M. (1992). "Retribution and Capital Punishment: Toward a Better Understanding of Death Penalty Opinion." *Journal of Criminal Justice*, **20**:227–236.

BOHM, ROBERT M., LOUISE J. CLARK, and ADRIAN F. AVENTI (1990). "The Influence of Knowledge on Reasons for Death Penalty Opinions: An Experimental Test." *Justice Quarterly* 7:175–188.

BOHM, ROBERT M., LOUISE J. CLARK, and ADRIAN F. AVENTI (1991). "Knowledge and Death Penalty Opinion: A Test of the Marshall Hypotheses." *Journal of Research in Crime and Delinquency* **28**:360–387.

BOHM, ROBERT M. and RONALD E. VOGEL (1994). "A Comparison of Factors Associated with Uninformed and Informed Death Penalty Opinions." *Journal of Criminal Justice* **22**:125–143.

BOND-MAUPIN, LISA, CAROL CHIAGO LUJAN, and M. A. BORTNER (1995). "Jailing of Americans Indian Adolescents: The Legacy of Cultural Domination and Imposed Law." *Crime Law and Social Change* **23**:1–16.

BOONE, HARRY N. JR. (1996). "Electronic Home Confinement: Judicial and Legislative Perspectives." *APPA Perspectives* 20:18–25.

BOTTCHER, JEAN (1993). *Dimensions of Gender and Delinquent Behavior: An Analysis of Qualitative Data on Incarcerated Youths and Their Siblings in Greater Sacramento.* Sacramento, CA: Research Division, California Department of the Youth Authority.

BOTTCHER, JEAN (1995). "Gender as Social Control: A Qualitative Study of Incarcerated Youths and Their Siblings in Greater Sacramento." *Justice Quarterly* **12**:33–57.

BOTTCHER, JEAN and TERESA ISORENA (1994). *LEAD: A Boot Camp and Intensive Parole Program: An Implementation and Process Evaluation of the First Year.* Sacramento, CA: Research Division, California Youth Authority.

BOURQUE, BLAIR B., MEL HAN, and SARAH M. HILL (1996). *A National Survey of Aftercare Provisions for Boot Camp Graduates.* Washington, DC: U.S. Department of Justice.

BOURQUE, BLAIR B. ET AL. (1996). *Boot Camps for Juvenile Offenders: An Implementation Evaluation of Three Demonstration Programs.* Washington, DC: U.S. National Institute of Justice.

BOWLING, LINDA R. (1987). "Day Treatment for Juveniles: A Book in Bluegrass County." *Corrections Today* **49**:104–106.

BRANDAU, TIMOTHY J. (1992). *An Alternative to Incarceration for Juvenile Delinquents: The Delaware Bay Marine Institute.* Ann Arbor, MI: University Microfilms International.

BRANTLEY, ALAN C. and ANDREW W. DIROSA (1994). "Gangs: A National Perspective." *FBI LAW Enforcement Bulletin* **63**:1–7.

BRANTLEY, ALAN C., ANTHONY SORRENTINO, and WAYNE C. TOROK (1994). "Focus on Gangs." *FBI Law Enforcement Bulletin* **63**:1–17.

BREED, ALLEN F. and BARRY KRISBERG (1986). "Juvenile Corrections: Is There a Future?" *Corrections Today* **48**:14–20.

BROOKS, JOHN H. and JOHN R. REDDON (1996). "Serum Testosterone in Violent and Nonviolent Young Offenders." *Journal of Clinical Psychology* **52**:475–483.

BROWN, J. W. (1985). *National Program Coordinator Jail Removal Initiative.* Urbana, IL: Community Research Center, University of Illinois.

BROWN, PAUL W. (1990). "Guns and Probation Officers: The Unspoken Reality." *Federal Probation* **54**:21–26.

BUMBY, KURT M. (1994). "Psychological Considerations in Abuse-Motivated Patricides: Children Who Kill Their Abusive Parents." *Journal of Psychiatry and Law* **22**:51–90.

BURNETT, RICHARD and CHERYL RATHBUN (1993). "Discovery and Treatment of Adolescent Sexual Offenders in a Residential Treatment Center." *Residential Treatment for Children and Youth* **11**:57–64.

BURTON, VELMER S., JR., EDWARD J. LATESSA, and TROY BARKER (1992). "The Role of Probation Officers: An Examination of Statutory Requirements." *Journal of Contemporary Criminal Justice* **8**:273–282.

BUSCH, KENNETH G. ET AL. (1990). "Adolescents Who Kill." *Journal of Clinical Psychology* **46**:472–485.

BUTTS, JEFFREY A. (1996a). *Offenders in Juvenile Court, 1994.* Washington, DC: Office of Juvenile Justice and Delinquency Prevention.

BUTTS, JEFFREY A. (1996b). "Speedy Trial in Juvenile Court." *American Journal of Criminal Law* **23**:515–561.

BUTTS, JEFFREY A. and PAUL DeMURO (1989). *Risk Assessment of Adjudicated Delinquents.* Ann Arbor, MI: Center for the Study of Youth Policy, University of Michigan.

BUTTS, JEFFREY A. and JEFFREY GABLE (1992). *Juvenile Detention in Cook County and the Feasibility of Alternatives.* Pittsburgh, PA: National Center for Juvenile Justice.

BUTTS, JEFFREY A. and GREGORY J. HALEMBA (1996). *Waiting for Justice: Moving Young Offenders through the Juvenile Court Process.* Pittsburgh, PA: National Center for Juvenile Justice.

BUTTS, JEFFREY A. and EILEEN POE (1993). *Offenders in Juvenile Court, 1990.* Washington, DC: Office of Juvenile Justice and Delinquency Prevention.

BUTTS, JEFFREY A. ET AL. (1996). *Juvenile Court Statistics 1993: Statistics Report.* Washington, DC: Office of Juvenile Justice and Delinquency Prevention.

BYRNE, JAMES M., ARTHUR J. LURIGIO, and JOAN PETERSILIA (EDS.) (1992). *Smart Sentencing: The Emergence of Intermediate Sanctions.* Thousand Oaks, CA: Sage.

CAETI, TORY J., CRAIG HEMMENS, and VELMER S. BURTON, JR. (1996). "Juvenile Right to Counsel: A National Comparison of State Legal Codes." *American Journal of Criminal Law* **23**:611–632.

CAHALAN, MARGARET W. (1986). *Historical Corrections Statistics in the United States, 1850–1984.* Washington, DC: U.S. Department of Justice.

CALDAS, STEPHEN J. (1990). "Intensive Incarceration Programs Offer Hope of Rehabilitation to a Fortunate Few: Orleans Parish Prison Does an 'About Face.'" *International Journal of Offender Therapy and Comparative Criminology* **34**:67–76.

CALIFORNIA DEPARTMENT OF THE YOUTH AUTHORITY (1984). *Adolescent Abuse: A Guide for Custody Personnel.* Sacramento, CA: California Department of the Youth Authority, Prevention and Community Corrections Branch.

CALIFORNIA LITTLE HOOVER COMMISSION (1994). *Putting Violence behind Bars.* Sacramento, CA: California Little Hoover Commission.

CAMBRIDGE SURVEY RESEARCH (1986). *An Analysis of Political Attitudes toward the Death Penalty in the State of Florida.* Cambridge, MA: Cambridge Survey Research.

CAMP, CAMILLE G. and GEORGE M. CAMP (1995a). *Adult Corrections.* South Salem, NY: Criminal Justice Institute.

CAMP, CAMILLE G. and GEORGE M. CAMP (1995b). *Jail Systems.* South Salem, NY: Criminal Justice Institute.

CAMP, CAMILLE G. and GEORGE M. CAMP (1995c). *Juvenile Corrections.* South Salem, NY: Criminal Justice Institute.

CAMP, CAMILLE G. and GEORGE M. CAMP (1995d). *Probation and Parole.* South Salem, NY: Criminal Justice Institute.

CAMP, CAMILLE G. and GEORGE M. CAMP (1996). *The Corrections Yearbook 1996.* South Salem, NY: Criminal Justice Institute, Inc.

CAMPBELL, ANNE (1984). *The Girls in the Gang: A Report from New York City.* Cambridge, MA: Blackwell.

CARCATERRA, LORENZO (1995). *Sleepers.* New York: Ballantine Books.

CARLSON, ERIC and EVALYN PARKS (1979). *Critical Issues in Adult Probation: Issues in Probation Management.* Washington, DC: U.S. Department of Justice.

CARRINGTON, PETER J. and SHARON MOYER (1990). "The Effect of Defence Counsel on Plea and Outcome in Juvenile Court." *Canadian Journal of Criminology* **32:**621–637.

CASTELLANO, THOMAS C. and IRINA R. SODERSTROM (1990). *Wilderness Challenges and Recidivism: A Program Evaluation.* Carbondale, IL: Center for the Study of Crime, Delinquency and Corrections, University of Southern Illinois.

CAVENDER, GRAY and PAUL KNEPPER (1992). "Strange Interlude: An Analysis of Juvenile Parole Revocation Decision Making." *Social Problems* **339:**387–399.

CENTER, TIM (1993). *Juvenile Records, Confidentiality and Interagency Cooperation or What You Are Entitled to Know and How to Get It.* Tallahassee, FL: Commission on Juvenile Justice, Florida Legislature.

CHALLEEN, DENNIS A. (1986). *Making It Right: A Common Sense Approach to Criminal Justice.* Aberdeen, SD: Melius and Peterson.

CHAMBERLAIN, PATRICIA (1994). *Family Connections: A Treatment Foster Care Model for Adolescents with Delinquency.* Eugene, OR: Castalia Publishing Company.

CHAMBERS, OLA R. (1983). *The Juvenile Offender: A Parole Profile.* Albany, NY: Evaluation and Planning Unit, New York State Division of Parole.

CHAMPION, DEAN J. (1988). *Felony Probation: Problems and Prospects.* Westport, CT: Praeger.

CHAMPION, DEAN J. (1989a). "Teenage Felons and Waiver Hearings: Some Recent Trends, 1980–1988." *Crime and Delinquency* **35:**577–585.

CHAMPION, DEAN J. (ED.) (1989b). *The U.S. Sentencing Guidelines: Implications for Criminal Justice.* Westport, CT: Praeger.

CHAMPION, DEAN J. (1990a). *Corrections in the United States: A Contemporary Perspective.* Upper Saddle River, NJ: Prentice Hall.

CHAMPION, DEAN J. (1990b). *Criminal Justice in the United States.* Columbus, OH: Merrill Publishing Company.

CHAMPION, DEAN J. (1992). *The Use of Attorneys in Juvenile Courts in Five States: A Trend Analysis, 1980–1989.* Pittsburgh, PA: National Center for Juvenile Justice.

CHAMPION, DEAN J. (1994). *Measuring Offender Risk: A Criminal Justice Sourcebook.* Westport, CT: Greenwood Press, 1994.

CHAMPION, DEAN J. (1996). *Probation, Parole and Community Corrections.* Upper Saddle River, NJ: Prentice Hall.

CHAMPION, DEAN J. (1997). *The Roxbury Dictionary of Criminal Justice: Key Terms and Leading Cases.* Los Angeles: Roxbury Press.

CHAMPION, DEAN J. and G. LARRY MAYS (1991). *Juvenile Transfer Hearings: Some Trends and Implications for Juvenile Justice.* Westport, CT: Praeger.

CHAMPION, DEAN J. and GEORGE E. RUSH (1997). *Policing in the Community.* Upper Saddle River, NJ: Prentice Hall.

CHARLES, MICHAEL T. (1989a). "The Development of a Juvenile Electronic Monitoring Program." *Federal Probation* **53**:3–12.

CHARLES, MICHAEL T. (1989b)."Electronic Monitoring for Juveniles." *Journal of Crime and Justice* **12**:147–169.

CHARLES, MICHAEL T. (1989c). "Research Note: Juveniles on Electronic Monitoring." *Journal of Contemporary Criminal Justice* **5**:165–172.

CHEATWOOD, DERRAL (1993). "Capital Punishment and the Deterrence of Violent Crime in Comparable Counties." *Criminal Justice Review* **18**:165–181.

CHESNEY-LIND, MEDA (1978). "Young Women in the Arms of the Law." In *Women, Crime and the Criminal Justice System,* L. H. Bowker (ed.). Lexington, MA: Lexington Books.

CHESNEY-LIND, MEDA (1987a). *Girls' Crime and Woman's Place: Toward a Feminist Model of Female Delinquency.* Honolulu, HI: Youth Development and Research Center and Women's Studies Program, University of Hawaii.

CHESNEY-LIND, MEDA (1987b). "Saving Girls: New Initiatives to Reinstitutionalize Status Offenders." Unpublished paper presented at the American Society of Criminology meetings, Montreal, Quebec, Canada (November).

CHESNEY-LIND, MEDA and WAYNE MATSUO (1995). *Juvenile Crime and Juvenile Justice in Hawaii.* Philadelphia: Center for the Study of Youth Policy, University of Pennsylvania.

CHESNEY-LIND, MEDA and RANDALL G. SHELDEN (1992). *Girls, Delinquency and Juvenile Justice.* Pacific Grove, CA: Brooks/Cole.

CHICAGO CRIME COMMISSION (1995). *Gangs: Public Enemy Number One.* Chicago: Chicago Crime Commission.

CHICAGO POLICE DEPARTMENT (1988). *Collecting, Organizing and Reporting Street Gang Crime.* Chicago: Gang Crime Section, Chicago Police Department.

CICOUREL, AARON V. (1995). *The Social Organization of Juvenile Justice.* New Brunswick, NJ: Transaction.

CLAGETT, ARTHUR F. (1989). "Effective Therapeutic Wilderness Camp Programs for Rehabilitating Emotionally-Disturbed, Problem Teenagers and Delinquents." *Journal of Offender Counseling, Services, and Rehabilitation* **14**:79–96.

CLARKE, STEVENS H. and AMY D. CRADDOCK (1987). *An Evaluation of North Carolina's Intensive Probation Program.* Chapel Hill, NC: Institute of Government, University of North Carolina at Chapel Hill.

CLARKSON, JOHN STANLEY and JAMES J. WEAKLAND (1991). "A Transitional Aftercare Model for Juveniles: Adapting Electronic Monitoring and Home Confinement." *Journal of Offender Monitoring* **4**:1–15.

CLEAR, TODD R. (1991). "Juvenile Intensive Probation Supervision: Theory and Rationale." In *Intensive Interventions with High-Risk Youths: Promising Approaches in Juvenile Probation and Parole,* Troy Armstrong (ed.). Monsey, NY: Criminal Justice Press.

COCHRAN, JOHN K., MITCHELL B. CHAMLIN, and MARK SETH (1994). "Deterrence or Brutalization? An Impact Assessment of Oklahoma's Return to Capital Punishment." *Criminology* **32**:107–134.

COHN, ALVIN W. (1994). "The Future of Juvenile Justice Administration: Evolution v. Revolution." *Juvenile and Family Court Journal* **45**:51–63.

COLLEY, LORI L. and ROBERT G. CULBERTSON (1988). "Status Offender Legislation and the Courts." *Journal of Offender Counseling, Services, and Rehabilitation* **12**:41–56.

COLLINS, JAMES J. ET AL. (1993). *Law Enforcement Policies and Practices Regarding Missing Children and Homeless Youth: Research Summary.* Washington, DC: U.S. Office of Juvenile Justice and Delinquency Prevention.

COLORADO SPRINGS POLICE DEPARTMENT (1988). *Juvenile Serious Habitual Offender/Directed Intervention Program.* Colorado Springs, CO: Colorado Springs Police Department.

CONLEY, DARLENE J. (1994). "Adding Color to a Black and White Picture: Using Qualitative Data to Explain Racial Disproportionality in the Juvenile Justice System." *Journal of Research in Crime and Delinquency* **31**:135–148.

CONLEY, JOHN A. (ED.) (1994). *The 1967 President's Crime Commission Report: Its Impact 25 Years Later.* Cincinnati, OH: Anderson Publishing Company.

CONNECTICUT GANG TASK FORCE (1994). *Report of the Gang Task Force to the Public Safety and Judiciary Committees.* Hartford, CT: Connecticut Legislature Judiciary and Public Safety Committees.

COSTANZO, MARK and LAWRENCE T. WHITE (EDS.) (1994). "The Death Penalty in the United States." *Journal of Social Issues* **50**:1–197.

COSTANZO, SAMUEL A. (1990). "Juvenile Academy Serves as Facility without Walls." *Corrections Today* **52**:112–126.

COSTIN, LELA B., HOWARD JACOB KARGER, and DAVID STOESZ (1996). *The Politics of Child Abuse in America.* New York: Oxford University Press.

COUMARELOS, CHRISTINE and DON WEATHERBURN (1995). "Targeting Intervention Strategies to Reduce Juvenile Recidivism." *Australian and New Zealand Journal of Criminology* **28**:35–72.

COX, STEPHEN M., WILLIAM S. DAVIDSON and TIMOTHY S. BYNUM (1995). "A Meta-analytic Assessment of Delinquency-Related Outcomes of Alternative Education Programs." *Crime and Delinquency* **41**:219–234.

CRAWFORD, J. (1988). *Tabulation of a Nationwide Survey of Female Inmates.* Phoenix, AZ: Research Advisory Services.

CRIPPEN, GARY (1990). *Valid Court Order Exception: Yes or No?* Ann Arbor, MI: Center for the Study of Youth Policy, University of Michigan.

CRISWELL, JOHN E. (1987). "Juvenile Detention Resource Centers: Florida's Experience Provides a Model for the Nation in Juvenile Detention." *Corrections Today* **49**:22–26.

CRONIN, ROBERTA C. (1994). *Boot Camps for Adult and Juvenile Offenders: Overview and Update.* Washington, DC: U.S. National Institute of Justice.

CURRAN, DANIEL J. (1984). "The Myth of a 'New' Female Delinquent." *Crime and Delinquency* **30**:386–399.

DALE, MICHAEL J. (1987). "The Burger Court and Children's Rights: A Trend toward Retribution." *Children's Legal Rights Journal* **8**:7–12.

DALE, MICHAEL J. (1988). "Detaining Juveniles in Adult Jails and Lockups: An Analysis of Rights and Liabilities." *American Jails* (Spring):46–50.

DATESMAN, SUSAN K. and MIKEL AICKIN (1985). "Offense Specialization and Escalation among Status Offenders." *Journal of Criminal Law and Criminology* **75:**1246–1275.

DAVIDSON, WILLIAM S. ET AL. (1987). "Diversion of Juvenile Offenders: An Experimental Comparison." *Journal of Consulting and Clinical Psychology* **55:**68–75.

DAVIS, AL (1993). *Montana: Moving toward Excellence.* Philadelphia, PA: Center for the Study of Youth Policy, University of Pennsylvania.

DAWSON, ROBERT O. (1992). "An Empirical Study of Kent Style Juvenile Transfers to Criminal Court." *St. Mary's Law Journal* **23:**975–1054.

DAWSON, ROBERT O. (1995). *State Bar Section Report on Juvenile Law: Special Legislative Issue.* Washington, DC: U.S. Government Printing Office.

DEAN, CHARLES W., J. DAVID HIRSCHEL, and ROBERT BRAME (1996). "Minorities and Juvenile Case Dispositions." *Justice System Journal* **18:**267–285.

DECKER, SCOTT H. and C. W. KOHFELD (1990). "The Deterrent Effect of Capital Punishment in the Five Most Active Execution States: A Time Series Analysis." *Criminal Justice Review* **15:**173–191.

DeCOMO, ROBERT E. (1993). *Juveniles Taken into Custody Research Program: Estimating the Prevalence of Juvenile Custody by Race and Gender.* San Francisco: NCCD Focus.

del CARMEN, ROLANDO V. (1985). "Legal Issues in Jail and Prison Privatization." Unpublished paper presented at the National Association of Juvenile Correctional Agencies, Las Vegas, NV (August).

DeZOLT, ERNEST M., LINDA M. SCHMIDT and DONNA C. GILCHER (1996). "The 'Tabula Rasa' Intervention Project for Delinquent Gang-Involved Females." *Journal of Gang Research* **3:**37–43.

DiCATALDO, FRANK and THOMAS GRISSO (1995). "A Typology of Juvenile Offenders Based on the Judgments of Juvenile Court Professionals." *Criminal Justice and Behavior* **22:**246–262.

DICKS, SHIRLEY (ED.) (1991). *Congregation of the Condemned: Voices Against the Death Penalty.* Amherst, NY: Prometheus Books.

DOERNER, WILLIAM G. (1987). "Child Maltreatment Seriousness and Juvenile Delinquency." *Youth and Society* **19:**197–224.

DOLIN, IRA H., DAVID B. KELLY and MARK T. BEASLEY (1992). "Chronic Self-Destructive Behavior in Normative and Delinquent Adolescents." *Journal of Adolescence* **15:**57–66.

DOOB, ANTHONY N. and LUCIEN A. BEAULIEU (1992). "Variation in the Exercise of Judicial Discretion with Young Offenders." *Canadian Journal of Criminology* **34:**35–50.

DOUGHERTY, JOYCE (1988). "Negotiating Justice in the Juvenile Justice System: A Comparison of Adult Plea Bargaining and Juvenile Intake." *Federal Probation* **52:**72–80.

Downs, William R. and Joan F. Robertson (1990). "Referral for Treatment among Adolescent Alcohol and Drug Abusers." *Journal of Research in Crime and Delinquency* **27:**190–209.

DuRANT, ROBERT H. ET AL. (1994). "Factors Associated with the Use of Violence among Urban Black Adolescents." *American Journal of Public Health* **84:**612–617.

DWYER, DIANE C. and ROGER B. McNALLY (1987). "Juvenile Justice: Reform, Retain, and Reaffirm." *Federal Probation* **51:**47–51.

ELLIOTT, DELBERT S. (1994a). "1993 Presidential Address: Serious Violent Offenders: Onset, Developmental Course, and Termination." *Criminology* **32:**1–21.

ELLIOTT, DELBERT S. (1994b). *Youth Violence: An Overview.* Boulder, CO: Center for the Study and Prevention of Violence.

ELLSWORTH, THOMAS (1988). "Case Supervision Planning: The Forgotten Component of Intensive Probation Supervision." *Federal Probation* **52**:28–33.

ELLSWORTH, THOMAS, MICHELLE T. KINSELLA, and KIMBERLEE MASSIN (1992). "Prosecuting Juveniles: Parens Patriae and Due Process in the 1990's." *Justice Professional* **7**:53–67.

EMERSON, ROBERT M. (1969). *Judging Delinquents.* Chicago: Aldine.

ENGLISH, KIM, SUSAN M. CHADWICK, and SUZANNE K. PULLEN (1994). *Colorado's Intensive Supervision Probation: Report of Findings.* Denver, CO: Division of Criminal Justice.

EPPS, KEVIN J. (1996). "Sexually Abusive Behavior in an Adolescent Boy with the 48,XXYY Syndrome: A Case Study." *Criminal Behavior and Mental Health* **6**:137–146.

ERWIN, BILLIE S. (1986). "Turning Up the Heat on Probationers in Georgia." *Federal Probation* **50**:70–76.

EVANS, DONALD (1996). "Electronic Monitoring: Testimony to Ontario's Standing Committee on Administration of Justice." *APPA Perspectives* **20**:8–10.

EWING, CHARLES PATRICK (1990). *When Children Kill: The Dynamics of Juvenile Homicide.* Lexington, MA: Lexington Books.

FAGAN, JEFFREY A. (1990). "Treatment and Reintegration of Violent Juvenile Offenders: Experimental Results." *Justice Quarterly* **7**:233–263.

FAGAN, JEFFREY A. and ELIZABETH PIPER DESCHENES (1990). "Determinants of Judicial Waiver Decisions for Violent Juvenile Offenders." *Journal of Criminal Law and Criminology* **81**:314–347.

FAGAN, JEFFREY A. and MARTIN GUGGENHEIM (1996). "Preventive Detention and the Judicial Prediction of Dangerousness for Juveniles: A Natural Experiment." *Journal of Criminal Law and Criminology* **86**:415–448.

FAGAN, JEFFREY and CRAIG REINARMAN (1991). "The Social Context of Intensive Supervision: Organizational and Ecological Influences on Community Treatment." In *Intensive Interventions with High-Risk Youths: Promising Approaches in Juvenile Probation and Parole*, Troy L. Armstrong (ed.). Monsey, NY: Criminal Justice Press.

FAMIGHETTI, ROBERT (ED.) (1996). *The World Almanac and Book of Facts, 1996.* Mahwah, NJ: World Almanac Books, an imprint of Funk & Wagnalls Corporation.

FAMULARO, RICHARD ET AL. (1988). "Advisability of Substance Abuse Testing in Parents Who Severely Maltreat Their Children: The Issue of Drug Testing before the Juvenile/Family Courts." *Bulletin of the American Academy of Psychiatry and the Law* **16**:217–223.

FAMULARO, RICHARD ET AL. (1992). "Differences in Neuropsychological and Academic Achievement between Adolescent Delinquents and Status Offenders." *American Journal of Psychiatry* **149**:1252–1257.

FARNWORTH, MARGARET, CHARLES E. FRAZIER and ANITA R. NEUBERGER (1988). "Orientations to Juvenile Justice: Exploratory Notes from a Statewide Survey of Juvenile Justice Decisionmakers." *Journal of Criminal Justice* **16**:477–491.

FEENEY, FLOYD (1987). "Defense Counsel for Delinquents: Does Quality Matter?" Unpublished paper presented at the American Society of Criminology meetings. Montreal, Quebec, Canada (November).

FEINBERG, NORMA (1991). "Juvenile Intensive Supervision: A Longitudinal Evaluation of Program Effectiveness." In *Intensive Interventions with High-Risk Youths: Promising Approaches in Juvenile Probation and Parole*, Troy L. Armstrong (ed.). Monsey, NY: Criminal Justice Press.

FELD, BARRY C. (1987a). "The Juvenile Court Meets the Principle of the Offense: Changing Juvenile Justice Sentencing Practices." Unpublished paper presented at the American Society of Criminology meetings, Montreal, Quebec, Canada (November).

FELD, BARRY C. (1987b). "The Juvenile Court Meets the Principle of the Offense: Legislative Changes in Juvenile Waiver Statutes." *Journal of Criminal Law and Criminology* **78**:471–533.

FELD, BARRY C. (1987c). "*In re Gault* Revisited: The Right to Counsel in the Juvenile Court." Unpublished paper presented at the American Society of Criminology meetings, Montreal, Quebec, Canada (November).

FELD, BARRY C. (1988a). "The Juvenile Court Meets the Principle of Offense: Punishment, Treatment, and the Difference It Makes." *Boston University Law Review* **68**:821–915.

FELD, BARRY C. (1988b). "*In re Gault* Revisited: A Cross-State Comparison of the Right to Counsel in Juvenile Court." *Crime and Delinquency* **34**:393–424.

FELD, BARRY C. (1988c). "The Right to Counsel in Juvenile Court: An Empirical Study of When Lawyers Appear and the Differences They Make." Unpublished paper presented at the American Society of Criminology meetings, Chicago (November).

FELD, BARRY C. (1989a). "Bad Law Makes Hard Cases: Reflections on Teen-Aged Axe-Murderers." *Law and Inequality: A Journal of Theory and Practice* **8**:1–101.

FELD, BARRY C. (1989b). "The Right to Counsel in Juvenile Court: An Empirical Study of When Lawyers Appear and the Difference They Can Make." *Journal of Criminal Law and Criminology* **79**:1185–1346.

FELD, BARRY C. (1993a). "Criminalizing the American Juvenile Court." In *Crime and Justice: A Review of Research*, Vol. 17, Michael Tonry (ed.). Chicago: University of Chicago Press.

FELD, BARRY C. (1993b). *Justice for Children: The Right to Counsel and the Juvenile Courts.* Boston: Northeastern University Press.

FELD, BARRY C. (1993c). "Juvenile (In)justice and the Criminal Court Alternative." *Crime and Delinquency* **39**:403–424.

FELD, BARRY C. (1995). "Violent Youth and Public Policy: A Case Study of Juvenile Justice Law Reform." *Minnesota Law Review* **79**:965–1128.

FERDINAND, THEODORE N. (1986). "A Brief History of Juvenile Delinquency in Boston and a Comparative Interpretation." *International Journal of Criminology* **24**:59–81.

FIELDS, CHARLES B. (ED.) (1994). *Innovative Trends and Specialized Strategies in Community-Based Corrections.* New York: Garland Publishing Company.

FINKEL, NORMAN J. ET AL. (1994). "Killing Kids: The Juvenile Death Penalty and Community Sentiment." *Behavioral Sciences and the Law* **12**:5–20.

FLANGO, VICTOR E. (1994a). "Court Unification and Quality of State Courts." *Justice System Journal* **16**:33–55.

FLANGO, VICTOR E. (1994b). "Federal Court Review of State Court Convictions in Noncapital Cases." *Justice System Journal* **17**:153–170.

FLEXNER, BERNARD and ROGER N. BALDWIN (1914). *Juvenile Courts and Probation.* New York: Harcourt.

FLORIDA ADVISORY COUNCIL ON INTERGOVERNMENTAL RELATIONS (1994). *Intergovernmental Impacts of the 1994 Juvenile Justice Reform Bill.* Tallahassee, FL: Florida Advisory Council on Intergovernmental Relations.

FLORIDA DEPARTMENT OF CORRECTIONS (1990). *Boot Camp: A Twenty-Five Month Review. Tallahassee,* FL: Florida Department of Corrections, Bureau of Planning, Research and Statistics.

FLORIDA GOVERNOR'S JUVENILE JUSTICE AND DELINQUENCY PREVENTION ADVISORY COMMITTEE (1994). *Non-delinquents Placed in Florida's Secure Juvenile Detention Facilities, 1991.* Tallahassee, FL: Florida Governor's Juvenile Justice and Delinquency Prevention Advisory Committee.

FLORIDA HOUSE COMMITTEE ON CRIMINAL JUSTICE (1994). *Juvenile Assessment Centers Generally.* Tallahassee, FL: Florida House Committee on Criminal Justice.

FLORIDA OFFICE OF THE AUDITOR GENERAL (1994). *Performance Audit of the Use of Non-prison Sanctions under Florida's Sentencing Guidelines in the Second Judicial District.* Tallahassee, FL: Florida Office of the Auditor General.

FLORIDA OFFICE OF PROGRAM POLICY ANALYSIS (1995). *Status Report on Boot Camps in Florida Administered by the Department of Corrections and Department of Juvenile Justice.* Tallahassee, FL: Florida Office of Program Policy Analysis and Government Accountability.

FLORIDA STATISTICAL ANALYSIS CENTER (1993). *A Study of Motor Vehicle Theft in Florida.* Tallahassee, FL: Florida Motor Vehicle Theft Prevention Authority.

FLORIDA SUPREME COURT (1990). *Where the Injured Fly for Justice: Reforming Practices which Impede the Dispensation of Justice to Minorities in Florida.* Tallahassee, FL: Florida Supreme Court Racial and Ethnic Bias Study Commission.

FLOWERS, R. BARRI (1994). *The Victimization and Exploitation of Women and Children: A Study of Physical, Mental and Sexual Maltreatment in the United States.* Jefferson, NC: McFarland and Company.

FOGEL, DAVID and JOE HUDSON (1981). *Justice as Fairness: Perspectives on the Justice Model.* Cincinnati, OH: Anderson Publishing Company.

FORD, MICHELLE E. and JEAN ANN LINNEY (1995). "Comparative Analysis of Juvenile Sexual Offenders, Violent Nonsexual Offenders, and Status Offenders." *Journal of Interpersonal Violence* **10**:56–70.

FORST, MARTIN L. (ED.) (1990). *Missing Children: The Law Enforcement Response.* Springfield, IL: Charles C Thomas.

FORST, MARTIN L. (1995). *The New Juvenile Justice.* Chicago: Nelson-Hall.

FORST, MARTIN L., Jeffrey Fagan, and T. Scott Vivona (1989). "Youth in Prisons and Training Schools: Perceptions and Consequences of the Treatment–Custody Dichotomy." *Juvenile and Family Court Journal* **40**:1–14.

FRASER, MARK and MICHAEL NORMAN (1988). "Chronic Juvenile Delinquency and the 'Suppression Effect': An Exploratory Study." *Journal of Offender Counseling, Services, and Rehabilitation* **13**:55–73.

FRAZIER, CHARLES E. (1991). *Teen and Juvenile Justice Placements or Transfer to Adult Court by Direct File?* Tallahassee, FL: Florida Commission on Juvenile Justice.

FULLER, JOHN R. and WILLIAM M. NORTON (1993). "Juvenile Diversion: The Impact of Program Philosophy on Net Widening." *Journal of Crime and Justice* **16**:29–45.

GABLE, RALPH KIRKLAND (1986). "Application of Personal Telemonitoring to Current Problems in Corrections." *Journal of Criminal Justice* **14**:167–176.

GALAWAY, BURT ET AL. (1995). "Specialist Foster Family Care for Delinquent Youth." *Federal Probation* **59**:19–27.

GARRETT, C. (1985). "Effects of Residential Treatment on Adjudicated Delinquents: A Meta-analysis." *Journal of Research on Crime and Delinquency* **22**:287–308.

GAVZER, B. (1986). "Must Kids Be Bad?" *Parade Magazine*, March 9, 1986:8–10.

GEIGER, BRENDA (1996). "Plato and Rawls on Correctional Rehabilitation of Juvenile Offenders." *Journal of Offender Rehabilitation* **23**:49–59.

GELBER, SEYMOUR (1988). *Hard-Core Delinquents: Reaching Out through the Miami Experiment.* Tuscaloosa, AL: University of Alabama Press.

GELBER, SEYMOUR (1990). "The Juvenile Justice System: Vision for the Future." *Juvenile and Family Court Journal* 41:15–18.

GELSTHORPE, LORAINE R. (1987). "The Differential Treatment of Males and Females in the Criminal Justice System." In *Sex, Gender and Care Work*, Gordon Horobin (ed.). Aberdeen, Scotland, UK: Department of Social Work, University of Aberdeen.

GERDES, KAREN E., M. MICHELLE GOURLEY and Monette C. Cash (1995). "Assessing Juvenile Sex Offenders to Determine Adequate Levels of Supervision." *Child Abuse and Neglect* 19:953–961.

GILLIARD, DARRELL K. and ALLEN J. BECK (1996). *Prison and Jail Inmates, 1995.* Washington, DC: U.S. Department of Justice.

GITTENS, JOAN (1994). *Poor Relations: The Children of the State of Illinois, 1818–1990.* Urbana, IL: University of Illinois Press.

GLICK, BARRY and ARNOLD P. GOLDSTEIN (eds.) (1995). *Managing Delinquency: Programs That Work.* Laurel, MD: American Correctional Association.

GODFREY, MICHAEL J. and VINCENT SCHIRALDI (1995). *How Have Homicide Rates Been Affected by California's Death Penalty?* San Francisco: Center on Juvenile and Criminal Justice.

GOLDSMITH, HERBERT R. (1995). "A Preliminary Analysis of the Effect of an Emergency Case Review Process on Per Diem Terminations." *Journal of Criminal Justice* 23:93–97.

GOLDSTEIN, ARNOLD P. and BARRY GLICK (1987). *Aggression Replacement Training: A Comprehensive Intervention for Aggressive Youth.* Champaign, IL: Research Press.

GOODSTEIN, LYNNE and HENRY SONTHEIMER (1987). "Evaluating Correctional Placements through the Use of Failure Rate Analysis." Unpublished paper presented at the American Society of Criminology meetings, Montreal, Quebec, Canada (November).

GOTTFREDSON, DENISE C. and WILLIAM H. BARTON (1993). "Deinstitutionalization of Juvenile Offenders." *Criminology* 31:591–610.

GOTTFREDSON, DON M. and MICHAEL TONRY (1987). *Prediction and Classification: Criminal Justice Decision-Making.* Chicago: University of Chicago Press.

GOTTFREDSON, STEPHEN D. and DON M. GOTTFREDSON (1988). *Decision Making in Criminal Justice: Toward the Rational Exercise of Discretion*, 2nd ed. New York: Plenum Press.

GOTTFREDSON, STEPHEN D. and DON M. GOTTFREDSON (1990). *Classification, Prediction, and Criminal Justice Policy: Final Report to the National Institute of Justice.* Washington, DC: U.S. National Institute of Justice.

GOTTLIEB, BARBARA (1984). *The Pretrial Processing of "Dangerous" Defendants: A Comparative Analysis of State Laws.* Washington, DC: Toborg Associates.

GOTTLIEB, BARBARA and PHILLIP ROSEN (1984). *Public Danger as a Factor in Pretrial Release: Summaries of State Danger Laws.* Washington, DC: Toborg Associates.

GOWAN, DARREN (1995). "Electronic Monitoring in the Southern District of Mississippi." *Federal Probation* 59:10–18.

GOWDY, VONCILE B. (1993). *Intermediate Sanctions.* Washington, DC: U.S. Department of Justice.

GRASMICK, HAROLD G., ROBERT J. BURSICK, JR., and BRENDA SIMS BLACKWELL (1993). "Religious Beliefs and Public Support for the Death Penalty for Juveniles and Adults." *Journal of Crime and Justice* 16:59–86.

GREEN, MAURICE (1984). "Child Advocacy: Rites and Rights in Juvenile Justice." In *Advances in Forensic Psychology and Psychiatry*, Vol. I, Robert W. Rieber (ed.). Norwood, NJ: Ablex.

GREENWOOD, PETER (1982). *Selective Incapacitation*. Santa Monica, CA: Rand Corporation.

GREENWOOD, PETER W. (1986a)."Differences in Criminal Behavior and Court Responses among Juvenile and Young Adult Defendants." In *Crime and Justice: An Annual Review of Research*, Vol. 7, Michael Tonry and Norval Morris (eds.). Chicago: University of Chicago Press.

GREENWOOD, PETER W. (ED.) (1986b). *Intervention Strategies for Chronic Juvenile Offenders: Some New Perspectives*. Westport, CT: Greenwood Press.

GREENWOOD, PETER W. (1986c). "Predictors of Chronic Behavior." In *Intervention Strategies for Chronic Juvenile Offenders: Some New Perspectives*, Peter Greenwood (ed.). Westport, CT: Greenwood Press.

GREENWOOD, PETER W. (1986d). "Promising Approaches for the Rehabilitation and Prevention of Chronic Juvenile Offenders." In *Intervention Strategies for Chronic Juvenile Offenders: Some New Perspectives*, Peter W. Greenwood (ed.). Westport, CT: Greenwood Press.

GREENWOOD, PETER W. (1990). "Reflections on Three Promising Programs." *Perspectives* **14**:20–24.

GREENWOOD, PETER W., ELIZABETH PIPER DESCHENES and JOHN ADAMS (1993). *Chronic Juvenile Offenders: Final Results from the Skillman Aftercare Experiment*. Santa Monica, CA: Rand Corporation.

GREENWOOD, PETER W. and SUSAN TURNER (1987). *The VisionQuest Program: An Evaluation*. Santa Monica, CA: Rand Corporation.

GREENWOOD, PETER W. and SUSAN TURNER (1993). "Evaluation of the Paint Creek Youth Center: A Residential Program for Serious Delinquents." *Criminology* **31**:263–279.

GRIFFIN, BRENDA S. and CHARLES T. GRIFFIN (1978). *Juvenile Delinquency in Perspective*. New York: Harper & Row.

GRISSO, THOMAS (1980). "Juveniles' Capacities to Waive Miranda Rights: An Empirical Analysis." *California Law Review* **68**:1134–1166.

GRISSO, THOMAS (1996). "Society's Retributive Response to Juvenile Violence: A Developmental Perspective." *Law and Human Behavior* **20**:229–247.

GRISSO, THOMAS, ALAN TOMKINS, and PAMELA CASEY (1988). "Psychosocial Concepts in Juvenile Law." *Law and Human Behavior* **12**:403–438.

GRISSOM, GRANT R. (1991). "Dispositional Authority and the Future of the Juvenile Justice System." *Juvenile and Family Court Journal* **42**:25–34.

GUARINO-GHEZZI, SUSAN (1989). "Classifying Juveniles: A Formula for Case-by-Case Assessment." *Corrections Today* **51**:112–116.

GUARINO-GHEZZI, SUSAN (1994). "Reintegrative Police Surveillance of Juvenile Offenders: Forging an Urban Model." *Crime and Delinquency* **40**:131–153.

GUGGENHEIM, MARTIN (1985a). "Incorrigibility Laws: The State's Role in Resolving Intrafamily Conflict." *Criminal Justice Ethics* **4**:11–19.

GUGGENHEIM, MARTIN (1985b). *The Rights of Young People*. New York: Bantam Books.

HAAS, KENNETH C. (1994). "The Triumph of Vengeance over Retribution: The United States Supreme Court and the Death Penalty." *Crime Law and Social Change* **21**:127–154.

HAGEDORN, JOHN (1988). *People and Folks: Gangs, Crime, and the Underclass in a Rustbelt City.* Chicago: Lake View Press.

HAGHIGHI, BAHRAM AND ALMA LOPEZ (1993). "Success/Failure of Group Home Treatment Programs for Juveniles." *Federal Probation* **57**:53–58.

HAHN, PAUL H. (1984). *The Juvenile Offender and the Law.* Cincinnati, OH: Anderson Publishing Company.

HALE, DONNA C. ET AL. (1991). "Juvenile Justice: History and Policy." *Crime and Delinquency* **37**:163–299.

HAMPARIAN, DONNA M. (1987). "Control and Treatment of Juveniles Committing Violent Offenses." In *Clinical Treatment of the Violent Person*, Loren H. Roth (ed.). New York: Guilford Press.

HAMPARIAN, DONNA M. and LYNN SAMETZ (1989). *Cuyahoga County Juvenile Court Intensive Probation Supervision.* Cleveland, OH: Federation for Community Planning.

HANCOCK, PAULA and KATHERINE TEILMANN VANDUSEN (1985). *Attorney Representation in Juvenile Court: A Comparison of Public Defenders and Privately Retained Counsel.* Washington, DC: U.S. Office of Juvenile Justice and Delinquency Prevention.

HANKE, PENELOPE J. (1996). "Putting School Crime into Perspective: Self-Reported School Victimizations of High School Seniors." *Journal of Criminal Justice* **24**:207–226.

HARADA, YUTAKA and SHINGO SUZUKI (1994). "An Analysis of the Recidivism of Juveniles Transferred to Family Court by Summary Referral." *Reports of the National Research Institute of Police Science* **35**:58–72.

HARDWICK, PETER J. and MARTYN A. ROWTON-LEE (1996). "Adolescent Homicide: Towards Assessment of Risk." *Journal of Adolescence* **19**:263–276.

HARRIS, PATRICIA M. (1988). "Juvenile Sentence Reform and Its Evaluation: A Demonstration of the Need for More Precise Measures of Offense Seriousness in Juvenile Justice Research." *Evaluation Review* **12**:655–666.

HARRIS, PATRICIA M. ET AL. (1993). "A Wilderness Challenge Program as Correctional Treatment." *Journal of Offender Rehabilitation* **19**:149–164.

HARTSTONE, ELIOT and KAREN V. HANSEN (1984). "The Violent Juvenile Offender: An Empirical Portrait." In *Violent Juvenile Offenders: An Anthology*, Robert A. Mathias, Paul DeMuro, and Richard S. Allinson (eds.). San Francisco: National Council on Crime and Delinquency.

HARTSTONE, ELIOT, ELLEN SLAUGHTER, and JEFFREY FAGAN (1986). *The Colorado Juvenile Justice System Processing of Violent, Serious and Minority Youths.* San Francisco: URSA Institute.

HASSENFELD, YEHESKEL and PAUL P. L. CHEUNG (1985). "The Juvenile Court as a People-Processing Organization: A Political Economy Perspective." *American Journal of Sociology* **90**:801–824.

HAWAII CRIME COMMISSION (1985). *The Serious Juvenile Offender in Hawaii.* Honolulu, HI: Hawaii Crime Commission.

HAWAII CRIMINAL JUSTICE COMMISSION (1986). *The Waivers of Juveniles in Hawaii.* Honolulu, HI: Hawaii Criminal Justice Commission.

HEIDE, KATHLEEN M. (1992). *Why Kids Kill Their Parents: Child Abuse and Adolescent Homicide.* Columbus, OH: Ohio State University Press.

HEIDE, KATHLEEN M. (1993). "Juvenile Involvement in Multiple Offender and Multiple Victim Patricides." *Journal of Police and Criminal Psychology* **9**:53–64.

HEIMER, KAREN (1996). "Gender, Interaction, and Delinquency: Testing a Theory of Differential Social Control." *Social Psychology* **59**:39–61.

HENDERSON, THOMAS A. ET AL. (1984). *The Significance of Judicial Structure: The Effect of Unification on Trial Court Operations.* Washington, DC: U.S. Government Printing Office.

HENGGELER, SCOTT ET AL. (1994). *Home-Based Services for Serious and Violent Juvenile Offenders.* Philadelphia, PA: Center for the Study of Youth Policy, University of Pennsylvania.

HEPBURN, JOHN R. ET AL. (1992). *The Maricopa County Demand Reduction Program: An Evaluation.* Phoenix, AZ: Maricopa County Sheriff's Department.

HIRSCHI, TRAVIS and MICHAEL GOTTFREDSON (1993). "Rethinking the Juvenile Justice System." *Crime and Delinquency* **39**:262–271.

HOFFMAN, ALLAN M. (ed.) (1996). *Schools, Violence and Society.* Westport, CT: Praeger.

HOFFMAN, PETER B. (1983). "Screening for Risk: A Revised Salient Factor Score (SFS 81)." *Journal of Criminal Justice* **11**:539–547.

HOGE, ROBERT D., D. A. ANDREWS, and ALAN W. LESCHIED (1995). "Investigation of Variables Associated with Probation and Custody Dispositions in a Sample of Juveniles." *Journal of Clinical Child Psychology* **24**:279–286.

HOLDEN, GWEN A. and ROBERT A. KAPLER (1995). "Deinstitutionalizing Status Offenders: A Record of Progress." *Juvenile Justice* **2**:3–10.

HOUK, JULIE M. (1984). "Electronic Monitoring of Probationers: A Step toward Big Brother?" *Golden Gate University Law Review* **14**:431–446.

HOWITT, PAMELA S. and EUGENE A. MOORE (1991). "The Efficacy of Intensive Early Intervention: An Evaluation of the Oakland County Probate Court Early Offender Program." *Juvenile and Family Court Journal* **42**:25–36.

HOWITT, PAMELA S. and EUGENE A. MOORE (1993). "Pay Now So You Won't Pay Later: The Effectiveness of Prevention Programming in the Fight to Reduce Delinquency." *Juvenile and Family Court Journal* **44**:57–67.

HUGHES, STELLA P. and ANNE L. SCHNEIDER (1989). "Victim–Offender Mediation: A Survey of Program Characteristics and Perceptions of Effectiveness." *Crime and Delinquency* **35**:217–233.

HUNTER, JOHN A., JR. and DENNIS W. GOODWIN (1992). "The Clinical Utility of Satiation Therapy with Juvenile Sexual Offenders: Variations and Efficacy." *Annals of Sex Research* **5**:71–80.

HURLEY, D. (1985). "Arresting Delinquency." *Psychology Today* **19**:63–66, 68.

HURST, HUNTER (1990a). "Juvenile Probation in Retrospect." *Perspectives* **14**:16–24.

HURST, HUNTER (1990b). "Turn of the Century: Rediscovering the Value of Juvenile Treatment." *Corrections Today* **52**:48–50.

HURST, HUNTER and PATRICIA McFALL TORBET (1993). *Organization and Administration of Juvenile Services: Probation, Aftercare and State Institutions for Delinquent Youth.* Pittsburgh, PA: National Center for Juvenile Justice.

HUSKEY, BOBBIE L. (1984). "Community Corrections Acts." *Corrections Today* **46**:45.

HUSKEY, BOBBIE L. (1990). "In Illinois: Law Forces Change in Juvenile Lockups." *Corrections Today* **52**:122–123.

ITO, JEANNE A. (1984). *Measuring the Performance of Different Types of Juvenile Courts.* Williamsburg, VA: National Center for State Courts.

JACKSON, JANET L., JAN W. deKEIJSER and JOHN A. L. MICHON (1995). "A Critical Look at Research on Alternatives to Custody." *Federal Probation* **59**:43–51.

JACOBS, SUSAN and DAVID C. MOORE (1994). "Successful Restitution as a Predictor of Juvenile Recidivism." *Juvenile and Family Court Journal* **45**:3–14.

JANUS, MARK-DAVID (1995). "Physical Abuse in Canadian Runaway Adolescents." *Child Abuse and Neglect* **19**:433–447.

JENSEN, ERIC L. and LINDA K. METSGER (1994). "A Test of the Deterrent Effect of Legislative Waiver on Violent Juvenile Crime." *Crime and Delinquency* **40**:96–104.

JESNESS, CARL F. (1987). "Early Identification of Delinquent-Prone Children: An Overview." In *The Prevention of Delinquent Behavior*, John D. Burchard and Sara N. Burchard (eds.). Thousand Oaks, CA: Sage.

JOHNSON, JAMES B. and PHILIP E. SECRET (1990). "Race and Juvenile Court Decision Making Revisited." *Criminal Justice Policy Review* **4**:159–187.

JOHNSON, JAMES B. and PHILIP E. SECRET (1995). "The Effects of Court Structure on Juvenile Court Decisionmaking." *Journal of Criminal Justice* **23**:63–82.

JONES, BERNADETTE (1990). "Intensive Probation Services in Philadelphia County." Unpublished paper presented at the American Society of Criminology meetings, Baltimore, MD (November).

JONES, MICHAEL A. and BARRY KRISBERG (1994). *Images and Reality: Juvenile Crime, Youth Violence and Public Policy*. San Francisco: National Council on Crime and Delinquency.

JOYCE, NOLA M. (1985). "Classification Research: Facing the Challenge." *Corrections Today* **47**:78–86.

KALINICH, DAVID B. and JEFFREY D. SENESE (1987). "Police Discretion and the Mentally Disordered in Chicago: A Reconsideration." *Police Studies* **10**:185–191.

KAMERMAN, SHEILA B. and ALFRED J. KAHN (EDS.) (1990). "Social Services for Children, Youth, and Families in the United States." *Children and Youth Services Review* **12**:170–184.

KANSAS JUVENILE JUSTICE TASK FORCE (1995). *Report on Juvenile Offenders*. Topeka, KS: Kansas Juvenile Justice Task Force.

KANSAS LEGISLATIVE DIVISION (1994). *Performance Audit Report: Reviewing Security and Management Issues at the Youth Center at Topeka*. Topeka, KS: Kansas Legislative Division of Post Audit.

KAPP, STEPHEN A., IRA SCHWARTZ, and IRWIN EPSTEIN (1994). "Adult Imprisonment of Males Released from Residential Childcare: A Longitudinal Study." *Residential Treatment for Children and Youth* **12**:19–36.

KARRAKER, N., D. E. MACALLAIR, and V. N. SCHIRALDI (1988). *Public Safety with Care: A Model for Juvenile Justice in Hawaii*. Alexandria, VA: National Center on Institutions and Alternatives.

KEARNEY, EDMUND M. (1994). "A Clinical Corrections Approach: The Failure of a Residential Juvenile Delinquency Treatment Center." *Juvenile and Family Court Journal* **45**:33–41.

KEARNEY, WILLIAM J. (1989). "Form Follows Function—And Function Follows Philosophy: An Architectural Response." *Juvenile and Family Court Journal* **40**:27–34.

KEARON, WILLIAM G. (1989). "Deinstitutionalization and Abuse of Children on Our Streets." *Juvenile and Family Court Journal* **40**:21–26.

KEARON, WILLIAM G. (1990). "Deinstitutionalization, Street Children, and the Coming AIDS Epidemic in the Adolescent Population." *Juvenile and Family Court Journal* **41**:9–18.

KEATING, J. MICHAEL (1984). *Public Ends and Private Means: Accountability among Private Providers of Public Support Services.* Pawtucket, RI: Institute of Conflict Management.

KEITH, RICHARD G. (1989). *Children and Drugs: The Next Generation.* Los Angeles: Los Angeles Unified School District Police Officers Association.

KENNEY, DENNIS JAY, ANTHONY MICHAEL PATE, and EDWIN HAMILTON (1990). *Police Handling of Juveniles: Developing Model Programs.* Washington, DC: Police Foundation.

KENNEY, JOHN P. and HARRY W. MORE (1986). *Patrol Field Problems and Solutions: 476 Field Situations.* Springfield, IL: Charles C Thomas.

KENOSHA COUNTY DEPARTMENT OF SOCIAL SERVICES (1990). "Monitoring Juvenile Offenders: The Kenosha County, Wisconsin Experience." *Journal of Offender Monitoring* **3**:1–7.

KLEIN, ANDREW R. (1989). "Developing Individualized Probationary Conditions." *Perspectives* **13**:6–11.

KLEIN, MALCOLM W. (1979). "Deinstitutionalization and Diversion of Juvenile Offenders: A Litany of Impediments." In *Crime and Justice*, Norval Morris and Michael Tonry (eds.). Chicago: University of Chicago Press.

KLEIN, MALCOLM W., L. ROSENZWEIG and M. BATES (1975). "The Ambiguous Juvenile Arrest." *Criminology* **24**:185–194.

KLEIN-SAFFRAN, JODY and FAITH LUTZE (1991). "The Effect of Shock Incarceration of Federal Offenders: Community Corrections and Post-Release Follow-Up." Unpublished paper presented at the annual meeting of the American Society of Criminology, San Francisco (November).

KNEPPER, PAUL and GRAY CAVENDER (1990). "Decision-Making and the Typification of Juveniles on Parole." Unpublished paper presented at the Academy of Criminal Justice Science meetings, Denver (April).

KNIGHT, KAREN WITCHCOFF and TONY TRIPODI (1996). "Societal Bonding and Delinquency: An Empirical Test of Hirschi's Theory of Control." *Journal of Offender Rehabilitation* **23**:117–129.

KNOX, GEORGE W., BRAD MARTIN, and EDWARD D. TROMANHAUSER (1995). "Preliminary Results of the 1995 National Prosecutor's Survey." *Journal of Gang Research* **2**:59–71.

KOEHLER, RICHARD J. and CHARLES LINDNER (1992). "Alternative Incarceration: An Inevitable Response to Institutional Overcrowding." *Federal Probation* **56**:12–18.

KRATCOSKI, PETER C. and LUCILLE DUNN KRATCOSKI (1986). *Juvenile Delinquency*, 2nd ed. Upper Saddle River, NJ: Prentice Hall.

KRAUSE, WESLEY and MARILYN D. MCSHANE (1994). "A Deinstitutionalization Retrospective: Relabeling the Status Offender." *Journal of Crime and Justice* **17**:45–67.

KRISBERG, BARRY (1988). *The Juvenile Court: Reclaiming the Vision.* San Francisco: National Council on Crime and Delinquency.

KRISBERG, BARRY and ROBERT DECOMO (1993). *Juveniles Taken into Custody: Fiscal Year Report.* Washington, DC: U.S. Office of Juvenile Justice and Delinquency Prevention.

KRISBERG, BARRY, IRA M. SCHWARTZ and EDMUND F. MCGARRELL (1993). "Reinventing Juvenile Justice: Research Directions." *Crime and Delinquency* **39**:3–124.

KRISBERG, BARRY ET AL. (1989). *Demonstration of Post-adjudication Non-residential Intensive Supervision Programs: Selected Program Summaries.* San Francisco: National Council on Crime and Delinquency.

KRISBERG, BARRY ET AL. (1993). *Juveniles in State Custody: Prospects for Community-Based Care of Troubled Adolescents.* San Francisco: National Center for Crime and Delinquency.

KRUTTSCHNITT, CANDACE and MAUDE DORNFELD (1993). "Exposure to Family Violence: A Partial Explanation for Initial and Subsequent Levels of Delinquency?" *Criminal Behaviour and Mental Health* **3:**61–75.

KUPFERSMID, JOEL and ROBERTA MONKMAN (eds.) (1987). "Assaultive Youth Responding to Physical Assaultiveness in Residential, Community, and Health Care Settings." *Child and Youth Services* **10:**155–163.

KURTZ, P. DAVID, MARTHA M. GIDDINGS, and RICHARD SUTPHEN (1993). "A Prospective Investigation of Racial Disparity in the Juvenile Justice System." *Juvenile and Family Court Journal* **44:**43–59.

KURZ, GWEN A. and LOUIS E. MOORE (1994). *The "8% Problem"—Chronic Juvenile Offender Recidivism: Exploratory Research Findings and Implications for Problem Solutions.* Santa Ana, CA: Orange County Probation Department.

LAB, STEVEN P., GLENN SHIELDS, and CONNIE SCHONDEL (1993). "Research Note: An Evaluation of Juvenile Sexual Offender Treatment." *Crime and Delinquency* **39:**543–553.

LAND, KENNETH C., PATRICIA L. MCCALL and KAREN F. PARKER (1994). "Logistic versus Hazards Regression Analyses in Evaluation Research: An Exposition and Application to the North Carolina Court Counselor's Intensive Protective Supervision Project." *Evaluation Review* **18:**411–437.

LARIVEE, JOHN (1990). "On the Outside: Corrections in the Community." *Corrections Today* **52:**84–106.

LATESSA, EDWARD J. and GENNARO F. VITO (1988). "The Effects of Intensive Supervision on Shock Probationers." *Journal of Criminal Justice* **16:**319–330.

LATTIMORE, PAMELA K., CHRISTY A. VISHER, and RICHARD L. LINSTER (1995). "Predicting Rearrest for Violence among Serious Youthful Offenders." *Journal of Research in Crime and Delinquency* **32:**54–83.

LAUB, JOHN H. and BRUCE K. MACMURRAY (1987). "Increasing the Prosecutor's Role in Juvenile Court Expectations and Realities." *Justice System Journal* **12:**196–209.

LAURENCE, S. E. and B. R. WEST (1985). *National Evaluation of the New Pride Replication Program: Final Report*, Vol. I. Lafayette, CA: Pacific Institute for Research and Evaluation.

LAWRENCE, RICHARD A. (1984). "The Role of Legal Counsel in Juveniles' Understanding of Their Rights." *Juvenile and Family Court Journal* **34:**49–58.

LAWRENCE, RICHARD A. (1985). "Jail Educational Programs: Helping Inmates Cope with Overcrowded Conditions." *Journal of Correctional Education* **36:**15–20.

LEE, LEONA (1996). "Predictors of Juvenile Court Dispositions." *Journal of Crime and Justice* **19:**149–166.

LEIBER, MICHAEL J. (1995). "Toward Clarification of the Concept of 'Minority' Status and Decision Making in Juvenile Court Proceedings." *Journal of Crime and Justice* **18:**79–108.

LEIBER, MICHAEL J. and TINA L. MAWHORR (1995). "Evaluating the Use of Social Skills Training and Employment with Delinquent Youth." *Journal of Criminal Justice* **23:**127–141.

LEMERT, EDWIN M. (1951). *Social Pathology.* New York: McGraw-Hill.

LEMERT, EDWIN M. (1967a). *Human Deviance, Social Problems and Social Control.* Upper Saddle River, NJ: Prentice Hall.

LEMERT, EDWIN M. (1967b). "The Juvenile Court—Quests and Realities." In *Task Force Report: Juvenile Delinquency and Youth Crime.* Washington, DC: President's Commission on Law Enforcement and the Administration of Justice.

LEVINE, IRENE (ed.) (1996). "Preventing Violence among Youth: Introduction." *American Journal of Orthopsychiatry* **66**:320–389.

LEWIS, DOROTHY OTNOW ET AL. (1991). "A Follow-Up of Female Delinquents: Maternal Contributions to the Perpetuation of Deviance." *Journal of the American Academy of Child and Adolescent Psychiatry* **30**:197–201.

LIEB, ROXANNE, LEE FISH and TODD CROSBY (1994). *A Summary of State Trends in Juvenile Justice.* Olympia, WA: Washington State Institute for Public Policy.

LILLY, J. ROBERT and RICHARD A. BALL (1987). "A Brief History of House Arrest and Electronic Monitoring." *Northern Kentucky Law Review* **13**:343–374.

LINDSTROM, PETER (1996). "Family Interaction, Neighborhood Context and Deviant Behavior: A Research Note." *Studies on Crime and Crime Prevention* **5**:113–119.

LIPSON, KARIN (1982). "Cops and TOPS: A Program for Police and Teens That Works." *Police Chief* **49**:45–46.

LISTUG, DAVID (1996). "Wisconsin Sheriff's Office Saves Money and Resources." *American Jails* **10**:85–86.

LITTLE HOOVER COMMISSION (1990). *Runaway/Homeless Youths: California's Efforts to Recycle Society's Throwaways.* Sacramento, CA: Little Hoover Commission.

LOCKE, THOMAS P. ET AL. (1986). "An Evaluation of a Juvenile Education Program in a State Penitentiary." *Evaluation Review* **10**:281–298.

LOCKHART, LETTIE L. ET AL. (1991). *Georgia's Juvenile Justice System: A Retrospective Investigation of Racial Disparity.* Athens, GA: School of Social Work, University of Georgia.

LOEBER, ROLF and THOMAS J. DISHION (1987). "Antisocial and Delinquent Youths: Methods for Their Early Identification." In *Prevention of Delinquent Behavior*, John D. Burchard and Sara Burchard (eds.). Thousand Oaks, CA: Sage.

LOGAN, CHARLES H. and SHARLA P. RAUSCH (1985). "Why Deinstitutionalizing Status Offenders is Pointless." *Crime and Delinquency* **31**:501–517.

LOMBARDO, RITA and JANET DiGIORGIO-MILLER (1988). "Concepts and Techniques in Working with Juvenile Sex Offenders." *Journal of Offender Counseling Services and Rehabilitation* **13**:39–53.

LONARDI, BARBARA M. (1987). "On-the-Job Training." *Corrections Today* **49**:142–144.

LONGMIRE, DENNIS R. (1985). "In Support of Privatization of America's Penal Facilities: Experimental, Economic, and Political Considerations." Unpublished paper presented at the National Association of Juvenile Correctional Agencies, Las Vegas, NV (August).

LUNDMAN, RICHARD J. (1984). *Prevention and Control of Juvenile Delinquency.* New York: Oxford University Press.

LYNN, CHERYL W. ET AL. (1993). *An Investigation of the Effectiveness of the Virginia Habitual Offender Act.* Richmond, VA: Research Council, Virginia Department of Transportation.

MACALLAIR, DAN (1994). "Disposition Case Advocacy in San Francisco's Juvenile Justice System: A New Approach to Deinstitutionalization." *Crime and Delinquency* **40**:84–95.

MACK, DENNIS E. (1992). "High Impact Incarceration Program: Rikers Boot Camp." *American Jails* **6**:63–65.

MacKenzie, Doris Layton and James W. Shaw (1993). "The Impact of Shock Incarceration on Technical Violations and New Criminal Activities." *Justice Quarterly* **10**:463–487.

MacKenzie, Doris Layton, James W. Shaw, and Voncile B. Gowdy (1993). *An Evaluation of Shock Incarceration in Louisiana.* Washington, DC: Office of Justice Programs, U.S. Department of Justice.

MacKenzie, Doris Layton and Claire Souryal (1994). *Multisite Evaluation of Shock Incarceration—A Final Summary.* Washington, DC: U.S. National Institute of Justice.

Maguire, Kathleen and Ann L. Pastore (1996). *Bureau of Justice Statistics Sourcebook of Criminal Justice Statistics, 1995.* Albany, NY: The Hindelang Criminal Justice Research Center, State University of New York at Albany.

Mahoney, Anne Rankin (1985). "Time and Process in Juvenile Court." *Justice System Journal* **10**:37–55.

Mahoney, Anne Rankin (1989). "Nonresident Delinquents: Whose Problem Are They?" *Journal of Juvenile Law* **10**:179–192.

Maine Juvenile Corrections Task Force (1993). *Determination and Recommendations to the Health and Social Services Transition Team Regarding Juvenile Correctional Services.* Augusta, ME: Maine Office of Policy and Legal Analysis.

Mainprize, Stephen (1992). "Electronic Monitoring in Corrections: Assessing Cost Effectiveness and the Potential for Widening the Net of Social Control." *Canadian Journal of Criminology* **34**:161–180.

Malmquist, Carl P. (1990). "Depression in Homicidal Adolescents." *Bulletin of the American Academy of Psychiatry and the Law* **18**:23–36.

Maloney, Dennis M., Dennis Romig, and Troy Armstrong (1988). "Juvenile Probation: The Balanced Approach." *Juvenile and Family Court Journal* **39**:1–63.

Maltz, Michael D. (1984). *Recidivism.* San Diego, CA: Academic Press.

Manikas, Peter M. et al. (1990). *Criminal Justice Policymaking: Boundaries and Borderlands.* Chicago: Criminal Justice Project of Cook County.

Mardon, Steven (1991). "Training America's Youth." *Corrections Today* **53**:32–65.

Martin, Joe R., Arnie D. Schulze, and Mike Valdez (1988). "Taking Aim at Truancy." *FBI Law Enforcement Bulletin* **57**:8–12.

Martinson, Robert (1974). "What Works? Questions and Answers about Prison Reform." *The Public Interest* **35**:22–54.

Maxson, Cheryl L., Margaret A. Little, and Malcolm W. Klein (1988). "Police Response to Runaway and Missing Children: A Conceptual Framework for Research and Policy." *Crime and Delinquency* **34**:84–102.

Mays, G. Larry and Joel Thompson (1991). *America's Small Jails.* Chicago, IL: Waveland Press.

McAnany, Patrick D., Doug Thomson, and David Fogel (eds.) (1984). *Probation and Justice: A Reconsideration of a Mission.* Boston: Oelgeschlager, Gunn & Hain.

McCarthy, Belinda R. (1985). "An Analysis of Detention." *Juvenile and Family Court Journal* **36**:49–50.

McCarthy, Belinda R. (1987a). *Intermediate Punishments.* Monsey, NY: Willow Tree Press.

McCarthy, Belinda R. (1987b). "Case Attrition in the Juvenile Court: An Application of the Crime Control Model." *Justice Quarterly* **4**:237–255.

McCarthy, Belinda R. (1989). "A Preliminary Research Model for the Juvenile and Family Court." *Juvenile and Family Court Journal* **40**:43–48.

McCarthy, Belinda R. and Bernard J. McCarthy (1997). *Community-Based Corrections.* Pacific Grove, CA: Brooks/Cole.

McCarthy, Belinda R. and B. L. Smith (1986). "The Conceptualization of Discrimination in the Juvenile Justice Process: The Impact of Administrative Factors and Screening Decisions on Juvenile Court Dispositions." *Criminology* **24:**41–64.

McCord, David M. (1995). "Toward a Typology of Wilderness-Based Residential Treatment Program Participants." *Residential Treatment for Children and Youth* **12:**51–60.

McDermott, M. Joan and John H. Laub (1987). "Adolescence and Juvenile Justice Policy." *Criminal Justice Policy Review* **1:**438–455.

McDonald, William F. (1985). *Plea Bargaining: Critical Issues and Common Practices.* Washington, DC: U.S. Department of Justice, National Institute of Justice.

McMillen, Michael J. (1987). "Bringing Flexibility to Juvenile Detention: The Minimum Security Approach." *Corrections Today* **49:**44–48, 105.

McNally, Roger B. (1984). "The Juvenile Justice System: A Legacy of Failure?" *Federal Probation* **48:**102–110.

Menard, Scott (1987). "Short-Term Trends in Crime and Delinquency: A Comparison of UCR, NCS, and Self-Report Data." *Justice Quarterly* **4:**455–474.

Mendel, Richard A. (1995). *Prevention or Pork? A Hard-Headed Look at Youth-Oriented Anti-crime Programs.* Washington, DC: American Youth Policy Forum.

Mennel, Robert M. (1983). "Attitudes and Policies toward Juvenile Delinquency in the United States: A Historiographical Review." In *Crime and Justice: An Annual Review of Research*, Michael Tonry and Norval Morris (eds.). Chicago: University of Chicago Press.

Mershon, Jerry L. (1991). *Juvenile Justice: The Adjudicatory and Dispositional Process.* Reno, NV: National Council of Juvenile and Family Court Judges.

MetaMetrics, Inc. (1984). *Evaluation of the Breakthrough Foundation Youth at Risk Program: The 10-Day Course and Followup Program: Final Report.* Washington, DC: MetaMetrics, Inc.

Miller, A. Therese, Colleen Eggertson-Tacon, and Brian Quigg (1990). "Patterns of Runaway Behavior with a Larger Systems Context: The Road to Empowerment." *Adolescence* **25:**271–289.

Miller, Darcy (1994). "Exploring Gender Differences in Suicidal Behavior among Adolescent Offenders: Findings and Implications." *Journal of Correctional Education* **45:**134–140.

Miller, Edward (1990). "Executing Minors and the Mentally Retarded: The Retribution and Deterrence Rationales." *Rutgers Law Review* **43:**15–52.

Miller, Larry and Michael Braswell (1993). *Human Relations and Police Work.* Prospect Heights, IL: Waveland Press.

Miller, Neal (1995). *State Laws on Prosecutors' and Judges' Use of Juvenile Records.* Washington, DC: U.S. National Institute of Justice.

Milton S. Eisenhower Foundation (1993). *Investing in Children and Youth, Reconstructing Our Cities: Doing What Works to Reverse the Betrayal of American Democracy.* Washington, DC: Milton S. Eisenhower Foundation.

Minnesota Criminal Justice Statistical Analysis Center (1989). *Violent and Chronic Juvenile Crime.* St. Paul, MN: Minnesota Criminal Justice Analysis Center.

Minnesota Department of Corrections (1993). *Short-Term Offender/Fee-for-Service Group 1994 Report to the Legislature.* St. Paul, MN: Minnesota Department of Corrections.

MINNESOTA OFFICE OF THE LEGISLATIVE AUDITOR (1995). *Residential Facilities for Juvenile Offenders.* St. Paul, MN: Minnesota Office of the Legislative Auditor Program Evaluation Division.

MINNESOTA SENTENCING GUIDELINES COMMISSION (1994). *Sentencing Practices: Juvenile Offenders Sentenced for Felonies in Adult Court.* St. Paul, MN: Minnesota Sentencing Guidelines Commission.

MINOR, KEVIN I. and H. PRESTON ELROD (1990). "The Effects of a Multi-faceted Intervention on the Offense Activities of Juvenile Probationers." *Journal of Offender Counseling, Services, and Rehabilitation* **15**:87–108.

MITCHELL, BILL and GENE SHILLER (1988). "Colorado's Shape-Up Program Gives Youth a Taste of the Inside." *Corrections Today* **50**:76–87.

MITCHELL, JOHN J. and SHARON A. WILLIAMS (1986). "SOS: Reducing Juvenile Recidivism." *Corrections Today* **48**:70–71.

MIXDORF, LLOYD (1989). "Pay Me Now or Pay Me Later." *Corrections Today* **51**:106–110.

MOLIDOR, CHRISTIAN E. (1996). "Female Gang Members: A Profile of Aggression and Victimization." *Social Work* **41**:251–257.

MONES, PAUL (1984). "Too Many Rights or Not Enough? A Study of the Juvenile Related Decisions of the West Virginia Supreme Court of Appeals." *Journal of Juvenile Law* **8**:32–57.

MONTGOMERY, IMOGENE M. and PATRICIA McFALL TORBET (1994). *What Works? Promising Interventions in Juvenile Justice Program Report.* Washington, DC: U.S. Office of Juvenile Justice and Delinquency Prevention.

MORASH, MERRY (1984). "Establishment of a Juvenile Police Record: The Influence of Individual and Peer Group Characteristics." *Criminology* **22**:97–111.

MURPHY, EDWARD M. (1985). "Handling Violent Juveniles." *Corrections Today* **47**:26–30.

MURPHY, J. MICHAEL ET AL. (1991). "Substance Abuse and Serious Child Mistreatment: Prevalence, Risk and Outcome in a Court Sample." *Child Abuse and Neglect* **15**:197–211.

MUSICK, DAVID (1995). *An Introduction to the Sociology of Juvenile Delinquency.* Albany, NY: State University of New York Press.

MUTCHNICK, ROBERT J. and MARGARET FAWCETT (1991). "Group Home Environments and Victimization of Resident Juveniles." *International Journal of Offender Therapy and Comparative Criminology* **35**:126–142.

MYERS, WADE C. (1992). "What Treatments Do We Have for Children and Adolescents Who Have Killed?" *Bulletin of the American Academy of Psychiatry and the Law* **20**:47–58.

MYERS, WADE C. (1994). "Sexual Homicide by Adolescents." *Journal of the American Academy of Child and Adolescent Psychiatry* **33**:962–969.

NAFFINE, NGAIRE and JOY WUNDERSITZ (1991). "Lawyers in the Children's Court: An Australian's Perspective." *Crime and Delinquency* **37**:374–392.

NAGOSHI, JACK T. (1986). *Juvenile Recidivism: Third Circuit Court.* Honolulu, HI: Youth Development and Research Center, University of Hawaii-Manoa.

NATIONAL ADVISORY COMMITTEE FOR JUVENILE JUSTICE AND DELINQUENCY PREVENTION (1980). *Standards for the Administration of Juvenile Justice.* Washington, DC: U.S. Government Printing Office.

NATIONAL ADVISORY COMMISSION ON CRIMINAL JUSTICE STANDARDS AND GOALS (1976). *Task Force Report on Juvenile Justice and Delinquency Prevention.* Washington, DC: Law Enforcement Assistance Administration.

NATIONAL CENTER FOR JUVENILE JUSTICE (1988). *Court Careers of Juvenile Offenders.* Pittsburgh, PA: National Center for Juvenile Justice.

NATIONAL COLLEGE OF JUVENILE AND FAMILY LAW (1989). "Court-Approved Alternative Dispute Resolution: A Better Way to Resolve Minor Delinquency, Status Offense, and Abuse/Neglect Cases." *Juvenile and Family Court Journal* **40**:51–98.

NATIONAL CONFERENCE OF STATE LEGISLATURES (1988). *Legal Dispositions and Confinement Policies for Delinquent Youth.* Denver, CO: National Conference of State Legislatures.

NATIONAL COUNCIL OF JUVENILE AND FAMILY COURT JUDGES (1986). "Deprived Children: A Judicial Response—73 Recommendations." *Juvenile and Family Court Journal* **37**:3–48.

NATIONAL COUNCIL ON CRIME AND DELINQUENCY (1990). *Development of Risk Prediction Scales for the California Youthful Offender Parole Board on Assessment of 1981–1982 Releasees.* San Francisco: National Council on Crime and Delinquency.

NATIONAL COUNCIL ON CRIME AND DELINQUENCY (1991). *Juvenile Justice Policy Statement.* San Francisco: National Council on Crime and Delinquency.

NEW JERSEY DIVISION OF CRIMINAL JUSTICE (1985). *Juvenile Waivers to Adult Court: A Report to the New Jersey State Legislature.* Trenton, NJ: New Jersey Division of Criminal Justice.

NEW JERSEY JUVENILE DELINQUENCY COMMISSION (1993). *Profile 93: A Sourcebook of Juvenile Justice Data and Trends in New Jersey.* Trenton, NJ: New Jersey Juvenile Delinquency Commission.

NEW YORK COMMISSION FOR THE STUDY OF YOUTH CRIME AND VIOLENCE AND THE REFORM OF THE JUVENILE JUSTICE SYSTEM (1994). *Preliminary Report to the Governor.* New York: New York Commission for the Study of Youth Crime and Violence and the Reform of the Juvenile Justice System.

NEW YORK STATE DEPARTMENT OF CORRECTIONAL SERVICES (1989). *Follow-Up Study of First Six Platoons of Shock Graduates.* Albany, NY: Division of Program Planning, New York State Department of Correctional Services.

NEW YORK STATE DEPARTMENT OF CORRECTIONAL SERVICES (1990). The Second Annual Report to the Legislature: *Shock Incarceration in New York.* Albany, NY: Division of Parole, New York State Department of Correctional Services.

NEW YORK STATE DEPARTMENT OF CORRECTIONAL SERVICES (1991). *The Third Annual Report to the Legislature: Shock Incarceration in New York.* Albany, NY: Division of Program Planning, New York State Department of Corrections.

NEW YORK STATE DEPARTMENT OF CORRECTIONAL SERVICES (1992). *Guidelines for Volunteer Services.* Albany, NY: New York State Department of Correctional Services.

NEW YORK STATE DIVISION OF CRIMINAL JUSTICE SERVICES (1994). *New York State's Agenda to Reduce and Prevent Violence.* Albany, NY: New York State Division of Criminal Justice Services.

NEW YORK STATE DIVISION OF PAROLE (1985). PARJO III: *Final Evaluation of the PARJO Pilot Supervision Program.* Albany, NY: New York State Division of Parole, Evaluation, and Planning.

NIARHOS, FRANCES JOHNSON and DONALD K. ROUTH (1992). "The Role of Clinical Assessments in the Juvenile Court: Predictors of Juvenile Dispositions and Recidivism." *Journal of Clinical Child Psychology* **21**:151–159.

NORMAN, MICHAEL D. (1986). "Discretionary Justice: Decision-Making in a State Juvenile Parole Board." *Juvenile and Family Court Journal* **37**:19–25.

NORMAN, MICHAEL D. and GEORGE S. BURBIDGE (1991). "Attitudes of Youth Corrections Professionals toward Juvenile Justice Reform and Policy Alternatives—A Youth Study." *Journal of Criminal Justice* **19**:81–92.

NORMAN, SHERWOOD (1970). *The Youth Service Bureau: A Key to Delinquency Prevention.* Hackensack, NJ: National Council on Crime and Delinquency.

NORTH CAROLINA ADMINISTRATIVE OFFICE OF THE COURTS (1994). *Interim Report on the Teen Court Program in the 12th Judicial District.* Raleigh, NC: North Carolina Administrative Office of the Courts.

NORTHRUP, GORDON (ed.) (1993). "Clinical Work." *Residential Treatment for Children and Youth* **10**:1–110.

O'NEIL, CARLE F. (1987). "Somebody Blew It: And We Let 'Em." *Corrections Today* **49**:140–192.

ONEK, DAVID (1994). *Pairing College Students with Delinquents: The Missouri Intensive Case Monitoring Program.* San Francisco: National Council on Crime and Delinquency.

ORLANDO, FRANK A., ALLEN F. BREED and ROBERT L. SMITH (1987). *Juvenile Justice Reform: A Critique of the A.L.E.C. Code.* Minneapolis, MN: Hubert Humphrey Institute of Public Affairs, University of Minnesota.

OSGOOD, D. WAYNE (1983). "Offense History and Juvenile Diversion." *Evaluation Review* **7**:793–806.

OSGOOD, D. WAYNE ET AL. (1987). "Time Trends and Age Trends in Self-Reported Illegal Behavior." Unpublished paper presented at American Society of Criminology meetings, Montreal, Quebec, Canada (November).

OSLER, MARK W. (1991). "Shock Incarceration: Hard Realities and Real Possibilities." *Federal Probation* **55**:34–42.

PACKER, HERBERT L. (1968). *The Limits of the Criminal Sanction.* Stanford, CA: Stanford University Press.

PAGE, ROBERT W. (1993). "Family Courts: An Effective Judicial Approach to the Resolution of Family Disputes." *Juvenile and Family Court Journal* **44**:3–60.

PALLONE, NATHANIEL J. (ed.) (1994). "Young Victims, Young Offenders: Current Issues in Policy and Treatment." *Journal of Offender Rehabilitation* **21**:1–237.

PALMER TED (1994). *A Profile of Correctional Effectiveness and New Directions for Research.* Albany, NY: State University of New York Press.

PALMER, TED and ROBERT WEDGE (1994). *California's Juvenile Probation Camps: A Validation Study.* Sacramento, CA: Research Division, California Department of the Youth Authority.

PAPY, JOSEPH E. (1994). "Electronic Monitoring Poses Myriad Challenges for Correctional Agencies." *Corrections Today* **56**:132–135.

PARENT, DALE G. (1989a). "Probation Supervision Fee Collection in Texas." *APPA Perspectives* **13**:9–12.

PARENT, DALE G. (1989b). *Shock Incarceration: An Overview of Existing Programs.* Washington, DC: Office of Justice Programs, U.S. Department of Justice.

PARENT, DALE G. (1991). "OJJDP Sponsors Conditions of Confinement Study." *Corrections Today* **53**:46,77.

PARENT, DALE G. (1993). "Conditions of Confinement." *Juvenile Justice* 1:3–23.

PARENT, DALE G. ET AL. (1994). *Conditions of Confinement: Juvenile Detention and Corrections Facilities Research Report.* Washington, DC: U.S. Office of Juvenile Justice and Delinquency Prevention.

PATTERSON, G. L., L. CROSBY and S. VUCHINICH (1992). "Predicting Risk for Early Police Arrest." *Journal of Quantitative Criminology* 8:335–355.

PEARSON, FRANK S. and DANIEL B. BIBEL (1986). "New Jersey's Intensive Supervision Program: What Is It Like? Is It Working?" *Federal Probation* 50:25–31.

PENNELL, SUSAN, CHRISTINE CURTIS and DENNIS C. SCHECK (1990). "Controlling Juvenile Delinquency: An Evaluation of an Interagency Strategy." *Crime and Delinquency* 36:257–275.

PETERSILIA, JOAN (1986). "Exploring the Option of House Arrest." *Federal Probation* 50:50–55.

PETERSILIA, JOAN AND SUSAN TURNER (1990). "Reducing Prison Admissions: The Potential of Intermediate Sanctions." *APPA Perspectives* 14:32–36.

PETERSON, MICHELE (1988). "Children's Understanding of the Juvenile Justice System: A Cognitive-Developmental Perspective." *Canadian Journal of Criminology* 30:381–395.

PILIAVIN, IRVING and SCOTT BRIAR (1964). "Police Encounters with Juveniles." *American Journal of Sociology* 70:206–214.

PINGREE, DAVID H. (1984). "Florida Youth Services." *Corrections Today* 46:60–62.

PIQUERO, ALEX and DORIS LAYTON MACKENZIE (1993). "The Impact of an Alternative Program on Bedspace." Unpublished paper presented at the annual meeting of the American Society of Criminology, Phoenix, AZ (October).

PLATT, ANTHONY N. (1969). *The Child Savers: The Invention of Delinquency.* Chicago: University of Chicago Press.

PODKOPACZ, MARCY RASMUSSEN (1994). *Juvenile Reference Study.* Minneapolis, MN: Hennepin County Department of Community Corrections.

PODKOPACZ, MARCY RASMUSSEN and BARRY C. FELD (1996). "The End of the Line: An Empirical Study of Judicial Waiver." *Journal of Criminal Law and Criminology* 86:449–492.

POLAN, SUSAN LORI (1994). *CSP Revisited: An Evaluation of Juvenile Diversion.* Ann Arbor, MI: University Microfilms International.

POLHILL, PAULA ET AL. (1994). *Juvenile Justice Detention Programs: Eight-Year Longitudinal Analysis.* Tallahassee, FL: Bureau of Research and Data, Florida Department of Juvenile Justice.

POLK, KENNETH (1984). "Juvenile Diversion: A Look at the Record." *Crime and Delinquency* 30:648–659.

POSNER, MARC (1992). *The Runaway Risk Reduction Project Assessment Report.* Newton, MA: Education Development Center, Inc.

POSNER, MARC (1994). *Working Together for Youth: A Guide to Collaboration between Law Enforcement Agencies and Programs That Serve Runaway and Homeless Youth.* Norman, OK: National Resource Center for Youth Services, University of Oklahoma.

POULOS, TAMMY MEREDITH and STAN ORCHOWSKY (1994). "Serious Juvenile Offenders: Predicting the Probability of Transfer to Criminal Court." *Crime and Delinquency* 40:3–17.

PROJECT NEW PRIDE (1985). *Project New Pride.* Washington, DC: U.S. Department of Justice.

QUINLAN, JUDITH and ELAINE MOTTE (1990). "Psychiatric Training for Officers: An Effective Tool for Increased Officer and Inmate Safety." *American Jails* 4:22–25.

RABINOWITZ, MARTIN (1992). *PINS Diversion in New York City: Research Findings*, Vol. 1. New York: Office of the Deputy Mayor for Public Safety.

RADELET, MICHAEL R., HUGO ADAM BEDAU, and CONSTANCE E. PUTNAM (1992). *In Spite of Innocence: The Ordeal of 400 Americans Wrongly Convicted of Crimes Punishable by Death*. Boston: Northeastern University Press.

RAIDER, MELVYN C. (1994). "Juvenile Electronic Monitoring: A Community-Based Program to Augment Residential Treatment." *Residential Treatment for Children and Youth* **12**:37–48.

RANS, LAUREL L. (1984). "The Validity of Models to Predict Violence in Community and Prison Settings." *Corrections Today* **46**:50–63.

RAPOPORT, ROBERT N. (1987). *New Interventions for Children and Youth: Action Research Approaches*. New York: Cambridge University Press.

RATLIFF, BASCOM W. (1988). "The Army Model: Boot Camp for Youthful Offenders." *Corrections Today* **50**:90–102.

REAVES, BRIAN A. (1993). *Census of State and Local Law Enforcement Agencies, 1992*. Washington, DC: U.S. Department of Justice.

REAVES, BRIAN A. (1996). *Local Police Departments, 1993*. Washington, DC: U.S. Department of Justice.

REDDINGTON, FRANCES P. (1992). *In the Best Interests of the Child: The Impact of Morales v. Turman on the Texas Youth Commission*. Ann Arbor, MI: University Microfilms International.

REED, DAVID (1983). *Needed: Serious Solutions for Serious Juvenile Crime*. Chicago: Chicago Law Enforcement Study Group.

REESE, WILLIAM A., III and RUSSELL L. CURTIS JR. (1991). "Paternalism and the Female Status Offender: Remanding the Juvenile Justice Double Standard." *Social Science Journal* **28**:63–83.

REINHARZ, PETER (1996). *Killer Kids: Bad Law and Tales of the Juvenile Court System*. New York: Barricade Books.

RHODE ISLAND GOVERNOR'S JUSTICE COMMISSION STATISTICAL ANALYSIS CENTER (1992). *Juveniles in Rhode Island: A Data Analysis and Statistical Study*. Warwick, RI: Rhode Island Governor's Justice Commission Statistical Analysis Center.

RHODE ISLAND STATE COUNCIL ON VOCATIONAL EDUCATION (1995). *Evaluation of Educational Services Provided for Incarcerated Juveniles*. Cranston, RI: Rhode Island State Council on Vocational Education.

RING, CHARLES R. (1987). *Contracting for the Operation of Private Prisons: Pros and Cons*. Laurel, MD: American Correctional Association.

RITTER, BRUCE (1987). Covenant House: *Lifeline to the Street*. New York: Doubleday.

RIVERA, BEVERLY and CATHY SPATZ WIDOM (1990). "Childhood Victimization and Violent Offending." *Violence and Victims* **5**:19–35.

ROBBINS, IRA P. (1986). "Privatization of Corrections: Defining the Issues." *Federal Probation* **50**:24–30.

ROBERTS, ALBERT R. (1989). *Juvenile Justice: Politics, Programs and Services*. Chicago: Dorsey Press.

ROBINSON, DINAH A. and OTIS H. STEPHENS (1992). "Patterns of Mitigating Factors in Juvenile Death Penalty Cases." *Criminal Law Bulletin* **28**:246–275.

Rodatus, Robert V. (1994). "Legal, Ethical and Professional Concerns When Representing Children in Abuse Cases in Juvenile Court." *Juvenile and Family Court Journal* **45**:39–50.

Rogers, Joseph W. (1990). "The Predisposition Report: Maintaining the Promise of Individualized Juvenile Justice." *Federal Probation* **54**:43–57.

Rogers, Joseph W. and G. Larry Mays (1987). *Juvenile Delinquency and Juvenile Justice.* New York: Wiley.

Rogers, Joseph W. and James D. Williams (1995). "The Predispositional Report, Decision Making, and Juvenile Court Policy." *Juvenile and Family Court Journal* **45**:47–57.

Romig, Dennis A. (1978). *Justice for Our Children.* Lexington, MA: Lexington Books.

Rosenbaum, Jill Leslie (1987). "Family Dysfunction and Female Delinquency." Unpublished paper presented at the American Society of Criminology meetings, Montreal, Quebec, Canada (November).

Rosenbaum, Jill Leslie (1996). "A Violent Few: Gang Girls in the California Youth Authority." *Journal of Gang Research* **3**:17–33.

Rosenbaum, Jill Leslie and Meda Chesney-Lind (1994). "Appearance and Delinquency: A Research Note." *Crime and Delinquency* **40**:250–261.

Rossum, Ralph A., Benedict J. Koller, and Christopher Manfredi (1987). *Juvenile Justice Reform: A Model for the States.* Claremont, CA: Rose Institute of State and Local Government and the American Legislative Exchange Council.

Rothstein, Natalie (1985). "Teen Court." *Corrections Today* **47**:18–22.

Rousch, David W. (1987). "Setting the Standard: National Juvenile Detention Resource Centers." Corrections Today **49**:32–34.

Rowan, Joseph R. (1989). "Suicide Detection and Prevention: A Must for Juvenile Facilities." *Corrections Today* **51**:218–223.

Rowe, David C., Alexander T. Vazsonyi and Daniel J. Flannery (1995). "Sex Differences in Crime? Do Means and Within-Sex Variation Have Similar Causes?" *Journal of Research in Crime and Delinquency* **32**:84–100.

Roy, Sudipto (1994). "Electronic Monitoring of Juvenile Offenders in Lake County, Indiana: An Exploratory Study." *Journal of Offender Monitoring* **7**:1–8.

Roy, Sudipto (1995). "Juvenile Restitution and Recidivism in a Midwestern County." *Federal Probation* **59**:55–62.

Rubel, Robert J. and Nancy L. Ames (1986). *Reducing School Crime and Student Misbehavior: A Problem-Solving Strategy.* Washington, DC: U.S. National Institute of Justice.

Rubin, H. Ted (1983). *Juvenile Justice and Delinquency Prevention: Viewpoints of Five Juvenile Court Judges.* Washington, DC: U.S. Office of Juvenile Justice and Delinquency Prevention.

Rubin, H. Ted (1985). *Behind the Black Robes: Juvenile Court Judges and the Court.* Thousand Oaks, CA: Sage.

Rubin, H. Ted (1988). "Fulfilling Juvenile Restitution Requirements in Community Correctional Programs." *Federal Probation* **52**:32–42.

Rush, Jeffrey P. (1992). "Juvenile Probation Officer Cynicism." *Corrections Today* **16**:1–16.

Russell, Robin and Ursala Sedlak (1993). "Status Offenders: Attitudes of Child Welfare Practitioners toward Practice and Policy Issues." *Child Welfare* **72**:13–24.

Ryan, C. I. and K. S. Williams (1986). "Police Discretion." Public Law (Summer):285–310.

RYAN, T. A. and K. A. McCABE (1993). "The Relationship between Mandatory vs. Voluntary Participation in a Prison Literacy Program and Academic Achievement." *Journal of Correctional Education* **44**:134–138.

SAGATUN, INGER J., LORETTA L. McCOLLUM and LEONARD P. EDWARDS (1985). "The Effect of Transfers from Juvenile to Criminal Court: A Log-Linear Analysis." *Journal of Crime and Justice* **8**:75–92.

SAKUMOTO, RAYMOND E. (1995). *Report of a Statistical Study and Evaluation of the Juvenile Intensive Supervision Program.* Honolulu, HI: University of Hawaii at Manoa.

SAMETZ, LYNN (1984). "Revamping the Adolescent's Justice System to Serve the Needs of the Very Young Offender." *Juvenile and Family Court Journal* **34**:21–30.

SAMETZ, LYNN, JOSEPH AHREN, and STEVEN YUAN (1994). "Rehabilitating Youth through Housing Rehabilitation." *Journal of Correctional Education* **45**:142–150.

SANBORN, JOSEPH B., JR. (1993). "Philosophical, Legal and Systemic Aspects of Juvenile Court Plea Bargaining." *Crime and Delinquency* **39**:509–527.

SANBORN, JOSEPH B., JR. (1994a). "Certification to Criminal Court: The Important Policy Questions of How, When and Why?" *Crime and Delinquency* **40**:262–281.

SANBORN, JOSEPH B., JR. (1994b). "Remnants of Parens Patriae in the Adjudicatory Hearing: Is a Fair Trial Possible in Juvenile Court?" *Crime and Delinquency* **40**:599–615.

SANBORN, JOSEPH B., JR. (1995). "How Parents Can Affect the Processing of Delinquents in the Juvenile Court." *Criminal Justice Policy Review* **7**:1–266.

SANDERS, WILEY B. (1945). *Some Early Beginnings of the Children's Court Movement in England.* New York: National Council on Crime and Delinquency.

SANDYS, MARLA and EDMUND F. McGARRELL (1995). "Attitudes toward Capital Punishment: Preference for the Penalty or Mere Acceptance?" *Journal of Research in Crime and Delinquency* **32**:191–213.

SARRI, R. C. (1983). "Gender Issues in Juvenile Justice." *Crime and Delinquency* **29**:381–397.

SARRI, R. C. (1988). "Keynote Remarks." Conference on Increasing Educational Equity for Juvenile Female Offenders. Washington, DC: Council of Chief State School Officers.

SARRI, R. C. and Y. HANSENFELD (eds.) (1976). *Brought to Justice? Juveniles, the Courts and the Law.* Ann Arbor, MI: National Assessment of Juvenile Corrections.

SCHACK, ELIZABETH T. and HERMINE NESSEN (1984). *The Experiment That Failed: New York Juvenile Offender Law—A Study Report.* New York: Citizen's Committee for Children of New York, Inc.

SCHIFF, ALLISON R. and DAVID B. WEXLER (1996). "Teen Court: A Therapeutic Jurisprudence Perspective." *Criminal Law Bulletin* **32**:342–357.

SCHLEUTER, MAX ET AL. (1994). *Developing a Youthful Offender System for the State of Vermont.* Montpelier, VT: Vermont Center for Justice Research.

SCHNEIDER, ANNE L. (1984a). "Deinstitutionalization of Status Offenders: The Impact of Recidivism and Secure Confinement." *Criminal Justice Abstracts* (September):410–432.

SCHNEIDER, ANNE L. (1984b). "Divesting Status Offenses from Juvenile Court Jurisdiction." *Crime and Delinquency* **30**:347–370.

SCHNEIDER, ANNE LARSON and PETER R. SCHNEIDER (1985). "The Impact of Restitution on Recidivism of Juvenile Offenders: An Experiment in Clayton County, Georgia." *Criminal Justice Review* **10**:1–10.

SCHNEIDER, ANNE LARSON and DONNA D. SCHRAM (1986). "The Washington State Juvenile Justice System Reform: A Review of Findings." *Criminal Justice Policy Review* **2:**211–235.

SCHNEIDER, ERIC C. (1992). *In the Web of Class: Delinquents and Reformers in Boston, 1810s–1930s.* New York: New York University Press.

SCHUR, EDWIN (1973). *Radical Nonintervention: Rethinking the Delinquency Problem.* Upper Saddle River, NJ: Prentice Hall.

SCHWARTZ, IRA M. (1989). *(In)Justice for Juveniles: Rethinking the Best Interests of the Child.* Lexington, MA: Lexington Books.

SCHWARTZ, IRA M. (ed.) (1992). *Juvenile Justice and Public Policy.* New York: Lexington Books.

SCHWARTZ, IRA M. and WILLIAM H. BARTON (eds.) (1994). *Reforming Juvenile Detention: No More Hidden Closets.* Columbus, OH: Ohio State University Press.

SCHWARTZ, IRA M. and CHANG MING HSIEH (1994). *Juveniles Confined in the United States, 1979–1991.* Philadelphia, PA: Center for the Study of Youth Policy, University of Pennsylvania.

SEIS, MARK C. and KENNETH L. ELBE (1991). "The Death Penalty for Juveniles: Bridging the Gap between an Evolving Standard of Decency and Legislative Policy." *Justice Quarterly* **8:**465–487.

SELLERS, CHRISTINE (1987). "Juvenile Dispositions: How Far Does Legalism Go?" Unpublished paper presented at the Academy of Criminal Justice Sciences meetings, St. Louis, MO (March).

SHAFFNER, PAULA D. (1985). "Around and Around on Pennsylvania's Juvenile Confession Carousel: This Time the Police Get the Brass Ring." *Villanova Law Review* **30:**1235–1266.

SHARLIN, SHLOMO A. and MICHAL MOR-BARAK (1992). "Runaway Girls in Distress: Motivation, Background, and Personality." *Adolescence* **27:**387–405.

SHAW, JAMES W. and DORIS LAYTON MACKENZIE (1991). "Shock Incarceration and Its Impact on the Lives of Problem Drinkers." *American Journal of Criminal Justice* **16:**63–96.

SHAW, JAMES W. and DORIS LAYTON MACKENZIE (1992). "The One-Year Community Supervision Performance of Drug Offenders and Louisiana DOC-Identified Substance Abusers Graduating from Shock Incarceration." *Journal of Criminal Justice* **20:**501–516.

SHELDEN, RANDALL G. (1987). "The Chronic Delinquent: Gender and Race Differences." Unpublished paper presented at the American Society of Criminology meetings, Montreal, Quebec, Canada (November).

SHELDEN, RANDALL G. and JOHN A. HORVATH (1987). "Intake Processing in a Juvenile Court: A Comparison of Legal and Nonlegal Variables." *Juvenile and Family Court Journal* **38:**13–19.

SHELDEN, RANDALL G., JOHN A. HORVATH, and SHARON TRACY (1989). "Do Status Offenders Get Worse? Some Clarifications on the Question of Escalation." *Crime and Delinquency* **35:**202–216.

SHELEY, JOSEPH F. and JAMES D. WRIGHT (1995). *In the Line of Fire: Youth, Guns and Violence in Urban America.* Hawthorne, NY: Aldine de Gruyter.

SHERRADEN, MICHAEL W. and SUSAN WHITELAW DOWNS (1984). "Institutions and Juvenile Delinquency in Historical Perspective." *Children and Youth Services Review* **6:**155–172.

SHICHOR, DAVID and CLEMENS BARTOLLAS (1990). "Private and Public Juvenile Placements: Is There a Difference?" *Crime and Delinquency* **36**:286–299.

SHINE, JAMES and DWIGHT PRICE (1992). "Prosecutors and Juvenile Justice: New Roles and Perspectives." In *Juvenile Justice and Public Policy: Toward a National Agenda*, I. M. Schwartz (ed.). New York: Lexington Books.

SICKMUND, MELISSA (1994). *How Juveniles Get to Criminal Court*. Washington, DC: Office of Juvenile Justice and Delinquency Prevention.

SIEGEL, LARRY J. and JOSEPH J. SENNA (1988). *Juvenile Delinquency: Theory, Practice, and the Law*, 3rd ed. St. Paul, MN: West Publishing Company.

SIMMONS, JOHN A. ET AL. (1995). *Punishment: A Philosophy and Public Affairs Reader*. Princeton, NJ: Princeton University Press.

SIMON, RITA J. and JUDITH D. SIMON (1988). "Female COs: Legitimate Authority." *Corrections Today* **50**:132–134.

SIMONE, MARGARET V. (1984). "Group Homes: Succeeding by Really Trying." *Corrections Today* **46**:110–119.

SIMPSON, SALLY S. and LORI ELIS (1995). "Doing Gender: Sorting Out the Caste and Crime Conundrum." *Criminology* **33**:47–81.

SINGER, SIMON I. (1985). *Relocating Juvenile Crime: The Shift from Juvenile to Criminal Justice*. Albany, NY: Nelson A. Rockefeller Institute of Government.

SINGER, SIMON I. (1993). "The Automatic Waiver of Juveniles and Substantive Justice." *Crime and Delinquency* **39**:253–261.

SINGER, SIMON I. and DAVID McDOWALL (1988). "Criminalizing Delinquency: The Deterrent Effects of the New York Juvenile Offender Law." *Law and Society Review* **22**:521–535.

SKOLNICK, JEROME H. and DAVID H. BAYLEY (1986). *The New Blue Line: Police Innovation in Six American Cities*. New York: Free Press.

SLONIM-NEVO, VERED ET AL. (1996). "The Long-Term Impact of AIDS-Preventive Interventions for Delinquent and Abused Adolescents." *Adolescence* **31**:409–421.

SLUDER, RICHARD D. and FRANCES P. REDDINGTON (1993). "An Empirical Examination of the Work Ideologies of Juvenile and Adult Probation Officers." *Journal of Offender Rehabilitation* **20**:115–137.

SMITH, DAVID JAMES (1994). *Beyond All Reason: The Crime That Shocked the World—The Story of Two British Ten-Year-Old Killers and Their Three-Year Old Victim*. New York: Donald I. Fine, Inc.

SMITH, GEORGE C. (1986). *Capital Punishment 1986: Last Lines of Defense*. Washington, DC: Washington Legal Foundation.

SMITH, J. STEVEN (1991). "A Lesson from Indiana: Detention Is an Invaluable Part of the System, But It's Not the Solution to All Youths' Problems." *Corrections Today* **53**:56–60.

SMITH, MELINDA (1990). "New Mexico Youths Use Mediation to Settle Their Problems Peacefully." *Corrections Today* **52**:112–114.

SMITH, M. DWAYNE (1996). "Sources of Firearm Acquisition among a Sample of Inner-City Youths: Research Results and Policy Implications." *Journal of Criminal Justice* **24**:361–367.

SNYDER, HOWARD N. (1988). *Court Careers of Juvenile Offenders*. Pittsburgh, PA: National Center for Juvenile Justice.

SNYDER, HOWARD N. and MELISSA SICKMUND (1995). *Juvenile Offenders and Victims: A Focus on Violence*. Washington, DC: U.S. Office of Juvenile Justice and Delinquency Prevention.

SNYDER, HOWARD N., MELISSA SICKMUND and EILEEN POE-YAMAGATA (1996). *Juvenile Offenders and Victims: 1996 Update on Violence: Statistics Summary*. Pittsburgh, PA: National Center for Juvenile Justice.

SNYDER, KEITH B. and CECIL MARSHALL (1990). "Pennsylvania's Juvenile Intensive Probation and Aftercare Programs." Unpublished paper presented at the American Society of Criminology meetings, Baltimore, MD (November).

Sommers, Ira and Deborah R. Baskin (1994). "Factors Related to Female Adolescent Initiation into Violent Street Crime." *Youth and Society* **25**:468–489.

SONTHEIMER, HENRY and LYNNE GOODSTEIN (1993). "An Evaluation of Juvenile Intensive Aftercare Probation: Aftercare Versus System Response Effects." *Justice Quarterly* **10**:197–227.

SONTHEIMER, HENRY, LYNNE GOODSTEIN and MICHAEL KOVACEVIC (1990). *Philadelphia Intensive Aftercare Probation Evaluation Project*. Harrisburg, PA: Pennsylvania Commission on Crime and Delinquency.

SORRENTINO, ANTHONY and DAVID WHITTAKER (1994). "The Chicago Area Project: Addressing the Gang Problem." *FBI Law Enforcement Bulletin* **63**:8–12.

SPERGEL, IRVING A. (1995). *The Youth Gang Problem: A Community Approach*. New York: Oxford University Press.

SPRINGER, CHARLES E. (1987). *Justice for Juveniles*. Rockville, MD: U.S. National Institute for Juvenile Justice and Delinquency Prevention.

SPRINGER, J. FRED (1991). "Selective Aftercare for Juvenile Parolees: Administrative Environment and Placement Decisions." In *Intensive Interventions with High-Risk Youths: Promising Approaches in Juvenile Probation and Parole*. Monsey, NY: Criminal Justice Press.

SPRINGER, MERLE E. (1976). "A Framework for the Public–Voluntary Collaboration in the Social Services—The Role of the Governmental Sector." In *The Social Welfare Forum*. New York: National Association of Social Welfare Organizations.

SPRINGER, MERLE E. (1988). "Youth Service Privatization: The Experience of a Provider." *Corrections Today* **50**:88–93.

STALANS, LORETTA J. and GARY T. HENRY (1994). "Societal Views of Justice for Adolescents Accused of Murder: Inconsistency between Community Sentiment and Automatic Legislative Transfers." *Law and Human Behavior* **18**:675–696.

STEFFENSMEIER, DARRELL and MILES D. HARER (1991). "Did Crime Rise or Fall during the Reagan Presidency? The Effects of an 'Aging' U.S. Population on the Nation's Crime Rate." *Journal of Research in Crime and Delinquency* **28**:330–359.

STEIN, ABBY, DOROTHY OTNOW LEWIS and CATHERINE A. YEAGER (1993). "The Juvenile Justice Assessment Instrument." *Juvenile and Family Court Journal* **44**:91–102.

STEINBERG, KAREN LESLIE, MURRAY LEVINE, and SIMON SINGER (1992). *All Things in Moderation: The ACD Adjudication among Status Offense Cases*. Buffalo, NY: Baldy Center for Law and Social Policy, SUNY at Buffalo.

STEINHART, DAVID (1988). *California Opinion Poll: Public Attitudes on Youth Crime*. San Francisco: National Council on Crime and Delinquency.

STEPHAN, JAMES J. and TRACY L. SNELL (1996). *Capital Punishment 1994*. Washington, DC: U.S. Department of Justice.

STITT, B. GRANT and SHELDON SIEGEL (1986). "The Ethics of Plea Bargaining." Unpublished paper presented at the Academy of Criminal Justice Sciences meetings, Orlando, FL (March).

STREIB, VICTOR L. (1987). *The Death Penalty for Juveniles*. Bloomington, IN: Indiana University Press.

STRONG, ANN (1981). *Case Classification Manual, Module One: Technical Aspects of Interviewing*. Austin, TX: Texas Adult Probation Commission.

STRUCKHOFF, DAVID R. (1987). "Selective Incapacitation." *Corrections Today* **49**:30–34.

STUTT, HOWARD (ED.) (1986). *Learning Disabilities and the Young Offender: Arrest to Disposition*. Ottawa, Ontario, Canada: Canadian Association for Children and Adults with Learning Disabilities.

SULLIVAN, PATRICK M. (1988). "Juvenile Facility Design: Unique Needs, Unique Construction." *Corrections Today* **50**:38–44.

SUTTON, JOHN R. (1985). "The Juvenile Court and Social Welfare: Dynamics of Progressive Reform." *Law and Society Review* **19**:107–145.

SWEET, JOSEPH (1985). "Probation as Therapy." *Corrections Today* **47**:89–90.

SWENSON, CYNTHIA CUPIT and WALLACE A. KENNEDY (1995). "Perceived Control and Treatment Outcome with Chronic Adolescent Offenders." *Adolescence* **30**:565–578.

TAYLOR, CARL S. (1986). *Black Urban Youth Gangs: Analysis of Contemporary Issues*. Unpublished paper presented at the American Society of Criminology meetings. San Francisco (November).

TAYLOR, WILLIAM J. (1992). "Tailoring Boot Camps to Juveniles." *Corrections Today* **54**:122–124.

TEDISCO, JAMES N. and MICHELE A. PALUDI (1996). *Missing Children: A Psychological Approach to Understanding the Causes and Consequences of Stranger and Non-stranger Abduction of Children*. Albany, NY: State University of New York Press.

TERRY, WALLACE (1997). "He Shows Them a Way Out of Violence." *Parade Magazine*, January 26:4–7.

TESS, GENE and KATHRYN BOGUE (1988). "Master Correctional Officer Program: An Idea with a Future." *American Jails* **1**:66–67.

TEXAS BILL BLACKWOOD LAW ENFORCEMENT MANAGEMENT INSTITUTE (1994). *Juvenile Curfews*. Huntsville, TX: TELEMASP.

TEXAS YOUTH COMMISSION (1990). *Independent Living: An Evaluation*. Austin, TX: Texas Youth Commission Department of Research and Planning.

THOMPSON, KEVIN M., DAVID BROWNFIELD, and ANN MARIE SORENSON (1996). "Specialization Patterns of Gang and Nongang Offending: A Latent Structure Analysis." *Journal of Gang Research* **3**:25–35.

THOMPSON, LINDA S. and JAMES A. FARROW (EDS.) (1993). *Hard Time, Healing Hands: Developing Primary Health Care Services for Incarcerated Youth*. Arlington, VA: U.S. National Center for Education in Maternal and Child Health.

THORNBERRY, TERENCE P., ROLF LOEBER, and DAVID HUIZINGA (1991). "Symposium on the Causes and Correlates of Juvenile Delinquency." *Journal of Criminal Law and Criminology* **82**:1–155.

THORNBERRY, TERENCE P., STEWART E. TOLNAY and TIMOTHY J. FLANAGAN (1991). *Children in Custody 1987: A Comparison of Public and Private Juvenile Custody Facilities.* Washington, DC: U.S. Office of Juvenile Justice and Delinquency Prevention.

THORNTON, WILLIAM E., JR., LYDIA VOIGT, and WILLIAM G. DOERNER (1987). *Delinquency and Justice.* New York: Random House.

THURMAN, QUINT C., ANDREW GIACOMAZZI, and PHIL BOGEN (1993). "Research Note: Cops, Kids and Community Policing: An Assessment of a Community Policing Project." *Crime and Delinquency* **39**:554–564.

TITTLE, CHARLES R. and ROBERT F. MEIER (1990). "Specifying the SES/Delinquency Relationship." *Criminology* **28**:271–299.

TOLAN, PATRICK and NANCY GUERRA (1994). *What Works in Reducing Adolescent Violence: An Empirical Review of the Field.* Boulder, CO: Center for the Study and Prevention of Violence, University of Colorado.

TOMSON, BARBARA and EDNA R. FIELDER (1975). "Gangs: A Response to the Urban World." In *Gang Delinquency*, Desmond S. Cartwright, Barbara Tomson, and Hershey Schwartz (eds.). Pacific Grove, CA: Brooks/Cole.

TONRY, MICHAEL and NORVAL MORRIS (eds.) (1986). *Crime and Justice: An Annual Review of Research*, Vol. 7. Chicago: University of Chicago Press.

TORBET, PATRICIA ET AL. (1996). *State Responses to Serious and Violent Juvenile Crime.* Washington, DC: Office of Juvenile Justice and Delinquency Prevention.

TORBET, PATRICIA McFALL (1987). *Organization and Administration of Juvenile Services: Probation, Aftercare, and State Delinquent Institutions.* Pittsburgh, PA: National Center for Juvenile Justice.

TOROK, WAYNE C. and KENNETH S. TRUMP (1994). "Gang Intervention: Police and School Collaboration." *FBI Law Enforcement Bulletin* **63**:13–17.

TOWBERMAN, DONNA B. (1992). "A National Survey of Juvenile Risk Assessment." *Juvenile and Family Court Journal* **43**:61–67.

TRACY, P., M. WOLFGANG, and R. FIGLIO (1985). *Delinquency in Two Birth Cohorts: Executive Summary.* Washington, DC: U.S. Department of Justice.

TRAVISONO, ANTHONY P. (1989). "Juvenile Corrections: What Road to the Future?" *Corrections Today* **51**:4.

TREANOR, WILLIAM W. and ADRIENNE E. VOLENIK (1987). *The New Right's Juvenile Crime and Justice Agenda for the States: A Legislator's Briefing Book.* Washington, DC: American Youth Work Center.

TREMBLAY, RICHARD E. (1992). *The Prediction of Delinquent Behavior from Childhood Behavior: Personality Theory Revisited.* New Brunswick, NJ: Transaction.

TRESTER, HAROLD B. (1981). *Supervison of the Offender.* Upper Saddle River, NJ: Prentice Hall.

TRIPLETT, RUTH and LAURA B. MYERS (1995). "Evaluating Contextual Patterns of Delinquency: Gender-Based Differences." *Justice Quarterly* **12**:59–84.

TROJANOWICZ, ROBERT and BONNIE BUCQUEROUX (1990). *Community Policing: A Contemporary Perspective.* Cincinnati, OH: Anderson Publishing Company.

TURNER, BOB (1988). "Cutting Red Tape: How Privatization Can Help the Public Sector Perform More Efficiently." *Corrections Today* **50**:74–87.

UNITED STATES CODE (1997). *United States Code Annotated.* St. Paul, MN: West Publishing Company.

UNIVERSITY OF HAWAII AT MANOA (1990). Gun Control: A Youth Issue. Honolulu, HI: Social Science Research Institute, Center for Youth Research, University of Hawaii at Manoa.

URSA INSTITUTE (1993). *Community Involvement in Mediation of First and Second Time Juvenile Offenders Project of the Community Board Program of San Francisco.* San Francisco: URSA Institute.

U.S. BUREAU OF JUSTICE STATISTICS (1988). *Criminal Justice Information Policy: Juvenile Records and Recordkeeping Systems.* Washington, DC: U.S. Bureau of Justice Statistics.

U.S. DEPARTMENT OF JUSTICE (1976). *Two Hundred Years of American Criminal Justice: An LEAA Bicentennial Study.* Washington, DC: Law Enforcement Assistance Administration.

U.S. DEPARTMENT OF JUSTICE (1988). *Report to the Nation on Crime and Justice.* Washington, DC: U.S. Government Printing Office.

U.S. DEPARTMENT OF JUSTICE (1996). *Probation and Parole Population Reaches About 3.8 Million.* Washington, DC: U.S. Department of Justice.

U.S. GENERAL ACCOUNTING OFFICE (1983). *Federally Supported Centers Provided Needed Services for Runaways and Homeless Youths.* Washington, DC: U.S. Government Printing Office.

U.S. GENERAL ACCOUNTING OFFICE (1991). *Noncriminal Juveniles: Detentions Have Been Reduced but Better Monitoring Is Needed.* Washington, DC: U.S. General Accounting Office.

U.S. GENERAL ACCOUNTING OFFICE (1994a). *Juvenile Justice: Admissions of Minors with Preadult Disorders to Private Psychiatric Hospitals.* Washington, DC: U.S. General Accounting Office.

U.S. GENERAL ACCOUNTING OFFICE (1994b). *Residential Care: Some High-Risk Youth Benefit, But More Study Needed.* Washington, DC: U.S. General Accounting Office.

U.S. GENERAL ACCOUNTING OFFICE (1995a). *Juvenile Justice: Minimal Gender Bias Occurred in Processing Noncriminal Juveniles.* Washington, DC: U.S. General Accounting Office.

U.S. GENERAL ACCOUNTING OFFICE (1995b). *Juvenile Justice: Representation Rates Varied as Did Counsel's Impact on Court Outcomes.* Washington, DC: U.S. General Accounting Office.

U.S. GENERAL ACCOUNTING OFFICE (1996). *At-Risk and Delinquent Youth: Multiple Federal Programs Raise Efficiency Questions.* Washington, DC: U.S. General Accounting Office.

U.S. SENATE JUDICIARY COMMITTEE (1984). *Deinstitutionalization of Juvenile Nonoffenders*: Hearing. Washington, DC: U.S. Government Printing Office.

VAN DEN HAAG, ERNEST (1986). "On Sentencing." In *Punishment and Privilege*, W. Bryon Groves and Graeme Newman (eds.). Albany, NY: Harrow & Heston.

VAN DINE, STEPHEN ET AL. (1977). "The Incapacitation of the Dangerous Offender: A Statistical Experiment." *Journal of Research on Crime and Delinquency* **14**:24–34.

VAN WORMER, KATHERINE (1990a). "The Hidden Juvenile Justice System in Norway: A Journey Back in Time." *Federal Probation* **54**:57–61 (reprinted from Corrections Today 52:106-116.).

VAN WORMER, KATHERINE (1990b). "Norway's Juvenile Justice System: A Journey Back in Time." *Corrections Today* **52**:106–116.

VIRGINIA COMMISSION ON YOUTH (1993). *Report on the Study ot Serious Juvenile Offenders.* Richmond, VA: Commonwealth of Virginia.

Virginia Commission on Youth (1994a). *Report of the Virginia Study of Confidentiality of Juvenile Records.* Richmond, VA: Virginia Commission on Youth.

Virginia Commission on Youth (1994b). *Report on the Study of Serious Juvenile Offenders.* Richmond, VA: Virginia Commission on Youth.

Virginia Department of Youth and Family Services (1995). *Reviewing Juvenile Probation toward Developing a Balanced Approach to Its Use in the Juvenile Justice System.* Richmond, VA: Commonwealth of Virginia.

Virginia State Crime Commission (1993). *Report on the Feasibility of Implementing Locally Operated Boot Camps for Juvenile Offenders.* Richmond, VA: Virginia State Crime Commission, Commonwealth of Virginia.

Visher, Christy A. (1987). "Incapacitation and Crime Control: Does a 'Lock 'Em Up' Strategy Reduce Crime?" *Justice Quarterly* **4**:513–543.

Visher, Christy A., Pamela K. Lattimore, and Richard L. Linster (1991). "Predicting the Recidivism of Serious Youthful Offenders Using Survival Models." *Criminology* **29**:329–366.

Vito, Gennaro F. (1984). "Developments in Shock Probation: A Review of Research Findings and Policy Implementations." *Federal Probation* **48**:22–27.

Vogel, Ron and Dean J. Champion (eds.) (1993). "Perspectives on Juvenile Delinquency." *Journal of Contemporary Criminal Justice* **9**:81–167.

Volenik, Adrienne E. (1986). *Sample Pleadings for Use in Juvenile Delinquency Proceedings.* Washington, DC: American Bar Association.

Waldorf, Dan et al. (1990). "Needle Sharing among Male Prostitutes: Preliminary Findings of the Prospero Project." Journal of Drug Issues *20:309–334.*

Walker, Robert N. (1995). *Psychology of the Youthful Offender,* 3rd ed. Springfield, IL: Charles C Thomas.

Walker, Samuel (1989). *Sense and Nonsense About Crime,* 2nd ed. Pacific Grove, CA: Brooks/Cole.

Wang, Zheng (1996). "Is the Pattern of Asian Gang Affiliation Different? A Multiple Regression Analysis." *Journal of Crime and Justice* **19**:113–128.

Washington State Task Force on Juvenile Issues (1992). *Interim Report.* Olympia, WA: Washington State Task Force on Juvenile Issues.

Watkins, John C., Jr. (1987). "The Convolution of Ideology: American Juvenile Justice from a Critical Legal Studies Perspective." Unpublished paper presented at the American Society of Criminology meetings, Montreal, Quebec, Canada (November).

Webb, David (1984). "More on Gender and Justice: Girl Offenders on Supervision." Sociology **18**:367–381.

Weber, Donald E. and William H. Burke (1986). "An Alternative Approach to Treating Delinquent Youth." *Residential Group Care and Treatment* **3**:65–86.

Weisheit, Ralph A. and Diane M. Alexander (1988). "Juvenile Justice Philosophy and the Demise of Parens Patriae." *Federal Probation* **52**:56–63.

Wells, L. Edward and *Joseph H. Rankin* (1995). "Juvenile Victimization: Convergent Validation of Alterative Measurements." *Journal of Research on Crime and Delinquency* **32**:287–307.

Welsh, Lesley A. et al. (1995). *Running for Their Lives: Physical and Sexual Abuse of Runaway Adolescents.* New York: Garland.

Whitehead, John T. and Charles Lindquist (1985). "Job Stress and Burnout among Probation/Parole Officers: Perceptions and Causal Factors." *International Journal of Offender Therapy and Comparative Criminology* **29**:109–119.

WIEBUSH, RICHARD G. (1990). "The Ohio Experience: Programmatic Variations in Intensive Supervision for Juveniles." *Perspectives* **14**:26–35.

WIEBUSH, RICHARD G. (1993). *At the Crossroads: Juvenile Corrections in the District of Columbia: Profiles of Committed Youth in Secure Care.* Washington, DC: Robert F. Kennedy Memorial.

WILKINSON, CHRISTINE and ROGER EVANS (1990). "Police Cautioning of Juveniles." *Criminal Law Review* (March):165–176.

WILLIAMS, KATHERINE and MARCIA I. COHEN (1993). *Determinants of Disproportionate Representation of Minority Juveniles in Secure Settings: Final Report, Preliminary Findings and Recommendations.* Fairfax, VA: Fairfax Juvenile and Domestic Relations District Court.

WILLIAMSON, DEBORAH, MICHELLE CHALK, and PAUL KNEPPER (1993). "Teen Court: Juvenile Justice for the 21st Century?" *Federal Probation* **57**:54–58.

WILLMAN, HERB C., JR. and RON Y. CHUN (1974). "Homeward Bound: An Alternative to the Institutionalization of Adjudicated Juvenile Offenders." In Alternatives to Imprisonment: Corrections and the Community, George C. Killinger and Paul F. Cromwell, Jr. (eds.). St. Paul, MN: West Publishing Company.

WOLFGANG, MARVIN, ROBERT M. FIGLIO, and THORSTEN SELLIN (1972). *Delinquency in a Birth Cohort.* Chicago: University of Chicago Press.

WOODWARD, BILL and KIM ENGLISH (1993). *Juvenile Intensive Supervision Probation Pilot Project: Phase One Study.* Denver, CO: Colorado Department of Public Safety.

WOOLDREDGE, JOHN ET AL. (1994). "Effectiveness of Culturally Specific Community Treatment for African American Juvenile Felons." *Crime and Delinquency* **40**:589–598.

WORDES, MADELINE, TIMOTHY S. BYNUM and CHARLES J. CORLEY (1994). "Locking Up Youth: The Impact of Race on Detention Decisions." *Journal of Research in Crime and Delinquency* **31**:149–165.

WORLING, JAMES R. (1995). "Adolescent Sex Offenders against Females: Differences Based on the Age of Their Victims." *International Journal of Offender Therapy and Comparative Criminology* **39**:276–293.

YEAGER, CLAY R., JOHN A. HERB, and JOHN H. LEMMON (1989). *The Impact of Court Unification on Juvenile Probation Systems in Pennsylvania.* Shippensburg, PA: Center for Juvenile Justice Training and Research, Shippensburg University.

YURKANIN, ANN (1989). "Trend toward Shock Incarceration Increasing among the States." *Corrections Today* **50**:87.

ZAZLOW, JAY G. (1989). "Stop Assaultive Children–Project SAC Offers Hope for Violent Juveniles." *Corrections Today* **51**:48–50.

ZIMET, GREGORY D. ET AL. (1995). "Sexual Behavior, Drug Use, and AIDS Knowledge among Midwestern Runaways." *Youth and Society* **26**:450–462.

ZIMMER, LYNN E. (1986). *Women Guarding Men.* Chicago: University of Chicago Press.

ZIMRING, FRANKLIN E. and GORDON HAWKINS (1995). *Incapacitation: Penal Confinement and the Restraint of Crime.* New York: Oxford University Press.

NAME INDEX

Binder, Arnold, 386, 391
Bishop, Donna M., 16, 70, 92, 136, 181
Black, Henry Campbell, 5, 13–14, 36, 274, 480
Blackmore, John, 42, 163
Blackwell, Brenda Sims, 365
Blustein, Jeffrey, 15
Bogen, Phil, 141
Bogue, Kathryn, 497
Bohm, Robert M., 365–367
Bolyard, Melissa, 453
Bond-Maupin, Lisa, 115, 121
Boone, Harry N. Jr., 444, 447–448
Bortner, M.A., 115, 121
Bottcher, Jean, 179, 455
Bourque, Blair B., 452
Bowling, Linda R., 397
Brame, Robert, 182
Brandau, Timothy J., 187, 383, 415
Brantley, Alan C., 119, 137–138
Braswell, Michael, 114
Breed, Allen F., 379, 414, 496, 522
Briar, Scott, 123
Brooks, John H., 179
Brown, J.W., 501
Brown, Marci, 42, 163
Brown, Paul W., 472
Brownfield, David, 196
Bucqueroux, Bonnie, 115, 137–138
Bumby, Kurt M., 62
Burbidge, George S., 49
Burke, William H., 483
Burnett, Richard, 503
Bursick, Robert J. Jr., 365
Burton, Velmer S. Jr., 352–353, 470
Busch, Kenneth G., 289
Butts, Jeffrey A., 35, 57, 92, 107, 131, 150, 206, 217, 220, 245, 249, 257, 259, 261–264, 266, 329, 420, 482
Bynum, Timothy S., 157–158, 175, 482–483, 501
Byrne, James M., 414, 417

C

Caeti, Tory J., 352–353
Cahalan, Margaret W., 241, 480–482

Caldas, Stephen J., 122, 453
California Department of the Youth Authority, 522
California Little Hoover Commission, 21
California Youth Authority, 299–300
Cambridge Survey Research, 367
Camp, Camille, 19, 64–65, 93, 106–108, 229, 362, 444, 452, 468–469, 472, 479, 482, 500
Camp, George M., 19, 64–65, 93, 106–108, 229, 362, 444, 452, 468–469, 472, 479, 482, 500
Campbell, Anne, 67
Carcaterra, Lorenzo, 484
Carlson, Eric, 431
Carrington, Peter J., 273
Casey, Pamela, 175, 177, 204
Cash, Monette C., 23–24
Castellano, Thomas C., 494
Cavender, Gray, 504, 506, 510, 516
Center, Tim, 128, 130
Chadwick, Susan M., 416
Chalk, Michelle, 396
Challeen, Dennis, 251
Chamberlain, Patricia, 457
Chambers, Ola R., 512
Chamlin, Mitchell B., 367
Champion, Dean J., 12, 16, 86, 90, 103, 114, 117, 124, 126, 128, 139, 153, 155, 158, 163, 175–176, 178, 184, 186, 209, 216, 226, 228, 231, 252, 270, 272–273, 283, 293, 296–297, 505
Charles, Michael T., 445–446
Cheatwood, Derral, 367
Chesney-Lind, Meda, 67, 69–70, 79, 133, 136, 157, 182–183, 386, 388
Cheung, Paul P.L., 99, 174, 330
Chicago Crime Commission, 117, 121, 123
Chicago Police Department, 61
Chun, Ron Y., 494
Cicourel, Aaron V., 114, 121
Clagett, Arthur F., 493
Clark, Louise J., 365, 367
Clarke, Stevens H., 415
Clarkson, John Stanley, 444, 496
Clear, Todd R., 423

Cochran, John K., 367
Cohen, Marcia I., 136–137, 142, 156, 183, 185
Cohn, Alvin W., 12
Colley, Lori L., 45, 47, 133
Collins, James J., 40, 131, 135
Colorado Springs Police Department, 21
Conley, Darlene J., 121–122, 126
Conley, John A., 48
Connecticut Gang Task Force, 121
Corley, Charles J., 157–158, 175, 482, 501
Costanzo, Samuel A., 366, 436–437
Coumarelos, Christine, 161–162, 328, 384, 386
Cox, Stephen M., 483
Craddock, Amy D., 415
Crippen, Gary, 131
Criswell, John E., 499, 523
Cronin, Robert C., 502
Crosby, L., 292
Crosby, Todd, 48, 134, 452
Culbertson, Robert G., 45, 47, 133
Curran, Daniel J., 69
Curtis, Christine, 160–161, 170, 185, 283
Curtis, Russell L. Jr., 136

D

Dale, Michael J., 94, 270, 526–527
Datesman, Susan K., 45, 62, 418, 524
Davidson, William S., 400, 483
Davis, Al, 496
Dawson, Robert O., 203, 234
Dean, Charles W., 182
Decker, Scott H., 365, 367
DeComo, Robert E., 500, 504
deKeijser, Jan W., 415
del Carmen, Rolando V., 522
DeMuro, Paul, 107, 420
Deschenes, Elizabeth Piper, 282, 510
DeMan, Anton, 158
DeZolt, Ernest M., 179–180
DiCataldo, Frank, 102, 105
Dicks, Shirley, 366
DiGiorgio-Miller, Janet, 23
DiRosa, Andrew W., 137–138
Dishion, Thomas J., 373

Doerner, William G., 188, 482
Dolin, Ira H., 70
Doob, Anthony N., 290
Dornfeld, Maude, 195, 373–374
Dougherty, Joyce, 150, 154–156, 227
Downs, William R., 161–162, 521
DuRant, Robert H., 195, 374
Dwyer, Diane C., 376, 521

E

Eason, Carol S., 527
Edwards, Leonard P., 92, 95
Eggertson-Tacon, Colleen, 162
Elbe, Kenneth L., 365
Elis, Lori, 179
Elliott, Delbert S., 58–59, 64, 195, 334, 368, 373
Ellsworth, Thomas, 16, 18, 21, 100, 157, 185, 266, 429–432
Elrod, H. Preston, 283
Emerson, Robert M., 255
English, Kim, 414, 416
Epps, Kevin J., 179
Epstein, Irwin, 150, 178, 490
Erwin, Billie S., 421
Evans, Donald, 447
Evans, Roger, 160
Ewing, Charles Patrick, 289

F

Fabelo, Tony, 181
Fagan, Jeffrey A., 183, 227, 282, 286, 423, 501
Famighetti, Robert, 33
Famularo, Richard, 39, 135, 188
Farnworth, Margaret, 169, 326
Farrow, James A., 503
Fawcett, Margaret, 489–490
Feeney, Floyd, 251, 328
Feinberg, Norma, 423
Feld, Barry C., 12–13, 16, 19, 25–26, 28, 100, 102, 135, 150, 153, 163–164, 176, 182, 211, 221–223, 228, 232, 240, 246, 249–252, 266–267, 270, 328, 339, 357, 377, 502
Ferdinand, Theodore N., 10
Fielder, Edna R., 123

Fields, Charles B., 188, 388
Figlio, Robert M., 296, 409
Fish, Lee, 48, 134, 452
Flanagan, Timothy J., 131, 135
Flango, Victor E., 21, 375, 377
Flannery, Daniel J., 179
Flexner, Bernard, 413
Florida Advisory Council on Intergovernmental Relations, 210, 222, 452
Florida Department of Corrections, 454
Florida Governor's Juvenile Justice and Delinquency Prevention Advisory Committee, 39, 42, 133
Florida House Committee on Criminal Justice, 150, 155, 178, 471
Florida Office of the Auditor General, 21
Florida Office of Program Policy Analysis, 452, 456
Florida Statistical Analysis Center, 116, 121
Florida Supreme Court, 121, 128
Flowers, R. Barri, 40
Fogel, David, 24, 25–26
Ford, Michelle E., 133
Forst, Martin L., 116, 227–228, 365
Fraser, Mark, 228
Frazier, Charles E., 16, 70, 92, 136, 169, 181, 206, 326
Fuller, John R., 25, 37, 42, 184, 284, 386

G

Gable, Jeffrey, 266, 482
Gable, Ralph Kirkland, 444
Galaway, Burt, 489
Garrett, C., 482
Gavzer, B., 494–495
Geiger, Brenda, 24
Gelber, Seymour, 167, 361, 373
Gelsthorpe, Loraine R., 67–69
Gerdes, Karen, 23–24
Giacomazzi, Andrew, 141
Giddings, Martha M., 136–137, 157
Gilcher, Donna C., 179–180
Gourley, M. Michelle, 23–24
Gilliard, Darrell K., 86, 93, 501
Gittens, Joan, 3, 13

Glick, Barry, 68, 70, 483, 502, 506, 528–529
Godfrey, Michael J., 367
Goldsmith, Herbert R., 506
Goldstein, Arnold P., 68, 70, 483, 502, 506, 528–529
Goodstein, Lynne, 24, 411, 430, 492
Goodwin, Dennis W., 394
Gottfredson, Denise C., 48
Gottfredson, Don M., 296–297, 418, 525
Gottfredson, Michael, 249
Gottfredson, Stephen D., 296–297, 418, 525
Gottlieb, Barbara, 94
Gowan, Darren, 447
Gowdy, Voncile B., 415, 454–456
Grasmick, Harold G., 365
Green, Maurice, 164
Greenwood, Peter W., 24–25, 42, 296, 484–485, 494–495, 510
Griffin, Brenda S., 8
Griffin, Charles T., 8
Grisso, Thomas, 92, 102, 105, 175, 177, 204, 353
Grissom, Grant R., 16
Guarino-Ghezzi, Susan, 122–123, 126, 128, 137, 525
Guerra, Nancy, 491
Guggenheim, Martin, 14, 155, 501

H

Haas, Kenneth C., 365–367
Hagedorn, John, 61
Haghighi, Bahram, 483
Halemba, Gregory J., 257, 263
Hahn, Paul H., 12, 482
Hale, Donna C., 13, 70, 417
Hamilton, Edwin, 128, 160, 172
Hamparian, Donna M., 185
Han, Mel, 452
Hancock, Paula, 251
Hanke, Penelope J., 3, 60–61
Hansen, Karen V., 62
Harada, Tutaka, 289, 386
Hardwick, Peter J., 500
Harer, Miles D., 55

Krisberg, Barry, 23–24, 42, 44, 105, 163, 167, 184, 187, 282–283, 289, 326, 330, 383, 386, 414, 416–417, 483, 496, 500, 522

Kruttschitt, Candace, 195, 373–374

Kupfersmid, Joel, 185

Kurtz, P. David, 136–137, 157

Kurz, Gwen A., 409–410

L

Lab, Steven P., 63, 411–412

Land, Kenneth C., 133

Lang, K., 180

Larivee, John, 397

Latessa, Edward J., 454, 470

Lattimore, Pamela K., 23, 282, 284, 289, 292

Laub, John H., 25, 248, 253–254, 378

Laurence, S.E., 442–443

Lawrence, Richard A., 157, 269, 336, 434

LeCroy, Winston, 330, 410, 504, 508–509

Lee, Leona, 106

Leiber, Michael J., 149, 152, 156, 226, 339, 410–411

Lemert, Edwin M., 154, 161–162

Lemmon, John H., 375

Leschied, Alan W., 106

Levine, Irene, 60–61

Levine, Murray, 135, 157

Lewis, Dorothy Otnow, 70, 502

Lieb, Roxanne, 48, 134, 452

Lilly, J. Robert, 448

Lindner, Charles, 188, 383, 388, 400, 415, 421

Lindquist, Charles, 472

Lindstrom, Peter, 39

Linney, Jean Ann, 133

Linster, Richard L., 23, 282, 284, 289, 292

Lipson, Karin, 139

Listug, David, 446

Little Hoover Commission, 130, 135

Little, Margaret A., 97

Locke, Thomas P., 25

Lockhart, Lettie L., 158, 184

Loeber, Rolf, 59, 373

Logan, Charles H., 45, 134

Lombardo, Rita, 23

Lonardi, Barbara M., 497

Longmire, Dennis R., 524

Lopez, Alma, 483

Lujan, Carol Chiago, 115, 121

Lundman, Richard J., 452

Luneburg, William V., 48, 131, 133

Lurigio, Arthur J., 414, 417

Lutze, Faith, 454

M

Macallair, Dan, 48

Macallair, D.E., 419

Mack, Dennis E., 454

MacKenzie, Doris Layton, 453–456

MacMurray, Bruce K., 253–254, 378

Maguire, Kathleen, 19, 33, 39–40, 57, 61, 65, 75, 92, 107, 116, 177, 224, 228, 281–282, 285, 329, 415, 479, 485, 500, 508

Mahoney, Anne Rankin, 171, 224

Maine Juvenile Corrections Task Force, 496

Mainprize, Stephen, 167, 444

Malmquist, Carl P., 283

Maloney, Dennis M., 106, 176, 377, 432, 502–503

Maltz, Michael D., 414, 511

Manfredi, Christopher, 25, 78, 164, 378

Manikas, Peter M., 121, 128

Mardon, Steven, 428

Marshall, Cecil, 421

Martin, Brad, 210

Martin, Joe R., 116–118

Martinson, Robert, 482

Massin, Kimberlee, 16, 18, 21, 100, 157, 185, 266

Matsuo, Wayne, 79, 133, 386, 388

Mawhorr, Tina L., 410–411

Maxfield, Michael G., 449

Maxson, Cheryl L., 97

Mays, G. Larry, 16, 37, 86, 90, 116, 155, 158, 166, 175–176, 186, 209, 241, 270, 338, 480, 486

McAnany, Patrick D., 22

McCabe, K.A., 503

McCall, Patricia L., 133

McCarthy, Belinda R., 90, 101–102, 104, 106, 172, 174, 176, 179–181, 222, 228, 262, 266, 330, 395, 405, 443, 492–494, 524, 527

McCarthy, Bernard J., 90, 101, 104, 106, 228, 405, 443, 492–494

McCollum, Loretta L., 92, 95

McCord, David M., 492

McDermott, M. Joan, 25, 248

McDonald, William F., 81, 154, 226

McDowell, David, 329

McGarrell, Edmund F., 365, 483

McMillen, Michael J., 528–529

McNally, Roger B., 376, 394, 521

McShane, Marilyn D., 47, 130–131, 134, 188–189, 386

Meier, Robert F., 182

Menard, Scott, 59–60

Mendel, Richard A., 117, 126

Mendelsohn, Robert, 449

Mennel, Robert M., 481

Mershon, Jerry L., 16, 135, 149, 158, 227, 269

MetaMetrics, Inc., 392

Metsger, Linda K., 209–210, 216, 220, 339

Michigan Law Review, 254

Michon, John A.L., 415

Miller, Darcy, 490

Miller, Edward, 366

Miller, Larry, 114

Miller, Neal, 130

Miller, A. Therese, 162

Milton S. Eisenhower Foundation, 139

Minnesota Criminal Justice Analysis Center, 42, 167, 288

Minnesota Department of Corrections, 500

Minnesota Sentencing Guidelines Commission, 206, 219, 221, 231

Minor, Kevin I., 283

Mitchell, Bill, 452

Mitchell, John J., 25, 392

Mixdorf, Lloyd, 94, 115

Molidor, Christian E., 122

Mones, Paul, 197

Monkman, Roberta, 185

Montgomery, Imogene M., 457

Moore, David C., 410, 418

Moore, Eugene A., 162–163, 374, 484

Moore, Louis E., 409–410

Morash, Merry, 123

Mor-Barak, Michal, 40–41

More, Harry W., 114

Morris, Norval, 42

Motte, Elaine, 497

Moyer, Sharon, 273

Murphy, Edward M., 283, 331, 437–442

Musick, David, 10

Mutchnick, Robert J., 489–490

Myers, Laura B., 179–180

Myers, Wade C., 62

N

Naffine, Ngaire, 274

Nagoshi, Jack T., 172, 418, 524

National Advisory Committee for Juvenile Justice and Delinquency Prevention, 384

National Center for Juvenile Justice, 57, 115

National College of Juvenile and Family Law, 330

National Conference of State Legislatures, 105

National Council of Juvenile and Family Court Judges, 377

National Council on Crime and Delinquency, 107, 135, 137, 331

Nessen, Hermine, 231

New Jersey Division of Criminal Justice, 232

New Jersey Juvenile Delinquency Commission, 504

New York Commission for the Study of Youth Crime and Violence and the Reform of the Juvenile Justice System, 139

New York State Department of Correctional Services, 454

New York State Division of Criminal Justice Services, 114, 117

New York State Division of Parole, 108

Niarhos, Frances Johnson, 172, 184

Neuberger, Anita R., 169, 326

Robinson, Dinah A., 62, 368

Rodatus, Robert V., 274

Rogers, Joseph W., 37, 116, 166, 241, 319–320, 326, 338, 384, 480, 486

Romig, Dennis A., 106, 176, 377, 389, 432

Rosen, Phillip, 94

Rosenbaum, Jill Leslie, 64, 122, 157, 182–183, 290, 367

Rosenzweig, L., 128

Rossum, Ralph, A., 25, 78, 164, 378

Rothstein, Natalie, 396

Rousch, David W., 499

Routh, Donald K., 172, 184

Rowan, Joseph R., 388

Rowe, David C., 179

Rowton-Lee, Martyn A., 500

Roy, Sudipto, 163, 328, 410, 443–448, 457, 459

Rubin, H. Ted, 106, 219, 231, 284, 329, 377, 458

Rush, George E., 114, 117, 124, 126, 139

Rush, Jeffrey P., 459

Russell, Robin, 135

Ryan, C.J., 93–94

Ryan, T.A., 503

S

Sagatun, Inger J., 92, 95

Sametz, Lynn, 377, 490

Sanborn, Joseph B. Jr., 14, 22, 202, 223, 226–227, 274–275, 336, 339

Sanders, Wiley B., 7

Sandys, Marla, 365

Sarri, R.C., 69–70, 395

Saunders, Elisabeth B., 196

Schack, Elizabeth T., 231

Scheck, Dennis C., 160–161, 170, 185, 283

Schiff, Allison R., 395–396

Schiraldi, Vincent N., 367, 419

Schleuter, Max, 210

Schmidt, Linda M., 179–180

Schneider, Anne Larson, 43–45, 47–48, 165, 251–252, 376, 388, 457

Schneider, Eric C., 5, 14

Schneider, Peter R., 457

Schondel, Connie, 411–412

Schram, Donna D., 47, 165, 251

Schulze, Arnie D., 116–118

Schur, Edwin, 162

Schwartz, Ira M., 16, 19, 150, 156, 172, 178, 386, 458, 483, 490

Secret, Philip E., 16, 504

Sedlak, Ursala, 135

Seis, Mark C., 365

Sellers, Christine, 164

Sellin, Thorsten, 296, 409

Senese, Jeffrey D., 93

Senna, Joseph J., 162

Seth, Mark, 367

Shaffner, Paula D., 164, 270

Sharlin, Shlomo A., 40–41

Shaw, Clifford, 143

Shaw, James W., 453–456

Shelden, Randall G., 64, 67, 70, 99, 164, 179–180

Sheley, Joseph F., 61

Sherraden, Michael W., 521

Shichor, David, 283

Shields, Glenn, 411–412

Shiller, Gene, 452

Shine, James, 263–264

Sickmund, Melissa, 62, 65, 100, 106, 115–116, 125, 133, 175, 195, 203, 206, 220, 223, 231, 289, 394

Siegel, Larry J., 162

Siegel, Sheldon, 154–155

Siler, T.R., 430

Simmons, John A., 366–367

Simon, Judith D., 497

Simon, Rita J., 497

Simone, Margaret V., 400

Simpson, Sally S., 179

Singer, Simon I., 135, 157, 206, 221, 231, 329

Skolnick, Jerome H., 95

Slaughter, Ellen, 183

Slonim-Nevo, Vered, 500

Sluder, Richard D., 459

Smith, B.L., 179, 181, 524

Smith, David James, 61–62

Smith, J. Steven, 388

Smith, Melinda, 399

Smith, M. Dwayne, 196
Smith, Robert L., 379
Snell, Tracy L., 229, 362
Snyder, Howard N., 62, 65, 100, 106,
    115–116, 125, 133, 175, 179–180,
    195, 220, 223, 231, 289, 394, 421
Soderstrom, Irina R., 494
Sommers, Ira, 70, 178–179, 195, 373
Sontheimer, Henry, 24, 411, 430, 492
Sorenson, Ann Marie, 196
Sorrentino, Anthony, 119, 143–144, 290
Souryal, Claire, 454
Spergel, Irving A., 61, 283, 291
Springer, Charles E., 24, 251
Springer, Fred J., 492
Springer, Merle E., 524
Stalans, Loretta J., 3, 62, 165, 167, 171,
    185, 374
Steffensmeier, Darrell, 55
Stein, Abby, 502
Steinberg, Karen Leslie, 135, 157
Steinhart, David, 16, 164, 250, 377
Stephan, James J., 229, 362
Stephens, Otis H., 62, 368
Stitt, B. Grant, 154–155
Streib, Victor L., 90, 362, 364, 373
Strong, Ann, 467
Struckhoff, David R., 296
Sullivan, Patrick M., 496
Sutphen, Richard, 136–137, 157
Sutton, John R., 339
Suzuki, Shingo, 289, 386
Sweet, Joseph, 414, 467
Swenson, Cynthia Cupit, 493

T

Taylor, Carl S., 118
Taylor, Michael C., 70
Taylor, William J., 453
Terry, Wallace, 144
Tess, Gene, 497
Texas Bill Blackwood Law Enforcement
    Management Institute, 115–117, 121
Texas Youth Commission, 491
Thompson, Joel, 86
Thompson, Kevin M., 196

Thompson, Linda S., 503
Thomson, Doug, 22
Thornberry, Terence P., 59, 131, 135
Thornton, William E. Jr., 482
Thurman, Quint C., 141
Tittle, Charles R., 182
Tolan, Patrick, 491
Tolnay, Stewart E., 131, 135
Tomkins, Alan, 175, 177, 204
Tomson, Barbara, 123
Tonry, Michael, 42, 418, 525
Torbet, Patricia McFall, 106, 117, 125,
    129–130, 284–285, 326, 327, 330,
    376–377, 457, 473, 500
Torok, Wayne C., 117, 119, 138
Towberman, Donna B., 252, 262, 266,
    283, 330
Tracy, P,. 64, 409
Travisono, Anthony P,. 484–485
Treanor, William W., 378–379
Tremblay, Richard E., 284, 292
Trester, Harold B., 320
Triplett, Ruth, 179–180
Tripodi, Tony, 286
Trojanowicz, Robert, 115, 137–138
Tromanhauser, Edward D., 210
Trump, Kenneth S., 117, 138
Turner, Bob, 524
Turner, Susan, 415, 484, 494–495

U

University of Hawaii at Manoa, 291
U.S. Bureau of Justice Statistics, 121, 128
U.S. Department of Justice, 10, 86, 88, 212
U.S. General Accounting Office, 33, 48,
    64, 100, 131, 133, 135–138, 149, 152,
    155, 163, 167, 171–172, 176, 178–179,
    182, 184–185, 226, 251, 273, 340, 394,
    400, 434, 491, 496, 501, 503–504, 521
U.S. Senate Judiciary Committee, 45
URSA Institute, 393

V

Valdez, Mike, 116–118
van den Haag, Ernest, 227
Van Dine, Stephen, 296
Van Dusen, Kathrine Teilmann, 251

Vazsonyi, Alexander T., 179
Virginia Commission on Youth, 21, 209–210, 216, 219–220, 222, 226–227, 231
Virginia Department of Youth and Family Services, 432–433, 483
Virginia State Crime Commission, 452
Visher, Christy A., 23, 274, 282, 289, 292, 297
Vito, Gennaro F., 25, 450–452, 454
Vivona, T. Scott, 227
Vogel, Ronald E., 367, 505
Voigt, Lydia, 482
Volenik, Adrienne E., 102, 378–379
Vuchinich, S., 292

W

Waldorf, Dan, 171
Walker, Robert N., 62
Walker, Samuel, 196, 296–297
Wang, Zheng, 61
Washington State Task Force on Juvenile Issues, 40
Watkins, John C. Jr., 15, 36, 386
Weakland, James J., 444, 496
Weatherburn, Don ,161–162, 328, 384, 386
Webb, David, 70
Weber, Donald E., 483
Wedge, Robert, 409, 411, 512
Weideranders, Mark R., 512
Weisheit, Ralph A., 337
Wells, L. Edward, 55
Welsh, Lesley A., 97
West, Barbara R., 442–443, 496
Wexler, David B., 395–396

White, Lawrence T., 366
Whitehead, John T., 472
Whiteside, Leanne, 39
Whittaker, David, 143–144, 290
Widom, Cathy Spatz, 196, 374
Wiebush, Richard G., 102, 105, 176, 421, 423–429, 504
Wilkinson, Christine, 160
Williams, James D., 319
Williams, K.S., 93–94
Williams, Katherine, 136–137, 142, 156, 183, 185
Williams, Sharon A., 25, 392
Williamson, Deborah, 396
Willman, Herb C. Jr., 494
Wolfgang, Marvin, 296, 409
Woodward, Bill, 414, 416
Wooldredge, John, 504
Wordes, Madeline, 157–158, 175, 482, 501
Worling, James R., 98, 100, 156, 179
Wright, James D., 61
Wundersitz, Joy, 274
Wylen, Jane, 512

Y

Yeager, Catherine A., 502
Yeager, Clay R., 375
Yuan, Stevan, 490
Yurkanin, Ann, 451

Z

Zazlow, Jay G., 186
Zimet, Gregory D., 40
Zimmer, Lynn E., 499
Zimring, Franklin E., 106

TEXT INDEX

Behavioral Studies Program of the Pines Treatment Center, 394
Bell Telephone Company, 447
Bench trials, 84
Bensalem Youth Development Center (Philadelphia), 411
Beyond a reasonable doubt, 19, 254–255
Birth cohorts, 63–64, 409–410
Blended sentencing statutes, 232–235
 criminal-exclusive blend, 234–235
 criminal-inclusive blend, 235
 defined, 232
 juvenile-contiguous blend, 234
 juvenile-exclusive blend, 232
 juvenile-inclusive blend, 232–234
Blood alcohol levels, 101
Bluegrass County, Kentucky Program, 397–398
Booking, 80–81, 129
 juveniles, 129
Boot camps, 452–456
 defined, 452–453
 examples, 455–456
 goals, 453–454
 profile of clients, 454–455
 rationale, 453
Boston Offender Project (BOP), 437–442
 defined, 437
Brace, Charles Loring, 241–242, 481
Breed v. Jones, 347–348
Bridewell Workhouse, 7
Brokers, 467–468
Brown, James, 144
Bureau of Justice Statistics, 57
Burnout, 472
Buss-Durkee Hostility Inventory, 156

C

California Department of Corrections, 90
"California girls," 122
California Youth Authority, 19, 48, 107, 122, 299–300, 348, 395, 455
 female gang members, 122
 recidivism, 107
 risk instrument, 299–300
Camp Monterey Shock Incarceration Facility, 455
Camps, 492–495
Campus Pride, 140–141

Capital punishment (*See also* Death Penalty for Juveniles), 229
 defined, 229
Career escalation, 60–64
 defined, 62
Caseload assignment models, 431–432
 conventional model, 431
 conventional model with geographic considerations, 431
 numbers-game model, 431
 specialized caseload model, 431
Caseloads, 472
Cases in juvenile law, 340–348
Cellular devices, 444–445
Certifications, 100, 202–236
 defined, 202
 reasons for using, 203
 types, 210–215
Chancellors, 6, 15
Chancery courts, 6, 15
Chicago Area Project (CAP), 143–144
Chicago Reform School, 11
Child Behavior Checklist, 493
Children in need of supervision (CHINS), 138, 188–189, 200, 383, 486
Children's tribunals, 12, 481
Childsavers, 9, 242
Childsaving movement, 9
Chronic offenders, 40, 115, 284–285
Chronic 6 percent 409–410
Citizen action model, 389–390
Civil War, 11, 246, 481
Clark County (Nevada) Juvenile Court, 99
Classification, 95–97, 302–303, 524–526
 functions, 302–303
Cleared by arrest, 54
Cleveland Police Department, 117
Client Management Classification (CMC) System, 107, 430–431
Clinical prediction, 298
Cohorts, 63–64
Collective incapacitation, 297
Combination sentences, 450
Common law, 4, 6, 36
 applications for juveniles, 36
 defined, 6
Community aid panels (CAPs), 384–386
Community-based alternatives, 434–452
Community Board Program, 393

National Crime Victimization Survey
(NCVS), 34, 54–57, 60
criticisms, 54–57
defined, 54
self-reports, 60
National Institute of Corrections (NIC) Model
Classification Project, 406
National Juvenile Court Data Archive, 57
National Juvenile Detention Directory, 459–460
National Prison Association, 22
National Runaway and Homeless Youth
Program, 48
National Youth Survey, 58–59
Nature of the offense, 281–283
Needs assessment, 295, 315–319
defined, 295, 315
examples, 315–319
Needs assessment instruments, 315–319
Net-widening, 45–46, 133–135
DSO, 45–46
New Jersey ISP Model, 421
New Mexico Center for Dispute Resolution,
399–400
New Mexico Supreme Court, 444
New York Children's Aid Society, 242
New York House of Refuge, 9–10, 241,
480–481
New York's Juvenile Offender Law, 329
No bills, 83
Nolle prosequi, 216, 227
Nominal dispositions, 103–104, 328, 383–400
defined, 383
Nonadjudicated status offense cases,
198–199
Noninterventionist model, 161–162
Nonsecure custody, 104–105, 485–495
defined, 485
North Dakota Classification/Risk Assessment
Form, 309–310
No true bills, 83
Numbers-game model of caseload assign-
ments, 430–431

O

Offense seriousness, 171, 195–197, 281–283
Office of Juvenile Justice and Delinquency
Prevention (OJJDP), 42–43, 57, 499,
508–509
Ohio Experience, 176, 423–429
basic parameters, 424
contact standards by type and phase, 427

control elements, 428
defined, 423
program size and requirements, 425
Oklahoma Regimented Inmate Discipline
Program (RID), 455–456
Omega Boy's Club, 48
Once waived/always waived provision,
214–215
Out-of-home placement, 198
Outward Bound, 493–494
Overcrowding, 105, 187
secure placement, 105

P

Parens patriae, 5, 14–18, 28, 133, 135,
156–157, 160–161, 164–165, 179, 240,
245, 249, 255, 266, 270, 274, 335–340,
351, 378–379, 480
defined, 14–15
essential elements, 339–340
intake, 156–157
medical model, 160–161
PARJO (New York), 108
Parole (*See also* Juvenile Parole), 88, 108
adults, 89
defined, 88
juveniles, 108
Parole boards, 88
Parole revocation, 511–520
defined, 511
Paternalistic period, 69
Perceived Contingency Behavioral Domain
Scale, 493
Perry Preschool Project, 484
Petit juries, 84
Petitions, 100–101, 127–128
defined, 100
example, 127
Philadelphia House of Refuge, 10
Philadelphia Juvenile Probation
Department's Intensive Aftercare
Probation (IAP Program), 411
Philadelphia Society for Alleviating the
Miseries of the Public Prisons, 8–9
Photographing juveniles, 129, 255
Piers-Harris Self-Concept Scale, 493
PINS Diversion Program (PINS), 391–392
Placement, 198–200
numbers, 199–200
Plea bargaining, 81–82, 154–155, 226–227,
274–275

Violent offenders, 284–285

Virginia Department of Criminal Justice Services, 136–137

Virginia Department of Youth and Family Services, 432

VisionQuest, 494–495

W

Waiver hearings, 216–217

Waiver of rights for juveniles, 351–356
nine-point standard, 351–352

Waivers, 202–236
decision making, 206–208
defined, 202
implications for juveniles, 217–223
patterns and trends, 229–232
reasons for using, 203
time standards governing, 217
types, 210–215

Walnut Street Jail, 9, 480–481
innovations, 9

Wilderness projects, 492–495

Wilding, 484

Wisconsin Case Classification System, 430–431

"Without prejudice," 262

"With prejudice," 259

Women's movement, 69

Workhouses, 7

Y

Young Adult Offenders Program Facility (Draper, UT), 496

Youth Assistance Program, 484

Youth at Risk Program, 392

Youth Center (Beloit, KS), 428

Youth centers, 486

Youth facilities, 486

Youthfulness as a mitigating factor, 364

Youth Gang Response System, 79

Youth gangs, 116, 118–122
corporate gangs, 118
female gang members, 122
minority status, 118–119
scavenger gangs, 118

Youth gang units, 116–117

Youth Self-Report, 156

Youth service bureaus (YSBs), 389–390
defined, 389

Youth Services/Diversion and Community Service Programs, Inc., 390–391

Youth Services/Diversion (YS/D) 390–391

Youth squads 117–118
proactive units 118
reactive units 118

Youth-to-Victim Restitution Project 410

Z

Zoot suits 116

CASE INDEX

United States v. Bernard S., 795 F.2d 749 (9th Cir.) (1986)

United States v. Salerno, 107 S.Ct. 2095 (1987)

West v. United States, 399 F.2d 467 (5th Cir.) (1968)

Wilkins v. Missouri, 109 S.Ct. 2969 (1989)

Williams v. Florida, 399 U.S. 78 (1970)

Woods v. Clusen, 794 F.2d 293 (7th Cir.) (1986)